fourth edition

Corporate Finance
Principles & Practice

Denzil Watson and Antony Head

Sheffield Hallam University

FT Prentice Hall
FINANCIAL TIMES

An imprint of **Pearson Education**

Harlow, England • London • New York • Boston • San Francisco • Toronto • Sydney • Singapore • Hong Kong
Tokyo • Seoul • Taipei • New Delhi • Cape Town • Madrid • Mexico City • Amsterdam • Munich • Paris • Milan

Tony would like to thank Aidan and Rosemary for their love and courage, and dedicates this book to the memory of Lesley Head (1952–2005), dear wife and mother.

Denzil would like to thank Dora, Hugh and Doreen for their support and care.

Pearson Education Limited

Edinburgh Gate
Harlow
Essex CM20 2JE
England

and Associated Companies throughout the world

Visit us on the World Wide Web at:
www.pearsoned.co.uk

First edition published under the Financial Times Pitman Publishing imprint in 1998.
Second edition published under the Financial Times Prentice Hall imprint in 2001
Third edition published 2004
Fourth edition published 2007

© Pearson Education Limited 2007

ISBN-13: 978-0-273-70644-1
ISBN-10: 0-273-70644-6

British Library Cataloguing-in-Publication Data
A catalogue record for this book is available from the British Library

Library of Congress Cataloging-in-Publication Data
A catalogue record for this book is available from the Library of Congress

10 9 8 7 6 5 4 3 2 1
10 09 08 07 06

Typeset in 10/13pt Sabon by 73
Printed and bound by Graficas Estella, Bilbao, Spain

The publisher's policy is to use paper manufactured from sustainable forests.

Contents

4 Long-term finance: equity finance

5 Long-term finance: debt finance, hybrid finance and leasing

6 An overview of investment appraisal methods — 152

7 Investment appraisal: applications and risk — 182

· 11 Mergers and takeovers

12 Risk management

13 International investment decisions

Preface

Introduction

Corporate finance is concerned with the financing and investment decisions made by the management of companies in pursuit of corporate goals. As a subject, corporate finance has a theoretical base which has evolved over many years and which continues to evolve as we write. It has a practical side too, concerned with the study of how companies actually make financing and investment decisions, and it is often the case that theory and practice disagree.

The fundamental problem that faces financial managers is how to secure the greatest possible return in exchange for accepting the smallest amount of risk. This necessarily requires that financial managers have available to them (and are able to use) a range of appropriate tools and techniques. These will help them to value the decision options open to them and to assess the risk of those options. The value of an option depends upon the extent to which it contributes towards the achievement of corporate goals. In corporate finance, the fundamental goal is usually taken to be to increase the wealth of shareholders.

The aim of this book

The aim of this text is to provide an introduction to the core concepts and key topic areas of corporate finance in an approachable, 'user-friendly' style. Many texts on corporate finance adopt a theory-based or mathematical approach which are not appropriate for those coming to the subject for the first time. This book covers the core concepts and key topic areas without burdening the reader with what we regard as unnecessary detail or too heavy a dose of theory.

Flexible course design

Many undergraduate courses are now delivered on a modular or unit basis over one teaching semester of 12 weeks' duration. In order to meet the constraints imposed by such courses, this book has been designed to support self-study and directed learning. There is a choice of integrated topics for the end of the course.

Each chapter offers:

- a comprehensive list of key points to check understanding and aid revision;
- self-test questions, with answers at the end of the book, to check comprehension of concepts and computational techniques;

- questions for review, with answers at the end of the book, to aid in deepening understanding of particular topic areas;
- questions for discussion, answers for which are available in the *Lecturer's Guide*;
- comprehensive references to guide the reader to key texts and articles;
- suggestions for further reading to guide readers who wish to study further.

A comprehensive glossary is included at the end of the text to assist the reader in grasping any unfamiliar terms that may be encountered in the study of corporate finance.

New for the fourth edition

The fourth edition has been extensively revised and updated in order to keep its content fresh and relevant. Apart from considerable revision of the text, many vignettes have been updated to reflect current events and developments in the financial world. The fourth edition has also benefited from a major restructuring in the chapter sequencing. This has brought a more logical flow to the book, not only in terms of the order in which the subject material is covered but also from the perspective of the complexity of the material. The number of questions for review and discussion at the end of each chapter has been increased. The Companion Website for the book has been reviewed and updated, with many more multiple choice questions provided to aid student learning. The PowerPoint slides offered to lecturers have also been revised to reflect the content of the fourth edition. We trust that our readers will find these changes useful and constructive.

Target readership

This book has been written primarily for students taking a course in corporate finance in their second or final year of undergraduate study on business studies, accounting and finance-related degree programmes. It may also be suitable for students on professional and postgraduate business and finance courses where corporate finance or financial management are taught at introductory level.

Author acknowledgements

We are grateful to our reviewers for helpful comments and suggestions. We are also grateful to the undergraduate and postgraduate students of Sheffield Hallam University who have taken our courses and, thereby, helped in developing our approach to the teaching and learning of the subject. We are particularly grateful to our editor Justinia Seaman of Pearson Education for her patience and encouragement and assistant editor Stephanie Poulter for providing invaluable review information and feedback on the book drafts. We also extend our gratitude to our many colleagues at Sheffield Hallam University, with special thanks going to Geoff Russell for those vital statistics we couldn't find ourselves.

Guided tour of the book

Learning objectives list the topics covered and what the reader should have learnt by the end of the chapter

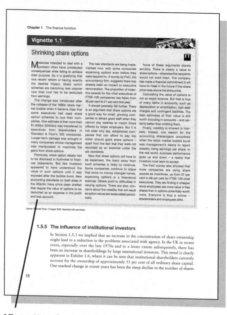

Vignettes feature extracts from topical news articles

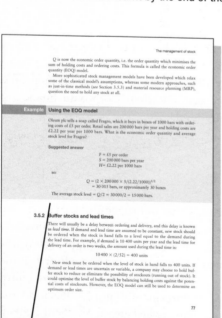

Examples appear throughout the text, giving worked examples and computational techniques

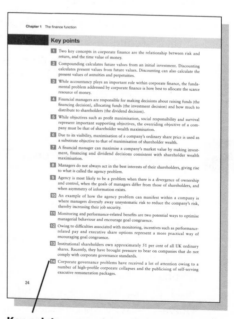

Key points summarise and recap the main points of the chapter, providing an important revision tool

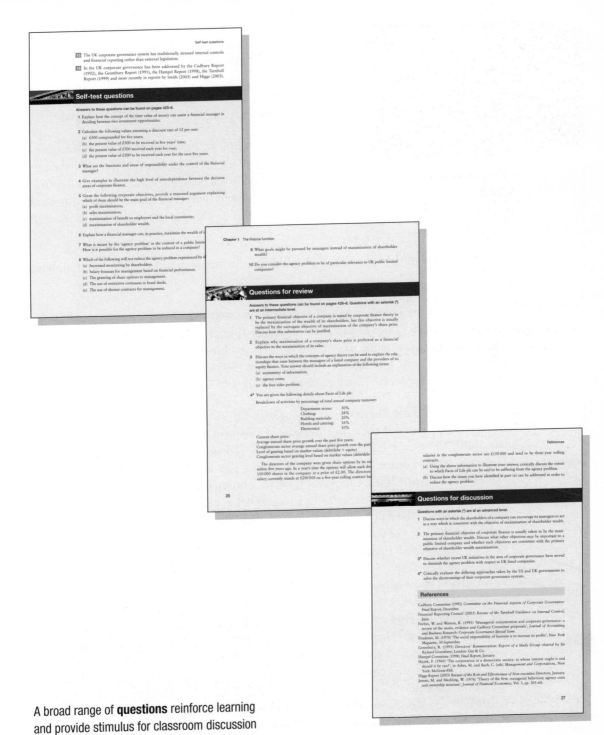

A broad range of **questions** reinforce learning and provide stimulus for classroom discussion

Publisher's acknowledgements

The publishers would like to thank all the reviewers who contributed to the development of this text, including Penny Belk from Loughborough University, Kerry Sullivan from the University of Surrey, Dr. M. J. Buckle from the University of Wales, Swansea and Richard Trafford from the University of Portsmouth.

We are grateful to the following for permission to reproduce copyright material:

Ex 7.6 from *A Survey of Management Accounting Practices in UK Manufacturing Companies'*. Certified Research Report 32, ACCA; Ex 9.3 from *FAME*, published by Bureau van Dijk Electronic Publishing; Ex 10.5 from *Sainsbury plc's Annual Reports*, reproduced by kind permission of Sainsbury's Supermarkets Ltd; Ex 12.2 from *Bank of England Quarterly Bulletin, Autumn 2005, The Determination of UK Corporate Capital Gearing*.

We are grateful to the Financial Times Limited for permission to reprint the following material:

Chapter 2 If only investors could compare like with like from *The Financial Times Limited*, 13 April 2006, © Martin Simons; Chapter 13 Europe is winning the war for economic freedoms from *The Financial Times Limited*, 31 March 2006, © Dan O'Brien, Economist Intelligence Unit; Chapter 13 Positive experience in difficult markets from *The Financial Times Limited*, 10 July 1997, © Jon Marks.

Chapter 1 Shrinking Share Options, © *Financial Times*, 13 August 2005; Chapter 1 Most companies 'flout code on corporate governance', © *Financial Times*, 20 December 1999; Chapter 1 Higgs review sets out boardroom code, © *Financial Times*, 20 January 2003; Chapter 1 Bonuses undermining pay link with performance, © *Financial Times*, 17 April 2005; Chapter 4 IPOs the chosen route as equity markets advance, © *Financial Times*, 3 January 2006; Chapter 4 Laura Ashley rights issue shunned, © *Financial Times*, 10 May 2003; Chapter 4 Nightfrieght to go private via £35m management buy-out, © *Financial Times*, 30 January 2001; Chapter 4 Opinions split over Pearson discounted rights issue, © *Financial Times*, 2 August 2000; Chapter 4 3i shareholders to reap £500m, © *Financial Times*, 31 March 2006; Chapter 5 Bayer's Euros 2bn in convertibles, © *Financial Times*, 30 March 2006; Chapter 5 Ahold looks for breathing space, © *Financial Times*, 1 March 2003; Chapter 5 Hellas' Euros 500m Pik, © *Financial Times*, 4 April 2006; Chapter 5 New issues: Denmark and VNU meet strong demand, © *Financial Times*, 8 May 2003; Chapter 5 Leasing looks like a worthwhile option, © *Financial Times*, 7 May 2003; Chapter 5 Independent's rights issue delivers a reality check, © *Financial Times*, 28 March 2003; Chapter 8 Sizing up the historical equity risk premium, © *Financial Times*, 21 February 2001; Chapter 9 Leeds defends Woodgate sale, © *Financial Times*, 1 February 2003; Chapter 10 Prudential falls 18% on dividend fears, © *Financial Times*, 26 February 2003; Chapter 10

M&S buoyed with relief, © *Financial Times*, 24 May 2000; Chapter 10 FT Money: Dubious dividend decisions that drive me to despair, © *Financial Times*, 4 June 2005; Chapter 10 Average dividend payout ratios for a selection of UK industries in 2003 and 2006, © *Financial Times*, 2 January and 3 February 2006; Chapter 10 Cadbury defends the bid price, © *Financial Times*, 27 January 1995; Chapter 10 Share buyback rise 92% in US, © *Financial Times*, 20 September 2005; Chapter 11 Water faces up to rising debt levels, © *Financial Times*, 5 April 2003; Chapter 11 Morrison bid value drops to £32bn, © *Financial Times*, 8 March 2003; Chapter 11 The Takeover Panel cracks down on Indigo, © *Financial Times*, 22 January 2003; Chapter 11 More EU member states opt for 'poison pill', © *Financial Times*, 1 March 2006; Chapter 11 No slanging match as BPB attempts to prove that its case is mathematically correct, © *Financial Times*, 15 September 2005; Chapter 11 Just a mention of spin-off can unlock value for shareholders, © *Financial Times*, 1 March 2006; Chapter 11 RSA's health insurer in £147m MBO, © *Financial Times*, 5 April 2003; Chapter 12 Balance sheets left reeling by the Real, © *Financial Times*, 26 November 2002; Chapter 12 Daimler increases hedging against dollar, © *Financial Times*, 3 June 2005; Chapter 12 Interest rate swaps: changing hopes boost volume, © *Financial Times*, 7 October 2002; Chapter 12 Companies 'too short sighted when hedging', © *Financial Times*, 27 January 2006; Chapter 13 National news: foreign direct investment almost trebles, © *Financial Times*, 14 December 2005; Chapter 13 Foreign investment: competitors turn up the heat, © *Financial Times*, 14 April 2003.

Chapter 1

The finance function

Learning objectives

After studying this chapter, you should have achieved the following learning objectives:

- an understanding of the time value of money and the relationship between risk and return;

- an appreciation of the three decision areas of the financial manager;

- an understanding of the reasons why shareholder wealth maximisation is the primary financial objective of a company, rather than other objectives a company may consider;

- an understanding of why the substitute objective of maximising a company's share price is preferred to the objective of shareholder wealth maximisation;

- an understanding of how agency theory can be used to analyse the relationship between shareholders and managers, and of ways in which agency problems may be overcome;

- an appreciation of the developing role of institutional investors in overcoming agency problems;

- an appreciation of how developments in corporate governance have helped to address the agency problem.

1

Introduction

Corporate finance is concerned with the efficient and effective management of the finances of an organisation in order to achieve the objectives of that organisation. This involves planning and controlling the *provision* of resources (where funds are raised from), the *allocation* of resources (where funds are deployed to) and finally the *control* of resources (whether funds are being used effectively or not). The fundamental aim of financial managers is the *optimal allocation* of the scarce resources available to them – the scarce resource being money. Corporate finance theory therefore draws heavily on the subject of economics.

The discipline of corporate finance is frequently associated with that of accounting. However, while financial managers do need to have a firm understanding of management accounting (in order to make decisions) and a good understanding of financial accounting (in order to be aware of how financial decisions and their results are presented to the outside world), corporate finance and accounting are fundamentally different in nature. Corporate finance is inherently forward-looking and based on cash flows: this differentiates it from financial accounting, which is historic in nature and focuses on profit rather than cash. Corporate finance is concerned with raising funds and providing a return to investors: this differentiates it from management accounting, which is primarily concerned with providing information to assist managers in making decisions within the company. However, although there are differences between these disciplines, there is no doubt that corporate finance borrows extensively from both.

While in the following chapters we consider in detail the many and varied problems and tasks faced by financial managers, the common theme that links these chapters together is the need for financial managers to be able to *value alternative courses of action* available to them. This allows them to make a decision on which is the best choice in financial terms. Therefore before we move on to look at the specific roles and goals of financial managers, we introduce two key concepts that are pivotal in financial decision-making.

1.1 Two key concepts in corporate finance

Two key concepts in corporate finance that are pivotal in helping managers to value alternative choices are the *relationship between risk and return* and the *time value of money*. Since these two concepts are referred to frequently in the following chapters, it is vital that you have a clear understanding of them.

1.1.1 The relationship between risk and return

This concept states that an investor or a company takes on more risk only if a higher return is offered in compensation. *Return* refers to the financial rewards gained as a result of making an investment. The nature of the return depends on the form of the investment. A company that invests in fixed assets and business operations expects returns in the form of *profit*, which may be measured on a before-interest, before-tax or an after-tax basis, and in the form of increased *cash flows*. An investor who buys ordinary shares expects returns in the form of *dividend payments* and *capital gains* (share price increases). An investor who buys corporate bonds expects regular returns in the form of *interest payments*. The meaning of risk is more complex than the meaning of return. An investor or a company expects or anticipates a particular return when making an investment. *Risk* refers to the possibility that the actual return may be different from the expected return. The actual return may be greater than the expected return: this is usually a welcome occurrence. Investors, companies and financial managers are more likely to be concerned with the possibility that the actual return is *less* than the expected return. A *risky investment* is therefore one where there is a significant possibility of its actual return being different from its expected return. As the possibility of actual return being different from expected return increases, investors and companies demand a higher expected return.

The relationship between risk and return is explored in a number of chapters in this book. In Chapter 7 we will see that a company can allow for the risk of a project by requiring a higher or lower rate of return according to the level of risk expected. In Chapter 8 we examine how an individual's attitude to the trade-off between risk and return shapes their utility curves; we also consider the capital asset pricing model which expresses the relationship between risk and return in a convenient linear form. In Chapter 9 we calculate the costs of different sources of finance and find that the higher the risk attached to the source of finance, the higher the return required by the investor.

1.1.2 The time value of money

The *time value of money* is a key concept in corporate finance and is relevant to both companies and investors. In a wider context it is relevant to anyone expecting to pay or receive money over a period of time. The time value of money is particularly important to companies since the financing, investment and dividend decisions made by companies result in substantial cash flows over a variety of periods of time. Simply stated, the time value of money refers to the fact that *the value of money changes over time*.

Imagine that your friend offers you either £100 today or £100 in one year's time. Faced with this choice, you will (hopefully) prefer to take £100 today. The question to ask yourself is *why* do you prefer £100 today? There are three major factors at work here.

- *Time*: if you have the money now, you can spend it now. It is human nature to want things now rather than to wait for them. Alternatively, if you do not wish to spend your money now, you will still prefer to take it now, since you can then invest it so that in one year's time you will have £100 plus any investment income you have earned.
- *Inflation*: £100 spent now will buy more goods and services than £100 spent in one year's time because inflation undermines the purchasing power of your money.
- *Risk*: if you take £100 now you definitely have the money in your possession. The alternative of the *promise* of £100 in a year's time carries the risk that the payment may be less than £100 or may not be paid at all.

1.1.3 Compounding and discounting

Compounding is the way to determine the *future value* of a sum of money invested now, for example in a bank account, where interest is left in the account after it has been paid. Since interest received is left in the account, interest is earned on interest in future years. The future value depends on the rate of interest paid, the initial sum invested and the number of years the sum is invested for:

$$FV = C_0(1 + i)^n$$

where: FV = future value
C_0 = sum deposited now
i = interest rate
n = number of years until the cash flow occurs

For example, £20 deposited for five years at an annual interest rate of 6 per cent will have a future value of:

$$FV = £20 \times (1.06)^5 = £26.76$$

In corporate finance, we can take account of the time value of money through the technique of discounting. Discounting is the opposite of compounding. While *compounding* takes us *forward* from the current value of an investment to its future value, *discounting* takes us *backward* from the future value of a cash flow to its *present value*. Cash flows occurring at different points in time cannot be compared directly because they have different time values; discounting allows us to compare these cash flows by comparing their present values.

Consider an investor who has the choice between receiving £1000 now and £1200 in one year's time. The investor can compare the two options by changing the future value of £1200 into a present value, and comparing this present value with the offer of £1000 now (note that the £1000 offered now is already in present value terms). The present value can be found by applying an appropriate *discount rate*, one which reflects the three factors discussed earlier: time, inflation and risk. If the best investment the investor can make offers an annual interest rate of 10 per cent, we can use this as the discount rate. Reversing the compounding illustrated above, the present value can be found from the future value by using the following formula:

$$PV = \frac{FV}{(1 + i)^n}$$

where: PV = present value
FV = future value
i = discount rate
n = number of years until the cash flow occurs

Inserting the values given above:

$$PV = 1200/(1.1)^1 = £1091$$

Alternatively, we can convert our present value of £1000 into a future value:

$$FV = 1000 \times (1.1)^1 = £1110$$

Whether we compare present values or future values, it is clear that £1200 in one year's time is worth more to the investor than £1000 now.

Discounting calculations are aided by the use of *present value tables*, which can be found at the back of this book. The first table, of present value factors, can be used to discount *single point* cash flows. For example, what is the present value of a single payment of £100 to be received in five years' time at a discount rate of 12 per cent? The table of present value factors gives the present value factor for 5 years (row) at 12 per cent (column) as 0.567. If we multiply this by £100 we find a present value of £56.70.

The next table, of cumulative present value factors, enables us to find the present value of an annuity. An *annuity* is a regular payment of a fixed amount of money over a finite period. For example, what is the present value of £100 to be received at the end of each of the next five years, if our required rate of return is 7 per cent? The table gives the cumulative present value factor (annuity factor) for 5 years (row) at a discount rate of 7 per cent (column) as 4.100. If we multiply this by £100 we find a present value of £410.

The present value of a *perpetuity*, the regular payment of a fixed amount of money over an infinite period, is even more straightforward to calculate. The present value of the payment is equal to the payment divided by the discount rate. The present value of a perpetuity of £100 at a discount rate of 10 per cent is £1000 (i.e. £100/0.1).

Discounted cash flow (DCF) techniques allow us to tackle far more complicated scenarios than the simple examples we have just considered. Later in the chapter we discuss the vital link that exists between shareholder wealth and *net present value*, the specific application of DCF techniques to investment appraisal decisions. Net present value and its sister DCF technique internal rate of return, are introduced in Chapter 6 (*see* Sections 6.3 and 6.4). The application of NPV to increasingly more complex investment decisions is comprehensively dealt with in Chapter 7. In Chapter 5 (*see* Section 5.6 onwards), DCF analysis is applied to the valuation of a variety of debt-related securities.

1.2 The role of the financial manager

While everybody manages their own finances to some extent, financial managers of companies are responsible for a much larger operation when they manage corporate funds. They are responsible for a company's *investment decisions*, advising on the allocation of funds in terms of the total amount of assets, the composition of fixed and current assets, and the consequent risk profile of the choices. They are also responsible for *raising funds*, choosing from a wide variety of institutions and markets, with each source of finance having different features as regards cost, availability, maturity and risk. The place where supply of finance meets demand for finance is called the financial market: this consists of the short-term money markets and the longer-term capital markets. A major source of finance for a company is internal rather than external,

Exhibit 1.1   **The role of the financial manager as the person central to a company's financing, investment and reinvestment decisions**

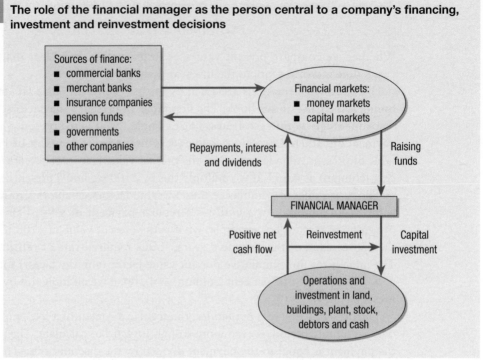

i.e. to retain part of the earnings generated by its business activities. The managers of the company, however, have to strike a balance between the amount of earnings they retain and the amount they pay out to shareholders as a dividend.

We can see, therefore, that a financial manager's decisions can be divided into three general areas: *investment* decisions, *financing* decisions and *dividend* decisions. The position of the financial manager as a person central to these decisions and their associated cash flows is illustrated in Exhibit 1.1.

While it is convenient to split a financial manager's decisions into three decision areas for discussion purposes, it is important to stress the high level of interdependence that exists between these areas. A financial manager making a decision in one of these three areas should always take into account the effect of that decision on the other two areas. Examples of possible knock-on effects of taking a decision in one of the three areas on the other two areas are indicated in Exhibit 1.2.

Who makes corporate finance decisions in practice? In most companies there will be no one individual solely responsible for corporate financial management. The more strategic dimensions of the three decision areas tend to be considered at board level, with an important contribution coming from the *finance director*, who oversees the finance function. Any financial decisions taken at this level will be after considerable consultation with accountants, tax experts and legal counsel. The daily cash and treasury management duties of the company and its liaison with financial institutions such

Exhibit 1.2	**The interrelationship between investment, financing and dividend decisions**

Investment: company decides to take on a large number of attractive new investment projects	**Finance**: company will need to raise finance in order to take up projects	**Dividends**: if finance is not available from external sources, dividends may need to be cut in order to increase internal financing
Dividends: company decides to pay higher levels of dividends to its shareholders	**Finance**: lower level of retained earnings available for investment means company may have to find finance from external sources	**Investment**: if finance is not available from external sources the company may have to postpone future investment projects
Finance: company finances itself using more expensive sources, resulting in a higher cost of capital	**Investment**: due to a higher cost of capital the number of projects attractive to the company decreases	**Dividends**: the company's ability to pay dividends in the future will be adversely affected

as banks will be undertaken by the *corporate treasurer*. It is common for both finance director and corporate treasurer to have an accounting background. An increasingly important responsibility for the corporate treasurer is that of hedging interest and exchange rate risk. An illustration of the various functions within the finance department of a large company is given in Exhibit 1.3.

Exhibit 1.3	**How the finance function fits within a company's management structure**

7

1.3 Corporate objectives

What should be the primary financial objective of corporate finance and, therefore, the main objective of financial managers? The answer is that their objective should be to make decisions that maximise the value of the company for its owners. As the owners of the company are its *shareholders*, the primary financial objective of corporate finance is usually stated to be *the maximisation of shareholder wealth*. Since shareholders receive their wealth through *dividends* and *capital gains* (increases in the value of their shares), shareholder wealth will be maximised by maximising the value of dividends and capital gains that shareholders receive over time. How financial managers go about achieving this objective is considered in the next section.

Owing to the rather vague and complicated nature of the concept of shareholder wealth maximisation, other objectives are commonly suggested as possible substitutes or surrogates. Alternative objectives to shareholder wealth maximisation also arise because of the existence of a number of other interest groups (stakeholders) within the company. All of these groups, such as employees, customers, creditors and the local community, will have different views on what the company should aim for. It is important to stress that while companies must consider the views of stakeholders other than shareholders, and while companies may adopt one or several substitute objectives over shorter periods, from a corporate finance perspective such objectives should be pursued only in support of the overriding long-term objective of maximising shareholder wealth. We now consider some of these other possible objectives for a company.

1.3.1 Maximisation of profits

The classical economic view of the firm, as put forward by Hayek (1960) and Friedman (1970), is that it should be operated in a manner that maximises its economic profits. The concept of *economic profit* is far removed from the *accounting profit* found in a company's profit and loss account. While economic profit broadly equates to cash, accounting profit does not. There are many examples of companies going into liquidation shortly after declaring high profits. Polly Peck plc's dramatic failure in 1990 is one such example. This leads us to the first of three fundamental problems with profit maximisation as an overall corporate goal. The first problem is that there are *quantitative difficulties* associated with profit. Maximisation of profit as a financial objective requires that profit be defined and measured accurately, and that all the factors contributing to it are known and can be taken into account. It is very doubtful that this requirement can be met on a consistent basis. If five auditors go into the same company, the chances are that each will come out with a different profit figure.

The second problem concerns the *timescale* over which profit should be maximised. Should profit be maximised in the short term or the long term? Given that profit considers one year at a time, the focus is likely to be on short-term profit maximisation at the expense of long-term investment, putting the long-term survival of the company into doubt.

The third problem is that profit does not take account of, or make an allowance for, *risk*. It would be inappropriate to concentrate our efforts on maximising accounting profit when this objective does not consider one of the key determinants of shareholder wealth.

Shareholders' dividends are paid with cash, not profit, and the timing and associated risk of dividend payments are important factors in the determination of shareholder wealth. When we consider this fact together with the problems just discussed, we can only conclude that maximisation of profit is not a suitable substitute objective for maximisation of shareholder wealth. That is not to say that a company does not need to pay attention to its profit figures, since falling profits or profit warnings are taken by the financial markets as a sign of financial weakness. In addition, profit targets can serve a useful purpose in helping a company to achieve short-term or operational objectives within its overall strategic plan.

1.3.2 Maximisation of sales

If a company were to pursue sales maximisation as its *only* overriding long-term objective, then it is likely to reach a stage where it is overtrading (*see* Section 3.4) and might eventually have to go into liquidation. Sales may not necessarily be at a profit and sales targets could be disastrous if products are not correctly priced. Maximisation of sales can be useful as a short-term objective, though. As an example, a company entering a new market and trying to establish sustainable market share could follow a policy of sales maximisation.

1.3.3 Survival

Survival cannot be accepted as a satisfactory long-term objective. Will investors want to invest in a company whose main objective is merely to survive? The answer has to be an emphatic no. In the long term, a company must attract capital investment by holding out the prospect of gains which are at least as great as those offered by comparable alternative investment opportunities. Survival may be a key short-term objective though, especially in times of economic recession. If a company were to go into liquidation, by the time assets have been distributed to stakeholders higher up the creditor hierarchy there may be little if any money to distribute to ordinary shareholders. If liquidation were a possibility, short-term survival as an objective *would* be consistent with shareholder wealth maximisation.

1.3.4 Social responsibility

Some organisations adopt an altruistic social purpose as a corporate objective. They may be concerned with improving working conditions for their employees, providing a healthy product for their customers or avoiding antisocial actions such as environmental pollution or undesirable promotional practices. While it is important not to upset stakeholders such as employees and the local community, social responsibility should play a supporting role within the framework of corporate objectives rather than acting as a company's primary goal. Although a company does not exist solely to please its employees, managers are aware that having a demotivated and unhappy workforce will be detrimental to its long-term prosperity. Equally, an action group of local residents unhappy with a factory's environmental impact can decrease its sales by inflicting adverse publicity on the company.

1.4 How is shareholder wealth maximised?

We have already mentioned that shareholder wealth maximisation is a rather vague and complicated concept. We have also stated that shareholders' wealth is increased through the cash they receive in dividend payments and the capital gains arising from increasing share prices. It follows that shareholder wealth can be maximised by maximising the purchasing power that shareholders derive through dividend payments and capital gains over time. From this view of shareholder wealth maximisation, we can identify three variables that directly affect shareholders' wealth:

- the *magnitude* of cash flows accumulating to the company;
- the *timing* of cash flows accumulating to the company;
- the *risk* associated with the cash flows accumulating to the company.

Having established the factors that affect shareholder wealth we can now consider what to take as an indicator of shareholder wealth. The indicator usually taken is a company's ordinary share price, since this will reflect expectations about future dividend payments as well as investor views about the long-term prospects of the company and its expected cash flows. The surrogate objective, therefore, is to *maximise the current market price* of the company's ordinary shares and hence to maximise the total market value of the company. The link between the cash flows arising from a company's projects all the way through to the wealth of its shareholders is illustrated in Exhibit 1.4.

At stage 1 a company takes on all projects with a positive net present value (NPV). By using NPV to appraise the desirability of potential projects the company is taking

Exhibit 1.4	**Diagram showing the links between the investment projects of a company and shareholder wealth**

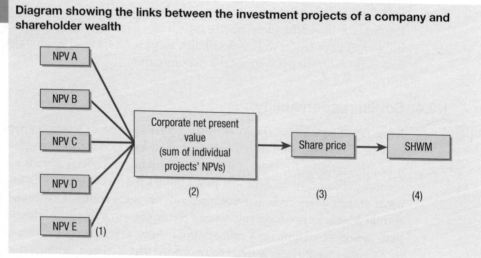

into account the three variables that affect shareholder wealth, i.e. the magnitude of expected cash flows, their timing (through discounting at the company's cost of capital) and their associated risk (through the selected discount rate). At stage 2, given that NPV is additive, the NPV of the company as a whole should equal the sum of the NPVs of the projects it has undertaken. At stage 3 the NPV of the company as a whole is accurately reflected by the market value of the company through its share price. The link between stages 2 and 3 (i.e. the market value of the company reflecting the true value of the company) will depend heavily upon the *efficiency* of the stock market and hence on the speed and accuracy with which share prices change to reflect new information about companies. The importance of stock market efficiency to corporate finance is considered in Chapter 2. Finally, at stage 4, the share price is taken to be a surrogate for shareholder wealth and so shareholder wealth will be maximised when the market capitalisation of the company is maximised.

Now that we have identified the factors that affect shareholder wealth and established maximisation of a company's share price as a surrogate objective for maximisation of shareholder wealth, we need to consider how a financial manager can achieve this objective. The factors identified as affecting shareholder wealth are largely under the control of the financial manager, even though the outcome of any decisions they make will also be affected by the conditions prevailing in the financial markets. In the terms of our earlier discussion, a company's value will be maximised if the financial manager makes 'good' investment, financing and dividend decisions. Examples of 'good' financial decisions, in the sense of decisions that promote maximisation of a company's share price, include the following:

- using NPV to assess all potential projects and then accepting all projects with a positive NPV;
- raising finance using the most appropriate mixture of debt and equity in order to minimise a company's cost of capital;
- adopting the most appropriate dividend policy, which reflects the amount of dividends a company can afford to pay, given its level of profit and the amount of retained earnings it requires for reinvestment;
- managing a company's working capital efficiently by striking a balance between the need to maintain liquidity and the opportunity cost of holding liquid assets;
- taking account of the risk associated with financial decisions and where possible guarding against it, e.g. hedging interest and exchange rate risk.

1.5 Agency theory

1.5.1 Why does agency exist?

While managers should make decisions that are consistent with the objective of maximising shareholder wealth, whether this happens in practice is another matter. The *agency problem* is said to occur when managers make decisions that are *not* consistent with the objective of shareholder wealth maximisation. Three important features that contribute to the existence of the agency problem within public limited companies are as follows:

- divergence of ownership and control, whereby those who own the company (shareholders) do not manage it but appoint agents (managers) to run the company on their behalf;
- the goals of the managers (agents) differ from those of the shareholders (principals). Human nature being what it is, managers are likely to look to maximising their own wealth rather than the wealth of shareholders;
- asymmetry of information exists between agent and principal. Managers, as a consequence of running the company on a day-to-day basis, have access to management accounting data and financial reports, whereas shareholders only receive annual reports, which may be subject to manipulation by the management.

When these three factors are considered together, it should be clear that managers are in a position to maximise their own wealth without necessarily being detected by the owners of the company. Asymmetry of information makes it difficult for shareholders to monitor managerial decisions, allowing managers to follow their own welfare-maximising decisions. Examples of possible management goals include:

- growth, or maximising the size of the company;
- increasing managerial power;
- creating job security;
- increasing managerial pay and rewards;
- pursuing their own social objectives or pet projects.

The potential agency problem between a company's managers and its shareholders is not the only agency problem that exists. Jensen and Meckling (1976) argued that the company can be viewed as a whole series of agency relationships between the different interest groups involved. These agency relationships are shown in Exhibit 1.5. The

Exhibit 1.5 The agency relationships that exist between the various stakeholders of a company

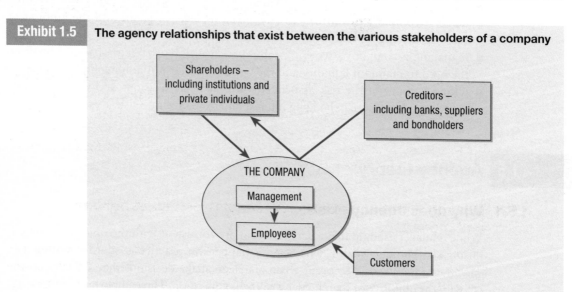

arrows point away from the principal towards the agent. For example, as customers pay for goods and services from the company, they are the principal, and the supplying company is their agent. While a company's managers are the agents of the shareholders, the relationship is reversed between creditors and shareholders, with shareholders becoming, through the actions of the managers they appoint and direct, the agents of the creditors.

From a corporate finance perspective an important agency relationship exists between shareholders, as agents, and the providers of debt finance, as principals. The agency problem here is that shareholders will have a preference for using debt for progressively riskier projects, as it is shareholders who gain from the success of such projects, but debt holders who bear the risk.

1.5.2 How does agency manifest with a company?

The agency problem manifests itself in the investment decisions managers make. Managerial reward schemes are often based on short-term performance measures and managers therefore tend to use the payback method when appraising possible projects, since this technique emphasises short-term returns. With respect to risk, managers may make investments to decrease unsystematic risk through diversification, in order to reduce the risk to the company. Unsystematic risk (*see* Section 8.2) is the risk associated with undertaking particular business activities. By reducing the risk to the company through diversification, managers hope to safeguard their own jobs. However, most investors will have already diversified away unsystematic risk themselves by investing in portfolios containing the shares of many different companies. Therefore shareholder wealth is not increased by the diversifying activities of managers. Another agency problem can arise in the area of risk if managers undertake low-risk projects when the preference of shareholders is for higher-risk projects.

The agency problem can also manifest itself in the financing decision. Managers will prefer to use equity finance rather than debt finance, even though equity finance is more expensive than debt finance, since lower interest payments mean lower bankruptcy risk and higher job security. This will be undesirable from a shareholder point of view because increasing equity finance will increase the cost of the company's capital.

Agency conflict arises between shareholders and debt holders because shareholders have a greater preference for higher-risk projects than debt holders. The return to shareholders is unlimited, whereas their loss is limited to the value of their shares, hence their preference for higher-risk (and hence higher-return) projects. The return to debt holders, however, is limited to a fixed interest return: they will not benefit from the higher returns from riskier projects.

1.5.3 Dealing with the agency problem between shareholders and managers

Jensen and Meckling (1976) suggested that there are two ways of seeking to optimise managerial behaviour in order to encourage *goal congruence* between shareholders and managers. The first way is for shareholders to *monitor* the actions of management.

There are a number of possible monitoring devices that can be used, although they all incur costs in terms of both time and money. These monitoring devices include the use of independently audited financial statements and additional reporting requirements, the shadowing of senior managers and the use of external analysts. The costs of monitoring must be weighed against the benefits accruing from a decrease in suboptimal managerial behaviour (i.e. managerial behaviour which does not aim to maximise shareholder wealth). A major difficulty associated with monitoring as a method of solving the agency problem is the existence of *free riders*. Smaller investors allow larger shareholders, who are more eager to monitor managerial behaviour owing to their larger stake in the company, to incur the bulk of monitoring costs, while sharing the benefits of corrected management behaviour. Hence the smaller investors obtain a free ride.

An alternative to monitoring is for shareholders to incorporate clauses into managerial contracts which encourage goal congruence. Such clauses formalise constraints, incentives and punishments. An *optimal contract* will be one which minimises the *total* costs associated with agency. These *agency costs* include:

- financial contracting costs, such as transaction and legal costs;
- the opportunity cost of any contractual constraints;
- the cost of managers' incentives and bonus fees;
- monitoring costs, such as the cost of reports and audits;
- the loss of wealth owing to suboptimal behaviour by the agent.

It is important that managerial contracts reflect the needs of individual companies. For example, monitoring may be both difficult and costly for certain companies. Managerial contracts for such companies may therefore include bonuses for improved performance. Owing to the difficulties associated with monitoring managerial behaviour, such incentives could offer a more practical way of encouraging goal congruence. The two most common incentives offered to managers are *performance-related pay* (PRP) and *executive share option schemes*. These methods are not without their drawbacks.

Performance-related pay (PRP)

The major problem here is that of finding an accurate measure of managerial performance. For example, managerial remuneration can be linked to performance indicators such as profit, earnings per share or return on capital employed (*see* Section 2.4). However, the accounting information on which these three performance measures are based is open to manipulation by the same managers who stand to benefit from performance-related pay. Profit, earnings per share and return on capital employed may also not be good indicators of wealth creation since they are not based on cash and hence do not have a direct link to shareholder wealth maximisation.

Executive share option schemes

Given the problems associated with performance-related pay, executive share option schemes represent an alternative way to encourage goal congruence between senior managers and shareholders. Share options allow managers to buy a specified number of their company's shares at a fixed price over a specified period. The options have value only when the market price of the company's shares exceeds the price at which they can be bought by using the option. The aim of executive share option schemes is to encourage managers to maximise the company's share price, and hence to maximise shareholder wealth, by making managers potential shareholders through their ownership of share options.

Share option schemes are not without their problems. First, while good financial management does increase share prices, there are a number of external factors that affect share prices. If the country is experiencing an economic boom, share prices will increase (a bull market). Managers will then benefit through increases in the value of their share options, but this is not necessarily down to their good financial management. Equally, if share prices in general are falling (a bear market), share options may not reward managers who have been doing a good job in difficult conditions. Second, problems with share option schemes arise because of their terms. Share options are not seen as an immediate cost to the company and so the terms of the options (i.e. the number of shares that can be bought and the price at which they can be bought) may sometimes be set at too generous a level. The difficulty of quantifying the cost of share options and the recent decline in their popularity due to the introduction of new accounting treatment of their costs is the subject of Vignette 1.1.

Shareholders, in addition to using monitoring and managerial incentives, have other ways of keeping managers on their toes. For example, they have the right to remove directors by voting them out of office at the company's annual general meeting (AGM). Whether this represents a viable threat to managers depends heavily on the ownership structure of the company, i.e. whether there are a few large influential shareholders holding over half of the company's ordinary shares. Alternatively, shareholders can 'vote with their feet' and sell their shares on the capital markets. This can have the effect of depressing the company's share price, making it a possible takeover target. The fact that target company managers usually lose their jobs after a takeover may provide an incentive for them to run their company more in the interests of shareholders.

1.5.4 The agency problem between debt holders and shareholders

The simplest way for debt holders to protect their investment in a company is to secure their debt against the company's assets. Should the company go into liquidation, debt holders will have a prior claim over assets which they can then sell in order to recover their investment.

An alternative way for debt holders to protect their interests and limit the amount of risk they face is for them to use restrictive covenants. These take the form of clauses written into bond agreements which restrict a company's decision-making process. They may prevent a company from investing in high-risk projects, or from paying out excessive levels of dividends, and may limit its future gearing levels. Restrictive covenants are discussed in Section 5.1.1.

Vignette 1.1

Shrinking share options

Measures intended to deal with a problem often have unintended consequences while failing to achieve their purpose. So it is gratifying that one recent reform is having exactly the desired impact. Share option schemes are becoming less popular now their cost has to be deducted from earnings.

The change was introduced after the collapse of the 1990s' stock market bubble when it became clear that some executives had used share option schemes to loot their companies. One estimate is that more than $1,000bn (£550bn) was transferred to executives from shareholders in Standard & Poor's 500 companies. Longer-term damage was wrought in many companies whose management was manipulated to maximise the gains from share options.

Previously, share option details had to be disclosed in footnotes to financial statements. But few investors appeared to have understood the value of such options until it was exposed after the bubble burst. New accounting standards on both sides of the Atlantic have since been drafted that require the value of options to be deducted as an expense in the profit and loss account.

The new standards are being implemented now, with some companies expensing options even before they were required to. A survey by PwC, the accountancy firm, suggests there has already been an impact on executive remuneration. The proportion of incentive awards for the chief executives of FTSE-100 companies has fallen from 36 per cent to 21 per cent this year.

It should probably fall further. There is an argument that share options are a good way for small, growing companies to attract good staff when they cannot pay salaries to match those offered by larger employers. But it is not clear why big, established companies that can afford to pay top dollar should grant share options – apart from the fact that they were not recorded as an expense under the old standards.

Now that share options will have to be expensed, the trend away from such schemes is likely to continue. Some companies continue to argue that since no money changes hands, expensing options is a theoretical exercise. Others point to difficulties in valuing options. There are also concerns about the volatility that will result as option values are recalculated periodically.

None of these arguments stands scrutiny. There is clearly a value to share options – otherwise the recipients would not want them. The company has made a financial commitment it will have to meet in the future if the share price rises above the strike price.

Calculating the value of options is not an exact science. But that is true of many items in accounts, such as depreciation or amortisation, bad debt charges and contingent liabilities. The best estimates of their value is still worth including in accounts – and certainly better than omitting them.

Finally, volatility is inherent in markets. Indeed, one reason for the accounting shenanigans uncovered when the stock market bubble burst was management's desire to report steadily rising earnings per share. In the real world, business performance goes up and down – a reality that investors must learn to accept.

The PwC survey also showed that more companies are using share awards as incentives, up from 57 per cent to 68 per cent for FTSE-100 chief executives. They are finding it cheaper since employees see more value in free shares than in options potentially worth more. Everyone is thus a winner – shareholders and employees alike.

Source: Financial Times, 13 August 2005. Reprinted with permission.

1.5.5 The influence of institutional investors

In Section 1.5.3 we implied that an increase in the concentration of share ownership might lead to a reduction in the problems associated with agency. In the UK in recent years, especially over the late 1970s and to a lesser extent subsequently, there has been an increase in shareholdings by large institutional investors. This trend is clearly apparent in Exhibit 1.6, where it can be seen that institutional shareholders currently account for the ownership of approximately 51 per cent of all ordinary share capital. One marked change in recent years has been the steep decline in the number of shares

Exhibit 1.6	The beneficial ownership of UK quoted ordinary shares in percentage terms according to classification of owner over the period 1969–2004

	1969 %	1975 %	1981 %	1990 %	1997 %	2001 %	2004 %
Insurance companies	12.2	15.9	20.5	20.4	23.5	20.0	17.2
Pension funds	9.0	16.8	26.7	31.7	22.1	16.1	15.7
Other financial institutions*	14.7	15.3	10.7	9.1	10.7	15.2	18.6
Institutional investors (total)	35.9	48.0	57.9	61.2	56.3	51.3	51.5
Industrial and commercial companies	5.4	3.0	5.1	2.8	1.2	1.0	0.6
Personal sector	47.4	37.5	28.2	20.3	16.5	14.8	14.1
Overseas sector	6.6	5.6	3.6	11.8	24.0	31.9	32.6
Other	4.7	5.9	5.2	3.9	2.0	1.0	1.2
Total	100.0	100.0	100.0	100.0	100.0	100.0	100.0

* includes banks, unit and investment trusts.

Source: National Statistics. © Crown Copyright 2004. Reproduced by the permission of the Office for National Statistics.

held by pension funds. This can be explained by the UK government's abolition in 1997 of the favourable tax treatment enjoyed by pension funds up to that date. They had been able to reclaim the tax paid on dividends; once this right was lost, ordinary shares became a less attractive investment.

In the past, while institutional investors had not been overtly interested in becoming involved with companies' operational decisions, they did put pressure on companies to maintain their dividend payments in an adverse macroeconomic environment. The irony is that, rather than reducing the agency problem, institutional investors may have been exacerbating it by pressing companies to pay dividends they could ill afford. However, recent years have seen institutional investors becoming more interested in corporate operational and governance issues. The number of occasions where institutional investors have got tough with companies in which they invest when they do not comply with companies' governance standards has steadily increased.

A recent development in the USA has been the increase in pressure on companies, from both performance and accountability perspectives, generated by shareholder coalitions such as the Council of Institutional Investors (CII) and the California Public Employees' Retirement System (CalPERS), which is the largest US pension fund. These organisations publish, on a regular basis, lists of companies which they consider to have been underperforming, due to bad management, over the preceding five years. The publication of these lists is a tactic to force such companies to take steps to improve their future performance. While this kind of shareholder 'vigilantism' has yet to take root in the UK, CalPERS is actively seeking to increase investments in Europe, and large investment companies such as UK-based Hermes Investment Management are both firm and outspoken about what they see as acceptable (and not acceptable) stewardship of the companies they invest in.

1.5.6 The influence of international investors

The pattern of UK share ownership over the past decade and a half has seen a steady increase in the proportion of shares held by overseas investors. Foreign investors now account for the ownership of one in three of the shares listed on the UK stock market, nearly three times the level it was back in 1990. The increase of UK share ownership by foreign investors has come predominantly from international fund management groups such as Fidelity and Capital. This increase has been at the expense of domestic pension funds, insurance companies and individual investors who have sought to diversify their share holdings internationally. This change in UK share ownership has made it more difficult for companies to identify and understand who their shareholders are and has led to a wider array of shareholder objectives for companies to consider.

1.6 Corporate governance

Until now we have only considered solutions to the agency problem at an individual company level. In recent years, however, a more general solution to the corporate governance problem has come through self-regulation. This approach has sought to influence the structure and nature of the mechanisms by which owners govern managers in order to promote fairness, accountability and transparency. The importance of good standards of corporate governance has been highlighted in the UK by recent concerns about the way in which remuneration packages for senior executives have been determined. This has been further reinforced by the collapse of a number of large companies, including Polly Peck in 1990, the Bank of Credit and Commerce International (BCCI) and Maxwell Communications Corporation in 1991, and more recently Enron and WorldCom in 2002. Doubts have been raised about whether the interests of shareholders are being met by executive remuneration packages which are not only complex but have been formulated by the very executives expected to enjoy their benefits.

The corporate governance system in the UK has traditionally stressed the importance of internal controls and the role of financial reporting and accountability, as opposed to a large amount of external legislation faced by US firms. The issue of corporate governance was first addressed in the UK in 1992 by a committee chaired by Sir Adrian Cadbury. The resulting Cadbury Report (1992) recommended a voluntary Code of Best Practice. The main proposals of this code were:

- the posts of chief executive officer and chairman, the two most powerful positions within a company, should not be held by the same person;
- company boards should include non-executive directors of sufficient calibre who are independent of management, appointed for specified terms after being selected through a formal process;
- executive directors' contracts should be for no longer than three years without shareholder approval;
- there should be full disclosure of directors' remunerations, including any pension contributions and share options;

- executive directors' pay should be subject to the recommendations of a remuneration committee made up wholly, or mainly, of non-executive directors;
- the relationship between a company and its auditor should be professional and objective;
- companies should establish an audit committee including at least three non-executive directors.

The committee recommended a greater role for non-executive directors on remuneration committees in order to avoid potential conflicts of interest. After Cadbury, the London Stock Exchange required its member companies to state in their accounts whether or not they complied with the Cadbury Code of Best Practice and, if not, to explain the reasons behind their non-compliance. The code also encouraged the 'constructive involvement' of institutional investors, suggesting they use their influence to ensure that companies comply with the code.

Many commentators were critical of the effectiveness of the Cadbury Report, focusing on the market-based nature of the proposed process of self-regulation. The efficacy of these proposals depended to a large extent on the manner in which non-executive directors were selected for appointment. In particular, the use of the 'old boy network' to select potential candidates ran contrary to the spirit of the Cadbury proposals. The effectiveness of the proposals was questioned by Forbes and Watson (1993), who argued that any scheme seeking to increase the accountability of senior management to shareholders would require the active involvement of institutional shareholders if it were to achieve its objectives.

The approach of the Cadbury Committee was reinforced by the Code of Best Practice produced as part of the Greenbury Report (1995). This report specifically criticised what it considered to be the overgenerous remuneration packages awarded to directors of the privatised utilities. Its recommendations were:

- directors' contracts should be reduced to one-year rolling contracts;
- remuneration committees, when setting pay levels, should be more sensitive to company-wide pay settlements and avoid excessive payments. These committees should consist exclusively of non-executive directors;
- companies should abandon directors' performance-related bonus schemes and phase out executive share option schemes. These should be replaced with long-term incentive plans which reward directors through the payment of shares if they reach stretching financial or share-price targets.

Investigation indicated that some elements of the Greenbury Report were being largely ignored by UK companies. According to research carried out in 1996 by the corporate governance consultancy Pension & Investment Research Consultants (PIRC), 60 per cent of the directors in the UK's 350 biggest companies had contracts in excess of one year. The research also showed that in approximately 50 per cent of companies surveyed long-term incentive plans had been *added* to existing executive share option schemes rather than replacing them. Further discussion of the non-compliance of companies with corporate governance codes can be found in Vignette 1.2.

Vignette 1.2

Most companies 'flout code on corporate governance'

Most companies are flouting the corporate governance code introduced last year to clean up the image of top executives riding roughshod over the wishes of their shareholders, according to a report published today by Pensions Investment Research Consultants (PIRC).

The worst case of non-compliance is over directors' pay. In a survey of 468 companies in the FTSE All Share Index, just nine – less than 2 per cent – put critical remuneration committee reports to the vote of shareholders at the annual general meetings. Almost half the companies have still not either imposed one-year contracts on executive directors, or adopted a policy of reducing contracts to this level.

The findings are likely to dismay the government, which has repeatedly urged companies to abide by the code, published by the London Stock Exchange following the recommendations of the committee on corporate governance chaired by Sir Ronald Hampel, former chairman of ICI. Earlier this year, [the government] called on companies to introduce voting on pay committee reports and one-year contracts for executives in a Department of Trade and Industry document.

PIRC found 27 per cent of companies were happy to disclose that they had considered putting pay committee reports to an AGM vote. Most of the companies, 69 per cent, gave no indication either way. Stuart Bell, PIRC research director, said: 'If they are not disclosing the information, shareholders can have little confidence that they are following the code.'

He said it was 'disappointing that compliance on some pay issues is relatively low', explaining that some – notably the recommendation to have one-year contracts – date back to the Greenbury Code of 1995, 'and so are not new requirements'.

Just 51 per cent of companies reported that their practice or policy was one-year, rolling contracts for all directors. Of the 77 FTSE 100 companies surveyed, 53 per cent admitted that one-year contracts were not even an objective, as against two-fifths of the 227 FTSE smallcap companies in the survey.

In other findings, PIRC reported that 77 per cent of companies staffed their remuneration committees with non-executives they themselves believed to be independent. The code says only independent non-executives should be appointed to pay committees.

Mr Bell said that the code 'represents a base-line standard'. He expected the best companies 'to go beyond it in providing better information to investors and improving their governance structure'. This was important because it 'will contribute to competitiveness in the long term'.

Source: Simon Targett, *Financial Times*, 20 December 1999. Reprinted with permission.

Continuing the three-year cycle, the Hampel Committee delivered its report on corporate governance in 1998. It established a 'super code' made up of a combination of its own recommendations and findings of the previous two committees. The new Combined Code on Corporate Governance was overseen by the London Stock Exchange, which included compliance with the provisions of the code in its listing requirements. The Hampel Committee sought to widen the governance debate by considering:

- the importance for companies of having a balanced board structure which accommodates both profitability and accountability;
- the role of independent non-executive directors as a link between the board and a company's shareholders;
- the importance of shareholder vigilance, especially institutional shareholders, in solving the governance problem.

While the Combined Code stated that companies' boards of directors should maintain sound systems of internal control, it did not offer specific guidelines. The Turnbull

Report, published a year later in September 1999, fleshed out the bones by considering the wide-ranging types of significant risk that companies need to control and the characteristics that an embedded control system should possess in order to control them. Companies had to be compliant with the Turnbull Report by December 2000, with auditors required to report non-compliance.

In 2002 the profile of corporate governance was raised for the wrong reasons with the sensational collapses of Enron Inc. and WorldCom, sending shock waves not only through the US financial system but through the major financial systems of the world as well. Despite the UK being considered by many commentators to be the best governed market in the world, the British government was sufficiently concerned by events in the USA that it established inquiries into the effectiveness of non-executive directors and into the independence of audit committees. Their findings were published in January 2003. The Higgs Report (the subject of Vignette 1.3) dealt with the first of these two issues and made a number of recommendations designed to enhance the independence, and hence effectiveness, of non-executive directors (NEDs). It also commissioned the Tyson Report to investigate how companies could recruit NEDs with varied backgrounds and skills to enhance board effectiveness. Although the Higgs Report was generally well received, some parties expressed their concerns that relationships between chairmen and chief executives may become less effectual, and others argued that compliance costs for smaller companies will be too onerous.

The Smith Report examined the role of audit committees and, while it stopped short of recommending that auditors should be rotated periodically (e.g. every five years), it gave authoritative guidance on how audit committees should operate and be structured. It recommended that audit committees be made up of at least three 'tough, knowledgeable and independent minded' non-executive directors to prevent relationships between auditors and companies becoming too 'cosy'. The recommendations of both Higgs and Smith were incorporated into an extended version of the Combined Code in July 2003. There have been no further reports since, although a June 2005 review by the Financial Reporting Council of Turnbull's 1999 guidance concluded that it continued to be appropriate and had contributed to improvements in the internal control of UK-listed companies. Only time will tell whether the Combined Code and any future revisions to the UK's corporate governance system will be sufficient to keep abreast of the changing demands made on it by stakeholders and society.

1.7 Conclusion

In this chapter we have introduced two key concepts in financial management: the relationship between risk and return, and the time value of money. We linked the time value to future values, present values, compounding and discounting. We clarified the role of the financial manager within a public company and established that his or her overriding aim should be to maximise the wealth of the company's shareholders; other objectives which are often cited, such as profit maximisation, survival and social

Vignette 1.3

Higgs review sets out boardroom code

Sweeping proposals to reform British boardrooms unveiled on Monday by a review led by Derek Higgs represented a 'determined and realistic agenda for change', the former investment banker said. Mr Higgs said he hoped the recommendations of his long-awaited review, focusing on an increased role for non-executive directors, would 'significantly raise the bar for board practice and corporate performance in the UK'. He said the review continued the 'comply or explain' approach of previous corporate governance reviews in the UK. Companies would be expected to comply with the revised code of corporate governance or explain why not.

'I do not presume that a one-size-fits-all approach to governance is appropriate. The review is not a blueprint for box-tickers but a counsel of best practice that can be intelligently applied,' Mr Higgs said.

The report dovetails with another published on Monday, conducted by Sir Robert Smith, chairman of Weir Group, which calls for an elevated status for audit committees to ensure sound financial reporting and an end to the cosy relationship between auditors and management.

Among the proposals of the Higgs report are the following recommendations:

- At least half the board should be independent non-executive directors. Appointments should be made through a nomination committee. All members of the audit and remuneration committees should also be independent and a majority on nomination committees.
- New definition of an independent director. 'A non-executive is considered independent when the board determines that the director is independent and there are no relationships which could affect, or appear to affect, the director's judgement,' the report concludes.
- Group led by Professor Laura D'Andrea Tyson, former senior adviser to US President Bill Clinton and Dean of London Business School, to draw up a list of potential non-executives from the non-commercial sector in order to widen the range of talents in the boardroom.
- Reaffirmation of existing best practice that the roles of chairman and chief executive should be separated. The chief executive of a company should also not go on to become chairman of the same company.
- Non-executive directors should meet at least once a year without the chairman or other executive directors present.
- Appointment of a 'senior independent director' to be shareholders' first point of contact should their concerns not be resolved through the chairman or chief executive.
- Induction programmes and extra training for executives, coupled with performance assessments conducted at least once a year. Time limit on non-executive directors' tenure of two three-year terms, except in exceptional circumstances.
- No full-time executive should hold more than one non-executive role, nor should an individual chair more than one major company. No limit set for number of non-executive roles an individual can hold, though care should be taken that individuals have enough time to do as is expected of them.
- Salaries should be bolstered to attract high-quality non-executives. Remuneration, however, should not ordinarily be paid in the form of share options.

The review has been broadly welcomed by business, shareholders and the government. Peter Montagnon, head of investment affairs at the Association of British Insurers, said: 'Strong boards make for strong companies that deliver value to their shareholders and prosperity to their employees. This report contains a number of common sense proposals to help independent directors maximize their contribution by supporting sound strategic development and ensuring proper oversight of key issues such as audit, remuneration and the nomination.'

Mr Montagnon played down concerns by some business groups that the recommendation of a senior non-executive director on a board should take part in discussions with shareholders. 'This is not about dividing boards, but making them work better together,' he said. 'It makes sense for the senior independent director to participate in meetings of the chairman and management with leading shareholders so that the board can take investor views fully into account.'

Source: Robert Orr and Tony Tassell, *Financial Times*, 20 January 2003. Reprinted with permission.

responsibility, are of secondary importance. Shareholder wealth is maximised through financial managers making sound investment, financing and dividend decisions. These decisions should take account of the amount, timing and associated risk of expected company cash flows, as these are the key variables driving shareholder wealth.

Unfortunately, managers are in a position to maximise their own wealth rather than that of shareholders. The agency problem can be tackled internally and externally. Internally, the two most common approaches are to offer performance-related pay or executive share option schemes to managers. These are far from perfect solutions, however. Externally, the terms and conditions of managers' pay and the topical issues of corporate governance have been the subject of reports by a number of committees including Cadbury, Greenbury, Hampel, Turnbull and Higgs. The recommendations of these committees are based on a principles-driven approach as opposed to the rule-based stance in the USA. While they have undoubtedly helped to reduce the problem of agency in the UK, as Vignette 1.4 illustrates, managerial remunerations continue to be an issue in the UK. 'Fat cat' headlines in the financial press are unlikely to become a thing of the past without a significant change in human nature.

Vignette 1.4

Bonuses undermining pay link with performance

The supposed link between executive pay and performance is being undermined by 'booming' bonuses and generous pensions, according to research published on Monday.

Following criticism of 'fat-cat' pay, companies are under investor pressure to ensure chief executive pay is tied to performance. Most claim to have achieved this through greater use of share-based incentive plans.

However, a study by Independent Remuneration Solutions, a consultancy, into the UK's 10 biggest quoted companies concludes the link remains a 'myth' because chief executives receive generous annual bonuses and pension awards that dwarf their salaries.

The survey shows the basic average salary of £968,000 was only 16 per cent of total pay. IRS said the award of various shares and share options, pen-sion, bonuses and benefits helped to lift the average total package to £5.9m, up 7 per cent on 2003.

The precise value of pension and share awards is not disclosed alongside salary, benefits and bonus in an annual report. IRS calculates the total package awarded into a single figure, which is not found in an annual report.

The consultancy said the average pension benefit in 2004 was £1.1m, or 118 per cent of salary. The average chief executive in the study boasts a pension pot of £7m, compared with shares and options worth £5.8m. Pension awards not linked to performance account for 20 per cent of annual pay. Cliff Weight, IRS director, said: 'Most CEOs have much more in their pension pot than they have invested in shares of their company. Should it not be the other way round?'

The survey shows the average bonus increased 28 per cent, to £1.3m. IRS said the companies' bonus plans paid out 121 per cent of the target, when their average share price went up 4 per cent. The survey covers disclosures for the chief executives of BP, Royal Dutch/Shell, Vodafone, GlaxoSmithKline, AstraZeneca, HSBC, HBOS, Barclays, Royal Bank of Scotland and Lloyds TSB. The 10 companies have a combined market capitalisation of £675bn, more than half the FTSE 100 by value. The study shows that Glaxo's Jean-Pierre Garnier was the UK's highest paid chief executive, with total remuneration awarded of £9.2m. However, £7.1m was variable compensation, with £800,000 going into his pension. IRS praised Glaxo for 'leading the way in terms of well-balanced incentives and linkage of wealth to company performance'.

Source: Sundeep Tucker, FT.com, 17 April 2005. Reprinted with permission.

Key points

1. Two key concepts in corporate finance are the relationship between risk and return, and the time value of money.

2. Compounding calculates future values from an initial investment. Discounting calculates present values from future values. Discounting can also calculate the present values of annuities and perpetuities.

3. While accountancy plays an important role within corporate finance, the fundamental problem addressed by corporate finance is how best to allocate the scarce resource of money.

4. Financial managers are responsible for making decisions about raising funds (the financing decision), allocating funds (the investment decision) and how much to distribute to shareholders (the dividend decision).

5. While objectives such as profit maximisation, social responsibility and survival represent important supporting objectives, the overriding objective of a company must be that of shareholder wealth maximisation.

6. Due to its visibility, maximisation of a company's ordinary share price is used as a substitute objective to that of maximisation of shareholder wealth.

7. A financial manager can maximise a company's market value by making investment, financing and dividend decisions consistent with shareholder wealth maximisation.

8. Managers do not always act in the best interests of their shareholders, giving rise to what is called the agency problem.

9. Agency is most likely to be a problem when there is a divergence of ownership and control, when the goals of managers differ from those of shareholders, and when asymmetry of information exists.

10. An example of how the agency problem can manifest within a company is where managers diversify away unsystematic risk to reduce the company's risk, thereby increasing their job security.

11. Monitoring and performance-related benefits are two potential ways to optimise managerial behaviour and encourage goal congruence.

12. Owing to difficulties associated with monitoring, incentives such as performance-related pay and executive share options represent a more practical way of encouraging goal congruence.

13. Institutional shareholders own approximately 51 per cent of all UK ordinary shares. Recently, they have brought pressure to bear on companies that do not comply with corporate governance standards.

14. Corporate governance problems have received a lot of attention owing to a number of high-profile corporate collapses and the publicising of self-serving executive remuneration packages.

15 The UK corporate governance system has traditionally stressed internal controls and financial reporting rather than external legislation.

16 In the UK corporate governance has been addressed by the Cadbury Report (1992), the Greenbury Report (1995), the Hampel Report (1998), the Turnbull Report (1999) and more recently in reports by Smith (2003) and Higgs (2003).

Self-test questions

Answers to these questions can be found on pages 425–6.

1 Explain how the concept of the time value of money can assist a financial manager in deciding between two investment opportunities.

2 Calculate the following values assuming a discount rate of 12 per cent:
   (a) £500 compounded for five years;
   (b) the present value of £500 to be received in five years' time;
   (c) the present value of £500 received each year for ever;
   (d) the present value of £500 to be received each year for the next five years.

3 What are the functions and areas of responsibility under the control of the financial manager?

4 Give examples to illustrate the high level of interdependence between the decision areas of corporate finance.

5 Given the following corporate objectives, provide a reasoned argument explaining which of them should be the main goal of the financial manager:
   (a) profit maximisation;
   (b) sales maximisation;
   (c) maximisation of benefit to employees and the local community;
   (d) maximisation of shareholder wealth.

6 Explain how a financial manager can, in practice, maximise the wealth of shareholders.

7 What is meant by the 'agency problem' in the context of a public limited company? How is it possible for the agency problem to be reduced in a company?

8 Which of the following will *not* reduce the agency problem experienced by shareholders?
   (a) Increased monitoring by shareholders.
   (b) Salary bonuses for management based on financial performance.
   (c) The granting of share options to management.
   (d) The use of restrictive covenants in bond deeds.
   (e) The use of shorter contracts for management.

9 What goals might be pursued by managers instead of maximisation of shareholder wealth?

10 Do you consider the agency problem to be of particular relevance to UK public limited companies?

Questions for review

Answers to these questions can be found on pages 426–8. Questions with an asterisk (*) are at an intermediate level.

1 The primary financial objective of a company is stated by corporate finance theory to be the maximisation of the wealth of its shareholders, but this objective is usually replaced by the surrogate objective of maximisation of the company's share price. Discuss how this substitution can be justified.

2 Explain why maximisation of a company's share price is preferred as a financial objective to the maximisation of its sales.

3 Discuss the ways in which the concepts of agency theory can be used to explain the relationships that exist between the managers of a listed company and the providers of its equity finance. Your answer should include an explanation of the following terms:

(a) asymmetry of information;

(b) agency costs;

(c) the free-rider problem.

4* You are given the following details about Facts of Life plc.

Breakdown of activities by percentage of total annual company turnover:

Department stores:	30%
Clothing:	24%
Building materials:	20%
Hotels and catering:	16%
Electronics:	10%

Current share price:	£2.34
Average annual share price growth over the past five years:	5%
Conglomerate sector average annual share price growth over the past five years:	9%
Level of gearing based on market values (debt/debt + equity)	23%
Conglomerate sector gearing level based on market values (debt/debt + equity)	52%

The directors of the company were given share options by its remuneration committee five years ago. In a year's time the options will allow each director to purchase 100 000 shares in the company at a price of £2.00. The directors' average annual salary currently stands at £200 000 on a five-year rolling contract basis, while average salaries in the conglomerate sector are £150 000 and tend to be three-year rolling contracts.

(a) Using the above information to illustrate your answer, critically discuss the extent to which Facts of Life plc can be said to be suffering from the agency problem.

(b) Discuss how the issues you have identified in part (a) can be addressed in order to reduce the agency problem.

Questions for discussion

Questions with an asterisk (*) are at an advanced level.

1 Discuss ways in which the shareholders of a company can encourage its managers to act in a way which is consistent with the objective of maximisation of shareholder wealth.

2 The primary financial objective of corporate finance is usually taken to be the maximisation of shareholder wealth. Discuss what other objectives may be important to a public limited company and whether such objectives are consistent with the primary objective of shareholder wealth maximisation.

3* Discuss whether recent UK initiatives in the area of corporate governance have served to diminish the agency problem with respect to UK listed companies.

4* Critically evaluate the differing approaches taken by the US and UK governments to solve the shortcomings of their corporate governance systems.

References

Cadbury Committee (1992) *Committee on the Financial Aspects of Corporate Governance: Final Report*, December.

Financial Reporting Council (2005) *Review of the Turnbull Guidance on Internal Control*, June.

Forbes, W. and Watson, R. (1993) 'Managerial remuneration and corporate governance: a review of the issues, evidence and Cadbury Committee proposals', *Journal of Accounting and Business Research: Corporate Governance Special Issue*.

Friedman, M. (1970) 'The social responsibility of business is to increase its profits', *New York Magazine*, 30 September.

Greenbury, R. (1995) *Directors' Remuneration: Report of a Study Group chaired by Sir Richard Greenbury*, London: Gee & Co.

Hampel Committee (1998) *Final Report*, January.

Hayek, F. (1960) 'The corporation in a democratic society: in whose interest ought it and should it be run?', in Asher, M. and Bach, C. (eds) *Management and Corporations*, New York: McGraw-Hill.

Higgs Report (2003) *Review of the Role and Effectiveness of Non-executive Directors*, January.

Jensen, M. and Meckling, W. (1976) 'Theory of the firm: managerial behaviour, agency costs and ownership structure', *Journal of Financial Economics*, Vol. 3, pp. 305–60.

Pension & Investment Research Consultants (1996) *After Greenbury: Contracts and Compensation*, August.

Smith Report (2003) *Audit Committees: Combined Code Guidance*, January.

Turnbull Report (1999) *Internal Control: Guidance for Directors on the Combined Code*, London: Institute of Chartered Accountants in England and Wales.

Tyson Report (2003) *Tyson Report on the Recruitment and Development of Non-Executive Directors,* June, London: London Business School.

Recommended reading

For an informative chapter which gives an American perspective on the problem of agency and how it can be solved by financial contracting see:

Emery, D., Stowe, J. and Finnerty, J. (2004) *Corporate Financial Management*, Harlow: FT Prentice Hall, chapter 9.

Important and informative papers and articles recommended for further reading include:

Andrews, G. (1982) 'What should a company's objectives be?,' *Managerial Finance*, Vol. 8, pp. 1–4.

Barfield, R. (1995) 'Shareholder value in practice,' *The Treasurer*, January, pp. 31–4.

Charkham, J. (1993) 'The Bank and corporate governance: past, present and future', *Bank of England Quarterly Bulletin*, August, pp. 388–92.

Fama, E. (1980) 'Agency problems and the theory of the firm,' *Journal of the Political Economy*, Vol. 88, April, pp. 288–307.

Gompers, P., Ishii, J. and Metrick, A. (2003) 'Corporate governance and equity prices', *Journal of Economics*, Vol. 118 (1), February, pp. 107–55.

Grinyer, J. (1986) 'Alternatives to maximization of shareholder wealth,' *Accounting and Business Research*, Autumn.

Marsh, P. (1998) 'Myths surrounding short-termism,' in *Mastering Finance*, London: FT Pitman, pp. 168–74.

Zingales, L. (1998) 'Why it's worth being in control,' in *Mastering Finance*, London: FT Pitman, pp. 43–8.

Chapter 2

Capital markets, market efficiency and ratio analysis

Learning objectives

After studying this chapter, you should have achieved the following learning objectives:

- an appreciation of the range of internal and external sources of finance available to a company, and of the factors influencing the relative proportions of internal and external finance used;

- an understanding of the significance of the capital markets to a company;

- a understanding of the importance of the efficient market hypothesis to corporate finance and an ability to explain the difference between the various forms of market efficiency;

- an appreciation of the empirical research that has been undertaken to establish the extent to which capital markets may be considered to be efficient in practice;

- the ability to calculate key ratios from corporate financial statements and an understanding of their significance in corporate finance;

- an appreciation of the difficulties relating to calculating and interpreting financial ratios;

- an appreciation of the concepts of economic profit and economic value added and their relationship with shareholder wealth.

Introduction

Capital markets are places where companies which need long-term finance can meet investors who have finance to offer. This finance may be equity finance, involving the issue of new ordinary shares, or debt finance, in which case companies can choose from a wide range of loans and debt securities. Capital markets are also places where investors buy and sell company and government securities. Their trading decisions reflect information on company performance provided by financial statements and financial analysis, dividend announcements by companies, market expectations on the future levels of interest rates and inflation, and investment decisions made by companies.

Both companies and investors want capital markets to assign fair prices to the securities being traded. In the language of corporate finance, companies and investors want the capital markets to be *efficient*. It is possible to describe the characteristics of an efficient capital market by considering the relationship between market prices and the information available to the market. Whether capital markets are in fact efficient is a question which has been studied extensively for many years and, in the first part of this chapter, we focus on the key topic of the efficient market hypothesis.

Shareholders make decisions on which shares to add or remove from their portfolios. Investors such as banks and other financial institutions make decisions about whether, and at what price, to offer finance to companies. Financial managers make decisions in the key areas of investment, financing and dividends. Shareholders, investors and financial managers can inform their decisions by evaluating the financial performance of companies using information from financial statements, financial databases, the financial press and the Internet. Ratio analysis of financial statements can provide useful historical information on the profitability, solvency, efficiency and risk of individual companies. By using performance measures such as economic profit and economic value added (EVA®), company performance can be linked more closely with shareholder value and shareholder wealth, and attention can be directed to ways in which companies can create more value for shareholders.

2.1 Sources of business finance

One of the key decision areas for corporate finance is the question of how a company finances its operations. If finance is not raised efficiently, the ability of a company to accept desirable projects will be adversely affected and the profitability of its existing operations may suffer. The aims of an efficient financing policy will be to raise the appropriate level of funds, at the time they are needed, at the lowest possible cost. There is clearly a link between the financing decisions made by a company's managers and the wealth of the company's shareholders. For a financing policy to be efficient, however, companies need to be aware of the sources of finance available to them.

2.1.1 Internal finance

Sources of finance can be divided into *external* finance and *internal* finance. By internal finance we mean cash generated by a company which is not needed to meet operating costs, interest payments, tax liabilities, cash dividends or fixed asset replacement. This surplus cash is called *retained earnings* in corporate finance. Retained earnings must not be confused with the accounting term 'retained profit', which is found in both profit and loss accounts and balance sheets. Retained profit in the profit and loss account may not be cash, and retained profit in the balance sheet does not represent funds that can be invested. Only *cash* can be invested. A company with substantial retained profits in its balance sheet, no cash in the bank and a large overdraft will clearly be unable to finance investment from retained earnings.

Another internal source of finance that is often overlooked is the savings generated by more efficient management of working capital. This is the capital associated with short-term assets and liabilities (*see* Section 3.3). More efficient management of debtors, stocks, cash and creditors can reduce bank overdraft interest charges, as well as increasing cash reserves.

2.1.2 External finance

There is a multitude of different types of external finance available which can be split broadly into debt and equity finance. External finance can also be classified according to whether it is short term (less than one year), medium term (between one year and five years), or long term (more than five years), and according to whether it is traded (e.g. ordinary shares) or untraded (e.g. bank loans). An indication of the range of financial instruments associated with external finance and their interrelationships is given in Exhibit 2.1. You will find it useful to refer back to this exhibit as you study this and subsequent chapters.

The distinction between equity finance and debt finance is of key importance in corporate finance and for this reason we devote whole chapters to these external sources of long-term finance: equity finance (ordinary shares and preference shares) is discussed in detail in Chapter 4 and debt finance (corporate bonds, bank debt and leasing) is discussed in Chapter 5. Short-term finance is discussed in Chapter 3.

2.1.3 The balance between internal and external finance

Retained earnings, the major source of internal finance, may be preferred to external finance by companies for several reasons:

- retained earnings are seen as a ready source of cash;
- the decision on the amount to pay shareholders (and hence on the amount of retained earnings) is an internal decision and so does not require a company to present a case for funding to a third party;
- retained earnings have no issue costs;
- there is no dilution of control as would occur with issuing new equity shares;
- there are no restrictions on business operations as might arise with a new issue of debt.

Exhibit 2.1 **An illustration of the variety of financial instruments that can be used by a company to raise finance**

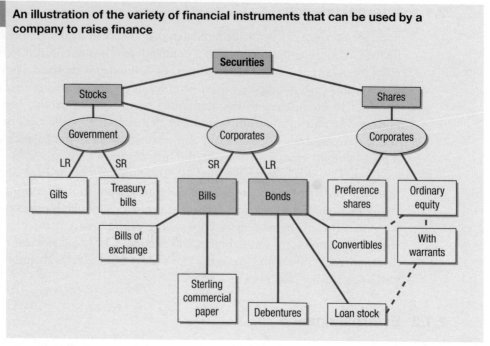

The amount of retained earnings available will be limited by the cash flow from business operations. Most companies will therefore need at some stage to consider external sources of finance if they need to raise funds for investment projects or to expand operating activities. The decision concerning the relative proportions of internal and external finance to be used for a capital investment project will depend on a number of factors.

The level of finance required

It may be possible for a company to finance small investments from retained earnings, for example refurbishing existing fixed assets or undertaking minor new investment projects. Larger projects are likely to require funds from outside the company.

The cash flow from existing operations

If the cash flow from existing operations is strong, a higher proportion of the finance needed for investment projects can be met internally. If the cash flow from existing operations is weak, a company will be more dependent on external financing.

The opportunity cost of retained earnings

Retained earnings are cash funds that belong to shareholders and hence can be classed as equity financing. This means they have a required rate of return which is equal to the best return that shareholders could obtain on their funds elsewhere in the financial markets. The best alternative return open to shareholders is called the *opportunity cost* of retained earnings and, as discussed in Sections 4.1.2 and 9.1.5, the required return on equity (the cost of equity) is greater than the required return on debt (the cost of debt).

The costs associated with raising external finance

By using retained earnings, companies can avoid incurring the issue costs associated with raising external finance and will not make commitments to servicing fixed interest debt.

The availability of external sources of finance

The external sources of finance available to a company depend on its circumstances. A company which is not listed on a recognised stock exchange, for example, will find it difficult to raise large amounts of equity finance, and a company which already has a large proportion of debt finance, and is therefore seen as risky, will find it difficult to raise further debt.

Dividend policy

As discussed in detail in Chapter 10, the dividend policy of a company will have a direct impact on the amount of retained earnings available for investment. A company which consistently pays out a high proportion of distributable profits as dividends will not have much by way of retained earnings and so is likely to use a higher proportion of external finance when funding investment projects.

2.2 Capital markets

Capital markets are markets for trading long-term financial securities. These securities were illustrated in Exhibit 2.1, but the most important ones for companies are ordinary shares, long-term debt securities such as debentures, unsecured loan stock and convertible bonds, and, to a much lesser extent, preference shares. Eurobonds and public sector securities, such as Treasury bills and gilts (gilt-edged stock), also trade on capital markets.

Capital markets have two main functions. First, they are a place where long-term funds can be raised by companies from those with funds to invest, such as financial institutions and private investors. In fulfilling this function, they are *primary markets* for new issues of equity and debt. Second, capital markets allow investors to sell their shares and bonds, or buy new ones to increase their portfolios. Here, capital markets act as *secondary markets* for dealing in existing securities. The secondary market plays a key role in corporate finance, because by facilitating the buying and selling of securities it increases their liquidity and hence their value. Investors would pay less for a security that would be difficult to sell at a later date. The secondary market is also a source of pricing information for the primary market and so helps to increase the efficiency with which the primary market allocates new funds to their best use.

The London Stock Exchange (LSE) is the main UK market for equity and bonds. Ways of obtaining a listing or quotation on this market are considered in Section 4.2.2. Exhibit 2.2 indicates that the number of companies listed on the London Stock Exchange has declined since 1996. The book value of their debt has declined since 1997. The total market value of equity reached a peak in 1999, before falling by 37 per cent up to 2002. Over the years 2003 and 2004, however, the total market value of

Exhibit 2.2	Companies listed on the UK stock market and the value of their equity and debt		

Year	Number of companies	Market value of equity (£bn)	Book value of debt (£bn)
1995	2078	900	25
1996	2171	1012	25
1997	2157	1251	30
1998	2087	1422	28
1999	1945	1820	22
2000	1904	1797	20
2001	1809	1523	19
2002	1701	1148	16
2003	1557	1336	16
2004	1465	1461	15

Source: London Stock Exchange Market Information and Analysis, 2006.

equity rose by 27 per cent, even though the number of companies (and the number of ordinary shares) continued to fall. The upward trend in total market value of equity can be linked to an improvement in prospects for economic growth both nationally and internationally.

Smaller companies which are unable to seek a listing on the main market of the LSE can apply for a listing on the Alternative Investment Market (AIM), which has been operated by the LSE since 1995. Market capitalisations on the AIM are typically between £2m and £100m. The AIM is both a primary and a secondary market for the shares of small and growing companies and has been quite successful to date. Unlike the LSE's main market, the AIM does not have any qualifying restrictions on market capitalisation, length of trading record or percentage of shares required to be held in public hands. The increasing importance of the AIM can be seen in Exhibit 2.3, which shows that the number of companies listed on the market has increased every year since its inception. One reason for this is companies transferring to the AIM from the main market. The total market value of equity peaked in 2000, declined by 31 per cent to 2002, and then increased by 79 per cent in 2003 and 73 per cent in 2004 to a new record value of £31753m. The book value of debt has tended to decline since 1999. The improvement in prospects for economic growth mentioned earlier is again a possible explanation for the upward trend in total market value of AIM equity.

2.3 Capital market efficiency

What are the desirable features of capital markets such as the LSE's main market and the AIM? Dixon and Holmes (1992) suggest that transaction costs should be as low as possible, so that barriers to trading on capital markets are reduced and *operational efficiency* is promoted. Primary markets should direct funds to their most productive

Exhibit 2.3	The growth of the Alternative Investment Market		
Year	Number of companies	Market value of equity (£m)	Book value of debt (£m)
1995	121	2 382	66
1996	252	5 298	82
1997	308	5 655	93
1998	312	4 438	94
1999	347	13 468	102
2000	524	14 935	69
2001	629	11 607	36
2002	704	10 252	39
2003	754	18 358	44
2004	1021	31 753	23

Source: London Stock Exchange Market Information and Analysis, 2006.

uses so that capital markets have *allocational efficiency*. This calls for fair prices to be provided by the secondary market, so activity on the primary market should have only a minimal effect on secondary market prices. This points to the need for *pricing efficiency*, which means that the prices of securities should reflect all relevant available information. Relevant information must be cheap to obtain and freely available to all, highlighting the need for *informational efficiency*.

2.3.1 Perfect markets and efficient markets

The are many references in corporate finance theory to perfect markets and efficient markets. According to Megginson (1997), a perfect market has the following characteristics:

- the absence of factors inhibiting buying and selling, such as taxes or transaction costs;
- all participants have the same expectations regarding asset prices, interest rates and other economic factors;
- entry to and exit from the market is free;
- information has no cost and is freely available to all market participants;
- a large number of buyers and sellers, none of whom dominates the market.

Clearly, no stock market anywhere in the world is a perfect market. However, companies and investors do not need capital markets to be perfect; rather, they need capital markets to be efficient and to offer fair prices so they can make reasoned investment and financing decisions. From our earlier discussion, we therefore expect an efficient capital market to have the following features:

- *Operational efficiency*: Transaction costs in the market should be as low as possible and required trading should be quickly effected.

■ *Pricing efficiency*: The prices of capital market securities fully and fairly reflect all information concerning past events and all events that the market expects to occur in the future. The prices of securities are therefore fair prices.

■ *Allocational efficiency*: The capital market, through the medium of pricing efficiency, allocates funds to where they can best be used.

The efficient market hypothesis is concerned with establishing the prices of capital market securities and states that the prices of securities fully and fairly reflect all relevant available information (Fama 1970). Market efficiency therefore refers to both the speed *and* the quality (i.e. direction and magnitude) of the price adjustment to new information. The testing of markets for efficiency has led to the recognition of three different levels or forms of market efficiency.

2.3.2 Different forms of market efficiency

Empirical tests of the efficiency of capital markets have investigated the extent to which share prices (security prices) reflect relevant information (i.e. pricing efficiency) because of a lack of data for testing allocational efficiency and operational efficiency. Many studies have investigated the extent to which it is possible for investors to make abnormal returns, which are returns in excess of expected returns, or returns in excess of those predicted by valuation methods such as the dividend growth model (*see* Section 10.4.3) and the capital asset pricing model (*see* Section 8.5).

Weak form efficiency

Capital markets are weak form efficient if current share prices reflect all historical information, such as past share price movements. This means it is not possible to make abnormal returns in such a market by using technical analysis to study past share price movements (*see* Section 2.3.5). Empirical evidence strongly supports the view that capital markets are weak form efficient.

Semi-strong form efficiency

Capital markets are semi-strong form efficient if current share prices reflect all historical information and all publicly available information, and if share prices react quickly and accurately to incorporate any new information as it becomes available. This means abnormal returns cannot be made in a semi-strong form efficient market by studying publicly available company information or by using fundamental analysis (*see* Section 2.3.5). Empirical studies support the proposition that capital markets are semi-strong form efficient.

Strong form efficiency

Capital markets are said to be strong form efficient if share prices reflect *all* information, whether it is publicly available or not. If markets are strong form efficient, *no one* can make abnormal returns from share dealing, not even investors who act on 'insider information'. Capital markets clearly do not meet all the conditions for strong form efficiency, since some investors do make abnormal returns by insider dealing, as shown by occasional prosecutions for this offence in recent years. However, these cases are few in number compared to the volume of transactions in the capital market as a whole.

2.3.3 Testing for market efficiency

Weak form tests

If a capital market is weak form efficient, so that share prices reflect completely all past information, it will not be possible for investors to predict future share prices by studying past share price movements. Share prices will change as new information arrives on the market and, since new information arrives at random, share price movements will also appear to be random (Samuelson 1965). Many empirical studies have supported the proposition that the movement of share prices over time represents a random walk. This *random walk hypothesis* suggests that, if we know the share price at the end of one time period, we cannot predict accurately the share price at the end of the next period. Empirical evidence strongly supports the view that the relationship between share prices in different periods is random, in which case we can say that research shows that capital markets are weak form efficient.

Empirical studies of weak form efficiency have used serial correlation tests, run tests and filter tests. One of the earliest studies testing for *serial correlation* looked for any correlation between security price changes at different points in time (Kendall 1953). The evidence from this and other studies tends to support the random walk hypothesis. Studies using *run tests* (e.g. Fama 1965) examine whether any significance can be attached to the direction of price changes by examining the length of the runs of successive price changes of the same sign. The empirical evidence indicated that the direction of price changes on any one day was independent of the direction of price changes on any other day. The distribution of directions was found to be based on pure chance, adding further support to the view that capital markets are weak form efficient. *Filter tests* try to identify any significant long-term relationships in security price movements by filtering out short-term price changes. One early study found that while filter tests could provide abnormal returns compared with a simple *buy and hold* strategy, gains were cancelled out when transaction costs were taken into account (Alexander 1961).

More recent studies have found weak evidence that a period of above-average returns may follow a long period of below-average returns (mean reversion), but the weak form of the efficient market hypothesis is still *broadly* supported (Megginson 1997; Beechey et al. 2000). It has also been argued from an insider perspective that trading strategies based on anomalies do not generate abnormal returns (Roll 1994).

Semi-strong form tests

Tests for semi-strong form efficiency look at the speed and accuracy of share price responses to new information (event studies). In general, event studies support the view that capital markets are semi-strong form efficient.

An examination of the adjustment of share prices to the release of information about share splits (*see* Section 4.4.1) found it was not possible to profit from the information because the market seemed to incorporate it efficiently and effectively (Fama et al. 1969). Similar findings were reached regarding earnings announcements (Ball and Brown 1968) and merger announcements (Keown and Pinkerton 1981). In fact, possible benefits arising from mergers were found to be anticipated by the capital market up to three months prior to any announcements (Franks et al. 1977). While event studies support the semi-strong form of the efficient market hypothesis, they also offer evidence of anomalies, such as the observation that share prices continue to rise (or fall) for a substantial period following the release of positive (or negative) information (Beechey et al. 2000). It has also been found that the more frequently a share is traded, the shorter the time required for its price to return to equilibrium having absorbed new information (Manganelli 2002).

Strong form tests

Because some people have access to information before other investors and so can make abnormal gains, it can be argued that capital markets are not strong form efficient. It is not possible to test for strong form efficiency *directly* by investigating the market's *use* of insider information, since by definition this information is unknown. Tests for strong form efficiency are therefore *indirect* in approach: they examine how *expert users* of information perform when compared against a yardstick such as the average return on the capital market.

Fund managers with resources to invest in discovering and analysing information may be in a better position than most to make abnormal gains. If their funds achieved above-average performances on a regular basis, this would be evidence that capital markets are not strong form efficient. A classic study of 115 mutual funds found that the majority did not make above-average returns when management costs were taken into account: in fact, their performance was inferior to a passive *buy-and-hold* strategy (Jensen 1968). Research continues to show that actively managed funds underperform the market after accounting for management costs, and in many cases before accounting for management costs as well (Megginson 1997; Beechey et al. 2000).

It has also been shown that investors could not benefit from the investment advice of financial tipsters (insider information becoming public information) due to the speed with which the market factored new information into share prices (Firth 1972).

2.3.4 Implications of the efficient market hypothesis

What are the implications for investors if the stock market is efficient?

- Paying for investment research will not produce above-average returns.
- Studying published accounts and investment tips will not produce above-average returns.
- There are no bargains (underpriced shares) to be found on the stock market.

   For a company and its managers, the implications of stock market efficiency are:

- The share price of a company fairly reflects its value and market expectations about its future performance and returns. The financial manager should therefore focus on making 'good' financial decisions which increase shareholder wealth as the market will interpret these decisions correctly and the share price will adjust accordingly.

- Cosmetic manipulation of accounting information, whether through window dressing of financial statements or by massaging earnings per share, will not mislead the market.
- The timing of new issues of shares is not important since shares are never underpriced.

2.3.5 Technical and fundamental analysis

The efficient market hypothesis suggests that future share prices cannot be predicted by studying past prices and, as we have seen, there is extensive evidence to support this view. Despite the evidence, investment strategies based on the study of past share prices, or on the analysis of published information such as annual accounts, are common, and the view held by many financial analysts seems to be therefore that capital markets are inefficient.

Technical analysis involves the use of charts (chartism) and other methods to predict future share prices and share price trends, clearly implying that a relationship exists between past and future prices. For technical analysis to lead to abnormal returns on a regular basis, capital markets cannot even be weak form efficient. *Fundamental analysis* uses public information to calculate a fundamental value for a share and then offers investment advice by comparing the fundamental value with the current market price. Fundamental analysis is not possible if capital markets are semi-strong form efficient, since all publicly available information will already be reflected in share prices.

Note that both technical analysis and fundamental analysis, by seeking abnormal returns, increase the speed with which share prices absorb new information and reach equilibrium, thereby preventing abnormal returns from being achieved.

2.3.6 Anomalies in the behaviour of share prices

Even though there is widespread acceptance that share prices respond quickly and accurately to new information, we have noted that research into market efficiency has produced evidence of anomalies in share price behaviour. Many such anomalies have been reported and investigated in the quest to understand the behaviour of share prices (Fama 1998), of which the following are examples.

Calendar effects

It has been reported that trading at particular times of the day can lead to negative or positive returns. For example, it appears that trading during the first 45 minutes on Monday mornings produces negative returns, whereas share prices tend to rise during the last 15 minutes of trading. While these effects have been reported, no satisfactory explanation has been offered. One suggestion is that investors evaluate their portfolios at weekends and sell on Monday mornings, whereas brokers initiate buy decisions regularly during the week.

High returns have also been noted in particular months, for example April in the UK and January in the USA. It is possible that these high returns are due to selling strategies designed to crystallise capital losses for tax purposes (known as *bed and breakfasting*) as the start of April is the end of the UK tax year. Share prices will be depressed at the start of April by such selling, but will recover as the new tax year begins. A trading strategy of buying at the start of the month and selling at the end may produce high returns in the UK in April.

Size anomalies

The returns from investing in smaller companies have been shown, in the long run, to be greater than the average return from all companies: one study, for example, found that small firms outperformed large firms by 6 per cent per year (Dimson and Marsh 1986). It has been suggested that above-average returns from small companies may compensate for the greater risk associated with them, such as the risk of financial distress (Beechey et al. 2000). It is possible that the growth prospects of smaller companies are better because they start from a lower base. However, it has been recognised that small companies account for only a small proportion of the equity trading on major stock exchanges and so studies of small-firm effects have little macroeconomic significance (Fama 1991).

Value effects

Above-average returns can apparently be gained by investing in *value stocks*, which are shares with high earnings, cash flows or tangible assets relative to current share price: i.e. by investing in shares with low price/earnings ratios, as summarised by Beechey et al. (2000). It has also been shown that abnormal returns can be gained by investing in a portfolio of shares with poor past returns (De Bondt and Thaler 1985).

2.3.7 Behavioural finance

Behavioural finance suggests that investors do not appear *in practice* to be consistently able to make decisions that have as their objective the maximisation of their own wealth. This may be because they fail to update their information correctly or because they do not make utility-maximising choices. Behavioural finance seeks to understand the market implications of the psychological factors underlying investor decisions and offers an alternative view of financial market activity to the efficient market hypothesis. It suggests that irrational investor behaviour can have significant and long-lasting effects on share price movements. While behavioural finance has not yet provided a unified theory of investor behaviour, it has had some success in explaining some anomalies in share price behaviour such as over-reaction to past price changes. A detailed discussion of behavioural finance is beyond the scope of this text; interested readers are referred to the excellent books by Haugen (1999) and Shleifer (2000), and to the survey by Barberis and Thaler (2002).

2.3.8 Summary

The existence of anomalies in share price behaviour suggests there are times when some share prices are not fair. Support for the efficient market hypothesis was almost universal before 1980. Since then, the theory has to some extent been regarded as an *incomplete* explanation of share price behaviour, with behavioural finance offering a growing challenge to the efficient marker hypothesis.

Research suggests that the UK and US stock markets, as well as a large number of other world-class stock markets, respond quickly and accurately to new information, and that only through insider dealing can investors make abnormal gains. Since such cases are small in number compared with the total volume of trading activity, and since legislation makes insider dealing illegal, it is likely that such capital markets are *at least* semi-strong form efficient. The continuing existence of anomalies in share price behaviour cannot be ignored, however, even though it has been suggested that some anomalies disappear when reasonable changes in research methodology are made (Fama 1998).

2.4 Assessing financial performance

In the introduction to this chapter, we mentioned that shareholders, investors and financial managers obtain a great deal of information about companies from their financial statements, financial databases, the financial press and the Internet. In this section we look at ratio analysis, which can be applied to financial statements and similar data in order to assess the financial performance of a company. In Section 2.4.10 we look at ways of assessing financial performance which have closer links to shareholder wealth maximisation.

Analysis of financial performance can provide useful financial information for a wide range of user groups.

Shareholders

Shareholders can use analysis of financial performance to assist them in making buy and sell decisions, comparing the performance of their investments with that of similar companies, and assessing whether managers as their agents (*see* Section 1.5) have been increasing shareholder wealth.

Investors

Investors such as banks and other financial institutions can use analysis of financial performance to inform decisions about whether to agree to requests for debt finance from companies and the terms and conditions to be attached to such finance.

Company managers

Managers can use analysis of financial performance to assess and compare the performance of different divisions and the performance of the company as a whole. They can compare their company's current performance with its performance in previous years, and against the performance of competitors.

Information sources for analysis of financial performance

Information for analysis of financial performance is initially derived from company financial statements (company accounts), but is now readily available through a variety of media. Financial databases are commonly used as a source of financial information on companies, for example, Datastream, Fame, Amadeus and LexisNexis. One advantage of using such databases is that ratio analysis can be performed by the software, although users must take care to ensure they are familiar with the definitions of the ratios provided. Useful company information can also be found by searching the Internet as most companies have their own websites. Free company accounts can be obtained from the FT World Investor Link for many companies listed on the London Stock Exchange.

Financial statements

Exhibit 2.4 shows two of the financial statements of Boater plc: a profit and loss account, and a balance sheet. The ability to calculate and understand accounting ratios rests on an understanding of financial statements such as these and what they represent.

The profit and loss account reports *financial performance* for an accounting period, which is usually one calendar year ending on the date given in the balance sheet. The profit and loss account begins with turnover (sales) and subtracts costs incurred in producing the goods sold or the services delivered (cost of sales) to give gross profit. Costs incurred by supporting activities such as administration and distribution are then subtracted to give operating profit, also known as *profit before interest and tax* (PBIT). This is the profit left after all operating costs have been deducted, hence the term operating profit.

The financial cost of meeting interest payments is subtracted to give profit before tax and the annual tax liability is subtracted to give profit after taxation (PAT). *Earnings* is the term given to profit that can be distributed to ordinary shareholders: in the absence of preference shares, earnings are equal to PAT; if preference shares have been issued, as in this case, earnings are equal to profit after tax and after preference dividends.

While the profit and loss account shows the financial performance of a company during an accounting period, the balance sheet shows the financial position of the company at the end of the accounting period. The balance sheet records the assets and liabilities of the company. Assets are divided into *fixed assets*, which are expected to be a source of economic benefit to the company over several accounting periods, and *current assets* (see Section 3.2.3), which are consumed or sold within an accounting period. These assets are balanced by current (short-term) liabilities, such as trade creditors and overdrafts, and long-term liabilities, such as debt, shareholders' funds and preference shares. Ordinary shareholders' funds are divided into the *ordinary share account* (ordinary shares), where the nominal or face value of issued shares is recorded; the *share premium account*, which records the difference between the nominal value of shares issued and the finance raised by selling shares; and reserves, the most common of which is the cumulative *profit and loss reserve*, which increases each year by the retained profit from the profit and loss account. If land and buildings are revalued, the gain in value is recorded in a *revaluation reserve*.

Another financial statement produced by UK companies, which is not illustrated in Exhibit 2.4, is the *cash flow statement*, which shows in a formal way the sources of and uses of cash during the accounting period. Financial statements are published at least once each year as part of company accounts. Vignette 2.1 discusses the importance of consistency in terms of the content of company accounts and the information they provide.

Exhibit 2.4	**Financial statements of Boater plc**

Profit and loss account for the year ended 31 December

	2006		2005	
	£000	£000	£000	£000
Turnover		5700		5300
Cost of sales		4330		4000
Gross profit		1370		1300
Administration cost		735		620
Operating profit		635		680
Interest		220		190
Profit before taxation		415		490
Taxation		125		147
Profit after taxation		290		343
Preference dividends	90		90	
Ordinary dividends	140	230	140	230
Retained profits		60		113

Balance sheet as at 31 December

	2006			2005		
	£000	£000	£000	£000	£000	£000
Fixed assets			5405			4880
Current assets:						
Stock		900			880	
Debtors		460			460	
Cash		55			60	
		1415			1400	
Creditors due within one year:						
Trade creditors	425			190		
Bank	nil			800		
Taxation	155			110		
Dividends	230			230		
		810			1330	
Net current assets			605			70
Total assets less current liabilities			6010			4950
Creditors due after one year:						
Debentures		1100			1100	
Bank loan		1000			0	
			2100			1100
			3910			3850
Capital and reserves:						
Ordinary shares, par value 100 pence			1500			1500
Preference shares, par value 100 pence			1000			1000
Share premium			500			500
Reserves			910			850
			3910			3850

Annual depreciation: £410 000 (2006) and 380 000 (2005)
Debenture market price: £102 (2006) and £98 (2005)
Ordinary share price: 135 pence (2006) and 220 pence (2005)

Vignette 2.1

If only investors could compare like with like

There is currently intense debate over proposed new rules to implement international harmonisation of annual accounting, management and audit reporting. But take the trouble to look at leading international and national companies, in all sectors, and you will see there are still significant reporting differences and shortcomings for both interim and annual reports that have generated scant discussion.

Differences in reporting standards and procedures are ever more important because of the internationalisation of capital markets. It is increasingly unacceptable that investors in continental Western Europe, the UK and the US are not similarly well informed.

US-quoted companies publish informative quarterly reports that are by and large better than those of Europe-listed companies. The American quarterly reports show gross margins, trade receivables (trade debtors) and trade payables (trade creditors); such information is unusual in interim reports of UK companies and patchy among those of continental Europeans.

When quarterly or half-yearly detailed working capital figures are published, users can assess much more effectively the company's ongoing performance and can make better judgments about any year-end 'window dressing' of figures. Such analysis, in turn, permits easier assessment of asset leverage and annual operating cash flows, which can influence performance bonuses.

In Europe, lack of interim information about costs of goods for big companies such as Cadbury-Schweppes, Nestlé and Unilever becomes particularly unfortunate for investors, analysts, bankers and those interested in macroeconomic performance. This is especially so when costs of raw materials, packaging or transport are volatile.

Cost-of-goods figures are key to assessing inflationary pressures. Their absence allows companies to disguise changes in their operating profit by temporarily reducing spending on marketing and other variable costs.

More frequent cost-of-sales information would be helpful for central banks, governments and equity and bond investors.

Hooray for the US – except that North American corporate performance reporting falls short of European practice in some important respects. While there is a wealth of information on the cost of capital and the effectiveness of management, there is no information on the cost of labour. This lack prevents effective comparisons of labour productivity trends among companies with similar activities. The travails of the US motor and air transport industries might have been identified earlier had adequate labour information been publicly available earlier.

The sparsity of employment statistics for Wal-Mart, by far the world's biggest retailer, is a telling example. The group reports that it has 1.8m employees, of whom 500,000 are abroad, but gives no information on full-time equivalents. Nor are employment costs published – although Asda, its UK subsidiary, provides full-time equivalent numbers and their costs. Leading European retailers, such as Metro of Germany and UK-based Tesco, publish comprehensive information.

Another difference in reporting is that UK-quoted companies publish detailed information on management rewards. In the US, such information is shown only in the proxy statement, a separate report.

There has been an exponential increase in US chief executives' pay, which rose 30 per cent in 2004, according to Corporate Library, a governance watchdog. Such rises have led the US Securities and Exchange Commission to press for pay to be covered in annual reports. There is even pressure in the US to have shareholder advisory votes on pay, which is now UK practice.

Success for the SEC would raise US practice to levels in the UK, which is well ahead of reporting in most of Western Europe.

Just as important as the inadequacy of some of the information published by quoted companies is the near total absence of financial information for huge private US and Canadian companies, including subsidiaries of quoted companies. It is surely unacceptable that there is such a big information lacuna regarding the performance of huge swaths of private manufacturing and financial groups, which play leading roles in the North American economy. They have sales of many billions and employ tens of thousands. Similar companies in France, Germany and the UK are required by law to file comprehensive financial statements in the public domain. Such information about US private companies would enhance competition at home and abroad.

Comparable key figures in reports are crucial for the proper allocation of resources.

Source: Martin Simons, FT.com, 13 April 2006. Reprinted with permission.

Profit, EBITDA and cash

In assessing financial performance, it is important to consider the quality of the returns generated by companies. While useful information is provided by the level of profit reported in the financial statements of a company, whether before or after tax, corporate finance tends to focus on cash flows. There is a fundamental difference between accounting profit and cash flows because accounting profit is prepared by applying *accruals accounting* and *accounting policies*. An example of the significance of accruals accounting here is that reported profit includes credit sales, which become cash flows only when debtors settle their accounts. The significance of accounting policies is that companies with similar cash flows can report different accounting profits if their accounting policies are different.

In order to remedy some of the deficiencies of accounting profit, it has become increasingly common for companies and analysts to consider earnings before interest, tax, depreciation and amortisation (EBITDA). Since EBITDA is in essence operating profit excluding non-cash expenses such as depreciation and amortisation (a regular provision writing down intangible assets such as goodwill), it is similar to cash flow from operating activities, ignoring the effect of changes in working capital. As a measure of financial performance, EBITDA eliminates the effects of financing and capital expenditure, and hence can indicate trends in sustainable profitability. EBITDA can be compared with capital employed, as well as indicating the cash flow available to meet interest payments. It has also been suggested that EBITDA can be compared with the market value of equity plus debt, less working capital (Rutterford 1998).

EBITDA can be criticised as a measure of cash flow since it ignores the fact that earnings and revenue are not cash flows. Simply adding back interest, depreciation and amortisation will not turn earnings back into cash. EBITDA also ignores the contribution to cash flow made by changes in working capital.

2.4.1 The need for benchmarks

When analysing financial performance, it is important to recognise that performance measures and financial ratios in isolation have little significance. In order to interpret the meaning of performance measures and ratios, they must be compared against appropriate benchmarks, of which the following are examples:

- financial targets set by a company's strategic plan, e.g. a target return on capital employed or economic profit;
- performance measures and ratios of companies engaged in similar business activities;
- average performance measures and ratios for the company's operations, i.e. sector averages;
- performance measures and ratios for the company from previous years, adjusted for inflation if necessary.

The benchmarks selected will depend on the purpose of the analysis. Comparing the calculated performance measures or ratios against appropriate benchmarks is not an end in itself – there is still the difficult task of interpreting or explaining any differences found.

2.4.2 Categories of ratios

When using ratios for analysing financial performance, computation and interpretation is assisted if the analyst uses some sort of analytical framework. Weetman (1999) suggests that a systematic approach to ratio analysis should initially establish a broad picture, before focusing on areas of concern. A systematic approach to ratio analysis is also facilitated by using a *ratio pyramid*. We have divided ratios into groups or categories which are linked to particular areas of concern. There is widespread agreement on the main ratios included in each category, even though the same category may be given different names by different authors.

- *Profitability ratios*: return on capital employed, net profit margin, net asset turnover, gross profit margin, etc.
- *Activity ratios*: debtor days, creditor days, stock days, sales/net current assets, etc. These ratios are important in the management of working capital.
- *Liquidity ratios*: current ratio, quick ratio, etc.
- *Gearing ratios*: capital gearing ratio, debt/equity ratio, interest cover, etc. These ratios are measures of financial risk (*see* Section 9.7).
- *Investor ratios*: return on equity, dividend per share, earnings per share, dividend cover, price/earnings ratio, payout ratio, dividend yield, earnings yield, etc.

A detailed introduction to ratio analysis can be found in Fraser and Ormiston (2004). Because some ratios can be defined in different ways, it is important when comparing ratios to make sure that they have been calculated on a similar basis. The golden rule is *always* to compare like with like.

The ratios discussed in the following sections are illustrated by calculations based on the accounts of Boater plc in Exhibit 2.4.

2.4.3 Profitability ratios

Profitability ratios indicate how successful the managers of a company have been in generating profit. Return on capital employed is often referred to as the *primary ratio*.

Return on capital employed (ROCE)

$$\frac{\text{Profit before interest and tax} \times 100}{\text{Capital employed}}$$

This ratio relates the overall profitability of a company to the finance used to generate it. It is also the product of net profit margin and asset turnover:

$$\text{ROCE} = \text{Net profit margin} \times \text{Asset turnover}$$

Profit before interest and tax is often called *operating profit*, as in Exhibit 2.4. The meaning of *capital employed* can cause confusion, but it is simply *total assets less current liabilities* (or shareholders' funds plus long-term debt, which has a similar meaning). Another definition of capital employed with the same meaning is *fixed assets plus net working capital*. This ratio is clearly sensitive to investment in fixed assets, to the age of fixed assets (since older assets will have depreciated more than young ones) and to when assets were last revalued. There is a close link between ROCE and accounting rate of return (*see* Section 6.2). For Boater plc:

$$\text{ROCE (2005)} = 100 \times (680/4950) = 13.7\%$$
$$\text{ROCE (2006)} = 100 \times (635/6010) = 10.6\%$$

Net profit margin

$$\frac{\text{Profit before interest and tax} \times 100}{\text{Sales or turnover}}$$

This ratio, also called *operating profit margin*, indicates the efficiency with which costs have been controlled in generating profit from sales. It does not distinguish between operating costs, administrative costs and distribution costs. A fall in ROCE may be due to a fall in net profit margin, in which case further investigation may determine whether an increased cost or a fall in profit margin is the cause. For Boater plc:

$$\text{Net profit margin (2005)} = 100 \times (680/5300) = 12.8\%$$
$$\text{Net profit margin (2006)} = 100 \times (635/5700) = 11.1\%$$

Net asset turnover

$$\frac{\text{Sales or turnover}}{\text{Capital employed}}$$

Capital employed is defined here in the same way as for ROCE, i.e. *total assets less current liabilities*, and so the asset turnover ratio is also sensitive to fixed asset values. This ratio gives a guide to productive efficiency, i.e. how well assets have been used in generating sales. A fall in ROCE may be due to a fall in asset turnover rather than a fall in net profit margin. For Boater plc:

$$\text{Asset turnover (2005)} = 5300/4950 = 1.07 \text{ times}$$
$$\text{Asset turnover (2006)} = 5700/6010 = 0.95 \text{ times}$$

Gross profit margin

$$\frac{\text{Gross profit} \times 100}{\text{Sales or turnover}}$$

This ratio shows how well costs of production have been controlled, as opposed to distribution costs and administration costs. For Boater plc:

$$\text{Gross profit margin (2005)} = 100 \times (1300/5300) = 24.5\%$$
$$\text{Gross profit margin (2006)} = 100 \times (1370/5700) = 24.0\%$$

EBITDA/capital employed

$$\frac{\text{EBITDA} \times 100}{\text{Capital employed}}$$

This ratio relates earnings before interest, tax, depreciation and amortisation to the equity and debt finance used to generate it. The meaning of *capital employed* is as for ROCE, i.e. *total assets less current liabilities*. For Boater plc:

$$\text{EBITDA (2005)} = (680 + 380) = £1\,060\,000$$
$$\text{EBITDA (2006)} = (635 + 410) = £1\,045\,000$$

$$\text{EBITDA/capital employed (2005)} = 100 \times (1060/4950) = 21.4\%$$
$$\text{EBITDA/capital employed (2006)} = 100 \times (1045/6010) = 17.4\%$$

2.4.4 Activity ratios

Activity ratios show how efficiently a company has managed short-term assets and liabilities, i.e. working capital, and they are closely linked to the liquidity ratios. With each ratio, the average value for the year should be used (e.g. average level of debtors should be used in calculating the debtors' ratio), but it is common for the year-end value to be used in order to obtain figures for comparative purposes. As ratios must be calculated on a consistent basis, either year-end values or average values must be used throughout your analysis.

Debtor days or debtors' ratio

$$\frac{\text{Debtors} \times 365}{\text{Credit sales}}$$

The value of credit sales is usually not available and it is common for sales or turnover to be used as a substitute. The debtor days ratio gives the average period of credit being taken by customers. If it is compared with a company's allowed credit period, it can give an indication of the efficiency of debtor administration (*see* Section 3.7). For Boater plc:

$$\text{Debtor days (2005)} = 365 \times (460/5300) = 32 \text{ days}$$
$$\text{Debtor days (2006)} = 365 \times (460/5700) = 29 \text{ days}$$

Creditor days or creditors' ratio

$$\frac{\text{Trade creditors} \times 365}{\text{Cost of sales}}$$

Trade creditors should be compared with credit purchases, but as this information is not always available, cost of sales is often used instead. The creditor days ratio gives the average time taken for suppliers of goods and services to receive payment. For Boater plc:

$$\text{Creditor days (2005)} = 365 \times (190/4000) = 17 \text{ days}$$
$$\text{Creditor days (2006)} = 365 \times (425/4330) = 36 \text{ days}$$

Stock days or stock turnover

$$\frac{\text{Stock or inventory} \times 365}{\text{Cost of sales}}$$

This ratio shows how long it takes for a company to turn its stocks into sales. Several other ratios can be calculated by separating the total stock figure into its component parts, i.e. raw materials, work-in-progress and finished goods (*see* Section 3.3). The shorter the stock days ratio, the lower the cost to the company of holding stock. The value of this ratio is very dependent on the need for stock and so will vary significantly depending on the nature of a company's business (*see* Section 3.5). For Boater plc:

$$\text{Stock days (2005)} = 365 \times (880/4000) = 80 \text{ days}$$
$$\text{Stock days (2006)} = 365 \times (900/4330) = 76 \text{ days}$$

Cash conversion cycle

The cash conversion cycle (also called the operating cycle or working capital cycle) is found by adding stock days and debtor days and then subtracting creditor days. It indicates the period of time for which working capital financing is needed (*see* Section 3.3). The longer the cash conversion cycle, the higher the investment in working capital. For Boater plc:

$$\text{Cash conversion cycle (2005)} = 32 \text{ days} + 80 \text{ days} - 17 \text{ days} = 95 \text{ days}$$
$$\text{Cash conversion cycle (2006)} = 29 \text{ days} + 76 \text{ days} - 36 \text{ days} = 69 \text{ days}$$

Fixed asset turnover

Net asset turnover (see above) is based on capital employed, but an alternative view of asset use can be found by separating fixed assets from capital employed.

$$\frac{\text{Sales or turnover}}{\text{Fixed assets}}$$

Fixed asset turnover indicates the sales being generated by the fixed asset base of a company. Like ROCE, it is sensitive to the acquisition, age and valuation of fixed assets. For Boater plc:

$$\text{Fixed asset turnover (2005)} = 5300/4880 = 1.09 \text{ times}$$
$$\text{Fixed asset turnover (2006)} = 5700/5405 = 1.05 \text{ times}$$

Sales/net current assets

The companion ratio to fixed asset turnover compares sales to net current assets (net working capital).

$$\frac{\text{Sales or turnover}}{\text{Net current assets}}$$

This ratio shows the level of working capital supporting sales. Working capital must increase in line with sales if undercapitalisation is to be avoided (*see* Section 3.4) and so this ratio can be used to forecast the level of working capital needed for a given level of sales when projecting financial statements. For Boater plc:

$$\text{Sales/net working capital (2005)} = 5300/(880 + 460 - 190) = 4.6 \text{ times}$$
$$\text{Sales/net working capital (2006)} = 5700/(900 + 460 - 425) = 6.1 \text{ times}$$

2.4.5 Liquidity ratios

Current ratio

$$\frac{\text{Current assets}}{\text{Current liabilities}}$$

This ratio measures a company's ability to meet its financial obligations as they fall due. It is often said that the current ratio should be around two, but what is normal will vary from industry to industry: sector averages are a better guide than a rule of thumb. For Boater plc:

$$\text{Current ratio (2005)} = 1400/1330 = 1.1 \text{ times}$$
$$\text{Current ratio (2006)} = 1415/810 = 1.8 \text{ times}$$

Quick ratio

$$\frac{\text{Current assets less stock}}{\text{Current liabilities}}$$

It is argued that the current ratio may overstate the ability to meet financial obligations because it includes stock in the numerator. This argument has merit if it takes more than a short time to convert stock into sales, i.e. if the stock days ratio is not small. It is not true, however, where stock is turned over quickly and where sales are mainly on a cash or near-cash basis, for example in the retail food trade. The quick ratio compares liquid current assets with short-term liabilities. While a common rule of thumb is that it should be close to one, in practice the sector average value should be used as a guide. For Boater plc:

$$\text{Quick ratio (2005)} = (1400 - 880)/1330 = 0.4 \text{ times}$$
$$\text{Quick ratio (2006)} = (1415 - 900)/810 = 0.6 \text{ times}$$

2.4.6 Gearing ratios

Gearing ratios or leverage ratios relate to how a company is financed with respect to debt and equity and can be used to assess the financial risk that arises with increasing debt (*see* Section 9.7 for a more detailed discussion of gearing and its implications).

Capital gearing ratio

$$\frac{\text{Long-term debt} \times 100}{\text{Capital employed}}$$

The purpose of this ratio is to show the proportion of debt finance used by a company. When comparing calculated values to benchmarks it is essential to confirm that the same method of calculation is used because other definitions of this ratio are found. One alternative replaces long-term debt capital with *prior charge capital*, which includes preference shares as well as debt.

A company may be thought *highly geared* if capital gearing is greater than 50 per cent using book values for debt and equity, but this is only a rule of thumb. For Boater plc:

$$\text{Capital gearing (2005)} = 100 \times (1100/4950) = 22.2\%$$
$$\text{Capital gearing (2006)} = 100 \times (2100/6010) = 35.0\%$$

It is usual in corporate finance to calculate gearing using market values for debt and equity. Reserves are not included in the calculation of the market value of equity. Note also that the 2006 market value of debt is the sum of the market value of the debentures and the book value of the bank loan because bank loans have no market value. For Boater plc:

Market value of equity (2005) = 1 500 000 × 2.2 = £3 300 000
Market value of equity (2006) = 1 500 000 × 1.35 = £2 025 000
Market value of debentures (2005) = 1 100 000 × 98/100 = £1 078 000
Market value of debentures (2006) = 1 100 000 × 102/100 = £1 122 000
Market value of debt (2006) = 1 122 000 + 1 000 000 = £2 122 000
Capital gearing (2005) = 100 × (1078/(1078 + 3300)) = 24.6%
Capital gearing (2006) = 100 × (2122/(2122 + 2025)) = 51.2%

Debt/equity ratio

$$\frac{\text{Long-term debt} \times 100}{\text{Share capital and reserves}}$$

This ratio serves a similar purpose to capital gearing. A company could be said to be highly geared if its debt/equity ratio were greater than 100 per cent using book values, but again this is only a rule of thumb. For Boater plc:

Debt/equity ratio (2005) = 100 × (1100/3850) = 28.6%
Debt/equity ratio (2006) = 100 × (2100/3910) = 53.7%

Using market values:

Debt/equity ratio (2005) = 100 × (1078/3300) = 32.7%
Debt/equity ratio (2006) = 100 × (2122/2025) = 104.8%

Interest cover and interest gearing

$$\frac{\text{Profit before interest and tax}}{\text{Interest charges}}$$

Interest cover shows how many times a company can cover its current interest payments out of current profits and indicates whether servicing debt may be a problem. An interest cover of more than seven times is usually regarded as safe, and an interest cover of more than three times as acceptable. These are only rules of thumb, however, and during periods of low and stable interest rates, lower levels of interest cover may be deemed acceptable. Interest cover is a clearer indication of financial distress than either capital gearing or the debt/equity ratio, since inability to meet interest payments will lead to corporate failure no matter what the level of gearing may be. For Boater plc:

$$\text{Interest cover (2005)} = 680/190 = 3.6 \text{ times}$$
$$\text{Interest cover (2006)} = 635/220 = 2.9 \text{ times}$$

The inverse of interest cover is known as interest gearing or income gearing and is preferred to interest cover by some analysts. For Boater plc:

$$\text{Interest gearing (2005)} = 100 \times (190/680) = 27.9\%$$
$$\text{Interest gearing (2006)} = 100 \times (220/635) = 34.7\%$$

2.4.7 Investor ratios

Investor ratios are used in corporate finance for a variety of purposes, including assessing the effects of proposed financing (e.g. on earnings per share); valuing a target company in a takeover (e.g. using the price/earnings ratio: *see* Section 11.4.3); analysing dividend policy (e.g. using the payout ratio: *see* Section 10.6); and predicting the effect of a rights issue (e.g. using earnings yield: *see* Section 4.3.4).

Return on equity

$$\frac{\text{Earnings after tax and preference dividends}}{\text{Shareholders' funds}}$$

Whereas ROCE looks at overall return to all providers of finance, return on equity compares the earnings attributable to ordinary shareholders with the book value of their investment in the business. *Shareholders' funds* are equal to ordinary share capital plus reserves, but exclude preference share capital. For Boater plc:

$$\text{Return on equity (2005)} = 100 \times ((343 - 90)/(3850 - 1000)) = 8.9\%$$
$$\text{Return on equity (2006)} = 100 \times ((290 - 90)/(3910 - 1000)) = 6.9\%$$

Dividend per share

$$\frac{\text{Total dividend paid to ordinary shareholders}}{\text{Number of issued ordinary shares}}$$

While the total dividend paid may change from year to year, individual shareholders will expect that dividend per share will not decrease (*see* Section 10.5). For Boater plc:

$$\text{Dividend per share (2005)} = 100 \times (140/1500) = 9.3 \text{ pence}$$
$$\text{Dividend per share (2006)} = 100 \times (140/1500) = 9.3 \text{ pence}$$

Earnings per share

$$\frac{\text{Earnings after tax and preference dividends}}{\text{Number of issued ordinary shares}}$$

Earnings per share is regarded as a key ratio by stock market investors. Take care when looking at this ratio in company accounts as there are several ways it can be calculated.

These complications are beyond the scope of this book: for further discussion, see for example Weetman (1999) and Fraser and Ormiston (2004). We shall calculate earnings per share by simply using earnings attributable to ordinary shareholders, so for Boater plc:

$$\text{Earnings per share (2005)} = 100 \times ((343 - 90)/1500)) = 16.9 \text{ pence}$$
$$\text{Earnings per share (2006)} = 100 \times ((290 - 90)/1500)) = 13.3 \text{ pence}$$

Dividend cover

$$\frac{\text{Earnings per share}}{\text{Dividend per share}}$$

Dividend cover indicates how safe a company's dividend payment is by calculating how many times the total dividend is covered by current earnings. The higher the dividend cover, the more likely it is that a company can maintain or increase future dividends. For Boater plc:

$$\text{Dividend cover (2005)} = 16.9/9.3 = 1.8 \text{ times}$$
$$\text{Dividend cover (2006)} = 13.3/9.3 = 1.4 \text{ times}$$

Price/earnings ratio

$$\frac{\text{Market price per share}}{\text{Earnings per share}}$$

Like earnings per share, the price/earnings ratio (P/E ratio) is seen as a key ratio by stock market investors. It shows how much an investor is prepared to pay for a company's shares, given its current earnings per share (EPS). The ratio can therefore indicate the confidence of investors in the expected future performance of a company: the higher the P/E ratio relative to other companies, the more confident the market is that future earnings will increase. A word of caution, though: a high P/E ratio could also be due to a low EPS, perhaps due to a one-off cost in the profit and loss account. The P/E ratio can also be used to determine the value of a company, as discussed in Section 11.4.3. For Boater plc:

$$\text{Price/earnings ratio (2005)} = 220/16.9 = 13.0$$
$$\text{Price/earnings ratio (2006)} = 135/13.3 = 10.2$$

Payout ratio

$$\frac{\text{Total dividend paid to ordinary shareholders} \times 100}{\text{Earnings after tax and preference dividends}}$$

The payout ratio is often used in the analysis of dividend policy. For example, some companies may choose to pay out a fixed percentage of earnings every year and finance any investment needs not covered by retained earnings from external sources. For Boater plc:

$$\text{Payout ratio (2005)} = 100 \times (140/(343 - 90)) = 55.3\%$$
$$\text{Payout ratio (2006)} = 100 \times (140/(290 - 90)) = 70.0\%$$

Dividend yield

$$\frac{\text{Dividend per share} \times 100}{\text{Market price of share}}$$

Dividend yield gives a measure of how much an investor expects to gain in exchange for buying a given share, ignoring any capital gains that may arise. It is commonly quoted on a gross (before tax) basis in the financial press. For Boater plc, on a net (after tax) basis:

$$\text{Net dividend yield (2005)} = 100 \times (9.3/220) = 4.2\%$$
$$\text{Net dividend yield (2006)} = 100 \times (9.3/135) = 6.9\%$$

Gross dividend yield is found by 'grossing up' net dividend yield at the basic rate of income tax. Assuming a tax rate of 20 per cent, for Boater plc, on a gross (before tax) basis:

$$\text{Gross dividend yield (2005)} = 4.2 \times (100/80) = 5.3\%$$
$$\text{Gross dividend yield (2006)} = 6.9 \times (100/80) = 8.6\%$$

Earnings yield

$$\frac{\text{Earnings per share} \times 100}{\text{Market price of share}}$$

Earnings yield gives a measure of the potential return shareholders expect to receive in exchange for purchasing a given share; it is the reciprocal of the price/earnings ratio. The return is a potential one since few companies pay out all of their earnings as dividends. Earnings yield can be used as a discount rate to capitalise future earnings in order to determine the value of a company, as discussed in Section 11.4.3. For Boater plc:

$$\text{Earnings yield (2005)} = 100 \times (16.9/220) = 7.7\%$$
$$\text{Earnings yield (2006)} = 100 \times (13.3/135) = 9.8\%$$

2.4.8 Interpreting the financial ratios of Boater plc

The ratios calculated for Boater plc are summarised in Exhibit 2.5. If there had been a particular focus to this analysis, only a selection of ratios would have been calculated. For example, if the focus had been on the efficiency of working capital management, no purpose would have been served by calculating the investor ratios. What is the overall assessment of financial performance indicated by Boater's ratios? The following comments are offered as a guide to some of the issues raised in each of the ratio categories, and should be studied in conjunction with Exhibit 2.5.

Profitability

Boater's overall profitability has declined, and this is due both to a decline in turnover in relation to capital employed and to a decline in profit margins. This decline has occurred despite an increase in turnover and seems to be partly due to a substantial increase in administration costs. The decline in ROCE and EBITDA/capital employed

Exhibit 2.5	Comparative financial ratios for Boater plc		
		2006	**2005**
Return on capital employed		10.6%	13.7%
Net profit margin		11.1%	12.8%
Asset turnover		0.95 times	1.07 times
Gross profit margin		24.0%	24.5%
EBITDA/capital employed		17.4%	21.4%
Debtor days		29 days	32 days
Creditor days		36 days	17 days
Stock days		76 days	80 days
Cash conversion cycle		69 days	95 days
Fixed asset turnover		1.05 times	1.09 times
Sales/net working capital		6.1 times	4.6 times
Current ratio		1.8 times	1.1 times
Quick ratio		0.6 times	0.4 times
Capital gearing (book value)		35.0%	22.2%
Capital gearing (market value)		51.2%	24.6%
Debt/equity ratio (book value)		53.7%	28.6%
Debt/equity ratio (market value)		104.8%	32.7%
Interest cover		2.9 times	3.6 times
Interest gearing		34.7%	27.9%
Return on equity		6.9%	8.9%
Dividend per share		9.3 pence	9.3 pence
Earnings per share		13.3 pence	16.9 pence
Dividend cover		1.4 times	1.8 times
Price/earnings ratio		10.2	13.0
Payout ratio		70.0 %	55.3%
Net dividend yield		6.9%	4.2%
Gross dividend yield		8.6%	5.3%
Earnings yield		9.8%	7.7%

can also be linked to replacement of the overdraft with a bank loan and substantial investment in fixed assets.

Activity and liquidity

The exchange of the overdraft for a long-term bank loan has improved both the current ratio and the quick ratio, but cash reserves have fallen. There has been little change in debtor days or stock days, but creditor days have more than doubled. Although Boater is no longer heavily reliant on an overdraft for working capital finance, the company has increased its dependence on trade creditors as a source of short-term finance.

Gearing and risk

The new loan has increased gearing substantially. Although gearing does not seem to be risky using book values, the change in gearing using market values is quite large. Interest cover now looks to be low and income gearing is increasing owing to the fall in operating profit and the increase in interest payments.

Investor interest

Even though earnings have fallen, the dividend has been maintained and, since the share price has fallen, dividend yield has increased as a result. The decrease in price/earnings ratio may indicate that investors feel that the company is unlikely to improve in the future.

2.4.9 Problems with ratio analysis

When using ratio analysis to evaluate financial performance, you must treat the results with caution for a number of reasons. One problem is that the balance sheet relates to a company's position on one day of the year. If the balance sheet had been prepared three months earlier, a different picture might have been presented and key financial ratios might have had different values. Tax payable and dividends due might not have been included in current liabilities, for example, and the current ratio could have looked much healthier. Should we exclude such temporary items when calculating working capital ratios?

It can be difficult to find a similar company as a basis for intercompany comparisons. No two companies are identical in every respect and so differences in commercial activity must be allowed for. As a minimum, differences in accounting policies should be considered.

The reliability of ratio analysis in the analysis of financial performance naturally depends on the reliability of the accounting information on which it is based. Financial statements have become increasingly complex and it is not easy to determine if *creative accounting* has taken place. Company accounting has been described as 'a jungle with many species of animal – some benign, some carnivorous – and its own rules' (Smith 1996). Care must be taken to identify *off-balance-sheet financing* or any complex financial instruments which may distort a company's true financial position. As shown by occasional high profile corporate failures, identifying the financial position of a company can be difficult, even for experts.

Ratio analysis, in conclusion, must be regarded as only the beginning of the analysis of financial performance, serving mainly to raise questions which require deeper investigation before understanding begins to appear. Shareholders, investors and company managers use ratio analysis as only one of many sources of information to assist them in making decisions.

2.4.10 Economic profit and economic value added (EVA®)

It has long been recognised that reported earnings are an incomplete measure of company performance, since positive earnings do not guarantee that a company is increasing shareholder wealth. What is missing is an opportunity cost for the capital employed in the business, since a company must earn at least the average required rate of return on its capital employed if it is going to create an increase in value for its shareholders. A performance measure which addresses this deficiency in reported earnings is economic profit, which can be defined as operating profit after tax less a cost of capital charge on capital employed.

$$\text{Economic profit} = (\text{Operating profit} \times (1 - t)) - (K_0 \times \text{CE})$$

where: t = company taxation rate
K_0 = average rate of return required by investors
CE = book value of capital employed

An almost identical concept which is familiar to management accountants is residual income, defined as controllable contribution less a cost of capital charge on controllable investment (Drury 2004), although contribution here is before taxation.

Economic profit as defined above corrects the deficiency in earnings of failing to allow for a charge on capital employed, but it still relies on accounting data, which is open to subjective adjustment and manipulation in its preparation. There is also the problem that the book value of capital employed fails to capture accurately the capital invested in a company. For example, research and development costs produce benefits for a company over several years, but are treated as an annual expense rather than a balance sheet asset. We cannot rely on a published balance sheet to give us an accurate measure of the tangible and intangible capital invested in a company. The difficulty of extracting a fair value for invested capital from financial statements is addressed by the topical performance measure known as EVA.

EVA was trademarked and introduced by the Stern Stewart company in the 1990s with the objective of providing an overall measure of company performance that would focus managers' attention on the drivers that lead to the creation of shareholder wealth. It refined and amended the information used in the calculation of economic profit so that the two terms have become largely synonymous (Hawawini and Viallet 2002). In fact, EVA can be seen as an attempt to measure a company's economic profit rather than its accounting profit (Keown et al. 2003). EVA calculates an adjusted value for invested capital by making rule-based changes to the book value of capital employed. For example, it capitalises expenditure on marketing and research and development, thereby treating these expenses as assets and spreading their costs over the periods benefiting from them. EVA also calculates an adjusted value for operating profit by making complementary changes to those it makes to the value of invested capital. For example, research and development expenses included in accounting profit must be reduced in order to balance the amount included in invested capital. By making these changes to invested capital and operating profit after tax, EVA corrects the effect of financial accounting rules that ignore the ways a company creates value for shareholders. EVA can be defined as:

$$\text{EVA} = (\text{AOP} \times (1 - t)) - (\text{WACC} \times \text{AVIC})$$

where: AOP   = adjusted operating profit
       t = company taxation rate
       WACC = weighted average cost of capital (*see* Section 9.2)
       AVIC   = adjusted value of invested capital

Alternatively:

$$EVA = (RAVIC - WACC) \times AVIC$$

where: RAVIC = required after-tax return on adjusted value of invested capital
       WACC = weighted average cost of capital
       AVIC   = adjusted value of invested capital

While open to criticism on the basis of the subjectivity of some of the adjustments it makes to accounting information, many large organisations have adopted EVA and some positive results have been claimed from its use as a performance measure (Leahy 2000).

The usefulness of EVA lies in the attention it directs towards the *drivers* of shareholder value creation. Reflecting on the definition of EVA points to several ways in which company managers can seek to generate increased value for shareholders. This leads on to the extensive topic of value management, which is beyond the scope of this book. Briefly, the value drivers that managers may be able to influence can be seen in the following value-creating strategies:

- look for ways to increase net operating profit after tax without increasing the amount of capital invested in the company;
- undertake investment projects which are expected to generate returns in excess of the company's cost of capital;
- take steps to reduce the opportunity cost of the capital invested in the company, either by reducing the company's cost of capital or by reducing the amount of invested capital.

You will find it useful to think of examples of how these value-creating strategies can be applied in practice. For example, net operating profit after tax can be increased by eliminating unnecessary costs. Undertaking projects which generate returns in excess of the company's cost of capital can be achieved by using net present value (NPV) and internal rate of return (IRR) as investment appraisal methods (*see* Sections 6.3 and 6.4). A company's cost of capital can be reduced by the sensible use of debt (*see* Section 9.15). The amount of invested capital can be reduced by disposing of unwanted assets and by returning unwanted cash to shareholders via a share repurchase scheme (*see* Section 10.7.2).

2.5 Conclusion

In this chapter, we have looked at some key aspects of the financing decision in corporate finance – the balance between internal and external finance, the different sources of finance available to a company, the importance of the capital markets – and we have also discussed at some length the key topic of capital market efficiency. The debate about market efficiency is a continuing one and it is recommended that you consider carefully the implications of market efficiency for corporate finance theory as you continue your studies.

The analysis of financial performance is a key activity providing financial information for a wide range of user groups, and we considered both ratio analysis and a currently topical performance measure, economic value added (EVA). Later chapters will discuss particular ratios in more detail, especially those concerned with working capital and gearing.

Key points

1 An efficient financing policy raises necessary funds at the required time and at the lowest cost.

2 Internal finance or retained earnings must not be confused with retained profit as only cash can be invested. Retained earnings are a major source of funds for investment.

3 The mix of internal and external finance depends on the amount of finance needed, the cash flow from existing operations, the opportunity cost of retained earnings, the cost and availability of external finance and the company's dividend policy.

4 There are many kinds of external finance available to a company, including ordinary shares, preference shares, debentures, loan stock and convertible bonds.

5 New issues of equity and debt are made in the primary market, while securities already in issue are traded in the secondary market, which is a source of pricing information.

6 Smaller companies not ready for the full market can obtain a listing on the Alternative Investment Market (AIM).

7 An efficient market needs operational efficiency, allocational efficiency and pricing efficiency: a perfect market requires the absence of factors inhibiting buying and selling, identical expectations of participants, free entry and exit, free and readily available information, and a large number of buyers and sellers, none of whom dominates.

8 Operational efficiency means that transaction costs should be low and sales executed quickly. Pricing efficiency means that share prices fully and fairly reflect all relevant information and so are fair prices. Allocational efficiency means that capital markets allocate funds to their most productive use.

9 Markets are weak form efficient if share prices reflect all past price movements. In such a market, abnormal returns cannot be made by studying past share price movements. Research suggests capital markets are weak form efficient.

10 The random walk hypothesis suggests there is no connection between movements in share price in successive periods. A substantial amount of research supports this view. Weak form tests include serial correlation tests, run tests and filter tests.

11 Markets are semi-strong form efficient if share prices reflect all past information and all publicly available information. In such a market, abnormal returns cannot be made by studying available company information. Research suggests capital markets are to a large extent semi-strong form efficient.

12 Tests for semi-strong form efficiency look at the speed and accuracy of share price movements to new information (event studies).

13 Markets are strong form efficient if share prices reflect *all* information. In such a market, no one can make abnormal returns. While capital markets are not totally strong form efficient, the inefficiency is perhaps limited and research suggests the UK and US stock markets have a high degree of efficiency.

14 Strong form efficiency can only be tested indirectly, for example by investigating whether fund managers can regularly make above-average returns.

15 The implications of capital market efficiency for investors are that research is pointless and no bargains exist.

16 The implications of capital market efficiency for companies are that share prices correctly value a company, manipulation of accounts is pointless and the timing of new issues is irrelevant.

17 Technical analysts try to predict share prices by studying their historical movements, while fundamental analysts look for the fundamental value of a share. Neither activity is worthwhile (theoretically) in a semi-strong form efficient market.

18 A significant body of research has examined anomalies in share price behaviour, such as calendar effects, size anomalies and value effects.

19 Behavioural finance seeks to understand the market implications of the psychological factors underlying investor decisions and has had some success explaining anomalies.

20 Shareholders, investors and financial managers can use analysis of financial performance to assist them in their decisions.

21 To remedy perceived deficiencies in accounting profit, reporting of earnings before interest, tax, depreciation and amortisation (EBITDA) has become more common.

22 Performance measures and ratios mean little in isolation, but must be compared with benchmarks such as financial targets, performance measures and ratios of similar companies, sector averages, or performance measures and ratios from previous years.

23 A systematic approach to ratio analysis could look at ratios relating to profitability, activity, liquidity, gearing and investment.

24 Problems with ratio analysis include the following: balance sheet figures are *single-point* values; similar companies for comparison are hard to find; accounting policies may differ between companies; creative accounting may distort financial statements; and complex financing methods can make accounts difficult to interpret.

25 The terms 'economic profit' and 'economic value added' (EVA) have a similar meaning. EVA is the difference between operating profit after tax and a cost of capital charge on invested capital. Many large companies use EVA.

26 EVA focuses attention on the drivers of shareholder value creation. Financial managers should seek to increase net operating profit, undertake projects with a return greater than the cost of capital, and reduce the opportunity cost and amount of invested capital.

Self-test questions

Answers to these questions can be found on pages 428–30.

1 Describe the factors that influence the relative proportions of internal and external finance used in capital investment.

2 What is the relevance of the efficient market hypothesis for the financial manager?

3 Which of the following statements about the efficient market hypothesis is *not* correct?

  (a) If the stock market shows weak form efficiency, chartists cannot make consistent abnormal returns.

  (b) If the market is strong form efficient, only people with insider information can beat the market.

  (c) In a semi-strong form efficient market, fundamental analysis will not bring abnormal returns.

  (d) If the market is semi-strong form efficient, all past and current publicly available information is reflected in the share price.

  (e) If the market is weak form efficient, all historical information about a share is reflected in its current market price.

4 Explain the meaning of the following terms: allocational efficiency, pricing efficiency and operational efficiency.

5 Why is it difficult to test for strong form efficiency?

6 Describe three anomalies in share price behaviour.

7 Describe benchmarks that can be used when assessing financial performance.

8 Describe the five categories of ratios, list and define the ratios in each category, and, without referring to the calculations in the text, calculate each ratio for Boater plc.

9 What are the potential problems associated with using ratio analysis to analyse the financial health and performance of companies?

10 Explain the meaning of economic value added (EVA). How can EVA help financial managers to create value for shareholders?

Questions for review

Answers to these questions can be found on pages 430–2. Questions with an asterisk (*) are at an intermediate level.

1 Distinguish between the primary and secondary capital markets in the UK and discuss the role played by these markets in corporate finance. What are the desirable features of primary and secondary capital markets?

2* While there is considerable evidence supporting the efficient market hypothesis, it has been suggested that this evidence shows only that it is not possible to prove that capital markets are inefficient. Recent research has explored anomalies in share price behaviour. Briefly describe some of these anomalies and suggest possible explanations.

3 The following financial statements are extracts from the accounts of Hoult Ltd:

Profit and loss accounts for years ending 31 December

	Year 1	Year 2	Year 3
	£000	£000	£000
Sales	960	1080	1220
Cost of sales	670	780	885
Gross profit	290	300	335
Administration expenses	260	270	302
Operating profit	30	30	33
Interest	13	14	18
Profit before taxation	17	16	15
Taxation	2	1	1
Profit after taxation	15	15	14
Dividends	0	0	4
Retained profit	15	15	10

Balance sheets for years to 31 December

	Year 1		Year 2		Year 3	
	£000	£000	£000	£000	£000	£000
Net fixed assets		160		120		100
Current assets:						
Stock	200		210		225	
Debtors	160		180		250	
Cash	0		0		0	
	360		390		475	

Balance sheets for years to 31 December

	Year 1		Year 2		Year 3	
	£000	£000	£000	£000	£000	£000
Current liabilities:						
Trade creditors	75		80		145	
Overdraft	70		80		110	
	145		160		255	
Net current assets		215		230		220
Total assets less current liabilities		375		350		320
8% debentures		120		80		40
		255		270		280
Capital and reserves:						
Ordinary shares		160		160		160
Profit and loss		95		110		120
		255		270		280

Annual depreciation was £18000 in year 1, £13000 in year 2 and £11000 in year 3. The 8 per cent debentures are redeemable in instalments and the final instalment is due in year 4.

The finance director is concerned about rising short-term interest rates and the poor liquidity of Hoult Ltd. After calculating appropriate ratios, prepare a report that comments on the recent performance and financial health of Hoult Ltd.

4 Comment on the following statement:
'It is not possible to test whether the capital markets are strong form efficient. In fact, the existence of insider trading proves otherwise.'

5* Comment on the following statement:
'Ratio analysis using financial statements is pointless. Only economic value added (EVA) gives a true measure of the financial performance of a company.'

Questions for discussion

Questions with an asterisk (*) are at an advanced level.

1* Dayton has asked you for advice about his investment portfolio. He is considering buying shares in companies listed on the Alternative Investment Market. Green, a friend of Dayton, has told him he should invest only in shares that are listed on an efficient capital market as otherwise he cannot be sure he is paying a fair price. Dayton has explained to you that he is not sure what an 'efficient' capital market is.

(a) Explain to Dayton what characteristics are usually required to be present for a market to be described as efficient.

(b) Discuss whether the Alternative Investment Market is considered to be an efficient market.

(c) Discuss the extent to which research has shown capital markets to be efficient.

2 Critically discuss the following statements about stock market efficiency:

(a) The weak form of the efficient market hypothesis implies that it is possible for an investor to generate abnormal returns by analysing changes in past share prices.

(b) The semi-strong form of the efficient market hypothesis implies that it is possible for an investor to earn superior returns by studying company accounts, newspapers and investment journals, or by purchasing reports from market analysts.

(c) The strong form of the efficient market hypothesis implies that, since security prices reflect all available information, there is no way investors can gain abnormal returns.

3 Discuss the importance of the efficient market hypothesis to the following parties:

(a) shareholders concerned about the maximisation of their wealth;

(b) corporate financial managers making capital investment decisions;

(c) investors analysing the annual reports of listed companies.

4* Mr Quilt has been attending a conference on market efficiency organised by his stockbroker. He prides himself on being a 'self-made man' and likes to boast that he has succeeded in business without having the benefit of a university education. His lack of education, however, meant that he was puzzled by some of the claims made by speakers at the conference. He has asked you, as his finance director, to help him to understand these matters. Critically discuss the following claims that Mr Quilt says were made by speakers at the conference.

(a) 'Pricing efficiency is the only kind of efficiency that is important in an analysis of stock market efficiency.'

(b) 'Only if stock markets are efficient is maximisation of shareholder wealth acceptable as a practical objective for financial managers.'

(c) 'Empirical research has shown again and again that capital markets are efficient.'

References

Alexander, S. (1961) 'Price movements in speculative markets: trends or random walks', *Industrial Management Review*, May, pp. 7–26.

Ball, R. and Brown, P. (1968) 'An empirical evaluation of accounting income numbers', *Journal of Accounting Research*, Autumn, pp. 159–78.

Barberis, N. and Thaler, R. (2002) 'A survey of behavioral finance', *Social Science Research Network Economic Library*, available at http://ssrn.com

Beechey, M., Gruen, D. and Vickery, J. (2000) 'The efficient market hypothesis: a survey', Research Discussion Paper, Economic Research Department, Reserve Bank of Australia.

De Bondt, W. and Thaler, R. (1985) 'Does the stock market overreact?', *Journal of Finance*, Vol. 40, pp. 793–805.

Dimson, E. and Marsh, P. (1986) 'Event study methodologies and the size effect: the case of UK press recommendations', *Journal of Financial Economics*, Vol. 17, No. 1, pp. 113–42.

Dixon, R. and Holmes, P. (1992) *Financial Markets: An Introduction*, London: Chapman & Hall.

Drury, C. (2004) *Management and Cost Accounting*, 6th edn, London: Thomson Learning Business Press.

Fama, E. (1965) 'The behaviour of stock market prices', *Journal of Business*, January, pp. 34–106.

Fama, E. (1970) 'Efficient capital markets: a review of theory and empirical work', *Journal of Finance*, Vol. 25, pp. 383–417.

Fama, E. (1991) 'Efficient capital markets: II', *Journal of Finance*, Vol. 46, pp. 1575–617.

Fama, E. (1998) 'Market efficiency, long-term returns and behavioural finance', *Journal of Financial Economics*, Vol. 49, pp. 283–306.

Fama, E., Fisher, L., Jensen, M. and Roll, R. (1969) 'The adjustment of stock prices to new information', *International Economic Review*, Vol. 10, February, pp. 1–21.

Firth, M. (1972) 'The performance of share recommendations made by investment analysts and the effects on market efficiency', *Journal of Business Finance*, Summer, pp. 58–67.

Franks, J., Broyles, J. and Hecht, M. (1977) 'An industry study of the profitability of mergers in the United Kingdom', *Journal of Finance*, Vol. 32, pp. 1513–25.

Fraser, L. and Ormiston, A. (2004) *Understanding Financial Statements*, 7th edn, Upper Saddle River, NJ: Prentice-Hall.

Haugen, R. (1999) *The New Finance: The Case Against Efficient Markets*, 2nd edn, Upper Saddle River, NJ: Prentice-Hall.

Hawawini, G. and Viallet, C. (2002) *Finance for Executives: Managing for Value Creation*, Cincinnati, Ohio: South-Western/Thomson Learning.

Jensen, M. (1968) 'The performance of mutual funds in the period 1945–64', *Journal of Finance*, May, pp. 389–416.

Kendall, R. (1953) 'The analysis of economic time series, part 1: prices', *Journal of the Royal Statistical Society*, Vol. 69, pp. 11–25.

Keown, A. and Pinkerton, J. (1981) 'Merger announcements and insider trading activity', *Journal of Finance*, Vol. 36, September, pp. 855–70.

Keown, A., Martin, J., Petty, J. and Scott, D. (2003) *Foundations of Finance: The Logic and Practice of Financial Management*, Upper Saddle River, NJ: Prentice-Hall.

Leahy, T. (2000) 'Capitalizing on economic value added', *Business Finance*, July.

Manganelli, S. (2002) 'Duration, volume and volatility impact of trades', European Central Bank Working Paper 125.

Megginson, W.L. (1997) *Corporate Finance Theory*, Reading, MA: Addison-Wesley.

Roll, R. (1994) 'What every CEO should know about scientific progress in economics: what is known and what remains to be resolved', *Financial Management*, Vol. 23, pp. 69–75.

Rutterford, J. (ed.) (1998) *Financial Strategy*, Chichester: Wiley.

Samuelson, P. (1965) 'Proof that properly anticipated prices fluctuate randomly', *Industrial Management Review*, Vol. 6, pp. 41–9.

Shleifer, A.S. (2000) *Inefficient Markets: An Introduction to Behavioural Finance*, Oxford: Oxford University Press.

Smith, T. (1996) *Accounting for Growth: Stripping the Camouflage from Company Accounts*, 2nd edn, London: Century Business.

Weetman, P. (1999) *Financial and Management Accounting: An Introduction*, Harlow: FT Prentice Hall.

Recommended reading

A lucid treatment of efficient markets is found in:

Arnold, G. (2005) *Corporate Financial Management*, 3rd edn, Harlow: FT Prentice Hall.

A practical and lucid discussion of ratio analysis can be found in:

Walsh, C. (2003) *Key Management Ratios*, 3rd edn, Harlow: FT Prentice Hall.

Useful journal articles and other material include the following:

Barberis, N. (1997) 'Markets: the price may not be right', in *Mastering Finance*, London: FT Pitman, pp. 163–7.

Fama, E. (1970) 'Efficient capital markets: a review of theory and empirical work', *Journal of Finance*, Vol. 25, pp. 383-417.

Fama, E. (1991) 'Efficient capital markets II', *Journal of Finance*, Vol. 46, pp. 1575–617.

Fraser, L. and Ormiston, A. (2004) *Understanding Financial Statements*, 7th edn, Harlow: FT Prentice Hall.

Free company annual reports and a wealth of other business information can be obtained from the FT.com homepage: http://news.ft.com/home/uk

Another useful website is:

LexisNexis: http://www.lexisnexis.co.uk/index.htm

Chapter 3

Short-term finance and the management of working capital

Learning objectives

After studying this chapter, you should have achieved the following learning objectives:

- an appreciation of the importance of working capital management in ensuring the profitability and liquidity of a company;

- the ability to describe the cash conversion cycle and to explain its significance to working capital management;

- an understanding of the need for working capital policies concerning the level of investment in current assets, and of the significance of aggressive, moderate and conservative approaches to working capital management;

- an understanding of the link between the sources of short-term finance available to a company and working capital policies concerning the financing of current assets;

- the ability to describe and discuss a range of methods for managing stock, cash, debtors and creditors;

- the ability to evaluate, at an introductory level, the costs and benefits of proposed changes in working capital policies;

- an understanding of how factoring and invoice discounting can assist in the management of working capital.

Introduction

Long-term investment and financing decisions give rise to future cash flows which, when discounted by an appropriate cost of capital, determine the market value of a company. However, such long-term decisions will only result in the expected benefits for a company if attention is also paid to short-term decisions regarding current assets and liabilities. *Current assets and liabilities*, that is assets and liabilities with maturities of less than one year, need to be carefully managed. *Net working capital* is the term given to the difference between current assets and current liabilities: current assets may include stocks of raw materials, work-in-progress and finished goods, debtors, short-term investments and cash, while current liabilities may include trade creditors, overdrafts and short-term loans.

The level of current assets is a key factor in a company's liquidity position. A company must have or be able to generate enough cash to meet its short-term needs if it is to continue in business. Therefore, working capital management is a key factor in the company's long-term success: without the 'oil' of working capital, the 'engine' of fixed assets will not function. The greater the extent to which current assets exceed current liabilities, the more solvent or liquid a company is likely to be, depending on the nature of its current assets.

3.1 The objectives of working capital management

To be effective, working capital management requires a clear specification of the objectives to be achieved. The two main objectives of working capital management are to increase the profitability of a company and to ensure that it has sufficient liquidity to meet short-term obligations as they fall due and so continue in business (Pass and Pike 1984). Profitability is related to the goal of shareholder wealth maximisation, so investment in current assets should be made only if an acceptable return is obtained. While liquidity is needed for a company to continue in business, a company may choose to hold more cash than is needed for operational or transaction needs, for example for precautionary or speculative reasons. The twin goals of profitability and liquidity will often conflict since liquid assets give the lowest returns. Cash kept in a safe will not generate a return, for example, while a six-month bank deposit will earn interest in exchange for loss of access for the period.

3.2 Working capital policies

Because working capital management is so important, a company will need to formulate clear policies concerning the various components of working capital. Key policy areas relate to the level of investment in working capital for a given level of operations and the extent to which working capital is financed from short-term funds such as bank overdrafts.

A company should have working capital policies on the management of stock, debtors, cash and short-term investments in order to minimise the possibility of managers making decisions which are not in the best interests of the company. Examples of such suboptimal decisions are giving credit to customers who are unlikely to pay and ordering unnecessary stocks of raw materials. Sensible working capital policies will reflect corporate decisions on: the *total* investment needed in current assets, i.e. the overall level of investment; the amount of investment needed in each *type* of current asset, i.e. the mix of current assets; and the way in which current assets are to be financed.

Working capital policies need to consider the nature of the company's business since different businesses will have different working capital requirements. A manufacturing company will need to invest heavily in spare parts and components and might be owed large amounts of money by its customers. A food retailer will have large stocks of goods for resale but will have very few debtors. The manufacturing company clearly has a need for a carefully thought out policy on debtor management, whereas the food retailer may not grant credit at all.

Working capital policies will also need to reflect the credit policies of a company's close competitors, since it would be foolish to lose business because of an unfavourable comparison of terms of trade. Any expected fluctuations in the supply of or demand for goods and services, for example due to seasonal variations in business, must also be considered, as must the impact of a company's manufacturing period on its current assets.

3.2.1 The level of working capital

An *aggressive* policy with regard to the level of investment in working capital means that a company chooses to operate with lower levels of stock, debtors and cash for a given level of activity or sales. An aggressive policy will increase profitability since less cash will be tied up in current assets, but it will also increase risk since the possibility of cash shortages or running out of stock (stockouts) is increased.

A *conservative* and more flexible working capital policy for a given level of turnover would be associated with maintaining a larger cash balance, perhaps even investing in short-term securities, offering more generous credit terms to customers and holding higher levels of stock. Such a policy will give rise to a lower risk of financial problems or stock problems, but at the expense of reducing profitability.

A *moderate* policy would tread a middle path between the aggressive and conservative approaches. All three approaches are shown in Exhibit 3.1.

It should be noted that the working capital policies of a company can be characterised as aggressive, moderate or conservative only by comparing them with the working capital policies of similar companies. There are no absolute benchmarks of what may be regarded as aggressive or otherwise, but these characterisations are useful for analysing the ways in which individual companies approach the operational problem of working capital management.

3.2.2 Short-term finance

Short-term sources of finance include overdrafts, short-term bank loans and trade credit.

An *overdraft* is an agreement by a bank to allow a company to borrow up to a certain limit without the need for further discussion. The company will borrow as much or as little as it needs up to the overdraft limit and the bank will charge daily interest

| Exhibit 3.1 | **Graph showing different policies regarding the level of investment in working capital** |

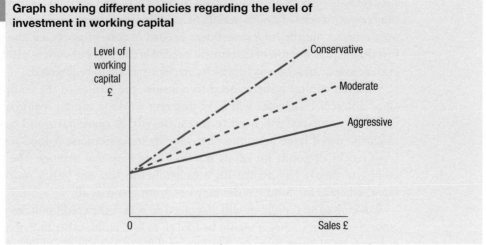

at a variable rate on the debt outstanding. The bank may also require security or collateral as protection against the risk of non-payment by the company. An overdraft is a flexible source of finance in that a company only uses it when the need arises. However, an overdraft is technically repayable on demand, even though a bank is likely in practice to give warning of its intention to withdraw agreed overdraft facilities.

A *short-term loan* is a fixed amount of debt finance borrowed by a company from a bank, with repayment to be made in the near future, for example after one year. The company pays interest on the loan at either a fixed or a floating (i.e. variable) rate at regular intervals, for example quarterly. A short-term bank loan is less flexible than an overdraft, since the full amount of the loan must be borrowed over the loan period and the company takes on the commitment to pay interest on this amount, whereas with an overdraft interest is only paid on the amount borrowed, not on the agreed overdraft limit. As with an overdraft, however, security may be required as a condition of the short-term loan being granted.

Trade credit is an agreement to take payment for goods and services at a later date than that on which the goods and services are supplied to the consuming company. It is common to find one, two or even three months' credit being offered on commercial transactions and trade credit is a major source of short-term finance for most companies.

Short-term sources of finance are usually *cheaper* and *more flexible* than long-term ones. Short-term interest rates are usually lower than long-term interest rates, for example, and an overdraft is more flexible than a long-term loan on which a company is committed to pay fixed amounts of interest every year. However, short-term sources of finance are riskier than long-term sources from the borrower's point of view in that they may not be renewed (an overdraft is, after all, repayable on demand) or may be renewed on less favourable terms (e.g. when short-term interest rates have increased). Another source of risk for the short-term borrower is that interest rates are more volatile in the short term than in the long term and this risk is compounded if floating rate short-term debt (such as an overdraft) is used. A company must clearly balance *profitability* and *risk* in reaching a decision on how the funding of current and fixed assets is divided between long-term and short-term sources of funds.

3.2.3 Financing working capital

The trade-off between risk and return which occurs in policy decisions regarding the level of investment in current assets is also significant in the policy decision on the relative amounts of finance of different maturities in the balance sheet, i.e. on the choice between short- and long-term funds to finance working capital. To assist in the analysis of policy decisions on the financing of working capital, we can divide a company's assets into three different types: fixed assets, permanent current assets and fluctuating current assets (Cheatham 1989). *Fixed assets* are long-term assets from which a company expects to derive benefit over several periods, for example factory buildings and production machinery. *Permanent current assets* represent the core level of investment needed to sustain normal levels of trading activity, such as investment in stocks and investment in the average level of a company's debtors. *Fluctuating current assets* correspond to the variations in the level of current assets arising from normal business activity.

A *matching funding policy* is one which finances fluctuating current assets with short-term funds and permanent current assets and fixed assets with long-term funds. The maturity of the funds roughly matches the maturity of the different types of assets. A *conservative funding policy* uses long-term funds to finance not only fixed assets and permanent current assets, but some fluctuating current assets as well. As there is less reliance on short-term funding, the risk of such a policy is lower, but the higher cost of long-term finance means that profitability is reduced as well. An *aggressive funding policy* uses short-term funds to finance not only fluctuating current assets, but some permanent current assets as well. This policy carries the greatest risk to solvency, but also offers the highest profitability and increases shareholder value. These three funding policies are illustrated in Exhibit 3.2.

| Exhibit 3.2 | Three graphs showing the (a) matching, (b) conservative and (c) aggressive approaches to the relative proportions of long- and short-term debt used to finance working capital |

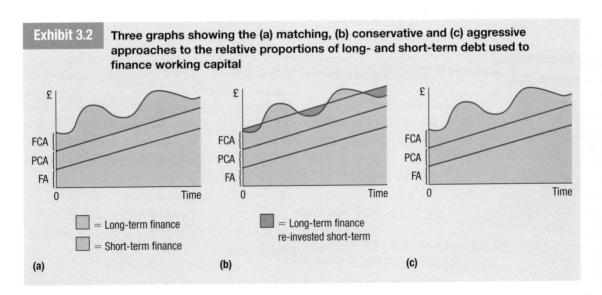

3.3 Working capital and the cash conversion cycle

Working capital can be viewed *statically* as the balance between current assets and current liabilities, for example by comparing the balance sheet figures for stock, trade debtors, cash and trade creditors. Alternatively, working capital can be viewed *dynamically* as an equilibrium between the income-generating and resource-purchasing activities of a company (Pass and Pike 1984), in which case it is closely linked to the cash conversion cycle (*see* Section 2.4.4).

The *cash conversion cycle*, which represents the interaction between the components of working capital and the flow of cash within a company, can be used to determine the amount of cash needed for any sales level. It is the *period of time* between the outlay of cash on raw materials and the inflow of cash from the sale of finished goods, and represents the number of days of operation for which financing is needed. The longer the cash conversion cycle, the greater the amount of investment required in working capital. The length of the cash conversion cycle depends on the length of:

- the stock conversion period;
- the debtor collection period;
- the creditor deferral period.

The *stock conversion period* is the average time taken to use up raw materials, plus the average time taken to convert raw materials into finished goods, plus the average time taken to sell finished goods to customers. The stock conversion period might be several months for an engineering or manufacturing company, but negligible for a service company. The *debtor collection period* is the average time taken by credit customers to settle their accounts. The *creditor deferral period* is the average time taken by a company to pay its trade creditors, i.e. its suppliers. If we approximate these three periods with the financial ratios of stock days, debtor days and creditor days (*see* Section 2.4.4), the length of the cash conversion cycle (CCC) is given by:

$$\text{CCC} = \text{Stock days} + \text{Debtor days} - \text{Creditor days}$$

Example | Calculating working capital required

The amount of working capital required by a company can be estimated from information on the value of relevant working capital inputs and outputs, such as raw material costs and credit purchases, together with information on the length of the components of the cash conversion cycle. Assume that Carmed plc expects credit sales of £18m in the next year and has budgeted production costs as follows:

	£m
Raw materials	4
Direct labour	5
Production overheads	3
Total production costs	12

Raw materials are in stock for an average of three weeks and finished goods are in stock for an average of four weeks. All raw materials are added at the start of the production cycle, which takes five weeks and incurs labour costs and production overheads at a constant rate. Suppliers of raw materials allow four weeks' credit, whereas customers are given 12 weeks to pay. If production takes place evenly throughout the year, what is the total working capital requirement?

Suggested answer

		£	£
Raw materials:	4m × (3/52) =		230 769
Work-in-progress:			
raw materials:	4m × (5/52) =	384 615	
labour costs:	5m × (5/52) × 0.5 =	240 385	
overheads:	3m × (5/52) × 0.5 =	144 231	
			769 231
Finished goods:	12m × (4/52) =		923 077
Debtors:	18m × (12/52) =		4 153 846
Creditors:	4m × (4/52) =		(307 692)
Working capital required:			5 769 231

In this calculation it has been assumed that all raw materials are added at the start of the production process, whereas labour costs and overheads are incurred evenly as production proceeds. If, on average, work-in-progress is half-finished, labour and overheads have to be multiplied by 0.5 as only half the amounts of these costs are present in finished goods.

On the information given, Carmed needs £5.77m of working capital. The proportions of long- and short-term finance used will depend on the working capital policies of the company. Note that Carmed's cash conversion cycle is (3 + 5 + 4) + 12 − 4 = 20 weeks.

3.3.1 The cash conversion cycle and working capital needs

Forecasts of working capital requirements can be based on forecasts of sales if a relationship between net working capital and sales is assumed to exist. Such a relationship is quantified by the *sales/net working capital ratio* described in Section 2.4.4, and made explicit by a policy on the level of investment in working capital (*see* Section 3.2.1). However, even with such a policy in place, the relationship between sales and working capital is unlikely to remain static as levels of business and economic activity change. Since budgeted production is based on forecast sales, care must be taken in periods of reduced economic activity to ensure that overinvestment in stocks of raw materials, work-in-progress and finished goods does not occur. Although the overall amount of working capital needed can be estimated from forecast sales and the cash conversion cycle, there is likely to be a difference between forecast activity and actual activity. There can be no substitute, then, for reviewing working capital needs regularly in the light of changing levels of activity.

The cash conversion cycle also shows where managers should focus their attention if they want to decrease the amount of cash tied up in current assets. Apart from reducing sales and reducing the cost per unit sold, cash invested in current assets can be reduced by shortening the cash conversion cycle (Cheatham 1989). This can be done by decreasing the stock conversion period (stock days), by reducing the debtor collection period (debtor days) or by increasing the creditor deferral period (creditor days).

The stock conversion period can be reduced by shortening the length of the production cycle, for example by more effective production planning or by out-sourcing part of the production process. The amount of stock within the production process can be reduced by using just-in-time (JIT) production methods (*see* Section 3.5.3) or by employing production methods which are responsive to changing sales levels.

The debtor conversion period can be shortened by offering incentives for early payment, by reducing the period of credit offered to customers, by chasing slow or late payers, and by more stringent assessment of the creditworthiness of customers to screen out slow payers. The minimum debtor conversion period is likely to be the credit offered by competitors.

The creditor deferral period is less flexible as it is determined to a large extent by a company's suppliers. While a company can delay payments to creditors past their due dates, it runs the risk of losing its suppliers or paying interest on overdue accounts.

3.4 Overtrading

Overtrading (also called undercapitalisation) occurs if a company is trying to support too large a volume of trade from too small a working capital base. It is the result of the supply of funds failing to meet the demand for funds within a company and it emphasises the need for adequate working capital investment. Even if a company is operating profitably, overtrading can result in a liquidity crisis, with the company being unable to meet its debts as they fall due because cash has been absorbed by growth in fixed assets, stock and debtors. Overtrading, therefore, can lead to serious, and sometimes fatal, problems for a company.

Overtrading can be caused by a rapid increase in turnover, perhaps as a result of a successful marketing campaign where provision for the necessary associated investment in fixed and current assets was not made. Overtrading can also arise in the early years of a new business if it starts off with insufficient capital. This may be due to a mistaken belief that sufficient capital could be generated from trading profits and ploughed back into the business, when in fact the early years of trading are often difficult ones. Overtrading may also be due to erosion of a company's capital base, perhaps due to the non-replacement of long-term loans following their repayment.

There are several strategies that are appropriate to deal with overtrading:

- *Introducing new capital*: this is likely to be an injection of equity finance rather than debt since, with liquidity under pressure due to overtrading, managers will be keen to avoid straining cash flow any further by increasing interest payments.
- *Improving working capital management*: overtrading can also be attacked by better control and management of working capital, for example by chasing overdue accounts. Since overtrading is more likely if an aggressive funding policy is being followed, adopting a matching policy or a more relaxed approach to funding could be appropriate.
- *Reducing business activity*: as a last resort, a company can choose to level off or reduce the level of its planned business activity in order to consolidate its trading position and allow time for its capital base to build up through retained earnings.

Indications that a company may be overtrading could include:

- rapid growth in sales over a relatively short period;
- rapid growth in the amount of current assets, and perhaps fixed assets;
- deteriorating stock days and debtor days' ratios;
- increasing use of trade credit to finance current asset growth (increasing creditor days);
- declining liquidity, indicated perhaps by a falling quick ratio;
- declining profitability, perhaps due to using discounts to increase sales;
- decreasing amounts of cash and liquid investments, or a rapidly increasing overdraft.

3.5 The management of stock

Significant amounts of working capital can be invested in stocks of raw materials, work-in-progress and finished goods. Stocks of raw materials and work-in-progress can act as a buffer between different stages of the production process, ensuring its smooth operation. Stocks of finished goods allow the sales department to satisfy customer demand without unreasonable delay and potential loss of sales. These *benefits* of holding stock must be weighed against any *costs* incurred, however, if optimal stock levels are to be determined. Costs which may be incurred in holding stock include:

- holding costs, such as insurance, rent and utility charges;
- replacement costs, including the cost of obsolete stock;
- the cost of the stock itself;
- the opportunity cost of cash tied up in stock.

3.5.1 The economic order quantity

This classical stock management model calculates an optimum order size by balancing the costs of holding stock against the costs of ordering fresh supplies. This optimum order size is the basis of a minimum cost procurement policy. The economic order quantity model assumes that, for the period under consideration (usually one year), costs and demand are constant and known with certainty. It is also called a *deterministic* model because it makes these steady-state assumptions. It makes no allowance for the existence of buffer stocks.

If we assume a constant demand for stock, holding costs will increase as average stock levels and order quantity increase, while ordering costs will decrease as order quantity increases and the number of orders falls. The total cost is the sum of the annual holding cost and the annual ordering cost. The total cost equation is therefore:

Total annual cost = Annual holding cost + Annual ordering cost

Algebraically:

$$TC = \frac{(Q \times H)}{2} + \frac{(S \times F)}{Q}$$

where: Q = order quantity in units
H = holding cost per unit per year
S = annual demand in units per year
F = ordering cost per order

The annual holding cost is the average stock level in units ($Q/2$) multiplied by the holding cost per unit per year (H). The annual ordering cost is the number of orders per year (S/Q) multiplied by the ordering cost per order (F). This relationship is shown in Exhibit 3.3.

The minimum total cost occurs when holding costs and ordering costs are equal (as can be shown by differentiating the total cost equation with respect to Q and setting to zero). Putting holding costs equal to ordering costs and rearranging gives:

$$Q = \sqrt{\frac{2 \times S \times F}{H}}$$

Exhibit 3.3 **The costs of holding stock and the economic order quantity model**

Q is now the economic order quantity, i.e. the order quantity which minimises the sum of holding costs and ordering costs. This formula is called the economic order quantity (EOQ) model.

More sophisticated stock management models have been developed which relax some of the classical model's assumptions, whereas some modern approaches, such as just-in-time methods (*see* Section 3.5.3) and material resource planning (MRP), question the need to hold any stock at all.

Example	Using the EOQ model

Oleum plc sells a soap called Fragro, which it buys in boxes of 1000 bars with ordering costs of £5 per order. Retail sales are 200 000 bars per year and holding costs are £2.22 per year per 1000 bars. What is the economic order quantity and average stock level for Fragro?

Suggested answer

$$F = £5 \text{ per order}$$
$$S = 200\,000 \text{ bars per year}$$
$$H = £2.22 \text{ per 1000 bars}$$

so:

$$Q = (2 \times 200\,000 \times 5/(2.22/1000))^{1/2}$$
$$= 30\,015 \text{ bars, or approximately 30 boxes}$$

The average stock level = $Q/2 = 30\,000/2 = 15\,000$ bars.

3.5.2 Buffer stocks and lead times

There will usually be a delay between ordering and delivery, and this delay is known as *lead time*. If demand and lead time are assumed to be constant, new stock should be ordered when the stock in hand falls to a level equal to the demand during the lead time. For example, if demand is 10 400 units per year and the lead time for delivery of an order is two weeks, the amount used during the lead time is:

$$10\,400 \times (2/52) = 400 \text{ units}$$

New stock must be ordered when the level of stock in hand falls to 400 units. If demand or lead times are uncertain or variable, a company may choose to hold buffer stock to reduce or eliminate the possibility of stockouts (running out of stock). It could optimise the level of buffer stock by balancing holding costs against the potential costs of stockouts. However, the EOQ model can still be used to determine an optimum order size.

Exhibit 3.4	**Average stock levels, reorder level and buffer stock**

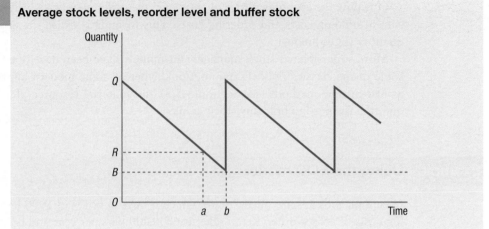

Exhibit 3.4 shows the pattern of stock levels where a company chooses to operate with buffer stock OB. Regular economic orders of size BQ are placed, based on average annual demand. Because lead time is known and is equal to ab, new orders are placed when stock levels fall to OR. The company can meet unexpected demand during the lead time from the buffer stocks held. The average stock level will be:

$$\text{Buffer stock} + \text{Half of regular order quantity} = OB + (BQ/2)$$

This can be used to calculate the expected holding cost for the year.

3.5.3 Just-in-time stock policies

Many companies in recent years have reduced stock costs by minimising stock levels. The main purpose of a just-in-time (JIT) *purchasing policy* is to minimise or eliminate the time which elapses between the delivery and use of stock. Such policies have been applied in a wide range of commercial operations and call for a close relationship between the supplier and the purchaser of both raw materials and bought components. The purchaser requires guarantees on both quality and reliability of delivery from the supplier in order to avoid disruptions to production. In return for these commitments, the supplier can benefit from long-term purchase agreements since a company adopting JIT purchasing methods will concentrate on dealing with suppliers who are able to offer goods of the required quality at the required time. The purchaser will benefit from a reduction in the costs of holding, ordering and handling stock since materials will move directly from reception to the production line.

The main purpose of a JIT *manufacturing policy* is to minimise stock acting as a buffer between different stages of production. Apart from developing closer relationships with suppliers, this can also be achieved by changing factory layout in order to reduce queues of work-in-progress and by reducing the size of production batches. Good production planning is also essential if a JIT manufacturing policy is to be successful.

3.6 The management of cash

Cash management, which is part of the wider task of treasury management, is concerned with optimising the amount of cash available, maximising the interest earned by spare funds not required immediately and reducing losses caused by delays in the transmission of funds. Holding cash to meet short-term needs incurs an opportunity cost equal to the return which could have been earned if the cash had been invested or put to productive use. However, reducing this opportunity cost by operating with small cash balances will increase the risk of being unable to meet debts as they fall due, so an optimum cash balance should be found.

3.6.1 The need for cash

There are three reasons why companies choose to hold cash.

Transactions motive

Companies need a cash reserve in order to balance short-term cash inflows and outflows since these are not perfectly matched. This is called the transactions motive for holding cash, and the approximate size of the cash reserve can be estimated by forecasting cash inflows and outflows and by preparing cash budgets. In addition to the cash reserve held for day-to-day operational needs, cash may be built up to meet significant anticipated cash outflows, for example arising from an investment project or the redemption of debt.

Precautionary motive

Forecasts of future cash flows are subject to uncertainty and it is possible that a company will experience unexpected demands for cash. This gives rise to the precautionary motive for holding cash. Reserves held for precautionary reasons could be in the form of easily realised short-term investments, which are discussed below.

Speculative motive

Companies may build up cash reserves in order to take advantage of any attractive investment opportunities that may arise, for example in the takeover market. Such reserves are held for speculative reasons. If a company has significant speculative cash reserves for which it cannot see an advantageous use, it may choose to enhance shareholder value by returning them to shareholders, for example by means of a share repurchase scheme or a special cash dividend (*see* Section 10.7).

3.6.2 Optimum cash levels

Given the variety of needs a company may have for cash and the different reasons it may have for holding cash, the optimum cash level will vary over time and between companies. The optimum amount of cash held by a company will depend on the following factors:

- forecasts of the future cash inflows and outflows of the company;
- the efficiency with which the cash flows of the company are managed;
- the availability of liquid assets to the company;
- the borrowing capability of the company;
- the company's tolerance of risk.

3.6.3 Cash flow problems

A company may experience cash flow problems for a number of reasons. It may, for example, be making losses: while this need not be a problem in the short term, making losses on a regular basis will lead to serious cash flow problems, and perhaps even liquidation or takeover. Inflation may also be a source of cash flow problems since historical profit may prove to be insufficient to fund the replacement of necessary assets. As we saw in our discussion of overtrading, growth requires investment in fixed assets and working capital; if the funds needed for this investment are not forthcoming, cash flows can be severely strained. Careful cash management is needed when dealing with a seasonal business as cyclical sales patterns can lead to cash flow imbalances. Finally, cash flow problems may arise due to sizable one-off items of expenditure, such as redemption of debt or investment in fixed assets. Companies could plan for the redemption of debt capital by setting up a *sinking fund* in which regular contributions of cash and accumulated interest combine to produce the required lump sum, although refinancing with new debt is more common.

When faced with cash flow shortages, a company may choose one or more of a number of possible remedies. It may, for example, postpone non-essential capital expenditure. It may be able to accelerate the rate at which cash flows into the business, for example by offering debtors discounts for early payment, by chasing overdue accounts or by having a sale to clear unwanted stock. If a company has investments, bought perhaps with surplus cash from an earlier period, it may choose to sell them in order to generate cash. Finally, a company may be able to identify ways to reduce or postpone cash outflows, for example by taking longer to pay suppliers or by rescheduling loan repayments. As a last resort, it may decide to reduce or pass a dividend payment, although this is usually seen as a sign of financial weakness by the capital markets (*see* Section 10.4.1).

3.6.4 Cash budgets

Cash budgets are central to the management of cash. They show expected cash inflows and outflows over a budget period and highlight anticipated cash surpluses and deficits. Their preparation assists managers in the planning of borrowing and investment and facilitates the control of expenditure. Computer spreadsheets allow managers to undertake 'what if' analysis to anticipate possible cash flow difficulties as well as to examine possible future scenarios. To be useful, cash budgets should be regularly updated by comparing estimated figures with actual results, using a *rolling cash budget* system. Significant variances from planned figures must always be investigated.

3.6.5 Managing cash flows

Cash flows must be managed efficiently. This means that debts should be collected in line with agreed credit terms and cash should be quickly banked. Prompt banking will either reduce the interest charged on an outstanding overdraft or increase the interest earned on cash deposits. Credit offered by suppliers should be used to the full and payments made as late as possible, provided the benefit of these actions is greater than the benefit of taking any early payment discounts available.

The *float* is the period of time between initiating payment and receiving cash in a company's bank account. The float can vary between four and nine days and consists of:

- transmission delay: time taken for a payment to pass from payer to payee;
- lodgement delay: delay in banking any payments received;
- clearance delay: time taken by a bank to clear a presented instruction to pay.

The float can be reduced by minimising lodgement delay and by simplifying and speeding up cash handling. Good cash management will seek to keep the float to a minimum.

3.6.6 Investing surplus cash

As discussed above, companies have several reasons for holding funds in liquid or near-liquid form. Cash which is surplus to immediate needs should earn a return by being invested on a short-term basis. There must be no risk of capital loss, since these funds are required to support a company's continuing working capital needs. To reduce the risk of loss, it is important for large companies to set limits on the amounts they deposit with individual banks (Leadill 1992) as banks can, and do, fail – two examples of bank failure from the 1990s would be the Bank of Credit and Commerce International (BCCI) and Barings Bank.

The factors which should be considered when choosing an appropriate investment method for short-term cash surpluses are:

- the size of the surplus, as some investment methods have minimum amounts;
- the ease with which an investment can be realised;
- when the investment is expected to mature;
- the risk and yield of the investment;
- any penalties which may be incurred for early liquidation.

Short-term methods that can be useful in managing corporate liquidity include money market deposits, sterling certificates of deposit, Treasury bills, sterling commercial paper and gilt-edged government securities.

Term deposits

Cash can be put on deposit with a bank to earn interest, with the interest rate depending on the size of the deposit, its maturity and the notice required for withdrawals. To maximise return, companies should obtain quotations from several banks before making a deposit since interest rates vary between banks as they compete for funds. Money market deposits are useful where cash flow needs are predictable with a high degree of certainty.

In the UK, large companies can lend directly to banks on the interbank market at rates close to the London Interbank Offered Rate (LIBOR). Smaller companies lend indirectly onto the market through term deposits with their banks.

Sterling certificates of deposit

Sterling certificates of deposit are negotiable bearer securities issued by banks and building societies. They are for amounts ranging from £500 000 to £1m and have maturities ranging from 28 days to five years. At maturity, the holder of a sterling certificate of deposit is entitled to receive both principal and interest.

Because certificates of deposit can be sold before maturity, and so are more liquid than money market deposits, they carry a lower rate of interest. They may be useful if a company's cash flows are not predictable enough for a money market deposit to be made. The anonymity of bearer securities makes them attractive to some investors.

Treasury bills

Treasury bills of two-, three- and six-month maturities are issued on a discounted basis by the UK government. They are bought and sold on the discount market (part of the London money market). The yield on Treasury bills is lower than on other money market instruments because of the lower default risk associated with government borrowing. In fact, the Treasury bill rate is often used as an approximation of the *risk-free rate* (*see* Section 8.6.2).

Sterling commercial paper

Sterling commercial paper refers to short-term promissory notes with a fixed maturity of between seven days and three months. They are unsecured bearer securities issued at a discount by companies, banks and building societies. The minimum amount of sterling commercial paper that can be issued is £100000 and issuing companies must be listed on the London Stock Exchange. Sterling commercial paper offers a higher return than government securities such as Treasury bills, however, since it has a higher default risk.

Gilt-edged government securities

Gilt-edged government securities (gilts) are the long-term equivalent of Treasury bills, with maturities usually greater than five years. Short-term cash surpluses should not be invested in newly issued gilts since their long maturities make their market prices sensitive to interest rate changes and the risk of capital loss in the short term could be high. Gilts close to maturity can be bought as short-term investments, however, and may be regarded as liquid assets similar to Treasury bills.

3.7 The management of debtors

A company's credit management policy should help it maximise expected profits. It will need to take into account its current and desired cash position, as well as its ability to satisfy expected demand. To put the credit management policy into effect successfully, managers and staff may need training or new staff may need to be recruited.

Key variables affecting the level of debtors will be the *terms of sale* prevailing in a company's area of business and the ability of the company to match and service comparable terms of sale. There is also a relationship between the level of debtors and a company's *pricing policy*: for example, it may choose to keep selling prices relatively high while offering attractive terms for early payment. The effectiveness of *debtor follow-up procedures* used will also influence the overall level of debtors and the likelihood of bad debts arising.

The debtor management policy decided upon by senior managers should also take into account the *administrative costs* of debt collection, the ways in which the policy could be implemented effectively, and the costs and effects of easing credit. It should balance the benefits to be gained from offering credit to customers against the costs of doing so. Longer credit terms may increase turnover, but will also increase the risk of bad debts. The cost of increased bad debts and the cost of any additional working capital required should be less than the increased profits generated by the higher turnover. In order to operate its debtor policy, a company needs to set up a credit analysis system, a credit control system and a debtor collection system.

3.7.1 Credit analysis system

To make a sensible decision about whether to trade with a company or not, information about the business is needed. The risk of bad debts can be minimised if the creditworthiness of new customers is carefully assessed before credit is granted and if the creditworthiness of existing customers is reviewed on a regular basis. Relevant information can be obtained from a variety of sources. New customers can be asked to provide *bank references* to confirm their financial standing, and *trade references* to indicate satisfactory conduct of business affairs. Published information, such as the audited annual report and accounts of a prospective customer, may also provide a useful indication of creditworthiness. A company's own experience of similar companies will also be useful in forming a view on creditworthiness, as will the experience of other companies within a group.

For a fee, a report may be obtained from a *credit reference agency*, such as Experian or Equifax. A credit report may include a company profile, recent accounts, financial ratios and industry comparisons, analysis of trading history, payment trends, types of borrowing, previous financial problems and a credit limit.

Bearing in mind the cost of assessing creditworthiness, the magnitude of likely regular sales could be used as a guide to determine the depth of the credit analysis.

3.7.2 Credit control system

Once creditworthiness has been assessed and a *credit limit* agreed, the company should take steps to ensure the customer keeps to the credit limit and the terms of trade. Customer accounts should be kept within the agreed credit limit and credit granted should be reviewed periodically to ensure that it remains appropriate. In order to encourage prompt payment, invoices and statements should be carefully checked for accuracy and despatched promptly. Under no circumstances should customers who have exceeded their credit limits be able to obtain goods.

3.7.3 Debtor collection system

Since the purpose of offering credit is to maximise profitability, the costs of debt collection should not be allowed to exceed the amounts recovered. A company should prepare regularly an *aged debtor analysis* and take steps to chase late payers. It is helpful to establish clear procedures for chasing late payers, to set out the circumstances under which credit control staff should send out reminders and initiate legal proceedings. Some thought could also be given to charging interest on overdue accounts to encourage timely payment, depending on the likely response of customers.

3.7.4 Insuring against bad debts

Although expensive, insurance against the risk of bad debts is available and can be arranged through brokers or intermediaries. *Whole turnover insurance* will cover any debt below an agreed amount against the risk of non-payment. *Specific account insurance* will allow a company to insure key accounts against default and may be used for major customers. Credit insurance is used more widely in continental Europe than in the UK (Williams 1994).

3.7.5 Discounts for early payment

Cash discounts may encourage early payment, but the cost of such discounts must be less than the total financing savings resulting from lower debtor balances, any administrative or financing savings arising from shorter debtor collection periods, and any benefits from lower bad debts.

Example	**Evaluating a change in debtor policy**

Mine plc has annual credit sales of £15m and allows 90 days' credit. It is considering introducing a 2 per cent discount for payment within 15 days, and reducing the credit period to 60 days. It estimates that 60 per cent of its customers will take advantage of the discount, while the volume of sales will not be affected. The company finances working capital from an overdraft at a cost of 10 per cent. Is the proposed change in policy worth implementing?

Suggested answer

	£000	£000
Current level of debtors: $15\,000 \times (90/365) =$		3699
Proposed level of debtors:		
$\quad 15\,000 \times (60/365) \times 40\% =$	986	
$\quad 15\,000 \times (15/365) \times 60\% =$	370	
		1356
Reduction in debtors		2343

	£
Saving in finance costs: $2343 \times 0.10 =$	234 300
Cost of discount: $15\,000 \times 2\% \times 60\% =$	180 000
Net benefit of proposed policy change	54 300

The policy change is financially attractive. However, the difficulty of forecasting accurately the effects of changes in debtor policy should be borne in mind when deciding whether or not to introduce it.

3.7.6 Factoring

Factoring companies offer a range of services in the area of sales administration and the collection of amounts due from debtors. A factor can take over the administration of sales invoicing and accounting for a client company, together with collecting amounts due from debtors and chasing up any slow payers. A factor can offer a cash advance against the security of debtors, allowing a company ready access to cash as soon as credit sales are made. For an additional fee, a factor can take on any bad debts that may arise through non-payment. Since here the factor does not have recourse to the company for compensation in the event of non-payment, this is called *non-recourse* factoring.

While a factor will advance up to 80 per cent of the face value of debts, interest will be charged on the sum advanced. In exchange for accelerated cash receipts, therefore, a company incurs an interest charge, which can be compared with the cost of short-term borrowings. This charge is in addition to the service fee levied by the factor, which is usually between 0.5 per cent and 2.5 per cent of gross annual turnover. There will be a reduction in administration costs, however, and the company will have access to the factor's expertise in credit analysis and control.

The advantages that factoring may offer to a company include the following:

- prompt payment of suppliers, leading perhaps to obtaining early payment discounts;
- a reduction in the amount of working capital tied up in debtors;
- financing growth through sales;
- savings on sales administration costs;
- benefits arising from the factor's experience in credit analysis and control.

3.7.7 Invoice discounting

Invoice discounting involves the sale of selected invoices to a third party while retaining full control over the sales ledger; it is a service often provided by factoring companies. The main cost of invoice discounting is a discount charge linked to bank base rates, although a fee of between 0.2 per cent and 0.5 per cent of turnover is often levied. Invoice discounting is useful to a company because it results in an improvement in cash flow.

Evaluating the costs and benefits of factoring and invoice discounting is similar to evaluating discounts for early payment, as discussed earlier.

| Example | **Cost–benefit analysis of factoring** |

Trebod has annual credit sales of £4.5m. Credit terms are 30 days, but its management of debtors has been poor and the average collection period is 50 days, with 0.4 per cent of sales resulting in bad debts. A factor has offered to take over the task of debt administration and credit checking, at an annual fee of 1 per cent of credit sales. Trebod plc estimates that it would save £35 000 per year in administration costs as a result. Due to the efficiency of the factor, the average collection period would fall to 30 days and bad debts would be eliminated. The factor would advance 80 per cent of invoiced debts at an annual interest rate of 11 per cent. Trebod plc currently finances debtors from an overdraft costing 10 per cent per year.

If credit sales occur smoothly throughout the year, determine whether the factor's services should be accepted.

Suggested answer

	£
Current level of debtors is £4.5m × (50/365) =	616 438
Under the factor, debtors would fall to £4.5m × (30/365) =	369 863

The costs of the current policy are as follows:

	£
Cost of financing current debtors: 616 438 × 10% =	61 644
Cost of bad debts: 4.5m × 0.4% =	18 000
Costs of current policy:	79 644

The costs under the factor are as follows:

	£
Cost of financing new debtors through factor:	
(£369 863 × 0.8 × 0.11) + (£369 863 × 0.2 × 0.10) =	39 945
Factor's annual fee: £4.5m × 0.01 =	45 000
Saved administration costs:	(35 000)
Net cost under factor:	49 945

Cost–benefit analysis shows the factor's services are cheaper than current practice by £29 699 per year. On financial grounds, the services of the factor should be accepted.

| 3.8 | **Conclusion** |

Effective working capital management lies at the heart of a successful company, playing a crucial role in the increase of shareholder wealth and the realisation of benefits from capital investment. In fact, poor management of working capital is one of the more common reasons for corporate failure. It is essential that company managers have an understanding of this key area of corporate finance.

Key points

1 The main objectives of working capital management are profitability and liquidity.

2 Short-term sources of finance include overdrafts, short-term bank loans and trade credit.

3 Companies may adopt aggressive, moderate or conservative working capital policies regarding the level and financing of working capital.

4 The cash conversion cycle can be used to determine the working capital requirement of a company as well as to help managers look for ways of decreasing the cash invested in current assets.

5 Overtrading can lead to business failure and must be corrected if found. Corrective measures include introducing new capital, improving working capital management and reducing business activity.

6 Because there can be significant amounts of cash tied up in stocks of raw materials, work-in-progress and finished goods, steps must be taken to question both the amount of stock held and the time it is held for.

7 The economic order quantity model can be used to determine an optimum order size and directs attention to the costs of holding and ordering stock. However, there is a growing trend for companies to minimise the use of stock.

8 Cash may be held for transactions, precautionary and speculative reasons, but companies should optimise holdings of cash according to their individual needs.

9 Cash flow problems can be anticipated by forecasting cash needs, for example by using cash flow forecasts and cash budgets.

10 Surplus cash should be invested to earn a return in appropriate short-term instruments.

11 The effective management of debtors requires assessment of the creditworthiness of customers, effective control of credit granted and efficient collection of money due. Effective management of debtors can be assisted by factoring and invoice discounting.

Self-test questions

Answers to these questions can be found on pages 432–3.

1 Explain the different strategies a company may follow in order to finance its cumulative working capital requirements.

2 Describe the cash conversion cycle and explain its significance in determining the working capital needed by a company.

3 Describe the main source of short-term finance for a company.

4 Describe the strategies that could be followed by a company seeking to deal with the problem of overtrading.

5 Discuss the possible reasons why a company might experience cash flow problems and suggest ways in which such problems might be alleviated.

6 Explain why a company may choose to have reserves of cash.

7 Discuss ways in which a company might invest its short-term cash surpluses, explaining briefly the factors which it should consider in making its selection.

8 How might the creditworthiness of a new customer be checked?

9 Is it worth offering discounts to debtors to encourage prompt payment?

10 Explain the difference between factoring and invoice discounting.

Questions for review

Answers to these questions can be found on pages 433–5. Questions with an asterisk (*) are at an intermediate level.

1* Sec uses a large quantity of salt in its production process. Annual consumption is 60 000 tons over a 50-week working year. It costs £100 to initiate and process an order and delivery follows two weeks later. Storage costs for the salt are estimated at £0.10 per ton per year. The current practice is to order twice a year when the stock falls to 10 000 tons (all orders are equal in size). Recommend an appropriate ordering policy for Sec and contrast its cost with the cost of the current policy.

2 MW has budgeted its sales to be £700 000 per annum. Its costs as a percentage of sales are as follows:

	%
Raw materials	20
Direct labour	35
Overheads	15

Raw materials are carried in stock for two weeks and finished goods are held in stock for three weeks. Production takes four weeks. MW takes four weeks' credit from suppliers and gives eight weeks' credit to its customers. If both overheads and production are incurred evenly throughout the year, what is MW's total working capital requirement?

3* MC has current sales of £1.5m per year. Cost of sales is 75 per cent of sales and bad debts are 1 per cent of sales. Cost of sales comprises 80 per cent variable costs and 20 per cent fixed costs, while the company's required rate of return is 12 per cent. MC currently allows customers 30 days' credit, but is considering increasing this to 60 days' credit in order to increase sales.

It has been estimated that this change in policy will increase sales by 15 per cent, while bad debts will increase from 1 per cent to 4 per cent. It is not expected that the policy change will result in an increase in fixed costs and creditors and stock will be unchanged. Should MC introduce the proposed policy?

4* A company is planning to offer a discount for payment within 10 days to its customers, who currently pay after 45 days. Only 40 per cent of credit customers would take the discount, although administrative cost savings of £4450 per year would be gained. If credit sales, which are unaffected by the discount, are £1 600 000 per year and the cost of short-term finance is 11 per cent, what is the maximum discount that could be offered?

Questions for discussion

Questions with an asterisk (*) are at an advanced level.

1* The finance director of Stenigot is reviewing the working capital management of the company. He is particularly concerned about the lax management of the company's debtors. The trade terms of Stenigot require settlement within 30 days, but its customers are taking an average of 60 days to pay their bills. In addition, out of total credit sales of £20m per year, the company suffers bad debts of £200 000 per year. Stenigot finances working capital needs with an overdraft at a rate of 10 per cent per year. The finance director is reviewing two options which have been suggested to him:

- *Option 1*: Offering a discount of 1 per cent for payment within 30 days. It is expected that 35 per cent of customers will take the discount, while the average time taken to pay by the remaining debtors will remain unchanged. Bad debts are expected to fall by £60000 per year and administration costs to fall by £20000 per year.

- *Option 2*: The debt administration and credit control of Stenigot could be taken over by Great Coates, a factoring company. The annual fee charged by Great Coates would be 1.75 per cent of sales. This would be offset by administration cost savings for Stenigot of £160 000 per year and by an 80 per cent reduction in bad debts. Great Coates would be able to reduce the average debtor days of Stenigot to 30 days and would advance 80 per cent of invoices at an interest rate of 15 per cent.

(a) Calculate the benefit, if any, to Stenigot of the two suggested options and, in the light of your findings, recommend an appropriate course of action to the finance director.

(b) Critically discuss whether it is possible for a company to optimise its working capital position. Your answer should include a discussion of the following matters:

(i) the risk of insolvency;

(ii) the return on assets;

(iii) the level, mix and financing of current assets.

2* Saltfleet, a wholesale merchant supplying the construction industry, has produced moderate profits for a number of years. It operates through a number of stores and depots throughout the UK and has a reputation in the sector as a steady if unspectacular performer. It has one subsidiary, Irby, which manufactures scaffolding and temporary security fences. The finance director of Saltfleet has been reviewing the way in which the company manages its working capital and has been discussing with you, a recently appointed graduate trainee in his department, a number of proposals which he hopes will lead to greater efficiency and effectiveness in this important area.

The proposals that the finance director has been discussing with you are:

- appointing a credit controller to oversee the credit management of the branches and depots;
- appointing a factoring company, Pyewipe, to take over the sales administration and debtor management of Irby;
- investing short-term cash surpluses on the London Stock Exchange. The finance director is especially interested in investing in the shares of a small company recently tipped by an investment magazine.

(a) Critically discuss the importance of credit management to a company like Saltfleet, explaining the areas to be addressed by a credit management policy.

(b) Distinguish between factoring and invoice discounting, and explain the benefits which Irby may receive from a factor such as Pyewipe.

(c) Discuss whether Saltfleet should invest short-term cash surpluses on the London Stock Exchange.

3* The following information has been extracted from the financial statements of Rowett by its finance manager:

Profit and loss account extracts

	£000	£000
Turnover		12 000
Cost of sales:		
Raw materials	5 800	
Labour	3 060	
		8 860
Gross profit		3 140
Administration/distribution		1 680
Operating profit		1 460

Balance sheet extracts

	£000	£000
Current assets:		
Stocks of raw materials	1 634	
Stocks of finished goods	2 018	
Debtors	1 538	
Cash and bank	500	
		5 690

Current liabilities:	
Trade creditors	1 092
Overdraft	300
Accrued expenses	76
	1 468
	4 222

Powell, a factoring company, has offered to take over the debt administration and credit control of Rowett on a non-recourse basis for an annual fee of 1.8 per cent of sales. This would save Rowett £160 000 per year in administration costs and reduce bad debts from 0.5 per cent of sales to nil. Powell would be able to reduce the credit period allowed to Rowett's customers to 40 days, and will advance 75 per cent of invoiced debts at an interest rate of 15 per cent.

Rowett finances working capital from an overdraft at 12 per cent.

(a) Calculate the length of the cash conversion cycle of Rowett and discuss its significance to the company.

(b) Discuss ways in which Rowett could improve the management of its debtors.

(c) Using the information given, assess whether Rowett should accept the factoring service offered by Powell. What use should the company make of any finance provided by the factor?

4 The finance director of Menendez is trying to improve the company's slack working capital management. Although the trade terms of Menendez require settlement within 30 days, its customers take an average of 45 days to pay their bills. In addition, out of total credit sales of £15m per year, the company suffers bad debts of £235 000 per year.

It has been suggested that the average settlement period could be reduced if a cash discount were given for early payment, and the finance director is considering offering a reduction of 1.5 per cent of the face value of the invoice for payment within 30 days. Informal discussions with customers have indicated to him that 40 per cent of customers would take advantage of the discount, but that the average time taken by the remaining customers would not be affected. It is also expected that, if the new credit terms are introduced, bad debts will fall by £60 000 per year and a small saving in credit administration costs of £15 000 per year will be made.

(a) If total sales are unchanged and if working capital is financed by an overdraft at 9 per cent per year, are the new credit terms of any benefit to Menendez?

(b) Discuss whether Menendez should finance its working capital needs from an overdraft.

(c) It has been suggested by the managing director of Menendez that the way to optimise the company's overall level of working capital is by minimising its cash conversion cycle. Critically discuss whether the finance director should follow this suggestion.

(d) Briefly discuss ways in which Menendez could use its debtors as a source of finance.

References

Cheatham, C. (1989) 'Economizing on cash investment in current assets', *Managerial Finance*, Vol. 15, No. 6, pp. 20–25.

Leadill, S. (1992) 'Liquidity and how to manage it', *Accountancy*, November, pp. 17–18.

Pass, C. and Pike, R. (1984) 'An overview of working capital management and corporate financing', *Managerial Finance*, Vol. 10, No. 3/4, pp. 1–11.

Williams, P. (1994) 'Who will you put your money on?', *Accountancy*, October, pp. 36–40.

Recommended reading

An interesting discussion of stock management methods can be found in:

Keown, A.J., Martin, J.D., Petty, J.W. and Scott, D.F. (2002) *Financial Management: Principles and Applications*, 9th edn, Harlow: Prentice Hall.

An excellent discussion of working capital management from an American perspective can be found in:

Gitman, L.J. (2006) *Principles of Managerial Finance*, 11th edn, Boston: Pearson Addison-Wesley.

Chapter 4

Long-term finance: equity finance

Learning objectives

After studying this chapter, you should have achieved the following learning objectives:

- a knowledge of the key characteristics of equity finance;

- an understanding of the different ways that a company can issue new equity finance and the reasons why a stock market quotation may or may not be desirable;

- an understanding of rights issues, their importance to companies and their effect on shareholder wealth;

- the ability to estimate the theoretical effect of rights issues on share prices;

- an appreciation of the difference between share splits, bonus issues, scrip dividends and share repurchases, and their importance to companies;

- an understanding of preference shares as a source of finance for a company.

Introduction

Ordinary share capital or equity finance is the foundation of the financial structure of a company and should be the source of most of its long-term finance. Since a company is owned by its ordinary shareholders, raising additional finance by issuing new ordinary shares has ownership and control implications which merit careful consideration.

In this chapter, we look at a number of the key areas concerning ordinary share capital, such as the ways in which a company can raise finance through issuing new shares and the implications for a company of obtaining a stock market listing. Rights issues (the issue of new shares to existing shareholders) are discussed, together with their impact on shareholder wealth. We examine some of the ways in which a company can increase or decrease the number of ordinary shares in issue, and their implications for both companies and investors. We also include a discussion of preference shares, which have characteristics in common with both equity and debt, and consider the relative merits of ordinary shares and preference shares.

4.1 Equity finance

Equity finance is raised through the sale of ordinary shares to investors. This may be a sale of shares to new owners, perhaps through the stock market as part of a company's initial listing, or it may be a sale of shares to existing shareholders by means of a rights issue. Ordinary shares are bought and sold regularly on stock exchanges throughout the world and ordinary shareholders, as owners of a company, want a satisfactory return on their investment. This is true whether they are the original purchasers of the shares or investors who have subsequently bought the shares on the stock exchange.

The ordinary shares of a company must have a *par value* (nominal value) by law, and cannot be issued for less than this amount. The nominal value of an ordinary share, usually 1p, 5p, 10p, 25p, 50p or £1, bears no relation to its *market value*, and ordinary shares with a nominal value of 25p may have a market price of several pounds. New shares, whether issued at the foundation of a company or subsequently, are almost always issued at a *premium* to their nominal value. The nominal value of shares issued by a company is represented in the balance sheet by the *ordinary share account*. The additional funds raised by selling shares at an issue price greater than the par value are represented by the *share premium account*. This means that the cash raised from the sale of shares on the asset side of the balance sheet is equally matched with shareholders' funds on the liability side of the balance sheet.

4.1.1 The rights of ordinary shareholders

Ownership of ordinary shares gives rights to ordinary shareholders on both an individual and a collective basis. From a corporate finance perspective, some of the most important rights of shareholders are:

- to attend general meetings of the company;
- to vote on the appointment of directors of the company;
- to vote on the appointment, remuneration and removal of auditors;
- to receive the annual accounts of the company and the report of its auditors;
- to receive a share of any dividend agreed to be distributed;
- to vote on important company matters such as permitting the repurchase of its shares, using its shares in a takeover bid or a change in its authorised share capital;
- to receive a share of any assets remaining after the company has been liquidated;
- to participate in a new issue of shares in the company (the pre-emptive right).

While individual shareholders have influence over who manages a company, and can express an opinion on decisions relating to their shares, it has been rare for shareholders to exercise their power collectively. This is due partly to the division between small shareholders and institutional shareholders, partly to real differences in opinion between shareholders and partly to shareholder apathy. There is evidence in recent years of an increasingly active approach by shareholders (*see* Section 1.5.5).

4.1.2 Equity finance, risk and return

Ordinary shareholders are the ultimate bearers of the risk associated with the business activities of the companies they own. This is because an order of precedence governs the distribution of the proceeds of liquidation in the event of a company going out of business. The first claims settled are those of *secured creditors*, such as debenture holders and banks, who are entitled to receive in full both unpaid interest and the outstanding capital or principal. The next claims settled are those of *unsecured creditors*, such as suppliers of goods and services. *Preference shareholders* are next in order of precedence and their claims are settled if any proceeds remain once the claims of secured and unsecured creditors have been met in full. *Ordinary shareholders* are not entitled to receive any of the proceeds of liquidation until the amounts owing to creditors, both secured and unsecured, and preference shareholders have been satisfied in full. The position of ordinary shareholders at the bottom of the *creditor hierarchy* means there is a significant risk of their receiving nothing or very little in the event of liquidation. This is especially true when it is recognised that liquidation is likely to occur after a protracted period of unprofitable trading. It is also possible, however, for ordinary shareholders to make substantial gains from liquidation as they are entitled to all that remains once the fixed claims of creditors and preference shareholders have been met.

Since ordinary shareholders carry the greatest risk of any of the providers of long-term finance, they expect the highest return in compensation. In terms of regular returns on capital, this means that ordinary shareholders expect the return they receive through capital gains and ordinary dividends to be higher than either interest payments or preference dividends. In terms of the cost of capital (*see* Chapter 9), it means that the cost of equity is always higher than either the cost of debt or the cost of preference shares.

4.2 The stock exchange

The ordinary shares of many large UK companies are traded on the London Stock Exchange. Companies pay an annual fee to have the price of their ordinary shares listed (quoted) on the stock exchange and undergo a rigorous financial assessment before being granted a listing. The London Stock Exchange is a market not only for ordinary shares, but also for bonds and depositary receipts. Bonds such as loan stock and debentures are discussed in Section 5.1. Depositary receipts, which are certificates representing ownership of a given company's shares that can be listed and traded independently of those shares, are not discussed in this book.

Trading on the London Stock Exchange is regulated by the Financial Services Authority under powers granted to it under the Financial Services and Markets Act 2000. In carrying out this regulatory role it is referred to as the UK Listing Authority (UKLA). The responsibilities of the UKLA include:

- admitting securities to listing;
- maintaining the Official List (also known as the Full List);
- the regulation of sponsors (*see* Section 4.2.1);
- imposing and enforcing continuing obligations on issuing companies;
- suspending and cancelling listings where necessary.

4.2.1 The new equity issues market

A company seeking a listing on the London Stock Exchange (LSE) or the Alternative Investment Market (AIM) will need to appoint a *sponsor* or *nominated adviser* in order to help it to meet and abide by all relevant regulations. A sponsor, usually a merchant bank, is an adviser who will be largely responsible for putting out the prospectus, managing the listing process and liaising with the LSE. The company will also need to appoint a *broker* to advise on an appropriate issue price for the new shares and to market the issue to institutional and other investors. The sponsor and the broker may in fact be the same firm. Sponsors are regulated by the UKLA.

Exhibit 4.1 illustrates the amount of funds raised on the UK stock market, both on the Official List and the AIM. The funds raised through issuing Eurobonds include funds raised by countries as well as companies: they do not tell us that UK companies are highly geared! Debt plays a smaller role than equity in financing UK companies, as illustrated by Exhibits 2.2 and 2.3 in Chapter 2.

4.2.2 New issue methods

A company may issue shares and/or obtain a listing on the London Stock Exchange and Alternative Investment Market by several methods. Issuing shares in order to obtain a listing is called an *initial public offering* (IPO) and, as indicated by Vignette 4.1, there is a high level of activity in this market at the present time.

Exhibit 4.1	Money raised on the UK stock market, 1995–2004

Year	New companies (£m)	Other issue (£m)	Eurobonds (£m)	Total (£m)	AIM (£m)
1995	2 962	9 855	24 766	37 573	95
1996	10 607	8 924	35 661	55 192	816
1997	7 100	6 649	43 644	57 393	694
1998	4 196	6 780	55 775	66 751	558
1999	5 353	9 917	85 515	100 785	933
2000	11 399	13 979	100 556	125 934	3 074
2001	6 922	14 824	83 342	105 088	1 128
2002	5 802	11 696	86 657	104 155	976
2003	2 445	4 920	119 798	127 163	2 095
2004	3 610	8 621	127 508	139 739	4 656

Source: London Stock Exchange Market Information and Analysis, 2006.

A placing

There are two main methods of issuing ordinary shares in the UK and the one used most frequently is called a *placing*. Here, the shares are issued at a fixed price to a number of institutional investors who are approached by the broker before the issue takes place. The issue is underwritten by the issuing company's sponsor. This issue method carries very little risk since it is in essence a way of distributing a company's shares to institutional investors. Consequently, it has a low cost by comparison with other issue methods.

A public offer

The other main method of raising funds by issuing shares is called a public offer for sale or *public offer* which is usually made at a fixed price. It is normally used for a large issue when a company is coming to the market (seeking a listing) for the first time. In this listing method, the shares are offered to the public with the help of the sponsor and the broker, who will help the company to decide on an issue price. The issue price should be low enough to be attractive to potential investors, but high enough to allow the required finance to be raised without the issue of more shares than necessary. The issue is underwritten, usually by institutional investors, so that the issuing company is guaranteed to receive the finance it needs. Any shares on offer which are not taken up are bought by the underwriters at an agreed price (*see* Section 4.2.5).

An introduction

A stock exchange listing may also be gained via an *introduction*. This is where a listing is granted to the existing ordinary shares of a company which already have a wide ownership base. It does not involve selling any new shares and so no new finance is

Vignette 4.1

IPOs the chosen route as equity markets advance

The decision by Drax Group, the owner of Europe's biggest coal-fired power plant, to list on the London Stock Exchange, in spite of receiving three takeover bids, highlights the strength of the market for initial public offerings in 2005. On the first day of trading, the listing generated more value for investors than if the company had been acquired, helping silence those who criticised the flotation.

Indeed, rising equity capital markets in 2005 have encouraged chief executives, governments and private equity owners to launch flotations. There were 307 new trading entrants to the main market and AIM, raising a combined total of more than £8.5bn, according to KPMG. This surpasses the 102 IPOs raising £7.8bn in 2001 and is close to the levels seen in 2000 when 251 IPOs raised just more than £9bn.

The biggest flotations of the year included RHM, the food group whose brands include Hovis, Mr Kipling, Sharwoods and Bisto; Inmarsat, the satellite group; Petrofac Resources, the oil services group; and IG, the spread-betting group. All four of these businesses were floated by private equity groups, including Doughty Hanson, CVC Capital, 3i, Apax and Permira. Shares in Petrofac, IG Group and Inmarsat have all outperformed the market since they floated. However, shares in RHM are currently trading below their float price of 275p each and have underperformed the food producers and processors sector as well as the wider market.

However, Tom Lamb, managing director at Barclays Private Equity, argues that for many private equity houses the secondary buy-out, where one group sells to a rival buy-out firm, has become a more attractive exit route than the IPO market.

'You can get better pricing, you can do it quicker and you can sell 100 per cent of the business in one go,' he said, adding: 'Five years ago, you often got a better valuation on a float than on a secondary. That is not the case now.'

Examples of large secondary buy-outs in 2005 and businesses that may one day look to float include Travelex, the foreign currency chain; Tussauds, the waxworks groups; and NCP, the car parks group. Mr Lamb said secondary buy-out activity was being driven by aggressive debt markets and the billions of capital sloshing around in private equity funds.

'If there is an attractive business up for sale, private equity groups will be trying very hard to buy it,' he notes.

As a result, many private equity firms are choosing to run informal dual-track processes, whereby they test the appetite of potential buyers of an investment while simultaneously preparing it for flotation.

Companies that have signalled that they may come to market in 2006 include Qinetiq, formerly the defence evaluation research agency, which is part-owned by Carlyle; Standard Life, the Edinburgh-based insurer which wants to demutualise; New Look, the retailer; United Biscuits, the owner of the Jaffa Cakes, McVitie's and Hula Hoops brands that was taken private in 2000; and General Healthcare, the private hospital chain owned by BC Partners.

Industry observers also believe Debenhams, the department store chain owned by CVC, Texas Pacific Group and Merrill Lynch Private Equity, could return to the market next spring, with a price tag of up to £3bn. Those that are unable to use the main market to raise funds have been turning to AIM.

By late December, 287 trading companies had raised £3.4bn on AIM, up from 243 IPOs raising £2.4bn in 2004, according to KPMG.

'Many more companies are considering listing on AIM, an increasingly attractive option due to the tax breaks and the lower costs of compliance with regulations in comparison with other markets,' said Gregory Ericksen at Ernst & Young.

However, any bankers preparing companies for flotation in 2006 – whether on AIM or the main market – would be wise to heed the concerns of the Financial Services Authority. In November, the UK market watchdog said the competitive process used by some companies to pick bookrunners for their IPOs could lead to conflicts of interest for banks. The FSA said the process in which a company chose its bank only after it had seen some research might encourage issuers to exert pressure on competing banks to produce analysis that was favourable or that justified a higher valuation price.

Competition among the banks for positions to lead manage IPOs has always been intensely fierce as they often lead to lucrative follow-on placings and other business. If UK equity markets continue to rise in 2006, the competition will increase further. Investors can only hope it is to their benefit.

Source: Lina Saigol and Peter Smith, FT.com, 3 January 2006. Reprinted with permission.

raised. A company may choose an introduction in order to increase the marketability of its shares, to obtain access to capital markets or simply to determine the value of its shares.

4.2.3 Listing regulations

New issues of unlisted ordinary shares are governed by the Financial Services and Markets Act 2000 and the Prospectus Regulations 2005, which require that a prospectus is issued, the contents of which comply with the regulations. Securities are admitted to the Official List by the UK Listing Authority, which is a division of the Financial Services Authority, and admitted to trading by the Stock Exchange itself under its own Admission and Disclosure Standards. The UKLA Listing Rules contain listing requirements that must be met by companies seeking a listing, some of which are as follows:

- Audited published accounts, usually for at least three years prior to admission.
- At least 25 per cent of the company's shares must be in public hands when trading in its shares begins.
- The company must be able to conduct its business independently of any shareholders with a controlling interest.
- The company must publish a prospectus containing a forecast of expected performance and other detailed information to assist investors in making an assessment of its prospects.
- The company must have a minimum market capitalisation of £700 000.

4.2.4 Relative importance of placing and public offer

Although placings are the most common method of obtaining a stock market quotation in the UK, they do not account for the majority of finance raised. Most of the new finance is raised by means of public offers, which tend to be much larger in value terms than placings.

The relative importance of public offers and placings varies between markets. In essence, placings are used more frequently in smaller markets where the amounts raised cannot usually justify the additional costs (e.g. marketing, advertising and underwriting costs) incurred by a public offer. The dominant position of placings in the Alternative Investment Market was confirmed by Corbett (1996), who reported that most AIM companies obtain a market listing by means of a placing. Public offers, though, still accounted for most of the funds raised. This data reflects the limitation of placings to smaller offers and the smaller size of AIM offers implied by Exhibit 4.1.

4.2.5 Underwriting

In the period between the announcement of a new equity issue and its completion, there is the possibility of adverse share price movements which may lead to the issue being unsuccessful. An unsuccessful equity issue is one where a company fails to raise the finance it is seeking or where it is left with shares that investors did not wish to

Vignette 4.2

Laura Ashley rights issue shunned

Laura Ashley revealed yesterday that only a third of its shareholders had responded to its £8.2m fundraising and a further 10 per cent [of offered shares] were sold in the market yesterday. As a result, the two underwriters were left with the bulk of the new shares in the rights issue. Bonham Industries, the investment vehicle of Dr Khoo Peng, Ashley's chairman, was left with an extra 27m shares on top of those it had agreed to take previously, and Bank of East Asia was left with 64m.

The blow came less than a month after the company was forced to revise the rights terms, cutting the price of the new shares by 25 per cent to 6p. At the time Malaysian United Industries (MUI), Ashley's biggest shareholder, also chose not to help underwrite the shares and said it might not take up its rights. Ashley announced the cash call in January to finance the closure of most of its poorly performing continental European stores.

MUI bought into Ashley in its previous emergency rights issue in 1998 and holds 43 per cent in the company. At that point, Ashley was in difficulty after an ill-fated foray into North America. Ashley also issued a trading statement that revealed sales dropped 1 per cent in the 14 weeks to May 3. The trading figures continued the poor trend outlined in the latest set of figures published this week. The full-year pre-tax loss of £14.1m was the worst performance by the company for four years.

Source: Peter John, FT.com, 10 May 2003. Reprinted with permission.

purchase. A company will wish to avoid an unsuccessful equity issue because of the damage it may cause to its reputation. An unsuccessful equity issue is also likely to make raising equity finance more expensive in the future. For these reasons, companies insure against the possibility of a new issue being unsuccessful by having it underwritten.

For each new issue, one or more main *underwriters* will be appointed, who will further spread the risk by appointing a number of *sub-underwriters*. While the main underwriter is usually the issuing house or merchant bank organising the equity issue, most underwriters are financial institutions such as insurance companies and pension funds. In return for a fee of about 1.25 per cent of the proceeds of the new equity issue (the total underwriting fee is about 2 per cent of proceeds), underwriters will accept the shares not taken up by the market, each underwriter taking unsold shares in proportion to the amount of fee income received. Through underwriting, therefore, a company is certain of raising the finance that it needs.

A new equity issue would still be regarded as unsuccessful, however, if most of the shares were taken up by underwriters rather than by the market. This has not been true with initial public offerings in recent years as most IPOs have been oversubscribed, but it is possible for a *rights issue*, where new ordinary shares are offered to existing shareholders, to be unsuccessful, as illustrated by Vignette 4.2.

4.2.6 Advantages of obtaining a stock exchange quotation

There are a number of benefits that may be obtained by a company through becoming listed on a stock exchange and any one of them may encourage the directors of a company to decide to seek a listing. Broadly speaking, these benefits include the raising of finance by coming to market, easier access to finance and the uses to which quoted shares can be put.

Raising finance through coming to market

The owners of a private company may decide to seek a listing so that, as part of the process of becoming listed, they can sell some of their shares and thereby realise some of the investment they have made in the company. An unquoted company whose growth has been due in part to an investment of venture capital may seek a stock market listing in order to give the venture capitalists an *exit route* by which to realise their investment. This is particularly true of management buyouts (*see* Section 11.7.3). In both of these situations, some or all of the funds raised by selling shares pass to a third party rather than to the company obtaining the listing. But a company may also decide to seek a listing primarily to raise funds for its own use, for example to fund an expansion of business activities.

Access to finance

By being listed on a recognised stock exchange, a company will have easier access to external sources of equity capital, whether through the new issues market or by a rights issue, since a listed company is likely to be more attractive to institutional investors. This means that a listed company can more easily obtain any long-term equity funds it needs for expansion. Unquoted companies, in contrast, may find their growth opportunities limited because of difficulties in raising the finance they need. This gap is filled to some extent by venture capitalists, who usually take an equity stake in companies they invest in. As far as debt finance is concerned, lenders tend to look on quoted companies more favourably since both credibility and reputation are enhanced by a listing, increasing a company's security and lowering its perceived risk. This may result in a lower cost of debt.

Uses of shares

Taking over another company can be a relatively easy way to achieve corporate growth and issuing new shares is a common way of financing a takeover. The shares of a listed company are more likely to be accepted by target company shareholders in exchange for their existing shares than shares in a private company. This is partly because the shares of listed companies are easier to sell: a ready market exists in them since, in order to satisfy listing rules, at least 25 per cent of their shares must be in public hands. The shares of a private company may not have a ready market. Marketability also increases the value of the shares and hence the value of the company. The use of shares as a means of payment for acquisitions is shown in Exhibit 11.2 in Chapter 11.

4.2.7 Disadvantages of obtaining a stock market quotation

The benefits derived from a listing naturally have a cost, and the disadvantages associated with being listed must be considered if a balanced view is to be presented. There are, after all, many other ways to obtain funds or to establish a reputation: seeking a stock market listing will not be the best option for all companies.

Costs of a quotation

Obtaining and maintaining a stock exchange quotation is a costly business. The costs of obtaining a listing will reduce the amount of finance raised by a new issue. Initial listing costs will include the admission fee (typically between £50 300 and £266 0000), the sponsor's fee (£200 000 minimum), legal fees (£100 000 minimum) and the reporting accountant's fee (£100 000 minimum). The ongoing annual costs of satisfying listing requirements must also be met. One of these costs is the cost of increased financial disclosure since stock exchange disclosure requirements are more demanding than those of company law. This will lead to increased public scrutiny of the company and its performance.

Shareholder expectations

The directors of a private company may have been used to satisfying their own needs but, once the company becomes listed, they will need to consider the expectations of new shareholders. These will include the expectations of institutional shareholders, which may include a focus on short-term profitability and dividend income. The possibility of being taken over is increased if the company fails to meet shareholder expectations since dissatisfied shareholders are likely to be more willing to sell their shares to a bidding company. The stock exchange is therefore seen as providing a *market for corporate control*, meaning that poor performance by a listed company may be corrected by removing its managers through a takeover. The increased financial transparency resulting from the stock exchange requirement to produce regular reports and accounts means that bidders are more easily able to select likely acquisition targets, whose shares they can then seek to acquire on the open market.

Dissatisfaction can arise with being listed on the stock market, as shown by Vignette 4.3.

Vignette 4.3

Nightfreight to go private via £35m management buy-out

Nightfreight has joined the stream of companies leaving the stock market after agreeing a £35m management buy-out. Ewenny, an MBO vehicle, has offered 69p a share for the logistics group – a 54 per cent premium to the company's valuation on December 14, when it first announced it was in talks. Yesterday, Nightfreight shares rose 5¼p to 67¾p. Ewenny said it had received irrevocable undertakings in respect of 27.8m shares, about 55 per cent of its issued capital.

Ronald Sullivan, chief executive, who is not part of the MBO team, said Nightfreight had been undervalued by the market.

Paul Hemming, at Arthur Andersen Corporate Finance, which advised on the MBO, described the deal as a 'good opportunity to move the business forward with private equity money'.

Nightfreight yesterday announced an increase in pre-tax profits to £4.51m (£4.12m) on turnover slightly ahead at £96m (£94m) for the year to November 30.

Consolidation in the parcel delivery sector is set to continue. Last week, Fastrack collapsed following problems integrating its parcel delivery and freight forwarding business. Mr Sullivan hoped Nightfreight would benefit from Fastrack's demise.

Ewenny comprises Craig Russell, Nightfreight finance director, and three senior Nightfreight managers: Robert Kelly, Paul Watson and John Miller. Earnings were 6.25p (5.48p). In light of the MBO, there is no dividend (2.4p).

Source: Lydia Adetunji, *Financial Times*, 30 January 2001. Reprinted with permission.

4.3 Rights issues

If a company wishes to issue new shares, it is required by law to offer them first to its existing shareholders, unless those shareholders have already agreed in a meeting of the company to waive the right for a period. Because of this legal right to be offered the shares before other investors, such an issue of new shares is called a *rights issue*. In order to preserve existing patterns of ownership and control, a rights issue is offered on a *pro rata basis*, such as one new share for every four existing shares (referred to as a *1 for 4* issue).

Rights issues are cheaper in terms of issuing costs than a public offer to the general public as a way of raising finance. In addition there is no dilution of ownership and control if the rights offered are fully taken up. But a rights issue is not appropriate if the amount of finance to be raised is large, as the funds available to individual shareholders are likely to be limited.

Rights issues are offered at a discount to the current market price, commonly in the region of 15 to 20 per cent. This discount makes the new shares more attractive to shareholders and also allows for any adverse share price movements prior to the issue. The current market price will normally be quoted *ex dividend*, which means that buying the share will not confer the right to receive a dividend about to be paid (*see* Section 10.1). The price of an already issued share may increase to reflect the value of the right to receive new shares at a discount; this new price is called the *cum rights* price. When buying shares on the open market no longer gives the buyer the right to participate in the rights issue because the list of shareholders has closed, the share price will fall as it goes *ex rights*. Exhibit 4.2 indicates that the number of rights issues has continued to decline from a peak of 98 issues in 1996 and the amount of finance raised has decreased significantly in recent years.

| Exhibit 4.2 | Money raised by rights issues on the UK stock market, 1998–2004 |

Year	Number of issues	Money raised (£bn)
1995	83	5.1
1996	98	4.7
1997	61	2.2
1998	39	1.2
1999	39	2.6
2000	33	3.9
2001	24	6.5
2002	23	6.4
2003	14	2.8
2004	17	0.2

Source: London Stock Exchange Market Information and Analysis, 2006.

4.3.1 The theoretical ex-rights price

After the issue, both old and new shares will trade at the *theoretical ex rights price*, which is a weighted average of the *cum rights price* and the *rights issue price*. We have:

$$P_e = P_P \frac{N_O}{N} + P_N \frac{N_N}{N}$$

where: P_e = the theoretical ex-rights price
P_p = cum-rights price
P_N = rights issue price
N_O = number of old shares
N_N = number of new shares
N = the total number of shares

Example | **Calculation of the theoretical ex rights price**

Nolig plc has in issue 2 million ordinary shares of par value £1.00, currently trading at £2.20 per share. The company decides to raise new equity funds by offering its existing shareholders the right to subscribe for one new share at £1.85 each for every four shares already held. After the announcement of the issue, the ordinary share price falls to £2.10 and remains at this level until the time of the rights issue. What is the theoretical ex rights price?

Suggested answer

Cum rights price, P_P =	£2.10
New issue price, P_N =	£1.85
Number of old shares, N_O =	2.0 million
Number of new shares, N_N =	0.5 million
Total number of shares, N =	2.5 million

and so:

$$\text{Theoretical ex rights price, } P_e = \frac{(2 \times 2.10) + (0.5 \times 1.85)}{2.5} = £2.05$$

Alternatively, using the terms of the 1 for 4 rights issue:

$$\text{Theoretical ex rights price, } P_e = \frac{(4 \times 2.10) + (1 \times 1.85)}{5} = £2.05$$

4.3.2 The value of the rights

An ordinary shareholder can *detach* the rights from the shares and sell them to other investors. There is an active market in rights, with prices quoted regularly in the financial press. The value of the rights is the maximum price that a buyer is prepared to pay for them: this will be the theoretical gain the buyer could make by exercising them. It is the difference between the theoretical ex-rights price and the rights issue price. Continuing the example of Nolig plc, the value of the rights attached to four Nolig shares is £2.05 − £1.85 = £0.20 or 20p. This is the amount that an investor would be prepared to pay in exchange for the rights attached to the four shares, as he could then pay £1.85 for a share which would be worth £2.05 on the equity market. The value of the rights can also be expressed as 20p/4 = 5p per existing share.

4.3.3 Rights issues and shareholder wealth

If we regard cash in a shareholder's bank account as equivalent in wealth terms to the ordinary shares that could be bought in exchange for it, then the wealth of the shareholder need not be affected by a rights issue. If shareholders subscribe for their full entitlement of new shares or if they sell all the rights attached to their existing shares (or any combination of these two alternatives), their wealth position will be unchanged. If they do nothing and allow their rights to lapse, however, their wealth will fall. We can show this with a simple example.

Example	Wealth effect of a rights issue

Nolig plc has 2 million ordinary shares of par value £1.00 in issue. The company decided (see above) to make a 1 for 4 rights issue at £1.85 per new share and the cum-rights share price was £2.10. The theoretical ex-rights price was found to be £2.05 and the value of the rights was found to be 5p per existing share. If Rosemary, a shareholder, owns 1000 shares in Nolig plc, she has the right to subscribe for 250 new shares and her shareholding is currently worth £2100 (1000 × £2.10). How will Rosemary's wealth be affected in each of the following scenarios?

1 Rosemary subscribes for 250 new shares.
2 Rosemary sells all her rights.
3 Rosemary takes no action over the rights issue.

1 Rosemary subscribes for 250 new shares

	£
1000 shares cum-rights @ £2.10 =	2100.00
Cash for 250 new shares @ £1.85 =	462.50
1250 shares ex-rights @ £2.05 =	2562.50

Rosemary's overall wealth position is unchanged if she subscribes for the new shares, even though some of her wealth has changed from cash into ordinary shares.

2 Rosemary sells her rights

	£
1000 shares ex-rights @ £2.05 =	2050.00
Sale of rights, 1000 @ 5 pence =	50.00
Wealth position after rights issue	2100.00

→

Rosemary's wealth position is also unchanged if she sells her rights: the effect here is that some of her wealth has changed from ordinary shares into cash.

3 Rosemary takes no action over the rights issue

	£
Initial position, 1000 shares @ £2.10 =	2100.00
Final position, 1000 shares @ £2.05 =	2050.00
Decline in wealth by doing nothing	50.00

Rosemary's wealth has declined because the price of her shares has fallen from the cum-rights value to the ex-rights value.

Choosing neither to subscribe for new shares offered, nor to sell the rights attached to existing shares held, will lead to a decrease in shareholder wealth, as this example shows. If appropriate action is taken, however, the effect on shareholder wealth is, in theory at least, a neutral one. This will be true no matter how great a discount is attached to the new shares.

4.3.4 Market price after a rights issue

The *actual* ex-rights price is likely to be different from the price predicted by theory. This is primarily due to differing investor expectations, which influence their buying and selling preferences and hence market prices. Investors will have expectations about the future state of the economy; they may be expecting interest rates or inflation to increase, for example, or may be anticipating a downturn in economic activity. Investors may also have formed opinions about the proposed use of the new funds by the company. If these opinions are favourable, the share price will increase accordingly.

As far as earnings are concerned, if these are expected to be maintained or increased after the new issue then the share price may be unchanged or even increase, in spite of there being more shares in circulation. This points to the need to consider the effect of a proposed rights issue on *earnings yield* (*see* Section 2.4.7) as well as earnings per share. If the earnings yield on existing funds remains unchanged, the key variable affecting the ex-rights price will be the expected earnings yield on the funds raised.

We can modify our original expression for the theoretical ex-rights price (P_e), given earlier in Section 4.3.1, to enable it to take into account the expected earnings yield on the new funds raised (γ_N), compared with the earnings yield on existing funds (γ_O). We have:

$$P_e = P_P \frac{N_O}{N} + P_N \frac{N_N \gamma_N}{N \gamma_O}$$

where: P_P = cum-rights price
$\quad\quad\quad P_N$ = rights issue price
$\quad\quad\quad N_O$ = number of old shares

$$N_N \quad = \text{number of new shares}$$

$N \quad = \text{total number of shares}$

$\gamma_N/\gamma_O = \text{ratio of earnings yield on new capital to earnings yield on old capital}$

If γ_N/γ_O is greater than one, corresponding to the situation where investors expect earnings to increase after the rights issue, the ex-rights share price will be greater than the price predicted by the simple weighted average considered in Section 4.3.1. If the issue is not seen as a positive move by the market, so that overall earnings are expected to fall, then γ_N/γ_O is less than one and the ex-rights share price will be less than a simple weighted average.

Returning to the earlier example of Nolig plc, you will recall that the theoretical ex-rights price was found to be £2.05. If we now assume that the earnings yield on existing funds is 18 per cent, but that the expected earnings yield on the funds raised by the rights issue is 25 per cent, we have:

$$\text{Ex-rights price, } P_e = \frac{(2 \times 2.10)}{2.5} + \frac{(0.5 \times 1.85) \times 25}{(2.5 \times 18)} = £2.19$$

The increased earnings expected from the new funds have led to a higher predicted ex-rights share price.

The ex-rights share price will also be affected by the expected level of dividends: if dividends are expected to fall, the share price will decline. While earnings from the new investment may take some time to come on stream, the decision on how much to pay out as dividends rests with the directors of the company. In order to reassure shareholders, who are being asked to subscribe further funds to the company, an announcement about the expected level of dividends often accompanies the announcement of a rights issue.

Empirical evidence suggests that the market assumes that companies will be able to maintain their level of dividend payments and that the formula for determining the theoretical ex-rights price is a reasonably accurate reflection of the true state of affairs.

4.3.5 Underwriting and deep discount rights issues

In theory, shareholder wealth is not affected by a rights issue since the value of the rights is equivalent to the difference between the value of the original shares held and the theoretical ex-rights price. We also noted that one of the reasons why a rights issue is issued at a discount to the current market price is in order to make it attractive to existing shareholders and thereby help to ensure the issue's success. Why, in that case, is it common for a company to seek a further guarantee of the success of a rights issue by having it underwritten? Since the size of the discount is irrelevant, the cost of underwriting could be avoided and the success of a rights issue could be assured by increasing the size of the discount, i.e. by offering the new shares at a *deep discount* to the current share price. Deep discount rights issues, however, are seldom encountered. An example of a recent one is the subject of Vignette 4.4.

An explanation of the rarity of deep discount rights issues has been sought in the role played by underwriters. It has been suggested that underwriting may act as a

Vignette 4.4

Opinions split on Pearson discounted rights issue

Institutional shareholders said yesterday they expected other companies to follow Pearson's move to fund a big acquisition by way of a deeply-discounted rights issue – a capital raising exercise not seen on a similar scale for more than 10 years. However, some investment bankers expressed doubt that Pearson, the media group that owns the Financial Times, would start a renewed trend.

On Monday, Pearson announced an offer for National Computer Systems of the US that would be funded by a £1.7bn 3-for-11 rights issue at half the market price. The large discount enabled Pearson to minimize the costs of underwriting the issue. Institutional investors backed the move, which they described as 'innovative' and 'cost-effective' and urged other companies to adopt the method.

One investor said yesterday: 'I have spoken to at least six investment bankers in the last year who were considering it as an option but their transactions went away. Pearson's didn't.'

The move caused confusion in the City about whether Pearson shareholders were worse or better off following Monday's 9 per cent fall in the share price. 'There is such a difference of opinion in the market,' said one analyst. 'Deeply-discounted rights issues are so rare that people have forgotten the mechanics of how they work.' The shares recovered much of the lost ground yesterday, closing up 117p at £19.45, compared with £20.10 before the issue was announced. But analysts expect the shares to fall when they go ex-rights on Tuesday.

Companies have tended to shy away from deeply-discounted rights issues for several reasons. Many believed they would be under pressure to maintain the level of dividends on the enlarged equity, increasing their cost of capital. But Pearson said it would scale back dividends on a pro forma basis.

Another concern has been the effect of deeply-discounted rights issues on private shareholders, who can face capital gains tax problems if they do not take up all their rights.

In spite of the warm reception to Pearson's move, Paul Thompson at Merrill Lynch did not expect a trend to emerge. 'The downside for companies looking to participate in globalization is that rights issues do not easily broaden your shareholder base.'

Analysts said the rise in the share price yesterday reflected the generally positive reaction to the NCS offer and the accompanying interim figures.

Analysts welcomed the statement that investment in the Financial Times Group's Internet operations had 'reached the high water mark'. The net figure was £64m in the first half.

Pearson, which leads the educational publishing market following the acquisition of Simon & Schuster's specialist publishing arm in 1998, said funding for online education activities would be stepped up in the second half.

Source: Ashling O'Connor, *Financial Times*, 2 August 2000. Reprinted with permission.

signalling device, giving assurance to shareholders that the risk associated with a rights issue is regarded as acceptable by the underwriters and hence by institutional investors. On this analysis, underwriting has a positive effect on both the rights issue and the company's market price.

4.4 Scrip issues, share splits, scrip dividends and share repurchases

4.4.1 Scrip issues and share splits

Scrip issues and share splits are both ways in which a company can increase the number of shares in issue, without raising any additional finance. A *scrip issue* (also known as a bonus issue) is a conversion of existing capital reserves or retained earnings into additional shares, which are then distributed pro rata to existing shareholders. It is in essence a balance sheet transfer from reserves to the ordinary share account. A *share split* (also known as a stock split in the USA) involves simultaneously reducing the nominal value of each share and increasing the number of shares in issue so that the balance sheet value of the shares is unchanged. For example, a company with 1 million shares of par value 50p could, as a result of a share split, have 2 million ordinary shares of par value 25p.

A number of possible explanations for share splits have been advanced. One common theory is that share splits increase the ease with which ordinary shares can be traded by moving them into a more favourable price range. More investors will be willing to buy shares trading at £5, it is argued, than shares trading at £10. Under this theory, share splits increase liquidity. Research by Copeland (1979), however, suggests that liquidity actually declines following a share split since trading volume is proportionately lower and transactions costs are proportionately higher.

Another common theory about why share splits occur is that they have, in some unexplained way, a positive effect on shareholder wealth. The effect of share splits on shareholder wealth has been the subject of much research, but the results are inconclusive. Some researchers, such as Firth (1973), have found that share splits do not have any beneficial effects resulting from share price movements. Other researchers, such as Grinblatt et al. (1984), have detected a positive effect on shareholder wealth and suggest that the announcement of a share split might be interpreted by investors as a favourable signal concerning a company's future cash flows. Grinblatt et al. (1984) also found that positive effects on shareholder wealth appeared to occur as a result of scrip issue announcements.

4.4.2 Scrip dividends

Another method of issuing new equity which does not result in the raising of additional finance is the issuing of a *scrip dividend* (also known as a share dividend). Here, a shareholder accepts more ordinary shares in a company as a partial or total alternative to a cash dividend (*see* Section 10.7.1).

There are cash flow advantages to the company in offering a scrip dividend, since if investors choose to take up the scrip dividend there will be less cash paid out by the company as dividends. A further benefit to the company is that, as a result of the increase in equity, there will be a small decrease in gearing (*see* Section 2.4.6). Since the scrip dividend replaces a cash dividend that would have been paid anyway, there is no reason why a scrip dividend should cause a share price fall in an efficient capital market.

If ordinary shareholders wish to increase their shareholdings, a scrip dividend allows them to do so cheaply, without incurring dealing costs. For a tax-paying ordinary shareholder, there is no difference in the UK between a scrip dividend and a cash dividend since a scrip dividend is taxed as though it were income. For tax-exempt ordinary shareholders, however, there is a difference. With a cash dividend, tax-exempt shareholders can benefit by reclaiming the tax paid by the company on the profits distributed. With a scrip dividend, this benefit is lost since no corporation tax liability arises when a scrip dividend is issued. As a cash dividend and any scrip dividend alternative offered by a company are required by regulation to be similar in value, there is a financial disincentive for tax-exempt ordinary shareholders to accept scrip dividends.

4.4.3 Share repurchases

Share repurchases (or share buybacks) are one way of returning cash to ordinary shareholders. A UK company can purchase its own shares provided that permission has been given by shareholders in a general meeting of the company. To protect the interests of creditors and the remaining shareholders, though, share repurchases are carefully regulated. By law, payment for repurchased shares can only be made from distributable profits (*see* Section 10.7.2).

There are several reasons for returning surplus capital to shareholders. One rationale is that shareholders will be able to invest the cash more effectively than the company. Another is that the value of the remaining shares will be enhanced after shares have been repurchased. Since the capital employed by a company is reduced by repurchasing shares, return on capital employed (*see* Section 2.4.3) will increase. The number of shares will fall, resulting in an increase in earnings per share. While share repurchases also lead to an increase in gearing, it is argued that any increase in financial risk is negligible and so, if the cost of equity is unaltered, the value of both shares and company will be increased. A recent example of a share repurchase programme is the subject of Vignette 4.5.

Vignette 4.5

3i shareholders to reap £500m

Private equity group 3i yesterday said it would return at least £500m to shareholders for the second year running. It came after the FTSE 100 group generated more than £1.8bn from selling, floating and refinancing companies in its portfolio in the first 11 months of its financial year. The cash is likely to be returned via share buybacks, with further details expected when 3i announces full-year results in May. Last July, 3i said it would return £500m to shareholders. It paid £250m via a special dividend and has to date bought shares in the market worth £220m.

In spite of expanding in markets such as India and establishing new business lines, including infrastructure, 3i is generating more cash than it needs. In the 11 months to February, it floated 13 businesses on seven different stock markets, including Petrofac, the oil services group, in London and Focus Media on Nasdaq. Further cash was generated by selling stakes in Travelex, the foreign exchange group, and Betapharm, the German drugs group.

Full-year profits on the disposal of investments were expected to be 'significantly higher' than last year, 3i said. The group made £1.82bn from selling assets in the 11 months, an increase of almost 60 per cent over the corresponding period in the previous year.

Philip Yea, chief executive, described the return of cash as 'a signal we need to make to the market today' but would not say how it would affect the group's gearing, which is currently well below its 30-40 per cent target.

Standard & Poor's, the credit ratings agency, said the decision would not affect its assessment of 3i and that it did not expect net leverage, last reported in September 2005 at 20 per cent, to approach the top end of the target range.

The company invested £1.18bn in the 11 months to February, up from £843m. 'We continue to be highly selective with respect to new business,' Mr Yea said, noting that the group had made its first deal in India and was expanding in the US.

Philip Middleton, an analyst at Merrill Lynch, said recently that 3i's expansion abroad and an apparent pick-up in its venture operations should suit current market conditions.

Shares in 3i, which have risen 40 per cent in the last year, added 3½p to close at 949½p, valuing the group at £5.2bn.

Source: Peter Smith and Delphine Strauss, *Financial Times*, 31 March 2006. Reprinted with permission.

4.5 Preference shares

Preference shares differ from ordinary shares in giving the holder preferential rights to receive a share of annual profits. An ordinary dividend cannot be paid unless all preference dividends due have been paid in full. Preference shares are also higher in the creditor hierarchy than ordinary shares, and have a preferential right to receive the proceeds of disposal of the assets in the event of a company going into liquidation. They are therefore less risky than ordinary shares, even though they are legally share capital as well. Like ordinary shares, preference shares are normally permanent (i.e. irredeemable) but, unlike ordinary shares, they do not normally carry voting rights. However, preference shares carry a higher risk than debt, for several reasons:

- preference shares, unlike debt, are not secured on company assets;
- preference dividends cannot be paid until interest payments on debt have been covered;
- in the event of liquidation, preference shareholders will not be paid off until the claims of debt holders have been satisfied.

Preference shares may be either non-cumulative or cumulative with respect to preference dividends, which like ordinary dividends are a distribution of taxed profits and not a payment of interest. With *non-cumulative* preference shares, if distributable profits are insufficient to pay the preference dividend, the dividend is lost; with *cumulative* preference shares, if distributable profits are insufficient to pay the preference dividend, the right to receive it is carried forward and unpaid preference dividends must be settled before any ordinary dividend can be paid in subsequent years. If preference shares are *non-participating*, the preference dividend represents the sole return to the holders of the shares, irrespective of the company's earnings growth. *Participating* preference shares, in addition to paying a fixed preference dividend, offer the right to receive an additional dividend if profits in the year exceed an agreed amount.

4.5.1 Variable rate preference shares

Preference shares commonly pay investors a fixed rate dividend, but preference shares paying a variable rate dividend have become more common in recent years. Two distinct methods of periodically resetting the preference dividend rate are used. In the first method, the preference dividend rate is a *floating rate* or an adjustable rate determined by adding a fixed percentage to a market interest rate such as the London Interbank Offered Rate (LIBOR). With the second method, the preference dividend rate is adjusted periodically to the rate which allows the preference shares to trade at a *constant stated market value*. An example of the second method of resetting the dividend rate is given by auction market preferred stock (AMPS).

4.5.2 Convertible preference shares

Other features may be added to preference shares to make them attractive or to satisfy particular company financing needs. Convertible preference shares, for example, give the holder the option to convert them into ordinary shares on prescribed terms in prescribed circumstances.

4.5.3 The popularity of preference shares

The cost disadvantage of preference shares relative to debt has led to a decline in their popularity in the UK. It is unlikely that the dividend rate on preference shares would be less than the after-tax interest cost of a debenture issue due to the relative risks associated with the two securities. Convertible redeemable preference shares have been a popular financing method with providers of venture capital, however. If the company supported by the venture finance is doing well, the preference shares can be converted into ordinary shares, leading to higher returns. If the company is not doing well, the preference shares can be redeemed. The 1980s saw preference shares growing in popularity with bank issuers, whereas AMPS proved attractive to corporate issuers in the 1990s.

4.5.4 The advantages and disadvantages of preference shares

One of the main advantages to companies of preference shares compared with debt – an advantage shared with ordinary shares – is that preference dividends do not need to be paid if profits are insufficient to cover them. This is less of a problem for holders of cumulative preference shares (although the real value of unpaid preference dividends will decline), but owners of non-cumulative preference shares will be unhappy about not receiving a dividend. For this reason, holders of non-cumulative preference shares will demand a higher return. Further advantages to companies of preference shares are:

- they do not carry general voting rights and so will not dilute ownership and control;
- they preserve debt capacity, since they are not secured;
- non-payment of preference dividends does not give preference shareholders the right to appoint a receiver.

The major disadvantage of preference shares to companies is their cost relative to, say, the cost of debentures. Because of the higher risk associated with preference shares the percentage dividend may, for example, be 12 per cent whereas the interest rate on debentures stands at 10 per cent. This cost differential is exacerbated when the favourable tax position of the interest paid on debentures is taken into consideration. Assuming that the issuing company is not in a tax-exhausted position, its after-tax cost of debt with a corporation tax rate of 30 per cent and an interest coupon rate of 10 per cent will be $10 \times (1 - 0.3)$, or 7 per cent. Given these relative costs, companies will choose debenture finance rather than preference shares.

4.6 Conclusion

In this chapter we have discussed a number of the important issues in connection with equity finance and preference shares. Equity finance gives a company a solid financial foundation, since it is truly permanent capital which does not normally need to be repaid. Ordinary shareholders, as the owners of the company and the carriers of the largest slice of risk, expect the highest returns. Their position and rights as owners are protected by both government and stock market regulations and any new issue of shares must take these into account.

Key points

1. Ordinary shares have a nominal value which is different from their market value, and are usually issued at a premium. They confer individual and collective rights on their owners.

2. Ordinary shareholders are the ultimate bearers of risk because, being at the bottom of the creditor hierarchy, they stand to lose everything in the event of company liquidation. They therefore expect the greatest return.

3. To help it to satisfy regulations governing new equity issues and to advise it on listing procedures, a company will appoint a sponsor, which is usually a merchant bank.

4. A placing involves issuing blocks of new shares at a fixed price to institutional investors. It is a low-cost issue method involving little risk.

5. A public offer is usually used for large issues of new equity and involves offering shares to the public through an issuing house or sponsoring merchant bank.

6. An introduction grants a listing to the existing shares of a company, and does not involve the issuing of new shares.

7. The UK Listing Authority enforces Listing Regulations which are designed to protect investors and screen companies seeking a listing.

8. Placings are the most common method of obtaining a stock market listing, but most of the new finance raised is by public offers.

9. Companies insure against the failure of a new equity issue through underwriting. The main underwriter is usually the issuing house: most underwriters are financial institutions.

10. The benefits arising from obtaining a listing are: raising finance by coming to market, easier access to equity and other finance, and uses to which listed shares can be put, including payment in a takeover bid.

11. The disadvantages of being listed include the costs of obtaining and maintaining a listing, increased financial transparency, the need to meet shareholder expectations, the need to maintain dividends and the risk of takeover.

12. A rights issue involves the issue of new shares to existing shareholders in proportion to their existing holdings. It can preserve existing patterns of ownership and control and is cheaper than a public offer, but is unsuitable for raising large amounts of finance.

13 Rights issue shares are usually offered at a 15 to 20 per cent discount to the current market price, making them more attractive to shareholders and allowing for any adverse share price movements.

14 After a rights issue, shares should trade at the theoretical ex-rights price.

15 Rights can be sold to investors: the value of rights is the difference between the theoretical ex-rights price and the rights issue price. If shareholders either buy the offered shares or sell their rights, there is no effect on their wealth.

16 The actual ex-rights price may be different from the theoretical ex-rights price because of market expectations. In particular, the share price will reflect the expected yield on existing and new funds.

17 A scrip issue is a conversion of existing reserves into additional shares. A share split involves reducing the nominal value of shares while at the same time increasing the number of shares in issue so that balance sheet value is unchanged.

18 It has been suggested that share splits increase liquidity, but research has not supported this view. It has also been suggested that share splits increase shareholder wealth, but the evidence is inconclusive.

19 A scrip dividend involves offering ordinary shares as an alternative to a cash dividend. It has cash flow advantages for a company.

20 Share repurchases are a way of returning cash to shareholders. They are carefully regulated in order to protect creditors.

21 Preference shares carry a right to receive a dividend before ordinary shareholders, but a dividend may not need to be paid if profits are low.

22 Preference shares are less risky than ordinary shares but are riskier than debt. They do not normally give voting rights and are unsecured. They preserve debt capacity, but are not tax efficient.

23 Preference shares may be either cumulative or non-cumulative with respect to preference dividends. It is also possible to issue variable rate preference shares, participating and non-participating preference shares, and convertible preference shares.

24 In practice, ordinary preference shares tend to be less attractive than debt.

Self-test questions

Answers to these questions can be found on pages 435–6.

1 Explain why the return required by ordinary shareholders is different from the return required by bondholders.

2 Briefly outline some of the important rights of ordinary shareholders.

3 Briefly explain the various ways in which a company may obtain a quotation for its ordinary shares on the London Stock Exchange.

4 Outline the advantages and disadvantages which should be considered by a currently unquoted company which is considering obtaining a listing on a recognised stock exchange.

5 What are pre-emptive rights and why are they important to shareholders?

6 Discuss the advantages and disadvantages of a rights issue to a company.

7 XTC is planning a 1 for 4 rights issue at a 20 per cent discount to the current market price of £2.50. If investors wish to sell their 'rights per existing share', how much should they sell them for?

(a) 10p (b) 20p (c) 30p (d) 40p (e) 50p

8 'A conversion of existing capital reserves into ordinary shares, which are then distributed pro rata to existing shareholders.' This statement best defines:

(a) scrip dividends

(b) a rights issue

(c) bonus bonds

(d) scrip issues

(e) share splits

9 Explain why preference shares are not popular as a source of finance for companies.

10 Which one of the following statements best describes a cumulative preference share?

(a) It has the right to be converted into ordinary shares at a future date.

(b) It entitles the shareholder to a share of residual profits.

(c) It carries forward to the next year the right to receive unpaid dividends.

(d) It entitles the shareholder to a fixed rate of dividend.

(e) It gives its holder voting rights at a company's annual general meeting.

Questions for review

Answers to these questions can be found on pages 437–8. Questions with an asterisk (*) are at an intermediate level.

1 Brand plc generates profit after tax of 15 per cent on shareholders' funds. Its current capital structure is as follows:

	£
Ordinary shares of 50p each	200 000
Reserves	400 000
	600 000

The board of Brand plc wishes to raise £160 000 from a rights issue in order to expand existing operations. Its return on shareholders' funds will be unchanged. The current ex-dividend market price of Brand plc is £1.90. Three different rights issue prices have been suggested by the finance director: £1.80, £1.60 and £1.40.

Determine the number of shares to be issued, the theoretical ex-rights price, the expected earnings per share and the form of the issue for each rights issue price. Comment on your results.

2* Maltby plc, a company quoted on the London Stock Exchange, has been making regular annual after-tax profits of £7 million for some years and has the following long-term capital structure.

	£000
Ordinary shares, 50p each	4 000
12 per cent debentures	9 000
	13 000

The debenture issue is not due to be redeemed for some time and the company has become increasingly concerned about the need to continue paying interest at 12 per cent when the interest rate on newly issued government stock of a similar maturity is only 6 per cent.

A proposal has been made to issue 2 million new shares in a rights issue, at a discount of 20 per cent to the current share price of Maltby plc, and to use the funds raised to pay off part of the debenture issue. The current share price of Maltby plc is £3.50 and the current market price of the debentures is £112 per £100 block.

Alternatively, the funds raised by the rights issue could be invested in a new project giving an annual after-tax return of 20 per cent. Whichever option is undertaken, the stock market view of the company's prospects and hence its P/E ratio will remain unchanged. Maltby plc pays corporation tax at a rate of 30 per cent.

By considering the effect on the share price of the two alternative proposals, discuss whether the proposed rights issue can be recommended as being in the best interests of the ordinary shareholders of Maltby plc. Your answer should include all relevant calculations.

3 It has become increasingly common for companies to offer their shareholders a choice between a cash dividend and an equivalent scrip dividend. Briefly consider the advantages of scrip dividends from the point of view of:

(a) the company;

(b) the shareholders.

Questions for discussion

Questions with an asterisk (*) are at an advanced level.

1 Hanging Valley plc has issued share capital of 2 million ordinary shares, par value £1.00. The board of the company has decided it needs to raise £1m, net of issue costs, to finance a new product.

(a) It has been suggested that the additional finance be raised by means of a 1 for 4 rights issue. The issue price will be at a 20 per cent discount to the current market price of £2.75 and issue costs are expected to be £50 000. Calculate and explain the following:

(i) the theoretical ex-rights price per share;

(ii) the net cash raised;

(iii) the value of the rights.

(b) Is the underwriting of rights issues an unnecessary expense?

2 Brag plc is raising finance through a rights issue and the current ex-dividend market price of its shares is £3.00. The rights issue is on a 1 for 6 basis and the new shares will be offered at a 20 per cent discount to the current market price.

(a) Discuss the relative merits of the following ways of raising new equity finance:

(i) a placing;

(ii) a public offer.

(b) Explain why, in general, rights issues are priced at a discount to the prevailing market price of the share.

(c) Calculate the theoretical ex-rights share price of Brag plc and the value of the rights per share using the above information.

(d) Discuss the factors that determine whether the actual ex-rights share price is the same as the theoretical ex-rights price.

3* Mansun plc is a listed company with the following capital structure.

	£000
Ordinary shares, £1 each	20 000
Reserves	10 000
8% unsecured loan stock 2016	2 000
13% debentures 2011	16 000
	48 000

The debentures give Mansun plc the right to redeem them at any time before maturity as long as full market value is paid to bondholders. The unsecured loan stock has just been issued and its cost is indicative of current financial market conditions. The current share price of Mansun plc is £4.27 and the current market price of the debentures is £105. Mansun plc has been making regular annual after-tax profits of £10m for some years and pays corporation tax at a rate of 30 per cent.

At a recent board meeting, the finance director suggested that 4 million new shares be issued in a rights issue, at a discount of 15 per cent to the company's current share price, and that the funds raised should be used to redeem part of the debenture issue. Issue costs are expected to be £660 000. The managing director, however, feels strongly that the proceeds of the rights issue should be invested in a project yielding an annual return before tax of 22 per cent.

The board agreed that the stock market view of the company's prospects would be unchanged whichever option were selected and agreed to proceed with the rights issue. One week later, the company announced the rights issue and explained the use to which the funds were to be put.

(a) If capital markets are semi-strong form efficient, determine the expected share price on the announcement of the rights issue under each of the two alternative proposals.

(b) Discuss, with the aid of supporting calculations, whether the rights issue is in the best interests of the shareholders of Mansun plc.

4 Freeze plc is a service company that has been listed for six years. Its merchant bank has advised the company's directors that their proposed 1 for 4 rights issue should be at a 15 per cent discount to their current ordinary share price of £4.20. The proposed rights issue is for £3m to expand existing business activities.

(a) Mr Tundra is a small investor who owns 10 000 shares of Freeze plc. Using the information provided, discuss the effect of the proposed rights issue on the personal wealth of Mr Tundra.

(b) Critically discuss the factors to be considered by Freeze plc in using a rights issue as a way of raising new equity finance. Your answer should include a discussion of the following points:

(i) the difference between actual and theoretical ex-rights price;

(ii) other ways in which Freeze plc could raise the new equity finance.

References

Copeland, T. (1979) 'Liquidity changes following stock splits', *Journal of Finance*, Vol. 34, March, pp. 115–41.

Corbett, P. (1996) 'Share ownership', *AIM News*, Issue 5, July.

Firth, M. (1973) 'Shareholder wealth attendant upon capitalization issues', *Accounting and Business Research*, Vol. 4, No. 13, pp. 23–32.

Grinblatt, M., Masulis, R. and Titman, S. (1984) 'The valuation effects of stock splits and stock dividends', *Journal of Financial Economics*, December, pp. 461–90.

Recommended reading

A useful discussion of equity finance, new issue methods and preference shares can be found in:

Arnold, G. (2005) *Corporate Financial Management*, 3rd edn, Harlow: FT Prentice Hall.

It is interesting to contrast the treatment of equity in the UK and the USA. See, for example:

Ross, S., Westerfield, R. and Jaffe, J. (2005) *Corporate Finance*, 7th edn, New York: McGraw Hill.

Useful articles include the following:

Blume, M. (1998) 'Stock exchanges: forces of change', in Dickson, T. and Bickerstaffe, G. (eds) *Mastering Finance*, London: FT Pitman, pp. 210–15.

Brealey, R. and Nyborg, K. (1998) 'New equity issues and raising cash', in Dickson, T. and Bickerstaffe, G. (eds) *Mastering Finance*, London: FT Pitman, pp. 65–75.

Myners, Paul (2004) 'The impact of shareholders' pre-emption rights on a public company's ability to raise new capital: an invitation to comment', *DTI Discussion Paper*, located at http://www.dti.gov.uk/cld/pdfs/11_02_discussion_paper.pdf.

Chapter 5

Long-term finance: debt finance, hybrid finance and leasing

Learning objectives

After studying this chapter, you should have achieved the following learning objectives:

- a knowledge of the key features of long-term debt finance;

- an appreciation of the kinds of long-term debt finance available to companies, including bank debt, ordinary loan stock, debentures, deep discount bonds, zero coupon bonds, convertible debt and Eurobonds;

- the ability to value redeemable debt, irredeemable debt, convertible debt and warrants;

- an understanding of the relative attractions of different kinds of long-term debt finance to a company, together with an appreciation of the relative attractions of debt and equity finance;

- an ability to compare leasing with borrowing to buy as a source of finance for a company and an appreciation of the way in which the financing decision can interact with the investment decision;

- an understanding of the reasons for the popularity of leasing as a source of finance in recent years.

Introduction

Long-term debt finance, for example fixed interest securities such as loan stock or debentures, has significant differences from equity finance. The interest paid on long-term debt finance is an allowable deduction from profit chargeable to tax, whereas dividends paid to ordinary and preference shareholders are not an allowable deduction from profit: dividends are in fact a share of the after-tax profit itself. Interest must be paid to providers of debt finance, but dividends are paid to shareholders only if managers elect to do so. In the event of liquidation, debt holders are paid off before shareholders because they rank higher in the creditor hierarchy. Thus, in liquidation, shareholders may receive only part-payment and in some cases nothing at all. Long-term debt finance therefore carries less risk for investors than equity finance and this is reflected in its lower required return. The future interest and capital payments from a debt security can be discounted by the rate of return required by providers of debt finance in order to estimate a fair price for the security.

Debt can be engineered to suit the requirements of issuing companies and investors. For example, a new issue of debt securities can be made more attractive to investors by attaching *warrants* to it: these give the holder the right to subscribe for ordinary shares at an attractive price in the future. Alternatively, debt securities may be convertible into ordinary shares at a future date, in which case they may pay a lower interest rate because of the higher capital and dividend returns that may be available following conversion.

A further source of finance discussed in this chapter is leasing, which can be seen as a substitute for debt finance and is a popular method of gaining access to a wide range of assets. We compare leasing with borrowing to buy and examine recent trends in lease finance.

5.1 Loan stock and debentures

Loan stock and debentures are long-term bonds or debt securities with a par value which is usually (in the UK) £100 and a market price determined by buying and selling in the bond markets. The interest rate (or coupon) is based on the par value and is usually paid once or twice each year. For example, a fixed interest 10 per cent debenture will pay the holder £10 per year in interest, although this might be in the form of £5 paid twice each year. Interest is an allowable deduction in calculating taxable profit and so the effective cost to a company of servicing debt is lower than the interest (or coupon) rate. On a fixed interest 10 per cent debenture with corporation tax at 30 per cent, for example, the servicing cost is reduced to 7 per cent per year ($10 \times (1 - 0.3)$). In corporate finance, this is referred to as the *tax efficiency* of debt. If the loan stock or debenture is redeemable, the principal (the par value) will need to be repaid on the redemption date.

While the terms *debenture* and *loan stock* can be used interchangeably, since a debenture is simply a written acknowledgement of indebtedness, a debenture is usually taken to signify a bond that is *secured* by a trust deed against corporate assets, whereas loan stock is usually taken to refer to an *unsecured* bond. The debenture trust deed will cover in detail such matters as: any charges on the assets of the issuing company (security); the way in which interest is paid; procedures for redemption of the issue; the production of regular reports on the position of the issuing company; the power of trustees to appoint a receiver; and any restrictive covenants intended to protect the investors of debt finance.

The debenture may be secured against assets of the company by either a fixed or a floating charge. A *fixed charge* will be on specified assets which cannot be disposed of while the debt is outstanding: if the assets are land and buildings, the debenture is called a mortgage debenture. A *floating charge* will be on a class of assets, such as current assets, and so disposal of some assets is permitted. In the event of default, for example non-payment of interest, a floating charge will crystallise into a fixed charge on the specified class of assets.

5.1.1 Restrictive covenants

Restrictive (or banking) covenants are conditions attached to loan stock and debentures as a means by which providers of long-term debt finance can restrict the actions of the managers of the issuing company. The purpose of restrictive covenants is to prevent any significant change in the *risk profile* of the company which existed when the long-term debt was first issued. This was the risk profile which was taken into account by the cost of debt (i.e. the required return) at the time of issue. For example, a restrictive covenant could limit the amount of additional debt that could be issued by the company, or it might require a target *gearing ratio* to be maintained (*see* Section 2.4.6). In order to guard against insolvency and liquidity difficulties, it is possible for a restrictive covenant to specify a target range for the *current ratio* (*see* Section 2.4.5) in the hope of encouraging good working capital management. If the terms agreed in the restrictive covenant are breached, disposal of assets may be needed in order to satisfy the debenture holders, although the actual course of events following such a breach is likely to be determined by negotiation.

5.1.2 Redemption and refinancing

The redemption of loan stock or debentures represents a significant demand on the cash flow of a company and calls for careful financial planning. Because of the large amount of finance needed, some companies may choose to invest regularly in a fund which has the sole purpose of providing for redemption. The regular amounts invested in such a *sinking fund*, together with accrued interest, will be sufficient to allow a company to redeem debt without placing undue strain on its liquidity position.

Alternatively, a company may replace an issue of long-term debt due for redemption with a new issue of long-term debt or a new issue of equity. This *refinancing* choice has the advantage that it allows the company to maintain the relationship between long-term assets and long-term liabilities, i.e. the matching principle is upheld (*see*

Section 3.2.3). Refinancing can also be used to change the amount, the maturity or the nature of existing debt in line with a company's corporate financial planning, as shown in Vignette 5.1.

The cash flow demands of redemption can also be eased by providing in the trust deed for redemption over a period of time, rather than redemption on a specific date. This *redemption window* will allow the company to choose for itself the best time for redemption in the light of prevailing conditions (e.g. the level of interest rates). A choice about when to redeem can also be gained by attaching a *call option* to the

---

Vignette 5.1

Bayer's €2bn in convertibles

FT

Bayer, the German pharmaceutical and chemicals company, yesterday issued the biggest European convertible bond in nearly three years to refinance its acquisition of Schering, its domestic peer.

The company sold €2bn bonds that will convert into ordinary Bayer shares in about three years. The transaction was the biggest in the European market since May 2003, when Siemens, the German technology company, sold €2.5bn of convertible bonds, according to data from Dealogic.

The new mandatory convertible bond was part of the €4bn of equity or equity-like instruments Bayer last week said it would issue to refinance the takeover. It indicated the company could issue about €2bn in shares at a later stage.

'It looks like they have made a good start to the refinancing process,' said Frances Hutt, credit analyst at BNP Paribas. 'It leaves about €2bn for the rights issue, which should be easily manageable for a company like Bayer.'

The new bond will convert into Bayer shares in June 2009. Citigroup and Credit Suisse lead-managed the sale. The bond will pay an annual coupon of 6.625 per cent with a minimum conversion price of €33.03 and a premium of 17 per cent, which gives a maximum conversion price of €38.64.

The bond was sold in a private placement to institutional investors only. The bonds will be subordinated to other debt of Bayer, including its existing hybrid bonds.

Bayer last week announced a €16.3bn agreed takeover of Schering, which trumped a €14.6bn hostile bid from Merck, another German pharmaceutical group. Bayer said it would finance the acquisition with €3bn of existing cash holdings and short-term loans provided by Citigroup and Credit Suisse. The loans will be refinanced with up to €4bn of equity, about $1.5bn (€1.25bn) of hybrid bonds and proceeds from the sale of two non-core assets.

Bank sources said last week that HC Starck and Wolff Walsrode, which are both part of Bayer's Material Science plastics and chemicals unit, could bring in €1.5bn–€2bn.

Werner Wenning, Bayer's chief executive, said last week the remaining €5bn–€6bn would be replaced with long-term bonds and loans. That would indicate that the company was seeking a price of at least €2bn for HC Starck and Wolff Walsrode.

Bayer also plans to issue hybrid bonds to refinance debt from the Schering takeover. Hybrid bonds combine features of debt and equity, which protects the borrower's credit ratings.

Bayer was one of the first companies to sell hybrid bonds last summer, after the credit rating agencies clarified how the bonds had to be structured to get as much as 75 per cent of the amount raised treated as equity for rating purposes.

Moody's Investors Service and Standard & Poor's last week warned they were likely to downgrade Bayer from A3 and A, respectively, to reflect its higher leverage. Ms Hutt forecast that Bayer's debt would increase by about €11bn as a result of the acquisition. Bond analysts expect any downgrades to be limited to a maximum of two notches. Mr Wenning said last week the company aimed to return to an A rating by 2009.

The company's €1.3bn hybrid notes weakened when the takeover was announced last week. Having already tapped demand in the euro market, Bayer said it planned to sell the new hybrid notes in the US. The yield spread on the existing Bayer hybrid bond yesterday tightened 4 basis points to 257bp above the 10-year Bund. Shares in Bayer fell 3.9 per cent to €32.76 in Frankfurt.

Source: Ivar Simensen, FT.com, 30 March 2006. Reprinted with permission.

debenture issue, as this gives the company the right, but not the obligation, to buy (i.e. redeem) the issue before maturity. Early redemption might be gained in exchange for compensating investors for interest forgone by paying a premium over par value. Redemption *at a premium* can also be used to obtain a lower interest rate (coupon) on a loan stock or debenture.

It is even possible for loan stock or debentures to be *irredeemable*, but this is rare. One example is the Permanent Interest Bearing Stock (PIBS) issued by some building societies.

5.1.3 Floating interest rates

While it is usual to think of loan stock and debentures as fixed interest securities, they may be offered with a *floating interest rate* linked to a current market interest rate, for example 3 per cent (300 basis points) over the three-month London Interbank Offered Rate (LIBOR) or 2 per cent (200 basis points) above bank base rate. A floating rate may be attractive to investors who want a return which is consistently comparable with prevailing market interest rates or who want to protect themselves against unanticipated inflation. A fixed interest rate protects investors against anticipated inflation since this was taken into account when the fixed rate was set on issue. Floating rate debt is also attractive to a company as a way of hedging against falls in market interest rates (*see* Section 12.1.1) since, when interest rates fall, the company is not burdened by fixed interest rates higher than market rates.

5.1.4 Bond ratings

A key feature of a bond is its rating, which measures its investment risk by considering the degree of protection offered on interest payments and repayment of principal, both now and in the future. The investment risk is rated by reference to a standard risk index. Bond rating is carried out by commercial organisations such as Moody's Investors Service, Standard & Poor's Corporation (both US companies) and FitchIBCA (a European company). The rating for a particular bond is based on detailed analysis of the issuing company's expected financial performance as well as on expert forecasts of the economic environment. Institutional investors may have a statutory or self-imposed requirement to invest only in *investment-grade* bonds; a downgrading of the rating of a particular bond to speculative (or junk) status can therefore lead to an increase in selling pressure, causing a fall in the bond's market price and an increase in its required yield (*see* Section 5.6). The standard ratings issued by Moody's Investor Service are given in Exhibit 5.1, while Vignette 5.2 illustrates the interaction between banking covenants, redemption, security and bond ratings.

5.1.5 Deep discount and zero coupon bonds

There is clearly a relationship between the terms of redemption, the coupon rate and the issue price of loan stock or debentures. This relationship is explored in more detail in Section 5.6, which deals with the valuation of debt securities. One possibility open

Exhibit 5.1	**Moody's Investors Service's bond ratings**
Aaa	Best quality bonds with the lowest degree of risk
Aa	High quality bonds with higher risk than Aaa
A	Upper medium-grade bonds with potential future impairment
Baa	Medium-grade bonds with adequate protection but some speculative aspects
Ba	Bonds with moderate protection and speculative elements
B	Bonds lacking desirable investment characteristics: low level of protection
Caa	Bonds of poor standing with danger to interest and principal: may be in default
Ca	Bonds that are highly speculative and often in default
C	The lowest grade of bonds, unlikely to achieve investment grade

Vignette 5.2

Ahold looks for breathing space

One big question over Ahold's future is whether the embattled Dutch retailer can repay the €3bn–€4bn ($3.2bn–$4.3bn) in debt maturing this year, or whether it will run out of cash. A €3.1bn rescue loan has been agreed in principle with five banks after revelations on Monday of at least $500m in accounting irregularities, but terms are still being thrashed out.

Ahold has received the €1.35bn needed to replace existing loans because this proportion is secured on some of its assets, believed to be the share capital of its main subsidiaries. But the €1.75bn unsecured portion has yet to be signed off. 'Until the new loan documentation is firmly in place, Ahold's liquidity position is precarious,' said Jens Jantzen, analyst at Bear Stearns.

Fitch, the credit rating agency, yesterday cut Ahold's bond ratings to junk, following similar moves in the week by Moody's Investors Service and Standard & Poor's. 'The level of liquidity available to Ahold is more constrained than originally thought,' said Fitch. 'It will be critical for Ahold to achieve the conditions set, including satisfactory sign-off on audited accounts for certain subsidiaries, in order to draw down the unsecured element of the hastily arranged financing package.'

This week Ahold's shareholders and bondholders suffered large losses. Shares are down 64 per cent, closing on Friday at €3.50. The €9bn of bonds that Ahold has outstanding in the dollar, euro and sterling markets have lost about 30 per cent of their value. Banks have so far not lost out because the €1.35bn extended is secured on assets. It may not be possible for Ahold to secure any more bank debt because of terms in the documentation of its bonds, so banks may still feel the pinch if Ahold does not sell assets quickly

enough or if it reveals more holes in its accounts.

Ahold has used €1.35bn of the emergency bank loan package to replace two other debt facilities – €550m which was outstanding under an existing $2bn bank facility, which is no longer accessible following the deterioration in its accounts, and €600m of borrowing through short-term credit lines. The company has €1.2bn of debt repayments due by December 2003, the biggest item being a €678m convertible bond due in September. It also has €850m of borrowings under a receivables-backed securitisation programme.

The 364-day bank rescue package was arranged by ABN Amro, Goldman Sachs, ING, JP Morgan and Rabobank. A requirement is that Ahold maintains a minimum interest cover ratio of 2.5 times, which gives little room to manoeuvre.

Source: Aline van Duyn, FT.com, 1 March 2003. Reprinted with permission.

to a company is to issue a bond at a price well below its par value in exchange for a lower interest rate coupled with redemption at par (or at a premium) on maturity. Such a security, referred to as a *deep discount bond*, will be attractive to investors who prefer to receive a higher proportion of their return in the form of capital gains, as opposed to interest income. Different personal taxation treatment of interest income and capital gains will also be a factor which will influence the preferences of individual investors.

The lower servicing cost of deep discount bonds may be attractive if cash flow problems are being experienced or are anticipated, for example if the cash raised by the new issue is to be used in an investment project whose returns are expected to be low in its initial years.

If no interest at all is paid on a bond issued at a deep discount, so that all of the return to investors will be in the form of capital appreciation, it is called a *zero coupon bond*. The general attractions of zero coupon bonds to the issuing company are similar to those of deep discount bonds. However, these advantages must be weighed against the high cost of redemption compared with the amount of finance raised.

An alternative to a zero coupon bond is one which offers additional bonds instead of interest, referred to as a payment in kind or PIK bond as illustrated in Vignette 5.3.

5.1.6 New issues

Debt finance is raised in the new issues market (the primary market) through a lead bank, which will seek to place blocks of new bonds with clients through advance orders prior to the issue date. This process is referred to as book building. An example of how companies and countries raise finance through bond issues is given in Vignette 5.4.

Vignette 5.3

Hellas' €500m Pik

FT

TIM Hellas, the Greek mobile phone operator, plans to sell €500m pay-in-kind notes to fund a special dividend to its private equity owners. The new issue will test investor appetite for risk, at a time when the performance of high-yield bonds and derivatives indices has diverged. While some of the recent new issues in the European high-yield market are trading at or below their launch price, the Itraxx Xover index, which covers issuers rated speculative grade, has tightened sharply.

Pik notes do not pay regular interest. Coupon payments are made in new notes and the whole amount is paid when the issue matures. The new TIM Hellas Pik note will pay a floating rate of interest, guaranteeing investors a premium over eurozone interest rates. The 2014 bond was on Tuesday offered to yield 825 basis points more than Euribor.

About €120m of the proceeds from the new issue will be used to repay an existing Pik loan, while the rest will be paid out to the shareholders. Deutsche Bank, Goldman Sachs and JPMorgan are lead-managing the sale.

Source: Ivar Simensen, FT.com, 4 April 2006. Reprinted with permission.

Vignette 5.4

New issues: Denmark and VNU meet strong demand

Investors, faced with a shortage of fresh bond issuance in recent months, continue to pounce on new deals, with a Triple A rated transaction from Denmark and a Triple B bond from the Dutch media group VNU both heavily oversubscribed. Denmark priced a €2.3bn five-year bond on Wednesday morning after finishing book building on Tuesday. It had taken five hours to sell, receiving a total of about €7.5bn in bids. The bond was priced to yield 18 basis points more than comparable German government debt. Germany's Obl 141 was yielding about 3.137 per cent on Wednesday.

'The original price guidance when we started book building was 19 to 21 basis points over the Obl 141. Within two hours, we changed our spread guidance because the order book had shot up to about €6bn,' said Hans den Hoedt at ABN Amro. The bond, which was lead-managed by ABN Amro, Deutsche Bank and JP Morgan, was trading about 2bp tighter in the secondary market on Wednesday.

VNU, the Netherlands based media group, made its first foray into the sterling market with a £250m bond, lead-managed by Barclays Capital and Morgan Stanley. The deal was a 14-year transaction with a put option after seven years, meaning investors can sell their bonds back to the borrower after seven years. The size was increased from £200m in response to demand after orders reached about £1.5bn.

'VNU's aim was to diversify its investor base into the sterling market,' said Marco Baldini, director at Barclays Capital. 'And, as well as getting strong participation from most of the largest UK investors there was also some good take-up from continental Europe.' VNU is rated BBB+ by Standard & Poor's and the equivalent by Moody's Investors Service.

Source: Adrienne Roberts, FT.com, 8 May 2003. Reprinted with permission.

5.2 Bank and institutional debt

Long-term loans are available from banks and other financial institutions at both fixed and floating interest rates, provided the issuing bank is convinced that the purpose of the loan is a good one. The cost of bank loans is usually a floating rate of 3–6 per cent above bank base rate, depending on the perceived risk of the borrowing company. The issuing bank charges an arrangement fee on bank loans, which are usually secured by a fixed or floating charge, the nature of the charge depending on the availability of assets of good quality to act as security. A *repayment schedule* is often agreed between the bank and the borrowing company, structured to meet the specific needs of the borrower and in accordance with the lending policies of the bank. Payments on long-term bank loans will include both interest and capital elements.

Example | Interest and capital elements of annual loan payments

Consider a £100 000 bank loan at 10 per cent per year, repayable in equal annual instalments over five years. The annual repayment can be found by dividing the amount of the loan by the cumulative present value factor for five years at 10%:

$$\text{Annual repayment} = 100\,000/3.791 = £26\,378.26$$

Exhibit 5.2	Interest elements of loan repayments

Year	Opening balance (£)	Add 10% interest (£)	Less repayment (£)	Closing balance (£)
1	100 000	10 000	26 378.26	83 621.74
2	83 621.74	8 362.17	26 378.26	65 605.65
3	65 605.65	6 560.57	26 378.26	45 787.96
4	45 787.96	4 578.79	26 378.26	23 988.50
5	23 988.50	2 398.85	26 378.26	(9.05)

The interest elements of the annual repayments are calculated in Exhibit 5.2. The capital elements are the difference between the interest elements and the annual repayments. The small residual difference is due to rounding of the cumulative present value factor.

Long-term bank loans cannot be sold on directly by the company to a third party. The growth of *securitisation*, however, means that banks, financial institutions and large companies can, in some circumstances, parcel up debts as securities and sell them on the securitised debt market.

The problems faced by small businesses in raising debt finance can be partially mitigated by government assistance, for example the Loan Guarantee Scheme operated by the UK government. This allows smaller companies to obtain bank loans without offering security.

5.3 International debt finance

The international operations of companies directly influence their financing needs. For example, a company may finance business operations in a foreign country by borrowing in the local currency in order to hedge against exchange rate losses (*see* Section 12.2.2). It may also borrow in a foreign currency because of comparatively low interest rates (although it is likely that exchange rate movements will eliminate this advantage). Foreign currency borrowing can enable a company to diminish the effect of restrictions on currency exchange. One way of obtaining long-term foreign currency debt finance is by issuing Eurobonds.

5.3.1 Eurobonds

Eurobonds are bonds which are outside the control of the country in whose currency they are denominated and they are sold in different countries at the same time by large companies and governments. A Eurodollar bond, for example, is outside of the jurisdiction of the USA. Eurobonds typically have maturities of 5 to 15 years and interest on them, which is payable gross (i.e. without deduction of tax), may be at either a fixed or a floating rate.

The Eurobond market is not as tightly regulated as domestic capital markets and so Eurobond interest rates tend to be lower than those on comparable domestic bonds.

Eurobonds are *bearer securities*, which means that their owners are unregistered, and so they offer investors the attraction of anonymity. Because Eurobonds are unsecured, companies that issue them must be internationally known and have an excellent credit rating. Common issue currencies are US dollars (Eurodollars), yen (Euroyen) and sterling (Eurosterling). The variety of Eurobonds mirrors the variety on domestic bond markets: for example, fixed-rate, floating-rate, zero coupon and convertible Eurobonds are available.

Companies may find Eurobonds useful for financing long-term investment, or as a way of balancing their long-term asset and liability structures in terms of exposure to exchange rate risk. Investors, for their part, may be attracted to Eurobonds because they offer both security and anonymity, but will be concerned about achieving an adequate return, especially as the secondary market for Eurobonds has been criticised for poor liquidity in recent years.

5.4 Convertible bonds

Convertible bonds are fixed interest debt securities which can be converted into ordinary shares of the company at the option of the holder, on a predetermined date and at a predetermined rate. If they are not converted, they are redeemed at a date which is usually several years after the conversion date. The conversion rate is stated either as a *conversion price* (the nominal value of the bond that can be converted into one ordinary share) or as a *conversion ratio* (the number of ordinary shares obtained from one bond). Conversion terms may be specified to vary over time, with the conversion ratio decreasing in line with the expected increase in the value of ordinary shares. For example, the conversion terms on 1 January 2007 may be that one bond can be converted into 35 ordinary shares, whereas on 1 January 2008, one bond may only be convertible into 30 ordinary shares.

Conversion value is the market value of ordinary shares into which one bond may be converted and is equal to the conversion ratio multiplied by the market price per ordinary share. When convertible bonds are first issued, the conversion value is less than the issue value of the bond. As the conversion date approaches, it is expected that the conversion value will have increased due to the growth of the ordinary share price so that converting into equity becomes an attractive choice for investors. The *conversion premium* (*see* Section 5.7.3) is the difference between the market price of the convertible bond and its conversion value. In Exhibit 5.3 on p. 135, the conversion premium is represented by the vertical distance between the lines MM' and CM'. The conversion premium is proportional to the time remaining before conversion takes place and, as conversion approaches, the market value and the conversion value converge and the conversion premium becomes negligible. The conversion premium is often expressed on a per share basis. The difference between the market value of a convertible bond and its value as straight debt is called the *rights premium*. In Exhibit 5.3, the rights premium is represented by the vertical distance between the lines MM' and LR.

Example	Convertible bond terms

Consider a 12 per cent convertible bond, redeemable at par in six years' time, which can be converted at any time in the next three years into 30 ordinary shares. The bond is currently trading ex-interest (buying the bond does not confer the right to receive the next interest payment) at £118.20 and the current ordinary share price is £3.20. The ex-interest market value of ordinary bonds of a similar risk class and maturity is £108.70.

Current conversion value:	30 × £3.20 = £96.00
Current conversion premium:	£118.20 − £96.00 = £22.20 or 74p per share
Current rights premium:	£118.20 − £108.70 = £9.50 or 32p per share

The interest on a convertible bond is less than that on an unconvertible bond (also called an ordinary, vanilla or straight bond) due to the value to the investor of the conversion rights. The minimum price or *floor value* of a convertible bond is equal to its value as an ordinary bond with the same interest rate, maturity and risk. The *actual* market value of a convertible bond will depend on:

- the current conversion value;
- the time to conversion;
- the expected conversion value;
- whether the market expects that conversion is likely.

We consider the valuation of convertible bonds in Section 5.7.

5.4.1 The attractions of convertible bonds to companies

Companies can view convertible bonds as *delayed equity*. Issuing such debt securities may be attractive when, in the directors' opinion, the company's ordinary share price is depressed and so does not reflect the true worth of the company. Alternatively, the directors may turn to convertible bonds as a way of raising finance because they feel that an immediate issue of new equity would cause an unacceptably large fall in earnings per share.

Convertible bonds are also attractive because they usually, like ordinary bonds, pay fixed interest, making financial forecasting and planning somewhat easier. Furthermore, issuing convertible bonds allows a company to pay a lower rate of interest than it would pay if it were to issue straight bonds of a similar maturity, therefore helping its cash flow situation. As interest payments on bonds are tax deductible, issuing convertible bonds may decrease the overall cost of capital. Convertible bonds also allow companies to push their gearing beyond a level normally considered acceptable by creditors, owing to the expectation that conversion, with a consequent reduction in gearing, is likely to occur. One of the main attractions of convertible bonds is that, if the conditions governing conversion were assessed correctly at the time of issue, they are *self-liquidating* in that the issuing company does not have to find cash to redeem them, whereas straight bonds must be redeemed or refinanced on maturity.

As for disadvantages, gearing will be increased while convertible bonds are outstanding, which will affect the overall risk profile of the company. Also, dilution of earnings per share may occur on conversion, as well as dilution of the control of existing shareholders.

5.4.2 The attractions of convertible bonds to investors

The convertible bond combination of fixed interest in the short term and the option to convert into equity in the longer term may be attractive to some investors, giving as it does a lower-risk investment in the short term with the possibility of greater gains in the longer term. This may be seen as a distinct advantage compared with ordinary bonds, as convertibles offer investors the opportunity to participate financially in the growth of the company, rather than receiving a fixed return. An advantage over ordinary equity is that holders of convertible bonds can evaluate the performance of a company and its shares before deciding whether to become ordinary shareholders by converting.

It is not certain, however, that bondholders will exercise their option to convert. They are under no obligation to do so if conversion is unattractive, for example if the expected share price growth has not occurred and so the conversion value is less than the floor value. This lack of growth may be due entirely to factors which are outside of the control of the company, for example a general downturn in overall economic conditions. If conversion does not occur, the bond will run its full term and will need to be redeemed at maturity.

5.5 Warrants

A warrant is the right to buy new ordinary shares in a company at a future date, at a fixed, predetermined price known as the *exercise price*. Warrants are usually issued as part of a package with loan stock as an *equity sweetener*, a phrase which signifies that attaching warrants to the bond issue can make it more attractive to investors. Warrants can be separated from the underlying loan stock, however, and traded in their own right, both before and during the specified exercise period. The buyer of loan stock with warrants attached can therefore reduce the investment cost by selling the warrants.

The *intrinsic value* of a warrant (V_w) is the current ordinary share price (P) less the exercise price (E), multiplied by the number of shares obtained for each warrant exercised (N):

$$V_w = (P - E) \times N$$

For example, if a warrant entitles the holder to purchase five ordinary shares at an exercise price of £1 and the ordinary share price is currently £1.25, the intrinsic value is:

$$V_w = (1.25 - 1.00) \times 5 = £1.25$$

The actual warrant price on the market will be higher than the intrinsic value owing to the possibility of future share price growth. The difference between the actual warrant price and the intrinsic value is called *time value* and so:

Actual warrant price = Intrinsic value + Time value

Warrants can therefore have a market value even when they have no intrinsic value.

Continuing our example, suppose that the ordinary share price increases from £1.25 to £2.50 over a six-month period. The intrinsic value of the warrant increases to:

$$V_w = (2.50 - 1.00) \times 5 = £7.50$$

The value of the underlying ordinary share increases by 100 per cent, but the value of the warrant increases by 500 per cent. This means that a greater proportionate gain can be obtained by buying and holding the warrant than by buying and holding the ordinary share. If the ordinary share price decreases from £1.25 to £1.00 over the six-month period, the intrinsic value of the warrant is zero. The value of the underlying share decreases by 20 per cent, but the value of the warrant decreases by 100 per cent. In this case a greater proportionate loss is sustained by holding the warrant than by holding the ordinary share. This phenomenon of proportionately higher gains and losses is known as the *gearing effect* of warrants. The absolute loss on the warrant is limited to £0.25, however, while the loss on the ordinary share can be as high as £1.00.

For investors, the attractions of warrants therefore include a low initial outlay, a lower loss potential than that entailed by purchasing ordinary shares, and a higher relative profit potential due to the gearing effect of warrants.

From a company point of view, the interest rate on sweetened loan stock will be lower than that on ordinary loan stock of similar maturity, while attaching warrants will make the issue more attractive to investors. Warrants may even make an issue of loan stock possible when the available security is insufficient. Unlike convertible bonds, warrants lead to the subscription of a small amount of additional equity funds in the future, provided that satisfactory share price growth is achieved and the warrants are exercised.

5.6 The valuation of fixed-interest bonds

5.6.1 Irredeemable bonds

Valuing irredeemable bonds, where the principal or capital amount is never repaid, is straightforward. It is the sum to infinity of the discounted future interest payments, as follows:

$$P_0 = \frac{I}{K_d}$$

where: P_0 = ex-interest market value (£)

I = annual interest paid (£)

K_d = rate of return required by debt investors (%)

Example	Valuation of an irredeemable bond

Consider the case of an 8 per cent irredeemable bond where debt investors require a return or yield of 11 per cent. The predicted market value of the bond will be:

$$P_0 = \frac{I}{K_d} = £8/0.11 = £72.73$$

The market price is considerably less than the par value of £100 because the bond offers annual interest of only 8 per cent when investors require a yield of 11 per cent. If the bond had offered more than 11 per cent interest, we would expect it to be trading at a premium to par.

It is important to remember that this valuation model gives the *ex-interest* market price of irredeemable bonds since it represents the present value of *future* cash flows. Any interest which is shortly to be paid is not included in the valuation. The rate of return (K_d) on bonds required by investors is the cost of debt (*see* Section 9.1.3) and is also known as the *yield* of the bond. If the current market value (P_0) and interest rate are known, therefore, the model can be used to calculate the current yield.

5.6.2 Redeemable bonds

Redeemable bonds can be valued by discounting the future interest payments and the future redemption value by the debt holders' required rate of return (K_d). Interest payments are usually made on an annual or semi-annual basis, while redemption value is usually at the par value of £100.

$$P_0 = \frac{I}{(1 + K_d)} + \frac{I}{(1 + K_d)^2} + \frac{I}{(1 + K_d)^3} + \cdots + \frac{I + RV}{(1 + K_d)^n}$$

where: P_0 = ex-interest market value
I = interest paid (£)
K_d = rate of return required by debt investors (%)
RV = redemption value (£)
n = time to maturity (years)

Example	Valuation of a redeemable bond with annual interest

Consider a bond that pays annual interest of 10 per cent and which is redeemable at par in four years' time, and let us suppose investors in this bond require an annual return of 12 per cent. Because the bond is redeemed at par and the required rate of return is greater than its interest rate, we would expect its market value to be less than its par value. We can calculate the predicted market value as follows:

$$P_0 = \frac{10}{(1.12)} + \frac{10}{(1.12)^2} + \frac{10}{(1.12)^3} + \frac{(10 + 100)}{(1.12)^4} = £93.93$$

If the interest on the bond is paid semi-annually, the valuation model can be modified by dividing both the annual discount rate and the annual interest rate by 2, while leaving the treatment of the redemption value unchanged. While not mathematically accurate, this approximation is good enough for most purposes.

Example | **Valuation of a redeemable bond with semi-annual interest**

We repeat our earlier calculation with semi-annual interest payments of £5 discounted at a six-monthly required rate of return of 6 per cent. The predicted market value now becomes:

$$P_0 = \frac{5}{(1.06)} + \frac{5}{(1.06)^2} + \cdots + \frac{5}{(1.06)^8} + \frac{(100)}{(1.12)^4} = £94.60$$

The increase in expected market value occurs because half of each year's interest payment is received sooner and therefore has a higher present value.

5.7 The valuation of convertible bonds

Because convertible bonds give the holder the option to convert them into ordinary equity at a future date, valuing them is more difficult than valuing ordinary bonds. The valuation can be carried out from two different perspectives:

- Convertible bonds can be valued as ordinary bonds, if conversion at some future date appears unlikely. The market value will be the sum of the present values of the future interest payments and the principal to be repaid on maturity.
- Alternatively, convertible bonds can be valued on the assumption that they will be converted into ordinary shares. The market value will be the sum of the present values of the future interest payments up to the conversion date and the present value of the shares into which each bond is converted.

Which perspective is adopted will depend on the expectations of investors with respect to the future price of the underlying ordinary share.

5.7.1 Conversion value

If investors expect the company's share price to increase at an average annual rate which will be sufficient to make future conversion into ordinary equity an attractive option, the current market value of a convertible bond depends primarily on its future conversion value. The conversion value depends on the estimated share price on the conversion date, as follows:

$$CV = P_0(1 + g)^n R$$

where: CV = conversion value of the convertible bond (£)
P_0 = current ex-dividend ordinary share price (£)
g = expected annual growth rate of ordinary share price (%)
n = time to conversion (years)
R = number of shares received on conversion

5.7.2 Market value

The current market value of a convertible bond where conversion is expected should be the sum of the present values of the future interest payments and the present value of the bond's conversion value, as follows:

$$V_0 = \frac{I}{(1 + K_d)} + \frac{I}{(1 + K_d)^2} + \frac{I}{(1 + K_d)^3} + \cdots + \frac{I + CV}{(1 + K_d)^n}$$

where: V_0 = ex-interest market value (£)
I = interest paid (£)
K_d = rate of return required by investors (%)
CV = conversion value of the convertible loan stock (£)
n = time to maturity (years)

This can also be expressed as follows:

$$V_0 = \sum_{i=1}^{i=n} \frac{I}{(1 + K_d)^i} + \frac{P_0(1 + g)^n R}{(1 + K_d)^n}$$

Example	Valuation of a convertible bond

How much would an investor be prepared to pay for a 10 per cent convertible bond, if it can be converted in four years' time into 25 ordinary shares or redeemed at par on the same date? His required return is 11 per cent and the current market price of the underlying share is £3.35: this is expected to grow by 5 per cent per year.

Suggested answer

The first step is to find the conversion value of the bond.

$$CV = P_0(1 + g)^n R = 3.35 \times 1.05^4 \times 25 = £101.80$$

The second step is to ask whether conversion is likely. The investor, faced by a choice between the conversion value of £101.80 and the par value of £100, will choose to convert.

The final step is to value the expected future cash flows. From discount tables, the cumulative present value factor (CPVF) for four years at 11 per cent is 3.102 and the present value factor (PVF) for four years at 11 per cent is 0.659. Using our valuation model, we have:

$$
\begin{aligned}
V_0 &= (I \times CPVF_{11,4}) + (CV \times PVF_{11,4}) \\
&= (10 \times 3.102) + (101.80 \times 0.659) \\
&= 31.02 + 67.09 \\
&= £98.11
\end{aligned}
$$

Note that if conversion were unlikely, redemption would still be guaranteed and the bond would be trading at its *floor value* of £96.92 $((10 \times 3.102) + (100 \times 0.659))$.

5.7.3 Factors influencing the market value of a convertible bond

The factors influencing the market value of a convertible bond are illustrated in Exhibit 5.3. The market value is shown by the dotted line MM'. Initially, the floor price of the convertible bond will be its redemption value. As the ordinary share price rises over time, however, the conversion value (CM') will become greater than the redemption value, and the conversion value will then become the floor price. The actual market value (MM') is greater than the conversion value (CM') because of the expectation of investors that the share price will increase even further in the future, therefore increasing the future conversion value.

The conversion premium is represented by the vertical distance between the curve MM' and the line CM', whereas the rights premium is represented by the vertical

Exhibit 5.3 **Factors influencing the market value of a convertible security**

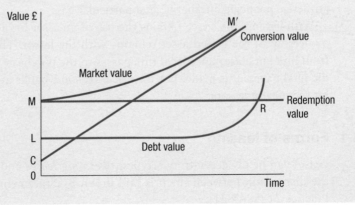

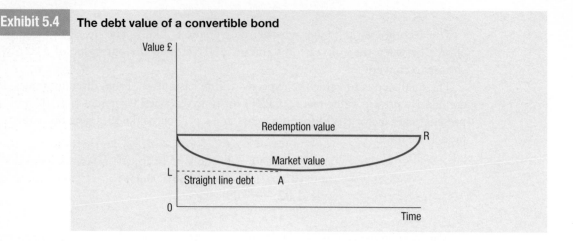

| Exhibit 5.4 | **The debt value of a convertible bond** |

distance between the curves MM′ and LR. Conversion should only take place after M′ since conversion before this point will result in a loss in potential profit to the investor.

If the underlying share price rises slowly or falls and conversion is not anticipated, the convertible bond will have value only as debt and its market value will fall to that of an ordinary bond, where it will remain until redemption at point R, as shown in Exhibit 5.4. At point A, the right to convert has ceased to have any value and the convertible bond is valued thereafter as ordinary debt.

5.8 Leasing

Leasing is a form of short- to medium-term financing which in essence refers to hiring an asset under an agreed contract. The company hiring the asset is called the *lessee*, whereas the company owning the asset is called the *lessor*. In corporate finance, we are concerned on the one hand with the reasons why leasing is a popular source of finance, and on the other with how we can evaluate whether leasing is an attractive financing alternative in a particular case.

With leasing, the lessee obtains the use of an asset for a period of time while legal ownership of the leased asset remains with the lessor. This is where leasing differs from hire purchase, since legal title passes to the purchaser under hire purchase when the final payment is made. For historical reasons, banks and their subsidiaries are by far the biggest lessors.

5.8.1 Forms of leasing

Leases can be divided into two types: *operating leases* and *finance leases*. In the UK, the distinction between them is laid down by Statement of Standard Accounting Practice 21 (SSAP 21).

Operating leases

Operating leases are in essence rental agreements between a lessor and a lessee in which the lessor tends to be responsible for servicing and maintaining the leased asset. The lease period is substantially less than the expected economic life of the leased asset so assets leased under operating leases can be leased to a number of different parties before they cease to have any further use. The types of asset commonly available under operating leases include cars, computers and photocopiers. Under SSAP 21, a company is required to disclose in its balance sheet only the operating lease payments that it is obliged to meet in the next accounting period. The leased asset does not appear in the company's balance sheet and for this reason operating leases are referred to as *off-balance-sheet financing*.

Finance leases

A finance lease is a non-cancellable contractual agreement between a lessee and a lessor and exists, according to SSAP 21, in all cases where the present value of the minimum lease payments constitutes 90 per cent or more of the fair market value of the leased asset at the beginning of the lease period. While this may seem a rather technical definition, the intent of SSAP 21 is to require accounting statements to recognise that the lessee owns the leased asset in everything but name. The *substance* of the finance lease agreement, in other words, is one of ownership, even though, under its *legal form*, title to the leased asset remains with the lessor. In consequence, SSAP 21 requires that finance leases be *capitalised* in the balance sheet of a company. This means that the present value of the capital part of future lease payments becomes an *asset* under the fixed assets heading, while the obligations to make future lease payments become a *liability* and appear under the headings of both current and long-term liabilities.

One example of the way in which the lessee enjoys 'substantially all the risks and rewards of ownership', in the words of the accounting standard, is that the lessee tends to be responsible for servicing and maintaining the leased asset under a finance lease agreement.

A finance lease usually has a primary period and a secondary period. The primary lease period covers most, if not all, of the expected economic life of the leased asset. Within this primary period, the lessor recovers from the primary lease payments the capital cost of the leased asset and his required return. Within the secondary period, the lessee may be able to lease the asset for a nominal or *peppercorn* rent.

5.8.2 Trends in leasing

The most significant economic factor in the growth of leasing before 1984 was taxation. If a company is not producing sufficient taxable profits at the time that a decision to acquire an asset is taken, it will not be able to take immediate advantage of available capital allowances. Leasing would be an attractive alternative to buying for a company in such circumstances, especially if a lessor with adequate profits were able to pass on the benefit of capital allowances in the form of lower lease payments. This was the situation in the late 1960s and early 1970s when leasing first experienced a rapid rise in popularity. Many clearing banks set up leasing subsidiaries to improve profitability by taking advantage of capital allowances. This early growth of leasing was stimulated by relatively high levels of corporation tax and by the introduction in 1972 of 100 per cent first-year capital allowances, leaving many companies in a tax-exhausted position.

The Finance Act 1984 introduced 25 per cent reducing balance capital allowances (*see* Section 7.2.1) as a replacement for 100 per cent first-year allowances, and reduced corporation tax over the same period from 50 per cent to 35 per cent. These changes reduced the taxation incentives to lease, as they led directly to fewer companies being in a tax-exhausted position and to more companies being in a position to take full advantage of capital allowances. Despite these changes to the tax system, leasing continued to grow in popularity, the reasons for which are explored in the next section.

5.8.3 Non-tax reasons for leasing

Drury and Braund (1990) suggested a number of possible reasons why companies choose to lease assets rather than buy them outright. It has been pointed out that leasing provides a source of finance if a company is short of liquidity. If a company has difficulty in borrowing to finance the acquisition of an asset because of a lack of good quality assets to offer as security, leasing can be used instead. Since legal title to the leased asset never passes to the lessee, the leased asset is itself security for the leasing contract and can be reclaimed in the event of default on lease payments. For this reason, leasing provides an attractive source of finance for small companies.

It should not be thought that all tax advantages disappeared after 1984: tax advantages can still occur if the tax-paying positions of the lessor and lessee are different. For example, a lessor in a tax-paying position could buy an asset, use the capital allowance and then lease the asset to the lessee in a non-tax-paying situation, setting the lease payments at a level where both lessor and lessee benefit. Tax benefits can also arise due to year-end effects as different accounting year-ends may allow a lessor to capture tax benefits more quickly than a lessee. This benefit can be enhanced by lessors having several subsidiaries with different year-ends.

In an era of fast-changing technology and rapid development, it is easy for some assets to become obsolete in a relatively short space of time. Leasing offers a solution to this *obsolescence problem* since assets leased under operating leases can be returned in exchange for a more up-to-date model. By leasing rather than buying, companies can ensure that they are using the most up-to-date equipment.

Before 1984, the distinction between operating and finance leases did not exist in the UK and, by tradition, leasing was seen as off-balance-sheet finance which did not interfere with a company's borrowing capacity. This changed with the publication in April 1984 of SSAP 21, which clarified the distinction between operating and finance leases, and which required capitalisation of finance leases. Operating leases remain off balance sheet, however, and the flexibility of lease contracts with respect to the choice of equipment and the scheduling of lease payments means that the popularity of leasing has continued to increase. The continuing attraction of leasing is illustrated by Vignette 5.5.

Vignette 5.5

Leasing looks like a worthwhile option

IT budgets are tighter than ever and finance directors are scouring balance sheets for under-performing assets. In such a climate, leasing rather than buying IT equipment looks like a winning move. But before taking the plunge, companies need to read the small print and weigh up a host of factors that can make leasing IT systems much more complicated than leasing a vehicle or building.

Technology evolves at a frightening pace and one of the strengths of leasing IT systems rather than buying them outright is that the customer has all the benefits of using the technology, but none of the complications of owning it.

At the end of most leases, customers have various options. HP Financial Services, the world's second largest IT leasing company, lets customers hand back their computers, upgrade them with a 'refresh' option, extend the lease at a lower rate or purchase the computers at their fair market value. This flexibility is one of the great benefits of leasing computers but it can make IT leasing contracts particularly difficult to understand, with myriad conditions and clauses hidden in the small print.

The basics of leasing are nevertheless easy to grasp. The big difference between a lease and a loan is that leases assume the equipment is worth something at the end of the lease term. This is called its residual value. The pace of innovation in the IT industry means residual values can drop rapidly and after five or six years a million-dollar computer may only have a scrap value on the open market. Nevertheless, its value to the customer might be much higher. Understanding residual values is critical to making a decision whether to lease or buy. Specialist companies such as IDC publish independent reports that calculate residual values for IT hardware.

A lease finances only the value of the equipment expected to be lost during the lease term, so that usually makes the lease payments lower than a loan. Also, while a loan typically requires a down payment to be made upfront, a lease requires only the first monthly instalment to be paid in advance. These advantages have an obvious appeal in today's cautious investment climate. Despite the clampdown on IT spending, many companies have IT projects that cannot be postponed forever. Leasing allows them to acquire much-needed equipment with predictable and affordable rental payments but without having to use their capital equipment budget. 'Customers are looking to start projects sooner rather than later and leasing can help them do things quicker,' says Keith Brewer, European marketing manager for IBM Global Financing.

There are two main types of leasing contract: operating leases and finance leases. With an operating lease, the leasing company or 'lessor' retains ownership of the system for tax purposes, and the customer or 'lessee' typically claims all lease payments as an operating expense or tax deduction. Operating leases, which typically last from 18 to 36 months, usually offer the lowest rates. 'Because of the residual value, an operating lease lowers the total cost of ownership,' says Mr Brewer.

This type of lease is also simplest to understand as the customer does not own the equipment being leased and so it never has to be shown on the balance sheet. Off-balance-sheet accounting has acquired sinister overtones since the collapse of Enron but experts say it is a perfectly legitimate strategy, particularly for companies with tight budgets or that frequently upgrade equipment.

At the end of the operating lease, the customer can walk away from the lease and give the equipment back, assuming it is in reasonable condition. Alternatively, the lessee may want to hang on to it for a few more months and extend the lease on a month-by-month basis. Other options include renegotiating a new lease for the existing equipment at a lower rate, or upgrading to a newer system and entering into a completely new lease.

A finance lease, also known as a capital lease, is primarily designed for customers who want to own the equipment at the end of the lease. The lease is structured in such a way that the lessee effectively owns the equipment for tax purposes and so can claim depreciation and interest payments. At the end of a finance lease, the lessee can buy the equipment for a bargain price – often $1 or €1.

Within these two broad categories of operating and finance leases there are a bewildering number of lease types and options, and making the right choice of leasing contract is rarely easy. It is not only the customers that can have difficulty understanding the implications of complicated leases. In the 1980s, UK leasing company Atlantic Computers thought it had revolutionised the leasing industry with a new type of leasing contract called a flexlease. Atlantic grew rapidly to become the third largest computer leasing company. But after British & Commonwealth, a major UK conglomerate, bought out Atlantic in 1988, the flexlease was revealed to be nothing more than a giant pyramid selling scheme. B&C collapsed in 1990 with debts of more than £1.5bn.

Novel leasing contracts also brought disaster to Comdisco, another former giant of the 1980s IT leasing industry. One of the factors behind Comdisco's recent downfall was its heavy exposure to dotcom companies via 'venture leasing'. In the Internet boom of the late 1990s, Comdisco saw a succulent market in leasing equipment to dotcoms that would otherwise be turned down by mainstream finance houses because of their chronic losses and short track record. As well as making monthly payments to Comdisco, these start-ups were required to surrender an equity stake – hence the name venture leasing. But the dotcom boom soon turned to bust, the leasing payments could no longer be made and the equity stakes proved worthless. Comdisco had to write off millions of dollars in bad debts and file for bankruptcy protection in 2001. It is currently in the process of winding down and selling all its activities to pay its creditors.

Source: Geoffrey Nairn, FT.com, 7 May 2003. Reprinted with permission.

5.8.4 Evaluating leasing as a source of finance

It is important to recognise that evaluating leasing as a source of finance may involve both an investment decision and a finance decision. The optimal overall decision can be reached in several ways, as follows:

- make the investment decision first, then optimise the financing method;
- make the financing decision first, and then evaluate the investment decision;
- combine the investment and financing decisions.

If the investment decision is made first, an investment project might be rejected which would have been accepted if the lowest-cost financing method had been taken into account. Combining the investment and financing decision involves investment appraisal methods beyond the scope of this book. For these reasons, the second method, where financing method is determined before the investment decision is evaluated, is recommended. This means that the financing decision can be divorced from the investment decision and we need consider the investment decision no further in this section.

If we assume that the debt capacity of a company is limited and recognise that the commitment to a series of regular payments arises under both leasing and borrowing, we can regard leasing as being equivalent to borrowing as a way of acquiring use of an asset (Myers et al. 1976). Discounted cash flow methods can then be used to compare the relative costs of the two financing alternatives. In order to perform this comparison, we need first of all to identify the relevant cash flows, as follows.

- *Taxation*: capital allowances are available to the buyer if an asset is purchased, while if an asset is leased, the lessee can set off lease payments against taxable profits. The relevant cash flows are therefore the tax benefits arising from capital allowances and lease payments, possibly taken one year in arrears.
- *Maintenance costs*: maintenance costs, which are an allowable deduction against profits for tax purposes, may be payable by the lessor under an operating lease, but by the lessee if the asset is leased under a finance lease or by the owner if the asset is purchased.
- *Lease payments*: lease payments may be payable in advance or in arrears, and their amount and timing are clearly important.

- *Purchase price and disposal value*: if the asset is purchased through borrowing, the purchase price (equivalent to the present value cost of the loan) must be considered, together with any disposal value. Balancing allowances or charges will be affected by any disposal value expected to arise at the end of the useful life of the purchased asset.

Before these cash flows can be discounted, an appropriate discount rate must be selected. Since leasing is seen as a direct substitute for borrowing as a source of finance, an appropriate discount rate to use is the cost of borrowing to the company. We could use, for example, the *before-tax interest rate* on the loan the company would need to take out in order to purchase the asset. This rate is appropriate if the company is tax exhausted and cannot take advantage of available tax benefits. If the company is profitable (i.e. not tax exhausted), the *after-tax interest rate* on the loan should be used as the discount rate.

If the net present value method is used to compare leasing with borrowing to buy, then cash flows can be discounted by the after-tax cost of borrowing. If the internal rate of return method is used, the IRR of leasing can be compared with the cost of borrowing (Tan 1992). Here, we shall consider only the net present value method.

| Example | Evaluation of leasing versus borrowing to buy |

Dadd Ltd is trying to decide whether to lease or to buy a machine with a useful life of six years. Dadd could borrow £90 000 to buy the machine or lease it for annual lease rentals of £20 000 per year for six years, payable at the start of each year. If the machine is bought, maintenance costs of £1000 per year will be incurred. These costs will not be incurred if the machine is leased. Dadd pays profit tax at a rate of 30 per cent one year in arrears and can claim capital allowances on a 25 per cent reducing balance basis. The company's before-tax cost of borrowing is 10 per cent. Should Dadd lease or buy the machine?

Suggested answer

As leasing is an alternative to borrowing, the relevant cash flows of the two alternatives can be compared using the after-tax cost of borrowing, i.e. $10 \times (1 - 0.30) = 7$ per cent.

The capital allowances are calculated as follows:

Year		£
1	$90\,000 \times 0.25 =$	22 500
2	$22\,500 \times 0.75 =$	16 875
3	$16\,875 \times 0.75 =$	12 656
4	$12\,656 \times 0.75 =$	9 492
5	$9\,492 \times 0.75 =$	7 119
6	(by difference)	21 358
		90 000

The tax benefits of borrowing to buy are calculated in Exhibit 5.5. Notice that the maintenance costs give rise to tax relief, a point that is often overlooked. →

| Exhibit 5.5 | **Tax relief computation for Dadd Ltd if buying is used** |

Year	Capital allowances (£)	Operating costs (£)	Total deductions (£)	30% tax relief (£)	Taken in year
1	22 500	1000	23 500	7 050	2
2	16 875	1000	17 875	5 363	3
3	12 656	1000	13 656	4 097	4
4	9 492	1000	10 492	3 148	5
5	7 119	1000	8 119	2 436	6
6	21 358	1000	22 358	6 707	7

| Exhibit 5.6 | **The present costs of leasing and borrowing to buy for Dadd Ltd** |

Present cost of leasing				
Years	Cash flow	(£)	7% discount factors	Present value (£)
0–5	lease payments	(20 000)	(4.100 + 1.000) = 5.100	(102 000)
2–7	tax relief	6 000	(5.389 − 0.935) = 4.454	26 724
				(75 276)

Present cost of borrowing to buy						
Year	Capital (£)	Operating costs (£)	Tax relief (£)	Net cash flow (£)	7% discount factors	Present value (£)
0	(90 000)			(90 000)	1.000	(90 000)
1		(1000)		(1 000)	0.935	(935)
2		(1000)	7 050	6 050	0.873	5 282
3		(1000)	5 363	4 363	0.816	3 560
4		(1000)	4 097	3 097	0.763	2 363
5		(1000)	3 148	2 148	0.713	1 532
6		(1000)	2 436	1 436	0.666	956
7			6 707	6 707	0.623	4 179
						(73 063)

We can now calculate the present costs of leasing and of borrowing to buy, as shown in Exhibit 5.6.

From Exhibit 5.6, we can see that the present cost of leasing (£75 276) is slightly higher than the present cost of borrowing (£73 063), and so on financial grounds we recommend that the machine should be bought. The present cost of borrowing to buy is included in the evaluation of the investment decision using the net present value method (*see* Section 6.3).

5.8.5 The distribution of financial benefits

For a leasing contract to go ahead, both parties to the lease must benefit. If both lessee and lessor pay taxes at the same rate, then from a taxation perspective there are no overall financial benefits to be distributed and leasing appears to be a *zero sum game* (Drury and Braund 1990). For tax benefits to arise, lessee and lessor must be faced to some extent with differences in their respective cash flow situations, arising as a result of some or all of the following factors:

- different costs of capital for the lessor and lessee;
- different tax rates between the lessor and lessee;
- different abilities to utilise the available capital allowances.

Different costs of capital may arise because the cost of equity and the cost of borrowing of a large leasing company are likely to be lower than those of a small company wishing to lease an asset from it. Different tax rates may arise because the UK tax system differentiates between small and large companies. Different abilities to utilise capital allowances can arise, for example if a lessor sets up multiple subsidiaries with different year-ends. Non-tax financial benefits can also lead to lower lease payments, for example if a discount is gained by a lessor making bulk purchases of assets to lease.

The distribution of financial benefits depends on the size and timing of lease payments. The lessor will have a minimum amount it wishes to receive and the lessee will have a maximum amount it is prepared to pay. The actual lease payments are likely to be between these limits and determined by the relative bargaining power of the two parties.

5.9 Conclusion

We have seen in this chapter that debt, hybrid finance and leasing can all be useful ways for a company to obtain the financing it needs to acquire assets for use in its business. Each of these financing methods has advantages and disadvantages which must be considered carefully by a company before a final decision is reached as to the most suitable method to use. In theory it should be possible, given the wide range of methods available, for a company to satisfy its individual financing requirements. The difficulties of satisfying these financing requirements in practice are illustrated by Vignette 5.6.

Key points

1 Loan stock and debentures are interest-paying debt securities which must be redeemed on maturity unless irredeemable. Interest paid is tax deductible, which reduces the cost of debt finance. Debentures are usually secured on assets of the company.

Vignette 5.6

Independent's rights issue delivers a reality check

It is a fair bet that a rights issue was the last option Sir Anthony O'Reilly would have gone for, when considering how to reduce debt at Independent News & Media. After all, the executive chairman of the Irish newspaper group owns 153m shares or 27 per cent. Even at the deeply discounted price of 70 cents, the 4-for-15 offering will require the former Irish rugby star to fork out €28m (£18m). But this week's announcement – coupled with the €88m realised from the sale of its UK regional titles – represents a badly needed reality check for the group.

Since 1992 it has spent €1.6bn establishing itself as a global media player in Ireland, UK, Australia, New Zealand and South Africa. Apart from a 1996 rights issue when it bought into Wilson & Horton in New Zealand, this expansion has been funded almost exclusively through borrowing. While earnings kept growing, the balance sheet was not a worry. But with the advertising recession, and less scope to raise cover prices to compensate for lower circulation, the rising debts have suddenly become more ominous.

In a report in February, Paul Sullivan, media analyst at Merrill Lynch, said the shares, which have fallen from more than €3 in 1999 to about €1.20, 'are unlikely to perform until refinancing risk subdues'. Net borrowings at the end of 2002 stood at €1.2bn, including just over €200m in lease liabilities on mastheads. In addition, the group had about €140m of convertible loans, issued by its Australian subsidiary Australian Provincial Newspapers, as well as about €170m of preference shares, which the group treats as a minority interest in its accounts.

Its options were limited. Taking out further bank debt would have compounded the problem. Its bonds are unrated. And with a yield of about 10 per cent, this looked an expensive route to raise extra funds. With such a large personal shareholding, Sir Anthony was unlikely to be keen to see the dividend cut. Disposals seemed the obvious choice, but Sir Anthony is said to be a natural accumulator of assets. At the half year, the group was adamant it had no plans for sales. Even at this week's press briefing, Ivan Fallon, chief executive of the UK division, was insisting the regional newspaper deal was at the instigation of the purchaser, the US company Gannett.

But with €170m of convertible debt falling due by November – and with operations throwing off insufficient free cash – it was clear that something had to be done.

With hindsight, it is easy to point to two events that led to the current financing squeeze. In August 2000, the group paid about €500m for the *Belfast Telegraph*, its largest deal. Few analysts question the business logic. It dominates the Northern Ireland market, generates strong earnings and enjoys a lucrative contract print business. It is also tax efficient, giving Independent a profits stream against which it can set off the losses it continues to incur at *The Independent* and *The Independent on Sunday* – Sir Anthony's calling cards, as he likes to call the UK national titles. But the purchase was carried out with cash – all short-term bank debt.

The other contributory factor was the failure to capitalise on the technology bubble to sell its 50 per cent stake in the Irish cable television company Chorus. The investment at one point was valued at €250m. This week Independent said it had written it down to zero, taking a €80m charge.

Donal Buggy, chief financial officer, indicated that in addition to the preference shares, the group was likely to pay down about €100m of short-term debt before the year-end, still outstanding from the €1bn five-year bank facility negotiated at the time of the *Belfast Telegraph* purchase. But he said the real concern in framing this week's announcement was to ensure attractive terms when the group comes to refinance the preference shares – about €108m of a 6.375 per cent cumulative redeemable preference share due in June and €66m in November, which were originally issued in 1996 as part of Independent's takeover of Wilson & Horton.

The longer-term ambition is to achieve investment grade, which would allow Independent to restructure its debt portfolio. Analysts believe they are some way from achieving that, particularly if the rating agencies consider preference shares and an APN convertible as group debt.

By the end of 2003, Mr Buggy expects net debt will have fallen to €900m – or €500m if the debts of the group's 45 per cent owned APN are excluded.

Gavin O'Reilly, the chairman's 36-year-old son who is group chief operations officer, described this week's announcement as a 'transformative' move. If Independent could bring its debts down to €500m – half the levels of 2000 – that would transform the group's fortunes.

Source: John Murray Brown, FT.com, 28 March 2003. Reprinted with permission.

2 Restrictive covenants are a way of protecting providers of debt finance and may, for example, limit how much further debt can be raised, set a target gearing ratio or set a target current ratio.

3 Redemption of bonds needs careful financial planning, and can be over a period of time rather than on a specific date. Companies may use a sinking fund or a new issue of long-term debt or equity to aid redemption. The latter choice upholds the matching principle.

4 Bond ratings measure the risk of bonds as an investment.

5 A deep discount bond is issued at a price well below par in exchange for a lower interest rate. It may attract investors who prefer capital growth to interest, and companies who prefer lower servicing costs to match expected returns on invested capital.

6 A zero coupon bond pays no interest and is issued at a deep discount to its par value.

7 Fixed and floating rate long-term loans are available from banks and other financial institutions, secured by either a fixed or a floating charge on the assets of a company.

8 Debt finance may be raised in a particular currency to hedge exchange rate risk, to exploit interest rate differentials or to get round restrictions on currency movements.

9 Eurobonds are long-term international debt finance issued as bearer securities, with fixed or floating rate interest that can be lower than domestic rates.

10 Eurobonds can be used to finance international investment or to hedge exchange rate risk. Investors may find them attractive because they offer anonymity.

11 Convertible bonds can be converted, on predetermined dates and at a predetermined rate, at the option of the holder, into ordinary shares of the company.

12 Conversion value is the market value of shares into which a bond can be converted. Conversion premium is the difference between a convertible's market price and its conversion value. Rights premium is the difference between a convertible's market value and its value as ordinary debt.

13 Convertible bond interest is usually lower than interest on unconvertible bonds.

14 The floor value of a convertible bond is its value as an ordinary bond. Its actual value depends on its current conversion value, the time to conversion and market expectations.

15 Issuing convertible bonds can be attractive if a company's share price is depressed or if dilution of EPS by new equity is unacceptable. It will also decrease the overall cost of capital. A major attraction of convertible bonds is that they can be self-liquidating.

16 Convertible bonds offer a lower-risk medium-term investment coupled with the possibility of greater long-term gains. Unlike ordinary bonds, they offer the opportunity to participate in company growth.

17 A warrant is the right to buy new shares at a future date, at a fixed, predetermined price. Warrants are often issued with bonds as an equity sweetener.

18 The gearing effect of warrants means that a greater proportionate gain can be obtained by holding the warrant than by holding the ordinary share. The initial outlay is also lower.

19 The interest rate on 'sweetened' loan stock will be lower than on ordinary loan stock, while the attached warrants may make it easier to sell.

20 The expected market value of a fixed interest bond can be found by discounting interest payments and redemption value by the cost of debt.

21 A convertible bond is valued in the same way as ordinary loan stock, except that its expected value is the greater of two possible values: its value as an ordinary redeemable bond and its value if converted into equity.

22 Leasing is a source of financing where the lessee obtains use of an asset for a period of time, while legal title of the asset remains with the lessor.

23 In the UK, SSAP 21 distinguishes operating leases from finance leases. Operating leases are in essence rental agreements. With a finance lease, the lessee has most of the risks and rewards of ownership and the leased asset must be capitalised in the balance sheet.

24 Tax-related reasons were mainly responsible for the growth of leasing before the Finance Act 1984, which introduced 25 per cent reducing balance capital allowances and cut corporation tax progressively from 50 per cent to 35 per cent, making other reasons for the growth of leasing more important.

25 Post-1984 reasons for the popularity of leasing in the UK include:

(a) leases can represent an off-balance-sheet source of finance;

(b) leasing is a source of finance if a company is short of liquidity;

(c) leasing allows small companies access to expensive assets;

(d) leasing allows a company to avoid obsolescence of some assets;

(e) the lessor may be able to borrow at a cheaper rate than the lessee;

(f) leases offer flexibility of payment and choice of equipment;

(g) year-end tax effects.

26 Leasing can be regarded as equivalent to borrowing as a way of acquiring assets. The two alternatives can be compared in present value terms by discounting using the after-tax cost or before-tax cost of borrowing.

27 For tax benefits to arise, the cash flows of lessee and lessor must be different due to different costs of capital, different tax rates, or different abilities to use capital allowances.

Self-test questions

Answers to these questions can be found on pages 438–40.

1 Discuss briefly the key features of debentures and ordinary loan stock.

2 Explain what is meant by the following terms that refer to fixed interest bonds:
   (a) restrictive covenant;
   (b) refinancing;
   (c) redemption window.

3 Explain the meaning of the following terms and state the circumstances under which their issue would be beneficial to (i) lenders and (ii) borrowers:
   (a) deep discount bonds;
   (b) zero coupon bonds;
   (c) warrants;
   (d) convertible bonds.

4 What are the advantages and disadvantages to a company of raising finance via Eurobonds?

5 Explain the difference between a conversion premium and a rights premium.

6 A company has in issue a 10 per cent bond, redeemable at the option of the company between one and five years from now. What factors do you think will be considered by the company in reaching a decision on when to redeem the bond?

7 Briefly outline the advantages and disadvantages to a company of issuing convertible bonds.

8 What is the gearing effect of warrants?

9 A company has in issue some 9 per cent debentures, which are redeemable at par in three years' time. Investors now require a yield of 10 per cent. What will be the current ex-interest market value of £100-worth of debentures? What would be the current ex-interest market value if the issue had been of irredeemable bonds?

10 Explain the difference between a finance lease and an operating lease, and discuss the importance of the distinction for corporate finance.

Questions for review

Answers to these questions can be found on pages 440–1. Questions with an asterisk (*) are at an intermediate level.

1 Bugle plc has some surplus funds that it wishes to invest in corporate bonds. It requires a return of 15 per cent on corporate bonds and you have been asked to advise on whether it should invest in either of the following bonds which have been offered to it.

(a) *Stock 1*: 12 per cent loan stock redeemable at par at the end of two more years, current market value per £100 debenture is £95.

(b) *Stock 2*: 8 per cent debentures redeemable at £110 at the end of two more years, current market value per £100 debenture is also £95.

2 Discuss, with the aid of a diagram, the relationship between the conversion premium, the rights premium and the market value of a convertible bond.

3* Laursen plc has in issue 10 per cent convertible bonds which will be redeemed in 10 years' time and which are currently selling at £93. Interest on the bonds is paid annually and each £100 bond is convertible into 25 shares at any time over the next two years. The current market price of Laursen plc's ordinary shares is £3.20 per share and this is expected to increase by 14 per cent per year for the foreseeable future. Bonds of a similar risk class are currently yielding 12 per cent.

(a) Advise an investor holding some of Laursen's convertible bonds as to which of the following courses of action to take:

(i)   sell the convertible bond now;

(ii) convert the bond now or within the next two years;

(iii) hold the bond to maturity.

(b) Explain the importance to an investor of the distinction between convertible bonds and loan stock with warrants attached.

4 Discuss the reasons for the popularity of leasing as a source of finance.

5 Turner plc is considering whether to buy a machine costing £1000 through a three-year loan with interest at 14 per cent per year. The machine would have zero scrap value at the end of its three-year life. Alternatively, the machine could be leased for £320 per year, payable in arrears. Corporation tax is payable at 30 per cent and capital allowances are available over the life of the machine on a 25 per cent reducing balance basis. Calculate whether Turner should lease or buy the machine.

Questions for discussion

Questions with an asterisk (*) are at an advanced level.

1 Tetney plc and Habrough plc have both issued 5 million ordinary shares. In addition, Tetney plc has issued £500 000 of 11 per cent convertible bonds, par value £100,

convertible into 40 ordinary shares in five years' time. If not converted, they will be redeemed at £105. Habrough plc has in issue 800 000 warrants, each with a subscription price of £2.50 for one ordinary share in Habrough plc. The warrants can be exercised in five years' time.

(a) Describe the circumstances under which issuing convertible bonds or warrants would be advantageous to a company.

(b) Calculate the value of each convertible bond and each warrant in five years' time, for the following situations:

(i) the share price of both companies in five years' time is £2;

(ii) the share price of both companies in five years' time is £3.

(c) For each situation, advise holders of the securities whether to exercise their respective conversion and/or warrant rights.

(d) Calculate the current market price of the convertible bond if the ordinary share price in five years' time is either £2 or £3, using a cost of debt of eight per cent per year.

2* (a) Discuss the factors which determine the market price of convertible bonds.

(b) Marlowe plc has in issue bonds which are convertible in three years' time into 25 ordinary shares per bond. If not converted, they will be redeemed in six years' time at par. The bond pays interest of 9 per cent per year and has a current market price of £90.01. Marlowe's current share price is £3.24. If holders of ordinary bonds of a similar risk class require a return of 13 per cent per annum, calculate:

(i) the minimum expected annual growth in Marlowe's share price that would be needed to ensure that conversion takes place in three years' time:

(ii) the implicit conversion premium.

3* Utterby Ltd was formed four years ago to manufacture decorative tableware and has relied upon trained artists to carry out the detailed finishing work on its hand-painted range of dinner sets, which sell at a premium to its budget product lines. The market for tableware is very competitive and Utterby Ltd's rivals have been cutting costs by investing in automated production methods. The finance director is therefore considering the purchase of the AutoDec, a recently developed machine which can reproduce the work of experienced finishing artists after scanning in a detailed original template. This would enable the company to reduce the number of trained artists in its employment, cutting its salaries bill by £130 000 per year.

The machine would cost £480 000 if bought from the manufacturers, Fotherby plc. Annual service costs, mainly the wages of a service engineer employed by Utterby Ltd, would be £14 500. The machine would need to be replaced after five years, but at that time could be sold on by Utterby Ltd for breaking up into spare parts. It is expected this sale for spare parts would realise 2.5 per cent of the purchase price of the AutoDec.

Fotherby plc has offered to lease the AutoDec to Utterby Ltd for a lease payment of £98 000 per year, payable in advance at the start of each year. This lease payment would also cover service costs, with the lease contract renewable on an annual basis.

Utterby Ltd could finance the purchase of the AutoDec by a medium-term bank loan from Laceby Bank plc at an interest rate of 11 per cent per year.

Utterby Ltd pays corporation tax at a rate of 30 per cent per year, one year in arrears, and has been making a small profit after tax in each of the last two years. Current legislation allows the company to claim 25 per cent reducing balance capital allowances on plant and machinery.

(a) The finance director of Utterby Ltd is not sure, because of the low profitability of the company, whether the tax benefits of leasing or buying would be significant or not. Using the net present value method, determine whether Utterby Ltd should buy through borrowing or lease the AutoDec, considering:

  (i) the case where tax benefits are utilised; and

  (ii) the case where tax benefits are ignored.

(b) Critically discuss the reasons why leasing has been a popular source of finance in recent years, illustrating your answer by referring to the information given about Utterby Ltd.

4* Cold plc has decided to acquire equipment with a current market value of £700 000 and has approached its bank in order to borrow this amount. The bank has indicated that it is prepared to offer a five-year loan at an interest rate of 13 per cent per year, provided it can reach agreement with Cold plc on ways to protect its investment. The equipment would be scrapped after five years and at that time would have negligible scrap value.

Cold plc could also lease the equipment for £180 000 per year, payable at the start of each year. The lessor would be responsible for servicing the equipment whereas, if the equipment were bought, Cold plc would incur annual servicing costs of £25 000.

Cold plc is a profitable company that pays corporation tax one year in arrears at an annual rate of 30 per cent and can claim annual capital allowances on a 25 per cent reducing balance basis.

(a) Discuss ways in which the bank could protect its loan of £700 000 to Cold plc for the equipment purchase.

(b) Determine the present value of the tax benefits arising on capital allowances if Cold plc decides to purchase the new equipment.

(c) Determine whether, on financial grounds, Cold plc should lease or buy the new equipment.

(d) Critically discuss what other factors may influence the decision of Cold plc to lease or buy the new equipment, apart from financial considerations.

5* Permafrost plc needs a new computer network but is uncertain whether to buy the system or to lease it from Slush plc. The system will cost £800 000 if bought and Permafrost plc would borrow to finance this. Information on the two options is as follows.

Option 1

If the system is leased, Slush plc will expect an annual lease payment of £150 000, payable in advance. Slush plc will be responsible for servicing the system, at no additional cost, over the eight-year life of the system.

Option 2

If the system is bought, Permafrost plc will be responsible for servicing the system at an annual cost of £10 000. It has a choice of three financing methods:

1 It could issue 12 per cent debentures, to be redeemed in eight years' time at par. The debentures will be secured on existing fixed assets.

2 It could raise an eight-year floating rate bank loan. This loan would be repaid in equal instalments over its life and secured on existing land and buildings.

3 It could issue zero coupon bonds, to be redeemed at par in eight years.

Permafrost plc pays tax one year in arrears at an annual rate of 30 per cent and can claim capital allowances on a 25 per cent reducing balance basis. The current after-tax cost of debt of the company is 10 per cent and this is not expected to change as a result of the financing choice made in connection with the new computer network.

(a) Determine the expected market values of the debenture issue and the zero coupon bond issue, and critically discuss the relative merits of these three debt finance methods to Permafrost plc.

(b) Using the information provided, write a report that advises Permafrost plc on whether it should lease or buy the new computer network.

References

Drury, C. and Braund, S. (1990) 'The leasing decision: a comparison of theory and practice', *Accounting and Business Research*, Vol. 20, No. 79, pp. 179–91.

Myers, S.C., Dill, D.A. and Bautista, A.J. (1976) 'Valuation of financial lease contracts', Vol. 31, *Journal of Finance*, June, pp. 799–819.

Tan, C. (1992) 'Lease or buy?', *Accountancy*, December, pp. 58–9.

Recommended reading

Ross, S.A., Westerfield, R.W. and Jaffe, J. (2005) *Corporate Finance*, 7th edn, New York: McGraw-Hill, Irwin International Edition, offers a useful discussion of leasing and adds an international perspective in Chapter 21.

Useful information on bond ratings can be obtained from the websites of the rating organisations themselves, for example:

Moody's Investors Service: www.moodys.com
Standard & Poor's Corporation: www.standardandpoors.com
FitchIBCA: www.fitchibca.com

Information on benchmark yields for short-term and long-term debt can be found on the website of the UK Government Debt Management Office: www.dmo.gov.uk/

A useful website for further information on leasing is that of the Finance and Leasing Association, found at www.fla.org.uk/fla/

Bonds trading on the London Stock Exchange can be searched at www. londonstockexchange. com/en-gb/pricesnews/prices/bonds.htm

Chapter 6

An overview of investment appraisal methods

Learning objectives

After studying this chapter, you should have achieved the following learning objectives:

- to be able to define and apply the four main investment appraisal methods of payback, return on capital employed, net present value and internal rate of return;

- to be able to explain the reasons why discounted cash flow methods are preferred to the more traditional techniques of payback and return on capital employed;

- to be able to explain why net present value is considered to be superior to internal rate of return as an investment appraisal method;

- an understanding of the techniques to be employed in order to arrive at the best investment decision if investment capital is rationed.

Introduction

Companies need to invest in wealth-creating assets in order to renew, extend or replace the means by which they carry on their business. Capital investment allows companies to continue to generate cash flows in the future or to maintain the profitability of existing business activities. Typically, capital investment projects will require significant cash outflows at the beginning and will then produce cash inflows over several years. Capital investment projects require careful evaluation because they require very large amounts of cash to be raised and invested, and because they will determine whether the company is profitable in the future.

A company seeks to select the best or most profitable investment projects so that it can maximise the return to its shareholders. It also seeks to avoid the negative strategic and financial consequences which could follow from poor investment decisions.

Since capital investment decisions affect a company over a long period of time, it is possible to view a company and its balance sheet as the sum of the previous investment and financing decisions taken by its directors and managers.

6.1 The payback method

While research has shown that payback is the most popular investment appraisal method, it suffers from such serious shortcomings that it should only really be regarded as a first screening method. The *payback period* is the number of years it is expected to take to recover the original investment from the net cash flows resulting from a capital investment project. The decision rule when using the *payback method* to appraise investments is to accept a project if its payback period is equal to or less than a predetermined target value. It is possible to obtain an estimate of the payback period to several decimal places if cash flows are assumed to occur evenly throughout each year, but a high degree of accuracy in estimating the payback period is not desirable since it does not offer information which is especially useful. A figure to the nearest year or half-year is usually sufficient.

6.1.1 Example of the payback method

Consider an investment project with the cash flows given in Exhibit 6.1.

The cash flows of this project are called *conventional* cash flows and the project is called a *conventional project*. A conventional project can be defined as one which

Exhibit 6.1	Simple investment project, showing a significant initial investment followed by a series of cash inflows over the life of the project

Year	0	1	2	3	4	5
Cash flow (£)	(450)	100	200	100	100	80

Exhibit 6.2	**Table of cumulative cash flows for the conventional project of the previous exhibit, showing that the payback period is between three and four years**

Year	Cash flow (£)	Cumulative cash flow (£)
0	(450)	(450)
1	100	(350)
2	200	(150)
3	100	(50)
4	100	50
5	80	130

requires a cash investment at the start of the project, followed by a series of cash inflows over the life of the project. We can see from Exhibit 6.1 that, after three years, the project has generated total cash inflows of £400. During the fourth year, the remaining £50 of the initial investment will be recovered. As the cash inflow in this year is £100, and assuming that it occurs evenly during the year, it will take a further six months or 0.5 years for the final £50 to be recovered. The payback period is therefore 3.5 years.

It can be helpful to draw up a table of cumulative project cash flows in order to determine the payback period, as shown in Exhibit 6.2.

6.1.2 The advantages of the payback method

The advantages of the payback method are that it is simple and easy to apply and, as a concept, it is straightforward to understand. The payback period is calculated using cash flows, not accounting profits, and so should not be open to manipulation by managerial preferences for particular accounting policies. If we accept that more distant cash flows are more uncertain and that increasing uncertainty is the same as increasing risk, it is possible to argue that a further advantage of the payback method is that it takes account of risk in that it implicitly assumes that a shorter payback period is superior to a longer one.

It has been argued that payback period is a useful investment appraisal method when a company is restricted in the amount of finance it has available for investment since the sooner cash is returned by a project, the sooner it can be reinvested into other projects. While there is some truth in this claim, it ignores the fact that there are better investment appraisal methods available to deal with capital rationing, as explained in Section 6.6.

6.1.3 The disadvantages of the payback method

There are a number of difficulties in using the payback method to assess capital investment projects and these are sufficiently serious for it to be generally rejected by corporate finance theory as a credible method of investment appraisal. One of the major disadvantages is that the payback method ignores the *time value of money* (see Section 1.1.2), so that it gives equal weight to cash flows whenever they occur within the payback period. We can illustrate this point by referring back to the example in Exhibit 6.1. You can see that the payback period remains 3.5 years even if the project generates no cash inflows in the first and second years, but then a cash inflow of £400 occurs in the third year. In fact, any combination of cash inflows in the first three years which totals £400 would give the same payback period.

The problem of ignoring the time value of money is partly remedied by using the *discounted payback method* discussed in Section 6.7.

Another serious disadvantage of the payback method is that it ignores all cash flows outside the payback period and so does not consider the project as a whole. If a company rejected all projects with payback periods greater than three years, it would reject the project given in Exhibit 6.1. Suppose that this project had been expected to generate a cash inflow of £1000 in year 4. This expected cash inflow would have been ignored if the sole investment appraisal method being applied was the payback method and the project would still have been rejected. Would this have been a wealth-maximising decision for the company concerned? Hardly! In fact, the choice of the maximum payback period acceptable to a company is an arbitrary one since it is not possible to say why one payback period is preferable to any other. Why should a project with a payback period of three years be accepted while one with a payback period of three-and-a-half years be rejected?

In fairness, we should recognise that in practice when the payback method is used, cash flows outside of the payback period are not ignored, but are taken into consideration as part of the exercise of managerial judgement. However, this only serves to reinforce the inadequacy of the payback method as the *sole* measure of project acceptability.

The general conclusion that can be drawn from this discussion is that the payback method does not give any real indication of whether an investment project increases the value of a company. For this reason it has been argued that, despite its well-documented popularity, the payback method is not really an investment appraisal method at all, but rather a means of assessing the effect of accepting an investment project on a company's liquidity position.

6.2 The return on capital employed method

There are several different definitions of return on capital employed (ROCE), which is also called return on investment (ROI) and accounting rate of return (ARR). All definitions relate accounting profit to some measure of the capital employed in a capital investment project. One definition that is widely used is:

$$\text{ROCE} = \frac{\text{Average annual accounting profit}}{\text{Average investment}} \times 100$$

The average investment must take account of any scrap value. Assuming straight-line depreciation from the initial investment to the terminal scrap value, we have:

$$\text{Average investment} = \frac{\text{Initial investment + Scrap value}}{2}$$

Another common definition of return on capital employed (*see* Section 2.4.3) uses the initial or final investment rather than the average investment, for example:

$$\text{ROCE} = \frac{\text{Average annual accounting profit}}{\text{Initial (or final) investment}} \times 100$$

It is important to remember that return on capital employed is calculated using accounting profits, which are operating cash flows adjusted to take account of depreciation. *Accounting profits are not cash flows*, since depreciation is an accounting adjustment which does not correspond to an annual movement of cash. The *decision rule* here is to accept an investment project if its return on capital employed is greater than a target or hurdle rate of return set by the investing company. If only one of two investment projects can be undertaken (i.e. if the projects are *mutually exclusive*), the project with the higher return on capital employed should be accepted.

Example │ Calculation of the return on capital employed

Carbon plc is considering the purchase of a new machine and has found two which meet its specification. Each machine has an expected life of five years. Machine 1 would generate annual cash flows (receipts less payments) of £210 000 and would cost £570 000. Its scrap value at the end of five years would be £70 000. Machine 2 would generate annual cash flows of £510 000 and would cost £1 616 000. The scrap value of this machine at the end of five years would be £301 000. Carbon plc uses the straight-line method of depreciation and has a target return on capital employed of 20 per cent.

Calculate the return on capital employed for both Machine 1 and Machine 2 on an average investment basis and state which machine you would recommend, giving reasons.

Suggested answer

	£
For Machine 1:	
Total cash profit = 210 000 × 5 =	1 050 000
Total depreciation = 570 000 − 70 000 =	500 000
Total accounting profit	550 000
Average annual accounting profit = 550 000/5 =	£110 000 per year
Average investment = (570 000 + 70 000)/2 =	£320 000
Return on capital employed = 100 × (110 000/320 000) =	34.4%

For Machine 2:	£
Total cash profit = $510\,000 \times 5$ =	2 550 000
Total depreciation = $1\,616\,000 - 301\,000$ =	1 315 000
Total accounting profit	1 235 000
Average annual accounting profit = $1\,235\,000/5$ =	£247 000 per year
Average investment = $(1\,616\,000 + 301\,000)/2$ =	£958 500
Return on capital employed = $100 \times (247\,000/958\,000)$ =	25.8%

Both machines have a return on capital employed greater than the target rate and so are financially acceptable, but as only one machine is to be purchased, the recommendation is that Machine 1 should be chosen, as it has a higher return on capital employed than Machine 2.

6.2.1 Advantages of the return on capital employed method

There are a number of reasons for the popularity of the return on capital employed method, even though it has little theoretical credibility as a method of making investment decisions. For example, it gives a value in percentage terms, a familiar measure of return, which can be compared with the existing ROCE of a company, the primary accounting ratio used by financial analysts in assessing company performance (*see* Section 2.4.3). It is also a reasonably simple method to apply and can be used to compare mutually exclusive projects. Unlike the payback method, it considers all cash flows arising during the life of an investment project and it can indicate whether a project is acceptable by comparing the ROCE of the project with a target rate, for example a company's current ROCE or the ROCE of a division.

6.2.2 Disadvantages of the return on capital employed method

While it can be argued that the return on capital employed method provides us with useful information about a project, as an investment appraisal method it has significant drawbacks. For example, it is not based on cash, but uses accounting profit, which is open to manipulation and is not linked to the fundamental objective of maximising shareholder wealth.

Because the method uses *average* profits, it also ignores the *timing* of profits. Consider the two projects A and B in Exhibit 6.3. Both projects have the same initial investment and zero scrap value and hence the same average investment:

$$£45\,000/2 = £22\,500$$

Both projects have the same average annual accounting profit:

$$\text{Project A: } (-250 + 1000 + 1000 + 20\,750)/4 = £5625$$
$$\text{Project B: } (6000 + 6000 + 5500 + 5000)/4 = £5625$$

Exhibit 6.3	Illustration of how return on capital employed, which uses average accounting profit, ignores the timing of project cash flows				

Year	0 £000	1 £000	2 £000	3 £000	4 £000
Project A					
cash flows	(45 000)	11 000	12 250	12 250	32 000
depreciation		11 250	11 250	11 250	11 250
accounting profit		(250)	1 000	1 000	20 750
Project B					
cash flows	(45 000)	17 250	17 250	16 750	16 250
depreciation		11 250	11 250	11 250	11 250
accounting profit		6 000	6 000	5 500	5 000

So their return on capital employed values are identical too:

$$\text{ROCE} = (100 \times 5625)/22\,500 = 25\%$$

But Project B has a smooth pattern of returns, whereas Project A offers little in the first three years and a large return in the final year. We can see that, even though they both have the same ROCE, Project B is preferable to Project A by virtue of the pattern of its profits.

A more serious drawback is that the return on capital employed method does not consider the time value of money and so gives equal weight to profits whenever they occur. It also fails to take into account the length of the project life and, since it is expressed in percentage terms and is therefore a relative measure, it ignores the size of the investment made. For these reasons, the return on capital employed method cannot be seen as offering sensible advice about whether a project creates wealth or not. In order to obtain such advice, we need to use discounted cash flow methods, the most widely accepted of which is net present value.

6.3 The net present value method

The net present value (NPV) method of investment appraisal uses *discounted cash flows* to evaluate capital investment projects and is based on the sound theoretical foundation of the investment–consumption model developed by Hirschleifer (1958). It uses a *cost of capital* (*see* Chapter 9) or target rate of return to discount all cash inflows and outflows to their *present values*, and then compares the present value of all cash inflows with the present value of all cash outflows. A *positive* net present value indicates that an investment project is expected to give a return in excess of the cost of capital and will therefore lead to an increase in shareholder wealth. We can represent the calculation of NPV algebraically as follows:

$$\text{NPV} = -I_0 + \frac{C_1}{(1 + r)} + \frac{C_2}{(1 + r)^2} + \frac{C_3}{(1 + r)^3} + \cdots + \frac{C_n}{(1 + r)^n}$$

where: I_0 is the initial investment

$C_1, C_2, \ldots, C_n$ are the project cash flows occurring in years $1, 2, \ldots, n$

r is the cost of capital or required rate of return

By convention, in order to avoid the mathematics of continuous discounting, cash flows occurring *during* a time period are assumed to occur at the *end* of that time period. The initial investment occurs at the start of the first time period. The NPV *decision rule* is to accept all independent projects with a positive net present value. If two capital investment projects are not independent but mutually exclusive, so that of the two projects available only one project can be undertaken, the project with the higher net present value should be selected.

Example	Calculation of the net present value

Carter Ltd is evaluating three investment projects, whose expected cash flows are given in Exhibit 6.4. Calculate the net present value for each project if Carter's cost of capital is 10 per cent. Which project should be selected?

Project A

The cash inflows of this project are identical and so do not need to be discounted separately. Instead, we can use the cumulative present value factor (CPVF) or annuity

Exhibit 6.4	Three investment projects with different cash flow profiles to illustrate the calculation of net present value

Carter Ltd: cash flows of proposed investment projects			
Period	Project A (£000)	Project B (£000)	Project C (£000)
0	(5000)	(5000)	(5000)
1	1100	800	2000
2	1100	900	2000
3	1100	1200	2000
4	1100	1400	100
5	1100	1600	100
6	1100	1300	100
7	1100	1100	100

factor for seven years at 10 per cent ($CPVF_{10,7}$), which is found from CPVF tables (see pages 487–8) to have a value of 4.868. We have:

	£000
Initial investment	(5000)
Present value of cash inflows = £1100 × 4.868 =	5355
Net present value	355

Project A has a positive net present value of £355 000.

Project B

Because the cash inflows of this project are all different, it is necessary to discount each one separately. The easiest way to organise this calculation is by using a table, as in Exhibit 6.5.

Using a table to organise net present value calculations is especially useful when dealing with the more complex cash flows which arise when account is taken of taxation, inflation and a range of costs or project variables. A tabular approach also aids clear thinking and methodical working in examinations. From Exhibit 6.5, we can see that Project B has a positive net present value of £618 000.

Project C

The cash flows for the first three years are identical and can be discounted using the cumulative present value factor for three years at 10 per cent ($CPVF_{10,3}$), which is found from cumulative present value factor (CPVF) tables to be 2.487. The cash flows for years 4 to 7 are also identical and can be discounted using a cumulative present value factor. To find this, we subtract the cumulative present value factor for three

Exhibit 6.5 Calculation of net present value of Project B using a tabular approach. This approach organises the calculation and information used in a clear, easily understood format which helps to avoid errors during the calculation process

Year	Cash flow (£000)	10% present value factors	Present value (£000)
0	(5000)	1.000	(5000)
1	800	0.909	727
2	900	0.826	743
3	1200	0.751	901
4	1400	0.683	956
5	1600	0.621	994
6	1300	0.564	733
7	1100	0.513	564
		Net present value	618

years at 10 per cent from the cumulative present value factor for seven years at 10 per cent. From the CPVF tables, we have:

$$\text{CPVF}_{10,7} - \text{CPVF}_{10,3} = 4.868 - 2.487 = 2.381$$

	£000
Initial investment	(5000)
Present value of cash inflows, years 1 to 3 = £2000 × 2.487 =	4974
Present value of cash inflows, years 4 to 7 = £100 × 2.381 =	238
Net present value	212

Project C has a positive net present value of £212 000. If the annual cash flows are discounted separately, as in Exhibit 6.9, the NPV is £209 000, the difference being due to rounding.

The decision on project selection

We can now rank the projects in order of decreasing net present value:

Project B	NPV of £618 000
Project A	NPV of £355 000
Project C	NPV of £212 000

Which project should be selected? If the projects are mutually exclusive, then Project B should be undertaken since it has the highest NPV and will lead to the largest increase in shareholder wealth. If the projects are not mutually exclusive and there is no restriction on capital available for investment, all three projects should be undertaken since all three have a positive NPV and will increase shareholder wealth. However, the cash flows in years 4 to 7 of Project C should be investigated; they are not very large and they are critical to the project, since without them it would have a negative NPV and would therefore lead to a decrease in shareholder wealth.

6.3.1 Advantages of the net present value method

The net present value method of investment appraisal, being based on discounted cash flows, takes account of the *time value of money* (*see* Section 1.1.2), which is one of the key concepts in corporate finance. Net present value uses cash flows rather than accounting profit, takes account of both the amount and the timing of project cash flows, and takes account of all relevant cash flows over the life of an investment project. For all these reasons, net present value is the *academically preferred method* of investment appraisal. In all cases where there are no constraints on capital, the net present value decision rule offers sound investment advice.

6.3.2 Disadvantages of the net present value method

It has been argued that net present value is conceptually difficult to understand, but this is hardly a realistic criticism. It has also been pointed out that it is difficult to estimate the values of the cash inflows and outflows over the life of a project which are needed in order to calculate its net present value, but this difficulty of forecasting future cash flows is a problem of investment appraisal in general and not one that is specific to any particular investment appraisal technique. A more serious criticism is that it is only possible to accept all projects with a positive NPV in a perfect capital market since only in such a market is there no restriction on the amount of finance available. In reality, capital is restricted or rationed (*see* Section 6.6) and this can limit the applicability of the NPV decision rule.

When calculating the NPV of an investment project, we tend to assume not only that the company's cost of capital is known, but also that it remains constant over the life of the project. In practice, the cost of capital of a company may be difficult to estimate (*see* Section 9.5) and so the selection of an appropriate discount rate for use in investment appraisal is also not straightforward (*see* Chapter 9). The cost of capital is also likely to change over the life of the project, since it is influenced by the dynamic economic environment within which all business is conducted. However, if these changes can be forecast the net present value method can accommodate them without difficulty (*see* Section 6.5.3).

6.4 The internal rate of return method

If the cost of capital used to discount future cash flows is increased, the net present value of an investment project with conventional cash flows will fall. Eventually, as the cost of capital continues to increase, the NPV will become zero, and then negative. This is illustrated in Exhibit 6.6.

 Exhibit 6.6 **The relationship between the net present values of a conventional project and the discount rate. The internal rate of return produces a net present value of zero**

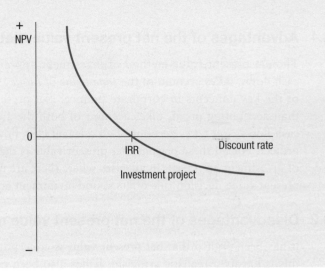

The *internal rate of return* (IRR) of an investment project is the cost of capital or required rate of return which, when used to discount the cash flows of a project, produces a net present value of zero. The internal rate of return method of investment appraisal involves calculating the IRR of a project, usually by linear interpolation, and then comparing it with a target rate of return or hurdle rate. The internal rate of return decision rule is to accept all independent investment projects with an IRR greater than the company's cost of capital or target rate of return.

We can restate the expression for net present value in terms of the internal rate of return as follows:

$$\frac{C_1}{(1 + r^*)} + \frac{C_2}{(1 + r^*)^2} + \frac{C_3}{(1 + r^*)^3} + \cdots + \frac{C_n}{(1 + r^*)^n} - I_0 = 0$$

where: $C_1, C_2, \ldots, C_n$ are the project cash flows occurring in years $1, 2, \ldots, n$
r^* is the internal rate of return
I_0 is the initial investment

Example | Calculation of internal rates of return

Carter Ltd is evaluating three investment projects, whose expected cash flows are given in Exhibit 6.4. Calculate the internal rate of return for each project. If Carter's cost of capital is 10 per cent, which project should be selected?

Project A

In the previous example we found that (all values in £000):

$$(£1100 \times CPVF_{10,7}) - £5000 = (1100 \times 4.868) - 5000 = £355$$

Where project cash inflows are identical, we can determine the cumulative present value factor for a period corresponding to the life of the project and a discount rate equal to the internal rate of return. If we represent this by $(CPVF_{r^*,7})$, then from our above expression:

$$(£1100 \times CPVF_{r^*,7}) - £5000 = 0$$

Rearranging:

$$CPVF_{r^*7} = 5000/1100 = 4.545$$

From CPVF tables (see pages 487–8), looking along the row corresponding to seven years, we find that the discount rate corresponding to this cumulative present value factor is approximately 12 per cent. Project A, then, has an internal rate of return of 12 per cent.

→

163

Project B

The cash flows of Project B are all different and so to find its IRR we need to use linear interpolation. This technique relies on the fact that, if we know the location of any two points on a straight line, we can find any other point which also lies on that line. The procedure is to make an estimate (R_1) of the internal rate of return, giving a net present value of NPV_1. We then make a second estimate (R_2) of the internal rate of return: if NPV_1 was positive, R_2 should be higher than R_1; if NPV_1 was negative, R_2 should be lower than R_1. We then calculate a second net present value, NPV_2, from R_2. The values of R_1, R_2, NPV_1 and NPV_2 can then be put into the following expression.

$$IRR = R_1 + \frac{(R_2 - R_1) \times NPV_1}{(NPV_1 - NPV_2)}$$

We calculated earlier that the NPV of Project B was £618 000 at a discount rate of 10 per cent. If we now make an estimate that the internal rate of return is 20 per cent, we can recalculate the NPV, as shown in Exhibit 6.7. The earlier NPV calculation is included for comparison.

Interpolating, using the method discussed earlier:

$$IRR = 10 + \frac{(20 - 10) \times 618}{618 - (-953)} = 10 + 3.9 \cong 13.9\%$$

So the internal rate of return of Project B is approximately 13.9 per cent.

We say 'approximately' since, in using linear interpolation we have drawn a straight line between two points on a project NPV line that is in fact a curve. As shown in Exhibit 6.8, the straight line will not cut the x-axis at the same place as the project NPV curve, so the value we have obtained by interpolation is not the actual value of the IRR, but only an estimated value (and, for conventional projects, an underestimate). We would have obtained a different value if we had used a different estimate for R_2;

Exhibit 6.7   **Calculation of the NPV of Project B at discount rates of 10 per cent and 20 per cent as preparation for determining its IRR by linear interpolation**

Year	Cash flow (£)	10% PV factors	Present value (£)	20% PV factors	Present value (£)
0	(5000)	1.000	(5000)	1.000	(5000)
1	800	0.909	727	0.833	666
2	900	0.826	743	0.694	625
3	1200	0.751	901	0.579	695
4	1400	0.683	956	0.482	675
5	1600	0.621	994	0.402	643
6	1300	0.564	733	0.335	436
7	1100	0.513	564	0.279	307
			618		(953)

Exhibit 6.8 **Illustration of why the IRR estimated by a single linear interpolation is only an approximation of the actual IRR of an investment project**

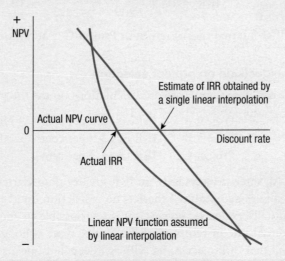

for example, if we had used $R_1 = 10$ per cent and $R_2 = 15$ per cent, we would have obtained a value for the IRR of 13.5 per cent. To determine the actual IRR the interpolation calculation must be repeated, feeding successive approximations back into the calculation until the value produced no longer changes significantly. A financial calculator or a computer spreadsheet can easily do this task.

Project C

The calculation of the NPV of Project C at Carter's cost of capital of 10 per cent and a first estimate of the project IRR of 15 per cent is given in Exhibit 6.9.

Exhibit 6.9 **Calculation of the NPV of Project C at discount rates of 10 per cent and 15 per cent as preparation for determining its IRR by linear interpolation**

Year	Cash flow (£)	10% PV factors	Present value (£)	15% PV factors	Present value (£)
0	(5000)	1.000	(5000)	1.000	(5000)
1	2000	0.909	1818	0.870	1740
2	2000	0.826	1652	0.756	1512
3	2000	0.751	1502	0.658	1316
4	100	0.683	68	0.572	57
5	100	0.621	62	0.497	50
6	100	0.564	56	0.432	43
7	100	0.513	51	0.376	38
			209		(244)

Interpolating:

$$\text{IRR} = 10 + \frac{(15 - 10) \times 209}{209 - (-244)} = 10 + 2.3 = 12.3 \text{ per cent}$$

The internal rate of return of Project C is approximately 12.3 per cent.

The decision on project selection

We can now summarise our calculations on the three projects:

Project A	IRR of 12.0 per cent	NPV of £355 000
Project B	IRR of 13.9 per cent	NPV of £618 000
Project C	IRR of 12.3 per cent	NPV of £209 000

All three projects have an IRR greater than Carter's cost of capital of 10 per cent, so all are acceptable if there is no restriction on available capital. If the projects are mutually exclusive, however, it is not possible to choose the best project by using the internal rate of return method. Notice that, although the IRR of Project C is higher than that of Project A, its NPV is lower. This means that the projects are ranked differently using IRR than they are using NPV. The problem of mutually exclusive investment projects is discussed in Section 6.5.1.

6.5 A comparison of the NPV and IRR methods

There is no conflict between these two discounted cash flow methods when a *single* investment project with *conventional* cash flows is being evaluated. In the following situations, however, the net present value method may be preferred:

- where mutually exclusive projects are being compared;
- where the cash flows of a project are not conventional;
- where the discount rate changes during the life of the project.

6.5.1 Mutually exclusive projects

Consider two mutually exclusive projects, A and B, whose cash flows are given in Exhibit 6.10. The net present value decision rule recommends accepting Project B, since it has the higher NPV at a cost of capital of 14 per cent. However, if the projects are compared using internal rate of return, Project A is preferred as it has the higher IRR. If the projects were independent so that both could be undertaken, this conflict of preferences would not be relevant. Since the projects are mutually exclusive, however, which should be accepted?

In all cases where this conflict occurs, the correct decision is to choose the project with the higher NPV. This decision supports the primary corporate finance objective of maximising shareholder wealth since selecting the project with the highest NPV leads to the greatest increase in the value of the company. Although Project A has the highest

Exhibit 6.10 | Table showing the cash flows, net present values at a cost of capital of 14 per cent and internal rates of return of two mutually exclusive projects

	Project A	Project B
Initial investment (£)	13 000	33 000
Year 1 net cash flow (£)	7 000	15 000
Year 2 net cash flow (£)	6 000	15 000
Year 3 net cash flow (£)	5 000	15 000
Net present value (£)	+1 128	+1 830
Internal rate of return (%)	19.5	17

Exhibit 6.11 | The net present values of two mutually exclusive projects at different discount rates

Discount rate (%)	12	14	16	18	20	22
Project A (£)	1593	1128	697	282	(113)	(473)
Project B (£)	3030	1830	690	(390)	(1410)	(2370)

IRR, this is only a *relative* measure of return. NPV measures the *absolute* increase in value of the company.

In order to illustrate the conflict between the two investment appraisal methods in more detail, Exhibit 6.11 shows the NPV of the two projects at different discount rates and Exhibit 6.12 displays the same information in the form of a graph.

From Exhibit 6.12, it can be seen that the two projects, A and B, have lines with different slopes. For costs of capital *greater* than the IRR of the intersection of the two

Exhibit 6.12 | Graph showing the calculated NPV of two mutually exclusive projects and the region of conflict

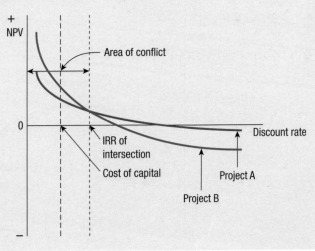

project lines, which occurs at approximately 16 per cent, the two methods give the same advice: accept Project A. For costs of capital *less* than the IRR of the inter-section, the advice offered by the two methods is in conflict and the net present value method is preferred.

6.5.2 Non-conventional cash flows

If an investment project has cash flows of different signs in successive periods (e.g. a cash inflow followed by a cash outflow, followed by a further cash inflow), it may have more than one internal rate of return. Such cash flows are called non-conventional cash flows, and the existence of multiple internal rates of return may result in incorrect deci-sions being taken if the IRR decision rule is applied. The NPV method has no difficulty in accommodating non-conventional cash flows, as can be seen from Exhibit 6.13.

The non-conventional project in Exhibit 6.13 has two internal rates of return, at IRR_1 and IRR_2. This kind of project is not unusual: for example, a mineral extrac-tion project, with heavy initial investment in land, plant and machinery and significant environmental costs towards the end of the project life, might have this kind of NPV profile. Using the internal rate of return method, which IRR should be used to assess the project?

If the cost of capital is R_A, the project would be accepted using the internal rate of return method, since both IRR_1 and IRR_2 are greater than R_A. If the net present value method is used, however, it will be rejected, because at this discount rate it has a negative NPV and would decrease shareholder wealth.

However, if the cost of capital used to assess the project is R_B, it will be accepted using the net present value method because at this discount rate it has a positive NPV. The internal rate of return method cannot offer any clear advice since R_B is between IRR_1 and IRR_2.

In each case, the net present value method gives the correct investment advice.

Exhibit 6.13 **Diagram of non-conventional project with multiple internal rates of return**

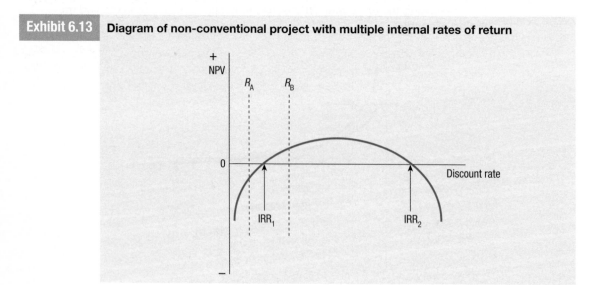

6.5.3 Changes in the discount rate

If there are changes in the cost of capital over the life of an investment project, the net present value method can easily accommodate them. Consider the net present value expression described earlier, with the symbols having the same meaning:

$$NPV = -I_0 + \frac{C_1}{(1 + r)} + \frac{C_2}{(1 + r)^2} + \frac{C_3}{(1 + r)^3} + \cdots + \frac{C_n}{(1 + r)^n}$$

If the discount rates in successive years are r_1, r_2, etc., we have:

$$NPV = -I_0 + \frac{C_1}{(1 + r_1)} + \frac{C_2}{(1 + r_1)(1 + r_2)} + \cdots$$

Consider the investment project in Exhibit 6.14, where the discount rate increases in year 3 from 10 per cent to 15 per cent. The present value factor for year 3 is the present value factor for two years at 10 per cent multiplied by the present value factor for one year at 15 per cent. Using present value tables (see pages 487–8), we have:

$$PVF_{10,2} \times PVF_{15,1} = 0.826 \times 0.870 = 0.719$$

The NPV of the project is £1807 while the IRR is approximately 18.8 per cent. The IRR, however, cannot take into account the fact that the discount rate in year 3 is different from that in years 1 and 2.

6.5.4 Reinvestment assumptions

The net present value method assumes that cash flows generated during the life of the project can be reinvested elsewhere at a rate equal to the cost of capital. This seems to be a sensible reinvestment assumption since the cost of capital represents an opportunity cost, i.e. the best return that could have been obtained on an alternative investment. The internal rate of return method, however, assumes that cash flows generated during the life of the project can be reinvested elsewhere at the internal rate of return. The more the IRR exceeds the cost of capital, the less likely it is that such alternative returns could be realised, and so the reinvestment assumption underlying the internal rate of return method is a doubtful one. The reinvestment assumption underlying the NPV method seems realistic.

Exhibit 6.14	Investment project in which the discount rate changes during the project life			
Year	0	1	2	3
Discount rate (%)		10	10	15
Cash flow (£)	(13 000)	7000	5000	6000
PV factors	1.000	0.909	0.826	0.719
Present value (£)	(13 000)	6363	4130	4314

6.5.5 The superiority of the net present value method

We can now summarise the arguments in favour of the net present value method of investment appraisal:

1 The NPV method gives correct advice about mutually exclusive projects.
2 The NPV method can accommodate non-conventional cash flows, when the internal rate of return method may offer multiple solutions.
3 The reinvestment assumption underlying the NPV method is realistic, but that underlying the internal rate of return method is not.
4 The NPV method can easily incorporate changes in the discount rate, whereas the internal rate of return method is unable to accommodate them.

For these reasons, the net present value method is held to be technically superior to the internal rate of return method.

The internal rate of return method, however, enjoys comparable popularity (*see* Section 7.5). It is obviously to be preferred to both payback period and accounting rate of return as an investment appraisal method since it takes account of the time value of money, is based on cash flows and considers the whole of the project. The IRR or *yield* of an investment project is also a concept widely understood by financial analysts, investors and managers, and indicates the extent to which a project offers returns in excess of a minimum required level, i.e. it indicates a margin of safety.

This chapter has argued that discounted cash flow investment appraisal methods (i.e. NPV and IRR) are superior to simplistic investment appraisal methods (i.e. payback and return on capital employed) and this is widely accepted. Companies using discounted cash flow (DCF) investment appraisal methods should therefore perform better than those using simplistic methods. Empirical research on this question has produced mixed results, however, and Haka et al. (1985) found evidence that adoption of sophisticated investment appraisal methods may not necessarily, in itself, lead to improved performance. Since most companies now use more than one investment appraisal method (*see* Section 7.5.1), it is in practice difficult to isolate any beneficial effects that may be solely due to using DCF methods. This does not invalidate the academic superiority of NPV and IRR.

6.6 The profitability index and capital rationing

If a company does not have sufficient funds to undertake all projects that have a positive net present value, it is in a *capital rationing* situation. It will need to find a way of choosing between investment opportunities which maximise the return on the funds invested, i.e. it needs to *rank* investment projects in terms of desirability. The NPV method, which requires a company to invest in *all* projects with a positive NPV in order to maximise shareholder wealth, calls for the existence of a perfect market to provide any investment funds that may be required. The NPV method cannot be used to rank investment projects if capital is rationed, however, since ranking by NPV may lead to incorrect investment decisions. This is because a *combination* of smaller projects may collectively offer a higher NPV than a single project in return for the available capital, even if, when ranked by NPV, the smaller projects are ranked below the larger one.

6.6.1 Hard and soft capital rationing

We can distinguish between hard and soft capital rationing. Hard capital rationing occurs when the limitation on investment funds is imposed externally by the capital market. Soft capital rationing occurs when the limitation on investment funds is imposed internally by a company's managers.

Hard capital rationing

A company may be unable to raise investment capital because capital markets are depressed or because investors consider the company to be too risky. If only a small amount of finance is needed, for example to satisfy a marginal funding requirement, issue costs might make raising this finance unacceptably expensive. It is unusual in practice for hard capital rationing to occur, however, and most capital rationing is self-imposed and therefore soft in nature.

Soft capital rationing

Investment funds may be restricted internally by managers for a number of reasons. They may decide against issuing more equity finance, for example, because they wish to avoid dilution (reduction) of control, or because they wish to avoid any potential dilution (reduction) of earnings per share (EPS). They may decide against raising additional debt finance through a desire to avoid increased interest payment commitments, perhaps because they are concerned about their company's existing level of gearing or financial risk. If a company is small or family-owned, its managers may limit the investment funds available as part of a policy of seeking steady growth through retained earnings, as opposed to a policy of rapid expansion.

It is possible that self-imposed capital rationing, by fostering a competitive *internal market* for available investment funds, will weed out marginal or borderline investment projects and encourage the generation of better, more robust, investment proposals.

6.6.2 Single-period capital rationing

In single period capital rationing the available funds are only restricted initially, i.e. in year 0. A company needs to choose the combination of projects which maximises the total NPV. Depending on the circumstances, this can be done either by ranking projects using the profitability index or by finding the NPV of possible combinations of projects.

Divisible, non-deferrable investment projects

To assist in clarifying the circumstances in which the profitability index can be used, we can define three kinds of investment project. A *divisible project* is one where any portion of the project may be undertaken; a *non-deferrable project* is one which, if it is not undertaken at the present time, cannot be undertaken later; a *non-repeatable project* is one that may be undertaken only once.

If the available investment projects are divisible, non-deferrable and non-repeatable and if capital is rationed in the initial period only, ranking projects by their absolute NPV will not lead to the correct decision since, as pointed out earlier, a project with a large NPV will be favoured over a combination of several smaller projects with a larger collective NPV. The correct approach here is to calculate a *profitability index* or benefit to cost ratio for each project and then to rank them using this measure. The profitability index tells us how much we can expect to receive, in present value terms, for each unit of currency invested in the project:

$$\text{Profitability index} = \frac{\text{Present value of future cash flows}}{\text{Value of initial capital invested}}$$

If there is no restriction on investment capital, all projects with a profitability index greater than one should be accepted. This corresponds to the NPV decision rule of accepting all projects with a positive NPV. If investment capital is restricted, the project with the highest profitability index should be undertaken, then the project with the next highest profitability index should have funds allocated to it, and so on until there is no longer a whole project that can be undertaken. As the projects are divisible, the remaining funds are invested pro rata in the next best project. The total NPV arising from this investment schedule is the sum of the NPV of the complete projects, added to the pro rata share of the NPV of the partly undertaken project. This procedure is illustrated in Exhibit 6.15.

From Exhibit 6.15 we can see that, if we have £1650 available to invest in the divisible Projects A, B, C and D, then the optimum investment is to undertake all of Projects A and B and 62.5 per cent of Project C, giving a total NPV of £1865. This is preferable to investing £1650 in Projects C and D, even though these have the highest

Exhibit 6.15 **Example of ranking of divisible projects by profitability index in order to derive the optimum investment schedule under single-period capital rationing. Note that the ranking by absolute NPV is quite different from the ranking by profitability index**

Project	A	B	C	D
Initial investment (£)	500	650	800	850
Net present value (£)	650	715	800	765
PV of future cash flows (£)	1150	1365	1600	1615
Profitability index	2.3	2.1	2.0	1.9
Ranking by NPV	4	3	1	2
Ranking by profitability index	1	2	3	4

Capital available = £1650

Optimum investment schedule:	NPV (£)	Cumulative investment (£)
£500 invested in Project A	650	500
£650 invested in Project B	715	1150
£500 invested in Project C	500	1650
Total NPV for £1650 invested:	1865	

NPV, since their total NPV is only £1565. If Project A had been repeatable, the optimum investment schedule would have been to repeat Project A 3.3 times, giving a total NPV of £2145.

The profitability index can also be defined as the ratio of net present value to initial capital invested: the optimum investment schedule decision process is the same regardless of the definition of profitability index used.

Indivisible, non-deferrable investment projects

If investment projects are not divisible, profitability indices still provide useful information, but the selection of projects can only be achieved by examining the total NPV of all possible combinations of projects. The combination with the highest NPV which does not exceed the available investment capital is optimal. Assuming that the projects in Exhibit 6.15 are now indivisible, the optimum investment schedule is a combination of Projects C and D.

Projects A and B	Total NPV = £1365
Projects A and C	Total NPV = £1450
Projects A and D	Total NPV = £1415
Projects B and C	Total NPV = £1515
Projects B and D	Total NPV = £1480
Projects C and D	Total NPV = £1565

6.6.3 Multiple-period capital rationing

If investment funds are expected to be restricted in more than one period, the decision about which projects to choose cannot be based on ranking projects by profitability index or by trying different combinations of projects since neither of these methods takes into account the restriction on finance in future periods. The complexity of the problem calls for the use of linear programming. With only two variables, the linear programming problem can be solved graphically, but, if there are more than two variables, the simplex method or a computer must be used. The solution of multiple-period capital rationing problems is not considered in this text (but see, for example, Drury 2004).

6.7 The discounted payback method

The payback method discussed in Section 6.1 can be modified by discounting the project cash flows by the company's cost of capital in order to take account of the time value of money. Consider the example given in Exhibit 6.16, where a company with a cost of capital of 15 per cent is evaluating an investment project.

The discounted payback period is approximately 3.5 years, compared with an undiscounted payback period of approximately 2.2 years. The discounted payback method has the same advantages and disadvantages as before except that the shortcoming of failing to account for the time value of money has been overcome.

Exhibit 6.16	Table showing how cumulative NPV can be used to determine the discounted payback period for a project

Year	Cash flow (£)	15% PV factor	Present value (£)	Cumulative NPV (£)
0	(5000)	1.000	(5000)	(5000)
1	2300	0.870	2001	(2999)
2	2500	0.756	1890	(1109)
3	1200	0.658	790	(319)
4	1000	0.572	572	253
5	1000	0.497	497	750

6.8 Conclusion

In this chapter, we have considered at an introductory level the methods used by corporate finance to evaluate investment projects. While there are a wide range of techniques that can be used, the net present value method enjoys the support of academics and is regarded as superior to the other investment appraisal methods discussed.

Key points

1 Payback period is the number of years it takes to recover the original investment from the cash flows resulting from a capital investment project.

2 Payback takes account of risk (if by risk we mean the uncertainty that increases as cash flows become more distant), and is a simple method to apply and understand. However, it ignores the time value of money, the timing of cash flows within the payback period and any cash flows after the payback period. It does not say whether a project is a 'good' one.

3 Return on capital employed is the ratio of average annual profit to capital invested. It is simple to apply, looks at the whole of an investment project and can be used to compare mutually exclusive projects. A project is acceptable if the ROCE exceeds a target value.

4 Return on capital employed ignores the time value of money, fails to take account of the size and timing of cash flows and uses accounting profits rather than cash flows.

5 Net present value is the difference between the present value of future benefits and the present value of capital invested, discounted at a company's cost of capital. The NPV decision rule is to accept all projects with a positive net present value.

6 The NPV method takes account of the time value of money and the amount and timing of all relevant cash flows over the life of the project.

7 The NPV method can take account of both conventional and non-conventional cash flows, can accommodate changes in the discount rate during the life of a project and gives an absolute rather than a relative measure of project desirability.

8 Difficulties with using the NPV method are: it is difficult to estimate cash flows over the project life; the cost of capital for a company may be difficult to estimate; and the cost of capital may change over the project life.

9 The internal rate of return method involves the calculation of the discount rate which gives an NPV of zero. The IRR decision rule is to accept all projects with an IRR greater than the company's target rate of return.

10 The NPV method gives correct investment advice when comparing mutually exclusive projects; IRR might not.

11 The NPV method assumes that cash flows can be reinvested at the cost of capital, while the IRR method assumes that cash flows are reinvested at the internal rate of return. Only the reinvestment assumption underlying the NPV method is realistic.

12 Capital rationing can be either hard (externally imposed) or soft (internally imposed).

13 Hard capital rationing might occur because capital markets are depressed or because a company is thought to be too risky.

14 Soft capital rationing might occur because a company wishes to avoid dilution of control, dilution of EPS or further fixed interest commitments. The company may wish to pursue a policy of steady growth or believe that restricting available funds will encourage better projects.

15 In single-period capital rationing, divisible, non-deferrable and non-repeatable investment projects can be ranked using the profitability index in order to find the optimal investment schedule. The profitability index is the ratio of the present value of future cash flows divided by the initial capital invested.

16 Multiple-period capital rationing requires the use of linear programming.

Self-test questions

Answers to these questions can be found on pages 442–4.

1 Explain why the payback method cannot be recommended as the main method used by a company to assess potential investment projects.

2 Calculate the return on capital employed (average investment basis) for the following projects, and show which would be chosen if the target ROCE is 12 per cent. Assume straight-line depreciation (equal annual amounts) over the life of the project, with zero scrap value.

	Project A (£)	Project B (£)	Project C (£)
Initial investment	10 000	15 000	20 000
Net cash inflows:			
Year 1	5 000	5 000	10 000
Year 2	5 000	5 000	8 000
Year 3	2 000	5 000	4 000
Year 4	1 000	10 000	2 000
Year 5		5 000	

3 Explain the shortcomings of return on capital employed as an investment appraisal method and suggest reasons why it may be used by managers.

4 Three investment projects have the following net cash flows. Decide which of them should be accepted using the NPV decision rule if the discount rate to be applied is 12 per cent.

Year (£)	Project A (£)	Project B (£)	Project C (£)
0	(10 000)	(15 000)	(20 000)
1	5 000	5 000	10 000
2	5 000	5 000	10 000
3	2 000	5 000	4 000
4	1 000	10 000	2 000
5		5 000	

5 List the advantages of the net present value investment appraisal method.

6 Explain how NPV and IRR deal with non-conventional cash flows.

7 Discuss the problem of choosing between mutually exclusive projects with respect to their net present values and internal rates of return.

8 Show with the aid of a numerical example how linear interpolation can be used to determine the internal rate of return of a project.

9 Explain the distinction between hard and soft capital rationing, and outline the reasons why these conditions might occur.

10 What techniques can be used to determine the optimum investment schedule for a company under conditions of capital rationing?

Questions for review

Answers to these questions can be found on pages 444–9. Questions with an asterisk (*) are at an intermediate level.

1* The expected cash flows of three projects are given below. The cost of capital is 10 per cent.

(a) Calculate the payback period, net present value, internal rate of return and return on capital employed of each project.

(b) Show the rankings of the projects by each of the four methods and comment on your findings.

Period	Project A (£)	Project B (£)	Project C (£)
0	(5000)	(5000)	(5000)
1	900	700	2000
2	900	800	2000
3	900	900	2000
4	900	1000	1000
5	900	1100	
6	900	1200	
7	900	1300	
8	900	1400	
9	900	1500	
10	900	1600	

2* Tarragon needs to choose between two mutually exclusive investment projects, each lasting for five years. The company uses the straight-line method of depreciation and its cost of capital is 15 per cent.

Project Alpha would generate annual cash inflows of £200 000 after the purchase of machinery costing £556 000, with a scrap value after five years of £56 000.

Project Beta would generate annual cash inflows of £500 000 after the purchase of machinery costing £1 616 000, with a scrap value after five years of £301 000.

(a) Calculate, for each project, the return on capital employed (ROCE), net present value (NPV), internal rate of return (IRR) and payback period.

(b) State which project, if any, you would recommend. Give your reasons.

3* Brown Ltd is considering buying a new machine which would have a useful economic life of five years, a cost of £125 000 and a scrap value of £30 000, with 80 per cent of the cost being payable at the start of the project and 20 per cent after one year. The machine would produce 50 000 units per year of a new product with an estimated selling price of £3 per unit. Direct costs would be £1.75 per unit and annual fixed costs, including depreciation calculated on a straight-line basis (equal annual amounts), would be £40 000 per annum.

In years 1 and 2, special sales promotion expenditure, not included in the above costs, would be incurred, amounting to £10 000 and £15 000, respectively.

Evaluate the project using the NPV method of investment appraisal, assuming the company's cost of capital is 10 per cent.

4* Better plc is comparing two mutually exclusive projects, whose details are given below. The company's cost of capital is 12 per cent.

	Project A (£m)	Project B (£m)
Year 0	(150)	(152)
Year 1	40	80
Year 2	50	60
Year 3	60	50
Year 4	60	40
Year 5	80	30

(a) Using the net present value method, which project should be accepted?

(b) Using the internal rate of return method, which project should be accepted?

(c) If the cost of capital increases to 20 per cent in year 5, would your advice change?

5 A company with a cost of capital of 10 per cent has non-deferrable investment opportunities with the estimated cash flows shown below.

Year	Project A (£)	Project B (£)	Project C (£)	Project D (£)	Project E (£)
0	(1000)	(800)	(750)	(500)	(800)
1		200	300	150	
2		300	300	150	350
3		400	300	150	350
4		400	300	150	350
5		300	300	150	350
6		200		150	350
7		(100)		150	350
8	3000				

Decide which projects should be accepted in the following circumstances:

(a) the company is not in a capital rationing situation;

(b) the projects are divisible and only £2500 of investment capital is available;

(c) the projects are not divisible and only £2500 of investment capital is available.

Questions for discussion

Questions with an asterisk (*) are at an advanced level.

1 The finance manager of Yates plc is preparing a report for the next board meeting on the proposed construction of a new factory at an estimated cost of £5m. The factory will produce the Turbojet Printer Mark 4, a state-of-the-art laserjet printer for business use. This project was sanctioned by the management of Yates plc prior to the takeover of the company by Smith Holdings plc and it appears that little in the way of financial analysis of the project was carried out before that decision was taken. The land needed for the new factory, costing £2.2m, has already been purchased. The factory cost, while additional to the cost of the land, does include £4m for the cost of plant, equipment and computerised control systems.

Net cash sales of £2m per year for three years are expected, with a decline to £1m in the fourth year due to increasing competition from more technologically advanced substitutes. The Turbojet Printer Mark 4 will be replaced in the fifth year by the more advanced Mark 5 model.

No decision has yet been taken as to where the Mark 5 model will be made, but it is likely that the site used to manufacture the Mark 4 model will be redeveloped. At the end of four years, the plant and equipment used to manufacture the Mark 4 model will have negligible value. The value of the factory at that time is uncertain, but it is anticipated that, if manufacture of the Mark 5 model takes place on the same site, the factory used for the Mark 4 will require demolition and replacement.

Smith Holdings plc requires its subsidiaries to evaluate new projects using its own overall required rate of return, which is 10 per cent. Taxation may be ignored.

(a) For the Turbojet Printer Mark 4 project, calculate the following, and for each investment appraisal method discuss whether your calculations show the project to be acceptable or not:

(i) the accounting rate of return, based on the average investment;

(ii) the net present value;

(iii) the internal rate of return.

(b) Discuss what other information might assist the board in reaching a decision on the acceptability of the Turbojet Printer Mark 4 project.

(c) Discuss the reasons why net present value is regarded as superior to internal rate of return as a method of investment appraisal.

2 The finance director of Rosad Meerhay plc is considering several investment projects and has collected the following information about them.

Projects D and E are mutually exclusive. The capital available for investment in these projects is limited to £1m in the first year. All projects are divisible and none may be postponed or repeated. The cost of capital of Rosad Meerhay plc is 15 per cent.

Project	Estimated initial outlay (£)	Cash inflow Year 1 (£)	Cash inflow Year 2 (£)	Cash inflow Year 3 (£)
A	200 000	150 000	150 000	150 000
B	450 000	357 000	357 000	357 000
C	550 000	863 000	853 000	853 000
D	170 000	278 000	278 000	nil
E	200 000	250 000	250 000	250 000
F	330 000	332 000	332 000	nil

(a) Discuss the possible reasons why Rosad Meerhay plc may be limited as to the amount of capital available for investment in its projects.

(b) Determine which investment projects the finance director of Rosad Meerhay plc should choose in order to maximise the return on the capital available for investment. If the projects were not divisible, would you change your advice to the finance director?

(c) Critically discuss the reasons why net present value is the method of investment appraisal preferred by academics. Has the internal rate of return method now been made redundant?

3 The finance manager of Wide plc is evaluating two capital investment projects which may assist the company in achieving its business objectives. Both projects will require an initial investment of £500 000 in plant and machinery but it is not expected that any additional investment in working capital will be needed. The expected cash flows of the two projects are as follows.

Period	Broad Project (£)	Keeling Project (£)
1	60 000	220 000
2	90 000	220 000
3	140 000	50 000
4	210 000	50 000
5	300 000	50 000
6	140 000	50 000
7	100 000	200 000

The weighted average cost of capital of Wide plc is 10 per cent while its after-tax cost of borrowing is 7 per cent. Taxation may be ignored.

(a) For both the Broad and Keeling projects, calculate the return on capital employed, based on the average investment, the net present value and the internal rate of return.

(b) If the Broad and Keeling projects are mutually exclusive, advise Wide plc which project should be undertaken.

(c) Critically discuss the advantages and disadvantages of return on capital employed as an investment appraisal method.

References

Drury, C. (2004) *Management and Cost Accounting*, 6th edn, London: Thomson, pp. 116–20.

Haka, S., Gordon, L. and Pinches, G. (1985) 'Sophisticated capital budgeting selection techniques and firm performance', *The Accounting Review*, Vol. 60, No. 4, pp. 651–69.

Hirschleifer, J. (1958) 'On the theory of optimal investment decisions', *Journal of Political Economy*, Vol. 66, pp. 329–52.

Recommended reading

Many textbooks offer the opportunity to read further on the topic of investment appraisal techniques. A useful text is:

Arnold, G. (2005) *Corporate Financial Management*, 3rd edn, Harlow: FT Prentice Hall.

Chapter 7

Investment appraisal:
applications and risk

Learning objectives

After studying this chapter, you should have achieved the following learning objectives:

- an understanding of the influence of taxation on investment decisions and a familiarity with the calculation of tax liabilities and benefits;

- an understanding of the influence of general and specific inflation on investment decisions;

- a familiarity with both the real-terms and nominal-terms approaches to investment appraisal under conditions of inflation;

- an understanding of the distinction between risk and uncertainty;

- a familiarity with the application of sensitivity analysis to investment projects;

- a general understanding of the ways in which risk can be incorporated into the investment appraisal process;

- an appreciation of the general results of empirical research into the capital investment decision-making process.

Introduction

To make optimal capital investment decisions, the investment appraisal process needs to take account of the effects of taxation and inflation on project cash flows and on the required rate of return since the influence of these factors is inescapable. In addition, expected future cash flows are subject to both risk and uncertainty. In this chapter we consider some of the suggested methods for the investment appraisal process to take them into account. Finally, we look at what research has to say about the way in which investment appraisal is conducted in the real world. Do companies take the advice of academics on the best investment appraisal methods to use, or do they have their own ideas about how to evaluate investment projects?

7.1 Relevant project cash flows

In Chapter 6 we gave little thought to which costs and revenues should be included in project appraisal, beyond emphasising the use of cash flows rather than accounting profits. A key concept to grasp is that only *relevant* cash flows should be included. One test of cash flow relevance is to ask whether a cash flow occurs as a result of undertaking a project. If the answer is no, the cash flow is not relevant. It is useful to think in terms of *incremental* cash flows, which are the changes in a company's cash flows that result directly from undertaking an investment project. Cash flows such as initial investment, cash from sales and direct cost of sales are clearly incremental. The following costs, however, need careful consideration.

7.1.1 Sunk costs

Costs incurred prior to the start of an investment project are called *sunk costs* and are not relevant to project appraisal, even if they have not yet been paid, since such costs will be incurred regardless of whether the project is undertaken or not. Examples of such costs are market research, the historical cost of machinery already owned, and research and development expenditure.

7.1.2 Apportioned fixed costs

Costs which will be incurred regardless of whether a project is undertaken or not, such as apportioned fixed costs (e.g. rent and building insurance) or apportioned head office charges, are not relevant to project evaluation and should be excluded. Only *incremental* fixed costs which arise *as a result* of taking on a project should be included as relevant project cash flows.

7.1.3 Opportunity costs

An *opportunity cost* is the benefit forgone in using an asset for one purpose rather than another. If an asset is used for an investment project, it is important to ask what benefit has thereby been lost since this lost benefit or opportunity cost is the relevant cost as far as the project is concerned. An example using raw materials will serve to illustrate this point.

Suppose we have in stock 1000 kg of raw material A, which cost £2000 when purchased six months ago. This bill has been settled and the supplier is now quoting a price of £2.20 per kg for this material. The existing stocks could be sold on the second-hand market for £1.90 per kg, the lower price being due to slight deterioration in storage. Two-thirds of the stock of material A is required for a new project which begins in three weeks' time. What is the relevant cost of material A to the project?

Since material A has already been bought, the original cost of £2000 is irrelevant: it is a sunk cost. If the company has no other use for material A and uses it for the new project, the benefit of reselling it on the second-hand market is lost and the relevant cost is the resale price of £1.90 per kg. If material A is regularly used in other production activities, any material used in the new project will have to be replaced and the relevant cost is the repurchase price of £2.20 per kg.

7.1.4 Incremental working capital

As activity levels rise as a result of investment in fixed assets, the company's levels of debtors, stocks of raw materials and stocks of finished goods will also increase. These increases will be financed in part by increases in trade creditors. This incremental increase in working capital will represent a cash outflow for the company and is a relevant cash flow which must be included in the investment appraisal process. Further investment in working capital may be needed, as sales levels continue to rise, if the problem of undercapitalisation or *overtrading* is to be avoided (*see* Section 3.4). At the end of a project, however, levels of debtors, stocks and trade creditors will fall (unless the project is sold as a going concern) and so any investment in working capital will be recovered. The recovery of working capital will be a cash inflow either in the final year of the project or in the year immediately following the end of the project.

7.2 Taxation and capital investment decisions

At the start of this chapter it was pointed out that the effect of taxation on capital investment decisions could not be ignored. In order to determine the net cash benefits gained by a company as a result of an investment project, an estimate must be made of the benefits or liabilities that arise as a result of corporate taxation. The factors to consider when estimating these benefits or liabilities are now discussed.

7.2.1 Capital allowances

In financial accounting, capital expenditure appears in the profit and loss account in the form of annual depreciation charges. These charges are determined by company management in accordance with relevant accounting standards. For taxation purposes, capital expenditure is written off against taxable profits in a manner laid

Taxation and capital investment decisions

down by government and enforced by the tax authorities. Under this system, companies write off capital expenditure by means of annual capital allowances (also known as writing down allowances or tax-allowable depreciation).

Capital allowances are a matter of government policy. In the UK the standard capital allowance on plant and machinery is 25 per cent on a reducing balance basis. In recent years, a 40 per cent first-year capital allowance (offered to medium-sized UK businesses) and a 50 per cent first-year capital allowance (offered to small UK businesses) have been available on purchased plant and machinery (followed by reversion to 25 per cent reducing balance capital allowances). UK businesses have also been offered 100 per cent first-year capital allowances (known as 'enhanced' capital allowances) for investments in technologies and products that save energy, reduce carbon emissions or save water (UK Government Business Link 2006). Enhanced capital allowances are clearly preferable in present value terms. The capital allowances on offer also depend on the type of asset for which capital expenditure is being claimed; on industrial buildings, for example, the allowance is limited to 4 per cent per year on a straight-line basis. A *balancing allowance* (or balancing charge) is needed in addition to a capital allowance in the last year of an investment project in order to ensure that the capital value consumed by the business over the life of the project (capital cost minus scrap value) has been deducted in full in calculating taxable profits.

The current (2006) UK corporation tax rate for small businesses is 19 per cent and the main corporation tax rate is 30 per cent.

It is useful to calculate taxable profits and tax liabilities separately before calculating the net cash flows of a project. Performing the two calculations at the same time can lead to confusion. Since a worked example makes these concepts easier to grasp, an example of the calculation of capital allowances on plant and machinery on a 25 per cent reducing balance basis, together with the associated tax benefits at a corporation tax rate of 30 per cent, is given in Exhibit 7.1.

7.2.2 Tax allowable costs

Tax liabilities will arise on the taxable profits generated by an investment project. Liability to taxation is reduced by deducting allowable expenditure from annual revenue when calculating taxable profit. Relief for *capital* expenditure is given by deducting capital allowances from annual revenue, as already discussed. Relief for *revenue* expenditure is given by deducting tax-allowable costs. Tax-allowable costs include the costs of materials, components, wages and salaries, production overheads, insurance, maintenance, lease rentals and so on.

7.2.3 Are interest payments a relevant cash flow?

While interest payments on debt are an allowable deduction for the purpose of calculating taxable profit, it is a mistake to include interest payments as a relevant cash flow in the appraisal of a domestic capital investment project. The reason for excluding interest payments is that the required return on any debt finance used in an investment project is accounted for as part of the cost of capital used to discount the project cash

---

Exhibit 7.1 Capital allowances on a 25 per cent reducing basis on a machine costing £200 000 which is purchased at year 0. The expected life of the machine is four years and its scrap value after four years is £20 000. Corporation tax is 30 per cent

	£	£
Calculation of capital allowances:		
Year 1: 200 000 × 0.25 =		50 000
Year 2: (200 000 − 50 000) × 0.25 =		37 500
Year 3: (200 000 − 50 000 − 37 500) × 0.25 =		28 125
Year 4: (200 000 − 50 000 − 37 500 − 28 125) × 0.25 =		21 094
Initial value =	200 000	
Scrap value =	20 000	
Value consumed by the business over 4 years =	180 000	
Sum of capital allowances to end of Year 4 =	136 719	
Year 4 balancing allowance =		43 281
Total capital allowances over 4 years =		180 000
Calculation of taxation benefits:	£	
Year 1 (taken in Year 2): 50 000 × 0.30 =	15 000	
Year 2 (taken in Year 3): 37 500 × 0.30 =	11 250	
Year 3 (taken in Year 4): 28 125 × 0.30 =	8 438	
Year 4 (taken in Year 5): (21 094 + 43 281) × 0.30 =	19 312	
Total benefits (should equal 180 000 × 0.30 = 54 000)	54 000	

flows. If a company has sufficient taxable profits, the tax-allowability of interest payments is accommodated by using the after-tax weighted average cost of capital (*see* Section 9.1.3) to discount after-tax net cash flows.

7.2.4 The timing of tax liabilities and benefits

UK corporation tax on taxable profits is payable nine months after the end of the relevant accounting year for companies with annual profits less than £1.5m (HM Revenue and Customs 2006). In investment appraisal, cash flows arising during a period are taken as occurring at the end of that period, so *tax liabilities* are taken as being paid one year after the originating taxable profits. Any *tax benefits*, for example from capital allowances, are also received one year in arrears. There is some variation in the way that different authors include the benefits arising from capital allowances in investment appraisal calculations. The method used here is as follows:

- Capital investment occurs at Year 0.
- The first capital allowance affects cash flows arising in Year 1.
- The benefit from the first capital allowance arises in Year 2.
- The number of capital allowances is equal to the number of years in the life of the project.

The UK has introduced a 'pay and file' tax system requiring large companies (those with annual taxable profits greater than £1.5m) to pay a proportion of their estimated tax liabilities during the accounting year in which they arise. This means that large UK companies essentially pay the bulk of their tax liabilities (on an average basis) close to the end of the relevant accounting year. For such companies, tax liabilities and benefits can be treated as occurring at the end of the year in which relevant profits and costs are generated.

| Example | NPV calculation involving taxation |

Lark plc is considering buying a new machine costing £200 000 which would generate the following pre-tax profits from the sale of goods produced.

Year	Profit before tax
1	85 000
2	65 000
3	75 000
4	70 000

Lark pays corporation tax of 30 per cent per year one year in arrears and is able to claim capital allowances on a 25 per cent reducing balance basis. The machine would be sold after four years for £20 000. If Lark's after-tax cost of capital is 10 per cent, should the company buy the machine in the first place?

| Exhibit 7.2 | Calculation of net cash flows and net present value for Lark plc |

Year	Capital (£)	Operating cash flows (£)	Taxation (£)	Net cash flows (£)
0	(200 000)			(200 000)
1		85 000		85 000
2		65 000	(10 500)	54 500
3		75 000	(8 250)	66 750
4	20 000	70 000	(14 062)	75 938
5			(1 688)	(1 688)

Year	Net cash flows (£)	10% discount factor	Present value (£)
0	(200 000)	1.000	(200 000)
1	85 000	0.909	77 265
2	54 500	0.826	45 017
3	66 750	0.751	50 129
4	75 938	0.683	51 866
5	(1 688)	0.621	(1 048)
		Net present value	23 229

$\rightarrow$

Suggested answer

The capital allowances were calculated in Exhibit 7.1. The tax liabilities can be found by subtracting the capital allowances from the profits before tax to give taxable profits and then multiplying taxable profits by the tax rate:

$$£$$

Year 1 (taken in Year 2): $(85\,000 - 50\,000) \times 0.30 = \quad 10\,500$

Year 2 (taken in Year 3): $(65\,000 - 37\,500) \times 0.30 = \quad 8\,250$

Year 3 (taken in Year 4): $(75\,000 - 28\,125) \times 0.30 = \quad 14\,062$

Year 4 (taken in Year 5): $(70\,000 - 64\,375) \times 0.30 = \quad 1\,688$

The calculations of the net cash flows and the net present value of the proposed investment are shown in Exhibit 7.2. The NPV is a positive value of £23 229 and so purchase of the machine by Lark is recommended on financial grounds.

7.2.5 Can taxation be ignored?

If an investment project is found to be viable using the net present value method, introducing tax liabilities on profits is unlikely to change the decision, even if these liabilities are paid one year in arrears (Scarlett 1993, 1995). Project viability can be affected, however, if the profit on which tax liability is calculated is different from the cash flows generated by the project. This situation arises when capital allowances are introduced into the evaluation, although it has been noted that the effect on project viability is still only a small one. The effect is amplified under inflationary conditions since capital allowances are based on historical investment costs and their real value will therefore decline over the life of the project. This decline in the real value of capital allowances is counteracted to some extent, in the case of plant and machinery, by the use of substantial (e.g. 100 per cent, 50 per cent or 40 per cent) first-year capital allowances.

We may conclude our discussion of taxation, therefore, by noting that, while introducing the effects of taxation into investment appraisal makes calculations more complex, it also makes the appraisal more accurate and should lead to better investment decisions.

7.3 Inflation and capital investment decisions

Inflation can have a serious effect on capital investment decisions, both by reducing the *real value* of future cash flows and by increasing their *uncertainty*. Future cash flows must be adjusted to take account of any expected inflation in the prices of goods and services in order to express them in *nominal* (or money) terms, i.e. in terms of the actual cash amounts to be received or paid in the future. Nominal cash flows are discounted by a nominal cost of capital using the net present value method of investment appraisal.

As an alternative to the nominal approach to dealing with inflation in investment appraisal, it is possible to deflate nominal cash flows by the general rate of inflation in

| Exhibit 7.3 | **Net operating cash flows and net present value for Wren plc** |

Year	1	2	3	4
Selling price per unit (£)	23.10	24.25	25.47	26.74
Variable cost per unit (£)	17.12	18.32	19.60	20.97
Contribution per unit (£)	5.98	5.93	5.87	5.77
Contribution per year (£)	717 600	711 600	704 400	692 400
Fixed costs per year (£)	384 800	400 192	416 200	432 848
Net operating cash flow (£)	332 800	311 408	288 200	259 552

Year	0	1	2	3	4
Capital (£)	(500 000)	(200 000)			
Working capital (£)	(330 000)	(23 100)	(24 717)	(26 447)	404 264
Operating cash flow (£)		332 800	311 408	288 200	259 552
Net cash flow (£)	(830 000)	109 700	286 691	261 753	663 816
14% discount factors	1.000	0.877	0.769	0.675	0.592
Present value (£)	(830 000)	96 207	220 465	176 683	392 979

NPV = 96 207 + 220 465 + 176 683 + 392 979 − 830 000 = £56 334

The contribution per unit is the difference between the sales price and the variable cost per unit, inflated by their respective inflation rates. The nominal net operating cash flow for each year is then the difference between the total contribution and the inflated fixed costs for that year, as shown in Exhibit 7.3.

Investment in working capital in Year 0 = £330 000
Cumulative investment in working capital in Year 1 = £353 100, an increase of £23 100
Cumulative investment in working capital in Year 2 = £377 817, a further increase of £24 717
Cumulative investment in working capital in Year 3 = £404 264, a further increase of £26 447
Cumulative investment in working capital recovered at the end of Year 4 = £404 264

We could deflate the nominal cash flows by the general rate of inflation to obtain real cash flows and then discount them by Wren's real cost of capital. It is simpler and quicker to inflate Wren's real cost of capital into nominal terms and use it to discount our calculated nominal cash flows. Wren's nominal cost of capital is 1.075 × 1.06 = 1.1395 ≈ 14 per cent.

The nominal (money terms) net present value calculation is given in Exhibit 7.3.

Since the NPV is positive, the project can be recommended on financial grounds. The NPV is not very large, however, so we must take care to ensure that forecasts and estimates are as accurate as possible. In particular, a small increase in inflation during the life of the project might make the project uneconomical. Sensitivity analysis (*see* Section 7.4.1) can be used to determine the key project variables on which success may depend.

7.4	**Investment appraisal and risk**

While the words *risk* and *uncertainty* tend to be used interchangeably, they do have different meanings. Risk refers to sets of circumstances which can be quantified and to which probabilities can be assigned. Uncertainty implies that probabilities cannot be assigned to sets of circumstances. In the context of investment appraisal, risk refers to the business risk of an investment, which increases with the variability of expected returns, rather than to financial risk, which since it derives from a company's capital structure is reflected in its weighted average cost of capital (*see* Section 9.2). Risk is thus distinct from uncertainty, which increases proportionately with project life. However, the distinction between the two terms has little significance in actual business decisions as managers are neither completely ignorant nor completely certain about the probabilities of future events, although they may be able to assign probabilities with varying degrees of confidence (Grayson 1967). For this reason, the distinction between risk and uncertainty is usually neglected in the practical context of investment appraisal.

A risk-averse company is concerned about the possibility of receiving a return less than expected, i.e. with *downside risk*, and will therefore want to assess the risk of an investment project. There are several methods of assessing project risk and of incorporating risk into the decision-making process.

7.4.1 Sensitivity analysis

Sensitivity analysis is a way of assessing the risk of an investment project by evaluating how responsive the NPV of the project is to changes in the variables from which it has been calculated. There are several ways this sensitivity can be measured. In one method, each project variable in turn is changed by a set amount, say 5 per cent, and the NPV is recalculated. Only one variable is changed at a time. Since we are more concerned with downside risk, the 5 per cent change is made so as to adversely affect the NPV calculation. In another method, the amounts by which each project variable would have to change to make the NPV become zero are determined. Again, only one variable is changed at a time.

Both methods of sensitivity analysis give an indication of the *key variables* associated with an investment project. Key variables are those variables where a relatively small change can have a significant adverse effect on project NPV. These variables merit further investigation, for example to determine the extent to which their values can be relied upon, and their identification will also serve to indicate where management should focus its attention in order to ensure the success of the proposed investment project.

Both methods suffer from the disadvantage that only one variable at a time can be changed. This implies that all project variables are independent, which is clearly unrealistic. A more fundamental problem is that sensitivity analysis is not really a method of assessing the risk of an investment project at all. This may seem surprising since sensitivity analysis is always included in discussions of investment appraisal and risk, but the method does nothing more than indicate *which* are the key variables. It gives no information as to the *probability of changes* in the key variables, which is the information that would be needed if the risk of the project were to be estimated. If the values of all project variables are certain, a project will have zero risk, even if sensitivity analysis has identified its key variables. In such a case, however, identifying the key variables will still help managers to monitor and control the project in order to ensure that the desired financial objectives are achieved.

Example	**Application of sensitivity analysis**

Swift has a cost of capital of 12 per cent and plans to invest £7m in an improved moulding machine with a life of four years. The garden ornaments produced will have a selling price of £9.20 each and will cost £6.00 each to make. It is expected that 800 000 ornaments will be sold each year. By how much will each variable have to change to make the NPV zero? What are the key variables for the project?

Suggested answer

The net present value of the project in terms of the project variables is as follows:

$$NPV = ((S - VC) \times N \times CPVF_{12,4}) - I_0$$

where: S = selling price per unit
VC = variable cost per unit
N = number of units sold per year or sales volume
$CPVF_{12,4}$ = cumulative present value factor for four years at 12 per cent
I_0 = initial investment

Inserting this information and finding the cumulative present value factor from the table on page 488, we have:

$$NPV = ((9.20 - 6.00) \times 800\,000 \times 3.037) - 7\,000\,000 = £774\,720$$

Alternatively:

	£
Present value of sales revenue = 9.20 × 800 000 × 3.037 =	22 352 320
Present value of variable costs = 6.00 × 800 000 × 3.037 =	14 577 600
Present value of contribution	7 774 720
Initial investment	7 000 000
Net present value	774 720

We can now calculate the change needed in each variable to make the NPV zero.

Initial investment

The NPV becomes zero if the initial investment increases by an absolute amount equal to the NPV (£774 720), which is a relative increase of 11.1 per cent:

$$100 \times (774\,720/7\,000\,000) = 11.1\%$$

$\rightarrow$

Sales price

The relative decrease in sales revenue or selling price per unit that makes the NPV zero is the ratio of the NPV to the present value of sales revenue:

$$100 \times (774\,720/22\,352\,320) = 3.5\%$$

This is an absolute decrease of £9.20 × 0.035 = 32 pence, so the selling price that makes the NPV zero is 9.20 − 0.32 = £8.88.

Variable cost

Since a decrease of 32 pence in selling price makes the NPV zero, an increase of 32 pence or 5.3 per cent in variable cost will have the same effect.

Sales volume

The relative decrease in sales volume that makes the NPV zero is the ratio of the NPV to the present value of contribution:

$$100 \times (774\,720/7\,774\,720) = 10.0\%$$

This is an absolute decrease of 800 000 × 0.1 = 80 000 units, so the sales volume that makes the NPV zero is 800 000 − 80 000 = 720 000 units.

Project discount rate

What is the cumulative present value factor that makes the NPV zero? We have:

$$((9.20 - 6.00) \times 800\,000 \times CPVF) - 7\,000\,000 = 0$$

and so:

$$CPVF = (7\,000\,000/(9.20 - 6.00) \times 800\,000) = 2.734$$

Using the table of cumulative present value factors on page 488, and looking along the row of values for a life of four years (as project life remains constant), we find that 2.734 corresponds to a discount rate of almost exactly 17 per cent, an increase in the discount rate of 5 per cent in absolute terms or 41.7 per cent in relative terms. Note that this is the method for finding the internal rate of return of an investment project described in Section 6.4.

Our sensitivity analysis is summarised in Exhibit 7.4. The project is most sensitive to changes in selling price and variable cost per unit and so these are the key project variables.

Exhibit 7.4	Sensitivity analysis of the proposed investment by Swift

Variable	Change to make NPV zero		Sensitivity
Selling price per unit	−32p	−3.5%	High
Sales volume	−80 000 units	−10.0%	Low
Variable cost per unit	+32p	+5.3%	High
Initial investment	+£774 720	+11.1%	Low
Project discount rate	+5%	+41.7%	Very low

7.4.2 Payback

The payback method discussed in Section 6.1 is the oldest and most widely used method of explicitly recognising uncertainty in capital investment decisions. It recognises uncertainty by focusing on the near future, thereby emphasising liquidity, and by promoting short-term projects over longer-term (and therefore perhaps riskier) ones. While it may be criticised for its shortcomings as an investment appraisal method, it is harder to criticise *shortening payback* as a way of dealing with risk. After all, since the future cash flows on which both payback and net present value are based are only estimates, it may be sensible to consider whether better advice can be offered by using discounted cash flow methods to incorporate risk. Furthermore, the effect of investment on liquidity cannot be ignored, especially by small firms. However, payback has such serious shortcomings as an investment appraisal method that its use as a method of adjusting for risk cannot be recommended.

7.4.3 Conservative forecasts

Also known as the *certainty-equivalents* method, this traditional way of reducing uncertainty, where estimated future cash flows are reduced to a more conservative figure 'just to be on the safe side', cannot be recommended. First, such reductions are subjective and may be applied differently between projects. Second, reductions may be anticipated by managers and cash flows increased to compensate for potential reduction before investment projects are submitted for evaluation. Finally, attractive investment opportunities may be rejected due to the focus on pessimistic cash flows, especially if further methods of adjusting for risk are subsequently applied.

7.4.4 Risk-adjusted discount rates using risk classes

It is widely accepted that investors need a return in excess of the risk-free rate to compensate for taking on a risky investment; this concept is used in both portfolio theory and the capital asset pricing model (*see* Chapter 8). The greater the risk attached to future returns, the greater the risk premium required. When using discounted cash flow investment appraisal methods, the discount rate can be regarded as having two components (Grayson 1967). The first component allows for *time preference* or *liquidity preference*, meaning that investors prefer cash now rather than later and want compensation for being unable to use their cash now. The second component allows for *risk preference*, meaning that investors prefer low-risk to high-risk projects and want compensation (a risk premium) for taking on high-risk projects. However, it is very difficult to decide on the size of the risk premium to be applied to particular investment projects.

One solution is to assign investment projects to particular *risk classes* and then to discount them using the discount rate selected as appropriate for that class. This solution gives rise to problems with both the assessment of project risk and the determination of appropriate discount rates for the different risk classes. Another solution is to assume that the average risk of a company's investment projects will be similar to the average risk of its current business. In these circumstances a single overall discount rate – typically the company's weighted average cost of capital – can be used.

The use of a risk-adjusted discount rate implicitly assumes *constantly increasing risk* as project life increases. This may accurately reflect the risk profile of an investment project. If, however, the assumption of increasing risk is not appropriate, incorrect decisions may result. There are situations where the use of a *constant risk* allowance could be appropriate, in which case the risk-adjusted discount rate should decline over time. With the launch of a new project, a *higher initial risk* premium may be appropriate, with progressive reduction as the product becomes established.

7.4.5 Probability analysis and expected net present value

So far, we have discussed investment projects with single-point estimates of future cash flows. If instead a probability distribution of expected cash flows can be estimated, it can be used to obtain an *expected net present value*. The risk of an investment project can be examined in more detail by calculating the probability of the worst case and the probability of failing to achieve a positive NPV. Probability analysis is increasing in popularity as a method of assessing the risk of investment projects (*see* Section 7.5.3).

In its simplest form, a probability distribution may consist of estimates of the probabilities of the best, most likely and worst cases, as follows.

Forecast	Probability	Net present value
Best case	0.2	£30 000
Most likely	0.7	£20 000
Worst case	0.1	£10 000

The expected net present value (ENPV) can then be determined:

$$(0.2 \times £30\,000) + (0.7 \times £20\,000) + (0.1 \times £10\,000) = £21\,000$$

It is argued that this approach may give more useful information than single-point NPV estimates, but it should be noted that the single point estimates represent future states that are expected to occur, while the ENPV value does not represent an expected future state. The calculations of the probability of the worst case and of the probability of failing to achieve a positive NPV are illustrated in Exhibit 7.5.

The probabilities being discussed here are the probability estimates made by managers on the basis of the project data available to them. While such estimates are subjective, this is not grounds for their rejection, since they only make explicit the assessments of the likelihood of future events which are made by managers in the normal course of business.

7.4.6 Simulation models

It may be possible to improve the decision-making process involving the calculation of NPV by estimating probability distributions for each project variable. Sensitivity analysis changes one project variable at a time, but some of the variables, for example,

Exhibit 7.5 **Example of the calculation of expected net present value**

Star has a cost of capital of 12 per cent and is evaluating a project with an initial investment of £375 000. The estimated net cash flows of the project under different economic circumstances and their respective probabilities are as follows.

Net cash flows for Year 1

Economic conditions	Probability	Cash flow (£)
Weak	0.2	100 000
Moderate	0.5	200 000
Good	0.3	300 000

Net cash flows for Year 2

Economic conditions	Probability	Cash flow (£)
Moderate	0.7	250 000
Good	0.3	350 000

If economic conditions in Year 2 are not dependent on economic conditions in Year 1, what is the expected value of the project's NPV? What is the risk that the NPV will be negative?

Suggested answer

The first step is to calculate the present values of each individual cash flow.

Year	Economic conditions	Cash flow (£000)	12% discount factor	Present value (£000)
1	Weak	100	0.893	89.3
1	Moderate	200	0.893	178.6
1	Good	300	0.893	267.9
2	Moderate	250	0.797	199.2
2	Good	350	0.797	279.0

The next step is to calculate the *total* present value of the cash flows of each *combination* of Year 1 and Year 2 economic conditions by adding their present values.

Year 1		Year 2		Overall
Economic conditions	Present value of cash flow (£000)	Economic conditions	Present value of cash flow (£000)	Total present value of cash flow (£000)
Weak	89.3	Moderate	199.2	288.5
Weak	89.3	Good	279.0	368.3
Moderate	178.6	Moderate	199.2	377.8
Moderate	178.6	Good	279.0	457.6
Good	267.9	Moderate	199.2	467.1
Good	267.9	Good	279.0	546.9

Exhibit 7.5 **continued**

The total present value of the cash flows of each combination of economic conditions is now multiplied by the joint probability of each combination of economic conditions, and these values are then added to give the expected present value of the cash flows of the project.

Total present value of cash flow (£000) A	Year 1 probability B	Year 2 probability C	Joint probability D = B × C	Expected present value of cash flows (£000) A × D
288.5	0.2	0.7	0.14	40.4
368.3	0.2	0.3	0.06	22.1
377.8	0.5	0.7	0.35	132.2
457.6	0.5	0.3	0.15	68.6
467.1	0.3	0.7	0.21	98.1
546.9	0.3	0.3	0.09	49.2
				410.6

	£
Expected present value of cash inflows	410 600
Less: Initial investment	375 000
Expected value of NPV	35 600

The probability that the project will have a negative NPV is the probability that the total present value of the cash flows is less than £375 000. Using the column in the table headed 'Total present value of cash flow' and picking out values less than £375 000, we can see that the probability that the project will have a negative NPV is 0.14 + 0.06 = 0.20, or 20 per cent.

costs and market share, may be interdependent. A simulation model can be used to determine, by repeated analysis, how simultaneous changes in more than one variable may influence the expected net present value. The procedure is to assign random numbers to ranges of values in the probability distribution for each project variable. A computer then generates a set of random numbers and uses these to randomly select a value for each variable. The NPV of that set of variables is then calculated. The computer then repeats the process many times and builds up a frequency distribution of the NPV. From this frequency distribution, the expected NPV and its standard deviation can be determined. This simulation technique is often referred to as the Monte Carlo method. Spreadsheet software and cheap computing power combine to make this approach more accessible for investment appraisal (Smith, 2000).

This simulation technique does not give clear investment advice. From a corporate finance point of view, managers must still decide whether an investment is acceptable or not, or whether it is preferable to a mutually exclusive alternative. They will be able to consider both the return of the investment (its expected NPV) and the risk of the investment (the standard deviation of the expected NPV). The rational decision (*see* Section 8.3) would be to prefer the investment with the highest return for a given level of risk or with the lowest risk for a given level of return.

7.5 Empirical investigations of investment appraisal

There have been a number of studies that help to build up a picture of the investment appraisal methods actually used by companies, such as Pike (1983, 1996), McIntyre and Coulthurst (1986), Lapsley (1986), Drury et al. (1993), and Arnold and Hatzopoulos (2000). Their findings can be summarised as follows:

- While for many years payback was the most commonly used investment appraisal method, discounted cash flow (DCF) methods now appear to be more popular.
- In large organisations, payback is used in conjunction with other investment appraisal methods. In smaller organisations, using payback as the sole investment appraisal method continues to decline.
- Internal rate of return is more popular than net present value in small companies, but net present value is now the most popular investment appraisal method in large companies.
- Use of experience and qualitative judgement is an important complement to quantitative methods.
- Although return on capital employed is the least popular investment appraisal method, it continues to be used in conjunction with other methods.
- Companies tend not to use sophisticated methods to account for project risk.
- Where companies do take account of risk, sensitivity analysis is most often used.

We have noted that the academically preferred approach is to use discounted cash flow methods, with net present value being preferred to internal rate of return. This conclusion is rooted in the fact that discounted cash flow methods take account of both the time value of money and corporate risk preferences. Earlier cash flows are discounted less heavily than more distant ones, while risk can be incorporated by applying a higher discount rate to more risky projects. There are a number of drawbacks with the payback and return on capital employed methods, as discussed earlier in Chapter 6.

7.5.1 Investment appraisal techniques used

Drury et al. (1993) found that payback was the most frequently used investment appraisal technique, followed by net present value and accounting rate of return, with internal rate of return the least popular. In contrast, Arnold and Hatzopoulos (2000) found that net present value and internal rate of return were almost equal in overall popularity, with both being more popular than payback, indicating that the gap between theory and practice in investment appraisal methods had diminished.

A similar change can be noted in the relative preferences of small and large companies for different investment appraisal methods. Drury et al. (1993) found that larger companies tended to prefer DCF methods to payback and accounting rate of return, with 90 per cent of larger companies using at least one DCF method compared with 35 per cent of smaller companies; smaller companies preferred payback. Arnold and Hatzopoulos (2000) found that acceptance of DCF methods by small companies had increased, with internal rate of return being more popular than payback (76 per cent compared with 71 per cent), and that large companies preferred internal rate of return (81 per cent) and net present value (80 per cent) to payback (70 per cent).

Drury et al. (1993) found that only 14 per cent of all companies used payback alone and suggested that, after using payback as an initial screening device to select suitable projects, companies then subjected those projects to a more thorough screening using net present value or internal rate of return. Arnold and Hatzopoulos (2000) found that 68 per cent of all companies used payback in conjunction with one or more investment appraisal methods. They also found that 90 per cent of companies used two or more investment appraisal methods.

Why should the vast majority of companies use multiple investment appraisal methods? One possible explanation is that using multiple evaluation techniques may reinforce the justification for the decision and increase the feeling of security or comfort derived from the use of analytical investment appraisal methods (Kennedy and Sugden 1986). Another possible explanation is that evaluating investment projects from a number of different perspectives compensates for the breakdown of some of the assumptions underlying the net present value method in real-world situations (Arnold and Hatzopoulos 2000).

7.5.2 The treatment of inflation

It is important to account for inflation in the investment appraisal process in order to prevent suboptimal decisions being made. The techniques to deal with the problem of inflation that were discussed earlier (*see* Section 7.3) are:

1 using nominal discount rates to discount nominal cash flows that have been adjusted to take account of expected future inflation (nominal-terms approach);
2 using real discount rates to discount real cash flows (real-terms approach).

The findings of Drury et al. (1993) on how inflation is dealt with are shown in Exhibit 7.6, from which we can see that the majority of companies applied a nominal discount rate to unadjusted cash flows and that, as a whole, only 27 per cent of all companies allowed for inflation using a theoretically correct method. The findings of this survey were consistent with those of earlier surveys, which indicated that most companies did not account for inflation in the investment appraisal process in an

| Exhibit 7.6 | How inflation is accommodated in investment appraisal |

Cash flow adjustment	Real discount rate (%)	Nominal discount rate (%)
By anticipated inflation	36	29
No adjustment	41	63
Expressed in real terms	23	8

Source: Drury et al. (1993), p. 44. Table from *A Survey of Management Accounting Practices in UK Manufacturing Companies,* Certified Research Report 32. This research was funded and published by the Association of Chartered Certified Accountants (ACCA). Table reproduced with the ACCA's kind permission.

appropriate manner. In contrast, Arnold and Hatzopoulos (2000) reported that 81 per cent of companies correctly accounted for inflation in investment appraisal, lending support to their overall conclusion that the gap between theory and practice in capital budgeting continues to narrow.

7.5.3 Risk analysis

It is generally agreed (*see* Section 7.4) that risk should be considered in the capital investment process and that project risk should be reflected in the discount rate. Prior to the 1970s, companies took account of risk by shortening the target payback period or by using conservative cash flows. Some companies used probability analysis and the Monte Carlo method. These models, while addressing the risk attached to future cash flows, gave no guidance on the selection of an appropriate discount rate. This problem was addressed by the capital asset pricing model (*see* Chapter 8), which enabled the systematic risk of a project to be considered and reflected in an appropriate discount rate.

Drury et al. (1993) found a very low level of use of the more sophisticated methods of allowing for risk, with 63 per cent of companies either very unlikely to use probability analysis or never having used it at all, and with more than 95 per cent of companies rejecting Monte Carlo simulation and the use of the capital asset pricing model. Sensitivity analysis, the most popular risk adjustment technique, was used by 82 per cent of all companies. Similar results were reported by Arnold and Hatzopoulos (2000), who found that 85 per cent of all companies used sensitivity analysis and that very few companies used the capital asset pricing model. They did find, however, that 31 per cent of companies used probability analysis; the increased use of this technique is perhaps a consequence of the increasing availability of information processing technology.

7.5.4 Conclusions of empirical investigations

We can conclude that the majority of companies use a combination of investment appraisal techniques and that there are differences between the practices of small and large companies, although these differences are not great. Most companies now deal with inflation correctly, removing possible distortions in DCF calculations and resulting in better investment decisions. As regards risk, companies were found to be more likely to use simple methods such as sensitivity analysis than theoretically correct methods such as the capital asset pricing model.

7.6 Conclusion

In this chapter we have considered some of the problems which arise when we evaluate 'real-world' investment projects, including the difficulties associated with allowing for the effects of taxation and inflation. We have considered the need to take account of project risk in the investment appraisal process, and examined a number of the different ways by which this has been attempted. Some of these methods were found to be more successful than others. We concluded our discussion by examining the investment appraisal methods used by companies in the real world, as revealed by empirical research, and noted that the gap between theory and practice appears to be diminishing.

Key points

1. Only relevant cash flows, which are the incremental cash flows arising as the result of an investment decision, should be included in investment appraisal. Relevant cash flows include opportunity costs and incremental investment in working capital.

2. Non-relevant cash flows, such as sunk costs and apportioned fixed costs, must be excluded from the investment appraisal.

3. Tax relief for capital expenditure is given through capital allowances, which are a matter of government policy and depend on the type of asset for which allowances are claimed.

4. Tax liability is reduced by expenses that can be deducted from revenue in calculating taxable profit. Relief for such expenses is given by allowing them to be deducted in full.

5. Tax liabilities are paid nine months after the end of the year in which taxable profits arise.

6. Taxation does not alter the viability of simple projects unless taxable profit is different from the cash flows generated by the project.

7. Inflation can have a serious effect on investment decisions by reducing the real value of future cash flows and by increasing their uncertainty.

8. Inflation can be included in investment appraisal by discounting nominal cash flows by a nominal cost of capital or by discounting real cash flows by a real cost of capital.

9. The real cost of capital can be found by deflating the nominal cost of capital by the general rate of inflation.

10. Both specific and general inflation need to be considered in investment appraisal.

11. Risk refers to situations where the probabilities of future events are known. Uncertainty refers to circumstances where the probabilities of future events are not known.

12. Sensitivity analysis examines how responsive the NPV of a project is to changes in the variables from which it has been calculated.

13 One problem with sensitivity analysis is that only one variable can be changed at a time, but project variables are unlikely to be independent in reality.

14 Sensitivity analysis identifies key project variables but does not indicate the probability that they will change. For this reason, it is not really a method of assessing project risk.

15 Payback reduces risk and uncertainty by focusing on the near future and by promoting short-term projects.

16 Conservative forecasts can be criticised because they are subjective, because they may be applied inconsistently, because cash flow reductions may be anticipated and because attractive investments may be rejected.

17 Despite difficulties in assessing project risk and determining risk premiums, risk-adjusted discounted rates are a favoured way of incorporating risk into investment appraisal.

18 Probability analysis can be used to find the expected NPV of a project, the probability of the worst case NPV and the probability of a negative NPV.

19 The Monte Carlo method can be used to obtain a frequency distribution of the NPV, the expected NPV and its standard deviation.

20 Research has shown that DCF methods are now the most common investment appraisal techniques, often used in conjunction with other methods.

21 Companies tend to use simple methods of assessing risk, such as sensitivity analysis, rather than sophisticated methods.

22 The majority of companies correctly account for inflation in investment appraisal.

Self-test questions

Answers to these questions can be found on pages 449–51.

1 Discuss which cash flows are relevant to investment appraisal calculations.

2 Illustrate with a simple example the calculation of 25 per cent reducing balance capital allowances.

3 Explain the difference between the nominal (or money) terms approach and the real terms approach to dealing with inflation in the context of investment appraisal.

4 Explain whether general or specific inflation should be taken into account in investment appraisal.

5 Explain the difference between risk and uncertainty.

6 Discuss how sensitivity analysis can help managers to assess the risk of an investment project.

7 Why is payback commonly used as a way of dealing with risk in investment projects?

8 Discuss the use of risk-adjusted discount rates in the evaluation of investment projects.

9 Explain the meaning of the term 'Monte Carlo simulation'.

10 Discuss whether all companies use the same investment appraisal methods.

Questions for review

Answers to these questions can be found on pages 451–3. Questions with an asterisk (*) are at an intermediate level.

1   A machine is to be purchased by Blake Ltd for £100 000. The expected life of the machine is four years, at the end of which it will have zero value and will be scrapped. Blake Ltd pays corporation tax at a rate of 30 per cent and its discount rate for investment purposes is 8 per cent. What are the present values of the tax benefits arising to Blake Ltd from the purchase of the machine in the following circumstances?

(a) First-year capital allowances of 100 per cent are available.

(b) Capital allowances are available on a straight-line basis over the asset's life.

(c) Capital allowances are available on a 25 per cent reducing balance basis.

2*   The financial manager of Logar is considering the purchase of a finishing machine which will improve the appearance of the company's range of decorated chocolates. She expects that the improved output will lead to increased sales of £110 000 per year for a period of five years. At the end of the five-year period, the machine will be scrapped. Two machines are being considered and the relevant financial information on the capital investment proposal form is as follows:

	Machine A	Machine B
Initial cost (£)	200 000	250 000
Labour cost (£ per year)	10 000	7 000
Power cost (£ per year)	9 000	4 000
Scrap value (£)	nil	25 000

The following forecasts of average annual rates of inflation have been prepared by the planning department of Logar:

Sales prices:	6% per year
Labour costs:	5% per year
Power costs:	3% per year

Logar pays corporation tax of 30 per cent one year in arrears and has a nominal after-tax cost of capital of 15 per cent. Capital allowances are available on a 25 per cent reducing balance basis.

Advise the financial manager of Logar on her choice of machine.

3* Mr Smart has £75 000 invested in relatively risk-free assets returning 10 per cent per year. He has been approached by a friend with a 'really good idea' for a business venture. This would take the whole of the £75 000. Market research has revealed that it is not possible to be exact about the returns of the project, but that the following can be inferred from the study:

■ There is a 20 per cent chance that returns will be £10 000 per year.

■ There is a 60 per cent chance that returns will be £30 000 per year.

■ There is a 20 per cent chance that returns will be £50 000 per year.

■ If returns are £10 000 per year, there is a 60 per cent chance that the life of the project will be five years and a 40 per cent chance that it will be seven years.

■ If returns are £30 000 per year, there is a 50 per cent chance that the life of the project will be five years and a 50 per cent chance that it will be seven years.

■ If returns are £50 000 per year, there is a 40 per cent chance that the life of the project will be five years and a 60 per cent chance that it will be seven years.

Assume that cash flows happen at the end of each year.

(a) Calculate the worst likely return and the best likely return on the project, along with the probabilities of these events happening.

(b) Calculate the expected net present value of the investment.

4 Buddington Ltd is evaluating the purchase of a new machine and has the following information:

Initial investment:	£350 000
Residual value:	nil
Expected life:	10 years
Sales volume:	20 000 units per year
Sales price:	£8.50 per unit
Variable cost:	£3.50 per unit
Fixed costs:	£24 875 per year
Cost of capital:	15 per cent

(a) Calculate the internal rate of return of the project.

(b) Assess the sensitivity of the purchase evaluation to a change in project life.

(c) Assess the sensitivity of the purchase evaluation to a change in sales price.

5 Discuss three methods that a company could use in order to take account of the risk of an investment project.

Questions for discussion

Questions with an asterisk (*) are at an advanced level.

1* Bald Eagle is considering whether to buy a licence to extract oil in Pond Gap. The £2m cost of the licence would be payable immediately, but oil extraction could not begin until one year later, following exploration and investigation. Geologists estimate the amount of oil to be found is as follows.

Quantity of oil	Probability
High	0.3
Low	0.5
Zero	0.2

The marketing director expects that annual cash sales will depend on the quantity of oil found and whether the demand for oil is strong or weak. If demand is strong:

Quantity of oil found	Annual cash sales
High	£10m
Low	£4m

If demand is weak:

Quantity of oil found	Annual cash sales
High	£3m
Low	£2m

The marketing director estimates a 35 per cent probability of strong demand and a 65 per cent probability of weak demand. Exploratory drilling will cost £1.5m, payable when the licence is bought. If exploratory drilling reveals oil, it will be extracted over 10 years, using extraction equipment and pipelines costing £8m payable one year after purchase of the licence. This equipment will not be purchased if no oil is discovered. Bald Eagle has a cost of capital of 14 per cent per year. Ignore taxation.

Calculate the expected net present value of the project, the best case net present value and the probability of a negative net present value, and comment briefly on the risk of the project.

2 Darla Kinsett is evaluating the purchase of a freeze dryer, which will allow it to move from the supply of raw food to local supermarkets into the more lucrative frozen foods market. Packets of frozen food will be sold in boxes of eight and the following information applies to each box:

	£ per box
Selling price	9.70
Packaging and labour	2.20
Frozen food and processing	4.80

The selling price and cost of the frozen food are expected to increase by 6 per cent per year, while packaging and labour costs are expected to increase by 5 per cent per year. Investment in working capital will increase by £90 000 during the first year. The freeze dryer will have a useful life of five years before being scrapped, the net cost of disposal being £18 000. Sales in the first year are expected to be 80000 boxes, but sales in the second and subsequent years will be 110000 boxes.

The manufacturer of the freeze dryer, in order to encourage Darla Kinsett to go ahead with the deal, has offered to defer payment of part of the purchase price. The total cost of the freeze dryer is £1m and the offer is for 60 per cent to be paid initially, with the remaining 40 per cent to be paid one year later. The company's nominal cost of capital is 14 per cent. Ignore taxation.

(a) Assess whether Darla Kinsett should invest in the freeze dryer.

(b) Explain your choice of discount rate in your answer to part (a).

3 Critically discuss the use of the following techniques as methods of dealing with risk in the appraisal of capital investment projects:

(a) Sensitivity analysis

(b) Risk-adjusted discount rates

(c) Adjusted payback

(d) Monte Carlo methods

4* Cryptic has recently completed a strategic evaluation of its products and has concluded that excellent prospects exist for an updated version of an existing product, the BookWorm, an electronic pocket-sized crossword solver. The development director feels that, with more powerful software, a redesigned shell and sophisticated marketing, sales could be quite healthy for a few more years until technological developments make the product relatively uncompetitive.

The software could be used under a licensing agreement requiring an initial fee of £250 000 and annual payments at the end of each year of 5 per cent of sales. The tax authorities have ruled that lump sum initial payments on such licensing agreements are of a capital nature, attracting 25 per cent per year reducing balance capital allowances, although they have stated that the annual payments are allowable against profit tax on a revenue basis only.

Sales of the BookWorm are expected to be £800 000 per year initially, with sales growth of 5 per cent per year expected over five years. At the end of five years, it is expected that technological obsolescence will cause sales to decline by 50 per cent per year. After three years of declining sales, the product will have to be withdrawn.

Redesign of the shell containing the electronics and the display screen will cost £200 000. The development director expects that working capital will increase by £68 000 during the first year and that this additional amount will grow by 5 per cent per year in line with sales. Once sales start to decline, this additional working capital will be released proportionately with the decline in sales.

Marketing the BookWorm will cost £300 000 spread evenly over the first three years of the project. Direct costs of production, including raw materials, are expected to be 65 per cent of sales. In order to maintain growth in sales, further redesign will be needed in year 4 at a cost of £200 000. The tax authorities have ruled that redesign costs will attract capital allowances at a rate of 25 per cent per year on a reducing balance basis. Profit tax is to be charged at a rate of 30 per cent.

(a) Calculate the internal rate of return of the BookWorm project.

(b) Discuss what other information might be useful in reaching a decision on whether to proceed with the project.

References

Arnold, G.C. and Hatzopoulos, P.D. (2000) 'The theory–practice gap in capital budgeting: evidence from the United Kingdom', *Journal of Business Finance and Accounting*, Vol. 27, No. 5.

Drury, C., Braund, S., Osborn, P. and Tayles, M. (1993) *A Survey of Management Accounting Practices in UK Manufacturing Companies*, Certified Research Report 32, ACCA.

Grayson, C. (1967) 'The use of statistical techniques in capital budgeting', in Robicheck, A. (ed.) *Financial Research and Management Decisions*, New York: Wiley, pp. 90–132.

HM Revenue and Customs (2006) at http://www.hmrc.gov.uk/ctsa/index.htm.

Kennedy, A. and Sugden, K. (1986) 'Ritual and reality in capital budgeting', *Management Accounting*, February, pp. 34–7.

Lapsley, I. (1986) 'Investment appraisal in UK non-trading organizations', *Financial Accountability and Management*, Summer, Vol. 2, pp. 135–51.

McIntyre, A. and Coulthurst, N. (1986) *Capital Budgeting in Medium-sized Businesses*, London: CIMA Research Report.

Mills, R. (1988) 'Capital budgeting: the state of the art', *Long Range Planning*, Vol. 21, No. 4, pp. 76–81.

Pike, R. (1983) 'A review of recent trends in formal capital budgeting processes', *Accounting and Business Research*, Summer, Vol. 13, pp. 201–8.

Pike, R. (1996) 'A longitudinal survey of capital budgeting practices', *Journal of Business Finance and Accounting*, Vol. 23, No. 1.

Scarlett, R. (1993) 'The impact of corporate taxation on the viability of investment', *Management Accounting*, November, p. 30.

Scarlett, R. (1995) 'Further aspects of the impact of taxation on the viability of investment', *Management Accounting*, May, p. 54.

Smith, D. (2000) 'Risk Simulation and the Appraisal of Investment Projects', *Computers in Higher Education Economic Review*, Vol. 14, No. 1.

UK Government Business Link (2006), *Corporation Tax Rates and Types of Allowance*, at http://www.businesslink.gov.uk/bdotg/action/home.

Recommended reading

A more detailed analysis of risk and uncertainty in the context of investment appraisal can be found in:

Arnold, G. (2005) *Corporate Financial Management*, 3rd edn., Harlow: FT Prentice Hall.

Chapter 8

Portfolio theory and the capital asset pricing model

Learning objectives

After studying this chapter, you should have achieved the following learning objectives:

■ an ability to calculate the standard deviation of an investment's returns and to calculate the risk and return of a two-share portfolio;

■ a firm understanding of both systematic and unsystematic risk and the concept of risk diversification using portfolio investment;

■ the ability to explain the foundations of Markowitz's portfolio theory and to discuss the problems associated with its practical application;

■ a critical understanding of the capital asset pricing model and the assumptions upon which it is based;

■ the ability to calculate the required rate of return of a security using the capital asset pricing model;

■ an appreciation of the empirical research that has been undertaken to establish the applicability and reliability of the capital asset pricing model in practice.

Introduction

Risk–return trade-offs have an important role to play in corporate finance theory – from both a company and an investor perspective. Companies face variability in their project cash flows whereas investors face variability in their capital gains and dividends. Risk–return trade-offs were met earlier in the book, in Chapter 7, in the form of risk-adjusted hurdle rates and will be met again later, in Chapter 9, where required rates of return for different securities will be seen to vary according to the level of risk they face. Until now, however, we have not given risk and return a formal treatment.

Assuming that companies and shareholders are rational, their aim will be to minimise the risk they face for a given return they expect to receive. In order for them to do this they will need a firm understanding of the nature of the risk they face. They will then be able to quantify the risk and hence manage or control it. Traditionally, risk has been measured by the standard deviation of returns, the calculation of which is considered in Section 8.1. In Section 8.2 we examine how investors, by 'not putting all their eggs in one basket', are able to reduce the risk they face given the level of their expected return. Next, in Section 8.3, we consider how an investor's attitude to risk and return is mirrored in the shape of their utility curves. The final part of the jigsaw is to introduce an investor's utility curves to the assets available for investment, allowing them to make an informed choice of portfolio – the essence of the portfolio theory developed by Markowitz in 1952 and the subject of Section 8.4.

Having considered portfolio theory, we turn to the capital asset pricing model developed by Sharpe in 1964 in Section 8.5 and subsequent sections. This provides us with a framework in which to value individual securities according to their level of 'relevant' risk, having already eradicated their 'non-relevant' risk through holding a diversified portfolio.

8.1   The measurement of risk

Risk plays a key role in the decision-making process of both investors and companies, so it is important that the risk associated with an investment can be quantified. Risk is measured by the *standard deviation* (σ) of returns of a share, calculated using either historical returns or the expected future returns.

8.1.1   Calculating risk and return using probabilities

Exhibit 8.1 gives the possible returns and associated probabilities of shares A and B, where:

$$P_A = \text{probability of return on A}$$
$$R_A = \text{the corresponding return on A}$$
$$P_B = \text{probability of return on B}$$
$$R_B = \text{the corresponding return on B}$$

Exhibit 8.1	The possible returns and associated probabilities of two shares, A and B

Share A		Share B	
P_A	$R_A(\%)$	P_B	$R_B(\%)$
0.05	10	0.05	12
0.25	15	0.25	18
0.40	22	0.40	28
0.25	25	0.25	32
0.05	30	0.05	38
1.00		1.00	

The mean returns and standard deviations of the two shares are given by the following formulae:

$$\text{Mean return of a share } \overline{R} = \sum_{i=1}^{n} P_i \times R_i$$

$$\text{Standard deviation } (\sigma) = \sqrt{\sum_{i=1}^{n} P_i \times (R_i - \overline{R})^2}$$

where: $P_1, \ldots, P_n$ = the probabilities of the n different outcomes

$R_1, \ldots, R_n$ = the corresponding returns associated with the n different outcomes

By using the above formulae and the information provided we can calculate the mean return and the standard deviation of returns for each share.

Mean return of share A
$(0.05 \times 10) + (0.25 \times 15) + (0.40 \times 22) + (0.25 \times 25) + (0.05 \times 30)$
$= 20.8$ per cent

Mean return of share B
$(0.05 \times 12) + (0.25 \times 18) + (0.40 \times 28) + (0.25 \times 32) + (0.05 \times 38)$
$= 26.2$ per cent

Standard deviation of share A
$((0.05 \times (10 - 20.8)^2) + (0.25 \times (15 - 20.8)^2) + (0.40 \times (22 - 20.8)^2)$
$+ (0.25 \times (25 - 20.8)^2) + (0.05 \times (30 - 20.8)^2))^{1/2} = 4.84$ per cent

Standard deviation of share B
$((0.05 \times (12 - 26.2)^2) + (0.25 \times (18 - 26.2)^2) + (0.40 \times (28 - 26.2)^2)$
$+ (0.25 \times (32 - 26.2)^2) + (0.05 \times (38 - 26.2)^2))^{1/2} = 6.60$ per cent

Here we can see that while share B has a higher mean return compared with A, it also has a correspondingly higher level of risk.

Exhibit 8.2	The historical returns of two shares, S and T	

Year (t)	S return (%)	T return (%)
−4	6.6	24.5
−3	5.6	−5.9
−2	−9.0	19.9
−1	12.6	−7.8
0	14.0	14.8

8.1.2 Calculating risk and return using historical data

The mean and standard deviation of the annual historical returns of a share can be found using the following equations.

$$\text{Mean return } \overline{R} = \frac{\sum\limits_{i=1}^{n} R_i}{n}$$

$$\text{Standard deviation } (\sigma) = \sqrt{\frac{\sum\limits_{i=1}^{n} (R_i - \overline{R})^2}{n}}$$

Exhibit 8.2 is a table of data detailing the historical returns of two shares, S and T, over the past five years.

Using the historical returns and the formulae above:

Mean return of share S
$$(6.6 + 5.6 + (−9.0) + 12.6 + 14.0)/5 = 5.96 \text{ per cent}$$

Mean return of share T
$$(24.5 + (−5.9) + 19.9 + (−7.8) + 14.8)/5 = 9.10 \text{ per cent}$$

Standard deviation of share S
$$(((6.6 − 5.96)^2 + (5.6 − 5.96)^2 + (−9.0 − 5.96)^2 + (12.6 − 5.96)^2 + (14.0 − 5.96)^2)/5)^{1/2} = 8.16 \text{ per cent}$$

Standard deviation of share T
$$(((24.5 − 9.10)^2 + (−5.9 − 9.10)^2 + (19.9 − 9.10)^2 + (−7.8 − 9.10)^2 + (14.8 − 9.10)^2)/5)^{1/2} = 13.39 \text{ per cent}$$

We can see that while share T has a higher mean return than security S, it also has a higher standard deviation of returns. In Exhibit 8.3 we can see a graphical representation of the distribution of the expected returns of the two shares. T has a higher mean return, but has a flatter normal distribution curve when compared with S, due to its higher standard deviation.

Exhibit 8.3	Graph showing the distribution of returns of securities S and T

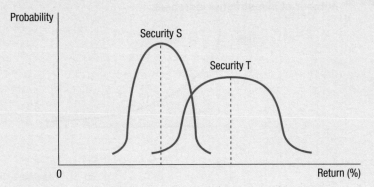

8.2 The concept of diversification

Earlier we mentioned that in order for investors to control and manage risk it is important for them to understand the *nature* of the risk they face. The overall risk that investors and companies face can be separated into systematic and unsystematic risk. *Systematic risk* (also known as non-diversifiable, non-specific, unavoidable or market risk) represents how a share's returns are affected by systematic factors such as business cycles, government policy and changes in interest rates. According to Solnik (1974), systematic risk accounts in the UK for roughly 34 per cent of an individual share's total risk.

Unsystematic risk (also known as diversifiable, specific, avoidable or non-market risk) is the risk specific to a particular share, i.e. the risk of the individual company performing badly or going into liquidation. While this type of risk accounts in the UK for approximately 66 per cent of an individual share's total risk, an investor can progressively reduce unsystematic risk by spreading their investments over a larger number of different securities. It is this possibility of reducing unsystematic risk through holding a *diversified portfolio* of shares that is the basis of Markowitz's portfolio theory. An illustration of the relationship between systematic and unsystematic risk relative to the number of investments held is shown in Exhibit 8.4.

There is no reason, however, why investors should limit their investment to UK shares. Investors who include in their portfolio shares from major stock exchanges around the world can further reduce unsystematic risk. While the fortunes of the world's stock exchanges are closely linked, there is significantly less than perfect correlation between many of them. This is particularly true for the stock exchanges of Europe and their South-East Asian counterparts. Solnik (1974) estimated that an internationally diversified portfolio reduced the proportion of systematic risk to a mere 11 per cent of total risk.

8.2.1 Diversifying unsystematic risk using a two-share portfolio

The simplest portfolio to consider is that containing two shares. The extent to which a two-share portfolio will reduce unsystematic risk depends on the correlation between

Exhibit 8.4 **Diagram showing the amount of unsystematic risk diversification obtained as the number of investments increases**

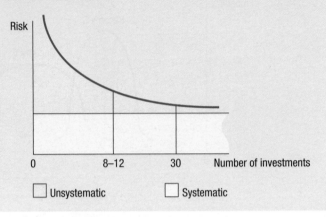

the two shares' returns. This correlation is quantified by the correlation coefficient (ρ) of the returns of the two shares, which can take any value in the range -1 to 1.

$$\text{If } \rho_{x,y} = 1 \quad \text{no unsystematic risk can be diversified away}$$
$$\text{If } \rho_{x,y} = -1 \quad \text{all unsystematic risk will be diversified away}$$
$$\text{If } \rho_{x,y} = 0 \quad \text{no correlation between the two securities' returns}$$

Therefore, when picking a two-share portfolio it is most beneficial to choose two shares whose correlation coefficient is as close to -1 as possible. However, as long as the correlation coefficient is less than $+1$, some unsystematic risk will be diversified away. In practice it is difficult to find two securities whose correlation coefficient is exactly -1, but the most commonly quoted example is that of an umbrella manufacturer and an ice cream company.

The *correlation coefficient* of two shares x and y ($\rho_{x,y}$) can be calculated by the formula:

$$\rho_{x,y} = \frac{\text{Cov}_{x,y}}{\sigma_x \sigma_y}$$

where $\text{Cov}_{x,y}$ is the covariance of returns of securities x and y.
If using expected return data, $\rho_{x,y}$ is given by:

$$\rho_{x,y} = \frac{\sum_{i=1}^{n} P_i (R_{ix} - \overline{R}_x) \times (R_{iy} - \overline{R}_y)}{\sigma_x \sigma_y}$$

and if using historical data, $\rho_{x,y}$ is given by:

$$\rho_{x,y} = \frac{\sum_{i=1}^{n} (R_{ix} - \overline{R}_x) \times (R_{iy} - \overline{R}_y)}{n \sigma_x \sigma_y}$$

The formulae to calculate the return and risk of a two-share portfolio are given below. The return of a two-share portfolio is the weighted average of the two shares' returns. The standard deviation formula is more complex owing to the diversification of unsystematic risk that occurs.

Return of a two-share portfolio (R_p):

$$R_p = (W_x R_x) + (W_y R_y)$$

Standard deviation of a two-share portfolio (σ_p):

$$\sigma_p = \sqrt{(W_x)^2(\sigma_x)^2 + (W_y)^2(\sigma_y)^2 + 2\,W_x W_y \sigma_x \sigma_y \rho_{x,y}}$$

where: W_x = percentage of funds invested in share x
W_y = percentage of funds invested in share y
R_x = mean return of share x (per cent)
R_y = mean return of share y (per cent)
σ_x = standard deviation of share x's returns (per cent)
σ_y = standard deviation of share y's returns (per cent)
$\rho_{x,y}$ = correlation coefficient between x and y's returns
σ_p = standard deviation of portfolio containing x and y (per cent)

Using annual returns of the two shares S and T from our earlier example, we can calculate the return and standard deviation (risk) of a series of portfolios consisting of differing amounts of S and T. First we calculate the correlation coefficient between the returns of the two shares:

$$\begin{aligned}
\rho_{S,T} &= ((6.6 - 5.96) \times (24.5 - 9.10) + (5.6 - 5.96) \times (-5.9 - 9.10) \\
&\quad + (-9.0 - 5.96) \times (19.9 - 9.10) + (12.6 - 5.96) \times (-7.8 - 9.10) \\
&\quad + (14.0 - 5.96) \times (14.8 - 9.10))/(5 \times 8.16 \times 13.39) \\
&= -0.389
\end{aligned}$$

The return and risk of a portfolio consisting of 80 per cent of S and 20 per cent of T are as follows:

$$\begin{aligned}
\text{Return of portfolio} &= (0.8 \times 5.96) + (0.2 \times 9.1) = 6.59 \text{ per cent} \\
\text{Risk of portfolio} &= ((0.8^2 \times 8.16^2) + (0.2^2 \times 13.39^2) \\
&\quad + (2 \times 0.8 \times 0.2 \times 8.16 \times 13.39 \times -0.389))^{1/2} \\
&= 6.02
\end{aligned}$$

The results of these calculations are given in Exhibit 8.5, where:

$$\begin{aligned}
A &= 80\% \text{ S} + 20\% \text{ T} \\
B &= 60\% \text{ S} + 40\% \text{ T} \\
C &= 40\% \text{ S} + 60\% \text{ T} \\
D &= 20\% \text{ S} + 80\% \text{ T}
\end{aligned}$$

Exhibit 8.5	Diversification of risk in a portfolio containing securities S and T					
	All S	**A**	**B**	**C**	**D**	**All T**
Mean	5.96	6.59	7.21	7.84	8.47	9.10
Standard deviation	8.16	6.02	5.68	7.40	10.18	13.39

Exhibit 8.6   **Graph showing the risk and return of portfolios consisting of different combinations of securities S and T**

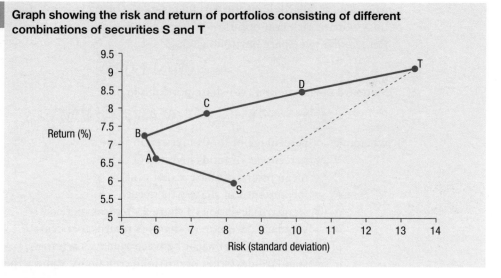

The results of these calculations are illustrated graphically in Exhibit 8.6. We can see that an investor can locate herself anywhere along the arc SABCDT according to how she divides her portfolio between the shares S and T. The points along the arc are *superior* to those on the straight line between security S and security T due to the diversification of unsystematic risk that occurs when more than one security is held.

8.2.2   Diversifying unsystematic risk using a three-share portfolio

With the introduction of an additional share into the portfolio there is even further scope for the diversification of unsystematic risk. The introduction of a higher risk and return share R into the earlier example is represented graphically in Exhibit 8.7, where:

    ST represents portfolios of securities S and T
    SR (dotted line) represents portfolios of securities S and R
    TR represents portfolios of securities T and R
    SR (bold line) represents portfolios of securities T, S and R

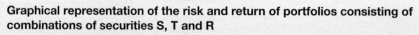

Exhibit 8.7   **Graphical representation of the risk and return of portfolios consisting of combinations of securities S, T and R**

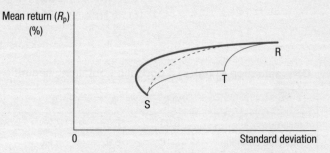

Here we can see that the optimal set of portfolios is achieved when all three shares are invested in (i.e. the bold line SR). This *optimal frontier* is superior to investing in just S and T owing to a greater ability to diversify away unsystematic risk when investing in all three shares. As more shares are added to the investment portfolio, progressively more and more unsystematic risk will be diversified away. This principle forms the basis of Markowitz's portfolio theory, where the investor's choice of investments is not limited to three shares but includes all available risky securities. Before we consider Markowitz's theory, however, let us consider investor attitudes to risk and return.

8.3 Investor attitudes to risk

How much risk will an investor accept in the first place? The answer to this question depends on how much utility an individual investor or company receives from taking risk. The attitudes that investors and companies have towards risk can be summarised as follows:

- *Risk-loving*: where the preference is for high return in exchange for a high level of risk.
- *Risk-neutral*: where the investor is indifferent to the level of risk faced.
- *Risk-averse*: where the preference is for low-risk, low-return investments.

While attitudes towards risk may differ, we expect that investors act rationally and do not expose themselves to higher risk without the possibility of higher returns. A common misconception often levelled at risk-loving investors is that they are acting irrationally. This is not the case, however, as investors with a preference for taking risks will be prepared to incur higher risk only if it is accompanied by correspondingly higher returns.

The attitude of an investor to different combinations of risk and return is reflected by the shape of their *utility curves* (indifference curves). These are adapted from microeconomics and the concept of *utility maximisation*, which uses utility curves to analyse consumer demand for different combinations of goods and services. Here, we apply utility curve analysis to portfolios rather than to goods and services, in terms of investors receiving positive utility from increasing returns and negative utility from increasing risk.

Utility curves are similar to contour lines on a map, but instead of joining up points of equal height, utility curves map out points of equal utility. Consider utility curve U_1 in Exhibit 8.8. At point A, the combination of expected return of er_0 and risk of r_0 gives the investor a certain level of utility that corresponds to utility curve U_1. If the investor is faced with an increased level of risk r_1, he would require an increase in the expected return equivalent to $er_1 - er_0$ in order to preserve his original level of utility – corresponding to point C on U_1. Utility curves slope upwards at an increasing rate because in order for an investor to be persuaded to take on progressively more risk, progressively higher rates of expected return are required to compensate and keep their utility constant. This is referred to as an *increasing marginal rate of substitution*.

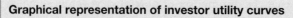

Exhibit 8.8   **Graphical representation of investor utility curves**

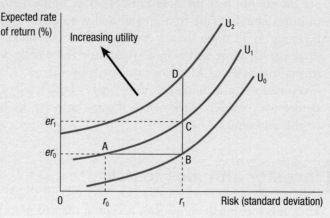

Rational investors will always try to increase their level of utility by seeking the highest return for a given level of risk, or by seeking the lowest risk for a given level of return. Hence moving from utility curve U_1 onto U_2 (i.e. from point C to point D) represents an increase in utility for the investor. Subsequent movements in a north-westerly direction will further increase investor utility. Conversely, a movement from point C to point B would represent a decrease in investor utility as they find themselves on U_0, which represents a lower utility curve compared with U_1.

Just as contour lines on a map differ with the type of terrain, utility curves differ in shape according to investors' differing preferences for risk and return. The key difference here is the slope of the utility curves. In Exhibit 8.9, V_0 represents the utility curve of risk-loving investor V while U_0 corresponds to investor U who is risk averse. Initially both investors are located at point D and derive an equal level of utility given an expected

Exhibit 8.9   **Comparison of a risk-averse investor's utility curve (U_0) with that of a risk-loving investor (V_0)**

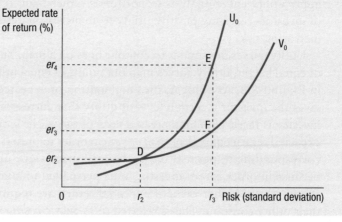

Exhibit 8.10 **Utility curves for risk-loving (I) and risk-averse (U) investors**

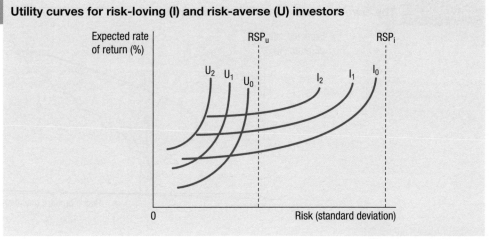

return of er_2 and risk of r_2. Assume both investors are faced with an increase in risk to point r_3. In order to maintain his utility, investor V requires an increase in expected return of $er_3 - er_2$. However, given investor U's risk aversion, he requires a much higher increase in expected return ($er_4 - er_2$) to maintain his utility.

Hence, as indicated in Exhibit 8.10, a risk-averse investor's utility curves (U_0, U_1 and U_2) quickly steepen at low levels of risk whereas the opposite is true for a risk-loving investor, whose curves (I_0, I_1 and I_2) are much flatter. The risk saturation point, i.e. the level of risk beyond which an investor will not go, is much lower for investor U (indicated by the vertical line RSP_U) when compared with that of investor I (RSP_I).

Having considered earlier the portfolio choices available to investors in Section 8.2, we are now in a position to combine these choices with the utility curves of investors, thereby allowing investors to select portfolios which satisfy their preference for risk and return.

8.4 Markowitz's portfolio theory

The cornerstone of Markowitz's seminal 1952 theory, for which he was awarded a Nobel Prize in Economics in 1990, is the ability of investors to diversify away unsystematic risk by holding portfolios consisting of a number of different shares. Markowitz's starting point is to construct what is known as the *envelope* curve. This represents the set of portfolio choices available to investors when investing in different combinations of risky assets. In Exhibit 8.11 the envelope curve is represented by the shaded area AEFCDG. Investors can construct portfolios anywhere in this shaded area by holding different combinations of available risky assets.

While investors are able to locate themselves anywhere within the envelope curve, rational investors will invest only in those portfolios on the *efficient frontier* represented by the arc AEF. It is called the efficient frontier because all portfolios on this arc are superior to (i.e. more efficient than) all other portfolios within the envelope curve,

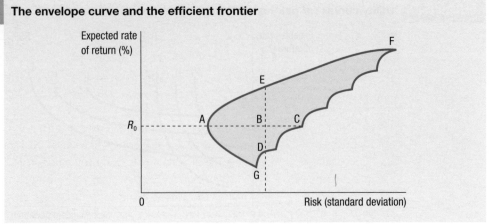

Exhibit 8.11 **The envelope curve and the efficient frontier**

giving either the *maximum return* for a given level of risk or the *minimum risk* for a given level of return. For example, if we compare portfolios B and E on the boundary of the envelope curve which both have the same level of risk, we can see that portfolio E offers a higher return without incurring any additional risk. Portfolio E is said to *dominate* portfolio B. Equally, while portfolio A has the same expected return as portfolios B and C, it dominates them as both B and C incur a higher level of risk. Using the same rationale, portfolios on the arc between A and G cannot be regarded as efficient as they are dominated by those on the arc AEF.

Investor choice, however, is not restricted solely to risky securities. Tobin (1958) recognised this in an important paper which further developed Markowitz's earlier work. By assuming that investors can both lend and borrow at a risk-free rate of return, we can construct what is known as the *capital market line* (CML), represented by the line R_fMN in Exhibit 8.12. The starting point is to estimate the rate of return on the risk-free asset, R_f. Traditionally the risk-free rate is approximated by using the rate of return (redemption yield) on government Treasury bills, which can be assumed

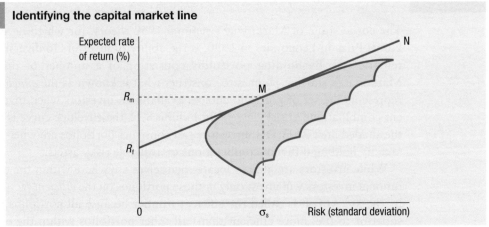

Exhibit 8.12 **Identifying the capital market line**

to be virtually risk-free. If a line pivoting about R_f is rotated clockwise until it reaches a point of tangency M with the efficient frontier, we locate what is known as the *market portfolio*. This portfolio represents the optimal combination of risky assets *given the existence of the risk-free asset*. Investors are able to move along the CML by changing the proportions of the risk-free asset and the market portfolio in what is in effect a two-share portfolio. This results in a straightforward linear trade-off between risk and return.

Investors will always choose a portfolio on the CML because the CML portfolios are more efficient than those on the efficient frontier (shown by AEF in Exhibit 8.11). The CML portfolio chosen by an investor will depend on the investor's risk preference. Risk-averse investors will choose portfolios towards R_f by investing most of their money in the risk-free asset; less risk-averse investors will choose portfolios closer to M, putting most of their funds into the market portfolio. The precise position that an investor will choose on the CML will be determined by the point of tangency of their utility curves with the CML. In Exhibit 8.13 we consider a moderately risk-averse investor with utility curves U_0, U_1, U_2 and U_3. He will locate at point P on utility curve U_2 by investing the majority of his funds into the risk-free asset and the remainder into the market portfolio (note that U_3 is out of the investor's grasp). If the risk-free asset was not available and hence the CML did not exist, the investor would choose portfolio Q on the efficient frontier and enjoy a lower level of utility U_1.

Risk-loving investors will choose portfolios on the CML to the right of point M. They do this by putting all their money into the market portfolio and, in addition, *borrowing at the risk-free rate* and investing their borrowings in the market portfolio.

The two-stage process of identifying the market portfolio (to diversify away unsystematic risk) and then combining this optimal portfolio of risky assets with lending or borrowing at the risk-free rate (to satisfy the individual investor's preference for risk and return) is often referred to as *Tobin's separation theory*.

| Exhibit 8.13 | **Graphical representation of Markowitz's theory** |

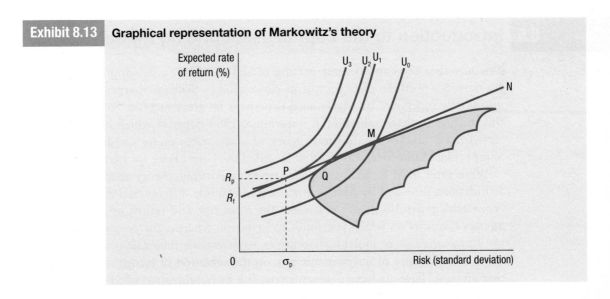

Furthermore, the risk-free asset is significant from the perspective of calculating the risk of a portfolio containing a large number of shares in order to facilitate an optimal investment decision. This calculation involves incorporating correlation coefficients for every possible pair of shares, with the number of correlation coefficients growing exponentially with the number of shares in the portfolio. The introduction of the risk-free asset simplifies enormously the calculation of portfolio risk since the returns of the shares are not correlated with the return on the risk-free asset.

8.4.1 Problems with the practical application of portfolio theory

There are problems associated with trying to apply portfolio theory in practice, some of which are as follows.

- It is unrealistic to assume that investors can borrow at the risk-free rate. Individuals and companies are not risk-free and will therefore not be able to borrow at the risk-free rate; they will be charged a premium to reflect their higher level of risk.
- There are problems with identifying the market portfolio as this requires knowledge of the risk and return of all risky investments and their corresponding correlation coefficients.
- Once the make-up of the market portfolio is identified it will be expensive to construct because of transaction costs. These costs will be prohibitive in the case of smaller investors.
- The composition of the market portfolio will change over time. This will be due to shifts both in the risk-free rate of return and in the envelope curve and hence the efficient frontier.

One way for smaller investors to overcome the problems mentioned above is by buying a stake in a large, diversified portfolio, for example by buying into unit trusts, investment trusts or *index tracker funds*.

8.5 Introduction to the capital asset pricing model

The fact that the capital asset pricing model (CAPM), a development based on Markowitz's portfolio theory, owes its conception to William Sharpe, a PhD student unofficially supervised by Markowitz, is perhaps no great surprise. Sharpe developed this method of share valuation in his seminal 1964 paper in which he attempted to 'construct a market equilibrium theory of asset prices under conditions of risk'. Sharpe, like Markowitz, was in 1990 awarded the Nobel Prize for Economics.

While the CAPM is the next logical step from portfolio theory and is based on the foundations provided by Markowitz, there are subtle differences between the two. *Normative* portfolio theory considers the *total* risk and return of portfolios and advises investors on which portfolios to invest in, whereas the *positive* CAPM uses the *systematic* risk of individual securities to determine their fair price. In order to ignore the influence of unsystematic risk on the valuation of securities, it is assumed that investors have eradicated unsystematic risk by holding diversified portfolios.

As with most academic models, the CAPM is based on a simplified world using the following assumptions:

- Investors are rational and want to maximise their utility; they do not take risk for risk's sake.
- All information is freely available to investors and, having interpreted it, investors arrive at similar expectations.
- Investors are able to borrow and lend at the risk-free rate.
- Investors hold diversified portfolios, eliminating all unsystematic risk.
- Capital markets are perfectly competitive. The conditions required for this are: a large number of buyers and sellers; no one participant can influence the market; no taxes and transaction costs; no entry or exit barriers to the market; and securities are divisible.
- Investment occurs over a single, standardised holding period.

While these assumptions are clearly at odds with the real world, we should refrain from dismissing the CAPM as unrealistic and impractical. As Sharpe (1964) observed: 'the proper test of a theory is not the realism of its assumptions but the acceptability of its implications'. The issue of the CAPM's applicability and usefulness is considered later in the chapter.

8.6 Using the CAPM to value shares

Central to the CAPM is the existence of a *linear relationship* between risk and return. This linear relationship is defined by what is known as the *security market line* (SML), where the systematic risk of a security is compared with the risk and return of the market and the risk-free rate of return in order to calculate a required return for the security and hence a fair price. A graphical representation of the SML is given in Exhibit 8.14. The equation of the SML can be defined as:

$$R_j = R_f + \beta_j(R_m - R_f)$$

where: R_j = the rate of return of security j predicted by the model
R_f = the risk-free rate of return
β_j = the beta coefficient of security j
R_m = the return of the market

In order for the CAPM to be used in the valuation of shares, we require an understanding of the components that make up the SML and how they can be calculated or approximated. First, we consider the beta coefficient, which is used to quantify a security's level of systematic risk.

8.6.1 The meaning and calculation of beta

The beta (β) of a security can be defined as an *index of responsiveness* of the changes in returns of the security relative to a change in the stock exchange or market. By

Exhibit 8.14 **The security market line indicating the relationship between systematic risk (measured by beta) and the required rate of return on capital assets**

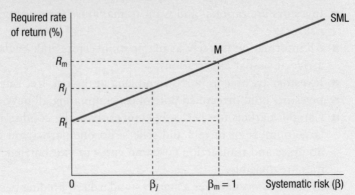

definition, the *beta of the market* is always 1 and acts as a benchmark against which the systematic risk of securities can be measured. The *beta of a security* measures the sensitivity of the returns on the security to changes in systematic factors. For example, if a security has a beta of 0.8 (i.e. less systematic risk than the market) and the market return *increases* by 10 per cent, the security's return will increase by 8 per cent. If the market return *decreases* by 10 per cent, the return of the security decreases by 8 per cent. This security represents what is known as a *defensive* security and is most attractive to investors when the stock exchange is falling. Alternatively, for a security with a beta of 1.5 (i.e. more systematic risk than the market), if the return of the market increases by 10 per cent, the security's return will increase by 15 per cent. If the market return decreases by 10 per cent, the return of the security decreases by 15 per cent. This is what is termed an *aggressive* security and is most attractive to investors when the market is rising.

As we will see later in Section 9.4.1, betas can be classified as either liability or asset betas. *Liability betas* (or equity betas as they are more commonly known) take into account a security's total systematic risk, i.e. risk arising from the nature of a company's business (business risk) and risk arising from the way in which the company finances itself (financial risk). *Asset betas* reflect only the former type of systematic risk. In subsequent paragraphs when we talk of beta we are in fact referring to equity betas.

The relationship between the beta of a security, and the risk and return of the security and the market is given by the following equation:

$$\beta_j = \frac{\mathrm{Cov}_{j,m}}{(\sigma_m)^2} = \frac{\sigma_j \times \sigma_m \times \rho_{j,m}}{(\sigma_m)^2} = \frac{\sigma_j \times \rho_{j,m}}{\sigma_m}$$

where: σ_j = standard deviation of security j's returns
σ_m = standard deviation of returns of the market
$\rho_{j,m}$ = correlation coefficient between the security's returns and the market returns
$\mathrm{Cov}_{j,m}$ = covariance of returns of security j and the market.

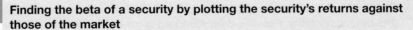

Exhibit 8.15 Finding the beta of a security by plotting the security's returns against those of the market

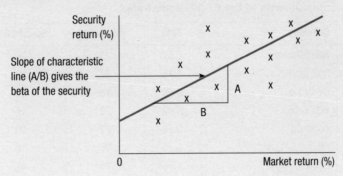

The calculation of a share's beta coefficient involves collecting data on the periodic returns of the market and the security under consideration. This data can then be plotted with the returns of the security on the vertical axis and the returns of the market on the horizontal axis. The slope of the line of best fit, or *characteristic line*, will then give the value of beta. This is illustrated in Exhibit 8.15. Here the gradient of the line is positive and less than 1, and the beta is approximately 0.5. Alternatively, beta can be determined using regression analysis.

If regression analysis is used, the *coefficient of variation* (R^2) gives an indication of the extent to which the regression equation, and hence the determined value of beta, explains the distribution of correlated returns. Put another way, the closer R^2 is to 100 per cent, the more of the total variability of a security's returns is explained by systematic risk as measured by beta, as opposed to other factors. Hence the higher the value of R^2, the stronger the case for a unifactor model like the CAPM, rather than multifactor models such as arbitrage pricing theory.

An easier way to find a security's beta is to leave it to the experts. The Risk Measurement Service of the London Business School publishes quarterly *beta books* of companies' equity beta coefficients. They calculate the betas of all major companies by regressing their monthly returns against the monthly returns of the FT actuaries' all-share index over the previous five years. An extract from one of the pages of the beta books is shown in Exhibit 8.16.

Not only do the beta books give equity betas, they also provide other important information. The *variability* column indicates the total variability of a share's returns (σ_j) as measured by standard deviation. The *specific risk* column gives the variability of a share's returns ($\sigma_{j\text{-sp}}$) which is explained by specific factors measured by standard deviation. The *standard error* column indicates the reliability of the beta coefficient calculated – the closer this is to zero the better. Finally, the *R-squared* column indicates the percentage of a share's total variability of returns that is explained by systematic factors as measured by beta. The relationship that exists between the total variability, the systematic variability (note σ_m^2 represents the variance of market returns) and

Exhibit 8.16	Extract from the beta books produced by the London Business School, showing the beta, variability, specific risk, standard error of beta and *R*-squared of the constituents of the FT-30 Share Index

Company	Beta	Variability	Specific risk	Std error	R sq.
Allied Domecq	0.57	21	20	0.15	16
BAE Systems	1.16	37	33	0.21	22
BG Group	0.58	18	16	0.13	28
BOC Group	0.82	20	16	0.13	36
Boots Co	0.68	22	20	0.15	20
BP	0.75	20	16	0.13	32
British Airways	1.65	48	41	0.23	26
British American Tobacco	0.59	23	22	0.16	14
BT Group	1.43	34	27	0.19	38
Cadbury-Schweppes	0.55	20	19	0.14	16
Compass Group	1.06	30	25	0.19	29
Diageo	0.32	20	19	0.15	6
EMI Group	1.22	45	41	0.23	16
GKN	1.15	33	28	0.19	27
GlaxoSmithKline	0.30	19	18	0.14	6
ICI	1.35	47	42	0.23	19
Invensys	1.36	69	66	0.27	8
ITV	1.57	43	36	0.22	30
Lloyds-TSB Group	1.18	28	22	0.16	39
LogicaCMG	1.45	54	49	0.25	16
Marks and Spencer	0.64	27	25	0.18	12
Peninsular and Orient	1.16	34	29	0.20	25
Prudential	1.54	35	26	0.18	43
Reuters Group	1.47	49	43	0.24	20
Royal Bank of Scotland	1.14	27	21	0.16	39
Royal & Sun Alliance	1.60	47	41	0.23	25
Scottish Power	0.45	23	22	0.16	8
Tate and Lyle	0.59	30	28	0.19	9
Tesco	0.49	23	21	0.16	10
Vodafone Group	1.13	34	30	0.20	24

Source: London Business School, Risk Measurement Service, April–June 2005.

the specific variability of a share's returns is:

Total variability of returns = Systematic variability + Specific variability

$$\sigma_j^2 = (\beta_j^2 \times \sigma_m^2) + \sigma_{j\text{-sp}}^2$$

Exhibit 8.17 Bar chart showing the frequency distribution of equity betas for the companies constituting the FTSE 100, June 2005

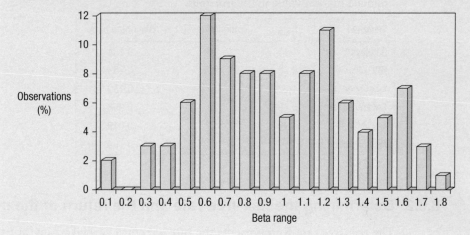

Algebraically, R-squared is represented by:

$$R^2 = \frac{\beta_j^2 \times \sigma_m^2}{\sigma_j^2}$$

A frequency distribution of FTSE 100 company betas is shown in Exhibit 8.17. It can be seen that the majority of company betas (61 per cent) lie in the range 0.6 to 1.2, with a beta of 0.6 being the most common. While it is mathematically possible for beta to be negative, it is very rare in practice as few companies experience increasing returns in times of economic downturn. The most important determinant of a company's beta is the industry in which it operates. Companies with betas greater than one tend to be those in industries such as consumer durables, leisure and luxury goods. Companies with betas less than one usually come from industries such as food retailers, utilities and other necessity goods producers. A useful exercise is to look through the industrial betas sections that the London Business School includes in its beta books.

An important use of equity betas is that they can be used to find the beta of a portfolio of shares. This allows the calculation of the required rate of return from the portfolio as a whole. An example is given in Exhibit 8.18.

The *portfolio beta* is obtained by weighting the individual security betas by their relative market value (i.e. the number of shares multiplied by their market price and divided by the total market value of the portfolio). In the example in Exhibit 8.18, the portfolio beta is 0.794, indicating that the portfolio has less systematic risk than the market portfolio (i.e. it is a defensive portfolio). It must be noted, however, that a portfolio of only five shares will not diversify away all unsystematic risk and therefore the risk of this portfolio will not consist solely of systematic risk.

Having now built up a firm understanding of what beta represents and how it can be determined, we can go on to consider the other variables used in the CAPM.

Exhibit 8.18	Calculating the beta of a portfolio by weighting the betas of its constituent securities according to their relative market value in the portfolio

Security	Beta	Weighting (%)	Weighted beta
Barclays	1.17	20	0.234
BP	0.75	35	0.263
Kingfisher	1.00	15	0.150
Severn Trent	0.49	20	0.098
Tesco	0.49	10	0.049
Portfolio beta		100	0.794

8.6.2 Determining the risk-free rate and the return of the market

The risk-free rate R_f represents the rate of return earned by investing in the risk-free asset. In reality, while no investments are risk-free, bonds issued by the governments of politically and economically stable countries are generally considered to be free from the risk of default. Therefore, the risk-free rate can be approximated by taking the current rate of return or yield on short-dated government bonds. In the UK this equates to the yield on short-dated Treasury bills, which is reported regularly in the *Financial Times*.

The return of the market, R_m, is more difficult to calculate. It is usually approximated by using *stock exchange indices* such as the FTSE 100 or the FT actuaries' All-Share Index, as a representation of the market. To find the return of the market, the capital gains of the chosen index over a period, say one year, should be added to the dividend yield of the shares in the index over the same period. This is given by the following formula, which allows us to approximate the return of the market over the period:

$$R_m = \frac{P_1 - P_0}{P_0} + \text{Div}$$

where: P_0 = the stock exchange index at the beginning of the period
P_1 = the stock exchange index at the end of the period
Div = average dividend yield of the stock exchange index over the period

Because of short-term fluctuations in stock exchange indices it is advisable to use a *time-smoothed average* in order to estimate the return of the market. For instance, if using monthly data, calculate the monthly return of the index over, say, a three-year period. Alternatively, if using annual data, we can calculate a moving average by shifting the year period back a month at a time to cover a number of years.

A large number of empirical studies have attempted to quantify the *market* or *equity risk premium* ($R_m - R_f$), which represents the excess of market returns over those associated with investing in risk-free assets. Results vary considerably according to the time period used as a basis, whether a geometric or arithmetic average is calculated (Jenkinson (1994) found that the latter tend to give higher results), and whether gilts or Treasury bills are used to represent the risk-free asset (again the latter give higher results).

Dimson and Brealey (1978), using historical market returns for the UK over the period 1918–77, found an average market risk premium of 9 per cent. A similar result (9.1 per cent) was obtained by Allan et al. (1986) taking a longer time period 1919–84. A more recent study by Dimson et al. (2002) yielded a range of results including a geometric market risk premium for the UK of 4.5 per cent based on the period of 1900–2001 and taking Treasury bills to represent risk-free assets. This increased significantly to 7.2 per cent when the period 1951–2001 was considered. Meanwhile in the USA, Ibbotson Associates (2003) arrived at an arithmetic market risk premium of 8.4 per cent using data over the period 1926–2002. Hence, while a market risk premium of between 8 and 9 per cent has traditionally been put forward by academics, others have argued that this represents an overstatement and that a figure of around 5 per cent provides a more appropriate current premium for equity risk. Barclays Global Investors went further, affirming their 10 year arithmetic market risk premium of 3.25 per cent to be more realistic for UK investors. The use of a lower premium is further supported if we consider the effects on equity returns of the tragic events of 11 September 2001. It is also interesting to note that UK industry watchdogs such as Ofwat, Ofgem and Ofcom apply an equity risk premium of between 3.5 and 5 per cent when making their weighted average cost of capital (WACC) calculations (see Section 9.6). The issue of the market risk premium is discussed further in Vignette 8.1.

8.6.3 A numerical example of the CAPM's use

Now that we have a firm understanding of the components of the CAPM, we can work through an example to illustrate its use. Consider the following data:

$$\text{Beta of British Airways plc } (\beta_j) \qquad = 1.65$$
$$\text{Yield of short-dated Treasury bills } (R_f) = 4.5\%$$
$$\text{Market risk premium } (R_m - R_f) \qquad = 5.0\%$$

Using $R_j = R_f + \beta_j(R_m - R_f)$ we have:

$$R_j = 4.5\% + (1.65 \times 5.0\%) = 12.8\%$$

From the data provided, the CAPM predicts that the required rate of return of British Airway's shareholders and hence British Airway's cost of equity is 12.8 per cent.

8.6.4 Summary of the implications of the CAPM

The implications of the CAPM when applying it to pricing shares can be summarised as follows:

- Investors calculating the required rate of return of a security will only consider systematic risk to be relevant, as unsystematic risk can be eradicated by portfolio diversification.
- Shares with high levels of systematic risk are expected, on average, to yield higher rates of return.
- There should be a linear relationship between systematic risk and return, and securities that are correctly priced should plot on the security market line (SML).

Vignette 8.1

Sizing up the historical equity risk premium

It seems to be the high season for long-term stock market performance analyses says Barry Riley. Last week's equity-gilt study from Barclays Capital, covering the UK and the US, was followed on Monday by the second edition of a comprehensive analysis from the London Business School in conjunction with ABN Amro. Elroy Dimson, Paul Marsh and Mike Staunton have produced Millennium Book II, a 284-page volume covering 101 years of investment returns in 15 countries.

The central topic is the size of the historical, or ex post, equity risk premium – the extra return that shareholders receive for investing in risky stocks rather than risk-free alternatives. According to Dimson, Marsh and Staunton: 'most finance professionals and financial economists regard the equity risk premium as the single most important number in finance.' Unfortunately, there is a lot of confusion about its calculation and estimates of its size have fallen significantly in recent years. The three academics conclude that many companies are living in the past and may be under-investing. This is because they do not understand that the cost of equity capital is lower than generally accepted, either because the risk premium has fallen, or because it was overestimated.

The subject is also addressed by Adrian Fitzgerald in Professional Investor, the journal of the UK Society of Investment Professionals. He says the expected, or ex ante, risk premium in the UK has always been low (usually under 2 per cent). However, ex post returns have been consistently boosted over the past 50 years by factors including equity re-rating, unexpectedly high dividend growth and high bond returns. The outcome, he says, has been an actual annual average risk premium during the second half of the 20th century of 6.7 per cent (though only 4.5 per cent during the past 20 years). But 'it would be difficult to arrive at a risk premium expectation above 3 per cent in the present environment'.

The Barclays study, published annually since 1956, was substantially revised last year. Previous indications of a risk premium typically between 6 and 8 per cent have been reduced. Factoring in a poor 2000 for equity returns, the annual UK risk premium emerges at 4.4 per cent over 101 years (and 5.3 per cent over 75 years in the US).

Millennium Book II arrives at a similar result, at 4.4 per cent for the UK and 5.0 per cent for the US. These seem fairly typical figures, because the study's average across all 15 countries was 4.7 per cent.

Statistical question marks remain. Equity index returns over a century may be misleading because extensive rebalancing of constituents is involved. Moreover, should the equity premium be measured relative to returns on government bills or bonds? I have selected the bond-related measure, which in the UK has been 0.3 percentage points lower than the premium against Treasury bills. Finally, should the arithmetic or geometric average of annual returns be used? I have used the numerically smaller geometric (or compound) figures. There is also the embarrassing point that the occasional hyperinflation, war or revolution can generate minus 100 per cent single year returns and thus wipe out century-long data sequences. Survivor bias is certainly a problem. Puzzlingly, France's long-term average equity risk premium is 7.5 per cent while Denmark's is 2.5 per cent.

The conclusion is that investors are confused by the past data, which have almost all been skewed in just one direction: upwards. Opinion surveys report very high expected premia, even by professional investors, often in the order of 10 per cent. This conflicts with the high valuation basis of equities, which perversely can only be justified if the expectations built into market prices are low. If future returns are to be high, equities must surely start off cheap.

The LBS team concludes that the expected annualised equity risk premium is 3–4 per cent. The Barclays Capital study notes that the ex post premium in the UK has been 2.4 per cent over the past decade, and rising technological risks and widening bond market spreads are threats to future returns on equities.

A huge asset management industry has developed globally to promote equities. Private and professional investors still retain high expectations. Could these be satisfied by a risk premium of 3 per cent, given the high level of portfolio management charges? Much may depend on whether the experience of 2000 turns out to be a healthy occasional rebalancing between bonds and equities, or the start of a lengthy period of low returns on the latter.

Source: Barry Riley, *Financial Times*, 21 February 2001. Reprinted with permission.

Exhibit 8.19 **The security market line (SML) showing an underpriced share (A), and overpriced share (C) and a correctly valued share (B)**

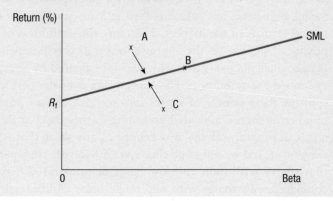

A graphical representation of the final implication is shown in Exhibit 8.19. Security B is correctly priced and plots on the SML. Security A is considered to be *underpriced*, giving higher returns compared with those required by investors given its level of systematic risk. Therefore investors will buy the share, causing its price to rise and its return to decrease, and the share to move onto the SML. Security C is *overpriced* and hence the opposite situation will occur. If securities take a long time moving onto the SML, the linear relationship between risk and systematic return will be weakened. Therefore we see the importance of the assumption made by the CAPM that capital markets are perfect as under these conditions a share's price will move accurately and quickly to reflect information about the share.

8.7 Empirical tests of the CAPM

Earlier in the chapter we acknowledged that the assumptions of the CAPM are unrealistic from a real-world perspective. In Section 8.5, for example, we noted that a key assumption of the CAPM is that capital markets are perfect; but capital markets are not perfect as transaction costs and taxes clearly do exist in practice. However, capital markets have been shown by empirical tests to exhibit high levels of efficiency. In fact, although the assumptions made by the CAPM do not totally mirror reality, reality may not be so far away from the assumptions as to invalidate the model. The model, therefore, should not be prejudged on its assumptions but assessed on the results of its application.

There have been a large number of tests on the validity of the CAPM's applications and uses. Research has concentrated on two main areas: the stability of beta coefficients over time, and the strength and nature of the linear relationship that exists between risk and return.

8.7.1 Tests of the stability of beta

While the CAPM is a forward-looking model, the availability of only historical data means that betas are calculated using historical returns of shares in relation to historical returns of the market. Therefore the usefulness of historical betas in both the pricing of shares and the appraisal of projects will depend heavily on the stability of beta coefficients over time. This was investigated by Sharpe and Cooper (1972), who examined the stability of US equity betas over the period 1931–67. They started by splitting their sample of shares into ten risk classes, each class containing an equal number of shares, allocated according to their beta at the start of the test period. As a rule of thumb, stability was defined as any share that either remained in its existing class or moved by only one class over a five-year time period. Their results suggested that shares with high and low betas demonstrated higher levels of stability when compared with shares with mid-range betas. Additionally they found that approximately 50 per cent of shares' betas could be considered stable (according to their earlier definition) over a five-year time period.

While empirical evidence on the stability of individual betas is inconclusive, there is general agreement that the betas of portfolios of shares exhibit much higher levels of stability over time. The most common reasons put forward to explain this are that any errors associated with the estimation of an individual share's beta or any actual changes in the systematic risk characteristics of individual shares will tend to average out when shares are combined in a portfolio.

8.7.2 Tests of the security market line

Many empirical tests have used regression analysis to derive a *fitted* security market line which is then compared with the *theoretical* SML. Deriving the fitted line involves a two-stage process. The first stage is to select a wide-ranging sample of shares and, using market returns and security returns over a specified period (say monthly data over a five-year period), calculate the average return of the securities and their beta coefficients using a series of regressions. The second stage is to regress the individual shares' beta coefficients against their average returns in order to derive a fitted SML. The theoretical SML is located by estimating the risk-free rate of return (R_f) to give the intercept on the vertical axis and then calculating the return of the market (R_m) and plotting it against a beta of one. Some of the best known tests include those carried out by Jacob (1971), Black et al. (1972) and Fama and Macbeth (1973). The conclusions of their tests can be summarised as follows:

- The intercept of the fitted line with the y-axis was above the one derived using the theoretical model, indicating that some other factor in addition to systematic risk was determining securities' rates of return.
- The slope of the fitted line was flatter than that suggested by the theoretical SML.
- The fitted line indicated the existence of a strong linear relationship between systematic risk and return, albeit different from the one suggested by the theoretical SML.

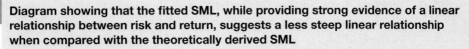

Exhibit 8.20 **Diagram showing that the fitted SML, while providing strong evidence of a linear relationship between risk and return, suggests a less steep linear relationship when compared with the theoretically derived SML**

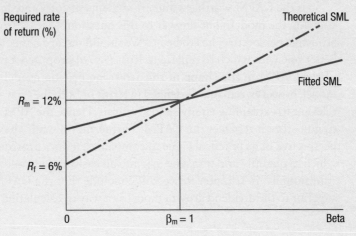

These points are illustrated in Exhibit 8.20.

The broad conclusion drawn from these tests is that the CAPM does not fully explain observed data, although systematic risk does go a long way towards explaining the expected returns of individual securities. More recent tests have been far less kind to the CAPM. Black (1993) considered the strength of the risk–return relationship in the USA over the periods 1931–65 and 1966–91. In his simulation he constructed ten portfolios, the first containing shares with beta values in the highest 10 per cent right down to the final portfolio made up of shares with betas in the lowest 10 per cent category. He then calculated the return for the ten portfolios over the previous five years. This process was repeated year on year with the ten portfolios' compositions changing to maintain their risk profile. When results for the period 1931–65 were examined, the ten portfolios plotted close to the theoretical SML with the highest risk portfolio yielding the highest return and the lowest risk portfolio the lowest return. However, when the period 1966–91 was considered, the relationship completely broke down. Fama and French (1992) also found against the CAPM. They too focused on US equity returns over the period 1963–90, concluding that no meaningful relationship could be found between average share returns and market betas. They did, however, find that average share returns were negatively correlated with company size and positively correlated with companies' book-to-market value. Comparative studies based on share returns from the major stock markets of Europe were equally unsupportive of the CAPM.

While recent tests question the validity of the CAPM, Roll (1977) argued that the CAPM is difficult, if not almost impossible, to test. The reason is that the stock exchange indices that are used to approximate the market return are poor surrogates. Not only do stock exchange indices fail to include all tradable shares, they also omit untradable shares and other financial and non-financial assets (such as bonds, property, land, antiques and so on). Roll therefore concluded that, without a market portfolio which accurately reflects all risky assets, it is impossible to test the validity of the CAPM.

So is the CAPM worthless and are students of corporate finance wasting their time by studying the model? The answer to this question, at least from an educational if not an academic perspective, has to be no. We should discard a theory or model only if there is a better one with which to replace it. Ross (1976) proposed a potential 'heir to the throne' of the CAPM in the shape of the arbitrage pricing model (APM). This multi-factor model, however, remains ill-defined in terms of both the type and the number of variables relevant to explaining equity shares' returns. Hence the APM has some considerable way to go before it replaces the CAPM. Furthermore, while the CAPM is limited from the perspective of its practical value to companies, it does provide us with a framework with which to quantify and translate risk into an easily understandable required rate of return. Additionally, in Chapter 9, we will conclude that the CAPM can be considered to be superior to the dividend growth model as a way of calculating a company's cost of equity.

8.8 Conclusion

In this chapter we considered the important relationship that exists between risk and return. We started by looking at how the risk and return of individual investments can be measured and then went on to demonstrate that investors, by holding well-diversified portfolios, can eradicate the unsystematic risk they face – the basis of Markowitz's portfolio theory. We then located the optimal portfolio of risky shares (the market portfolio) when risk-free assets are available to investors, identifying the linear relationship between risk and return known as the capital market line. Investors can select portfolios on the line according to their risk preferences.

Sharpe's capital asset pricing model is a development of Markowitz's portfolio theory. The model identifies a linear relationship between the return of individual securities and their systematic risk as measured by their beta factor. This relationship allows investors to calculate the required return for a security given its systematic risk and hence determine whether it is fairly priced or not. While the assumptions on which the model is based are not realistic, empirical tests do provide evidence of the existence of a linear relationship between systematic risk and return, albeit one which is slightly different from that suggested by theory.

Key points

1 The relationship between risk and return plays an important role in corporate finance. Risk is measured by the standard deviation of an investment's returns and can be calculated using either historical returns or expected future returns.

2 The risk of an investment can be split into systematic and unsystematic risk. Unsystematic risk can be diversified away by investing in a number of different shares.

3 The simplest form of diversification is to invest in a two-share portfolio. The key determinant of the amount of risk that can be diversified away is the degree of correlation between the two shares' returns.

4 The greater the variety of shares in a portfolio, the more unsystematic risk will be eradicated.

5 Markowitz's portfolio theory provides the basis from which investors can combine the most efficient portfolio of risky assets with the risk-free asset in order to construct a portfolio which satisfies their risk and return requirements and hence maximises their utility.

6 One of the difficulties associated with using portfolio theory in practice for smaller investors is that the transaction costs can be prohibitive. However, they can overcome this problem by buying into diversified portfolios, i.e. investment trusts and unit trusts.

7 The CAPM, which builds on portfolio theory, defines a linear relationship between the systematic risk of a security and its required rate of return. This linear relationship is represented by the security market line (SML).

8 Systematic risk is measured by beta, which indicates the sensitivity of a security's returns to systematic factors, relative to the market return and the risk-free rate of return.

9 If securities are correctly priced they should plot on the security market line.

10 While empirical tests do not reinforce the validity of the CAPM, the model does provide a useful aid to understanding the relationship between systematic risk and the required rate of return of securities.

Self-test questions

Answers to these questions can be found on pages 453–5.

1 Explain why certain levels of risk cannot be avoided even in a well-diversified portfolio.

2 Discuss whether diversification at company level has any value to a company's ordinary shareholders.

3 Distinguish between an efficient portfolio and an optimal portfolio.

4 Explain the importance of risk-free assets to portfolio theory.

5 How do we approximate the risk-free rate in practice? In reality, will the capital market line be a straight line?

6 List the limitations of portfolio theory as an aid to investment decisions.

7 Explain whether you consider the assumptions upon which the capital asset pricing model is based to be unrealistic.

8 Explain what is measured by beta.

9 Identify the problems associated with determining the equity risk premium.

10 The market currently yields a return of 10 per cent whereas Treasury bills yield 4 per cent. Shares of Lime Spider plc have a covariance of 7.5 with the market whereas the market has a variance of 4.5. What is the required rate of return for Lime Spider plc's shares?

Questions for review

Answers to these questions can be found on pages 455–7. Questions with an asterisk (*) are at an intermediate level.

1 Discuss how portfolio theory can help individual investors maximise their utility.

2 You are considering investing in two securities, X and Y, and have the following information:

Security	Possible return (%)	Probability
X	30	0.3
	25	0.4
	20	0.3
Y	50	0.2
	30	0.6
	10	0.2

(a) Calculate the expected return for each security separately and for a portfolio of 60 per cent X and 40 per cent Y.

(b) Calculate the expected risk of each security separately and of the portfolio as defined above if the correlation coefficient of the two returns is +0.15.

3* Brown plc has been investing surplus funds in a small portfolio of equity shares over the past few years. Details of the portfolio are as follows.

Company	No. shares	Beta	Share price (£)	Dividend yield (%)	Expected return (%)
Rasiak	70 000	1.27	3.75	5.6	12
Johnson	150 000	1.53	4.25	3.5	16
Smith	100 000	1.01	2.50	4.2	14
Bisgaard	80 000	0.95	4.50	6.2	9.5
Idiakez	130 000	0.82	3.50	4.8	15

The current market return is 12 per cent and the yield on Treasury bills is 5 per cent.

(a) Is Brown's portfolio more or less risky than that of the market portfolio? Support your answer with appropriate calculations.

(b) Give Brown plc advice on how it should change the composition of its portfolio, giving a rationale for the changes that you recommend.

4 You are given the following data which refers to the performance of the FTSE 100 and two companies over the last financial year.

FTSE 100 Index at the end of 2004:	4753
FTSE 100 Index at the end of 2005:	5153
Dividend yield on the FTSE 100 for 2005:	4.55%
Current redemption yield for 7% Treasury Bills:	3.78%

	Aardvark plc	Bear plc
Share price at 31 December 2004	201p	260p
Share price at 31 December 2005	224p	307p
Total dividend payment	8p	9p
Equity beta	1.3	0.87

Required:

(a) Using the data above, calculate whether or not a diversified investor with share-holdings in the two companies will be satisfied with the returns they are receiving.

(b) Critically discuss how useful you consider the analysis in part (a) to be when making portfolio management decisions.

Questions for discussion

Questions with an asterisk (*) are at an advanced level.

1 The securities of companies Z and Y have the following expected returns and standard deviations:

	Z	Y
Expected return (%)	15	35
Standard deviation (%)	20	40

If the correlation coefficient between the two securities is +0.25, calculate the expected return and standard deviation for the following portfolios:

(a) 100 per cent Z;

(b) 75 per cent Z and 25 per cent Y;

(c) 50 per cent Z and 50 per cent Y;

(d) 25 per cent Z and 75 per cent Y;

(e) 100 per cent Y.

2* Mr. Moroley has just finished reading a textbook about portfolio theory and he is keen to put his new-found knowledge into action with respect to savings of £1000 he wishes to invest. He has identified the efficient frontier for portfolios of risky assets according to the following table.

Portfolio	Expected return (%)	Standard deviation (%)
A	4	5
B	6	4
C	8	5
D	10	8
E	10.6	11
F	11	14

He has also estimated that the redemption yield on short-dated Treasury bills is 7 per cent and has identified the shape of a typical utility curve given his own attitude towards risk. Points that plot on this utility curve are as follows.

Expected return (%)	Standard deviation (%)
8.8	1
9.0	3
9.5	5
10.2	6
11.2	7

Using this information, construct an appropriate diagram that enables you to identify how Mr. Moroley will split his investment between Treasury bills and the market portfolio.

3 Loring plc has paid the following dividends in recent years:

Year	2002	2003	2004	2005	2006
Dividend per share	64p	nil	7p	69p	75p

The dividend for 2006 has just been paid. The risk-free rate of return is 6 per cent and the market rate of return is 15 per cent.

(a) If Loring plc has an equity beta of 1.203, what will be the market price of one of its shares?

(b) Discuss the meaning of the term 'equity beta' and explain how the equity beta of a public limited company may be determined.

4* Critically discuss whether the CAPM makes portfolio theory redundant.

5 You have the following information about the returns for the securities of Super Lux plc and the returns for the market:

Time	Return of Super Lux (%)	Return of the market (%)
t_1	18	10
t_2	21	11
t_3	20	8
t_4	25	12
t_5	26	14

Given that the rate of return on Treasury bills is 8 per cent and that the correlation coefficient between the security and the market is +0.83, calculate the required rate of return on Super Lux's shares using the CAPM.

References

Allan, D., Day, R., Hirst, I. and Kwiatowski, J. (1986) 'Equity, gilts, treasury bills and inflation', *Investment Analyst*, Vol. 83, pp. 11–18.

Black, F. (1993) 'Beta and returns', *Journal of Portfolio Management*, Vol. 20, pp. 8–18.

Black, F., Jensen, M. and Scholes, M. (1972) 'The capital asset pricing model: some empirical tests', in Jensen, Frederick A. (ed.) *Studies in the Theory of Capital Markets*, New York: Praeger.

Dimson, E. and Brealey, R. (1978) 'The risk premium on UK equities', *Investment Analyst*, Vol. 52, pp. 14–18.

Dimson, E., Marsh P. and Staunton, M. (2002) *Triumph of the Optimists: 101 Years of Global Investment Returns*, Princetown, NJ, and Oxford: Princetown University Press.

Fama, E. and French, K. (1992), 'The cross-section of expected stock returns', *Journal of Finance*, Vol. 47, pp. 427–65.

Fama, E. and Macbeth, J. (1973) 'Risk, return and equilibrium: empirical tests', *Journal of Political Economy*, Vol. 81, May/June, pp. 607–36.

Ibbotson Associates (2003) *Stocks, Bonds, Bills, and Inflation Yearbook: Valuation Edition*, Chicago: Ibbotson Associates.

Jacob, N. (1971) 'The measurement of systematic risk for securities and portfolios: some empirical results', *Journal of Financial and Quantitative Analysis*, Vol. 6, pp. 815–33.

Jenkinson, T. (1994) 'The equity risk premium and the cost of capital debate in the UK regulated utilities', University of Oxford, mimeo.

Markowitz, H. (1952) 'Portfolio selection', *Journal of Finance*, Vol. 7, pp. 13–37.

Roll, R. (1977) 'A critique of the asset pricing theory's tests, part 1: on past and potential testability of the theory', *Journal of Financial Economics*, Vol. 4, pp. 129–76.

Ross, S. (1976) 'The arbitrage theory of capital asset pricing', *Journal of Economic Theory*, Vol. 13, pp. 341–60.

Sharpe, W. (1964) 'Capital asset prices: a theory of market equilibrium under conditions of risk', *Journal of Finance*, Vol. 19, pp. 768–83.

Sharpe, W. and Cooper, G. (1972) 'Risk–return classes of New York Stock Exchange common stocks 1931–67', *Financial Analysts Journal*, Vol. 28, pp. 46–54.

Solnik, B. (1974) 'Why not diversify internationally rather than domestically?', *Financial Analysts Journal*, Vol. 30, July/August, pp. 48–54.

Tobin, J. (1958) 'Liquidity preference as behaviour towards risk', *Review of Economic Studies*, February, 26, pp. 65–86.

Recommended reading

For an in-depth account of risk and return, portfolio theory and the CAPM see:

Arnold, G. (2005) *Corporate Financial Management*, 3rd edn, Harlow: FT Prentice Hall, chapters 7 and 8.

For one of the most definitive accounts of portfolio theory, the CAPM and their application see:

Elton, E., Gruber, M., Brown, S. and Goetzmann, W. (2003) *Modern Portfolio Theory and Investment Analysis*, 6th edn, New York: Wiley.

The following book includes a number of very readable and interesting articles, including both Markowitz's and Sharpe's seminal articles and an excellent overview article of the CAPM by Mullins:

Ward, K. (ed.) (1994) *Strategic Issues in Finance*, Oxford: Butterworth-Heinemann.

The next publication gives an interesting overview of the CAPM and the challenges associated with its use. It also considers Fama and French's enhanced CAPM, which includes variables to allow for the effect of small companies and firms with low book-to-market equity values:

Davies, R., Unni, S., Draper, P. and Paudyal, K. (1999) *The Cost of Equity Capital*, London: CIMA Publishing, chapters 2–4.

Important and informative papers, reports and articles recommended for further reading include the following:

Appleyard, A. and Strong, N. (1989) 'Beta geared and ungeared: the case of active debt management', *Accounting and Business Research*, Vol. 19, No. 74, pp. 170–74.

Barclays Capital (2005) *Barclays Capital Equity Gilt Study: 50th Edition*, London: Barclays Capital.

Dimson, E. (1998) 'Capital budgeting: a beta way to do it', in *Mastering Finance*, London: FT Pitman, pp. 17–23.

Dimson, E., Marsh, P. and Staunton, M. (2003) 'Global evidence on the equity risk premium', *Journal of Applied Corporate Finance*, Vol. 15, No. 4, pp. 27–38.

Fielding, J. (1989) 'Is beta better?' *Management Accounting*, November, pp. 38–40.

Gregory, A. (1990) 'The usefulness of beta in the investment-appraisal process', *Management Accounting*, January, pp. 42–3.

Chapter 9

The cost of capital
and capital structure

Learning objectives

After studying this chapter, you should have achieved the following learning objectives:

- a firm understanding of how to calculate a company's cost of capital and how to apply it appropriately in the investment appraisal process;

- the ability to calculate the costs of different sources of finance used by a company and to calculate the weighted average cost of capital of a company;

- an appreciation of why, when calculating the weighted average cost of capital, it is better to use market values than book values;

- an understanding of how the capital asset pricing model can be used to calculate risk-adjusted discount rates for use in investment appraisal;

- the ability to discuss critically whether or not a company can, by adopting a particular capital structure, influence its cost of capital.

Introduction

The concept of the cost of capital, which is the rate of return required on invested funds, plays an important role in corporate finance theory and practice. A company's cost of capital is (or could be) used as the discount rate in the investment appraisal process when using techniques such as net present value and internal rate of return. If we assume that a company is rational, it will seek to raise capital by the cheapest and most efficient methods, thereby minimising its average cost of capital. This will have the effect of increasing the net present value of the company's projects and hence its market value. For a company to try to minimise its average cost of capital, it first requires information on the costs associated with the different sources of finance available to it. Second, it needs to know how to combine these different sources of finance in order to reach its optimal capital structure.

The importance of a company's capital structure, like the importance of dividend policy, has been the subject of heated academic debate. As with dividends, Miller and Modigliani argued, somewhat against the grain of academic thought at the time, that a company's capital structure was irrelevant in determining its average cost of capital. They later revised their views to take account of the tax implications of debt finance. If market imperfections are also considered, it can be argued that capital structure does have relevance to the average cost of capital. In practice, calculating a company's cost of capital can be extremely difficult and time-consuming; it is also difficult to identify or prove that a given company has an optimal financing mix.

9.1 Calculating the cost of individual sources of finance

A company's overall or weighted average cost of capital can be used as a *discount rate* in investment appraisal and as a *benchmark* for company performance, so being able to calculate it is a key skill in corporate finance. The first step in calculating the weighted average cost of capital (WACC) is to find the cost of capital of each source of *long-term* finance used by a company. That is the purpose of this section.

9.1.1 Ordinary shares

Equity finance can be raised either by issuing new ordinary shares or by using retained earnings. We can find the cost of equity (K_e) by rearranging the dividend growth model which is considered later in the book in Section 10.4.3:

$$K_e = \frac{D_0(1 + g)}{P_0} + g$$

where: K_e = cost of equity
D_0 = current dividend or dividend to be paid shortly
g = expected annual growth rate in dividends
P_0 = ex dividend share price

Retained earnings have a cost of capital equal to the cost of equity. A common misconception is to see retained earnings as a source of finance with no cost. It is true that retained earnings do not have servicing costs, but they do have an *opportunity cost* equal to the cost of equity since if these funds were returned to shareholders they could have achieved a return equivalent to the cost of equity through personal reinvestment.

An alternative and arguably more reliable method of calculating the cost of equity is to use the *capital asset pricing model* (CAPM), considered earlier in Chapter 8. The CAPM allows shareholders to determine their required rate of return, based on the risk-free rate of return plus an equity risk premium. The *equity risk premium* reflects both the systematic risk of the company and the excess return generated by the market relative to risk-free investments.

Using the CAPM, the cost of equity finance is given by the following linear relationship:

$$R_j = R_f + [\beta_j \times (R_m - R_f)]$$

where: R_j = the rate of return of security j predicted by the model
         R_f = the risk-free rate of return
         β_j = the beta coefficient of security j
         R_m = the return of the market

9.1.2 Preference shares

Calculating the cost of preference shares is usually easier than calculating the cost of ordinary shares. This is because the dividends paid on preference shares are usually constant. Preference shares are, generally speaking, irredeemable and preference dividends are not tax-deductible since they are a distribution of after-tax profits. The cost of irredeemable preference shares (K_{ps}) can be calculated by dividing the dividend payable by the ex dividend market price as follows:

$$K_{ps} = \frac{\text{Dividend payable}}{\text{Market price (ex dividend)}}$$

When calculating the cost of raising new preference shares, the above expression can be modified, as can the dividend growth model, to take issue costs into account.

9.1.3 Debentures, loan stock and convertibles

There are three major types of bonds: irredeemable bonds, redeemable bonds and convertible bonds. The cost of irredeemable bonds is calculated in a similar way to that of irredeemable preference shares. In both cases, the model being used is one that values a perpetual stream of cash flows (a perpetuity). Since the interest payments made on irredeemable bonds are tax-deductible, it will have both a before- and an after-tax cost of debt. The *before-tax* cost of irredeemable bonds (K_{id}) can be calculated as follows:

$$K_{id} = \frac{\text{Interest rate payable}}{\text{Market price of bond}}$$

The *after-tax* cost of debt is then easily obtained if the corporation taxation rate (C_T) is assumed to be constant:

$$K_{id} \text{ (after tax)} = K_{id}(1 - C_T)$$

To find the cost of redeemable bonds we need to find the overall return required by providers of debt finance, which combines both revenue (interest) and capital (principal) returns. This is equivalent to the *internal rate of return* (K_d) of the following valuation model:

$$P_0 = \frac{I(1 - C_T)}{(1 + K_d)} + \frac{I(1 - C_T)}{(1 + K_d)^2} + \frac{I(1 - C_T)}{(1 + K_d)^3} + \cdots + \frac{I(1 - C_T) + RV}{(1 + K_d)^n}$$

where: P_0 = current market price of bond
I = annual interest payment
C_T = corporation taxation rate
RV = redemption value
K_d = cost of debt after tax
n = number of years to redemption

Note that this equation will give us the after-tax cost of debt. If the before-tax cost is required, I and not $I(1 - C_T)$ should be used. Interpolation can be used to estimate K_d (*see* Section 6.4).

Alternatively, instead of using interpolation, K_d can be estimated using the bond yield approximation model developed by Hawawini and Vora (1982):

$$K_d = \frac{I + \left[\dfrac{P - NPD}{n}\right]}{P + 0.6(NPD - P)}$$

where: I = annual interest payment
P = par value or face value
NPD = net proceeds from disposal (market price of bond)
n = number of years to redemption

The after-tax cost of debt can be found using the company taxation rate (C_T):

$$K_d \text{ (after tax)} = K_d(1 - C_T)$$

The cost of capital of convertible debt is more difficult to calculate. To find its cost we must first determine whether conversion is likely to occur (*see* Section 5.7). If conversion is *not* expected, we ignore the conversion value and treat the bond as redeemable debt, finding its cost of capital using the linear interpolation or bond approximation methods described above.

If conversion *is* expected, we find the cost of capital of convertible debt using linear interpolation and a *modified* version of the redeemable bond valuation model given earlier. We modify the valuation model by replacing the number of years to redemption (n) with the number of years to conversion, and replacing the redemption value (RV) with the expected future conversion value (CV) (*see* Section 5.7.2).

It must noted that an *after-tax* cost of debt is appropriate only if the company is in a profitable position, i.e. it has taxable profits against which to set its interest payments.

9.1.4 Bank borrowings

The sources of finance considered so far have all been in tradable security form and have a market price to which interest and dividend payments can be related in order to calculate their cost. This is not the case with bank borrowings, which are not in tradable security form and which do not have a market value. To approximate the cost of bank borrowings, therefore, the *average* interest rate paid on the loan should be taken, making an appropriate adjustment to allow for the tax-deductibility of interest payments. The average interest rate can be found by dividing the interest paid on bank borrowings by the average amount of bank borrowings for the year. Alternatively, the cost of debt of any bonds or traded debt issued by a company can be used as an approximate value for the cost of debt of bank borrowings.

9.1.5 The relationship between the costs of different sources of finance

When calculating the costs of the different sources of finance used by a company, a logical relationship should emerge between the *cost* of each source of finance on the one hand and the *risk* faced by each supplier of finance on the other. Equity finance represents the highest level of risk faced by investors. This is due both to the *uncertainty* surrounding dividend payments and capital gains, and to the *ranking* of ordinary shares at the bottom of the creditor hierarchy should a company go into liquidation. New equity issues therefore represent the most expensive source of finance, with retained earnings working out slightly cheaper owing to the savings on issue costs over a new equity issue.

The cost of preference shares will be less than the cost of ordinary shares for two reasons. First, preference dividends must be paid before ordinary dividends, hence there is less risk of their not being paid. Second, preference shares rank higher in the creditor hierarchy than ordinary shares and so there is less risk of failing to receive a share of liquidation proceeds.

There is no uncertainty with respect to interest payments on debt, unless a company is likely to be declared bankrupt. Debt is further up the creditor hierarchy than both preference shares and ordinary shares, implying that debt finance has a lower cost of capital than both. Whether bank borrowings are cheaper than bonds will depend on the relative costs of obtaining a bank loan and issuing bonds, on the amount of debt being raised, and on the extent and quality of security used. Generally speaking, the longer the period over which debt is raised, the higher will be its cost: this is because lenders require higher rewards for giving up their purchasing power for longer periods of time. The cost of convertible debt depends on when and whether the debt is expected to convert into ordinary shares. If convertible debt is *not* expected to convert, its cost will be similar to the cost of redeemable bonds of a similar maturity. If convertible debt *is* expected to convert, its cost will be between that of redeemable bonds and ordinary shares. The longer the time period before conversion, the closer will be the cost of convertible debt to that of redeemable bonds.

The relationships discussed above are evident in the example of a WACC calculation given in Section 9.2.

9.2 Calculating the weighted average cost of capital

Once the costs of a company's individual sources of finance have been found, the overall weighted average cost of capital (WACC) can be calculated. In order to calculate the WACC, the costs of the individual sources of finance are weighted according to their relative importance as sources of finance. The WACC can be calculated either for the existing capital structure (average basis) or for additional incremental finance (marginal basis). The problem of average versus marginal basis WACC is discussed in Section 9.3.

The WACC calculation for a company financed solely by debt and equity finance is represented by:

$$\text{WACC} = \frac{K_e \times E}{(D + E)} + \frac{K_d(1 - C_T) \times D}{(D + E)}$$

where: K_e = cost of equity
E = value of equity
K_d = before-tax cost of debt
C_T = corporation taxation rate
D = value of debt

This equation will expand in proportion to the number of different sources of finance used by a company. For instance, for a company using ordinary shares, preference shares and both redeemable and irredeemable bonds, the equation will become:

$$\text{WACC} = \frac{K_e \times E}{E + P + D_i + D_r} + \frac{K_{ps} \times P}{E + P + D_i + D_r} + \frac{K_{id}(1 - C_T)D_i}{E + P + D_i + D_r} + \frac{K_{rd}(1 - C_T)D_r}{E + P + D_i + D_r}$$

where P, D_i and D_r are the value of preference shares, irredeemable bonds and redeemable bonds, respectively.

9.2.1 Market value weightings or book value weightings?

We now need to determine the weightings to be attached to the different costs of finance. The weightings allow the calculated average to reflect the relative proportions of capital used by a company. We must choose between book values or market values. Book values are easily obtained from a company's accounts whereas market values can be obtained from the financial press and from a range of financial databases.

While book values are easy to obtain, using them to calculate the WACC cannot be recommended. Book values are based on historical costs and rarely reflect the current required return of providers of finance, whether equity or debt. The nominal value of an ordinary share, for example, is usually only a fraction of its market value. In the following example, an ordinary share with a nominal value of 25p has a market value of £1.76. Using book values will therefore seriously understate the impact of the cost of equity finance on the average cost of capital. Since the cost of equity is *always* greater than the cost of debt, this will lead to the WACC being underestimated. This can clearly be seen in the following example by comparing the WACC calculated using market values with the WACC calculated using book values. If the WACC is underestimated, unprofitable projects will be accepted.

Example	Calculation of the weighted average cost of capital

Strummer plc is currently trying to calculate its weighted average cost of capital. As the company's finance director, you have been asked to perform the necessary calculations, using both book values and market values. You have the following information:

Balance sheet as at 31 December

	£000
Fixed assets	445
Current assets	185
Current liabilities	(110)
11% bonds (redeemable in 5 years)	(80)
10% irredeemable bonds	(95)
Bank loans	(60)
	285
Ordinary shares (25p par value)	90
9% preference shares (£1 par value)	50
Reserves	145
	285

1 The current dividend, shortly to be paid, is 20p per share. Dividends in the future are expected to grow at a rate of 5 per cent per year.
2 Corporation tax currently stands at 30 per cent.
3 The interest rate on bank borrowings currently stands at 12.6 per cent.
4 Stock market prices as at 31 December (all ex-dividend or ex-interest):

Ordinary shares:	£1.76
Preference shares:	67p
11% bond:	£95 per £100 bond
10% irredeemable bond:	£72 per £100 bond

→

Step one: Calculate the costs of the individual sources of finance

1 *Cost of equity*: using the dividend growth model:

$$K_e = [D_0(1 + g)/P_0] + g$$
$$= [20 \times (1 + 0.05)/176] + 0.05$$
$$= 16.9\%$$

2 *Cost of preference shares*:

$$K_{ps} = 9/67 = 13.4\%$$

3 *Cost of redeemable bonds (after tax)*: using the Hawawini–Vora bond yield approximation model:

$$K_{rd} = \frac{11 + \left(\dfrac{100 - 95}{5}\right)}{100 + 0.6(95 - 100)}$$

$$K_{rd} = 12.4\%$$

$$K_{rd}(\text{after tax}) = 12.4 \times (1 - 0.30) = 8.7\%$$

4 *Cost of irredeemable bonds (after tax)*:

$$K_{id} = 10 \times (1 - 0.30)/72 = 9.7\%$$

5 *Cost of bank loans (after tax)*:

$$K_{bl} = 12.6 \times (1 - 0.30) = 8.8\%$$

Step two: Calculate the book and market values of the individual sources of finance

Source of finance	Book value (£000)	Market value (£000)
Equity	90 + 145 = 235	90 × ④ × 1.76 = 633.6
Preference shares	50	50 × 0.67 = 33.5
Redeemable bonds	80	80 × 95/100 = 76.0
Irredeemable bonds	95	95 × 72/100 = 68.4
Bank loans	60	60.0
Total	520	871.5

Step three: Calculate the WACC using both book values and market values

$$\text{WACC (book values)}: = (16.9\% \times 235/520) + (13.4\% \times 50/520)$$
$$+ (8.7\% \times 80/520) + (9.7\% \times 95/520)$$
$$+ (8.8\% \times 60/520)$$
$$= 13.1\%$$

$$\text{WACC (market values)}: = (16.9\% \times 633.6/871.5) + (13.4\% \times 33.5/871.5)$$
$$+ (8.7\% \times 76/871.5) + (9.7\% \times 68.4/871.5)$$
$$+ (8.8\% \times 60/871.5)$$
$$= 14.9\%$$

9.3 Average and marginal cost of capital

As mentioned earlier, the cost of capital can be calculated in two ways. If it is calculated on an average basis using balance sheet data and book values or market values as weightings, as in the above example, it represents the *average cost of capital* currently employed. This cost of capital represents historical financial decisions. If it is calculated as the cost of the next increment of capital raised by a company, it represents the *marginal cost of capital*. The relationship between average (AC) cost of capital and marginal (MC) cost of capital is shown in Exhibit 9.1.

The relationship between the average cost and marginal cost curves can be explained as follows. When the marginal cost is less than the average cost of capital, the average cost of capital will fall. Once the marginal cost rises above the average cost of capital, however, the marginal cost of capital will pull up the average cost of capital, albeit at a slower rate than that at which the marginal cost is rising.

Should we use the marginal or the average cost of capital when appraising investment projects? Strictly speaking, the marginal cost of capital raised to finance a project should be used rather than an average cost of capital. One problem with calculating the marginal cost of capital, however, is that it is often difficult to allocate particular funding to a specific project. Furthermore, companies which have a target capital structure will often raise marginal finance by utilising only one source of finance at a time. For example, suppose that a company aims to finance itself equally with equity and debt. If the company requires £10m, it might prefer to raise this as debt finance, incurring one issue fee, rather than split the finance equally between debt and equity. The next year, the company can raise £10m of equity finance to restore its desired financing mix. The problem here is that the marginal cost of capital will fluctuate from a low level when marginal debt financing is used to a high level when marginal equity financing is used. It could be argued therefore that a *rolling average* marginal cost of capital is more appropriate than an *incremental* marginal cost of capital.

 Exhibit 9.1 **The marginal cost and average cost of capital**

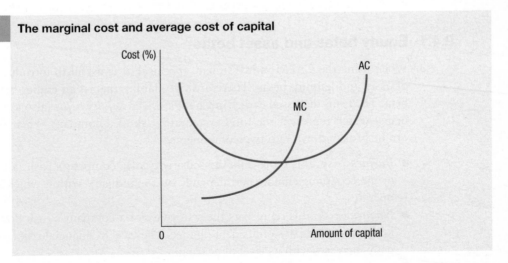

Using an average cost of capital as the discount rate in investment appraisal is appropriate only if several restrictive assumptions are satisfied. These restrictive assumptions are:

■ the business risk of an investment project is similar to the business risk of the company's current activities;
■ incremental finance is raised in proportions which preserve the existing capital structure of the company;
■ the incremental investment project does not disturb the existing risk/return relationships between providers of finance, whether by synergy, scale economies or other effects.

If these restrictive assumptions are *not* satisfied, a cost of capital calculated on a marginal basis may be more appropriate. Any effect on the existing average cost structure must also be reflected in the marginal cost of capital.

9.4 The CAPM and investment appraisal

In Chapter 8 we discussed using the CAPM in security valuation and saw that the model can be used by investors to calculate the required return on a security. For shareholders, this required return is the company's cost of equity finance and it can therefore be used in calculating a company's weighted average cost of capital (WACC). The WACC calculated using a CAPM-derived cost of equity finance can be used as the required rate of return for a company's investment projects. However, the CAPM can also be used to find a required rate of return which *directly* reflects the risk of a *specific* project.

In practice the business risk of new investment projects *rarely* mirrors the business risk of the company's current activities. Using the CAPM in the investment appraisal process is especially useful when a company is evaluating a project which has significantly different risk characteristics to those of the company as a whole. The CAPM will lead to better investment decisions, because it takes into account the risk of the project, than the company's existing WACC, which ignores project risk.

9.4.1 Equity betas and asset betas

When using the CAPM in investment appraisal, it is useful to introduce the concept of asset and liability betas. There are two liability betas: an equity beta and a debt beta. The betas discussed earlier in Chapter 8 were *equity betas* (also known as geared betas) which represent the total systematic risk of a company. This systematic risk can be broken down into two components:

■ *Business risk*: this represents the sensitivity of a company's cash flows to changes in the economic climate and depends on the industry within which the company operates.
■ *Financial risk*: this represents the sensitivity of a company's cash flows to changes in the interest it pays on its debt finance. The level of financial risk faced by a company increases with its level of gearing.

Both types of risk are reflected in a company's equity beta. The *asset beta* or *ungeared beta*, however, reflects only a company's business risk. A company's asset beta is the weighted average of the asset betas of a company's individual projects. For example, a company with only two projects, both equal in value, one with an asset beta of 1.2 and the other with an asset beta of 0.8, will have an overall company asset beta of 1.

A company's asset beta is also the weighted average of its liability betas, weighted to reflect the market values of its liabilities, whether debt or equity finance. This is represented by the following equation:

$$\beta_a = \left[\beta_e \times \frac{E}{E + D(1 - C_T)} \right] + \left[\beta_d \times \frac{D(1 - C_T)}{E + D(1 - C_T)} \right]$$

where: β_a = asset or ungeared beta
β_e = equity or geared beta
E = market value of equity
D = market value of debt
C_T = corporate tax rate
β_d = debt beta

We can see from this equation that a company's equity beta will always be greater than its asset beta, unless of course a company is all-equity financed, in which case its equity beta is equal to its asset beta. If we assume that companies do not default on their interest payments we can take the beta of debt to be zero. The last term of the equation therefore disappears to leave the following equation (the ungearing formula):

$$\beta_a = \beta_e \times \frac{E}{E + D(1 - C_T)}$$

Rearranging gives the following alternative equation (the regearing formula):

$$\beta_e = \beta_a \times \frac{E + D(1 - C_T)}{E}$$

9.4.2 Using the CAPM to calculate a project's hurdle rate

Using the CAPM in investment appraisal is very similar to using it in security valuation. Once again only the systematic risk of a project is relevant since shareholders of the company are assumed to have diversified portfolios. In order to use the CAPM to find a discount rate to use in investment appraisal, we need estimates of the risk-free rate and the equity risk premium (*see* Section 8.6.2.) and, in addition, the *beta of the project*. It is the last of these three components which is the most difficult to find. We now outline the steps involved in using the CAPM to derive a discount rate for using in investment appraisal.

1 Identify quoted companies engaged mainly or entirely in the same type of business operation as the project under appraisal. These companies will have similar systematic

risk characteristics to the project and so their equity betas can be used as suitable surrogates or *proxies* for the project beta.

2 Once the proxy companies and their equity betas have been identified, these betas must be adjusted to eliminate gearing effects (i.e. financial risk) and hence give proxy *asset* betas. This is because the proxy companies' gearing will be different from the gearing of the appraising company and is therefore not relevant. The formula to *ungear* an equity beta was given earlier.

3 The next step is either to calculate an average of the proxy asset betas or to select the proxy asset beta considered most appropriate. This beta must then be *regeared* to reflect the financial risk of the appraising company. The formula to regear an asset beta was given earlier in Section 9.4.1.

4 The *regeared equity beta* will now reflect the *business risk* of the project and the *financial risk* of the appraising company. This beta can now be inserted into the CAPM to yield a required rate of return which reflects the project's systematic risk.

The required rate of return on equity calculated by this method is an appropriate discount rate for appraising the new project if financing is wholly from retained earnings or from a new equity issue. If the project is financed by a mixture of debt and equity, however, the required rate of return on equity will need to be combined with the cost of new debt finance to give a *project-specific* weighted average cost of capital.

9.4.3 The benefits of using the CAPM instead of the WACC

We suggested earlier that using the CAPM in project appraisal would lead to better investment decisions. This is illustrated in Exhibit 9.2.

Consider two projects, A and B, where X marks the plot of their expected level of return and level of systematic risk as measured by beta. Project A would be rejected using the WACC since its expected return to less than the company's WACC. However, using the CAPM, which takes into account the low-risk nature of the project, Project A

 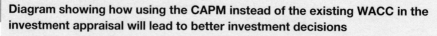

Exhibit 9.2 **Diagram showing how using the CAPM instead of the existing WACC in the investment appraisal will lead to better investment decisions**

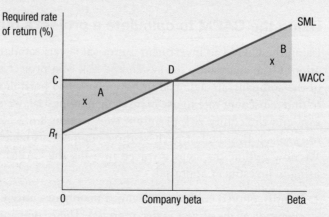

would be accepted since it is above the Security Market Line. The opposite is true of Project B. This would be accepted using the WACC but rejected using the CAPM. Therefore using the CAPM, which takes account of the systematic risk of projects, leads to better investment decisions in two areas:

■ the area shaded in pink, where we find low-risk, low-return projects, previously rejected using the WACC, but which will now be accepted;

■ the area shaded in blue, where we find high-risk, high-return projects, previously accepted using WACC, but which will now be rejected.

9.4.4 Problems using the CAPM in investment appraisal

While the CAPM leads to better investment decisions, there are many practical problems associated with using it in investment appraisal, as follows:

■ the CAPM's general assumptions are not applicable to the real world and hence may undermine the applicability of the model;

■ the problem of identifying suitable surrogate companies with similar levels of systematic risk to the project under consideration. Companies often undertake a diversified range of activities rather than undertaking only the activity specific to the project being appraised;

■ companies may have difficulty identifying relevant capital structure data with which to ungear surrogate companies' equity betas;

■ the CAPM assumes that transactions take place over a single period of time, which is usually taken to be no more than a year.

Clearly, the last point represents a difficulty as investments span multiple time periods. Two problems arise. First, equity betas calculated using historical data may not be appropriate for making future decisions, as they often exhibit instability over long time periods. This problem can be reduced by taking the betas of a number of surrogate companies and averaging them (*see* Section 9.4.2, step 3). Second, using the yield of short-dated government securities to approximate the risk-free rate of return will no longer be appropriate. The rate used will need to be tailored to the duration of the project under consideration. For example, if the project spans five years, the yield on gilts maturing in five years could be used to approximate the risk-free rate of return.

Example **The CAPM in the investment appraisal process**

Arclight plc, a company involved in producing high-quality household lighting products, is considering diversifying into the furniture business. The new venture has an expected return of 15 per cent. Arclight plc will use the CAPM to establish an appropriate discount rate to apply to the new venture and has the following information about suitable proxy companies.

Furnisure plc

This company has an equity beta of 1.23 and is wholly involved in furniture making. It is financed 35 per cent by debt and 65 per cent by equity.

Home Furnish plc

This company has an equity beta of 1.27 and is also wholly involved in furniture making. It is financed 40 per cent by debt and 60 per by cent equity.

Lux Interior plc

This company has an equity beta of 1.46 and is financed 30 per cent by debt and 70 per cent by equity. It is split into two divisions of equal size: one division produces furniture and the other produces luxury wallpaper. The wallpaper division is seen as 50 per cent more risky than the furniture division.

Other information

- Arclight plc has traditionally adopted a financing mix of 33 per cent debt and 67 per cent equity, although the project, if accepted, will be financed entirely by equity.
- The current yield on Treasury bills stands at 4 per cent and the return on the stock market is 10 per cent.
- The corporation tax rate is 30 per cent for all companies.
- Corporate debt can be assumed to be risk-free.

Using the above information, calculate an appropriate discount rate to apply to the new venture and decide whether it should be accepted.

Suggested answer

1 Extract the appropriate asset betas by ungearing the proxy companies' equity betas using the equation:

$$\beta_a = \beta_e \times \left[\frac{E}{E + D(1 - C_T)} \right]$$

Furnisure plc

$$\beta_a = 1.23 \times 65/(65 + 35 \times (1 - 0.30)) = 0.89$$

Home Furnish plc

$$\beta_a = 1.27 \times 60/(60 + 40 \times (1 - 0.30)) = 0.87$$

Lux Interior plc

$$\beta_a = 1.46 \times 70/(70 + 30 \times (1 - 0.30)) = 1.12$$

We have to make a further calculation here as Lux Interior's asset beta partly reflects the business risk of its wallpaper division, which is of no relevance to the project under consideration. Since the wallpaper division is 50 per cent more risky than the furniture division, its asset beta is 1.5 times the asset beta of the furniture division. We can find the asset beta of its furniture division (β_{af}) as follows:

Lux Interior asset beta = (0.5 × Wallpaper asset beta) + (0.5 × Furniture asset beta)

$$1.12 = (0.5 \times 1.5 \times \beta_{af}) + (0.5 \times \beta_{af})$$

Hence:

$$\beta_{af} = 1.12/1.25 = 0.90$$

2 Take an average of the three asset betas:

Proxy asset beta = (0.89 + 0.87 + 0.90)/3 = 0.89

3 Regear the proxy asset beta to reflect Arclight's financial risk using the equation:

$$\beta_e = \beta_a \times \left[\frac{E + D(1 - C_T)}{E}\right]$$

Proxy equity beta = 0.89 × (67 + 33 × (1 − 0.30))/67 = 1.20

4 Insert the proxy equity beta into the CAPM to calculate the discount rate:

$$R_j = 0.04 + 1.20 \times (0.10 - 0.04) = 0.112, \text{ i.e. } 11.2\%$$

The expected rate of return of the project (15 per cent) is greater than the discount rate (11.2 per cent) and so Arclight plc should accept the project.

9.5 Practical problems with calculating WACC

In addition to the problem of deciding whether an average or a marginal cost of capital is appropriate, there are a number of practical difficulties in calculating and using a company's WACC.

9.5.1 Calculating the cost of sources of finance

Calculating the cost of a particular source of finance is not always straightforward. For example, certain securities may not be traded regularly and therefore do not have a market price. This is particularly true for the ordinary shares of private companies. One way to overcome this problem is to calculate the cost of equity for a listed company in a similar line of business and then add a premium to reflect the higher level of risk of the private company. A similar problem may be experienced with obtaining the market value of bonds, even when the issuing company is listed. One solution is to find the market value of a bond issued by another company, with similar maturity, risk and interest rate, and use this market value as a substitute or proxy.

The cost of convertible bonds can be very difficult to calculate owing to their complex nature. Convertible bonds start life as debt and so initially have a cost of capital in line with ordinary bonds of a similar coupon and maturity. Later in their life, however, they are likely to convert into ordinary shares and hence have an equity-related cost of capital. If convertible bonds are likely to convert in the near future, the current market value will reflect the value of the ordinary shares to be gained on conversion and not redemption value: this current market value should not be used to calculate the cost of the convertible debt based on the assumption that redemption will occur as this will understate the cost of debt of ordinary bonds.

Leasing can also provide problems when we wish to calculate the average cost of capital. Many leases provide finance on a medium- to long-term basis and therefore should be included in average cost of capital calculations. While it may be relatively easy to identify the lease payments, which should be taken after tax due to their tax deductibility, the capital value to which these payments should be related is more difficult to determine. As leasing is seen as an alternative to debt finance, however, it may be appropriate to treat the cost of leasing as similar to that of secured debt finance given that leases are secured on the leased assets.

Another complication with respect to the cost of sources of finance relates to debt where interest payments are subject to swap agreements (see Section 12.6.1). The main issue here is whether the cost of the debt should reflect the interest rate when the loan was first raised or the interest rate agreed in the swap. There is no clear answer to this problem.

Finally, the accuracy of the calculated cost of equity depends heavily on the reliability and applicability of the models used. For example, if a company increases its dividends at a very low but constant rate, perhaps as a result of a low payout ratio, the cost of equity calculated by the dividend growth model is likely to be greatly understated. Alternatively, if a company's beta is unstable and unreliable, the cost of equity calculated using the capital asset pricing model will also be unstable and unreliable. The authors recommend using the CAPM for calculating the cost of equity, not only because it is more theoretically sound than the dividend growth model, but also because it does not depend on estimating the dividend growth rate of a company. It is very difficult to predict a dividend growth rate for an individual company with any real credibility.

9.5.2 Which sources of finance should be included in the WACC?

A major issue is which sources of finance should be included in the weighted average cost of capital calculation and which should not. The rule of thumb is that, if finance is being used to fund the long-term investments of a company, it should be included in the calculation. Equity finance, preference shares, medium- and long-term debt and leasing should all therefore be included. Generally speaking, short-term trade debt should not be included in the WACC calculation as it is connected with the financing of short-term rather than long-term assets. However, if a short-term source of finance, for example, a bank overdraft, is used on an ongoing basis, it can be argued that it is being used to finance long-term assets and hence *should* be included in the WACC calculation.

9.5.3 Problems associated with weighting the sources

Difficulties in finding the market values of securities will also have an impact on cost of capital through the weightings that are applied to the costs of the different sources of finance. Market values are preferred to book values, as discussed in Section 9.2.1. However, market values may be hard to find or, in the case of bank loans, may simply not exist. In practice, therefore, both market values and book values are used as weightings when calculating the weighted average cost of capital.

Additional problems will be experienced by companies that have raised debt finance denominated in foreign currencies. The values of these debts will have to be translated into sterling in order to include them in the WACC calculation. Two problems arise here. First, at which exchange rate should they be converted into sterling? Second, as exchange rates move, the sterling value of the weightings will also move.

9.5.4 WACC is not constant

The weighted average cost of capital is not static. As the market values of securities change, so will a company's average cost of capital. Not only will weightings change, but the costs of the different sources of finance will also change as macroeconomic conditions and the preferences and attitudes of investors change. It is therefore both advisable and necessary for companies to recalculate their cost of capital frequently in order to reflect such changes. We usually assume that the WACC is constant in future periods in investment appraisal, but this is clearly not true: while the assumption makes calculations easier, we should be aware that it is one of the reasons why investment appraisal is an imperfect mirror of the real world.

One thing that should be apparent from this section is that the weighted average cost of capital is in practice both hard to calculate and difficult to apply to the investment appraisal process. The application of WACC in the real world is the subject of the next section.

9.6 WACC in the real world

Given the difficulties and problems associated with calculating the weighted average cost of capital, do companies calculate their WACC in practice? Increasingly, the answer to this question is yes. Whereas few companies include cost of capital calculations in their financial statements, more and more attention is being paid to the value of WACC due to its close association with concepts such as economic value added (EVA© – *see* Section 2.4.10), an overall measure of company performance linked to shareholder wealth.

In recent years, WACC has also received attention from national regulatory bodies such as the UK Competition Commission (*see* Section 11.6.1) and industry-specific regulatory bodies such as Oftel and Ofgem, the regulators of the UK telecommunications, and UK gas and electricity-generating industries respectively. WACC is increasingly used in the regulatory process to help determine what is considered to be a 'fair' level of profit. Predictably, this has led to many companies claiming that the cost of capital calculated by a regulatory body underestimates their true cost of capital. In 1998 the Competition Commission (or Monopolies and Mergers Commission as it was then called) investigated the price of calls to mobile telephones. It estimated Vodaphone's nominal before-tax WACC to be between 14.9 and 17.8 per cent, whereas Vodafone estimated it to be 18.5 per cent. Given the subjectivity surrounding many of the key variables used in calculating the WACC, these differences should not be surprising. To their credit, UK regulatory bodies and the Office of Fair Trading jointly commissioned an independent report, published in February 2003 (*see* Wright et al. 2003) which sought to establish the best and most consistent approach to determining the cost of capital for regulated utility companies.

An extensive sector-by-sector survey of US companies' costs of capital by Damodaran (2005) found an average nominal after-tax WACC of 7.91 per cent using a sample of 7091 companies. Unsurprisingly, utility companies were found to have the lowest WACC, with natural gas distributors providing the lowest sector average (5.5 per cent). It was also not surprising that, given their high business risk and low gearing, e-commerce companies were found to have the highest sector average (18.14 per cent).

9.7 Gearing: its measurement and significance

The term *gearing* in a financial context refers to the amount of debt finance a company uses relative to its equity finance. A company with a high level of debt finance relative to equity finance is referred to as highly geared, and vice versa. The term *leverage* is used interchangeably with gearing, more often in the USA. The gearing of a company can be measured using a number of financial ratios. These include:

- debt/equity ratio (long-term debt/shareholders' funds);
- capital gearing ratio (long-term debt/capital employed).

The debt/equity ratio and the capital gearing ratio are both examples of balance sheet gearing ratios, as opposed to income gearing ratios such as interest cover (*see* Section 2.4.6). It is possible to include short-term debt as well as long-term debt when calculating balance sheet gearing ratios, especially if it is an overdraft which persists from year to year. As with the WACC, both the debt/equity ratio and capital gearing ratio can be calculated using market values and book values. It is often argued that book values should be used rather than market values since book values are less volatile. The problem, though, is that in most cases book values for securities, especially ordinary shares, are significantly different from their true or market value. As with the calculation of WACC, market values (rather than book values) are considered to be both more appropriate and useful when calculating gearing ratios.

The nature of the industry within which a particular company operates is a major factor in determining what the market considers to be an appropriate level of gearing. Industries with lower levels of business risk, such as utilities, typically have higher levels of gearing than industries associated with high levels of business risk, such as

Exhibit 9.3	Selected UK industrial sectors' capital gearing ratios (defined as preference shares plus short- and long-term debt/total capital employed plus short-term debt)

Industrial sector	Capital gearing ratio (%)
Transport (passenger)	70
Construction	56
Hotels	53
Food producers	52
Transport (road freight)	47
Pharmaceuticals	46
Retailers	44
Gas distribution	32
Engineering and contractors	32
Clothing	31

Source: FAME, published by Bureau van Dijk Electronic Publishing.

retailers of luxury goods. The difference in average gearing levels between industries is apparent in Exhibit 9.3. It must be appreciated, however, that gearing levels within a particular industry are not static, but change in response to changing economic conditions. A good example of this was the trend, up until the late 1990s, for firms in the energy and water sectors to gear up after their privatisation in the early 1990s.

When discussing the significance of gearing, it is usual to focus on the implications of high gearing rather than low gearing. The implications of high gearing are described below.

9.7.1 Increased volatility of equity returns

The higher a company's level of gearing, the more sensitive its profitability and earnings are to changes in interest rates. This sensitivity will be accentuated if the company has most of its debt based on floating interest rates.

If a company is partly financed by debt, its profits and distributable earnings will be at risk from increases in the interest rate charged on the company's debt. This risk will be borne by shareholders (and not debt holders) as the company may have to reduce dividend payments in order to meet its interest payments as they fall due. This kind of risk is referred to as financial risk. The more debt a company has in its capital structure, the higher will be its *financial risk*.

9.7.2 Increased possibility of bankruptcy

At very high levels of gearing, shareholders will start to face *bankruptcy risk*. This is defined as the risk of a company failing to meet its interest payment commitments and hence putting the company into liquidation. Interest payments may become unsustainable if profits decrease or interest payments on variable rate debt increase. From the shareholders' point of view, bankruptcy risk is the risk that they might lose the value of their initial investment owing to the position they occupy in the hierarchy of creditors. Debt holders face bankruptcy risk too, but, as we shall see later on in the chapter, at a much reduced level.

9.7.3 Reduced credibility on the stock exchange

Because of the extensive information requirements accompanying a stock exchange listing it is relatively straightforward for investors to calculate a company's level of gearing. Investors who have made this calculation may feel a company has too high a level of gearing, resulting in what they see as an unacceptable level of financial risk or bankruptcy risk. They will be reluctant to buy the company's shares or to offer it further debt; this reluctance to finance the company is a loss of *financial credibility* that will exert downward pressure on its share price.

9.7.4 The encouragement of short-termist behaviour

If a company has a high level of gearing its primary financial objective may shift from that of shareholder wealth maximisation to that of generating enough cash flow to meet its interest commitments and thereby staving off possible bankruptcy. Managers

Vignette 9.1

Leeds defends Woodgate sale

Managers at Leeds United, the debt-laden Premiership football club, yesterday defended their unpopular decision to sell Jonathan Woodgate, one of the team's star players, saying it was for the long-term stability of the club. Peter Ridsdale, chairman, said the decision to sell Woodgate to Premiership rivals Newcastle United for £9m was 'the only [one] that could have been taken to give us all peace of mind for the future. Woodgate was a player we did not want to sell,' he said. 'We are, however, a public company. An offer of £9m is significant when your company is valued at £15m on the stock exchange.'

Leeds has been paying the price for an ambitious but expensive push to establish itself as one of the best sides in Europe. But two consecutive failures to qualify for the UEFA Champions League have left it with unsustainably high overheads. The result was a pre-tax loss of £33.9m in the latest financial year. This all but wiped out shareholders' funds, which stood at £1.4m on June 30, against net debt of £77.9m.

Mr Ridsdale yesterday put the cost of two seasons without Champions League football at about £30m. He said, however, that the club was now 'on a financially sound footing assuming we are not in the Champions League'. The club also offloaded

Robbie Fowler, another England star, this week for £6m. It had earlier sold controversial midfielder Lee Bowyer to West Ham and loaned Olivier Dacourt to Roma of Italy. In the summer, it sold Rio Ferdinand to Manchester United for £30m – more than double its present market capitalisation – and Robbie Keane to Tottenham Hotspur.

Meanwhile uncertainty surrounds the futures of both Mr Ridsdale and Terry Venables, the club's manager. Mr Venables appeared yesterday to be veering towards a decision to stay. The future of his chairman, however, may depend on his ability to persuade fans that the disposals really are in the club's best interests.

Source: David Owen, FT.com, 1 February 2003. Reprinted with permission.

therefore focus on the short-term need to meet interest payments rather than the longer-term objective of wealth maximisation: this behaviour is termed short-termist or *short-termism*.

The difficulties associated with the combination of excessive levels of debt finance and the uncertainty of income streams, and a consequent need to sell off company assets at less than market price to rectify these difficulties, are the subject of Vignette 9.1.

9.8 The concept of an optimal capital structure

Earlier in the chapter we looked at how a company can determine its average cost of capital by calculating the costs of the various sources of finance it uses and weighting them according to their relative importance. The market value of a company clearly depends on its weighted average cost of capital. The lower a company's WACC, the higher the net present value of its future cash flows and therefore the higher its market value.

One issue that we have not considered so far is whether financing decisions can have an effect on investment decisions and thereby affect the value of the company. Put another way, will the way in which a company finances its assets (i.e. how much debt a company uses relative to equity) affect the company's average cost of capital and hence the company's value? If an optimum financing mix exists (i.e. one that gives a minimum WACC), then it would be in a company's best interests to locate it and move towards this *optimal capital structure*. There has been a large amount of academic discussion on the subject of whether or not an optimal capital structure exists for individual companies. Before we go on to discuss the differing views on capital structure, we shall first consider the factors that determine the rate of return required by shareholders and debt holders.

9.8.1 Gearing and the required rate of return

The rate of return required by shareholders and debt holders on their investments reflects the risk they face. Consequently the required rate of return of shareholders will *always* be higher than that of debt holders since shareholders face higher levels of risk. We shall now consider in detail the factors that determine the shape of the cost of debt curve and the cost of equity curve faced by a company, i.e. the relationship between these costs of capital and the level of gearing.

Let us consider first the cost of equity curve. Exhibit 9.4 summarises the factors that determine the shareholders' required rate of return. As a minimum, shareholders require the *risk-free rate of return*, which can be approximated by the yield on short-dated government debt (Treasury bills). In addition to this, shareholders require a *premium for business risk*, which is the risk associated with a company's profits and earnings varying due to systematic influences on that company's business sector. The level of business risk faced by shareholders will clearly vary from company to company and so therefore will the required premium. The combination of the risk-free rate and the business risk premium represents the cost of equity of a company financed entirely by equity.

As a company starts to gear up by taking on debt finance, its distributable profits will be reduced by the interest payments it is required to make, although this reduction

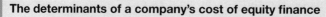

The determinants of a company's cost of equity finance

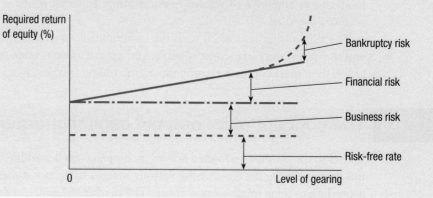

in profitability is lessened by the tax shield on debt. Any volatility in operating profits will be accentuated by the need to meet interest payments since these payments represent an additional cost. Further volatility in distributable profits arises if some or all of the interest payments are on floating rate rather than fixed rate debt since the size of such payments will be determined by prevailing market interest rates. The volatility of distributable profits arising from the need to meet interest payments, which is called *financial risk*, will get progressively higher as a company's gearing level increases. Shareholders require a premium for facing financial risk and this premium increases with the level of a company's gearing.

Finally, at very high levels of gearing, the possibility of the company going into liquidation increases due to its potential inability to meet interest payments. At high levels of gearing, shareholders require compensation for facing *bankruptcy risk* in addition to compensation for facing financial risk, resulting in a steeper slope for the cost of equity curve.

Turning to the cost of debt curve, we note that the situation of debt holders is different from that of shareholders. The returns of debt holders are fixed in the sense that they do not vary with changes in a company's profit level. By definition, therefore, debt holders do not face financial risk. They do, however, face bankruptcy risk at very high levels of gearing, but they face a lower level of bankruptcy risk than shareholders since debt holders have a preferential position in the creditor hierarchy and are able to secure debts against corporate assets.

9.9 The traditional approach to capital structure

The first view of capital structure we are going to consider is usually called the traditional approach. This view or model, like those that follow it, relies on a number of simplifying assumptions which are:

- no taxes exist, either at a personal or a corporate level;
- companies have two choices of finance: perpetual debt finance or ordinary equity shares;

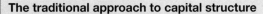

Exhibit 9.5	The traditional approach to capital structure

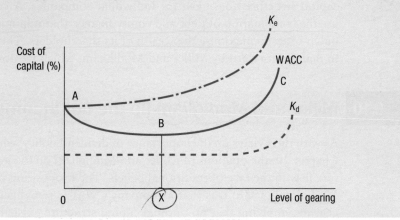

- companies can change their capital structure without issue or redemption costs;
- any increase in debt finance is accompanied by a simultaneous decrease in equity finance of the same amount;
- companies pay out all distributable earnings as dividends;
- the business risk associated with a company is constant over time;
- companies' earnings and hence dividends do not grow over time.

The proposition of the traditional approach to capital structure is that an optimal capital structure does exist and that a company can therefore increase its total value by the sensible use of debt finance within its capital structure. The traditional approach is illustrated in Exhibit 9.5.

Exhibit 9.5 can be explained as follows. The cost of equity curve (K_e) rises with increased gearing due to the increasing level of financial risk being faced by shareholders. The curve rises at a steeper rate at high gearing levels due to the risk of bankruptcy threatening the value of shareholders' investments. The cost of debt curve (K_d) will rise only at high levels of gearing, where bankruptcy risk threatens the value of debt holders' investments. A company financed entirely by equity will be located at point A in Exhibit 9.5. As a company starts to replace more expensive equity with cheaper debt finance, shareholders are initially indifferent to the introduction of a small amount of financial risk: their response to increasing financial risk is not a linear one. The WACC of the company will fall initially due to the benefit of the cheaper debt finance outweighing any increase in the cost of the company's remaining equity finance. Hence the company's WACC will fall to B, to give an optimal capital structure represented by the point X. If the company continues to gear up, increasing its gearing past X, the benefits associated with using cheaper debt finance are outweighed by the increase in the cost of the company's remaining equity finance. The company's WACC curve will therefore start to rise. At very high levels of gearing, bankruptcy risk causes the cost of equity curve to rise at a steeper rate and also causes the cost of debt to start to rise. At very high levels of gearing, therefore, the company's WACC curve will rise at an even faster rate.

The conclusion of the traditional approach to capital structure is that an optimal capital structure *does* exist for individual companies. A company should therefore use the combination of debt and equity finance that minimises its overall cost of capital in order to maximise the wealth of its shareholders. This view is in sharp contrast to that put forward by Miller and Modigliani, which we now consider.

9.10   Miller and Modigliani (I): the net income approach

As with their views on the importance of dividend policy, which are considered later in Chapter 10, the opinions of Miller and Modigliani on the importance of capital structure flew in the face of traditional beliefs. The proposition put forward by Miller and Modigliani (1958) was that a company's WACC remains unchanged at all levels of gearing, implying that no optimal capital structure exists for a particular company. They argued that the market value of a company depends on its expected performance and commercial risk: the market value of a company and its cost of capital are independent of its capital structure. They came to this conclusion using a model based on the assumptions outlined in the previous section, but added the extra assumption that capital markets were perfect. The assumption that capital markets are perfect was central to their model as it implies that bankruptcy risk could be ignored. Companies in financial distress could always raise additional finance in a perfect capital market. A diagrammatic representation of their model is shown in Exhibit 9.6.

The relationship between the curves in Exhibit 9.6 can be explained as follows. The cost of equity curve (K_e) increases at a constant rate in order to reflect the higher financial risk faced by shareholders at higher levels of gearing: there is a *linear relationship* between the cost of equity and financial risk (level of gearing). As debt holders do not face bankruptcy risk, the cost of debt curve (K_d) is horizontal and the cost of debt does not increase at high levels of gearing: the cost of debt is *independent* of the level of gearing. A company financed entirely by equity is represented by point A in Exhibit 9.6. As the company gears up by replacing equity with an equivalent amount of debt, the benefit of using an increased level of cheaper debt finance is

Exhibit 9.6   Miller and Modigliani's net operating income approach to capital structure

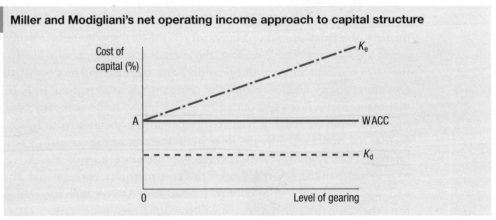

exactly offset by the increasing cost of the company's equity finance. The company's WACC therefore remains constant and, since its net income or earnings is constant, so is its market value. Miller and Modigliani therefore state that the WACC of a geared company is identical to the cost of equity the company would have if it were financed entirely by equity. This cost of equity is determined by the risk-free rate of return and the business risk of the company; it is independent of financial risk (level of gearing).

Miller and Modigliani supported their argument that capital structure was irrelevant in determining the market value and average cost of capital of a company by using arbitrage theory.

9.10.1 The arbitrage approach to capital structure

Arbitrage theory states that goods which are perfect substitutes for each other should not sell at different prices in the same market. Applying this to companies, Miller and Modigliani argued that two companies identical in every way except for their gearing levels should have *identical average costs of capital* and hence should not have different market values. This argument is best illustrated with an example.

Example | **Arbitrage process using two companies**

Two companies, A and B, are identical in every respect but one. Both companies have similar net operating incomes (i.e. gross income less operating expenses) and levels of business risk. The only difference is that Company A is not geared, whereas Company B is partly financed by £3000 of debt with an interest rate of 5 per cent. Financial data for the two companies are as follows:

	Company A	Company B
Net operating income (£)	1 000	1 000
Interest on debt (5% × £3000)	nil	150
Earnings available to shareholders (£)	1 000	850
Cost of equity	10%	11%
Market value of equity (£)	10 000	7 727
Market value of debt (£)	nil	3 000
Total value of company (£)	10 000	10 727
WACC	10%	9.3%

Note: market value of equity = earnings/cost of equity, e.g. 850/0.11 = £7 727

Company B has a higher cost of equity but a lower overall WACC and a higher market value. This is consistent with the traditional view of capital structure. Miller and Modigliani, however, would argue that, since the two companies have the same business risk and net operating income, they must have the same market values and WACC. Since this is not the case, they would consider Company A to be undervalued and Company B to be overvalued, and that arbitrage will cause the values of the two →

companies to converge. Using Miller and Modigliani's assumptions, which imply that companies and individuals can borrow at the same rate, we can illustrate how an investor can make a profit by exploiting the incorrect valuations of the two companies.

If a 'rational' investor owned 1 per cent of the equity of the geared firm, Company B, i.e. £77.27, he could:

- sell his shares in Company B for £77.27;
- borrow £30 at 5 per cent. Here the investor emulates Company B's level of financial risk by making his personal gearing equal to the company's gearing (30/77.27 = 3000/7727);
- buy 1 per cent of the shares in Company A (the ungeared firm) for £100 thus leaving a surplus of £7.27.

If we compare the investor's income streams, we have the following results:

Original situation

Return from Company B shares = 11% × 77.27 = £8.50

New situation

Return from Company A shares	= 10% × £100 =	£10.00
Less: Interest on debt	= 5% × £30 =	(£1.50)
Net return		£8.50

We see that by selling shares in Company B and buying shares in Company A, the investor obtains the same annual income and generates a surplus of £7.27. This risk-free surplus of £7.27 is called an *arbitrage profit*. A rational investor would repeat this process until the opportunity to create a profit disappears. The consequence of this repetition would be the following sequence of events:

- Company B's share price will fall due to pressure to sell its shares.
- Since returns to its shareholders remain the same, its cost of equity will rise.
- Since its cost of equity increases, its WACC will increase.

For Company A the opposite would happen. This process of *arbitrage* would stop when the companies' WACCs were equal.

There are, however, serious flaws in Miller and Modigliani's arbitrage argument, owing mainly to the unrealistic nature of their assumptions. First, the assumption that individuals can borrow at the same rate as companies can be challenged. The costs of personal debt and corporate debt cannot be the same, because companies have a higher credit rating than the majority of individuals. Personal borrowing is therefore seen as riskier, and hence more costly, than corporate borrowing. Second, their assumption that there are no transaction costs associated with the buying and selling of shares is clearly untrue. Higher personal borrowing rates and transaction costs both undermine the ability of investors to make risk-free profits from arbitrage, therefore creating the possibility of identical companies being overvalued and undervalued. Miller and

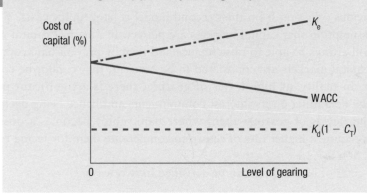

| Exhibit 9.7 | Miller and Modigliani (II), incorporating corporate taxation |

Modigliani (1958) acknowledged the rather unrealistic nature of their assumptions in their paper, stating that: 'These and other drastic simplifications have been necessary in order to come to grips with the problem at all. Having served their purpose they can now be relaxed in the direction of greater realism and relevance.'

Another simplification made by Miller and Modigliani was to ignore the existence of taxation. They amended their model to take into account corporation tax in a later paper, which is the subject of the next section.

9.11 Miller and Modigliani (II): corporate tax

In their second paper on capital structure, Miller and Modigliani (1963) amended their earlier model by recognising the existence of corporate tax. Their acknowledgement of the existence of corporate tax and the tax deductibility of interest payments implies that, as a company gears up by replacing equity with debt, it shields more and more of its profits from corporate tax. The tax advantage enjoyed by debt finance over equity finance means that a company's WACC decreases as gearing increases; this suggests that the optimal capital structure for a company is 100 per cent debt finance. This is illustrated in Exhibit 9.7. The cost of debt curve (K_d) from Miller and Modigliani's first model shifts downwards to reflect the lower after-tax cost of debt finance ($K_d(1 - C_T)$). As a company gears up its WACC curve now falls.

9.12 Market imperfections

There is clearly a problem with the model proposed in Miller and Modigliani's second paper since in practice companies do not adopt an all-debt capital structure. This indicates the existence of factors which *undermine* the tax advantages of debt finance and which Miller and Modigliani failed to take into account. These factors are now considered.

9.12.1 Bankruptcy costs

The obvious omission from their second model is bankruptcy costs. This stems from their assumption that capital markets are perfect. In a perfect capital market, a company will always be able to raise finance and thereby prevent bankruptcy. In practice, while capital markets are considered to be efficient, they cannot be considered to be perfect. In reality, at high levels of gearing, there is a significant possibility of a company defaulting on its interest commitments and hence being declared bankrupt. At higher levels of gearing, then, where bankruptcy becomes a possibility, shareholders require a higher rate of return to compensate them for facing bankruptcy risk (*see* Section 9.7.2).

The costs of bankruptcy can be classified in two ways:

■ *Direct bankruptcy costs*: includes the costs of paying lenders higher rates of interest to compensate them for higher risk and, if forced into liquidation, the cost of employing lawyers and accountants to manage the liquidation process.
■ *Indirect bankruptcy costs*: includes loss of sales and goodwill as a consequence of operating the company at extreme levels of financial distress and, if forced into liquidation, the cost of having to sell assets at below their market value.

If we now combine the tax shield advantage of increasing gearing with the bankruptcy costs associated with very high levels of gearing (in effect Miller and Modigliani's 1963 view modified to take into account bankruptcy risk) we again see an optimal capital structure emerging. This is illustrated in Exhibit 9.8.

Exhibit 9.8 can be explained in the following manner. As a company financed entirely by equity increases its gearing by replacing equity with debt, its market value increases due to the increasing value of its tax shield. This is given by the vertical distance between the dotted line DA and the line DC. Bankruptcy becomes a possibility when the gearing level increases beyond X and consequently the company's cost of equity starts to rise more steeply to compensate shareholders for facing bankruptcy

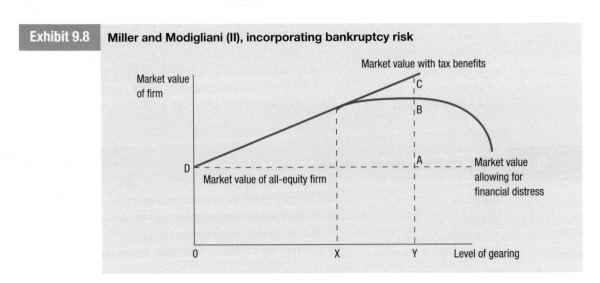

Exhibit 9.8   **Miller and Modigliani (II), incorporating bankruptcy risk**

risk, eating into the benefit of the tax shield. Beyond gearing level Y the marginal benefit of the tax shield is outweighed by the marginal increase in the cost of equity due to higher bankruptcy risk. An optimal gearing level therefore exists at gearing level Y where:

AC = value of the tax shield
BC = cost of bankruptcy risk
AB = net benefit of the geared company.

Gearing levels beyond Y will increase the value of the tax shield but this is more than cancelled out by increasing bankruptcy costs, leading to a decline in the value of the company.

While there is little doubt about the existence of bankruptcy costs at high gearing levels, the size of such costs and the level of gearing at which they become relevant (indicated by point X in Exhibit 9.8.) are less clear. Very little research has been done in the area of bankruptcy costs. Baxter (1967) made a study of individual and small US company liquidations, and found bankruptcy costs to be of sufficient magnitude to warrant consideration. Warner (1977) considered the bankruptcy of large public limited companies and found that direct bankruptcy costs were insignificant. Research by Altman (1984) into the bankruptcy of industrial companies found that the combined direct and indirect costs at the time of filing for bankruptcy averaged 16.7 per cent of a company's value. More recently Andrade and Kaplan (1998) estimated the combined effect of both economic and financial stress led to an average loss of 38 per cent of company value, based on 31 highly geared US companies over the period 1980–89. Financial distress accounted for 12 per cent of the total loss of value. These figures are clearly significant, even after allowing for the probability of bankruptcy occurring and its time of occurrence.

9.12.2 Agency costs

At higher levels of gearing, in addition to bankruptcy costs, there are costs associated with the problem of agency. If gearing levels are high, shareholders have a lower stake in a company and have fewer funds at risk if the company fails. They will therefore prefer the company to invest in high-risk/high-return projects since they will enjoy the benefit of the higher returns that arise. Providers of debt finance, however, will not share in the higher returns from such high-risk projects since their returns are not dependent on company performance. Hence they will take steps to prevent the company from undertaking high-risk projects which might put their investment at risk. They may, for example, impose restrictive covenants on the management (*see* Section 5.1.1). Such covenants could restrict future dividend payments, place restrictions on ways of raising finance or impose minimum levels of liquidity. Alternatively, debt holders may increase the level of management monitoring and require a higher level of financial information with respect to the company's activities. These agency costs will eat further into the tax shield benefits associated with increasing gearing levels.

9.12.3 Tax exhaustion

Another explanation of why companies fail to adopt higher levels of gearing is that many companies have insufficient profits from which to derive all available tax benefits as they increase their gearing level (often referred to as being in a 'tax-exhaustive' position). This will prevent them from enjoying the tax shield benefits associated with high gearing, but still leave them liable to incur bankruptcy costs and agency costs.

The existence of bankruptcy costs and agency costs, and the fact that companies may become tax exhausted at high gearing levels, explain why companies do not adopt 100 per cent debt capital structures, in contradiction to Miller and Modigliani's second paper.

9.13 Miller and personal taxation

Although Miller and Modigliani amended their earlier paper to take into account the effects of corporate taxation in 1963, it was left to Miller (1977) to integrate the effects of personal taxes into their model. Miller's complex model considers the relationship between gearing levels, corporate taxation, the rate of personal taxation on debt and equity returns, and the amount of debt and equity available for investors to invest in. The following explanation represents a simplification of his model.

Investors will choose investments in companies that suit their personal taxation situation, taking into account a company's capital structure and the amount of debt finance and equity finance that it and other companies have issued. For example, investors who pay income tax will be inclined to invest in equity rather than debt, due to the capital gains tax allowance associated with ordinary shares and the later payment date of capital gains tax compared with income tax. When the economy is in equilibrium, therefore, all investors will be holding investments that suit their personal tax situation.

In order for a company to increase its debt finance and take advantage of the associated tax benefits, it will have to persuade equity holders to swap ordinary shares for debt securities. Because this will involve investors moving to a less favourable personal tax position, they will have to be 'bribed' by the company through a higher, more attractive interest rate on the new debt. According to Miller's model, this higher interest rate will cancel out the tax benefits of the additional debt, leaving the average cost of capital unchanged. The result is a horizontal WACC curve similar to that in Miller and Modigliani's first model (*see* Exhibit 9.6). As with both Miller and Modigliani's previous models, Miller's 1977 paper did not take into account bankruptcy risk. If his model is modified to take into account the bankruptcy costs which exist at high levels of gearing, we arrive at the WACC curve illustrated in Exhibit 9.9.

Miller's paper was applicable to the tax regime prevalent in the USA during the 1970s. Since then the US tax regime has changed so that, as in the UK, there is now only a small difference in the personal tax treatment of debt and equity returns. This implies that introducing personal tax into the capital structure debate reduces, but does not eradicate, the corporate tax savings associated with an increase in gearing level.

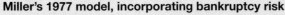

Exhibit 9.9 | **Miller's 1977 model, incorporating bankruptcy risk**

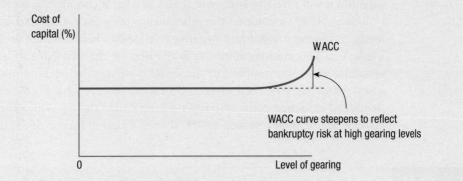

9.14 Pecking order theory

Pecking order theory (Donaldson 1961) goes against the idea of companies having a unique combination of debt and equity finance which minimises their cost of capital. The theory suggests that when a company is looking at financing its long-term investments, it has a well-defined order of preference with respect to the sources of finance available to it. Its first preference is to use internal finance or retained earnings rather than external sources of finance. If internal finance proves insufficient, bank borrowings and corporate bonds are the preferred source of external source of finance. After exhausting both of these possibilities, the final and least preferred source of finance is issuing new equity capital.

The initial explanation of these preferences involves issue costs and the ease with which sources of finance are accessed. Retained earnings are readily accessible, have no issue costs and do not involve dealing or negotiating with third parties such as banks. As for the choice between debt and equity finance, the cost of issuing new debt is much smaller than the cost of issuing new equity; it is also possible to raise small amounts of debt, whereas it is not usually possible to raise small amounts of equity. Additionally the issue of debt avoids the potential ownership issues associated with the issue of new equity.

A more sophisticated explanation for the existence of a pecking order was put forward by Myers (1984). He suggested that the order of preference stemmed from the existence of asymmetry of information between the company and the capital markets. For example, suppose that a company wants to raise finance for a new project and the capital market has underestimated the benefit of the project. The company's managers, with their inside information, will be aware that the market has undervalued the company. They will therefore choose to finance the project through retained earnings so that, when the market sees clearly the true value of the project, existing shareholders will benefit. If retained earnings are insufficient, managers will choose debt finance in preference to issuing new shares as they will not want to issue new shares if they are undervalued by the market. The opposite is true if the company considers the capital market to be overvaluing its shares in the light of the new project they are about to accept. In this situation it will prefer to issue new shares at what it considers to be an overvalued price.

Baskin (1989) examined the relationship between profits and companies' gearing levels and found a significant negative relationship between high profits and high gearing levels. This finding contradicts the idea of the existence of an optimal capital structure and gives support to the insights offered by pecking order theory. Subsequent evidence has been mixed. US-based research by Frank and Goyal (2003) produced evidence contradicting pecking order theory while Watson and Wilson (2002), basing their research on UK shares, found in favour of the theory.

9.15   Does an optimal capital structure exist? A conclusion

In this chapter we have shown that gearing is an important consideration for companies. Some academic theories support the existence of an optimal capital structure (i.e. the traditional approach, and Miller and Modigliani (II) with bankruptcy costs). Others argue that one capital structure is as good as another (Miller and Modigliani (I), and Miller). When considering the market imperfections that exist, such as corporate and personal taxation, and bankruptcy and agency costs, we tend towards accepting the existence of an optimal capital structure. In practice, though, it is more likely that there exists a range of capital structures with which a company can minimise its WACC (i.e. between P and Q in Exhibit 9.10) rather than one particular combination of debt and equity finance (i.e. optimal capital structure) that academic theories such as the traditional approach suggest. This implies that the WACC curve will be flatter in practice than the U-shaped curve put forward by academic theories.

In conclusion, it appears that by integrating sensible levels of debt into its capital structure a company can enjoy the tax advantages arising from debt finance and thereby reduce its weighted average cost of capital, as long as it does not increase its gearing to levels that give rise to concern among its investors about its possible bankruptcy.

 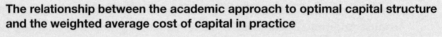

Exhibit 9.10   **The relationship between the academic approach to optimal capital structure and the weighted average cost of capital in practice**

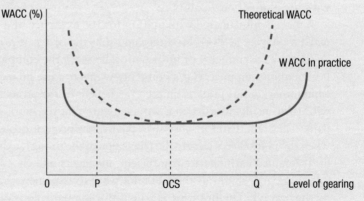

Key points

1 A company's average cost of capital is a fundamental determinant of its market value, since its cost of capital is used as the discount rate in investment appraisal methods such as net present value and internal rate of return.

2 A major determinant of a company's average cost of capital is its cost of equity, which can be calculated using either the dividend growth model or the capital asset pricing model.

3 The cost of preference shares and irredeemable bonds can be calculated by dividing the dividend or interest payment by the security's market value.

4 The cost of debt of redeemable bonds can be found by using an internal rate of return calculation or a bond approximation formula.

5 The cost of bank loans, which have no market value, is approximated by the interest rate paid on them or by the cost of debt of traded bonds.

6 If a company is in a tax-paying position, the cost of debt finance must be adjusted to take into account the tax deductibility of interest payments.

7 The costs of the individual sources of finance must be weighted according to their relative importance using either market or book values.

8 While book values are stable and easy to find, it is better to use market values as they reflect the true value of a company's securities.

9 A company can calculate its average cost of capital, representing the cost of existing finance, or its marginal cost of capital, representing the cost of incremental capital raised.

10 A company's average cost of capital is only appropriate for appraising new projects if they are financed in similar proportions to its existing capital structure and have similar levels of risk to that of the company as a whole.

11 When new projects have significantly different risk characteristics to that of the company as a whole the CAPM can be used in investment appraisal. If an appropriate project beta can be estimated, then a discount rate for appraising a project can be tailored to reflect its risk.

12 It is difficult in practice to calculate a company's WACC. Problems include dealing with the wide variety of sources of finance used by a company, the existence of complex instruments such as convertibles and the volatility of a company's cost of capital.

13 The optimal capital structure debate addresses the question of whether a company can minimise its cost of capital by adopting a particular combination of debt and equity.

14 The traditional approach to the optimal capital structure question argued that an optimal capital structure did exist for companies.

15 Miller and Modigliani's first paper argued that a company's market value depends on its expected performance and commercial risk; market value and average cost of capital are therefore independent of capital structure, as shown by arbitrage theory. Their model was academically sound, but based on a number of restrictive and unrealistic assumptions.

16 Miller and Modigliani later modified their earlier model to take account of corporate tax and argued that companies should gear up in order to take advantage of the tax shield of debt. If this later model is modified to take into account the existence of bankruptcy and agency costs at high levels of gearing, an optimal capital structure emerges.

17 Miller amended their earlier model to take into account differences in the personal tax treatment of equity and debt returns. He argued that the need to 'bribe' investors into holding more debt cancels out the tax benefits to companies of issuing extra debt, and concluded that all combinations of debt and equity finance were optimal.

18 Pecking order theory suggests that companies, rather than seeking an optimal capital structure, prefer retained earnings to external funds and prefer new debt to new equity.

19 In practice it seems plausible that companies can reduce their cost of capital by integrating sensible levels of debt finance into their balance sheet. Whether a company can accurately locate its range of optimal capital structures is open to debate.

 **Self-test questions**

Answers to these questions can be found on pages 458–60.

1 Gorky has in issue 500 000 £1 ordinary shares whose current ex-dividend market price is £1.50 per share. The company has just paid a dividend of 27p per share and dividends are expected to continue at this level for some time. If the company has no debt capital, what is its weighted average cost of capital?

2 Five years ago, Eranio plc issued 12 per cent irredeemable debentures at their par value of £100. The current market price of these debentures is £94. If the company pays corporation tax at a rate of 30 per cent, what is its current cost of debenture capital?

3 Pollock has in issue 1 million ordinary shares, par value 25p and £100 000 of 10 per cent irredeemable debentures. The current ex-dividend market price of the ordinary shares is 49p per share and the current ex-interest market price of the debentures is £72 per £100 par. The company has just paid a dividend of 9p per share and dividends are expected to continue at this level indefinitely. If the company pays corporation tax at a rate of 30 per cent, what is its weighted average cost of capital?

4 Should companies use their weighted average cost of capital as the discount rate when assessing the acceptability of new projects?

5 Explain why the asset beta of a company will always be lower than its equity beta unless the company is all-equity financed.

6 Which of the following companies is likely to have the highest equity beta?
   (a) A highly geared supermarket company
   (b) A low-geared electricity generating company
   (c) A highly geared building materials company
   (d) A low-geared retail bank
   (e) An industrial conglomerate financed entirely by equity

7 For which of the following reasons might a company considered to be risky have a lower beta factor than an equivalent company that is perceived as less risky?
   (a) The risky company has a lower financial gearing level
   (b) Inaccuracies in the estimation of beta by linear regression
   (c) The risky company has lower systematic risk but higher unsystematic risk
   (d) The risky company is larger in size
   (e) The two companies have differing asset betas

8 A firm has an equity beta of 1.30 and is currently financed by 25 per cent debt and 75 per cent equity. What will be the company's new equity beta if the company changes its financing to 33 per cent debt and 67 per cent equity? Assume corporation tax is 30 per cent.

9 A company incorporates increasing amounts of debt finance into its capital structure while leaving its operating risk unchanged. Assuming that a perfect capital market exists with no taxation, will the company's weighted average cost of capital:
   (a) fall slowly?
   (b) fall quickly?
   (c) remain the same?
   (d) fall to a minimum and then rise?
   (e) rise steadily?

10 One-third of the total market value of Johnson plc consists of loan stock with a cost of 10 per cent. York plc is identical in every respect to Johnson except that its capital structure is all equity and its cost of equity is 16 per cent. According to Modigliani and Miller, if we ignored taxation and tax relief on debt capital, what would be the cost of equity of Johnson plc?

11 Which of the following statements concerning capital structure is *not* correct?
   (a) Bankruptcy risk is ignored in Miller and Modigliani's first model.
   (b) Debt holders are not subject to the effects of financial risk.

(c) The traditional approach assumes that capital markets are perfect.

(d) Miller and Modigliani's second paper takes into account the effects of corporate taxation.

(e) Miller and Modigliani's first paper argues that no optimal capital structure exists and supports this proposition with arbitrage theory.

12 If a company finds that its cost of capital has changed, does this affect the company's profitability?

13 Briefly explain the traditional view of capital structure.

14 What is the significance of the arbitrage proof for Miller and Modigliani's first paper on capital structure?

Questions for review

Answers to these questions can be found on pages 460–2. Questions with an asterisk (*) are at an intermediate level.

1 Calet plc, which pays corporation tax at 30 per cent, has the following capital structure:

- *Ordinary shares*: 1 000 000 ordinary shares of nominal value 25p per share. The market value of the shares is 49p per share. A dividend of 7p per share has just been paid and dividends are expected to grow by 8 per cent per year for the foreseeable future.

- *Preference shares*: 250 000 preference shares of nominal value 50p per share. The market value of the shares is 32p per share and the annual net dividend of 7.5 per cent has just been paid.

- *Debentures*: £100 000 of irredeemable debentures with a market price of £92 per £100 par. These debentures have a coupon rate of 10 per cent and the annual interest payment has just been made.

Calculate the weighted average after-tax cost of capital of Calet plc.

2 Smith plc has the following capital structure:

	£000
Ordinary shares, 50p each	4 000
16% debentures	9 000
	13 000

The current share price of Smith plc is £3.50 per share and the current market price of the debentures is £112 per £100 par.

Calculate the capital gearing of Smith plc based on (a) market values, and (b) book values, and discuss why a market-based estimate of capital gearing is generally considered to be superior.

3* Icicle Works plc is a frozen food packaging company that intends to diversify into electronics. The project has a return of 18 per cent and Icicle Works is trying to decide whether it should be accepted. To help it decide it is going to use the CAPM to find a proxy beta for the project and has the following information on three electronics companies:

(a) *Supertronic plc*
    This company has an equity beta of 1.33 and is financed by 50 per cent debt and 50 per cent equity.

(b) *Electroland plc*
    This company has an equity beta of 1.30, but it has just bought a non-electronics company with an asset beta of 1.4 that accounts for 20 per cent of the company's value. The company is financed by 40 per cent debt and 60 per cent equity.

(c) *Transelectro plc*
    This company has an equity beta of 1.05 and is financed by 35 per cent debt and 65 per cent equity.

Assume that all debt is risk-free and that corporation tax is at a rate of 30 per cent. Icicle Works plc is financed by 30 per cent debt and 70 per cent equity. The risk-free rate of return is 10 per cent and the return on the market portfolio is 14 per cent. Should the company accept the project?

4* Carbon and Short plc both operate in the same industry with the same business risk. Their earnings, capital structure, share prices and other data are as follows:

	Carbon plc £000	Short plc £000
Annual operating income	500	1000
Annual interest	nil	200
Annual cash flow	500	1200
Equity market value	3125	6000
Debt market value	nil	2000
Total market value	3125	8000
Cost of equity capital	16%	16.6%
Cost of debt capital		10%
WACC	16%	15%
No. of shares in issue	3.25m	5m
Market price per share	96p	120p

Kitson holds £1000 worth of shares in Short and can borrow at the same rate as Short. Show how Kitson can increase his wealth through arbitrage. Ignore taxes and transaction costs.

5 Paisley Brothers plc, a company producing loud paisley shirts, has net operating income of £2000 and is faced with three options of how to structure its debt and equity:

(a) to issue no debt and pay shareholders a return of 9 per cent;

(b) to borrow £5000 at 3 per cent and pay shareholders an increased return of 10 per cent;

(c) to borrow £9000 at 6 per cent and pay a 13 per cent return to shareholders.

Assuming no taxation and a 100 per cent payout ratio, determine which financing option maximises the market value of the company.

6 The calculation of the WACC is straightforward in theory, but difficult in practice. Outline any possible difficulties that might be experienced when trying to calculate the WACC.

7 Discuss problems that may be encountered in applying the CAPM in investment appraisal.

Questions for discussion

Questions with an asterisk (*) are at an advanced level.

1 You are given the following information about Jordan plc:

Balance sheet at January 20X0

	£000	£000
Fixed assets		1511
Current assets	672	
Current liabilities	323	349
Total assets less current liabilities		1860
7% preference shares (£1)	300	
9% debentures (redeemable January 20X8)	650	
9% bank loans	560	1510
		350
Ordinary shares (50p)		200
Reserves		150
		350

You are also given the following information:

Yield on government Treasury bills	7%
Company equity beta	1.21
Market risk premium	9.1%
Current ex-div ordinary share price	£2.35
Current ex-div preference share price	66p
Current ex-interest debenture market value	£105
Corporation tax rate	30%

Calculate the company's WACC using market weightings.

2* The following information has been extracted from the accounts of Merlin plc:

Balance sheet as at 30 June 20XX

	Notes	£000	£000	£000
Fixed assets:				
Freehold property				712
Plant and equipment				160
				872
Current assets:				
Stocks			240	
Debtors			300	
Cash			33	
			573	
Current liabilities:				
Trade creditors		120		
Bank overdraft		200		
			320	
Net current assets				253
Total assets less current liabilities				1125
Long-term liabilities:				
12% debentures	(i)		500	
9% convertible loan stock	(ii)		250	
				750
				375
Capital and reserves:				
Ordinary shares, £1 each	(iii)			225
Reserves				150
				375

Notes

i   The 12 per cent debentures are redeemable in five years' time at par. Annual interest has just been paid. The current ex-interest market price of the debentures is £114.

ii   The 9 per cent loan stock is convertible in three years' time into 40 ordinary shares of Merlin plc per bond or in four years' time into 35 ordinary shares per bond. The current ex-interest market price of the convertible loan stock is £119.

iii The current ex-dividend market price of the ordinary shares of Merlin is £3.14. Both dividends and share price are expected to increase by 7 per cent per year for the foreseeable future.

iv   Corporation tax is at a rate of 30 per cent.

(a) Calculate the cost of debt of the straight debentures.

(b) If ordinary loan stock of a similar risk class is expected to be trading at £125 in three years' time and at £128 in four years' time, calculate the cost of debt of the convertible loan stock.

(c) If a dividend of 35p per ordinary share has just been paid, calculate the cost of equity.

(d) Calculate the weighted average after-tax cost of capital of Merlin plc.

3 Critically discuss whether you consider that companies, by integrating a sensible level of gearing into their capital structure, can minimise their weighted average cost of capital.

4* The finance director of Kingsize plc is currently reviewing the capital structure of his company. He is convinced that the company is not financing itself in a way that minimises its cost of capital (WACC). The company's financing as at 1 January 2006 is as follows:

	£000
Ordinary shares, £1 each	15 000
Reserves	10 000
7% preference shares, £1 each	10 000
10% debentures (redeemable 1 January 2013)	15 000
	50 000

Other information (as at 1 January 2006):

Ordinary share price (ex-div)	£2.65
Preference share price (ex-div)	75p
Bond price for 10% debentures	£102
Last 5 years' dividends (most recent last)	22p, 23p, 25p 27p, 29p

The finance director feels that by issuing more debt the company will be able to reduce its cost of capital. He proposes the issue of £15m of 11 per cent debentures. The debentures will be sold at a 5 per cent premium to their par value and will mature after seven years. The funds raised will be used to repurchase ordinary shares which the company will then cancel. He expects the repurchase will cause the company's share price to rise to £2.78 and the future dividend growth rate to increase by 20 per cent (in relative terms). He expects the price of the 10 per cent debentures to be unaffected, but the price of the preference shares to fall to 68p. Corporation tax stands at 30 per cent.

(a) Calculate the *current* cost of capital (WACC) for Kingsize plc.

(b) Given the proposed changes to Kingsize's capital structure, *recalculate* the company's cost of capital to reflect these changes and comment on the finance director's projections.

(c) Identify and discuss possible inaccuracies that may occur with the finance director's estimates.

References

Altman, E. (1984) 'A further empirical investigation of the bankruptcy cost question', *Journal of Finance*, Vol. 39, pp. 1067–89.

Andrade, G. and Kaplan, S. (1998) 'How costly is financial (not economic) distress? Evidence from highly leveraged transactions that became distressed', *Journal of Finance*, Vol. 53, October, pp. 1443–93.

Baskin, J.B. (1989) 'An empirical investigation of the pecking order hypothesis', *Financial Management*, Vol. 18, pp. 26–35.

Baxter, N. (1967) 'Leverage, risk of ruin and the cost of capital', *Journal of Finance*, Vol. 26, pp. 395–403.

Damodaran, A. (2005) 'The cost of capital by sector', available at http://pages.stern.nyu.edu/~adamodar/New_Home_Page/datafile/wacc.htm

Donaldson, G. (1961) *Corporate Debt Capacity*, Boston, MA: Harvard University Press.

Frank, M. and Goyal, V. (2003) 'Testing the pecking order theory of capital structure', *Journal of Financial Economics*, Vol. 67, pp. 217–48.

Hawawini, G. and Vora, A. (1982) 'Yield approximations: an historical perspective', *Journal of Finance*, Vol. 37, March, pp. 145–56.

Miller, M. (1977) 'Debt and taxes', *Journal of Finance*, Vol. 32, pp. 261–75.

Miller, M. and Modigliani, F. (1958) 'The cost of capital, corporation finance and the theory of investment', *American Economic Review*, Vol. 48, pp. 261–96.

Miller, M. and Modigliani, F. (1963) 'Taxes and the cost of capital: a correction', *American Economic Review*, Vol. 53, pp. 433–43.

Myers, S. (1984) 'The capital structure puzzle', *Journal of Finance*, Vol. 39, pp. 575–92.

Warner, J. (1977) 'Bankruptcy costs: some evidence', *Journal of Finance*, Vol. 26, pp. 337–48.

Watson, R. and Wilson, N. (2002) 'Small and medium size enterprise financing: some of the empirical implications of a pecking order', *Journal of Business Finance and Accounting*, Vol. 29 (April), pp. 557–78.

Wright, S., Mason, R. and Miles, D. (2003) 'A study into certain aspects of the cost of capital for regulated utilities in the U.K.', *Smithers and Co Ltd*, downloadable from http://www.ofgem.gov.uk/temp/ofgem/cache/cmsattach/2012_jointregscoc.pdf

Recommended reading

This text is dedicated to the subject of the cost of capital and its calculation. Useful despite being eleven years out of date.

Alexander, I. (1995) *Cost of Capital*, Oxford: Oxera Press.

Another text totally dedicated to the subject of the cost of capital. Up to date and extremely enlightening.

Armitage, S. (2005) *Cost of Capital: Intermediate Theory*, Cambridge University Press.

This text critically discusses alternative models for estimating the cost of equity, including recent developments with respect to the capital asset pricing model.

Davies, R., Unni, S., Draper, P. and Paudyal, K. (1999) *The Cost of Equity Capital*, London: CIMA Publishing.

A book in FT Prentice Hall's Corporate Financial Manual series dedicated to determining the cost of capital and including a useful interactive software package.

Johnson, H. (1999) *Determining Cost of Capital: The Key to Firm Value*, London: FT Prentice Hall.

An extensive US text focusing on the calculation and application of cost of capital.

Pratt, S. (2002) *Cost of Capital: Estimation and Applications*, 2nd edn, CPE Self-Study Examination.

These texts collect together a number of very readable and interesting articles on the capital structure debate, including (in Ward) reprints of Miller and Modigliani's two seminal papers.

Stern, J. and Chew, D. (eds) (2003) *The Revolution in Corporate Finance*, 4th edn, Malden, MA: Blackwell.

Ward, K. (ed.) (1994) *Strategic Issues in Finance*, Oxford: Butterworth-Heinemann.

Important and informative papers and articles recommended for further reading on the subject of cost of capital and capital structure include the following:

Brierley, P. and Bunn, P. (2005) 'The determination of UK corporate capital gearing', Bank of England Quarterly Bulletin, Summer, pp. 354–66.

Neish, S. (1994) 'Building the best balance sheet', *Corporate Finance*, March, pp. 26–31.

Rajan, R. and Zingales, L. (1998) 'Debt, folklore and financial structure', in *Mastering Finance*, London: FT Pitman, pp. 53–8.

Wilson, S.A. (1991) 'Industrial and commercial companies' gearing', *Bank of England Quarterly Bulletin*, May, pp. 228–33.

Chapter 10

Dividend policy

Learning objectives

The key question this chapter sets out to answer is whether or not the dividend policy adopted by a company affects its share price and hence the value of the company; this chapter also examines the factors which determine a company's dividend policy. After studying this chapter, you should have achieved the following learning objectives:

- an understanding of the arguments put forward by the 'dividend irrelevance' school;

- a general understanding of the arguments put forward by those who believe that dividends are relevant to share valuation due to their informational, liquidity and taxation implications;

- the ability to discuss the reasons why a financial manager disregards the importance of the dividend decision at his or her peril;

- an appreciation of the alternative dividend policies that companies can operate and their significance to investors;

- the ability to describe alternatives to cash dividends such as share repurchases, scrip dividends and non-pecuniary benefits.

Introduction

Traditionally, corporate finance was seen to involve two distinct areas of decision-making: the investment decision, where investment projects are evaluated and suitable projects selected; and the finance decision, where finance is raised to enable the selected projects to be implemented. The dividend decision, which considers the amount of earnings to be retained by the company and the amount to be distributed to shareholders, is closely linked to both the investment and financing decisions. For example, a company with few suitable projects should return unused earnings to shareholders via increased dividends. A company with several suitable projects that maintains high dividends will have to find finance from external sources.

In recent years, the decision on the amount of earnings to retain and the amount to pay out has become an increasingly important decision in its own right to the extent that it is now usual to talk about the three decision areas of corporate finance, as we did in Chapter 1. Managers need to take into account the views and expectations of shareholders and other providers of capital when making dividend decisions. The attitude of shareholders to changes in the level of dividend paid must be balanced against the availability and cost of internal and external sources of finance (*see* Section 2.1).

10.1 Dividends: operational and practical issues

A dividend is a cash payment made on a quarterly or semi-annual basis by a company to its shareholders. It is a distribution of after-tax profit. The majority of UK companies pay dividends semi-annually, while US companies pay them on a quarterly basis. The UK *interim dividend*, paid midway through the company's financial year (and after the publication of the interim results), tends to be smaller than the *final dividend*. The final dividend requires shareholder approval at the company's annual general meeting (AGM) and so is paid after the end of the financial year to which the annual accounts relate. The size of the interim dividend relative to the final dividend can be explained in part by the need for the company to link dividend payments with overall profitability for the period. At the end of the financial year the company is in a far better position to assess the level of dividend it can afford to pay.

The delay between the announcement of a dividend and the actual cash payment gives rise to the terms *cum dividend* and *ex dividend* when quoting share prices. When a dividend is announced, a company's share price will change. This change will reflect the market's attitude to the dividend that has just been declared. The share price will then continue to be cum dividend for a short period of time, meaning that anyone purchasing the share during this period is entitled to receive the dividend when it is paid. When the share price goes ex dividend, anyone purchasing the share on or after this date will not be entitled to the dividend payment, even though the payment has yet to be made. The entitlement to the dividend will remain with the previous owner of the share. The share price will change on the ex dividend date, falling by the value of the dividend to be paid, to reflect the intrinsic change in the value of the share. Suppose,

Exhibit 10.1 **Diagram showing the relationship between cum dividend and ex dividend share prices**

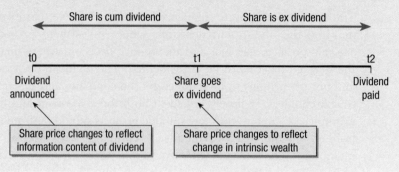

for example, that a share is currently trading at a cum dividend price of £3.45 and the recently announced dividend is 23p per share: when the share goes ex dividend, the share price will fall by 23p to £3.22.

The timings of dividend announcement and payment and the corresponding cum dividend and ex dividend periods are illustrated in Exhibits 10.1 and 10.2.

There are a number of practical constraints that companies must consider when paying dividends to shareholders. These are described below.

10.1.1 Legal constraints

Companies are bound by the Companies Act 1985 to pay dividends solely out of *accumulated net realised profits*. This includes profits that have been realised in the current

Exhibit 10.2 **Diagram showing how a company's share price changes over time. The long-term upward trend is punctuated by falls in the share price on the company's ex dividend dates**

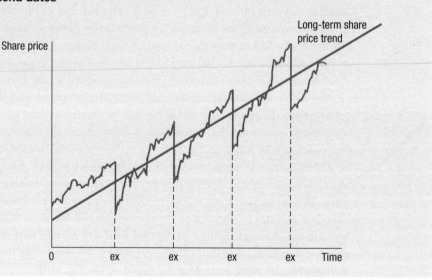

year and those that have been realised historically. The Act unfortunately fails to define clearly how accumulated net realised profit should be calculated. However, the Consultative Committee of Accountancy Bodies (CCAB) has issued guidance stating that dividends can be paid out of profit calculated using Accounting Standards after taking into account any accumulated losses.

On occasions in the past, the UK government has imposed direct restrictions on the amount of dividends that companies can pay. One example occurred in the 1960s when the Labour government, as part of its prices and incomes policy, placed restrictions on the percentage increase that companies could make on their dividend payments. These restrictions were lifted after the Conservative government came to power in 1979.

Companies must also adhere to any restrictions imposed on dividend policy by loan agreements or covenants which seek to protect the interests of the company's creditors.

10.1.2 Liquidity

Since dividends and their associated tax liabilities are cash transactions, managers need to consider carefully the effect on the company's liquidity position of any proposed dividends. A common misconception is that a company with high levels of profits can afford to pay high dividends. As stressed in Chapter 1, profit is not the same as the cash available to the company and so the amount of dividends paid must reflect not just the company's profits but also its ability to pay dividends.

10.1.3 Interest payment obligations

Dividends are paid out of profits remaining after interest and taxation liabilities have been accounted for. A company's level of gearing and its interest commitments are therefore a major constraint on its dividend policy. A highly geared company with high interest payments will have lower profits from which to pay dividends than a company with low gearing and similar overall profit levels. However, if a highly geared company has fewer issued shares than a low-geared company with similar overall profits, the highly geared company may actually pay a higher dividend per share.

10.1.4 Investment opportunities

Retained earnings are a major source of finance for UK companies. Hence, when companies are faced with a number of attractive projects, there is pressure to reduce dividends in order to finance such projects as much as possible from retained earnings. Whether a company will choose to reduce dividend payments to finance new projects will depend on a number of factors. These will include:

- the attitude of shareholders and capital markets to a reduction in dividends;
- the availability and cost of external sources of finance;
- the amount of funds required relative to the available distributable profits.

The effect of dividends on shareholder wealth

The objectives of a company's dividend policy should be consistent with the overall objective of maximisation of shareholder wealth. Therefore, a company should pay a dividend only if it leads to such an increase in wealth. A simple model for analysing dividend payments was put forward by Porterfield (1965), who suggested that paying a dividend will increase shareholder wealth only when:

$$d_1 + P_1 > P_0$$

where: d_1 = cash value of dividend paid to shareholders
P_1 = expected ex-dividend share price
P_0 = market price before the dividend was announced

It is important to consider the factors which influence these variables. For example, the value of d_1 is influenced by the marginal income tax rate of individual shareholders, while P_0 will reflect market expectations of the company's performance before the dividend is paid. P_1 will be influenced by any new information about the future prospects of the company which the market sees as being signalled by the dividend decision. Porterfield's expression is consistent with dividend relevance which is considered in Section 10.4. If the expression is modified to:

$$d_1 + P_1 = P_0$$

it implies that dividends do not affect shareholder wealth and hence are irrelevant. Dividend irrelevance is discussed in the next section.

Dividend irrelevance

The question of the effect of dividends on share prices has been a controversial one for many years. The dividend irrelevance school originated with a paper published by Miller and Modigliani (1961). They argued that share valuation is a function of the level of corporate earnings, which reflects a company's investment policy, rather than a function of the proportion of a company's earnings paid out as dividends. They further argued that, given the irrelevancy of a company's capital structure (*see* Section 9.10 earlier), investment decisions were responsible for a company's future profitability and hence the only decisions determining its market value. Miller and Modigliani conclude that share valuation is *independent* of the level of dividend paid by a company.

In order for us to fully understand the workings of their model we must first identify the assumptions upon which it was based:

- there are no transactions costs associated with converting shares into cash by selling them;
- firms can issue shares without incurring flotation or transactions costs;
- there are no taxes at either a corporate or a personal level;
- capital markets are perfectly efficient (*see* Section 2.3.1 for the required characteristics).

Miller and Modigliani pointed out that investors who are rational (i.e. they always make the choice that maximises their wealth) are indifferent to whether they receive capital gains or dividends on their shares. What does matter, however, from the perspective of maximising shareholder utility, is that a company maximises its market value by adopting an optimal investment policy.

An *optimal investment policy* requires a company to invest in all projects with a positive net present value and hence maximises the net present value of the company as a whole. Given the assumption that capital markets are perfect, capital rationing is eliminated and no longer a hindrance to such an investment policy. A company with insufficient internal funds can raise funds on the capital markets, allowing it to finance all desirable projects. Alternatively, a company already investing in all projects with positive net present values available to it and with internal funds (retained earnings) left over could pay them out as a residual dividend. A graphical representation of dividends as a *residual payment* is given in Exhibit 10.3. Here, a company is faced with six projects. Only the first three are attractive to the company, i.e. they have an internal rate of return greater than its cost of equity. The amount of investment required therefore is OA. If the company has profits OP then OA is retained and AP could be paid as a residual dividend. If the profits are only OP*, however, OP* is retained, no dividend is paid and P*A is raised as equity finance from the capital markets.

Miller and Modigliani were not arguing that dividends are a residual payment. They were arguing was that as long as a company followed its optimal investment policy, its value was completely unaffected by its dividend policy. Hence, according to Miller and Modigliani, the investment decision is separate from the dividend decision; or, more precisely, a company's choice of dividend policy, given its investment policy, is really a choice of financing strategy.

Exhibit 10.3   **Graphical representation of dividends as a residual payment**

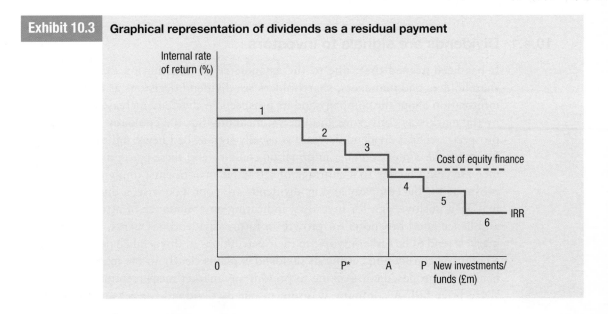

287

Miller and Modigliani also did not argue, as is often assumed, that investors were not concerned whether they received a dividend or not. Rather, they argued that shareholders were indifferent to the *timing* of dividend payments. If no dividends were paid, because all earnings had been consumed by the company's optimum investment schedule, the market value of the company would increase to reflect the expected future dividend payments or increasing share prices resulting from the investment returns. Shareholders who wanted cash when no dividend had been paid could, it was argued, generate a 'home-made' dividend by selling some of their shares.

10.4   Dividend relevance

In contrast to the theory advanced by Miller and Modigliani is the school of thought which argues that companies' dividend policies *are* relevant to their share valuations. This was the prevailing belief at the time that Miller and Modigliani published their paper, with the case for dividend relevance being put forward by Lintner (1956) and Gordon (1959). They argued that dividends are preferred to capital gains due to their certainty. This is often referred to as the *bird in the hand* argument and means that an investor will prefer to receive a certain dividend payment now rather than leaving the equivalent amount in an investment whose future value is uncertain. Current dividends, on this analysis, represent a more reliable return than future capital gains.

If dividends are preferred to capital gains by investors, dividend policy has a vital role to play in determining the market value of a company. Companies that pay out low dividends may experience a fall in share price as investors exchange their shares for those of a different company with a more generous dividend policy.

There are a number of other arguments that have been put forward in support of dividend relevance. These are now considered in turn.

10.4.1   Dividends are signals to investors

It has been argued that, due to the asymmetry of information existing between shareholders and managers, shareholders see dividend decisions as conveying new information about the company and its prospects. A dividend increase is usually seen by the market as conveying good news, meaning that the company has favourable prospects, while a dividend decrease is usually seen as bad news, indicating a gloomy future for the company. Fuller information could reverse these perceptions. A dividend increase could be due to a shortage of attractive investments, implying that growth prospects for the company and its dividends are poor. Likewise, a dividend decrease may be a positive sign for investors, indicating an abundance of attractive projects and hence good prospects for growth in future dividend payments. Unfortunately, markets tend to be rather myopic in their perceptions of dividend changes, even when a company considering cutting its dividend explains clearly to the market the reason behind the proposed cut, seeking to prevent any market misperception and resulting share price fall. A company wanting to cut its dividend for reasons of financial

Vignette 10.1

Prudential down 18% on dividend fears

Fears of a dividend cut by Prudential, the UK's second-biggest insurer, caused its shares to fall 18 per cent on Tuesday and sent shock waves through the European insurance sector. Prudential's announcement that it would abandon its commitment to steady dividend increases came as Credit Suisse, Switzerland's second-biggest bank, and Sampo, the Finnish bancassurer, cut their dividends.

The news rattled investors who have come to rely on steady dividend income to offset capital losses from plunging markets. The FTSE Eurotop 300 index was down 3 per cent at a six-year low of 753.62 yesterday, and in London the FTSE 100 index fell 2.2 per cent to

3,621.5. Prudential shares closed down 69 ¼p at 323 ¾p.

The group's statement came just four months after it had reassured investors there was no change in policy. Prudential said it wanted 'financial flexibility', given the continuing economic uncertainty. David Clementi, who took over as chairman of the insurer in December, said: 'While recognising the importance of cash payments to shareholders, the board believes it would be inappropriate to recommit at this time to the current dividend policy.'

The dividends of financial stocks, such as banks and insurers, are seen as among the market's most vulnerable.

The group infuriated some shareholders and analysts by saying it would not be able to give any guidance on its future intention until its interim results in July. Roman Cizdyn, an analyst at Commerzbank, said: 'This solves nothing: what the market hates most is uncertainty.'

The row over dividends overshadowed a strong set of results from Prudential, which managed to increase operating profit by 2 per cent to £1.13bn despite 'some of the most volatile markets we have seen for decades'. However, the slump in investment returns caused Prudential to cut bonuses for 2.1m UK with-profits policyholders for the fourth time in the last 12 months.

Source: Andrew Bolger, *Financial Times*, 26 February 2003. Reprinted with permission.

prudence often faces a significant decrease in its share price. British Steel plc and Trafalgar House plc experienced this in 1991, while a similar dilemma faced Barclays Bank in March 1993. Vignette 10.1 describes Prudential's experiences in 2003.

Miller (1986) argued that it was not so much the *direction* of a dividend change that mattered, but more the *difference* between the actual dividend payment and the market's expectations of what the dividend would be. The market, for instance, may be expecting a drop in a company's dividend payment, but if the *actual* decrease is greater than the *expected* decrease, this will lead to a fall in the company's share price. Vignette 10.2 provides an illustration of Marks and Spencer's dividend cut in 1999, which did not adversely affect its share price because the market anticipated the cut.

Empirical evidence on the signalling properties of dividends will be considered in Section 10.7.

10.4.2 The clientele effect

It has been argued that shareholders are not indifferent as to whether they receive dividends or capital gains. Preferences for one or the other can arise for two main reasons.

First, some shareholders require dividends as a source of regular income. This is true of small shareholders such as pensioners and institutional investors such as pension funds and insurance companies: both have regular liabilities to meet. This need is

Vignette 10.2

M&S buoyed by relief

Relief together with simple good fortune helped M&S sparkle as the group posted full-year figures that were better than many had anticipated. Although the company slashed the final dividend from 14.4p to 9p (representing a cut of 37.5 per cent), investors and market specialists had anticipated the move.

After a bumpy ride over the last two years, one analyst said: 'We are aware expectations have been managed but in truth we were simply relieved that for once the company did not present us with any nasty surprises.' Although the market was encouraged by better-than-anticipated margins and cost savings by the company, concern surrounding like-for-like sales remained.

But bulls of the stock that have held faith through its recent plunge in fortunes were determined this was going to be their day, and from the outset the shares raced ahead. They eventually closed 40 pence ahead, or just over 18 per cent, to 260.75p, the best performer in the FTSE 100. Dealers attributed much of the buying interest to US investors.

Several analysts indicated plans to upgrade current-year profit expectations, although doubts remain about the company's long-term future. One specialist said: 'I remain unconvinced. The shares will recover in the short-term but we have yet to see a strategy that addresses the company's problems in the long term.'

Source: *Financial Times*, 24 May 2000. Reprinted with permission.

balanced by stock exchange dealers, who over a small holding period prefer capital gains to dividend payments.

Second, preferences for dividends or capital gains may arise due to their different tax treatment. Currently, UK capital gains tax is equal to the marginal income tax rate. For private investors who have used up their income tax allowances, capital gains will initially be more attractive than dividends due to an annual capital gains allowance (£8500 for the 2005/06 tax year) on which tax is not paid. Dividends are treated as taxable income and are paid to investors net of tax at a rate of 10 per cent (with a 10 per cent dividend tax credit attached). Investors who pay income tax at the basic rate (i.e. those with taxable earnings under £32,400 for the 2005/06 tax year) have no more tax to pay. However, investors paying income tax at the higher rate pay tax on dividend income at a rate of 32.5 per cent, and hence have a further 22.5 per cent to pay. Consequently, higher income tax bracket investors who have exhausted their capital gains allowance tend to prefer further investment income in the form of dividends (taxed at 32.5 per cent) rather than capital gains (taxed at 40 per cent). Pension funds and charities, while tax exempt, had their right to reclaim the dividend tax credit removed by the UK government's June 1997 budget. This blow was softened for charities by allowing them to continue to claim the dividend tax credit until April 1999, when a five-year transition period began. The relative tax treatment of dividends and capital gains is clearly a matter of government policy.

The existence of preferences for either dividends or capital gains means that investors will be attracted to companies whose dividend policies meet their requirements. Each company will therefore build up a clientele of shareholders who are satisfied by its dividend policy. The implication for a company is that a significant change in its dividend policy could give rise to dissatisfaction among its shareholders, resulting in downward pressure on its share price.

Empirical evidence on the clientele effect is considered in Section 10.8.

10.4.3 The dividend growth model

The dividend growth model is a mathematical model that calculates the present value of a constantly increasing stream of cash flows (a perpetuity), allowing us to predict the value of ordinary shares. The model links the value of a share to the present value of the future dividend payments accruing to that share, and hence lends support to the dividend relevance view. The model holds that a share's market price is equal to the sum of that share's discounted future dividend payments. Algebraically, we have:

$$P_0 = \frac{D_1}{(1+r)} + \frac{D_1(1+g)}{(1+r)^2} + \frac{D_1(1+g)^2}{(1+r)^3} + \cdots + \frac{D_1(1+g)^{n-1}}{(1+r)^n}$$

where: P_0 = current ex dividend market price of the share
D_1 = declared dividend at time t_1
g = expected future growth rate of dividends
n = number of years for which the share is held
r = shareholders' required rate of return

This equation can be simplified by assuming that the share is held for a long time since as n tends towards infinity we have:

$$P_0 = \frac{D_0(1+g)}{(r-g)} = \frac{D_1}{(r-g)}$$

This equation is called the *dividend growth model*, although it is occasionally referred to as the *Gordon growth model*.

How can we find the information needed by the right-hand side of the equation? The current year's dividend D_0 is usually known. The shareholders' required rate of return r (also called the cost of equity, K_e) can be calculated using the capital asset pricing model (*see* Chapter 8). The expected future growth rate of dividends g is difficult to estimate. One method of predicting it is by looking at historical dividend growth rates.

Example Calculation of share price using dividend growth model

Shareholders require a 15 per cent return on their shares and a company has just paid a dividend of 80p per share. Over the past four years, the company has paid dividends of 68p, 73p, 74p and 77p per share (most recent dividend last). What is a fair price for the share using the dividend growth model?

Suggested answer

We need to make an estimate of g. Over the four-year period, dividends have grown from 68p to 80p per share and so:

$$68(1 + g)^4 = 80$$

Rearranging:

$$1 + g = \sqrt[4]{\frac{80}{68}}$$

hence:

$$g = 4.1\%$$

Inserting D_0, g and r into the Gordon growth model:

$$P_0 = \frac{80(1 + 0.041)}{(0.15 - 0.041)} = \frac{83.28}{(0.15 - 0.041)} = £7.64$$

A number of problems are commonly mentioned in connection with using the dividend growth model to value shares. These include the following:

- It has been noted that dividends do not grow smoothly in reality and so g is only an approximation of the future dividend growth rate. This is a valid point and care must be taken, when estimating g by calculating the historic dividend growth rate (on the assumption that the future dividend growth rate is the same as the historical dividend growth rate), that the sample of dividend payments used shows a stable trend. Drawing a graph can help the analyst to get an approximate idea of the historical pattern of dividend growth.

- The model implies that if D_0 is zero, the share is worthless. This is not really a problem, since, presumably, dividend payments will begin at some point in the future. The dividend growth model can be applied to the future dividend stream and the calculated future share price can be discounted to give a current share price.

- It is often said that the dividend growth model fails to take capital gains into account, i.e. it assumes investors buy shares and hold them for an infinite period of time. Again this is not really a problem since, if a share is sold, the price paid will be the present value of its expected future dividends on the selling date. The dividend stream, and hence its present value, is not affected by the change in ownership.

- It has been noted that the dividend growth model makes no allowance for personal or other taxation. While this is true, the model can be modified to incorporate such tax effects.

In the model's favour though, if dividends have followed a particular growth path in the past there may be no reason to assume it will change in the future, especially if a company is following a declared dividend policy. As dividends become distant (especially when the discount rate is high), small errors in dividend estimation become less significant due to the progressively higher discount being applied.

10.5 Dividend relevance or irrelevance?

Who is right? It is possible to criticise a number of the assumptions made by Miller and Modigliani as being unrealistic. Transaction costs are *not* zero and so there is a price to be paid by investors who try to sell their shares to create a 'home-made' dividend; this means that capital gains are not a perfect substitute for dividends in cash flow terms. Taxation *does* exist in the real world, at both a corporate and a personal level, further distorting the required equivalence of dividends and capital gains. Securities *do* incur issue costs and information is *not* necessarily freely available: investors will have to expend time and money in acquiring it.

While these shortcomings undermine Miller and Modigliani's argument, they do not totally invalidate it. In fact, empirical research since Miller and Modigliani published their paper has tended to support the dividend irrelevance school, for example research by Black and Scholes (1974) and by Miller and Scholes (1978). Further empirical evidence with respect to dividend policy is reviewed in Section 10.8.

Ultimately it is the attitude of a company's shareholders that will determine whether or not dividends are paid. Hence the company's dividend policy is an important factor in determining the market price of its shares. Certainly in the current financial climate, where roughly half of all ordinary shares are owned by institutional investors, the reactions of these shareholders to proposed dividend cuts indicate that they consider dividend payments to be very important. Because of their need for a constant stream of dividends from their shares, institutional investors have occasionally been accused of putting pressure on companies to maintain dividends they can ill afford to pay. The irony here is that institutional investors might potentially be restricting future dividends by limiting the amount of retained earnings available for reinvestment. The importance of dividend payments to shareholders is further considered in Vignette 10.3.

10.6 Dividend policies

There are a number of different dividend policies or payout strategies that companies can adopt. These are considered in turn, as are the relative advantages and disadvantages of each policy.

10.6.1 Fixed percentage payout ratio policy

Here the company pays out a fixed percentage of annual profits as dividends, i.e. it maintains a constant *payout ratio* (*see* Section 2.4.7). The advantages of this policy from the company's point of view are that it is relatively easy to operate and sends a clear signal to investors about the level of the company's performance. The disadvantage for a company is that it imposes a constraint on the amount of funds it is able to retain for reinvestment. This dividend policy is unsuitable for companies with volatile profits which have shareholders requiring a stable dividend payment.

Vignette 10.3

FT MONEY: dubious dividend decisions that drive me to despair

Against a' rather grey economic backdrop, with capital growth difficult to achieve, a defensive value investor like myself places even greater emphasis on dividends. So far most of my small cap holdings reporting in 2005 have delivered.

A number show double digit dividend increases – Air Partner, James Fisher, Fountains, Lookers, Parkdean Holidays, Pochins, Treatt, United Drug and WH Ireland, with shipbroker Clarkson taking first prize with a 43 per cent increase in total dividend.

Virtually all other holdings have either maintained dividend rates or modestly increased them – thankfully the importance of dividends has got through to most boards of established listed companies. However, two decisions surprised and angered me – leisure industry business services/software group Christie's mere maintenance of its dividend and electrical products manufacturer/distributor GET Group's slashing of its interim dividend.

Subsequent communication with both companies left me with the impression that the full implications of both decisions had perhaps not been fully thought through. Dividends should not be an afterthought. They are a prime responsibility of a listed company's board, recognising that it is the shareholders who own the company. It is their risk capital which sustains it and they are entitled to an annual return on

their investment which grows over the years. Only in exceptional circumstances should dividends be cut.

Of course a company needs a certain capital retention for future developments and all businesses do go through difficult periods, but a balance has to be struck between the obligations of today and the growth of tomorrow. With Christie it was the lack of logic in dividend policy that irritated me. Last year, good results rewarded investors with a 20 per cent dividend increase. So one might have expected this year's results in April – turnover, operating profit, net assets all up, and gearing eliminated – also to trigger an increase. The company's statement – 'We ended 2004 with a much strengthened balance sheet and with the prospect of good growth opportunities in all divisions in the UK and overseas' – should have pointed to at least a modest increase. But what we got was no comment other than to state a maintenance of its dividend rate. While this is not a disaster, it is a missed opportunity and wrong.

However, GET's justification of the bizarre cut to its interim from 2.85p to 0.5p is arguably the worst dividend decision I have experienced in a lifetime of investment: 'The board has decided to reduce its interim dividend to ensure the group has a stronger balance sheet to maximise the opportunities that should arise within our sector.'

I have been – and remain – an admirer of GET, with its emphasis on attractively designed, value for money, electrical products for the home. It has had an enviable record of growth in recent years with annual dividend increases. Then early last month came a trading statement: half year results in line with forecasts but since then a weaker retailing environment. This naturally resulted in a sharp fall in its shares; then three weeks later came the interims – turnover, profits, net assets all up, gearing 'relatively stable' – and this statement: 'Notwithstanding the current weakening in demand, we are confident in our strategy to increase shareholder value over the coming years.'

How can all this explain and justify the near elimination of the interim dividend, and no comment on the final dividend? This absurd action – shooting itself in the foot – knocked a further 20p off the share price.

By additional explanation the company said: 'Once the uncertainty within our market reduces it is the board's intention to resume its historic dividend policy.'

Playing ducks and drakes with shareholders' dividends is totally unacceptable – investors require continuity and certainty of dividend flow. Any advisers or non-executive directors who went along with this nonsense should have their roles and judgment seriously questioned. Sometimes I just despair.

Source: John Lee, *Financial Times*, 4 June 2005. Reprinted with permission.

10.6.2 Zero dividend policy

A company could decide to pay no dividend at all. Such an extreme policy is likely to be highly beneficial to a small minority of investors while being totally unacceptable to the majority. Such a policy is easy to operate and will not incur the administration costs associated with paying dividends. A zero dividend policy will allow the company to reinvest all of its profits and so will be attractive to investors who, from a personal tax perspective, prefer capital gains to dividends.

Given that the majority of ordinary shareholders are institutional investors who rely on dividend payments for income, a zero dividend policy is hardly likely to be acceptable on an ongoing basis. A zero dividend policy, however, is often adopted by new companies which require large amounts of reinvestment in the first few years of their existence. Eurotunnel plc, for instance, which floated in 1987, indicated that a payment of dividends was not likely to occur before 2005, although this was due to a large extent to the high level of interest payments arising out of inaccurate cost and revenue projections.

10.6.3 Constant or steadily increasing dividend

A company may choose to pay a constant or steadily increasing dividend in either *money terms* or in *real terms* (i.e. with the effects of inflation removed: *see* Section 7.3). A constant or increasing dividend in money terms may result in a declining or increasing dividend in real terms, depending on the level of inflation (or deflation). A constant or increasing dividend in real terms will usually result in an increasing dividend in money terms. In both policies, dividend increases are kept in line with long-term sustainable earnings. As mentioned in Section 10.4.2, it is important for a company to avoid volatility in dividend payments as doing so can help to maintain a stable share price. Cuts in dividends, however well signalled or justified to the markets, are usually taken to mean financial weakness and result in downward pressure on a company's share price.

The drawback of keeping dividends constant or of steadily increasing them is that investors may expect that dividend payments will continue on this trend indefinitely. This can cause major problems when companies wish to reduce dividend payments, either to fund reinvestment or in the name of financial prudence. Because of the reaction of the market to a dividend cut, companies experiencing increases in profit tend to be cautious about a dividend increase. Rarely will a 20 per cent increase in profits lead to a 20 per cent dividend increase. This is reinforced by the fact that a certain level of profit rarely equates to an equal amount of cash, which is ultimately what dividends are paid out of. Companies tend to increase dividends slowly over time, to reflect the new profit level, when they are confident that the new level is sustainable.

10.6.4 Dividend policies in practice

The dividend policies adopted by companies tend in practice to be influenced by two readily identifiable factors. The first factor is the industry or commercial sector within which a company operates. Companies operating in industries that require large amounts of long-term reinvestment are usually found to have lower payout ratios in order to facilitate higher levels of reinvestment. Companies operating in industries associated with high business risk, or industries susceptible to large cyclical swings in profit, tend to pay lower dividends and have lower payout ratios to avoid the risk of

Exhibit 10.4 **Average dividend payout ratios for a selection of UK industries in 2003 and 2006**

Industry	Payout ratio in 2003 (%)	Payout ratio in 2006 (%)
Electronics	38	67
Utilities (water)	80	57
Tobacco	59	53
Chemicals	53	52
General retail	48	51
Pharmaceuticals	50	50
Banks (retail)	63	50
Food retailers	46	50
Building and construction	32	50
Telecommunications	71	38
Leisure and hotels	48	35
Information technology	34	24
Extractive industries	53	23

Source: *Financial Times*, 02 January 2003 and 03 February 2006. Reprinted with permission.

having to reduce dividend payments in the future. This view was supported by Rozeff (1986) in a paper that examined how companies determined their payout ratios. The wide variation in payout ratios between different industries can clearly be seen in Exhibit 10.4. Remember, however, that these ratios are merely snapshots: in a poorly performing sector, a high payout ratio may be a short-term phenomenon as companies with lower profits maintain their dividend payments, causing a temporary increase in payout ratio. In general it can be seen from Exhibit 10.4 that payout ratios have fallen between 2003 and 2006, the one exception being the electronics industry. Here, the sector payout ratio has increased dramatically from 38 per cent to 67 per cent due to electronics companies trying to maintain dividend levels in the face of reduced profits resulting from high levels of competition.

The second factor that affects companies' dividend policies is the nature of the company and its individual characteristics. For example, a company which has reached the mature stage of its life cycle may choose to adopt a high payout ratio owing to its minimal reinvestment requirement. Alternatively, a company which has a high level of bank borrowings relative to the rest of the companies in its sector may, in response to an increase in interest rates, choose to decrease its level of dividend payout in order to meet its interest commitments.

These two factors will combine to influence what a company decides to pay out in dividends. An example of an individual company's dividend history is given in Exhibit 10.5. Here we can see that between the years 1996 and 1999, J Sainsbury plc kept its annual nominal dividend per share rising steadily. The dividend per share was maintained but not increased between 1999 and 2001, even though profitability fell

| Exhibit 10.5 | Dividend policy of J Sainsbury plc, 1996–2005 |

	1996	1997	1998	1999	2000	2001	2002	2003	2004	2005
EPS (p)	28.3	23.4	26.6	26.8	20.5	18.8	21.5	24.2	23.4	9.0
Nominal DPS (p)	12.1	12.3	13.9	14.3	14.3	14.3	14.8	15.6	15.7	7.8
Growth rate (%)		1.6	13.0	2.9	nil	nil	3.5	5.4	0.6	−50.0
Payout ratio (%)	42.8	52.6	52.3	53.4	69.8	76.1	68.8	64.5	67.1	86.7
Inflation (%)		3.3	3.5	1.3	3.3	1.6	1.5	3.1	3.0	2.9
Real DPS (p)	12.1	11.9	13.0	13.2	12.8	12.6	12.8	13.1	12.8	6.2
Growth rate (%)		−1.7	9.2	1.5	−3.0	−1.6	1.6	2.3	−2.3	−51.6

Note: inflation is taken from July to July to reflect the final dividend date
Source: J Sainsbury plc annual reports. Reproduced by kind permission of Sainsbury's Supermarkets Ltd.

sharply: this policy resulted in a significant increase in payout ratio in these years. In 2002, J Sainsbury plc increased its dividend per share as profitability improved, and maintained the upward trend in dividend per share in 2003 and 2004. However, in 2005 profits crashed and the company had no choice but to slash its nominal dividend.

Between 1996 and 1999, with the exception of 1997, J Sainsbury plc maintained a regular increase in real dividend per share (DPS). Since 1999, as the company came under increased financial pressure, it has been unable to maintain the real value of its dividend payments.

As can be seen from the example in Exhibit 10.5, companies tend to change their dividend policies over time to accommodate changes in their individual financial situation as well as changes in the economic environment in which they operate.

10.7 Alternatives to cash dividends

In addition to paying cash dividends, there are a number of other ways in which companies can reward their shareholders.

10.7.1 Scrip dividends

Scrip dividends involve the offer of additional ordinary shares to equity investors, in proportion to their existing shareholding (e.g. 1 for every 20 shares held), as a partial or total alternative to a cash dividend. Usually, shareholders are given the choice of taking either the declared cash dividend or the scrip alternative, allowing them to choose the alternative that best suits their liquidity and tax position.

The major advantage with paying a scrip dividend is that it allows a company to keep the cash that would have been paid out in cash dividends. From a personal taxation point of view, the scrip dividend received is treated as income, with tax deemed to have been paid at the basic rate of personal income tax. Unfortunately, scrip dividends will be unattractive to investors who are exempt from paying tax on dividends as they are not able to reclaim tax which is only 'deemed' to have been paid. Sometimes a scrip

Vignette 10.4

Cadbury defends the bid price

Funding for Dr Pepper buy to come in part from £395m rights issue

Cadbury went to great lengths yesterday to try to reassure shareholders it could afford the deal, stressing the combined group's interest cover of more than 4.5 times in the current year and strong cash flow.

It also sought to enlist shareholders' support not only for the 1-for-7 two-part rights issue but also for an innovative underwritten enhanced scrip dividend. The first tranche of the rights will raise £280m if it is completed.

The scrip dividend will improve cash flow by up to £111m in the first half of 1995, thanks to Cadbury saving on cash dividends and unrelieved advance corporation tax (ACT). The less desirable alternative was a large rights issue, but that would have required dividend payments on the new shares and exacerbated unrelieved ACT.

'This buys us time to manage our way through the long-term ACT problem,' Mr Kappler, Cadbury Schweppes finance director, said.

For the second interim dividend, shareholders can choose either an 11p cash payment per share or 0.0432432 of a new Cadbury share, worth about 16.5p. The enhanced scrip also carries a cash alternative of not less than 14.7p underwritten by Kleinwort Benson, Cadbury's advisor.

Source: Roderick Oram, *Financial Times*, 27 January 1995. Reprinted with permission.

issue may be *enhanced*, meaning that the value of the scrip dividend is in excess of the cash dividend alternative as a way of making it a more attractive choice to shareholders. If the enhancement is more than 15 per cent of the cash alternative though, shareholders may be liable to pay additional tax.

Another possible advantage associated with paying a scrip dividend is that it allows a company to decrease its gearing ratio slightly. It should also be noted that, if the capital market is efficient, the share price will not be depressed since the scrip dividend merely replaces a cash dividend which would have caused the price to fall anyway.

Cadbury plc's 1995 bid for Dr Pepper/7-UP, the US soft drinks manufacturer, is the subject of Vignette 10.4. Here, Cadbury proposed the use of an enhanced scrip dividend to allow it to retain cash to finance its proposed takeover.

10.7.2 Share repurchases

Share repurchases have become an increasingly common way of returning value to ordinary shareholders in the UK, following their adoption by a number of leading companies in recent years. Such companies include Reuters plc, which repurchased £350m of its shares in 1993, representing nearly 6 per cent of its total ordinary share capital; BP Amoco with two 'buybacks' in 2000 that amounted to £1993m in total; and, more recently, Vodafone plc who instigated an aggressive buyback programme in 2003 which by March 2005 had reached £4bn of repurchases. An estimated £34bn of 'buybacks' occurred between 1995 and 2000, with £9bn occurring in 2000 alone. Share repurchases have been commonplace in the USA over a much longer time period and continue to be popular, as Vignette 10.5 shows, with companies such as Dell Inc

Vignette 10.5

Share buybacks rise 92% in US

Leading US companies continued to buy back their own shares at a rapid pace during the second quarter.

Standard & Poor's, the index provider, said buyback activity in the second quarter grew 92 per cent compared with the same period last year for companies in the S&P 500 index, the most widely used gauge for the world's largest stock market.

S&P 500 buybacks totalled $82bn in the second quarter, from $42bn in the second quarter of last year.

Companies buying back their own stock also appear to be reducing their share count at a higher rate than in the past by buying back more stock than they issue, S&P said. This has the potential to boost earnings per share and represents a shift from previous quarters when buybacks would typically be used as a countermeasure to the issuance of stock options to employees and management.

Howard Silverblatt, equity market analyst at S&P, said: '[We're] seeing an increase in companies actually reducing their share count, which directly benefits existing shareholders . . . companies are actively trying to reduce their share count to assist in boosting earnings per share, as growth and comparisons become difficult.'

While the announcement of a buyback tends to boost a company's share price in the short term, some stock market observers have noted that in the past many companies have not reduced the number of total shares outstanding. Instead, the purchased shares were equal to the stock options issued to employees, keeping the number of shares outstanding the same.

As a result, earnings per share do not benefit from the buyback, because the total earnings number is divided by the same number of shares. S&P said share count reductions grew by 33 per cent in the second quarter while notable increases in share count fell by 36 percent.

'Reducing share count is the new trend that is growing fast [and] adds to equity, increases earnings per share, answers investor demand for companies to spend their enormous cash reserves, and still gives management the ability to reissue the shares at a later time for merger and acquisition,' Mr Silverblatt said.

The requirement for US companies to treat stock options as expenses, set to take effect next year, is expected to decrease option issuance and still boost share count reduction at a time when Corporate America has record amounts of cash on its balance sheet.

Source: Andrei Postelnicu *Financial Times*, 20 September 2005. Reprinted with permission.

and Time Warner Inc heavily involved in repurchasing their own shares. In the UK the Companies Act 1981 first opened the way for British companies to repurchase their own shares. Before any repurchase takes place, however, a company must obtain approval from both its current shareholders and any warrant, option and convertible holders it may have and is limited to repurchasing up to 15 per cent of its total share capital in any twelve-month period.

The main benefit to shareholders of a share repurchase is that they receive surplus funds from the company which they use more effectively. The main benefit for a company of a share repurchase is that it enhances the value of the remaining shares. In addition, since capital employed is reduced by repurchasing shares, return on capital employed (ROCE) will increase, as will earnings per share (EPS). While this has to be balanced against an increase in gearing, it is argued that the increase in financial risk associated with a share repurchase is negligible and so, since the cost of equity is unaltered, the value of shares and the company will increase. Many commentators put the late 1990s' boom in share repurchases down to the abolition of dividend tax credits in 1997 and the removal of advance corporation tax (ACT) in 1999. However, the more cynical among them believe that managers with EPS-based performance measures were using share repurchases as a way of increasing EPS and hence enhancing executive rewards.

There are three ways for a company to repurchase its shares. A *tender offer* to all shareholders is where shareholders are invited to offer their shares to be sold back at the price set by the company. The main advantage with this method is that it allows all shareholders to participate in the repurchase. Alternatively, a company can use a *stock market purchase*. This is more flexible than a tender offer as there is no one unique price at which the shares have to be repurchased and, in addition, less documentation is required. Finally, a company may repurchase its shares *by arrangement* with individual shareholders. Often companies employ a broker as an agent to organise the repurchase of its shares from institutional shareholders who are clients of the broker. Hence, this method of repurchase is sometimes known as an *agency buy back*.

As with scrip dividends, share repurchases have tax implications for both companies and investors. In the case of tender offers and repurchases by private arrangement, the capital amount (equivalent to the current market price of the shares) is taxed as capital gains. Any payment in excess of the current market price of the share is treated as a net dividend payment and therefore carries a tax credit, which tax-exempt shareholders cannot reclaim from the Inland Revenue. With stock market repurchases, the whole payment is treated as a capital gain and taxed accordingly. We can conclude that shareholders with differing tax situations will have different preferences for how a company should go about repurchasing its shares.

10.7.3 Special dividends

Occasionally, companies return surplus funds to shareholders by making a special dividend payment. A *special dividend* is a cash payout far in excess of the dividend payments usually made by a company. If a company has funds surplus to its investment requirements, paying out these funds via a special dividend enables shareholders to reinvest them according to their preferences. A special dividend scheme was used by East Midlands Electricity plc in October 1994 to return £186.5m of surplus funds to its shareholders. In subsequent years, special dividends have become a less frequent occurrence, although there has been a recent upsurge in special dividend activity. The London Stock Exchange paid a special dividend worth 55 pence per ordinary share (or total cash of £162m) in 2004 and, in 2005, De Vere plc announced a special dividend of £1.59 following the sale of the De Vere Belfrey.

10.7.4 Non-pecuniary benefits

Also referred to as shareholder perks, these can take the form of discounts on a company's goods and services and/or the offer of complimentary goods and services. Hilton Group plc, for instance, currently gives discounts on its hotels, restaurants and health clubs, regardless of the size of their shareholding. To qualify for most non-pecuniary benefits, however, shareholders usually have to hold a specified minimum number of the company's shares. British Airways plc, for instance, currently gives a 10 per cent discount on flights for shareholders with 200 or more of its shares. Meanwhile, shareholders with 200 or more shares in Thorntons plc receive annual discount vouchers to the value of £34.

10.8 Empirical evidence on dividend policy

Dividend policy is an area of corporate finance that has been the subject of extensive empirical research. This is due in no small part both to the continuing debate on whether dividend payments are relevant in determining the share price of a company and to the readily available supply of data on corporate dividend payments.

Before Miller and Modigliani's paper in 1961, the generally held belief of both academics and the business community was that dividends were preferred by investors to capital gains because of their certainty. The implication of this belief is that companies could increase their share prices by generous dividend policies. Lintner (1956) surveyed the financial managers of 28 US companies and concluded that the dividend decision was seen as an important one, with dividend payments being determined independently from companies' investment decisions. He found that companies changed dividend payments gradually towards their desired payout ratio as earnings increased, in order to reduce the need for subsequent dividend reductions should earnings decrease. A later study by Fama and Babiak (1968) of 201 US companies came to similar conclusions.

Gordon (1959) found that companies with high payout ratios also had high price/earnings ratios, implying that investors valued companies with high payout ratios more highly than companies with low payout ratios. However, this research has now been thoroughly discredited. First, price/earnings ratios and payout ratios tend to move together as earnings fluctuate, since both ratios have earnings per share as a denominator. Second, the relationship between price/earnings ratios and payout ratios may be explained *by the level of risk* of companies, rather than by shareholders preferring companies with high payout ratios. Companies with volatile earnings tend to have lower price/earnings ratios as a result of their higher risk; they usually pay out a lower proportion of their earnings as dividends to reflect the volatility of their earnings.

After Miller and Modigliani's 1961 paper on dividend policy a large amount of empirical research focused on dividends and their tax implications. Seminal work carried out by Brennan (1970) in the USA put forward the proposition that the market price of a company's shares would change in order to give the same after-tax rate of return regardless of its dividend policy. For example, if a company were to distribute a higher level of earnings, thereby increasing the amount of tax paid by its shareholders, its share price would fall to reflect the increase in tax liability. The implication of Brennan's proposition was that companies could increase their share price by adopting lower levels of earnings distribution.

Black and Scholes (1974) tested Brennan's proposition by examining whether companies with high dividend yields gave greater before-tax returns to compensate investors for the undesirable tax implications of high dividend distribution. Their results were inconclusive and they failed to find any positive relationship between dividend yields and before-tax returns. In contrast, Litzenberger and Ramaswamy (1979) did find a statistically significant relationship between dividend yields and before-tax returns. The findings of Litzenberger and Ramaswamy were later discredited by Miller and Scholes (1982), who repeated Litzenberger and Ramaswamy's analysis and concluded that the relationship between high dividend yields and high before-tax returns could be explained by dividend information effects rather than by dividend tax effects.

Elton and Gruber (1970) investigated the existence of tax clienteles by examining share price falls at the time when share prices went ex dividend. By looking at the magnitude of the share price fall they inferred the average marginal rate of income tax that a company's shareholders were paying. They concluded that high dividend shares were associated with lower marginal rates of income tax, hence supporting the proposition of the existence of a tax clientele. Subsequent investigations by Pettit (1977) in the USA and by Crossland et al. (1991) in the UK have given further support to the existence of a clientele effect.

Miller and Scholes (1978) showed that US shareholders could negate less preferential tax rates on dividends compared with capital gains by the appropriate use of tax planning, hence lending support to Miller and Modigliani's dividend irrelevance theory. However, Feenberg (1981) concluded that very few investors had taken advantage of the tax planning suggested by Miller and Scholes. This was, in some part, due to the transaction costs associated with such a course of action. More recently Bond et al. (1996) examined the effects of the now defunct advance corporation tax (ACT) system on dividend policy in the UK. They concluded that for companies with surplus (unrelieved) ACT, the higher tax cost of paying dividends exerted a significant downward pressure on their dividends.

Research into the effect on share prices of the information content of dividends has been carried out by Pettit (1972), Watts (1973), Aharony and Swary (1980) and Kwan (1981). All of these studies, apart from that of Watts, concluded that dividend changes *do* convey new information to shareholders.

10.9 Conclusion

In recent years corporate dividend policy has become an important decision area in its own right. A large number of factors influence the dividend policy of a company: these include the levels of personal and corporate taxation, the number of reinvestment opportunities available to the company relative to its distributable earnings, the company's liquidity position and the characteristics and composition of a company's shareholders. Broadly speaking, companies have the choice of three types of dividend policy: paying no dividend at all; paying out a fixed proportion of earnings; and paying a constant or slightly increasing dividend. In addition to cash dividends, companies are also able to use scrip dividends, share repurchases and non-pecuniary benefits as ways of rewarding shareholders.

The debate over whether dividend policy affects the value of a company is a continuing one. While Miller and Modigliani's argument for dividend irrelevance is logical within the restrictive assumptions they made, recent trends in corporate dividend policies lend more support to the relevance school. Given that over half of ordinary shares are now owned by large institutional investors looking for a regular income stream, only a naïve financial manager would fail to appreciate that the dividend decision of his or her company might affect its share price.

Key points

1 A company's dividend decision has important implications for both its investment and its financing decisions.

2 Dividends in the UK are paid on a semi-annual basis, net of tax deducted at the standard personal income tax rate for dividends (10 per cent currently).

3 Generally speaking, interim dividends are smaller than final dividends because of cash flow and financial planning considerations.

4 When a share passes from being cum dividend to ex dividend, its price will fall by the value of the net dividend forgone to reflect a change in the intrinsic value of the share.

5 Legal constraints on the payment of dividends include the Companies Act 1985, which states that dividends must be paid out of 'accumulated net realised profits', and restrictive loan agreements or covenants.

6 Other restrictions on a company's dividend policy include its liquidity position, its interest payment obligations and the number of attractive investment opportunities available.

7 A dividend should be paid only if it increases the wealth of the company's shareholders, i.e. if $d_1 + P_1 > P_0$.

8 Miller and Modigliani argued that dividend payments are irrelevant to the valuation of ordinary shares. The value of a company is maximised if it follows its optimum investment policy. A dividend might be a residual payment after all attractive investment projects have been accepted. Shareholders requiring dividends who did not receive them could make 'home-made' dividends by selling shares.

9 While the Miller and Modigliani model is academically sound, the assumptions that underpin it are not applicable to the real world.

10 Lintner and Gordon argued that investors preferred dividends to capital gains because of their certainty.

11 Dividend relevance to share valuation is further supported by the argument that dividends are seen by investors as signals of a company's future profitability.

12 The existence of taxation at both a personal and corporate level further undermines Miller and Modigliani's dividend irrelevance theory.

13 Companies have several dividend policies to choose from. These include paying no dividend, adopting a fixed payout ratio and maintaining a constant or steadily increasing dividend in nominal or real terms.

14 In practice most companies try to keep dividends rising smoothly by accommodating temporary drops in earnings through a higher payout ratio and by increasing dividends only gradually in response to an increase in earnings.

15 Payout ratios vary from industry to industry and depend on the risk and level of required reinvestment associated with each industry.

16 Scrip dividends, where new shares are offered as an alternative to cash dividends, allow companies to retain money for reinvestment.

17 Share repurchases and special dividends are sometimes used by companies to return surplus cash to shareholders.

18 Empirical research on the importance of dividends is by no means clear-cut. While Miller and Modigliani's model has not been totally discredited, there is substantial evidence to support the existence of tax clienteles and to support the view that dividends are seen by investors as signalling new information about a company's future prospects.

Self-test questions

Answers to these questions can be found on pages 462–4.

1 Discuss the practical issues to be considered by a company when deciding on the size of its dividend payment.

2 Which of the following statements lends support to dividend irrelevance rather than to dividend relevance theory?

(a) Investors prefer the certainty of dividends to the uncertainty of capital gains.

(b) Certain companies may build up a clientele of shareholders due to their dividend policy.

(c) Dividends are believed by many investors to signal information about the company.

(d) The existence of taxes distorts the desirability of dividends relative to capital gains.

(e) Shareholders can manufacture their own dividends by selling some of their shares.

3 XYZ's current cum dividend share price is £3.45 and the company has just announced a dividend per share of 20p. At what rate do investors expect dividends to grow in the future if the current share price is considered to be fair and if shareholders require a rate of return of 15 per cent?

4 The ordinary shares of Chock-stock plc are currently quoted at 200p per share and the company has been paying a dividend of 30p per share for 10 years. The company is planning to retain the next three years' dividends to invest in a new project. The project cash flows will begin in year 4, allowing the company to pay an increased dividend of 40p per share from that year onwards. What is the increase in wealth for the shareholders?

(a) −24.4p per share

(b) −14.2p per share

(c) 5.8p per share

(d) 10.2p per share

(e) 17.6p per share?

5 Which of the following statements best sums up recent trends in corporate dividend payments?

  (a) Nominal dividends per share have remained constant or slightly increased.

  (b) Companies have made large increases in real dividends per share.

  (c) Companies have decreased payout ratios to stabilise nominal dividends per share.

  (d) Nominal dividends per share have decreased on the whole.

  (e) Nominal dividends per share have slightly increased in order to increase dividend cover.

6 Given the assumptions made by Miller and Modigliani's dividend irrelevance theory, do you consider their conclusions to be logical?

7 Discuss whether the assumptions made by Miller and Modigliani's dividend irrelevance theory fail to mirror the real world. If you agree that they fail to mirror the real world, does that invalidate the usefulness of their theory?

8 How do you consider the increased ownership of shares by institutional shareholders has affected the dividend policies of UK public limited companies?

9 Explain the following terms:

  (a) the residual theory of dividends;

  (b) the clientele effect;

  (c) the signalling properties of dividends;

  (d) the 'bird in the hand' argument.

Questions for review

Answers to these questions can be found on pages 464–6. Questions with an asterisk (*) are at an intermediate level.

1 The decision about how much earnings to retain and how much to return to ordinary shareholders as a dividend is a key financial management decision. Discuss some of the factors that should be considered by the senior managers of a listed company in making a decision on the size of the annual dividend to pay to its shareholders.

2 (a) Stant has just announced an ordinary dividend per share of 20p. The past four years' dividends per share have been 13p, 14p, 17p and 18p (most recent dividend last) and shareholders require a return of 14 per cent. What is a fair price for Stant's shares?

  (b) Stant now decides to increase its debt level, thereby increasing the financial risk associated with its equity shares. As a consequence, Stant's shareholders increase their required rate of return to 15.4 per cent. Calculate a new price for Stant's shares.

  (c) Outline any problems with using the dividend growth model as a way of valuing shares.

3 It has become increasingly common for companies to offer their shareholders a choice between a cash dividend and an equivalent scrip issue of shares. Briefly consider the advantages of scrip dividends from the points of view of both the company and the shareholders.

4* The managing directors of three profitable companies were discussing their companies' dividend policies over lunch. Each managing director is certain that their company's policy is maximising shareholder wealth.

- Company A has deliberately paid no dividends for the last five years.
- Company B always pays a dividend of 50 per cent of earnings after taxation.
- Company C maintains a low but constant dividend per share and offers regular scrip issues and shareholder concessions.

(a) What are the advantages and disadvantages of the alternative dividend policies of the three companies?

(b) Discuss the circumstances under which each managing director might be correct in their belief that the company's dividend policy is maximising shareholder wealth. State clearly any assumptions that you make.

(ACCA 1987)

5* Ropeonfire is currently deciding on the level and form of its next dividend. It is considering three options:

(i) a cash dividend payment of 20p per share;

(ii) a 6 per cent scrip dividend;

(iii) a repurchase of 15 per cent of ordinary share capital at the current market price.

The company's financial statements are given below:

Profit and loss account	£ million	£ million
Operating profit		18.0
Net interest earned		5.0
		23.0
Taxation		7.3
Distributable earnings		15.7
Balance sheet		
Fixed assets		70
Current assets: Debtors	22	
Stock	21	
Cash	41	84
Current liabilities		(31)
		123
Financed by:		
Ordinary share capital (50p shares)		20
Reserves		103
		123

(a) If the current cum dividend share price is 420p, calculate the effect of the three options on the wealth of a shareholder owning 1000 shares in Ropeonfire.

(b) Explain briefly how the company's decision will be influenced by the opportunity to invest £60m in a project with a positive net present value.

Questions for discussion

Questions with an asterisk (*) are at an advanced level.

1 The ordinary shares of ZZZ are currently trading at 80p. The last dividend per share was 15p and its dividends have been constant for 10 years. The company plans to finance a new investment project out of retained earnings and so for the next two years the dividend per share will fall to 10p. Benefits from the investment project will be gained from year three onwards and so ZZZ will pay a dividend of 18p per share in that and subsequent years. Assuming that shareholders have all the above information, what would be a fair price for the shares of ZZZ?

2* (a) It is said that financial management is concerned with investment decisions, dividend decisions and financing decisions. Critically discuss why financial management theory has claimed that only investment decisions have any importance, and that decisions about financing and dividends depend upon a firm's optimal investment schedule.

(b) In the context of dividend policy, discuss the meaning of the following terms:

(i) asymmetric information;

(ii) scrip dividends;

(iii) shareholder perks.

(c) Discuss whether a policy of paying out no dividends means that a company has no value.

3* Pavlon plc has recently obtained a listing on the stock exchange. Previously, 90 per cent of the firm's shares were owned by members of one family, but since the listing about 60 per cent of the issued shares have been owned by other investors. Pavlon's earnings and dividends for the five years prior to the listing are detailed below:

Years prior to listing	Profit after tax (£)	Dividend per share (pence)
5	1 800 000	3.60
4	2 400 000	4.80
3	3 850 000	6.16
2	4 100 000	6.56
1	4 450 000	7.12
Current year	5 500 000 (estimate)	

The number of issued ordinary shares was increased by 25 per cent three years prior to the listing and by 50 per cent at the time of listing. The company's authorised capital is currently £25m in 25p ordinary shares, of which 40 million have been issued. The market value of the company's equity is £78m.

The board of directors is discussing future dividend policy. An interim dividend of 3.16p per share was paid immediately prior to the listing and the finance director has suggested a final dividend of 2.34p per share. The company's declared objective is to maximise shareholder wealth.

(a) Comment upon Pavlon's dividend policy prior to listing and discuss whether such a policy is likely to be suitable for a listed company.

(b) Discuss whether the proposed final dividend of 2.34p is likely to be an appropriate dividend if:

  (i) the majority of the shares are owned by institutional investors;

  (ii) the majority of shares are owned by wealthy individuals.

(c) Pavlon's profit after tax is expected to grow by 15 per cent per year for three years, and by 8 per cent per year after that. Pavlon's cost of equity is estimated to be 12 per cent per year. Dividends may be assumed to grow at the same rate as profits.

  (i) Using the dividend valuation model, calculate whether Pavlon's shares are currently undervalued or overvalued.

  (ii) Briefly outline the weaknesses of the dividend valuation model.

(ACCA)

4 Christie is a company that has been listed on the London Stock Exchange since 2001. Institutional investors own approximately 45 per cent of the ordinary shares of the company. The recent financial performance of the company is shown below. Using the information provided, comment on the dividend policy of Christie and critically discuss whether this dividend policy is likely to be acceptable to its institutional investors.

Year	2006	2005	2004	2003	2002	2001
Turnover (£ million)	3.3	3.1	2.7	2.6	2.5	2.0
Earnings per share (pence)	34.2	33.0	29.2	28.6	27.6	25.4
Dividend per share (pence)	11.4	11.1	9.9	9.6	9.2	8.5
Annual inflation (%)	3.1	3.4	3.1	2.4	3.4	2.5

5* It is 31 January 2006 and the managers of Dilbert are considering a change in the company's dividend policy. Earnings per share for 2005 for the company were 22.8 pence, and the finance director has said that he expects this to increase to 25.0 pence per share for 2006. The increase in earnings per share is in line with market expectations of the company's performance. The pattern of recent dividends, which are paid each year on 31 December, is as follows:

Year	2005	2004	2003	2002	2001	2000
Dividend per share (pence)	11.4	11.1	9.6	9.6	9.2	8.5

The managing director has proposed that 70 per cent of earnings in 2005 and subsequent years should be retained for investment in new product development. It is expected that, if this proposal is accepted, the dividend growth rate will be 8.75 per cent. Dilbert's cost of equity capital is estimated to be 12 per cent.

Calculate the share price of Dilbert in the following circumstances.

(a) The company decides not to change its current dividend policy.

(b) The company decides to change its dividend policy as proposed by the Managing Director and announces the change to the market.

References

Aharony, J. and Swary, I. (1980) 'Quarterly dividend and earnings announcements and stock holders' returns: an empirical analysis', *Journal of Finance*, Vol. 35, March, pp. 1–12.

Black, F. and Scholes, M. (1974) 'The effects of dividend yield and dividend policy on common stock prices and returns', *Journal of Financial Economics*, Vol. 1, pp. 1–22.

Bond, S., Chennells, L. and Devereux, M. (1996) 'Company dividends and taxes in the UK', *Fiscal Studies*, Vol. 16, pp. 1–18.

Brennan, M. (1970) 'Taxes, market valuation and corporate financial policy', *National Tax Journal*, Vol. 23, pp. 417–27.

Crossland, M., Dempsey, M. and Mozier, P. (1991) 'The effect of cum and ex dividend changes on UK share prices', *Accounting and Business Research*, Vol. 22, No. 85, pp. 47–50.

Elton, E. and Gruber, M. (1970) 'Marginal stockholder tax rates and the clientele effect', *Review of Economics and Statistics*, Vol. 52, pp. 68–74.

Fama, E. and Babiak, H. (1968) 'Dividend policy: an empirical analysis', *Journal of the American Statistical Association*, Vol. 63, pp. 1132–61.

Feenberg, D. (1981) 'Does the investment interest limitation explain the existence of dividends?', *Journal of Financial Economics*, Vol. 9, No. 3, pp. 265–9.

Gordon, M. (1959) 'Dividends, earnings and stock prices', *Review of Economics and Statistics*, Vol. 41, pp. 99–105.

Kwan, C. (1981) 'Efficient market tests of the information content of dividend announcements: critique and extension', *Journal of Financial and Quantitative Analysis*, Vol. 16, June, pp. 193–206.

Lintner, J. (1956) 'Distribution of incomes of corporations among dividends, retained earnings and taxes', *American Economic Review*, Vol. 46, pp. 97–113.

Litzenberger, R. and Ramaswamy, K. (1979) 'The effect of personal taxes and dividends on common stock prices and returns', *Journal of Financial Economics*, Vol. 7, June, pp. 163–95.

Miller, M. (1986) 'Behavioural rationality in finance: the case of dividends', *Journal of Business*, Vol. 59, pp. 451–68.

Miller, M. and Modigliani, F. (1961) 'Dividend policy, growth and the valuation of shares', *Journal of Business*, Vol. 34, pp. 411–33.

Miller, M. and Scholes, M. (1978) 'Dividends and taxes', *Journal of Financial Economics*, Vol. 6, pp. 333–64.

Miller, M. and Scholes, M. (1982) 'Dividends and taxes: some empirical evidence', *Journal of Political Economy*, Vol. 90, pp. 1118–41.

Pettit, R. (1972) 'Dividend announcements, security performance and capital market efficiency', *Journal of Finance*, Vol. 27, pp. 993–1007.

Pettit, R. (1977) 'Taxes, transaction cost and clientele effects of dividends', *Journal of Financial Economics*, Vol. 5, December, pp. 419–36.

Porterfield, J. (1965) *Investment Decisions and Capital Costs*, Englewood Cliffs, NJ: Prentice-Hall.

Rozeff, M. (1986) 'How companies set their dividend payout ratios', reprinted in Stern, J. and Chew, D. (eds) (2003) *The Revolution in Corporate Finance*, 4th edn, Oxford: Basil Blackwell.

Watts, R. (1973) 'The information content of dividends', *Journal of Business*, Vol. 46, pp. 191–211.

Recommended reading

This title has a comprehensive and very well written chapter on dividend policy from a US perspective.

Damodaran, A. (2001) *Corporate Finance, Theory and Practice*, 2nd edn, New York: Wiley.

A comprehensive guide to all you need to know about dividend policy.

Frankfurter, A. and Wood, B. (2003) *Dividend Policy: Theory and Practice*, London: Academic Press.

These titles collect together a number of interesting and very readable articles on dividend policy.

Stern, J. and Chew, D. (eds) (2003) *The Revolution in Corporate Finance*, 4th edn, Malden, MA: Blackwell

Ward, K. (ed.) (1994) *Strategic Issues in Finance*, Oxford: Butterworth-Heinemann.

Important and informative papers and articles recommended for further reading on the subject of dividend policy include:

Bank of England (1988) 'Share repurchase by quoted companies', *Bank of England Quarterly Bulletin*, August, pp. 382–8.

Barker, R. (1993) 'The future of dividends', *Professional Investor*, September, pp. 37–9.

Goodhart, W. (1991) 'Dividend dilemma', *Corporate Finance*, March, pp. 17–21.

Pettit, A. (2001) 'Is share buyback right for your company?', *Harvard Business Review*, April 2001, Vol. 79, No. 40, pp. 141–7.

Shaw, A. (1995) 'Share repurchases: a new fashion in corporate finance?', *The Treasurer*, January, pp. 35–6.

Chapter 11

Mergers and takeovers

Learning objectives

After studying this chapter, you should have achieved the following learning objectives:

- a familiarity with the different types of merger and takeover;

- an understanding of the justifications and motives behind merger and takeover activity;

- the ability to value target companies using a range of valuation techniques and to decide on an appropriate valuation;

- an awareness of the ways in which mergers and takeovers can be financed;

- an understanding of the strategies and tactics employed in the takeover process by bidding and target companies;

- an understanding of why a company may choose to divest part of its operations and an awareness of the different routes to divestment available;

- an appreciation of the effects of merger and takeover activity on stakeholder groups.

Introduction

Mergers and takeovers play a vital role in corporate finance. For many companies, mergers and takeovers are a source of external growth when organic growth is not possible, whereas to other companies they represent a constant threat to their continuing independent existence.

In practice, acquiring another company is a far more complex process than simply buying a machine or building a factory. First, valuing a target company and estimating the potential benefits of acquiring it are more difficult propositions than valuing a simple investment project. Second, the takeover process is often complicated by bids being resisted by the target company and hence acquisition may become a long and unpleasant contest. This contest often results in the bidder paying a price considerably higher than it had anticipated. Third, due to the size of many takeover deals, there are often serious financial implications for the acquiring company after it has paid for its acquisition. We must also recognise the amount of valuable senior management time absorbed by the takeover process.

The subject of mergers and takeovers is large and many books have been written on it. In this chapter, therefore, we cannot give the subject a detailed treatment, but you will obtain more than simply a general understanding of this fascinating area of corporate finance.

11.1 The terminology of mergers and takeovers

Although the terms 'merger' and 'takeover' tend to be used synonymously, in practice there is a narrow distinction between them. A merger can be defined as a friendly reorganisation of assets into a new organisation, i.e. A and B merge to become C, a new company, with the agreement of both sets of shareholders. Mergers involve similar-sized companies, reducing the likelihood of one company dominating the other. A takeover is the acquisition of one company's ordinary share capital by another company, financed by a cash payment, an issue of securities or a combination of both. Here, the bidding company is usually larger than the target company. In practice, most acquisitions are takeovers rather than mergers since one of the two parties is dominant. Perhaps the closest thing to a true merger in recent years was the joining of Lattice and National Grid in October 2002 to form National Grid Transco.

Takeovers can be classified into three broad types:

- *Horizontal takeover*: the combination of two companies operating in the same industry and at a similar stage of production.
- *Vertical takeover*: the combination of two companies operating at different stages of production within the same industry. A vertical takeover can involve a move forward in the production process to secure a distribution outlet, or a move backward in the production process to secure the supply of raw materials.
- *Conglomerate takeover*: the combination of two companies operating in different areas of business.

Exhibit 11.1	Major UK takeovers including total value of bid and classification			
Date	Bidder	Target	Deal value (£m)	Classification of takeover
1988	BP	Britoil	2 323	Vertical backwards
1988	Nestlé	Rowntree	2 666	Horizontal
1995	Glaxo	Wellcome	9 150	Horizontal
1995	Hanson	Eastern Electric	2 400	Conglomerate
1996	Granada	Forte	3 600	Horizontal
2000	GlaxoWellcome	SmithKline Beecham	38 600	Horizontal
2002	National Grid	Lattice Group	8 400	Horizontal merger
2004	Morrisons	Safeway	2 900	Horizontal
2005	Telefónica SA	O$_2$	17 700	Horizontal cross-border

Examples of these different types of business combinations are shown in Exhibit 11.1. Takeovers with an international dimension are called *cross-border* acquisitions. An example of a cross-border horizontal takeover was Hong Kong and Shanghai Bank Corporation's takeover of Midland Bank plc in 1992.

11.2 Justifications for acquisitions

Although company managers may offer many justifications for takeovers, an acquisition can be financially justified only if it increases the wealth of the acquiring company shareholders. Similarly, a merger can be financially justified only if the wealth of the shareholders of both companies increases. Justifications or motives for acquisitions are generally considered to be economic, financial or managerial in origin. These motives are now discussed.

11.2.1 Economic justifications

The economic justification for takeovers is that shareholder wealth will be increased by the transaction as the two companies are worth more combined than as separate companies. This can be shown algebraically as:

$$PV_{X+Y} > (PV_X + PV_Y)$$

Here, PV represents present value and X and Y are the two companies involved. Economic gains may be generated for a number of reasons, as follows.

Synergy

Synergy occurs when the assets and/or operations of two companies complement each other, so that their combined output is more than the sum of their separate outputs once merged. For example, a company may have to buy in an expensive service which it cannot provide for itself. By acquiring a company which can supply this service it may be able to reduce its costs. The problem with this justification is that synergy is difficult to *quantify* before companies combine, and difficult to *realise* once combination has occurred since this realisation depends on a high degree of post-merger corporate integration.

Economies of scale

Economies of scale are similar to synergy benefits and occur because the scale of operations is larger after a takeover. Economies of scale are most likely to arise in horizontal acquisitions but may also arise in vertical acquisitions, in areas such as production, distribution, marketing, management and finance. An example of a production economy is where two companies, producing the same good from similar machines, produce their combined output from a single, larger, cheaper machine after merging. An example of a distribution economy is where two companies, distributing their products in small vans, distribute their combined output using a large lorry after merging. Another example of an economy of scale is where a company gains the ability to enjoy bulk-buying discounts following an acquisition because of the larger scale of its operations.

Elimination of inefficient management

A company may be poorly run by its current managers, perhaps because they are pursuing their own objectives rather than those of their shareholders. The company's declining share price will attract potential bidders who believe they can manage the company more efficiently. If a takeover bid is successful, inefficient managers will be replaced by more efficient personnel who can deliver a better level of performance. Eliminating inefficient managers through a takeover may be more attractive to shareholders than voting them out of office (which may be difficult to achieve for practical reasons) or suffering a decrease in wealth in a liquidation.

Entry to new markets

Companies may want to expand into new geographical and business areas in order to meet their strategic objectives. Organic or internal growth may be deemed to be too slow or too costly and so acquisition may be chosen as a more efficient route to expansion. This is particularly true of the retail trade, where starting operations from scratch is both costly and time consuming. The costs involved will result from purchasing and fitting out premises, hiring and training personnel, and building up market share. Iceland plc's acquisition of Bejam in 1987 is an example of a company using acquisition to break into a new market; as a result, Iceland established a retail presence in the north of England. Building market share by competing with Bejam and other retailers in the area from a zero base would have been prohibitively expensive.

To provide critical mass

Smaller companies may experience a lack of credibility because of their size. In addition, owing to the increasing importance of research and development and brand investment, merging companies can pool resources to establish the critical mass required to provide sufficient cash flows to finance such requirements.

As a means of providing growth

Once a company reaches the mature stage of its growth cycle it will find organic growth difficult. Acquisitions provide a quick solution for a company following a growth strategy that finds itself in this position.

Market power and share

Horizontal acquisitions increase market share and hence increase a company's ability to earn *monopoly profits*, whereas vertical acquisitions increase a company's power in raw material or distribution markets. One problem for UK companies here is the risk of referral to the Competition Commission, a risk which is highest in horizontal acquisitions. A referral can be expensive for a company and can potentially damage its reputation (*see* Sections 11.2.4 and 11.6.1).

There is no doubt about the general validity of these economic justifications for acquisition in terms of their ability to increase shareholder wealth. The potential for economic gains in specific cases is not guaranteed and if such potential exists, it is not certain that economic gains can be realised during the post-takeover integration process. This issue is considered further in Section 11.8.

11.2.2 Financial justifications

Acquisitions can also be justified on the grounds of the financial benefits they bring to the shareholders of the companies involved. These are now considered in turn.

Financial synergy

Financial synergy is said to occur if a company's cost of capital decreases as a direct result of an acquisition. One way in which financial synergy can occur is through a conglomerate takeover, where the lack of correlation between the cash flows of the different companies will reduce cash flow volatility. A reduction in cash flow volatility represents a decrease in business risk and the cost of capital of the company may therefore decrease. Managers may therefore justify a conglomerate takeover by claiming it reduces the risk faced by shareholders.

This risk reduction cannot be justified from a shareholder wealth perspective since shareholders are in theory assumed to have eliminated unsystematic risk by holding a diversified portfolio of shares (*see* Section 8.2). Diversifying operations at the company level will therefore have little impact on the level of unsystematic risk faced by shareholders.

Financial synergy can also occur because of increased size following an acquisition, since a larger company can expect to have a lower interest rate on new debt. A larger company can also gain economies of scale in new finance issue costs (e.g. brokers' fees).

Target undervaluation

This justification for an acquisition suggests that some target companies may be bargain buys, in the sense that their shares are undervalued by the market. The implication here is that capital markets are not efficient since the idea of companies being undervalued for more than a short period is not consistent with pricing efficiency. Whether a takeover can be justified on these grounds, therefore, depends on the view taken towards stock market efficiency. While the evidence strongly supports market efficiency (*see* Section 2.3), companies are in practice difficult to value with certainty, which leaves scope for undervalued companies to exist.

Tax considerations

It may be beneficial for a tax-exhausted company to take over a company that is not tax exhausted so it can bring forward the realisation of tax-allowable benefits. This may apply to companies with insufficient profits against which to set off capital allowances and interest.

Increasing earnings per share

If a bidding company has a higher price/earnings ratio than its target company, it can increase its overall earnings proportionally more than it has to increase its share capital if the takeover is financed by a share-for-share issue. Its post-acquisition earnings per share (EPS) will therefore be higher than its pre-acquisition earnings per share: its EPS has been boosted through acquisition. This boosting can be beneficial to the company as EPS is seen as a key ratio by market analysts and an increase in EPS can, potentially, lead to a share price rise.

The process whereby companies seek to increase their EPS through acquisitions is known as *boot-strapping*. This process cannot be used to justify an acquisition in shareholder wealth terms, however, since changes in EPS do not indicate whether an acquisition is wealth creating. There are many drawbacks associated with using EPS alone as a guide to company performance, including the fact that it ignores both cash flow and risk, and that it uses historical numbers based on accounting profit, which is subject to both arbitrary accounting policies and possible manipulation by company management. In fact, boot-strapping may be considered as merely an exercise in creative accounting.

Example	**Boot-strapping**

Big plc is to take over Little plc and intends to offer its shares in payment for Little's shares.

	Big plc	Little plc
Number of shares	200m	25m
Earnings	£20m	£5m
Earnings per share	10p	20p
Price/earnings ratio	25	5
Share price	£2.50	£1
Market value	£500m	£25m

If we assume that Big has to pay £25m (market value) to take over Little, Big must issue 10 million new shares. Details of the enlarged company are as follows:

Number of shares = (200 + 10) = 210m
Earnings = (20 + 5) = £25m
EPS = (25/210) = 11.9p

We can see that Big has manufactured an increase in its EPS. Big plc hopes that the market will apply its original price/earnings ratio of 25 to its higher post-takeover EPS. If this is the case, then Big's shares and hence its market value will increase:

EPS	11.9p
P/E ratio	25
Share price	£2.97
Market value	£623.7m

Whether in practice the market applies a P/E ratio of 25 will depend on its expectations of the performance of Little once it has been taken over by Big. If there is an expectation that Big will pull Little's performance up to its own level, the market may well apply a P/E ratio of 25 to Big's EPS. A more likely scenario, though, is for the market to apply some other P/E ratio to the earnings of the enlarged company. We should note, however, that in practice it is the market price of the share that determines the P/E ratio, not the other way round.

11.2.3 Managerial motives

Takeovers can also arise because of the agency problem that exists between shareholders and managers, whereby managers are more concerned with satisfying their own objectives than with increasing the wealth of shareholders. From this perspective, the motives behind some acquisitions may be to increase managers' pay and power. Managers may also believe that the larger their organisation, the less likely it is to be taken over by another company and hence the more secure their jobs will become. Takeovers made on these grounds have no shareholder wealth justification since managers are likely to increase their own wealth at the expense of the shareholders.

11.2.4 The case against acquisition

So far we have discussed only the justifications offered for mergers and takeovers. A more balanced picture arises if we consider the arguments *against* growth by acquisition.

Possible referral to the Competition Commission

A referral to the Competition Commission, which replaced the Monopolies and Mergers Commission in 1999, can be very damaging to both the image of a bidding company and to its pocket. A formal investigation resulting from a referral may delay the proposed takeover for a considerable time. Depending on the result of the investigation, the takeover may not even be allowed to proceed.

The bid is contested

If a bid is contested, the bidding company may pay a large premium on the original market price in order to acquire its target. Indeed, with takeover premiums between 30 and 50 per cent, acquisition is viewed by many as a relatively expensive way of expanding.

Are mergers and takeovers beneficial?

Research on post-merger performance (*see* Section 11.8) suggests that the expected benefits arising from synergy and economies of scale rarely materialise and that, in general, the only beneficiaries from takeovers are the target company's shareholders and the bidding company's management.

The cost of financing a takeover

If a takeover bid is financed by a share-for-share offer, the bidding company will have to find money to pay dividends on the new shares that have been issued. There will also be changes in the bidding company's ownership structure. Conversely, if a takeover bid is financed by debt, it may increase the bidding company's gearing to levels where it may have difficulties meeting interest payments in the future. Consideration must also be given to the arrangement and issue fees that will be incurred by issuing securities to finance the takeover.

Other difficulties

There are a number of other difficulties that acquiring companies may encounter. Cultural problems are likely to exist, especially when the two companies are in different industries or in different countries if the takeover is a cross-border one. Cross-border takeovers are also subject to exchange rate risk, from both a transaction and a translation perspective (*see* Section 12.1.3). Takeovers can involve complicated taxation and legal issues and may incur large advisory fees. Finally, in some cases, the quality of the assets purchased may turn out to be lower than initially expected. An example of this occurred following the purchase of the US Crocker Bank by Midland Bank plc in the early 1980s, when a large amount of the advances previously made by the Crocker Bank turned out to be bad debts rather than assets.

11.3   Trends in takeover activity

It is apparent from Exhibit 11.2, which gives information on the number of takeovers and the total outlay involved, that merger and takeover activity tends to occur in *waves*. Such waves, which have all been different in nature, occurred in 1972–73, the late 1970s, the end of the 1980s and the mid-1990s. This final wave was by far the largest in terms of total outlay.

The late 1980s saw high levels of takeover activity by conglomerate companies, which purchased what they considered to be underpriced targets in a diverse range of

Exhibit 11.2 **The scale and method of financing takeover activity in the UK between 1970 and 2005**

Year	Number acquired	Outlay £m	Cash (%)	Shares (%)	Debt and preference shares (%)
1970	793	1 122	22	53	25
1971	884	911	31	48	21
1972	1210	2 532	19	58	23
1973	1205	1 304	53	36	11
1974	504	508	69	22	9
1975	315	291	59	32	9
1976	353	448	71	27	2
1977	481	824	62	37	1
1978	567	1 140	57	41	2
1979	534	1 656	56	31	13
1980	469	1 475	52	45	3
1981	452	1 144	67	30	3
1982	463	2 206	58	32	10
1983	568	5 474	53	34	13
1984	447	2 343	44	54	2
1985	474	7 090	40	53	7
1986	842	15 370	26	57	17
1987	1528	16 539	35	60	5
1988	1499	22 839	70	22	8
1989	1337	27 250	82	13	5
1990	779	8 329	77	18	5
1991	506	10 434	70	29	1
1992	432	5 941	63	36	1
1993	526	7 063	80	17	3
1994	674	8 269	64	34	2
1995	505	32 600	78	20	2
1996	584	30 457	63	36	1
1997	506	26 829	41	58	1
1998	635	29 525	53	45	2
1999	493	26 166	62	37	1
2000	587	106 916	37	62	1
2001	492	28 994	79	13	8
2002	430	25 236	69	27	4
2003	558	18 679	86	9	5
2004	741	31 408	63	33	4
2005	735	24 776	88	11	1

Source: Business Monitor and *Financial Statistics.* National Statistics. © Crown Copyright 2006. Reproduced by permission of the Offiice for National Statistics

Vignette 11.1

Water faces up to rising debt levels

FT

Increasing reliance on debt, by companies such as AWG, could have serious implications for large investment programmes to improve water quality and protect the environment demanded by government and the EU. These thoughts are already occupying the mind of industry regulator, Philip Fletcher, who last week warned that customers could face higher bills from April 2005.

Tough price cuts imposed three years ago by the industry regulator have triggered a series of takeover bids and financial restructuring among British water companies.

Failed diversification strategies and, in some cases, over-ambitious investment by large foreign utilities have further stretched balance sheets prompting changes in ownership and the way in which the industry is financed. The regulator, announcing reference terms for the next five-year price review, said: 'I shall ensure that customers face no higher burden than is necessary. But it would be unwise, in the light of likely pressures on most companies, for customers to expect real term reductions in bills from the new price limits.'

Sir Ian Byatt, his predecessor, cut customers' bills by an average of 12 per cent in 1999. Within two years, Hyder, owner of Welsh Water had collapsed under the burden of mounting debts caused by the company's expensive purchase of Swalec, the south Wales electricity company.

Hyder was forced to sell the electricity business and was replaced by Glas Cymru, a pioneering not-for-profit company funded totally by debt. Other financial restructurings – albeit maintaining at least a thin layer of equity – have followed at Mid-Kent, Portsmouth and Dee Valley water companies.

Anglian Water, owned by AWG, has become more than 80 per cent debt-financed following a financial restructuring last year that has already returned £500m to shareholders. Water company shares, nonetheless, have outperformed the FTSE All-Share Index by about 50 per cent since the last price review – regaining almost all of the ground the sector lost in the late 1990s.

It would also be wrong to blame regulatory price cuts for all of the industry's ills. AWG's problems have as much to do with a series of ill-judged diversifications, which last month prompted non-executive directors to ask chief executive, Chris Mellor, to resign. The company has begun legal proceedings to claim £130m in damages, following its £263m purchase of Morrison Construction in 2000 which has since produced losses and write-downs of £100m.

Other factors have also encouraged bid activity. Regulatory opposition to mergers between domestic water companies may have prevented industry consolidation, but has left the door open to foreign companies to enter the British market.

Thames, Britain's biggest water company in 2000 succumbed to a £4.3bn bid from RWE, the large German multi-utility. Bill Alexander, Thames chief executive, complained that merger policies had restricted Thames from growing and competing in international markets against larger French rivals such as Suez and Vivendi.

Suez, which badly needs to cut borrowings, is currently seeking buyers for Northumbrian Water, valued at about £2bn and supplying 4.3m people. A sale of Northumbrian is likely to involve further financial restructuring and increased debt, say analysts. The Royal Bank of Scotland meanwhile last month joined forces with Vivendi, as part of a highly-leveraged deal to buy Southern Water for £2.05bn.

The regulator remains concerned that equity should continue to play a strong part in water industry financing. Whether it does may depend upon his decisions on future pricing, say companies.

Source: Andrew Taylor, *Financial Times*, 5 April 2003. Reprinted with permission.

industries, in many cases subjecting them to restructuring and break-up. In contrast, the most recent wave, which began in the mid-1990s and peaked in 2000, involved horizontal acquisitions concentrated in a number of specific industries such as electrical distribution, pharmaceuticals and financial services. Here, acquiring companies sought to create economies of scale and synergy in areas such as research and development and marketing by acquiring businesses with similar operations. Most recently, a combination of factors have stimulated a wave of takeover bids amongst UK water companies, as illustrated by Vignette 11.1.

Why do mergers and takeovers tend to occur in waves? A number of reasons have been advanced in an attempt to answer this question, but no consensus has been reached. The combination of a booming stock exchange (enabling companies to use shares to finance acquisitions) and an increase in companies' real liquidity and profitability levels is often cited as a factor encouraging takeover activity. This argument is contradicted, though, when we consider that one of the biggest booms in takeover activity followed the 1987 stock exchange crash. There can be no doubt, however, that certain factors have helped to accommodate the financing side of takeovers. Deregulation in the capital markets, for example, making external sources of finance such as debt more available, in combination with low levels of corporate gearing in the early 1980s, certainly increased the capacity of companies to acquire debt for the purpose of financing takeovers and to accommodate borrowings on their balance sheets.

11.4 Target company valuation

Valuing a potential target company is a key stage in the takeover process. The feasibility of the bidder's strategy will not become clear until the target's value has been established and compared with the expected cost of the acquisition. Unfortunately, valuing the target company is a complicated process, partly because of the wide range of valuation methods available. In this sense, business valuation is considered by many to be more of an art than a science.

There are two broad approaches to valuing a company. *Asset-based valuations* focus on the value of the company's assets. *Income-based valuations*, sometimes referred to as *going concern valuations*, consider the future earnings or cash flows expected to be obtained by gaining control of the target company. Owing to the existence of many different techniques within these two broad approaches, it is possible to come up with multiple valuations of a company. Indeed, two bidding companies can produce different valuations of the same target company because each has different plans for it. Each valuation method has its associated advantages and disadvantages and will be more or less appropriate according to the intentions of the acquirer towards its target; for example, does the buyer want to break up its acquisition or does it want to integrate it into its own operations?

The different company valuation methods are now considered in turn and illustrated with the help of a numerical example.

Example   Takeover (Simpson and Stant)

Simpson plc has distributable earnings of £72.70m, a weighted average cost of capital of 14 per cent and a P/E ratio of 18.7. It is in the process of taking over Stant plc whose financial details are as follows:

Stant plc key financial data

Profit before interest and tax (PBIT)	£66.00m
Interest paid	£7.20m

→

Corporation tax	£17.64m
Distributable earnings	£41.16m
Current dividend	16p
Last 4 years' dividends	12p, 13p, 14p, 15p
Earnings per share (EPS)	16.7p
P/E ratio	12.87
Market price of ordinary shares	£2.15
Equity beta	1.17

Stant plc balance sheet

	£m	£m
Fixed assets		265
Current assets	60	
Current liabilities	43	
		17
		282
10% debentures (redemption 2016)		72
		210
Financed by:		
ordinary shares (50p)		123
reserves		87
		210

Simpson plc is optimistic that it will be able to maintain an annual increase in distributable earnings of 5 per cent due to anticipated synergy as a result of the takeover. The company will also be able to sell duplicated assets, realising £60m in one year's time. The risk-free rate of return is 4 per cent and the return on the market as a whole is 10 per cent.

11.4.1 Stock market valuation

Stock market value or market capitalisation is the number of issued ordinary shares of the target company multiplied by their market price. Whether stock market value is a fair value will depend on the efficiency of the stock market. It provides a guide to the bidding company of the minimum likely *purchase price* of the target company. It does not give an estimate of how much the target company is *worth* to the bidder since it does not reflect bidder's post-acquisition intentions. It is therefore a useful starting point for estimating the price that will be paid for the target company as it represents the minimum that target shareholders will accept, but a substantial *premium* will need to be added as an incentive to persuade the shareholders to relinquish their shares.

It must also be recognised that a company's quoted share price does not reflect the value of all of its shares. Since only a small proportion of them are traded at any one time, the quoted share price reflects only *marginal* trading. This reduces the reliance that can be placed on the stock market value and suggests the need to investigate the movement of the target company's share price over a period of time. A further limitation of stock market value is that it has limited applicability if the ordinary shares of the target company are not frequently traded or if the shares of the target company are not listed on a stock exchange.

For Stant plc:

$$\text{Number of ordinary shares of Stant} = \text{Balance sheet value/Par value} = \frac{123m}{0.5} = 246m$$

Therefore:

$$\text{Stock market valuation} = 246m \times £2.15 = £529m$$

11.4.2 Asset-based valuation methods

There are several different ways in which a company's assets can be valued.

Net asset value (book value)

The most straightforward net asset valuation is the *balance sheet* or *book value* of a company's assets. This can be defined as:

Net asset value (book value) = Fixed assets + Net current assets − Long-term debt

In our example, using Stant's balance sheet values:

$$\text{NAV (book value)} = 265m + 17m - 72m = £210m$$

While this valuation method has the advantage that it uses historical costs that are both factual and easily available, it has several disadvantages. For example, historical cost balance sheet values do not reflect current asset valuations: debtor and stock figures may be unreliable, and intangible assets such as goodwill, human capital and brands are ignored. Even at its most reliable, therefore, net asset value offers only a lower limit for the target company's value.

Net asset value (net realisable value)

Assets can be valued using their *net realisable value* rather than their book value. Net realisable value is the amount that could be gained by selling the target company's assets on the open market. It can be defined as the residual value after selling assets, deducting liquidation costs and paying off liabilities: this is often called *liquidation value*. In theory, the market value of the target company should be higher than its net realisable value; if it is not, the target company is by implication undervalued, perhaps owing to stock market inefficiency, and a bidding company can make a risk-free gain by buying the company and liquidating it.

However, calculating the net realisable value of a target company is not easy. The book values of its assets are unlikely to be indicative of their market values as they are largely based on historical cost. The balance sheet value of property tends to underestimate its true value. The balance sheet value of stock is likely to overestimate its net realisable value if items need to be sold quickly or have become obsolete, even though

UK accounting standards require that stock is valued at the lower of cost and net realisable value. The assets of some companies are unique and resale values for such assets may be unavailable; the net realisable values of such assets can only ever be estimates. A further problem is that the net realisable value of a target company will need to include provisions for unforeseen liabilities.

The net realisable value or liquidation value is not the most appropriate valuation method in most takeovers since very few takeovers involve the total break-up of the target company. This method may be useful if the bidder intends to sell off part of the target and integrate the remainder into its existing business operations.

Net asset value (replacement cost)

Replacement cost seeks to determine the cost of acquiring the separate assets of a target company on the open market. Replacement cost has an advantage over book value in that replacement cost estimates of asset values are more relevant than historical cost estimates. Unfortunately, replacement costs, like realisable values, do not take account of goodwill. The bidding company also has the difficulty of identifying the target company's separate assets and determining their replacement costs.

Due to a lack of information, we have not calculated the realisable and replacement values of Stant's assets. This is likely to be the case for most bidding companies which, while being able to obtain the book values of a company's assets from its published accounts, will have great difficulty in determining their replacement costs and realisable values because they lack access to the necessary inside information.

11.4.3 Income-based valuation methods

Valuing a target company as a going concern is appropriate if the bidding company intends to continue its business operations for the foreseeable future, as opposed to liquidating it or selling some of its assets (asset-stripping) after acquisition. The many ways to calculate the going concern value of a target company are all based on valuing the additional income which the bidding company expects to gain from the acquisition.

Capitalised earnings valuation

Here a value is calculated by *capitalising* (discounting) a company's annual maintainable expected earnings by an appropriate required earnings yield or return on investment. *Annual maintainable expected earnings* can be estimated by taking an average of historical earnings, weighted or otherwise, and allowing for any expected future increase in earnings due to synergy or economies of scale. The *capitalisation rate* used to discount this earnings stream should reflect factors such as the size of the company and the industry in which it is operating. The valuation using this method is as follows:

$$\text{Capitalised earnings value} = \frac{\text{Annual maintainable expected earnings}}{\text{Required earnings yield}}$$

In our example, the approximated capitalisation rate is as follows:

$$\text{Required earnings yield} = \text{EPS/share price} = (16.7/215) \times 100 = 7.8\%$$

This is also the reciprocal of the P/E ratio:

$$(1/12.87) \times 100 = 7.8\%$$

We only have the current distributable earnings, but if we assume that they are equivalent to the annual maintainable expected earnings, we have:

$$\text{Capitalised earnings value} = £41.16m/0.078 = £528m$$

Because of the way we determined the required earnings yield, this is the same as the stock market value obtained earlier (the slight difference is due to rounding). An advantage of using this method is that it is a forward-looking measure (it uses *expected* earnings) and it therefore encourages forecasting of future performance. A disadvantage of using this method is the uncertainty surrounding the accuracy of the earnings figure, which may be subject to differing accounting policies and to different treatments of exceptional and extraordinary items.

Price/earnings ratio valuation

This valuation method involves multiplying the target company's distributable earnings by an appropriate price/earnings ratio (P/E ratio) where:

$$\text{P/E ratio} = \frac{\text{Market value of company}}{\text{Distributable earnings}}$$

A major factor in this valuation method is the P/E ratio used. Possible P/E ratios include the bidder's P/E ratio, the target company's P/E ratio, a weighted average of these or, alternatively, an appropriate sector average P/E ratio. If the target company's P/E ratio is used, we obtain the following result for Stant:

$$\text{P/E ratio value} = 12.87 \times £41.16m = £528m$$

This yields a figure similar to the capitalised earnings valuation since, as mentioned earlier, the P/E ratio of a company is the reciprocal of its earnings yield. Alternatively, if the bidding company is sure that it will be able to bring the performance of the target company up to its own performance level, it is more appropriate to use its own P/E ratio. In our example, if Simpson is convinced that it can improve Stant's performance, then:

$$\text{P/E ratio value} = 18.70 \times £41.16m = £770m$$

If the future performance of neither bidding nor target company is expected to change, logic suggests that we apply a weighted average of the two companies' P/E ratios. If we weight the P/E ratios of Stant and Simpson by their current earnings, we obtain:

$$(12.87 \times (41.16/113.86)) + (18.70 \times (72.7/113.86)) = 16.59$$
$$\text{P/E ratio value} = 16.59 \times £41.16m = £683m$$

While this valuation method is straightforward in terms of calculation, it can be seen from the examples given that the values produced fluctuate widely according to the P/E ratio applied. In addition to the problems associated with using distributable earnings, therefore, there is the difficulty of estimating an appropriate post-merger P/E ratio to apply.

Dividend growth model

The value of a target company can be estimated by using the dividend growth model (*see* Section 10.4.3) to calculate the present value of future dividends accruing to its shares. Here:

$$P_0 = \frac{D_0(1 + g)}{(r - g)}$$

where: D_0 = current total dividend payment

g = expected annual growth rate of dividends

r = required rate of return of the company's shareholders

In order to apply this model to Stant, we need to calculate a value for the annual dividend growth rate, g. The average geometric growth rate of historical dividends is as follows:

$$12 \times (1 + g)^4 = 16$$

Hence:

$$g = \sqrt[4]{\frac{16}{12}} - 1 = 7.5\%$$

We can find the total amount of dividends paid recently (D_0) by multiplying the dividend per share by the number of Stant's shares:

$$£0.16 \times 246\text{m shares} = £39.4\text{m}$$

We now require a value for the cost of equity, r. The required return of Stant's shareholders should be used, rather than the required rate of return of the bidding company shareholders since it is the target company shareholders who are being asked to give up their future dividends by selling their shares. We can calculate the required return of Stant's shareholders by using the CAPM and the data supplied earlier:

$$r = 4\% + 1.17 \times (10\% - 4\%) = 11\%$$

If we put our calculated data into the dividend growth model we obtain:

$$\text{Company value} = \frac{£39.4\text{m} \times (1 + 0.075)}{(0.11 - 0.075)} = £1210\text{m}$$

The limitations of this model were discussed earlier in the book (*see* Section 10.4.3). The major drawback noted here is the sensitivity of the model to the value of g, the expected dividend growth rate. Additionally, in our example, the close proximity of cost of equity, r, to the annual dividend growth rate, g, gives us a company value which can be considered to be on the high side.

Discounted cash flow valuation

The maximum amount that Simpson (Y) should be prepared to pay for Stant (X), in theory, is given by the difference between the present values of its pre- and post-acquisition cash flows:

$$PV_{X+Y} - PV_Y$$

Determining these present values requires estimating relevant cash flows and calculating an appropriate discount rate. While a discounted cash flow valuation is in theory preferred, it throws up a number of problems which must be dealt with before any useful information is obtained from this approach to valuing a target company. These include:

- the difficulty of quantifying and incorporating into future cash flow predictions any expected synergy benefits or economies of scale, and deciding upon the rate at which these cash flows are expected to grow in the future;
- deciding upon on an appropriate period over which to estimate future cash flows and determining a terminal value for the company at the end of this period. Corporate forecasting is usually geared to a five-year time horizon and so, as a rough guideline, a five-year time span may be most appropriate;
- determining which discount rate should be used. The most appropriate discount rate is likely to be the bidding company's cost of capital, but the difficulties of calculating it must be overcome. There are certain situations, however, where the bidding company's WACC is not appropriate, for example when the target company possesses significantly different risk characteristics from those of the bidder. In such circumstances, the CAPM can be used to determine a discount rate that takes into account the target company's systematic risk.

Referring back to the example of Stant, we have insufficient information to determine the difference between the pre- and post-acquisition cash flows of the company. However, if we use distributable earnings as an approximate substitute, we have:

Current distributable earnings	£72.70m
Stant's distributable earnings	£41.16m
Total post-acquisition earnings	£113.86m

Simpson expects to be able to increase earnings by 5 per cent per year. It also expects to be able to sell surplus assets for £60m in one year's time. In the absence of a better alternative, we can use Simpson's WACC as the discount rate:

Present value of post-acquisition earnings	
= ((113.86 × 1.05)/(0.14 − 0.05)) + (60/1.14) =	£1381m
Present value of pre-acquisition earnings = (72.70/0.14) =	£519m
Maximum price that Simpson should pay =	£862m

This value, which uses an adaptation of the dividend growth model, assumes that growth in distributable earnings will occur only if the acquisition goes ahead.

11.4.4 Summary of valuation methods

We stated earlier that company valuation was considered to be more of an art than a science and that a wide range of valuation methods can be applied to a target company. The range of different methods has been illustrated by calculating values for Stant plc in our example that range from £210m to £1210m. The accuracy of these values depends on the reliability of the data used. The valuation method deemed most appropriate will depend on the information available to the bidding company and its intentions for the target company.

A summary of the values of Stant plc that have been obtained:

	£m
Stock market valuation	529
Net asset value (using book values)	210
Capitalised earnings valuation	528
P/E ratio valuation	528 or 683 or 770
Gordon growth model valuation	1210
DCF valuation	862

11.5 The financing of acquisitions

Owing to their size, takeovers have significant financial implications for the companies involved. These implications depend on the financing methods used to achieve the takeover. Ultimately, when deciding on its financing method, the bidding company must recognise that the needs of both sets of shareholders involved must be satisfied if its bid is to be successful.

Referring back to Exhibit 11.2, we can see that the ways in which takeovers have been financed have changed significantly over time. A large percentage of takeovers between 1985 and 1987 were financed through share-for-share offers, primarily due to a bullish stock market during this period. However, in the wake of the stock market crash of October 1987, cash offers have proved more popular than share-for-share offers.

11.5.1 Cash offers

Here the target company's shares are purchased by the bidding company using a cash consideration. A cash offer is attractive to the target company's shareholders because the compensation they receive for selling their shares is certain. This is not the case with a share-for-share offer since the value of the bidding company's shares is not constant, but is likely to change during the course of the takeover. With a cash offer, target company shareholders can adjust their portfolios without incurring selling costs. These advantages must be balanced against the disadvantage that if target shareholders sell their shares to the bidding company at a higher price than they originally paid for them, they may be liable to pay capital gains tax on their disposals. Clearly, this will be unattractive to shareholders with large portfolios as they are more likely to have used up their annual UK capital gains allowance (*see* Section 10.4.2). From the point of view of large institutional investors, cash offers are more attractive since pension funds and unit trusts are exempt from paying capital gains tax. The differing tax positions of small and large private and institutional investors help to explain why *mixed offers*, which involve cash and a share-for-share alternative, have grown in popularity. These are considered in Section 11.5.5.

Cash offers also have significant advantages to the bidding company and its shareholders. First, it allows them to see exactly how much is being offered for the target company. Second, cash offers will not affect the number of ordinary shares the bidding company has in issue and so will not alter its ownership structure nor lead to a dilution of its earnings per share.

The major issue surrounding cash issues is *where* the cash is raised from. In many cases, owing to the size of the transaction, the bidding company does not have to hand sufficient cash generated from retained earnings and it will need to raise cash from external sources. This may include debt finance, raised either through borrowing from banks (often in the form of *mezzanine* finance) or through the issue of bonds. Where large amounts of cash are borrowed in order to make a cash offer, the takeover is referred to as a *leveraged takeover*. A problem for bidding companies with high levels of gearing is that they may experience difficulty in finding a sufficient number of banks or other financial intermediaries prepared to supply them with the large amounts of debt finance they require.

Because of the undesirable side-effects associated with high gearing (*see* Section 9.7), many bidders that become highly geared as a result of financing a takeover subsequently sell off parts of the acquired business in order to bring their gearing down to a more manageable level.

In the UK during 1988 there was a large increase in the number of cash-offer takeovers financed by debt (*see* Exhibit 11.2). At the time, high levels of gearing were not seen as being problematic as interest rates were at a relatively low level. As the 1980s drew to a close, however, interest rates increased rapidly and the gearing levels of these highly leveraged companies became a cause for concern. As a result, a number of companies that had borrowed heavily to finance acquisitions had to reduce their gearing, for example through rights issues, in order to repair their balance sheets.

There were also a large number of leveraged takeovers in the USA during the 1980s. A common occurrence was for small companies to borrow massive amounts of cash from banks or to issue unsecured, high-risk, high-return *junk bonds* in order to take over companies much larger than themselves. A high profile example was the $25bn takeover of RJR Nabisco in 1988 by the small private company Kohlberg, Kravis and Roberts (KKR). KKR financed the transaction through borrowing and issuing junk bonds, and subsequently sold off part of RJR Nabisco to reduce its gearing.

11.5.2 Share-for-share offers

Here, the target company's shareholders are offered a fixed number of shares in the bidding company in exchange for the shares they hold in their own company. From the target company shareholders' perspective, one advantage of a share-for-share offer is that they still have an equity interest in the company they originally invested in, even

Vignette 11.2

Morrison bid value drops to £2bn

The value of the Wm Morrison Supermarkets bid for Safeway yesterday fell close to £2bn – a fresh low for the all-share offer launched two months ago. The news came as the Takeover Panel effectively froze the bid timetable to take account of the competition investigation into the battle for the group.

Shares in Morrison fell 3 ½p to 147p, valuing its offer for each Safeway share at 194p and the group at £2.05bn. People close to Morrison said the market was reflecting ongoing uncertainty over the bid, which is being considered by the Office of Fair Trading. When Sir Ken Morrison announced his agreed bid on January 9, he said it valued the group at £2.9bn, or 277 ½p a share.

As Sir Ken's move flushed out other potential bidders the Safeway share price has remained stubbornly high – but his shares have come under pressure and the Safeway board dropped its recommendation. Shares in Safeway last night closed down 5 ½p at 282 ½p.

The move by the Takeover Panel was prompted by the fact that next Tuesday would have been day 39 of the bid process – the last day for publication by Safeway of important new information in the context of the Morrison offer. The Panel said that it would push the date back, because a ruling on whether Morrison's bid would face a referral would not be announced by Tuesday. Day 39 will now be the second day after the announcement of any decision on the competition issues made by Patricia Hewitt, the trade and industry secretary. The rest of the bid timetable will be pushed back accordingly.

The OFT is also considering whether the Morrison bid should be referred to the Competition Commission. It is also considering potential bids from J Sainsbury, Asda/Wal-Mart and Tesco and from Philip Green.

Source: Susanna Voyle, *Financial Times*, 8 March 2003. Reprinted with permission.

though it is now part of a larger concern. In addition, they do not incur the transaction costs of reinvesting any cash received, nor do they incur any capital gains tax liability arising from a share disposal.

A disadvantage to both the acquiring company and its shareholders is that equity payments tend to work out more expensive than cash offers. Because the value of the shares being offered will vary over time (*see* Vignette 11.2), the share-for-share offer made will have to err on the side of generosity in order to prevent it becoming unattractive should the bidding company's share price fall during the offer period. There are also possible disadvantages arising from the bidding company increasing the number of its shares it has in circulation. The effect on the company's share price is unknown, although a fall in price is likely, which will be unpopular with its shareholders. The issue of the new shares will also lead to a dilution of control. On a more subtle level, the decrease in gearing that results from issuing more shares may move the bidding company away from its optimal capital structure and therefore increase its cost of capital. Equally, though, a share-for-share offer may move the bidding company *towards* its optimal cost of capital if it has too much debt finance.

Share-for-share offers can be used by bidding companies with high P/E ratios to engineer an increase in their earnings per share if the target company has a lower P/E ratio. This was dismissed in Section 11.2.2 as an acceptable justification for acquisition since the increase in the bidding company's earnings per share may not involve any intrinsic or real increase in the wealth of its shareholders.

11.5.3 Vendor placings and vendor rights issues

With a *vendor placing*, the bidding company offers shares to target company share-holders, giving them the option to continue their shareholding. However, the bidding company simultaneously arranges for the new shares to be placed with institutional investors and for the cash to be paid to the target company's share-holders. A *vendor rights issue* works in a similar manner, differing only with respect to the final destination of the offered shares. Instead of being placed with institutio-nal investors, the shares are offered to the acquiring company's shareholders. If they are accepted, the cash is then paid to the target company's shareholders. Any rights shares not taken up are placed with institutional investors.

11.5.4 Security packages

The use of securities other than the ordinary shares of the bidder as a means of pay-ment to target company shareholders is now rare. It can be seen from Exhibit 11.2 that the use of security packages, which can include bonds, convertibles and prefer-ence shares, has played only a minor role in the financing of takeovers since the mid to late 1980s, although it represented a popular financing choice for companies up until the late 1960s. The popularity of the use of debt security packages was severely damaged by the high levels of inflation (and the correspondingly higher levels of inter-est) caused by the oil crises of the 1970s.

The problems of using these securities as a method of payment are now considered.

Debentures and loan stock

A major problem with using ordinary bonds as a means of payment is their accept-ability to the target company's shareholders. Investors who previously purchased shares to satisfy their preferences for high risk and high return are unlikely to exchange their shares in the target company for low risk, low return bonds. Issuing bonds will also increase the bidding company's gearing. On the plus side, issuing debt will not necessarily dilute the bidding company's earnings per share, and interest payments are also tax efficient.

Convertible bonds

Some of the problems associated with the use of ordinary bonds may be partially resolved by offering convertible bonds to the target company's shareholders. Convert-ibles are attractive because they offer their holders a means of benefiting from future corporate growth on conversion. Considerable advantages exist from the bid-ding company's point of view (*see* Section 5.4.1). When convertibles rather than ordinary shares are used as a method of payment, dilution of earnings per share will be delayed until the securities are converted. Also, owing to their relative attractive-ness when compared with ordinary bonds, convertible bonds tend to pay a lower interest rate which can greatly ease the cash flow situation of the bidder. Even though banks may not be prepared to lend money to a bidding company because of the high post-acquisition gearing level that would arise, target shareholders may be prepared to accept convertibles as payment in the expectation that, at some future date, the company's gearing level will be reduced as conversion into ordinary equity occurs.

Preference shares

Using preference shares as a means of financing a takeover is even less common than using bonds. For the bidding company, preference shares are less attractive than ordinary shares because preference dividends are less flexible than ordinary dividends. Preference dividends are paid out of after-tax profit and so are not an allowable deduction against taxable profit. Preference shares offer target company shareholders neither the ownership aspects of ordinary shares nor the security of a cash offer.

11.5.5 Mixed bids

Mixed bids refer to a share-for-share offer with a cash alternative. They have become an increasingly popular method of financing takeovers in the UK for two reasons. First, they are perceived as being more acceptable to target company shareholders as they can select the method of payment that best suits their liquidity preferences and tax positions. Second, Rule 9 of the City Code on Takeovers and Mergers requires companies acquiring 30 per cent or more of a target company's shares to make a cash offer (or offer a cash alternative if a share-for-share payment is being used) at the highest price paid by the bidding company for the target company's shares over the previous twelve-month period.

11.6 Strategic and tactical issues

When a company is seeking acquisitions it is vital that it considers the strategy and tactics it is going to employ. It must satisfy itself that acquisition represents a more efficient alternative than organic growth or the independent purchase of required assets *before* it becomes involved in takeover activity. Once the company is satisfied on this count, the strategic process of acquiring a target company can be summarised as follows.

1 Identify suitable target companies.
2 Obtain as much information about the target companies as possible.
3 Using the information obtained, value each target company and decide on the maximum purchase price that should be paid for each alternative.
4 Decide which of the potential target companies is most appropriate.
5 Decide on the best way to finance the acquisition, taking into account which methods of payment are acceptable to both sets of shareholders.

Once an acquiring company has completed this process it must decide on the tactics it will use. Failing to use the right tactics can result in a bidding company paying over the odds or, in the worst-case scenario, failing to acquire its target altogether. Companies must also be aware of the rules and regulations governing mergers and takeovers.

Before we look in more detail at the regulatory environment governing merger and takeover activity, it is important to establish the significance, both legal and otherwise,

Exhibit 11.3	The implications associated with different proportions of shareholding

Voting rights held (%)	Implications and legal obligations of shareholding level
90 and over	Once 90 per cent of shares are held, the company has a right to purchase compulsorily the remaining shares
75 and over	The acquiring company can change the Articles of Association of the company taken over and put it into liquidation
50 and over	The company can influence dividend policy and appoint directors
30 and over	Implies effective control with respect to public companies and hence requires the launch of a formal takeover bid
25 and over	Minority influence to dividend policy and management and an ability to block changes to the company's articles
20 and over	According to the Companies Act 1981, implies related company status
10 and over	Can prevent a complete takeover
3 and over	Taking a holding over 3 per cent in a company requires formal notification

attached to various levels of shareholding. A summary of levels of shareholding and their associated implications is given in Exhibit 11.3.

The most significant level of shareholding from an acquisition perspective is that associated with holding 50 per cent of a company's voting rights. Once a bidding company has more than 50 per cent of its target company's ordinary shares, it has the power to dismiss and appoint directors and in effect has control of the target company's decision-making process.

11.6.1 Merger regulation and control

Broadly speaking, there are two types of regulation that govern merger and takeover activity. Legal controls, often referred to as *antitrust regulation*, consider from a public interest perspective whether mergers and takeovers should be allowed to proceed in the first place. In addition, *self-regulatory controls* focus on the regulation of the bid process itself.

Legal controls

Takeover activity is subject to a number of statutory controls, the most important of which is the Fair Trading Act 1973. Under this Act, the Director General of Fair Trading is required to review all mergers and takeovers which involve the formation of a company that accounts for greater than a 25 per cent share of a particular market or the purchase of assets that amount to over £70m. The Director General collects information on mergers and takeovers that meet these criteria and, after reviewing the evidence, approaches the Secretary of State to determine if a merger or takeover should be investigated by the Competition Commission (CC). Investigations by the CC usually take up to six months, during which time the Commission considers if the merger or takeover is in the public interest. If it decides that it is not, it can prohibit the transaction. The criteria that are considered in deciding whether a merger or takeover should be referred are meant to indicate whether it will maintain or promote the public interest as regards:

■ effective competition within the industry;
■ the interests of consumers, purchasers and users of the goods and services of that industry with respect to quality, price and choice;
■ the reduction of costs and the introduction of new products and techniques.

Historically, only a small number of mergers and takeovers reviewed by the Director General are referred and an even smaller proportion is found by the CC to be against the public interest. In 1997, only 10 out of 186 mergers that qualified for referral were investigated by the Competition Commission (then known as the Monopolies and Mergers Commission). Between 1998 and the end of 2002, 57 transactions were referred. Of these, 24 were deemed to have an adverse effect on competition and were subsequently blocked or had conditions attached to them before they could proceed. Of the remaining transactions, 21 were allowed to proceed as they were not deemed to be against public interest and 12 were 'laid aside'. The latter refers to cases where companies received an informal indication as to whether their takeover activities were likely to be referred. On finding out that they were likely to be referred, the majority of companies subsequently dropped their proposed transaction due to the delay and potentially adverse publicity associated with an investigation by the CC. During 2005, 197 transactions in total were screened by the Director General. Of these, 116 were cleared, 62 were found not to qualify leaving 19 that were referred to the CC.

Self-regulatory controls

In the UK the bid process falls under the non-statutory regulation of the Takeover Panel through its enforcement of the City Code on Takeovers and Mergers. The City Code is based on 10 general principles and 38 more specific rules, and applies to all listed and unlisted public companies resident in the UK. Its aim is to ensure that target company shareholders are treated fairly and equally during the bidding process and it lays down a strict timetable which must be followed by all takeover bids. While the principles and rules of the City Code are not legally enforceable, non-compliance can result in public reprimands along the lines of the one discussed in Vignette 11.3. The City Code has been developed by other self-regulatory organisations, including the London Stock Exchange and the Bank of England, and so for a company to be regarded as reputable in the UK financial system, it must comply with it.

11.6.2 The bidding process

When a predator launches a bid, it is often carried out in consultation with financial advisers such as merchant banks and, as mentioned earlier, it is important for the company to consider carefully the tactics it employs. Having decided on a maximum price that it is prepared to pay, the acquiring company aims to pay as far below this price as possible. The market price of the shares of the target company will act as a lower limit,

Vignette 11.3

The Takeover Panel cracks down on Indigo

Censure fully deserved

Whatever Robert Bonnier, the youthful businessman behind little-known Indigo Capital, learnt back when he was a trainee corporate financier with Swiss Bank Corporation, the finer points of Britain's takeover code do not appear to have figured on the list. Nor does the ability to listen to authority figures. The Takeover Panel yesterday publicly censured both Mr Bonnier and Indigo for their behaviour since January 7, when the company became subject to the takeover code by announcing it was considering a bid for Regus, the office services business.

The language used by the panel may sound mild – Mr Bonnier and Indigo are 'hereby criticised' for conduct falling 'well short of the standards required of parties in takeovers' – but this is the strongest action the panel can take short of a call (extremely rare) for the City to cold-shoulder a party, and the censure is thoroughly deserved.

It is a fundamental panel rule, designed to prevent false markets, that dealings by a bidder in the shares of a target company must be publicly disclosed by the following day. But on six occasions Indigo failed to do so, and three of the rule breaches are particularly bad.

Mr Bonnier twice bought parcels of shares in Regus in direct contravention of panel instructions that it must clear dealings in advance. He appears to have been attempting to rectify an inaccurate statement given to the market, declaring that Indigo held Regus shares when in fact it owned none.

The third deal involved the closing out of a contract for difference, which the panel regards as equivalent to a sale of shares. And before selling shares in a target, a predator must both warn the market and get the approval of the panel. Indigo did neither.

Its immediate punishment is that it will not be allowed to buy any more shares in Regus or exercise a right to take ownership of a near-13 per cent stake tied up in contracts for difference. But since Regus cannot be taken over without the approval of Mark Dixon, chief executive and holder of 63 per cent of the shares, this may not matter too much. Despite Mr Bonnier's apology to the panel, after this fiasco few will regard Indigo as a serious bidder or will take anything it says on trust.

The panel has done its job in maintaining the rules of the takeover game. The focus now passes to the Financial Services Authority, which was already investigating whether pre-January 7 statements by Indigo might have created a 'false and misleading' impression in the market. It will doubtless study the panel's statement carefully. If it uncovers actions that are sinister rather than stupid, it should crack down hard.

Source: Martin Dickson, *Financial Times*, 22 January 2003. Reprinted with permission.

on top of which the acquiring company can expect to pay a premium. Jensen (1993) found that, historically, the premiums paid in successful takeovers tended to be no less than 30 per cent and averaged approximately 50 per cent. Major determinants of the acquisition price finally paid include whether or not a takeover is contested and whether the predator employs the most appropriate tactics during the takeover process.

As mentioned earlier, the City Code must be adhered to during the bidding process. The Code, designed to protect the interests of the various groups of shareholders involved, includes the following procedures.

- The acquiring company must notify its potential target five days after it has built up a 3 per cent holding of its shares. This reduces the possibility of what are known as *dawn raids*, where predators sneak up on their targets before they have had time to organise their defences. Predators can get round this by using *concert parties*, where friendly companies form a coalition in which no one company holds more than the notifiable 3 per cent level of shareholding.

- Once 30 per cent of the target company's shares are held, the predator has to make a cash offer to all remaining shareholders at a price no less than the highest price paid in the preceding twelve-month period.
- When the predator makes the offer, it must first inform the board of the target company of the nature and terms of its offer. This information must then be passed on by the target company's board to its shareholders. The predator then has to post the terms of its offer to the target company's shareholders 28 days after its announcement.
- Once the offer has been received, the target company's board will express their views as to the acceptability of the offer. The predator may also be required by the stock exchange rule book to get approval from its own shareholders with respect to the proposed bid. Once offers have been posted they are open for 21 days. This is extended by 14 days if any amendments are made to the initial offer.
- An offer becomes unconditional when the acquiring company has obtained more than 50 per cent of the target company's shares. Once the offer has become unconditional, existing shareholders have 14 days either to sell their shares or to become minority shareholders in the new company.
- Partial bids, where the predator bids for a specific percentage of the target company's share capital, are allowed only in certain circumstances and require prior approval from the Takeover Panel. Permission is usually given only for partial bids of less than 30 per cent of the target company's overall equity.

11.6.3 Bid defences

When a company receives a bid for its shares, the managers must decide whether or not they will contest the bid. If they decide to contest the bid, they should make this decision purely on the grounds that the offer is not in the best interests of their shareholders and not because they do not wish to lose their jobs. They must communicate their decision to contest the bid to their shareholders. It may be difficult for them to convince shareholders to reject the bid if it appears to be in the financial interests of shareholders to accept it. They may seek to convince shareholders that the acquiring company's share price is artificially inflated and will drop after the proposed takeover, or perhaps argue that their own shares are currently undervalued by the market. Bid defences can be conveniently grouped into two types according to whether they were employed before or after a bid was received.

Pre-bid defences

The simplest and most *constructive* form of pre-bid defence is to make a company too - expensive to take over in the first place. This form of defence is consistent with the objective of shareholder wealth maximisation and can be achieved through the following means.

- *Improving operational efficiency*: rationalising production, cutting overheads and improving labour productivity can raise a company's EPS and share price, making a potential takeover both more expensive and less likely.
- *Examining asset portfolios and making necessary divestments*: managers can sell off non-core, low-growth business and concentrate on the markets in which they have

relative strengths. Again, this should lead to higher profits and a higher EPS and share price.

■ *Ensuring good investor relations*: maintaining good relations with both investors and analysts can make a takeover both more difficult and more expensive. Companies should keep investors well informed about company strategy, policies and performance and also try to satisfy investors' risk–return preferences.

Less desirable types of pre-bid defences are those put into place with the sole purpose of making a company both difficult and expensive to take over. These *obstructive* defences are often at odds with shareholder wealth maximisation and include the following techniques.

■ *Restructuring of equity*: a number of tactics are available within this area. For example, companies can repurchase their own shares to make it more difficult for predators to build up a controlling position, or they can increase their gearing level in order to make themselves less attractive to bidding companies. More intriguingly, companies can plant *poison pills* within their capital structure, for example options giving rights to shareholders to buy future loan stock or preference shares. If a bidding company tries to take over the company before the rights have to be exercised, it is obliged to buy up the securities, hence increasing the cost of the acquisition. The European Union's lengthy and troubled campaign to outlaw poison pills is the subject of Vignette 11.4.

■ *Management retrenchment devices*: the best known of these are *golden parachutes*, which give extremely generous termination packages to senior managers and thereby increase the cost of the takeover as substantial amounts of money are needed to remove incumbent managers. However, this form of takeover defence is becoming increasingly unpopular with institutional investors.

■ *Strategic defence via cross-holdings*: this defence ensures that a significant proportion of equity is in friendly hands through companies arranging to take a mutual shareholding in each other in order to block potential takeover bids.

Post-bid defences

Post-bid defences are used by target companies to repel a bid once one has been made. Post-bid defences that are often used include the following.

■ *Rejection of the initial offer*: when a takeover bid is made, the bid is attacked to signal to the predator that the target company will contest the takeover. In some cases, this may be sufficient to scare the predator off.

■ *A pre-emptive circulation to shareholders*: target companies can appeal to their own shareholders, explaining why the bid is not in their favour from both a logical and price perspective.

■ *Formulation of a defence document*: the board of the target company can prepare a formal document for circulation among its own shareholders which praises the company's performance and criticises the bidding company and its offer. Defence documents are the subject of Vignette 11.5.

■ *Profit announcements and forecasts*: the defending company can produce a report which indicates that its forecast profits for the future will be much better than those

Vignette 11.4

More EU member states opt for 'poison pill'

The European Union's long and troubled campaign against 'poison pills' and other takeover defences is heading for a further setback, with more and more member states deciding not to apply key provisions of the EU takeover directive.

National governments have until May 20 to implement the directive, adopted in 2004 after more than 14 years of fierce controversy. The law was originally intended to make it much harder for companies facing a bid to use 'poison pill' tactics such as issuing new shares or entering into complex joint ventures. It would also have curbed the use of shares with multiple voting rights – which can also act as a deterrent to bidders.

However, strong opposition from member states such as Germany and Sweden and lack of support in the European parliament ensured the draft law was severely watered down.

The directive now allows member states to 'opt out' of the key rules on takeover defences and, according to two new surveys, most states are doing just that. 'We cannot say that this directive is a step back, but we are still disappointed. We were hoping for a gold medal but we are only going to get a bronze,' said Philippe Bodson, the president of the European Group for

Investor Protection, which drafted one of the studies.

Julian Francis, a London-based partner at law firm Freshfields and the author of a similar study, agreed: 'From an investors' point of view this is without doubt a disappointment. There will be no single European takeover code and there is not much investor protection.'

Stung by Mittal Steel's recent takeover bid for Arcelor, the Luxembourg-based steel group, some countries are using the adoption of the directive to introduce new hurdles. France, for example, will give companies facing a hostile bid the right to issue warrants convertible into shares at a discounted price to existing shareholders – making any takeover more expensive.

Such moves may violate the spirit of the directive, but are almost certainly allowed under the weak compromise that the EU eventually agreed two years ago. Crucially, the law left member states free to decide whether to apply its core provisions relating to 'poison pill' defences. These stipulate that:

■ The board of the target company must seek authorisation from shareholders before taking any action that may frustrate the bid, and in

particular before issuing new shares (Article 9).

■ Defences against takeovers already laid out in the company's articles of association or in agreements with shareholders do not apply vis-a-vis a new takeover bid (Article 11).

Countries that decide to opt out of Article 9 leave management free to introduce poison pills after a bid is announced – without consulting shareholders. Countries opting out of Article 11 leave companies free to pre-empt possible bids by putting in place defences before bids are announced.

The Egip study said at least 15 out of 25 EU member states had decided to opt out of Article 11 or were likely to, including Italy, Germany, France, Britain, Spain, Poland, the Netherlands and Sweden. Only Latvia, Lithuania and Greece indicated they would ban pre-bid takeover defences.

Many member states are planning to exempt companies from these strictures in cases where they face takeover bids from companies that do not apply them in the first place. The inclusion of this 'reciprocity clause' reflects fears that heavily protected groups could go on a buying spree across the EU while being shielded from hostile bids itself.

Source: Tobias Buck, *Financial Times*, 1 March 2006. Reprinted with permission.

expected by the market. If these revised forecasts are accepted by the market, this acceptance will force up the market price and make the proposed takeover more expensive. A major problem here is that, if the company does not meet these increased forecasts, its share price is likely to fall, putting it at risk from another takeover bid and making it less likely that such a defence will be successful when used again.

■ *Dividend increase announcements*: a company can announce an increase in current dividend and an intention to pay increased dividends in the future. This expected increase in shareholder returns may dissuade them from selling their shares.

Vignette 11.5

No slanging match as BPB attempts to prove that its case is mathematically correct

Yesterday it all came down to money – as if it had ever been about anything else.

In its 41-page defence document, BPB attempted to prove mathematically that the cash price of 720p offered by Saint-Gobain was simply too low.

The company chose to steer clear of offering any more cash to shareholders – it has already promised a capital return of 70p and an increased full-year dividend of 23p. Instead, it focused on the growth potential in the business.

Based on a series of nine assumptions ranging from selling prices to the cost of the bid defence, the company put out a forecast for its full-year profit to March 2006. BPB believes that, barring natural disaster, extreme weather, industrial disruption, civil disturbance or government action, it ought to produce a 24 per cent rise in underlying profit to about £350m.

That profit rise – calculated before the effect of the return of capital to shareholders already announced – would give underlying diluted earnings per share of 50p. By applying BPB's peer group price-earnings ratio multiple of 14.3 to the earnings per share, the company believes that the implied trading value for a BPB share, without an

offer but including the 70p per share return to shareholders, is 715p.

But BPB's calculation was best described as cautious. Seldom does a company produce a lower trading value for its shares than is being offered during a hostile bid.

Richard Cousins, chief executive, admitted that the document was perhaps not as bullish as some had expected. 'We think it is an analytical, credible and cautious assessment of the business. We can all invent some maths and come up with a number like £9.'

Rather, Mr Cousins said the report should be seen less as a defence document but more as fundamental industrial assessment of the company's strength. Mr Cousins pointed to BPB's strong growth prospects. 'We think Europe as we look forward is a simply stunning business which is simply not reflected by the financial markets. It has not been adequately valued in our view. Our emerging markets are a huge driver of profits going forward.'

However, Mr Cousins said the company might have been guilty of underselling its advantages so far.

He said: 'We were trying to earn a re-rating step by step. We were due to

make a number of presentations in October and we think the company was due for a major re-rating over the next six to 12 months. We are trying to shout a bit louder now but still be credible.'

Essentially, BPB believes that, if Saint-Gobain walks away, there is no reason why its shares should not fall below 700p. But, predictably, Saint-Gobain disagreed.

The French company took issue with the way that BPB reached a valuation of 715p, saying it was using too high a multiple, and disagreed with BPB's statement that the premium offered was only 1 per cent.

It pointed out that 720p was a 40 per cent premium to the price at which BPB's shares were trading before it made an offer.

However, both sides worked hard to stop the tussle for control degenerating into a slanging match.

Saint-Gobain is known to be convinced of BPB's growth potential and the strength of its management.

For his part, Mr Cousins said: 'It is not personal. We actually think Saint-Gobain have been rather clever, to see the value in this company before the market did.'

Source: Lucy Smy, *Financial Times*, 15 September 2005. Reprinted with permission.

Equally, they may query why increased returns were not paid prior to the arrival of a takeover bid.

- *Revaluation of assets*: before or after a bid is made a company can revalue certain assets on its balance sheet, such as land and buildings, or capitalise intangible assets in its balance sheet, such as brands and goodwill, in order to make the company look stronger or more valuable. While this may lead to the predator having to make an increased offer, it could be argued that, if capital markets are efficient, no new information is being offered to the market and the existing share price is a fair one.

- *Searching for a white knight*: the target company can seek a more suitable company to take it over, although this tactic tends to be used only as a last resort. The City Code allows this tactic, but if the target company passes any information to the 'white knight' it must also be passed to the initial predator. A variation of this technique is to issue new shares to a 'white knight' in order to dilute the predator company's holdings. The defending company must get its shareholders' approval before it defends the takeover bid in this way, however.
- *Pac-man defence*: this defence involves the target company making a counter-bid for the shares of the predator. This option is difficult to organise and expensive to carry out, but it has been used on occasion in the USA.
- *Acquisitions and divestments*: the target company can either buy new assets or companies that are incompatible with its predator's business or sell the 'crown jewels' or assets that the predator company is particularly interested in. This tactic is more common in the USA than in the UK since, in the UK, the City Code restricts the sale of assets once a takeover bid has been made.

11.7   Divestment

So far we have considered only transactions that expand the size of a company. In practice, the majority of acquisitions are followed by a period of divestment or *asset stripping*, where predators sell off parts of the acquired company considered to be surplus to requirements. The past two decades have also witnessed prominent conglomerates dismantling themselves through divestments, such as the high-profile 1996 dissolution of Hanson plc. In addition, the 1980s and 1990s saw a number of companies divesting peripheral operations to focus on their core business in order to survive in an increasingly competitive commercial environment. Research by Comment and Jarrell (1995) concluded that, 'greater corporate focus through divesting activities is consistent with shareholder wealth maximization'. Examples of major divestments involving UK companies are shown in Exhibit 11.4.

| Exhibit 11.4 | Major UK divestments including total value and classification |

Date	Divestor	Divested	Value (£m)	Classification of divestment
1987	Asda	MFI	620	MBO (by MFI's management)
1997	British Gas	Centrica	2 900	Spin-off
2001	Kingfisher	Woolworth	424	Spin-off
2001	P&O	P&O Princess Cruise	2 000	Spin-off
2001	BT	Various properties	2 000	Sell-off
2004	Saga	N/A	1 350	MBO (by incumbent management)
2005	Rentokil	Style Conferences	325	Sell-off
2005	GUS	Burberry	1 150	Spin-off

11.7.1 Reasons for divestment

A number of arguments have been advanced to explain why companies divest themselves of part of their business. These include the following reasons.

- Divestment allows significant amounts of cash to be raised which can then be used to ease a company's liquidity situation or to reduce its level of gearing.
- It allows companies to concentrate on core activities, which they can then expand and use to generate benefits such as economies of scale.
- Synergy may be generated by selling off part of the business as the divested assets may be worth more in the hands of management specialising in that line of business.
- The company, on rare occasions, could be divesting its *crown jewels* in order to dissuade an unwanted predator company from taking it over.

11.7.2 Divestment strategies

Different divestment strategies can have markedly different characteristics and implications for the parties involved.

Sell-offs

Here a company sells off part of its operations to a third party, normally for a cash settlement. Research has indicated that a sell-off is most likely to occur in a multi-product company. A company may sell off a division or subsidiary that is peripheral to its main business in order to raise cash and ease any management control problems. The decision on whether to sell a part of the business should ideally be based on net present value (NPV) considerations (*see* Section 6.3). If selling off part of the business yields a positive NPV and hence adds to shareholder wealth, then the company should go through with the proposed divestment.

Spin-offs

A spin-off is another name for a *demerger*. The formal definition is 'a pro rata distribution of subsidiary shares to the shareholders of the parent'. The structure of the parent company changes but, unlike a sell-off, the ownership of the assets remains with the parent and no cash is raised. Where, before, there was one company, now there are two or more companies, one with a majority shareholding in the other. The new company *may* have different management from the original company but will still be owned by the same set of shareholders. The benefits put forward to justify this type of reconstruction are as follows.

- It results in a clearer management structure, which may lead to a more efficient use of the assets of the demerged company and of the assets remaining in the original company.
- A spin-off might facilitate future merger and takeover activity with respect to the demerged company.
- It may enhance the value of the company as a whole as the demerged company's assets may not have been fully appreciated within the original company. The company may currently be valued at what is referred to as a *conglomerate discount*, where investors cannot see the wood for the trees. Once spun off, the assets stand alone and hence are more visible to the market. The benefits of spin-offs are the subject of Vignette 11.6.

Vignette 11.6

Just a mention of spin-off can unlock value for shareholders

Spin-offs are becoming an increasingly popular theme driving the stock selection strategies of some funds. The most recent research into the phenomenon suggests that news of a corporate break-up could provide a valuable investment opportunity.

When Pfizer said last month that it planned to hive off its consumer products business, valued at about $10bn, it was the largest of recent US break-up announcements. The trend is in contrast to the wave of mergers and acquisitions sweeping Europe.

Pfizer said its objective was to 'unlock the value of the business for shareholders at a time when market valuations are attractive'. Pfizer climbed 6 per cent on the day of the announcement.

A spin-off is the sale or distribution to shareholders of new shares in a division of a parent company.

A sample compiled by Lehman Brothers shows that since 1990, the average spin-off has outperformed the S&P 500 by 13.3 per cent in its first year as a stand-alone company. The average parent company has outperformed by 14.4 per cent in the 12 months before the spin-off is completed.

'Most of the time, parent firms are seeking an increase in operational and strategic focus in order to unlock value,' says Henry Chip Dickson, of Lehman. 'In such cases, parents believe the sum of the parts is greater than the whole, and through greater focus they can increase shareholder returns.'

Shareholders gain confidence in the ability of the leaner parent company to improve operations following the spin-off, while the new company, once free of the parent's apron strings, becomes more focused. Fortunes of the spin-off may also depend, to some extent, on its attractiveness as a takeover target. David Williams, portfolio manager of the Excelsior Value and Restructuring Fund, looks for opportunities when companies break up. He sees potential in Tyco, the conglomerate that is splitting into three separate companies.

'I like the sum of the parts, and can see around 50 per cent upside from Tyco's current price,' Mr Williams says.

He also backed Centex Corp, the fourth-biggest US homebuilder, which rose nearly 90 per cent in the year before the February 2004 spin-off of Eagle Materials, the cement and plasterboard maker.

Eagle jumped 50 per cent the following year. Although this performance can be explained in part by the buoyant state of the housing market at that time, there have been other strong examples.

Barnes and Noble, the bookseller, spun off its video game retailing unit in November 2004. In the year or so between its announcement and the date of transaction, its shares gained 16 per cent. A year after, the shares of GameStop, the spin-off company, were up more than 80 per cent, and currently trade 94 per cent higher.

But results vary. Shares of Kimberly-Clark, the papermaker, rose handsomely after it announced the December 2004 spin-off of Neenah Paper. Neenah has since fallen 14.5 per cent amid plant closures and strikes. In 2005, aluminium producer Alcan spun off Novelis, the aluminium sheet maker, to similar effect.

Among companies that have recently announced spin-offs, Agilent Technologies, the maker of scientific testing equipment, said in August that its semiconductor testing unit would stand alone. Agilent has since risen 33 per cent. First Data, the payment services company, has risen 6 per cent since it announced a spin off of Western Union in January.

Sprint Nextel, however, has underperformed since announcing it was planning to spin off its local telephone network operations this year. But Sprint has been struggling to break into profit after its acquisition of Nextel last August. Mr Williams says companies will often announce spin-offs in weak periods to try to boost their share prices.

Lehman's research looks compelling, as did similar studies by Penn State in 1993 and McKinsey Quarterly in 1999. As in all investment theories, there is no simple formula to picking winners, but spin-offs are increasingly popular in stock selection in funds such as Investec's Global Strategic Value Fund and hedge fund Gotham Capital.

Source: Neil Dennis, *Financial Times*, 1 March 2006. Reprinted with permission.

Management buyouts

A management buyout (MBO) is the purchase of part or all of a business from its parent company by the existing management of the business, for example the purchase of a subsidiary company from the parent by the subsidiary's management. Sometimes, however, there may be insufficient skills among subsidiary managers and the

Vignette 11.7

RSA's health insurer in £147m MBO

Royal & Sun Alliance yesterday sold its UK healthcare business to management for £147m, continuing the programme of disposals launched last year to rebuild its finances. RSA said that the deal would release about £250m of capital to be redirected into its general insurance business. The healthcare unit, which provides private medical insurance and personal accident services and wrote £273m of premiums last year, was a non-core business, the group said. 'This is a significant step forward in our capital restructuring,' RSA said. The company's shares rose more than 3 per cent to 83 ¾p.

Oxfordway, the buy-out vehicle, is headed by Tim Ablett, a former chief executive of the healthcare business and managing director of Groupama in the UK. The consortium is backed by Barclays Private Equity, which is investing £87m for a 90 per cent stake in the venture, and Bank of Scotland. The move into the healthcare market, worth an estimated £5bn, is Barclays Private Equity's biggest investment to date.

The sale is the latest part of RSA's survival plan, which involved reducing its global workforce by more than 12000, withdrawing from underperforming lines and shedding non-core businesses. Earlier this week, RSA unveiled plans for the initial public offering of Promina, its business in Australia and New Zealand, which could raise between £500m and £800m.

Source: Robert Orr and Elizabeth Rigby, *Financial Times*, 5 April 2003. Reprinted with permission.

subsidiary may be sold to an external management team through a management buy-in (MBI). MBOs and MBIs are widespread phenomena and are considered in more detail in the next section. They are the subject of Vignette 11.7.

11.7.3 Management buyouts

The motivation behind MBOs usually comes from the parent company's board of directors. The reasons behind their desire to sell the subsidiary are usually similar to those attributed to sell-offs. However, an MBO may be preferred to a sell-off as a divestment strategy as the divesting company is more likely to get the co-operation of the subsidiary's management if it sells using an MBO. Additionally, if the subsidiary is loss-making, the current management may be more optimistic that they can turn the situation round than an outside buyer may be. Alternatively, the motivation may come from the managers of the subsidiary as they may be finding it difficult to obtain funds from the parent company and feel marginalised from the decision-making process in the group as a whole.

The financing of MBOs

Third-party financing is crucial in order for most MBOs to proceed as existing managers are unlikely to have sufficient funds at their disposal to finance the purchase. The management buyout team requires a well-thought-out business plan, incorporating future cash flow projections, as a prerequisite to obtaining the external finance it needs. Without such a business plan, the MBO team is unlikely to win the confidence of funding institutions such as venture capitalists.

MBOs are normally financed using a mixture of debt and equity, although there has been a trend towards *leveraged* MBOs (known as Leveraged Buyouts or LBOs) that use very high levels of debt, with in some cases as much as 90 per cent of the finance in debt form. How much debt is used in practice will depend on the amount of debt that can be supported by the MBO, given its line of business, perceived risk, existing level of gearing and quality of assets. Typically, the finance for an MBO will be drawn from the following sources.

■ *Ordinary equity*: the small amounts of equity finance issued tend to be bought by the management team themselves, except where venture capitalists purchase large amounts of equity in the new company. The management of the company might be reticent to use a large amount of equity finance, though, because of the loss of control it may bring. Venture capitalists normally look to hold on to their shares in the medium term, selling them off after about five years in order to realise their investment. Many MBOs therefore have flotation on, say, the Alternative Investment Market as a medium-term goal in order to provide an *exit route* for venture capitalists.

■ *Debt finance*: this can be obtained from a number of sources, including clearing, merchant and overseas banks, in addition to venture capitalists specialising in financing MBOs. Debt finance can take a number of forms, including term loans and debentures.

■ *Mezzanine finance*: the name given to unsecured debt finance that, while possessing less risk than ordinary equity, is more risky than secured debt and hence offers a return somewhere between the two.

In many cases, major suppliers of finance will require representation at board level because of the large stake they have in the business. This allows them to have a say in the long-term strategic decisions of the board; they will have no significant interest in the operational aspects of the company.

The difficulties faced by MBOs

As mentioned earlier, the suppliers of finance will have to assure themselves that an MBO will be a success. To this end, they will consider the quality and expertise of the management, the reasons behind the sale of the assets, the future prospects for the company and the stake the management team is taking in the venture. They will also be aware that certain types of company and product are more suitable to MBOs than others, for instance those with good cash flows and stable technology.

MBOs will clearly face a number of problems that managers will need to negotiate if their venture is to be successful. A major problem for MBOs when they sever links with their parent is how to provide, internally, services previously provided by the parent. For example, MBOs may have to develop their own financial management and financial accounting systems since their managers, while knowledgeable in the operational areas of their business, may not have the required knowledge and experience in these important financial areas. Other problems are likely to include the following:

■ determining a fair price for the MBO. The sale price will be in excess of the liquidation value of the division's assets but the final price will be determined by negotiation;

■ the complicated tax and legal considerations surrounding the MBO;

■ maintaining relationships with previous customers and suppliers;

■ generating reinvestment funds if refurbishment or replacement of assets is required;

- maintaining the pension rights of both managers and employees;
- inducing changes in work practices in order to turn company performance around.

Despite their problems, MBOs play an important role in corporate restructuring strategy. By the third quarter of 2005, for example, over 501 deals, totalling £18bn, were completed in the UK alone, compared with deals worth £20bn in 2004.

11.8 Empirical research on acquisitions

A large number of empirical investigations into the performance of acquisitions have considered the impact of acquisitions on the wealth of the various interest groups involved. Between 1971 and 2001 no fewer than 130 such studies were carried out. It is difficult to establish whether acquisitions have been successful, however, as evaluation of success or failure involves, in many cases, a series of subjective judgements. In theory, benefits such as economies of scale and synergy are available to companies involved in acquisition. Whether companies manage to crystallise these potential gains in practice is another matter and will depend heavily upon post-merger planning and management. Grubb and Lamb (2000) had no such doubts about the benefits of acquisitions, stating that: 'the sobering reality is that only about 20 percent of all mergers really succeed. Most mergers typically erode shareholder wealth.'

There is also a large body of information and research on how companies can increase the chances of successful acquisitions, as well as studies of post-merger integration. De Noble et al. (1988) cite a number of lessons for merger success, including involving line managers in takeover activity, searching out any hidden costs that takeovers incur, management being aware of the existence of culture differences and appreciating the vital link between corporate structure and strategy.

The best way to build up a picture of whether acquisitions are beneficial as a whole is to identify the groups affected and then to consider the evidence regarding the impact of acquisitions on them.

11.8.1 The economy

The important question here is whether or not acquisitions produce a social gain for the economy as a whole. The answer to this question, in theory, is 'possibly, yes'. This is because the potential for acquisitions to create an economy-wide gain does exist if, as a consequence of acquisitions, assets are transferred from the control of inefficient managers to the control of efficient managers. Unfortunately, the motives behind acquisitions often owe more to managerial self-interest than to the more efficient use of assets.

The weight of empirical evidence suggests that acquisitions have at best a neutral effect and that there are no extreme efficiency gains. Cowling et al. (1980) used cost–benefit analysis to examine nine mergers that occurred between 1965 and 1970 in the UK in order to determine whether increased efficiency through economies of scale outweighed the welfare loss from increased industrial concentration. They concluded that no real efficiency gains were made and that in the UK, where most takeovers were of a horizontal nature, any such gains were neutralised by increased monopoly power. They did, however, identify benefits in one or two instances where superior management gained control. Subsequent research has echoed the findings of Cowling et al. that the effect of acquisitions on the economy is, by and large, neutral. Although the economic wealth to be shared out between parties may not increase, scope still exists for certain parties to benefit at the expense of others.

11.8.2 The shareholders of the companies involved

The impact of acquisitions can be assessed at a company level by examining the effect of acquisitions on the wealth of acquiring and target company shareholders. Two broad approaches can be used here.

The first method is to use accounting and financial data to assess the performance of companies pre- and post-acquisition. The results of such surveys, including those carried out by Singh (1971) in the UK between 1955 and 1960 and Kelly (1967) in the USA between 1946 and 1960, concluded that acquisitions have proved unprofitable from the acquiring company's viewpoint. It must be noted, however, that the results of such investigations rely heavily on the quality and reliability of the accounting data used.

The second and more commonly used method to quantify the benefits of mergers to the two shareholder groups is to examine pre- and post-bid share prices. Research in this area uses the capital asset pricing model or CAPM (*see* Section 8.5) to calculate expected returns for both acquiring and target companies' shares before and after the announcement of a takeover bid. These are then compared with actual returns to allow the identification of any abnormal returns generated during the takeover period.

The results of empirical studies employing this methodology have concluded that *target company shareholders* tend to enjoy significant positive abnormal returns whereas *acquiring company shareholders* experience statistically insignificant negative or positive abnormal returns. Following on from this, many surveys conclude that, in the majority of cases, the gain made by the target company's shareholders outweighed the loss made by the acquiring company. A study by Jensen and Ruback (1983) in the USA showed average abnormal returns to acquiring company shareholders of 4 per cent for successful bids, compared with a 1 per cent loss for failed bids. This contrasted heavily with shareholders of the target company, who on average experienced benefits of 30 per cent for successful bids and losses of 3 per cent for failed bids. In the UK, studies by Franks et al. (1988) and Firth (1980) found that acquiring companies experienced little or no abnormal gain during the takeover period. One, however, must not lose sight of the *size* effect. Even if there is a significant improvement in the performance of the target company, when this is spread over the larger share base of the acquiring company, the gain will always be less significant in percentage terms.

A likely explanation of the benefits that accrue to target company shareholders is that they represent a bid premium which must be paid in order for target company shareholders to be persuaded to part with their shares. The observed lack of benefits to acquiring company shareholders at the time of takeover may be explained by the efficiency of capital markets, i.e. the market predicts takeovers long before they actually occur and consequently impounds the benefits of the takeover into the acquiring company's share price a number of months before its announcement. This explanation was supported by Franks et al. (1977) who found evidence that the market began to anticipate acquisitions at least three months before they were announced.

Some surveys have considered the abnormal returns of acquiring and target companies over periods starting well before takeovers were made. The results suggest that acquirers, on average, earned positive abnormal returns over these periods whereas their target companies experienced negative abnormal returns. This may give support to the idea that acquisitions facilitate the transfer of assets and resources from less efficient to more efficient management.

While most empirical studies have tended to reach the same broad conclusion, some have reported a number of more specific findings which are summarised here.

- Diversification destroys value whereas increasing focus conserves value. This conclusion was supported by, among others, Berger and Ofek (1995). Meanwhile, DeLong (2001) found this to be particularly true of takeovers involving banks.
- Acquisitions aimed at building monopoly power were found not to enhance acquiring company performance by Eckbo (1992).
- Healey et al. (1997) found that value was more likely to be created when managers had their own wealth at stake.
- Travlos (1987) found that paying for takeovers with shares was more expensive for acquirers than using cash.
- Rau and Vermaelen (1998) and Sudarsanam and Mahate (2003) concluded that 'glamour' buying acquiring companies were more likely to destroy wealth compared to acquirers who acquired under-performing target companies.

Concluding this section, empirical studies appear to be in agreement that substantial benefits accrue to target company shareholders. There is less agreement over the benefits to acquiring company shareholders: some surveys found no gains, others found small but statistically insignificant gains and losses. Many surveys concluded that acquisitions are not wealth *creating*, but rather involve the *transfer* of wealth from acquiring company shareholders to target company shareholders.

11.8.3 Managers and employees of acquiring and target companies

It is generally agreed that acquiring company managers benefit from successful takeovers. This is due to the increased power and status of running a larger company, which is often reflected by an increase in financial rewards. In addition, managers' jobs become more secure as it is more difficult for other companies to acquire the enlarged company. In contrast, target company managers lose out. In the majority of cases they are dismissed, either because they are deemed to be inefficient or because they are surplus to the acquirer's requirements. The same is true of target company employees as redundancies tend to follow the vast majority of acquisitions. An obvious way to achieve economies of scale is streamlining business operations by reducing the number of employees in duplicated functions and by closing down unwanted parts of the acquired business.

11.8.4 Financial institutions

Financial institutions, predominantly merchant banks, are involved in fee-making advisory roles in the merger and takeover process as advisers to both acquiring and target companies. They help in many aspects, from advising on bid values and organising defence tactics, to the arrangement of financing for mergers and acquisitions. In the takeover boom year of 1995, it has been estimated that City of London merchant banks were paid total advisory fees in the region of £950m, demonstrating clearly that they are major beneficiaries of acquisitions. Malcolm Glazier's £790m acquisition of Manchester United in 2005 generated advisory and bankers' fees of £22m. Defending takeover bids comes at a price too: the same year Rentokil paid out £20m in bid defences to a variety of advisors.

11.8.5 Summary of research on acquisitions

The clear winners from acquisitions appear to be target company shareholders, who receive substantial premiums over and above pre-bid share prices. Other parties that benefit from acquisitions are investment banks, lawyers and accountants, who earn substantial fee income from offering advice, and acquiring company managers, who experience increased job security and remuneration. Evidence suggests that little or no benefit arises for acquiring company shareholders, especially when acquisitions are contested and the acquiring company pays over the odds for its target as a result. There appears to be no clear evidence of any general economic benefits of acquisitions; if individual acquisitions transfer assets to more efficient use, however, society will ultimately gain. The clear losers are target company managers and employees, who may well lose their jobs once their company has been acquired.

11.9 Conclusion

In this chapter we have given a thorough consideration to acquisitions, an area that continues to maintain a high profile in modern corporate finance and has implications for corporate dividend, financing and investment policies. Many justifications have been offered for acquisitions, not all of which have been accepted as valid by academics. The existence of many company valuation methods illustrates the fact that determining a fair price for a target company is a very imprecise science. The financing implications of takeovers are also far from straightforward and can have serious implications for a company's balance sheet. The methods most commonly used are share-for-share offers, cash offers and mixed bids.

Takeovers can take months to complete, especially if the target company considers the bid to be hostile and tries to repel it, and, once completed, acquiring company shareholders rarely benefit from the acquisitions. This is not only because of the payment of substantial bid premiums, but also because of the failure of acquiring companies to obtain the expected post-acquisition benefits. These benefits tend not to materialise owing to the difficulties faced by the acquirer in achieving a successful integration of the assets of the two companies. Parties that do tend to gain from acquisitions are acquiring company managers and target company shareholders.

On the opposite side of the takeover coin is divestment. If used sensibly, companies can use divestments to increase shareholders' wealth. Acquiring companies often follow acquisitions with a series of divestments as they sell off parts of the target company that do not figure in their long-term plans. There are three major divestment strategies: sell-offs, spin-offs and management buyouts. The choice of strategy depends very much on the individual circumstances involved.

Key points

1. Acquisitions have significant effects on companies' assets and financial structures.

2. Acquisitions tend to be far more common than mergers owing to the relative sizes of the companies involved.

3. Acquisitions can be classified as being vertical, horizontal or conglomerate.

4. The motives put forward by companies to justify acquisitions can be economic, financial and managerial in nature.

5. Economies of scale and synergy are the economic benefits most frequently cited to justify acquisitions, especially those which are horizontal in nature.

6. When a company is considering entering into an acquisition it is important for it to consider the associated costs and disadvantages as well as the benefits.

7. Acquisitions tend to come in waves, usually coinciding with booms in the economy and times of high corporate liquidity.

8. An accurate valuation of the target company is crucial to the success of an acquisition.

9. The two broad approaches that can be used to value a company are based either on the value of the assets of the company itself or on the income associated with the ownership of the assets.

10. The most common ways for companies to finance acquisitions are by using share-for-share offers, cash offers or mixed offers.

11. It is important that companies consider the implications of their chosen method of financing on their shareholders' wealth, their level of gearing, their liquidity and their ownership structure.

12. Companies must have an understanding and an awareness of the regulatory framework that governs acquisitions.

13 Strategic and tactical aspects of acquisitions play an important part in determining whether bids are successful or not.

14 Target companies have a number of ways to defend themselves against an unwanted takeover bid once it has materialised. A better strategy, though, is to use pre-bid defences to dissuade potential acquirers from making a bid in the first place.

15 A company can also influence the wealth of its shareholders through a well-thought-out divestment strategy.

16 Companies should dispose of under-performing and peripheral businesses through the use of either a spin-off, a sell-off or a management buyout.

17 Empirical evidence suggests that acquisitions have a neutral effect on the economy as a whole while benefiting target company shareholders and acquiring company managers.

Self-test questions

Answers to these questions can be found on pages 466–7.

1 Briefly outline the economic reasons used to justify acquisitions.

2 Briefly outline the financial reasons used to justify acquisitions.

3 Why might growth by acquisition not be in the best interests of a company?

4 Explain why acquisitions occur in waves.

5 Discuss the use of the P/E ratio and dividend growth methods of determining the value of a target company.

6 Explain why the DCF valuation method is preferred by academics.

7 Briefly discuss the advantages and disadvantages of financing a takeover by an issue of convertible debentures.

8 Briefly describe four defences that could be used by a company after its board has received a takeover bid.

9 Explain why a company may look to divest part of its operations.

10 Describe briefly some of the important contributing factors which explain why shareholders of acquiring companies rarely benefit from takeovers.

Questions for review

Answers to these questions can be found on pages 468–70. Questions with an asterisk (*) are at an intermediate level.

1 Explain the major justifications likely to be put forward to explain the following types of acquisitions:

(a) horizontal acquisitions;

(b) vertical backwards and forwards acquisitions;

(c) conglomerate acquisitions.

2* Restwell plc, a hotel and leisure company, is currently considering taking over a smaller private limited company, Staygood Ltd. The board of Restwell is in the process of making a bid for Staygood but first needs to place a value on the company. Restwell has gathered the following data:

Restwell

Weighted average cost of capital	12%
P/E ratio	12
Shareholders' required rate of return	15%

Staygood

Current dividend payment	27p
Past five years' dividend payments	15p, 17p, 18p, 21p, 23p
Current EPS	37p
Number of ordinary shares in issue	5m

It is estimated that the shareholders of Staygood require a rate of return 20 per cent higher than that of the shareholders of Restwell owing to the higher level of risk associated with Staygood's operations. Restwell estimates that cash flows at the end of the first year will be £2.5m and these will grow at an annual rate of 5 per cent. Restwell also expects to raise £5m in two years' time by selling off hotels of Staygood that are surplus to its needs.

Given the earlier information, estimate values for Staygood using the following valuation methods:

(a) price/earnings ratio valuation;

(b) dividend growth model;

(c) discounted cash flow valuation.

3 Carsley plc and Powell plc are planning to merge to form Stimac plc. It has been agreed that Powell's shareholders will accept three shares in Carsley for every share in Powell they hold. Other details are as follows:

	Carsley plc	Powell plc
Number of shares	40m	10m
Annual earnings	£10m	£5.8m
Price/earnings ratio	8	10

Post-merger annual earnings of the enlarged company are expected to be 8 per cent higher than the sum of the earnings of each of the companies before the merger, due to economies of scale and other benefits. The market is expected to apply a P/E ratio of 9 to Stimac plc.

Determine the extent to which the shareholders of Powell will benefit from the proposed merger.

4 What are the major considerations that an acquiring company has to take into account when deciding how to finance a proposed takeover?

5* It is currently 1 January 2007 and Lissom plc is looking to divest itself of one of its subsidiaries in order to focus on its core business activities. Financial information relevant to the divestment is given below. Lissom plc has been negotiating the disposal with the subsidiary's current management team.

Turnover and profit after tax of the subsidiary over the last five years:

Year ending December:	2003	2004	2005	2006
Turnover (£m)	40.0	41.6	42.8	43.7
Profit after tax (£m)	6.0	6.2	6.3	6.3

Other financial information:
Current liquidation value of subsidiary: £42m
Cost of capital of Lissom plc: 14%
Long-term debt of subsidiary: £10m of 13% debenture repayable in 2009

(a) Using the information provided, determine a purchase price for the subsidiary that could be acceptable to both Lissom plc and the management buyout team. All relevant supporting calculations must be shown.

(b) Discuss any financial aspects of the proposed buyout that you feel should be brought to the attention of the management buyout team.

(c) Discuss the stages that will theoretically be followed by the management buyout of the subsidiary of Lissom plc.

(d) Critically discuss the financing of management buyouts.

Questions for discussion

Questions with an asterisk (*) are at an advanced level.

1 The board of Hanging Valley plc wishes to take over Rattling Creek Ltd. Shown below are summarised financial data for the two companies:

	Hanging Valley	*Rattling Creek*
Profit before interest and tax	£420 000	£200 000
Ordinary share dividends	6.9p	14.0p
Corporation tax rate	35%	35%

Balance sheet extracts:

	Hanging Valley	Rattling Creek
Net fixed assets	1 750 000	800 000
Current assets	800 000	500 000
Current liabilities	(450 000)	(200 000)
Total assets less current liabilities	2 100 000	1 100 000
Long term debt at 10% per year		
Long term liabilities		(200 000)
	2 100 000	900 000
Financed by:		
ordinary shares, £1	1 500 000	500 000
reserves	600 000	400 000
	2 100 000	900 000

Hanging Valley's earnings and dividends have been increasing at approximately 15 per cent per year in recent times, while over the same period the earnings and dividends of Rattling Creek have remained static. The current market price of Hanging Valley's ordinary shares is £1.60. The board of Hanging Valley considers that the shareholders of Rattling Creek will accept a share-for-share offer in the proportion of four shares in Hanging Valley for every five shares in Rattling Creek.

(a) Using three different valuation methods, determine the effect on the wealth of Hanging Valley plc's shareholders if Rattling Creek Ltd's shareholders accept the proposed share exchange.

(b) Critically discuss the *economic* reasons why one company may seek to take over another.

2* Two companies called Blur plc and Oasis plc are considering a merger. Financial data for the two companies are given below:

	Blur	Oasis
Number of shares issued	3m	6m
Distributable earnings	£1.8m	£0.5m
P/E ratio	12.0	10.3

The two companies have estimated that, due to economies of scale, the newly merged company would generate cost savings of £200 000 per year.

(a) It is initially suggested that 100 per cent of Oasis's shares should be exchanged for shares in Blur at a rate of one share in Blur for every three shares in Oasis. What would be the expected dilution of EPS of the merger from the point of view of Blur's shareholders?

(b) An alternative to this is for Blur's shares to be valued at £7.20 and for the total share capital of Oasis to be valued at £10.5m for merger purposes. A certain percentage of Oasis's shares would be exchanged for shares in Blur, while the remaining shares of Oasis would be exchanged for 6.5 per cent loan stock (issued at £100 par value) in the new company. Given that the corporation tax rate is 30 per cent, how much 6.5 per cent loan stock would be issued as part of the purchase consideration in order for there to be no dilution of EPS from Blur's existing shareholders' point of view?

3 The managing directors of Wrack plc are considering what value to place on Trollope plc, a company which they are planning to take over in the near future. Wrack plc's share price is currently £4.21 and the company's earnings per share stand at 29p. Wrack's weighted average cost of capital is 12 per cent.

The board estimates that annual after-tax synergy benefits resulting from the take-over will be £5m, that Trollope's distributable earnings will grow at an annual rate of 2 per cent and that duplication will allow the sale of £25m of assets, net of corporation tax (currently standing at 30 per cent), in a year's time. Information referring to Trollope plc, including the current balance sheet and profit and loss account, is as follows:

Balance sheet of Trollope plc

	£m	£m
Fixed assets		296
Current assets	70	
Current liabilities	52	
		18
		314
Financed by:		
ordinary shares (£1)		156
reserves		75
Net equity interest		231
7 per cent debentures		83
		314

Profit and loss account (extracts)

	£m
Profit before interest and tax	76.0
Interest payments	8.3
	67.7
Corporation tax payments	20.3
Distributable earnings	47.4

Other information:

Current ex-div share price	£2.25
Latest dividend payment	16p
Past four years' dividend payments	13p, 13.5p, 14p, 15p
Trollope's equity beta	1.15
Treasury bill yield	5%
Return of the market	12%

(a) Given the above information, calculate the value of Trollope plc using the following valuation methods:

(i) price/earnings ratio;

(ii) dividend valuation method;

(iii) discounted cash flow method.

(b) Discuss the problems associated with using the above valuation techniques. Which of the values would you recommend the board of Wrack to use?

(c) Critically discuss which factors will influence a company to finance a takeover by either a share-for-share offer or a cash offer financed by an issue of debentures.

4* Goldblade plc is about to launch a bid for Membrane plc. Both companies are in the light manufacturing industry. Goldblade plc is currently in the process of deciding how it will go about financing the takeover. You are provided with information on the two companies below:

Profit and loss accounts for year ended 31 December 2006

	Goldblade plc £m	Membrane plc £m
Profit before interest and tax	122	48
Interest payments	49	18
Profit before tax	73	30
Tax (at 30%)	22	9
Profit after tax	51	21
Dividends	18	8
Retained profit	33	13

Balance sheets as at 31 December 2006

	£m	£m
Fixed assets	508	228
Stocks	82	34
Debtors	66	30
Cash	59	25
Current liabilities	(138)	(64)
Long-term bank loans	(353)	(121)
	224	132
Financed by		
Ordinary shares (50p)	80	46
Reserves	144	86
	224	132
Current share price (31/12/06)	£3.65	£2.03
Year low:	£3.12	£1.85
Year high:	£3.78	£2.47
Average industry gearing level:	40%	

(debt divided by debt plus equity; equity at market value, debt at book value)

Goldblade expects that in order to secure a controlling share in Membrane it will have to offer a premium of 20 per cent on the current market price of Membrane's shares. Goldblade's long-run cost of borrowing currently stands at 10 per cent. The company is considering whether to finance the deal using a share-for-share offer or a cash purchase.

(a) If the company were to finance the takeover using a share-for-share offer, advise Goldblade plc on what form the offer should take and the number of shares it will issue.

(b) In the light of the information given above, critically evaluate whether a cash offer or a share-for-share offer would be more appropriate for Goldblade plc.

5 It is 1 January 2007 and Magnet plc is in the process of divesting part of its operations via a proposed management buyout (MBO). The buyout team is currently looking for venture capital to finance the MBO. They have agreed a price of £25m with Magnet and have proposed that the financing will involve their putting up £5m of their personal funds to purchase an equity stake in the business with the remaining funds (£20m) coming from the venture capitalist in the form of long-term unsecured mezzanine debt finance.

The venture capitalist has indicated that it will require an interest rate on its debt investment of 11 per cent given that its finance will be unsecured. The four members of the MBO team have indicated that they intend to draw an annual salary of £150 000 each. The MBO team has just presented the venture capitalist company with the following five-year cash flow predictions (excluding directors' salaries) which they consider to be on the pessimistic side:

Year ending	2007	2008	2009	2010	2011
Predicted sales	£6.78m	£6.82m	£7.23m	£7.51m	£8.02m
Cash outflows	£3.39m	£3.34m	£3.47m	£3.53m	£3.84m
Reinvestment			£1.5m		

The new entity will pay corporation tax at a rate of 20 per cent in the year that profits arise. The reinvestment of £1.5m in 2009 will not qualify for capital allowances.

On the basis of this information, critically evaluate whether the proposed MBO is viable from a cash flow perspective in light of the two parties' financial requirements and the predicted sales and costs. Support your answer with appropriate calculations.

References

Berger, P. and Ofek, E. (1995) 'Diversification's effect on firm value', *Journal of Financial Economics*, Vol. 37, pp. 39–65.

Comment, R. and Jarrell, G. (1995) 'Corporate focus and stock returns', *Journal of Financial Economics*, Vol. 37, pp. 67–87.

Cowling, K., Stoneman, P., Cubbin, J., Cable, J., Hall, G. and Dutton, P. (1980) *Mergers and Economic Performance*, Cambridge: Cambridge University Press.

DeLong, G. (2001) 'Stockholder gains from focusing versus diversifying bank mergers', *Journal of Financial Economics*, Vol. 59, pp. 221–52.

De Noble, A., Gustafson, L. and Hergert, M. (1988) 'Planning for post-merger integration: eight lessons for merger success', *Long Range Planning*, Vol. 2, No. 4, pp. 82–5.

Eckbo, B.E. (1992) 'Mergers and the value of antitrust deterrence', *Journal of Finance*, Vol. 47, pp. 1005–29.

Firth, M. (1980) 'Takeovers, shareholders' returns and the theory of the firm', *Quarterly Journal of Economics*, Vol. 94 (2), March, pp. 235–60.

Franks, J., Broyles, J. and Hecht, M. (1977) 'An industry study of the profitability of mergers in the United Kingdom', *Journal of Finance*, Vol. 32, December, pp. 1513–25.

Franks, J., Harris, R. and Mayer, C. (1988) 'Means of payment in takeovers: results for the UK and US', in Avernick, M. (ed.) *Corporate Takeovers: Causes and Consequences*, Chicago, IL: University of Chicago Press.

Grubb, M. and Lamb, R. (2000) *Capitalize on Merger Chaos*, New York: Free Press.

Healy, P., Palepu, K. and Ruback, R. (1997) 'Which takeovers are profitable: strategic or financial?', *Sloan Management Review*, Vol. 38, Summer, pp. 45–57.

Jensen, M. (1993) 'The takeover controversy: analysis and evidence', in Chew, D. (ed.) *The New Corporate Finance: Where Theory Meets Practice*, New York: McGraw-Hill.

Jensen, M. and Ruback, R. (1983) 'The market for corporate control: the scientific evidence', *Journal of Financial Economics*, Vol. 11, pp. 5–50.

Kelly, E. (1967) *The Profitability of Growth Through Mergers*, Pennsylvania: Pennsylvania State University.

Rau, P. and Vermaelen, T. (1998) 'Glamour, value and the post-acquisition performance of acquiring firms', *Journal of Financial Economics*, 49 (2), pp. 223–53.

Singh, A. (1971) *Takeovers: Their Relevance to the Stock Market and the Theory of the Firm*, Cambridge: Cambridge University Press.

Sudarsanam, S. and Mahate, A. (2003) 'Glamour acquirers, method of payment and post-acquisition performance: the UK evidence', *Journal of Business Finance and Accounting*, 30 (1 & 2), pp. 299–341.

Travlos, N. (1987) 'Corporate takeover bids, method of payment, and bidding firms' stock returns', *Journal of Finance*, Vol. 42, September, pp. 943–63.

Recommended reading

For a book totally dedicated to the topic of mergers and takeovers with a UK focus see:

Sudarsanam, S. (2003) *Creating Value from Mergers and Acquisitions*, Harlow: FT Prentice-Hall.

For two more advanced books on mergers and takeovers with a US focus see:

Bruner, R. (2004) *Applied Mergers and Acquisitions*, John Wiley and Sons Inc.

Weston, J., Mitchell, M. and Mulherin, H. (2003) *Takeovers, Restructuring and Corporate Governance*, 4th edn, Harlow: FT Prentice Hall.

The following books collect together a series of readable and interesting articles on the subject of mergers and takeovers and help to bridge the gap between theory and practice:

Chew, D. (ed.) (2000) *The New Corporate Finance: Where Theory Meets Practice*, 2nd edn, New York: McGraw-Hill.

Stern, J. and Chew, D. (eds) (2003) *The Revolution in Corporate Finance*, 4th edn, Malden, MA: Blackwell.

The following article gives an excellent summary and overview of the research done into the success of mergers and takeovers:

Bruner, R. (2002) 'Does M&A pay? A review of the evidence for the decision-maker', *Journal of Applied Finance*, Vol. 12, pp. 48–68.

Important and informative papers and articles recommended for further reading include the following:

Benzie, R. (1989) 'Takeover activity in the 1980s', *Bank of England Quarterly Bulletin*, Vol. 29, pp. 78–85.

Borstadt, L., Zwirlein, T. and Brickley, J. (1991) 'Defending against hostile takeovers: impact on shareholder wealth', *Managerial Finance*, Vol. 17, No. 1, pp. 25–33.

Ravenscraft, D. (1991) 'Gains and losses from mergers: the evidence', *Managerial Finance*, Vol. 17, No. 1, pp. 8–13.

Severiens, T. (1991) 'Creating value through mergers and acquisitions: some motivations', *Managerial Finance*, Vol. 17, No. 1, pp. 3–7.

Sudarsanam, P.S. (1991) 'Defensive strategies of target firms in UK contested takeovers', *Managerial Finance*, Vol. 17, No. 6, pp. 47–56.

Useful websites giving information on UK antitrust legislation and UK bid regulation, respectively, are:

http://www.competition-commission.org.uk/
http://www.thetakeoverpanel.org.uk/

Chapter 12

Risk management

Learning objectives

After studying this chapter, you should have achieved the following learning objectives:

■ an understanding of the theoretical and practical issues relating to interest rate and exchange rate risk;

■ an understanding of the internal and external methods of managing interest rate and exchange rate risk;

■ the ability to select and evaluate appropriate risk management techniques according to the nature of the risk being faced;

■ an appreciation of the benefits and costs of risk management techniques.

Introduction

Exchange rate and interest rate risk management are of key importance to companies that operate internationally or that use debt finance. Many currencies now float freely against each other and exchange rates can be volatile as a result. The seriousness of the impact that exchange rate risk can have on a company is the subject of Vignette 12.1. The need for hedging interest rate risk arises from the size and complexity of company borrowing.

In this chapter we consider the different types of exchange rate and interest rate risk that are faced by companies. We also consider the techniques available to control and manage such risk, including the increasingly complex derivatives available for external hedging of interest and exchange rate exposures.

12.1 Interest and exchange rate risk

Recent years have seen increased awareness by companies of the potential benefits of managing or *hedging* their interest and exchange rate risk exposures. The importance of hedging to companies depends largely on the magnitude of the potential losses that may result from unfavourable movements in interest and exchange rates. With interest rate exposures, the magnitude of such losses depends on the volatility of interest rates, the level of companies' gearing and the proportion of floating rate corporate debt. Short-term interest rate yields were relatively volatile during the 1970s and 1980s, as shown in Exhibit 12.1, and the need for companies to manage their interest rate exposures increased as a consequence. Exhibit 12.1 also shows that interest rates peaked in 1989 and 1990 before declining in the period to 1993 and then stabilizing between 4 and 7 percent. The impact of these interest rate changes on corporate sector *gearing* (debt as a percentage of debt plus equity at market values) can be seen in Exhibit 12.2.

Exchange rate risk has increased greatly since the early 1970s, when the collapse of the Bretton Woods exchange rate regime led the major currencies to float against each other. This is clearly illustrated by Exhibit 12.3 which shows the volatility of sterling–dollar exchange rates over the period 1962–2005. Furthermore, world trade has grown significantly over the past 25 years so that now virtually all companies are involved in some transactions denominated in a foreign currency. Increasing exchange rate risk and growing world trade mean that foreign exchange risk management has become of increasing importance to companies. Adverse exchange rate movements that are not hedged can eliminate profits on foreign deals or, even worse, drive a company into bankruptcy. The increased visibility of foreign exchange gains and losses has also been cited as a reason for the increasing importance of exchange rate risk management (Demirag and Goddard 1994). The importance of exchange rate risk to individual companies is illustrated in Vignette 12.2.

One of the easiest ways to understand interest and exchange rate management is to see them as a form of insurance whereby companies insure themselves against adverse exchange and interest rate movements in the same way that we insure ourselves against personal injury or loss of personal possessions.

Vignette 12.1

Balance sheets left reeling by the Real

FT

It has been a bizarre year for Brazilian companies. Whether or not they supported the campaign of president-elect Luiz Inácio Lula da Silva – and many did – senior executives have felt the impact of his election even though he does not take office until January 1. Concern among investors that a left-wing government under Lula – as he is universally known – might presage a default on Brazil's debts has caused the currency to shed more than 40 per cent of its value to the end of September, wreaking havoc on companies' balance sheets.

There were a few extraordinary winners. Eletrobrás, the electricity utility, made an accumulated net profit of R$4.01bn (US$1.03bn at September 30 exchange rates) during the first nine months of the year, including a spectacular R$3.4bn in the third quarter alone. This was thanks mostly to its share in the Itaipu hydro-electric power station, a Brazilian–Paraguayan joint venture that sells energy at prices set in dollars. But for most big companies, many of which borrow in dollars but make their income in Reals, the devaluation has been little short of calamitous.

In contrast to other periods of sharp devaluation, such as in 1999, the situation has been exacerbated because the economy is at a virtual standstill. According to Fernando Exel of Economática, a firm of business analysts in São Paulo, the value of sales among 193 publicly traded companies was R$215.1bn during the first nine months, an increase of just 0.7 per cent over the same period last year. To make matters far worse, he says, 70 per cent of those companies' debts are denominated in foreign currencies.

'They are extremely vulnerable,' he says. 'Even if only a small part of a company's debt is not hedged, a devaluation on this scale causes an enormous disaster.'

Many Brazilian companies began hedging their dollar debts when the Real began to slide during the second quarter, as opinion polls showed Lula leading the presidential campaign. But few imagined that the Real would fall so far. As the situation worsened and international banks began reducing their exposure to Brazil, the cost of hedging became increasingly prohibitive. Many concluded – incorrectly, as it turned out – that hedging was not worth the expense. Even those who took exemplary precautions were not immune.

'In our opinion, the most perfect hedge so far was that done by VCP [Votorantim Celulose e Papel, one of Latin America's biggest paper and pulp producers],' says Thomas Souza of Merrill Lynch in São Paulo. VCP produced operating profits of R$170m during the third quarter, up from R$130m a year earlier, and financial gains of R$10m, up from R$8m, thanks to its prudent hedging. But it recorded a net loss of R$25m, after profits last time of R$91m, because a subsidiary company was not as well-protected.

As with VCP, many companies in the steel sector protected operating income by switching sales to the export market and raising prices at home. Usiminas, one of Brazil's biggest steel producers, saw the value of its sales rise by 37 per cent in the third quarter over last year, to R$1.68bn. Nevertheless, it recorded a net loss of R$684m, because both the operating company and, especially, Cosipa, a subsidiary, were not fully hedged.

'Cosipa is one of the most leveraged companies in the industry. Hedging just became too expensive,' says Katia Brullo of Corretora Unibanco, a São Paulo brokerage.

One of the few sectors to show bigger profits was telecommunications. One reason is that in 2002 many began to see the results of investments made since the industry was privatised in 1998. Another is that companies such as Telemar and Brásil Telecom were aggressively hedged from an early stage. Nevertheless, says Carlos Constantini of Banco BBA in São Paulo, the sector suffered from the devaluation. 'You can point to one or other company and say they were winners or did better than others, but there's no doubt that the whole industry lost out,' he says.

The upside to all this is that it seems most unlikely that things will get worse. In spite of the heavy bottom-line impact on many companies, the effect on cash flow has been much less severe, because accounting practices demand that companies value all debt at current exchange rates, even though those debts may not have to be paid for several years.

As investors get used to the idea of a Lula government and as Lula and his advisers show increasing commitment to meeting fiscal targets and keeping inflation under control, the exchange rate has begun to fall back. Fourth-quarter results could even show some extraordinary financial gains.

Source: Jonathan Wheatley, FT.com, 26 November 2002. Reprinted with permission.

Exhibit 12.1 **Annual average yield on three-month Treasury bills over the period 1970–2005**

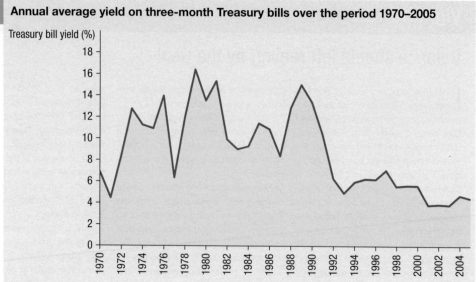

Source: National Statistics. © Crown Copyright 2006. Reproduced by permission of the Office for National Statistics.

Exhibit 12.2 **UK corporate sector aggregate capital gearing ratio over the period 1970–2004**

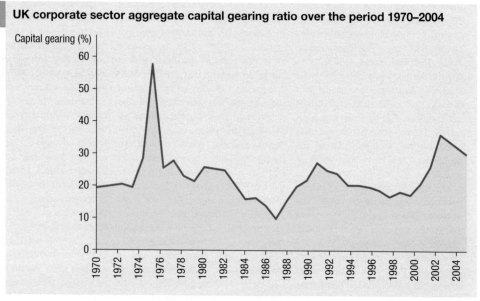

Source: Bank of England Quarterly Bulletin, Autumn 2005. The determination of UK corporate capital gearing. Reproduced by permission of the Bank of England.

12.1.1 Interest rate risk

The form of interest rate risk most commonly faced by a company is that associated with having a high proportion of floating interest rate debt. One consequence of interest rate volatility in this case is that forecasting and planning future cash flows becomes more difficult. More seriously, a company with a high proportion of floating rate debt

Exhibit 12.3 Quarterly average sterling–dollar exchange rate over the period 1962–2005.

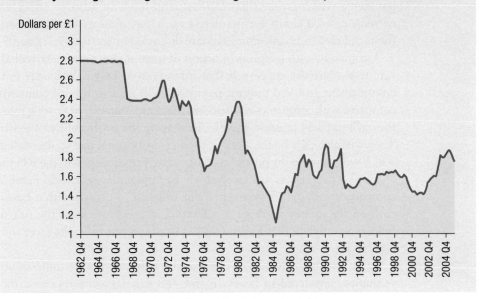

Vignette 12.2

Daimler increases hedging against dollar

DaimlerChrysler has taken advantage of the slide in the euro after the French and Dutch rejection of the European constitution to increase its financial hedging against the dollar, a move which mirrors that by rival German carmaker Volkswagen.

Daimler, which has estimated net exposure to the US dollar of €6bn–€7bn ($7.3bn–$8.5bn) because of exports of Mercedes cars from Europe, said it had increased hedging out until 2007.

Financial hedging locks in future sales at current exchange rates, protecting the company against a drop in the dollar.

The euro has fallen to eight-month lows after referenda in France and the Netherlands this week rejected the proposed constitution. 'We have used the euro's weakness of the past few days to increase our hedging for the years 2005, 2006 and 2007,' Daimler said.

The company refused to say how much extra protection it had put in place, but it is thought to be at least one percentage point more, worth at least €60m. The company was 80 per cent protected against dollar moves for this year already.

Volkswagen yesterday confirmed it has already carried out some extra hedging for this year, and is considering further hedging operations to take advantage of the euro's lower level.

The company is understood to be considering adding five percentage points of hedging, which would leave it 75 per cent protected against changes in the dollar/euro rate.

The level of hedging has been a key determinant of profitability at the German carmakers – and other big exporters – because of the steep rise in the euro over the past two years.

Companies such as Porsche, which locked in more advantageous rates against the dollar for several years, have been able to maintain higher earnings, while VW, which only increased its hedging recently, lost almost €1bn in the US last year.

Audi, VW's luxury division, yesterday revealed that every one cent drop in the euro against the dollar increased annual profits €20m.

will be afraid of interest rates increasing sharply since significantly increased interest payments will increase *financial risk* and have an adverse effect on cash flow. In extreme cases, a sharp rise in interest rates may increase the likelihood of bankruptcy (financial risk and bankruptcy risk are discussed in Sections 9.7.1 and 9.7.2).

A company with a high proportion of fixed interest rate debt will also face interest rate risk. Here the concern is that interest rates may *fall* sharply in the future. The commitment to fixed interest payments will lead to loss of competitive advantage compared with companies whose borrowings are primarily at floating rates. Such competitors will pay less interest, thereby increasing the profitability of existing operations. They will also experience a fall in their cost of capital due to decreasing financial risk, which will increase the portfolio of attractive projects open to them in the future.

Interest rate risk is not faced solely by companies with debt liabilities, but also by companies with debt investments. For example, a company that has invested surplus cash on the money markets at a floating interest rate faces the risk of interest rates falling; a company that has purchased fixed interest rate gilts faces the risk of interest rates rising.

In reality, the incidence of interest rate risk may not be quite as obvious as in the examples considered so far. *Basis risk* and *gap exposure* represent more subtle types of interest rate risk exposure that companies may encounter.

Basis risk

A company may have assets and liabilities of similar sizes, both with floating interest rates, and so will both receive and pay interest. At first sight it may not appear to have any interest rate risk exposure. However, if the two floating rates are not determined using the same basis (e.g. one is linked to LIBOR but the other is not), it is unlikely that they will move perfectly in line with each other: as one rate increases, the other rate might change by a different amount.

Gap exposure

Even more subtle is the situation where a company has assets and liabilities which are matched in terms of size, and where the floating interest rates on each are determined on the same basis, for example by reference to LIBOR. It is still possible for interest rate risk to exist as the rates on loans may be revised on a three-monthly basis, whereas the rates on assets may be revised on a six-monthly basis.

12.1.2 Spot and forward rates

Before we consider the different types of exchange rate risk we need to discuss *exchange rates* themselves. In practice, many exchange rates exist, not only the buy and sell rates between different currencies, but also for the same currency over different time horizons. The different rates can be illustrated by considering the exchange rate between sterling and the dollar:

$ spot rate	1.7368 − 1.7372
One-month $ forward rate	1.7445 − 1.7455
Three-month $ forward rate	1.7580 − 1.7597

The *spot rate* refers to the rate of exchange if buying or selling the currency immediately. The higher of the two spot rates (1.7372) is the *buy rate* (the number of dollars you have to give up to receive one pound), whereas the lower spot rate (1.7368) is the *sell rate* (the number of dollars you receive for giving up one pound). The difference between the two spot rates is called the *spread*. For frequently traded major currencies the spread is often *very* narrow.

The rates below the spot rate are called *forward rates* and these allow the fixing of buy and sell rates for settlement and delivery at a specific date in the future. The forward rates are in fact a consensus estimate of the future spot rate, and their accuracy depends on how efficiently the foreign exchange market forecasts future spot rates.

Forward rates can be at either a *premium* or a *discount* to the current spot rate. In our example, the one- and three-month rates are higher than the spot rate. Because the future value of the dollar is expected to be less, the forward rates are at a discount to the current spot rate. Hence we can see that the foreign exchange market is expecting an *appreciation* of the pound against the dollar (i.e. the market expects that you will be able to buy more dollars for your pound in the future).

12.1.3 What is meant by exchange rate risk?

Exchange rate risk can be divided into transaction risk, translation risk and economic risk.

Transaction risk

Companies expect either to pay or to receive amounts of foreign currency in the future as a result of either importing or exporting raw materials, goods or services. *Transaction risk* is the risk that the amount of domestic currency either paid or received in these foreign currency transactions may change due to movements in the exchange rate.

Consider a UK company which sells a car to a German customer for €22 000 and gives three months' credit, with payment to be received in euros. At the current spot rate of €1.434/£ the company expects to receive 22 000/1.434 = £15 342. If the German customer takes three months' credit and in the interim the exchange rate has moved to €1.496/£, the UK company will receive only £14 706 when it exchanges euros into sterling. This is approximately 4 per cent less than expected.

Companies expecting to *receive* foreign currency in the future will therefore be concerned about the possibility of the domestic currency *appreciating* against the foreign currency, whereas companies expecting to *pay* foreign currency in the future are concerned about the possibility of the domestic currency *depreciating* against the foreign currency.

Translation risk

As part of the process of producing consolidated accounts, the balance sheet values of the assets and liabilities of overseas subsidiaries, denominated in a foreign currency, need to be translated into the domestic currency. The foreign currency denominated profit and loss account will also need to be translated and consolidated. *Translation risk* refers to the possibility that, as a result of the translation of overseas assets, liabilities and profits into the domestic currency, the holding company may experience a loss or a gain due to exchange rate movements. Additionally, consolidation of accounts may lead to companies being in breach of loan covenants (e.g. a maximum gearing ratio). While translation losses or gains only appear on paper and do not represent *actual* cash flows, they may affect the perceptions and opinions of investors and financial institutions regarding a company's well-being. However, as Buckley (2003) points out, translation risk is simply a function of the accounting treatment of foreign assets and liabilities on consolidation, and does not give any indication of the real effect of currency fluctuations on the value of a company.

Translation risk can be illustrated by considering a UK company that buys a hotel in the USA and finances the purchase with sterling debt. The hotel costs $1.5m, which at the prevailing exchange rate of $1.737/£ gives a sterling value of £863 558. A year later, the hotel is still valued at $1.5m but the exchange rate now stands at $1.796/£. The sterling value of the debt used to finance the hotel will be the same (£863 558), but the value of the hotel, translated into sterling for consolidation purposes, has fallen to £835 189.

Economic risk

Economic risk refers to the risk of long-term movements in exchange rates undermining the international competitiveness of a company or reducing the net present value of its business operations. Economic risk is a more general type of exchange rate risk than transaction and translation risk. While companies can avoid transaction risk and translation risk by avoiding foreign currency transactions and not engaging in overseas operations, economic risk is almost impossible to avoid. It is also difficult to hedge against due to its ongoing nature.

Consider a company, based solely in the UK, which buys all its raw material and sells all its finished goods in the domestic market. While not facing any transaction risk or translation risk, it faces domestic competition from a US company. If the pound appreciates against the dollar, reducing the sterling cost of the US company's dollar-denominated imports, the UK company will lose its competitive edge.

Now that we have examined the different types of interest rate and exchange rate risk to which companies can be exposed, we can consider the methods companies use to manage these risks.

12.2 Internal risk management

Internal risk management refers to the hedging of either interest rate or exchange rate risk by the way in which a company structures its assets and liabilities. Internal risk management is cheaper than external hedging since using external hedging methods incurs a range of costs and arrangement fees, as we shall see later. Unfortunately, there are a number of factors which limit the amount of risk that can be hedged internally.

12.2.1 Internal management of interest rate risk

There are two general methods of internal hedging that can be used to manage interest rate exposure within a company's balance sheet.

Smoothing

Smoothing is where a company maintains a balance between its fixed rate and floating rate borrowing. If interest rates *rise*, the disadvantage of the relatively expensive floating rate loan will be cancelled out by the less expensive fixed rate loan. If interest rates *fall*, the disadvantage of the relatively expensive fixed rate loan will be cancelled out by the less expensive floating rate loan. One drawback of this hedging method is that it reduces the *comparative advantage* a company may gain by using fixed rate debt in preference to floating rate debt or vice versa (*see* Section 12.6.1 for further discussion on comparative advantage). On top of this, the company may incur two lots of transaction and arrangement costs.

Matching

This hedging method involves the internal matching of liabilities and assets which both have a common interest rate. Consider a decentralised group which has two subsidiaries. One subsidiary may be investing in the money markets at LIBOR, while the other is borrowing through the same money market at LIBOR. If LIBOR rises, one subsidiary's borrowing cost increases while the other's returns increase: the interest rates on the assets and liabilities are matched. One problem with this method is that it may be difficult for commercial and industrial companies to match the magnitudes and characteristics of their liabilities and assets as many companies, while paying interest on their liabilities, do not receive income in the form of interest payments. Matching is most widely used by financial institutions such as banks, which derive large amounts of income from interest received on advances.

12.2.2 Internal management of exchange rate risk

There are a number of techniques that can be used to hedge exchange rate risk internally. It is easier to hedge transaction and translation risk internally than economic risk owing to the difficulties associated with quantifying economic risk and the long period over which economic risk exposure occurs.

Matching

Matching can be used to reduce the amount of translation or transaction risk that a company faces. For example, in order to reduce *translation risk*, a company acquiring a foreign asset should borrow funds denominated in the currency of the country in which it is purchasing the asset, matching if possible the term of the loan to the expected economic life of the asset. As the exchange rate varies, the translated values of the asset and liability increase and decrease in concert. To mitigate *transaction risk*, a company selling goods in the USA with prices denominated in dollars could import raw materials through a supplier that invoices in dollars.

Netting

This internal hedging technique calls for companies to net off their foreign currency transactions and then to hedge any remaining exchange rate risk. The technique is used by multinationals with overseas subsidiaries and by large organisations with decentralised financial transactions.

Consider a UK company with a French subsidiary. The UK company expects to pay $5m to a supplier in three months' time, whereas the French subsidiary expects to receive $7m in three months' time in payment for goods supplied. If this information is centralised at a group level, the net exposure of $2m to be received in three months' time ($7m − $5m) can be identified and hedged externally. This will be cheaper than the UK company and its French subsidiary hedging their respective currency exposures of $5m and $7m independently.

Leading and lagging

This technique involves settling foreign currency accounts either at the beginning (leading) or after the end (lagging) of the allowed credit period. The choice of whether to lead or lag the settlement will depend on the company's expectations of future exchange rate movements. For example, a UK-based company paying for goods in dollars that expects the pound to appreciate against the dollar will lag its payment. While *leading* and *lagging* payments is not strictly a hedging technique, it can be used by companies facing transaction risk due to foreign-currency-denominated overseas creditors.

Invoicing in the domestic currency

A company exporting goods could invoice its buyers in its domestic currency rather than in the currency of the company to which it is exporting. The transaction risk is then transferred to the foreign buying company. The drawback of this method is that it may deter potential customers as they may transfer their orders to companies that invoice in their own currency.

12.3 External risk management

Having recognised that companies are limited in the amount of risk they can hedge using internal methods, we now turn our attention to the many types of external hedging available to them. Over the past 30 years the choice of external hedging methods has increased dramatically. Two of the longest-standing external methods of hedging interest rate and exchange rate risk are *forward contracts* and *money market hedges* (borrowing and lending in the money markets). Companies can also choose from a wide variety of *derivative* instruments, including futures contracts, swaps and options. Derivatives can also be divided according to whether they are standardised *traded* derivatives or bank-created *over-the-counter* derivatives.

12.3.1 Hedging using forward contracts

There are two types of forward contract. *Forward rate agreements* (FRAs) enable companies to fix, in advance, either a future borrowing rate or a future deposit rate, based on a nominal principal amount, for a given period. While the contracts themselves are binding, the company taking out the FRA is not bound by contract to take out a loan with the provider of the FRA. *Forward exchange contracts* (FECs) enable companies to fix, in advance, future exchange rates on an agreed quantity of foreign currency for delivery or purchase on an agreed date. Forward contracts are generally set up via banking institutions and are non-negotiable, legally binding contracts.

An advantage of forward contracts is that they can be tailor-made with respect to maturity and size in order to meet the requirements of the company. In this sense, they are different from their traded equivalent, *financial futures contracts*. Forward contracts cannot be traded owing to their lack of standardisation. While there will be an initial arrangement fee, forward contracts do not require the payment of *margin*, as with financial futures, nor do they require the payment of a *premium*, as with traded options. Cash flows occur only on the execution date of the agreement. While a company gains protection from any adverse interest rate or exchange rate movements, the binding nature of a forward contract means that the company must forgo any potential benefit from favourable movements in exchange rates and interest rates.

Example	**Forward rate agreement**

A company wants to borrow £5.6m in three months' time for a period of six months. Interest rates are standing at 6 per cent and the company, being afraid that in three months' time the interest rate may have increased, decides to hedge using an FRA. The bank guarantees the company a rate of 6.5 per cent on a notional £5.6m for six months starting in three months' time (known as a 3 v 9 FRA). If interest rates have *increased* after three months to, say, 7.5 per cent, the company will pay 7.5 per cent interest on the £5.6m loan that it takes out: this is 1 per cent more than the rate agreed in the FRA. The bank will make a compensating payment of £28 000 (1 per cent × £5.6m × 6/12) to the company, covering the higher cost of its borrowing. If interest rates have decreased after three months to, say, 5 per cent (1.5 per cent below the agreed rate), the company will have to make a £42000 payment to the bank.

12.3.2 Hedging using the money markets and eurocurrency markets

Companies can also hedge interest and exchange rate risk by using the money markets and the eurocurrency markets. These types of transaction are sometimes referred to as *cash market* hedges. Consider a company that wants to borrow £1m in three months' time for six months, but is afraid that interest rates will rise. The company can use the money markets to borrow £1m now for nine months and then deposit this on the money markets for three months. If interest rates rise in the three months before the loan is needed, the company will pay more on the loan but will benefit by receiving a higher rate of interest on the money market deposit.

Using the eurocurrency markets to hedge exchange rate risk is more complex: it involves setting up the opposite foreign currency transaction to the one being hedged. It is best illustrated with a numerical example.

Example	**Money market hedge**

A company expects to receive \$180 000 in three months' time and wants to lock into the current exchange rate of \$1.65/£. It is afraid that the pound will appreciate against the dollar. To set up a money market hedge, the company sets up a dollar debt by borrowing dollars now. It converts them to sterling at the current spot rate and deposits the sterling proceeds on the sterling money market. When the dollar loan matures, it is paid off by the expected dollar receipt. If the *annual* dollar borrowing rate is 7 per cent, the three-month dollar borrowing rate is 1.75 per cent i.e. $1 + (7\% \times 3/12)$: if Z is the amount of dollars to be borrowed now, then:

$$Z \times 1.0175 = \$180\,000$$

and so:

$$Z = \$180\,000/1.0175 = \$176\,904$$

The sterling value of these dollars at the current exchange rate is:

$$\$176\,904/1.65 = £107\,215$$

If the *annual* sterling deposit rate is 6 per cent, the three-month sterling deposit rate is 1.5 per cent and the value in three months' time will be:

$$£107\,214 \times 1.015 = £108\,822$$

This three-month sterling value achieved by using a money market hedge can be compared with the expected sterling receipt using a forward exchange contract to determine which is the cheapest hedging method. The cost of different hedging methods must always be compared from the same point in time.

12.4 Futures contracts

A futures contract can be defined as an agreement to buy or sell a standard quantity of a specified financial instrument or foreign currency at a future date at a price agreed between two parties. Financial futures resemble *traded options* (*see* Section 12.5.2) in that both are standardised contracts, but financial futures are a binding contract locking both buyer and seller into a particular amount and rate: there is no option on the part of the buyer not to proceed. When a company takes out a futures contract it has to place an *initial margin*, which represents between 1 and 3 per cent of the contract value, with the clearing house of the futures exchange. On £500 000 three-month sterling interest rate contracts, this could be a margin of £1500 per contract. As the interest or exchange rate specified in the futures contract changes on a daily basis, money is either credited to or debited from the company's margin account, depending on whether the rate change is favourable or adverse. The cash flow movements of a margin account are often referred to as accounts being *marked to market*. If the initial margin drops below a certain safety level, *variation margin* will be called for from the party concerned in order to top up the account.

Financial futures were first traded in the USA on the Chicago Mercantile Exchange (CME) in 1972. In the UK, the London International Financial Futures Exchange (LIFFE) was set up in 1982 to trade futures contracts. LIFFE merged with the London Traded Options Market (LTOM) in 1992 to form a single unified UK market for trading derivative securities. More recently, in 2002, LIFFE was bought by Euronext and renamed Euronext.liffe.

The mechanics of hedging interest rate and exchange rate risk using financial futures are illustrated below.

12.4.1 Using futures contracts to hedge interest rate risk

When hedging interest rate risk, companies must *buy* futures contracts if they want to guard against a *fall* in interest rates and *sell* futures contracts to guard against a *rise* in interest rates. Interest rate futures contracts run in three-month cycles and have a nominal value of £500 000. The two most useful contracts for hedging sterling interest rate risk are the three-month LIBOR sterling and long gilt contracts. Futures contracts are priced in nominal terms by subtracting the value of the specified interest rate from 100 (e.g. a futures contract price of 93 corresponds to an interest rate of 7 per cent). Profits or losses made on a futures contract are determined by reference to changes in this nominal price. Contract price changes are given in *ticks*, a tick being equal to a movement of one basis point or 0.01 per cent of the contract price. In value terms on a three-month £500 000 short sterling contract, a movement of one tick is worth £12.50 (i.e. £500 000 $\times$ 0.0001 $\times$ 3/12).

| Example | Using interest rate futures |

A company wants to borrow £500 000 in three months' time for a period of three months, but is expecting interest rates to rise above the current level of 10 per cent. In order to hedge its position, it therefore *sells* one £500 000 interest rate contract at 90 (i.e. 100 − 10).

Suppose that, after three months, the interest rate has gone up by 3 per cent and the contract price has moved by the same amount. The seller of the contract now *buys* a contract at 87 (i.e. 100 − 13), thereby *closing out* his position. The contract price movement in terms of ticks is 3/0.01 = 300 ticks.

Profit made by selling and buying futures = 300 $\times$ £12.50 = £3750

The profit compensates the company for the higher cost of borrowing £500 000 in three months' time. This higher cost is £3750 (500 000 $\times$ 0.03 $\times$ 1/4). Because the contract price movement exactly matched the change in the interest rate, the company has exactly offset its higher borrowing cost and hence constructed a perfect hedge for its interest rate risk.

The example above makes the unrealistic assumption that changes in interest rates exactly match changes in futures prices. In practice this is unlikely to be the case as the futures market, like any other financial market, is subject to pricing inefficiencies. Hence futures contracts suffer from what is known as *basis risk*. Take, for example, a three-month LIBOR futures contract with three months to maturity. The current futures contract price is 93.46 and three-month LIBOR stands at 6 per cent. Here we would expect the futures contract to be priced at 94.00. The difference between 94.00 and 93.46 represents the basis risk – in this case 0.54 per cent or 54 basis points. This basis risk will taper away over the next three months (at a rate of 18 basis points a month if we assume a linear decline) until it has disappeared as the contract matures. Clearly this will affect the efficiency of a hedge. Returning to the earlier example, assume now that the futures contract was actually priced at 89.54 rather than 90. If interest rates rose by 3 per cent the futures contract price will have dropped to 87. Here the investor will have made a gain of 254 ticks (89.54 − 87), giving a value of £3175. This is against a loss of £3750 in the cash market, giving a *hedge efficiency* of (3175/3750) × 100 = 85 per cent. Equally, basis risk can work the other way round, making the hedge efficiency greater than 100 per cent.

12.4.2 Using futures contracts to hedge exchange rate risk

Sterling-denominated currency futures contracts were discontinued by LIFFE in 1990 due to a lack of demand. However, the takeover of LIFFE by Euronext has seen the introduction of both €/US$ and US$/€ currency futures. While the Singapore Exchange (SGX) has also followed suit in discontinuing sterling-denominated currency futures contracts, they are still available on the Chicago Mercantile Exchange (CME).

| **Example** | **Using US currency futures** |

It is 1 January and a UK company expects to receive $300 000 in three months' time. Being concerned about the pound strengthening against the dollar, it decides to use CME traded currency futures to hedge its transaction risk.

Current spot rate:	$1.54 − $1.55
Sterling futures price (1 April):	$1.535
Standard size of futures contracts:	£62 500

The first thing to establish is whether the company should buy or sell futures contracts. Given that holding a futures contract (often referred to as *taking a long position*) allows future delivery of a *foreign* currency, and that in this case *sterling* is the foreign currency, the company should *buy* US sterling futures. This allows the company to take delivery of sterling in return for the dollars it expects to receive. The futures price quoted is the amount of US dollars needed to buy one unit of the foreign currency. Translating the expected dollar receipt into sterling at the exchange rate implicit in the currency future, we have:

$$\$300\,000/1.535 = £195\,440$$
$$\text{Number of contracts required} = 195\,440/62\,500 = 3.13$$

The company therefore buys three contracts, allowing it to take delivery of £187 500 (62 500 × 3) in return for a payment of $287 813 (187 500 × 1.535). Given that the company is to receive $300 000, it will have to sell the $12 187 surplus, either at the spot in the foreign exchange market in three months' time or now via a forward exchange contract. We can see that the company has locked into a particular exchange rate ($1.535/£1) and knows how much sterling it will receive from its future dollar receipts, except (perhaps) for the $12 187 surplus. In this example the company has *under-hedged* by using 3 contracts when it needed 3.13 contracts for a perfect hedge.

12.4.3 Advantages and disadvantages of using futures to hedge risk

An informed decision on hedging with financial futures will consider the advantages and disadvantages of choosing this risk management method. One advantage of futures is that, unlike options, there is no up-front premium to be paid, although money must be put into the margin account. Another advantage is that, unlike forward contracts, futures are tradable and can be bought and sold on a secondary market. This provides *pricing transparency* since prices are set by the futures market rather than by a financial institution. Finally, because contracts are marked to market on a daily basis, favourable movements in interest rates and exchange rates are immediately credited to a company's margin account.

Arguably the biggest drawback associated with futures is that, unlike options, they do not allow a company to take advantage of favourable movements in interest and exchange rates. A further problem is that, because contracts are standardised, it is difficult to find a perfect hedge with respect to the principal to be hedged and its maturity. This is illustrated in our earlier example, where four currency futures would over-hedge the exposure and three currency futures would under-hedge it. As regards cost, while there are no premiums to be paid with futures contracts, the initial margin must still be found. *Variation margin* may also be required as interest or exchange rates move adversely. Finally, as mentioned earlier, *basis risk* may exist if changes in exchange and interest rates are not perfectly correlated with changes in the futures prices contracts, which in turn affects the hedge efficiency of the futures contracts.

12.5 Options

Currency and interest rate options give their holders the right, but not the obligation, to borrow or lend at a specific interest rate, or to buy or sell foreign currency at a specific exchange rate. This gives option users the flexibility to take advantage of favourable interest rate and exchange rate movements. A price is paid for this flexibility, however, in the form of an *option premium*. This is a non-refundable fee paid when the option is acquired. There are two distinct categories of options available to companies to hedge their exposures: over-the-counter options and traded options.

12.5.1 Over-the-counter options

Over-the-counter (OTC) options can be purchased from financial institutions such as banks and can be tailor-made to meet company requirements. OTC options, which can be subdivided into caps, floors and collars, specify a principal amount, a time period over which the option runs and a particular currency or interest rate.

With an *interest rate cap*, if the specified interest rate goes above a predetermined level the financial institution pays the excess, thereby guaranteeing or *capping* the interest rate to be paid by the company. Alternatively, a UK company wanting to convert an amount of dollars into sterling at some future date can purchase an *exchange rate cap*. The company will be guaranteed a certain rate of exchange, say $1.5/£. If the exchange rate increases to $1.67/£, the company can use the cap to exchange at the more favourable rate of $1.5/£ with the bank from which it purchased the cap.

With an *interest rate floor*, if a specified interest rate falls below a certain rate, the financial institution pays the company the difference. Interest rate floors allow companies receiving floating rate interest income to guarantee a minimum level of receipts. Correspondingly, an *exchange rate floor* guarantees a UK company wanting to buy foreign currency in the future a minimum rate of exchange should the pound depreciate against the specified currency.

A *collar* is the combination of a floor and a cap and it is used by a company wanting to keep an interest rate or exchange rate between an upper and lower limit. Using a collar works out cheaper for companies compared with using caps or floors on their own. Take, for example, a company with floating rate income that takes out a collar to keep the interest rate between 6 per cent and 8 per cent. It is paying a premium to buy a floor of 6 per cent from the bank and at the same time it receives a premium for selling the bank a cap of 8 per cent. A collar will also work out cheaper than a floor since any beneficial interest rate changes over and above 8 per cent are paid to the bank. Conversely, a collar for a company wanting to keep its borrowing rate between an upper and lower limit combines buying a cap with selling a floor.

12.5.2 Traded options

Traded options are similar to over-the-counter options except that they are standardised with respect to the principal amount and the maturity date specified by the contract. The standardised nature of these contracts allows them to be bought and sold on a secondary market. The world's largest options market is the Chicago Board Options Exchange (CBOE) which trades share, interest and currency options. In the UK, currency, equity and interest rate options trade on Euronext.liffe.

Traded options mature in three-month cycles (March, June, September and December) and the standard size of a three-month sterling interest rate option on Euronext.liffe, for instance, is £500000. Traded options are of two kinds: *put* options carry the right to *sell* currency or to *lend* at a fixed rate; whereas *call* options carry the right to *buy* currency or to *borrow* at a fixed rate. Puts and calls can be further divided into *American options*, which are exercisable up to and on their expiry date, and *European options*, which are exercisable only on their expiry date.

12.5.3 Using traded options to hedge interest rate risk

Interest option contracts traded on Euronext.liffe use futures contracts as the underlying asset rather than cash market transactions because futures positions can be closed out by buying or selling contracts whereas cash market transactions require delivery. The diagrams in Exhibit 12.4 show the profit or loss associated with buying or selling put and call interest rate options, where K represents the *strike price* at which futures can be bought or sold and P represents the premium paid if the option is bought or the premium received if the option is sold.

It can be seen from Exhibit 12.4 that when selling or *writing* call and put options, the downside risk (i.e. the risk of loss) is unlimited. For this reason, only the buying of puts and calls is recommended for hedging commercial transactions (with the exception of collars), since this limits the downside risk for a company to the loss of the option premium paid.

| Exhibit 12.4 | Diagrams showing the pay-offs associated with buying and selling interest rate options that use futures as the underlying asset |

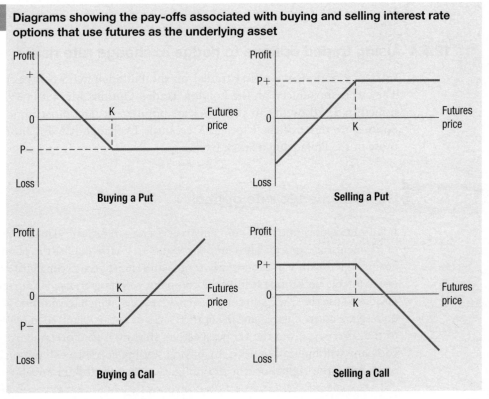

| Example | **Using interest rate options** |

It is 15 December and a company wants to borrow £2m, for a period of three months, in three months' time. The three-month LIBOR rate stands at 6 per cent and the company wants to guard against any increase in interest rates. To give the company the option to borrow at an effective rate of 6 per cent, it can purchase four 15 March LIBOR sterling put option contracts of £500 000 each with a strike price of 94. The price the company has been quoted for these option contracts is 0.17 per contract. This signifies a cost of 17 ticks per option contract. Given that ticks have a predetermined value of £12.50, this represents a cost per contract of £212.50 (17 × £12.50). The cost of four option contracts to the company is therefore £850.

If interest rates have increased to 8 per cent on 15 March, the company exercises its option contracts, allowing it to sell futures contracts at 94. The futures price, assuming no basis risk (*see* Section 12.4.1), will have dropped to 92 (i.e. 100 − 8), so the company makes a 2 per cent gain on its futures transactions by buying futures at 92 and selling them at 94. This represents a gain of 200 ticks at £12.50 each per contract, giving a total gain on the options of 200 × £12.50 × 4 = £10 000. This exactly balances the 2 per cent increase in its cost of borrowing, which is 2 per cent × £2m × 1/4 = £10 000. In exchange for an option premium of £850, the company has guaranteed a maximum borrowing rate of 6 per cent. If interest rates had dropped to 5 per cent on 15 March, the company would let its option contracts expire and borrow at the lower market rate of 5 per cent. Its loss would be the premium of £850 paid.

12.5.4 Using traded options to hedge exchange rate risk

Currency options were first traded on the Philadelphia Stock Exchange in 1982. They were introduced on the London Traded Options Market in 1985, but discontinued in 1990 owing to their lack of popularity. The most important currency options are those of the Chicago Mercantile Exchange (CME), closely followed by those of the Philadelphia Stock Exchange.

| Example | **Using exchange rate options** |

It is 19 December and a UK company is expecting to receive $1m in three months' time in payment for exports. The company wants to guard against the pound appreciating against the dollar, which currently stands at $1.65/£. As sterling currency options are not available on Euronext.liffe, the company will have to use US currency options. It decides to use the CME's sterling currency options, which have futures contracts as the underlying asset. These come in contract sizes of £62 500 and require physical delivery of the currency. From the US perspective, sterling is the foreign currency and so the company will buy call options. By buying sterling currency call options, the company can obtain the right but not the obligation to sell dollars and buy sterling at an exchange rate of $1.65 to the pound. To find the appropriate number of contracts required, the dollar amount to be received must be translated into pounds at the option strike price, giving £606 061 (i.e. $1m/$1.65). This is then divided by the standard contract size to give the number of contracts required as 9.7 (i.e. £606 061/£62 500). In this situation it is impossible to get a perfect hedge owing to the standard size of the contracts. The company will therefore have either to under-hedge by buying nine contracts or to over-hedge by buying ten contracts. Any shortfalls or excess amounts of dollars can be corrected by using forward exchange contracts or currency market transactions when the options are exercised. Assume that the company decides to purchase ten contracts.

If March sterling currency call options with a $1.65 strike price are currently trading at a premium of 7 cents (per pound of contract) then the total cost of ten contracts is given by:

$$62\,500 \times 10 \times 0.07 = \$43\,750$$

By purchasing March sterling currency call options with a $1.65 strike price the company will, in the worst-case scenario, exchange its dollars at a rate of $1.72 to the pound (i.e. $1.65 plus the 7 cents premium). If, in three months' time, the spot rate is below $1.65/£, the company will allow the option to expire and exchange its dollars in the spot market.

Conversely, if the company had imported goods and therefore needed to buy dollars in three months' time, it would purchase US sterling currency put options, giving it the option to sell sterling and receive dollars at a predetermined rate.

As with over-the-counter options, traded options can be combined to create collars and so decrease the costs of hedging with options. The combinations of put and call options required to create various interest rate and currency collars are shown in Exhibit 12.5.

Exhibit 12.5 — **The combinations of put and call options required to create interest and currency collars**

Using Euronext.liffe interest rate options on interest futures	
Borrower's collar: to keep interest rate between an upper and lower limit	Buy a put option and sell a call option
Lender's collar: to keep interest rate between an upper and lower limit	Buy a call option and sell a put option
Using US sterling currency options	
Exporter's collar: to keep exchange rate between an upper and lower limit	Buy a call option and sell a put option
Importer's collar: to keep exchange rate between an upper and lower limit	Buy a put option and sell a call option

12.5.5 Factors affecting the price of traded options

The determination of option premiums is a complex process owing to the large number of factors influencing the price of traded options. These factors are as follows.

Strike price

The higher the strike price specified in an interest rate option contract, the lower the price of a call option and the higher the price of the corresponding put option. A put option to lend at 10 per cent, for example, will cost more than a put option to lend at 8 per cent. Similarly, a put option to sell the dollar at a rate of $1.5 to £1 will cost less than a put option to sell the dollar at a rate of $1.3 to £1.

Changes in interest and exchange rates

Rising interest rates will increase the value of interest rate call options but decrease the value of interest rate put options. A call option to borrow at 12 per cent, for example, will become more valuable if interest rates rise from, say, 11 per cent to 13 per cent. Similarly, a US sterling put option to sell sterling at $1.5/£ will increase in value if the pound depreciates against the dollar.

Volatility of interest rates and exchange rates

Both call and put options will have a higher value if interest rates and exchange rates are volatile as greater volatility means a greater potential gain for the option holder and a greater potential loss for the option writer; a higher premium is therefore charged.

Time to expiry of the option

The longer the time an option has to go before its expiry date, the more valuable it will be as it can be used by a company to hedge unfavourable movements in exchange or interest rates for a longer period of time. Like a warrant, the value of an option can be split into two parts:

$$\text{Intrinsic value} + \text{Time value} = \text{Total value}$$

The *intrinsic value* of an option represents the value of an option if it is exercised immediately. If the current exchange rate between the dollar and the pound is $1.5/£, then a US sterling currency put option with a strike price of $1.7/£ will have intrinsic value, whereas a similar option with a strike price of $1.3/£ will not. The first option is *in the money* whereas the second option is *out of the money*.

If an option is out of the money and thus has no intrinsic value, it may still possess *time value*. Take the put option with a strike price of $1.3/£. This option has no intrinsic value but, if it has three months before expiry, there is time for the exchange rate to fall from its current rate of $1.5/£ to below the option's $1.3/£ strike price. Time value, therefore, is proportionate to the time left before the option expires and is at a maximum when a contract starts and at a minimum (i.e. zero) when the contract expires.

12.5.6 Advantages and disadvantages of hedging with options

While not the cheapest method of hedging owing to the premiums payable on them, options have the great advantage of offering the holder the opportunity to benefit from favourable movements in exchange and interest rates.

There are two situations where using options to hedge exposures is likely to be advantageous. The first is where a company is expecting to make a transaction, but is not certain that it will occur. For example, it may be expecting to borrow money in the future or may be tendering for an overseas contract. If the transaction does not occur, the company can either let the option expire or, due to the tradability of options, sell it on to another party if it has any value. The second situation is where a company expects interest or exchange rates to move in a certain direction but, in addition, believes there is a chance that rates might move in the opposite direction. By using options, the company is in a position to take advantage of any favourable movements in rates should they arise.

In addition to the disadvantage of their expense, using options makes it difficult to create a hedge which matches perfectly both the duration and size of a company's exposure. As with futures, this problem is due to the standardisation of traded option contracts. Using over-the-counter options may be a more appropriate choice than traded options for hedging significant non-standard exposures.

12.6 Swaps

The currency swaps market was developed in the early 1980s to facilitate access to international capital markets by multinational companies. In these markets, companies raise funds in *vehicle currencies* (in which they can borrow relatively cheaply but which are not the currency in which the debt is required) and swap into the preferred currency at a lower rate than if they borrowed the funds directly. The development of interest rate swaps followed closely on the heels of currency swaps and the market in interest rate swaps is now larger in terms of both size and importance. By 2004 the notional amounts outstanding on interest rate swaps stood at $184 trillion. The continuing success of the swaps market, the subject of Vignette 12.3, prompted Euronext.liffe (then known as LIFFE) to introduce in 2002 futures contracts based on two-, five- and ten-year interest rate swaps.

Swaps are used extensively by companies and banks to capitalise on their comparative advantages in the different debt markets and to hedge their interest and exchange rate exposures. The counterparties (companies) in a swap deal are normally brought together by a dealer (usually a bank) acting as an intermediary. Where a swap partner cannot be found immediately, banks can *warehouse* swaps by acting as a temporary swap partner until an appropriate counterparty is found. Banks benefit, through acting as swap brokers, from the arrangement fees they receive from the counterparties.

A major advantage of swaps over other derivatives such as traded options, forward rate agreements and financial futures is that they can be used to lock into interest and exchange rates for much longer periods, and do not require frequent monitoring and reviewing.

Vignette 12.3

Interest rate swaps: changing hopes boost volume

Interest rate swaps are among the most traded instruments in the international capital markets. An estimated $59 000bn changed hands every day last year, according to the Bank for International Settlements. And, by all accounts, the supremacy of interest rate swaps – derivatives contracts based on the direction of interest rates – has increased over the course of 2002. The main reason is rapidly shifting interest rate expectations.

Derivatives contracts often thrive when volatility affects the underlying commodity. Between late 2001, when the US economy looked set for recovery and economists were anticipating quick moves to tighten monetary policy by the US Federal Reserve, and September 2002, when the economic outlook had deteriorated so significantly that no rise in interest rates was in sight, activity in the swaps market picked up. Dealers and investors used swaps to adapt to the changed environment.

Rob Standing, head of European rates at JP Morgan, says there has been a lot of activity in US dollar swaps and other structures. 'This is because there is a disconnection between people's perceptions of when rates will rise in the US and the course of interest rates implied by the yield curve,' he adds.

Investment banks and trading platforms affected by the bursting of the dotcom bubble and the collapse of mergers and acquisitions activity are obtaining some relief from increased activity in swaps. 'Revenues on the business side of our interest rate operations have remained at the levels of the 2000 peak, unlike other sectors of investment banking, which have declined,' says Mr Standing.

Analysts estimate changing interest rate expectations have had a greater impact in the US than in Europe, but the use of interest rate derivatives in Europe is growing well, albeit for different reasons.

European pension and insurance funds that need to extend debt maturities to match assets with liabilities are using the interest rate swaps market to do so. This is because the swaps market can provide protection against falling equity markets and declining interest rates – both of which have occurred since the bursting of the dotcom bubble.

In a similar vein, government debt management agencies are using interest rate swaps to reduce maturities to cut borrowing costs. France, for example, began receiving interest rate swaps in October last year, and by the end of 2002 it will have moved as much as €100bn in the market.

'Interest rate swaps have become the most accepted instrument to hedge credit duration risk, as an increasing number of actors in the market want to customize their liability portfolio,' says Ed Eisler, head of European interest rate products at Goldman Sachs.

While most interest rate swaps products are traded through large inter-dealer brokers such as Icap and Cantor Fitzgerald, traditional exchanges have also been trying to capitalize on the growing market by launching futures contracts based on interest rate swaps. Last year, Liffe, the derivatives exchange that merged with Euronext, launched futures contracts based on two-year, five-year and 10-year interest rate swaps. The Chicago Board of Trade more recently launched five-year and 10-year contracts in the US. The main advantages of swap futures for traders, they say, is in hedging credit risk and relative value trading.

Amanda Sudworth, director of interest rate products at Euronext.liffe, believes swap futures will be a successful strategic move for the exchange. 'When products are so innovative it takes a long, long time for them to blossom,' she says. 'Swap futures are very attractive as a means of removing counterparty credit risk.'

But until today, the levels of liquidity enjoyed by these contracts have not been encouraging. At the CBOT, daily average volumes this year have not exceeded 3000 contracts a day on the 10-year note and 500 contracts a day since the June launch of the five-year note. Average daily volumes for this year at Euronext.liffe range from 8400 for the 10-year Swapnote to 3500 for Liffe's two-year note.

At JP Morgan, which is one of the largest users of interest rate swap futures, Mr Standing remains relatively unenthusiastic. 'There is a chance that they will be successful, but they are not offering the market something powerful that it has not seen before.'

Source: James Politi, *Financial Times*, 7 October 2002. Reprinted with permission.

12.6.1 Interest rate swaps

Winstone (1995) offers a definition of an interest rate swap as an exchange between two parties of interest obligations or receipts in the same currency on an agreed amount of notional principal for an agreed period of time. Interest rate swaps can be used to hedge against adverse interest rate movements or to achieve a chosen blend of fixed and floating rate debt. Companies may become involved in swap agreements because their borrowing or lending requirements do not coincide with their comparative advantages with respect to fixed and floating rate borrowing or lending. The most common type of interest rate swap is a *plain vanilla swap*, where fixed interest payments based on a notional principal are swapped with floating interest payments based on the same notional principal. The swap agreement will include the following details:

- the start and end dates of the swap;
- the notional principal on which the swap is based (amount and currency);
- which party is paying floating interest and receiving fixed interest in return, and vice versa;
- the level of the fixed rate and the basis of the floating rate (e.g. one-, three- or six-month LIBOR) upon which the agreement is based.

Example	**Plain vanilla interest rate swap**

Consider two companies, A and B. The interest rates at which they can borrow are shown in the first part of Exhibit 12.6.

Company A, with a better credit rating, can borrow at a lower fixed and a lower floating rate than Company B. We refer to A as having an *absolute advantage* over B. However, B has a *comparative advantage* over A with floating rate borrowing as its floating rate is proportionately less expensive than its fixed rate when compared with A's rates. If, for example, LIBOR stands at 5 per cent, then B's floating rate is 4 per cent

Exhibit 12.6	An example of a plain vanilla interest rate swap between two companies, A and B

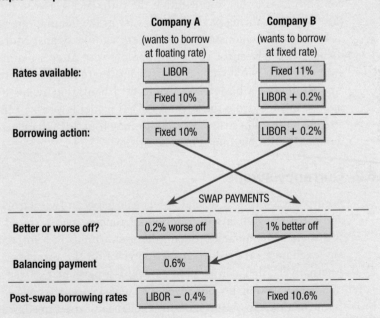

more expensive than A's floating rate (i.e. 0.2 per cent/5 per cent). This compares with B's fixed rate being 10 per cent more expensive (i.e. 1 per cent/10 per cent) than A's. Conversely, A has a comparative advantage in fixed rate borrowing.

The prerequisite for a swap agreement to proceed is for both companies to be able to benefit from it. For this to be the case, the companies must want to raise funds by borrowing at the rate in which they do not possess a comparative advantage. In our example, this means that A must want to borrow at a floating rate and B must want to borrow at a fixed rate.

If A raises a fixed rate loan at 10 per cent and B raises a floating rate loan at LIBOR plus 0.2 per cent, and they swap interest payments, then B is 1 per cent better off whereas A is 0.2 per cent worse off. If B makes a payment of 0.2 per cent to A, then A is neither better nor worse off, whereas B is still 0.8 per cent better off. If the benefits of the swap agreement are to be split evenly between the two parties, then B will have to make a further payment of 0.4 per cent to A. The post-swap borrowing rates are shown in Exhibit 12.6, where A ends up with a floating rate of LIBOR minus 0.4 per cent and B with a fixed rate of 10.6 per cent.

In practice, as swaps are arranged through the intermediation of a bank, the bank's arrangement fee will decrease the benefit that companies derive from the transaction. In our example, if the arranging bank took a fee of 0.2 per cent, equally divided between the two parties, the post-swap rates would become LIBOR minus 0.3 per cent for Company A and 10.7 per cent for Company B. Furthermore, companies will not swap interest payments, but make a balancing payment from one company to another, representing the difference between the fixed and the floating rate. These balancing payments will vary as the floating rate varies.

Here we have considered only plain vanilla swaps. More complex swap agreements exist. The most common type of swap after a plain vanilla swap is a *basis* swap in which two floating rate payments determined on different bases are exchanged. An example of a basis swap would be a bank that swaps its base-rate-determined interest income (from the advances it has made) for, say, a LIBOR-determined income stream. This allows the company to match its LIBOR-related cost of raising funds with a LIBOR-determined income stream.

12.6.2 Currency swaps

A currency swap is a formal agreement between two parties to exchange principal and interest payments in different currencies over a stated time period. Currency swaps enable companies to gain the use of funds in a foreign currency but to avoid any exchange rate risk (transaction risk) on the principal or servicing payments. Alternatively, they can be used to obtain a particular currency at a more favourable rate than if a company borrowed the currency itself.

Currency swaps begin with the exchange of the agreed principal amounts at a par exchange rate (usually the prevailing spot rate), followed by the exchange of interest payments over the life of the swap. When the swap matures, the principal amounts are re-exchanged at the par exchange rate agreed earlier. An alternative to the initial exchange of the principal is for both counterparties to make the appropriate spot market transactions, then to exchange interest payments over the duration of the swap and re-exchange principals on maturity.

The information included in currency swap contracts is similar to the information included in an interest rate swap agreement. In addition, though, it will specify which currency is to be paid, which currency is to be received and the exchange rate to be used as the par rate.

Implicit within currency swaps is an interest rate swap. The simplest form of currency swap is a *fixed to fixed* agreement, where the interest payments to be exchanged on the two currencies are both fixed. If the swap involves exchanging fixed and floating interest rates it is then called a *fixed to floating* or *currency coupon* swap.

An example of how currency swaps can be used to hedge exchange rate risk is explained in the following example.

Example	Fixed to floating currency swap

A UK airline is to purchase a new aeroplane. This has to be paid for in US dollars, so the airline will finance its purchase with a fixed interest dollar loan from a US bank (stage 1 in Exhibit 12.7). Owing to the company's income being received predominantly in sterling, the airline has approached another bank to arrange a currency swap. Within this swap will be a par exchange rate which is used to convert dollar cash flows into pounds. It will be used to convert the dollar loan into a sterling principal on which to determine the sterling LIBOR payments the airline will make to the bank (stage 2), in return for the bank paying to the airline the dollar interest payments on the airline's dollar loan (stage 3). These dollar interest payments will then be paid to the US bank by the airline (stage 4). When the swap matures the airline will pay the sterling principal to the bank (stage 5) and in return will receive a dollar payment (stage 6) with which to pay off its maturing dollar loan (stage 7). Looking at the swap as a whole, we can see that the airline has paid off a sterling loan principal and sterling LIBOR-determined interest payments, hence avoiding the possibility of exchange rate risk.

12.6.3 Swaptions

As the name suggests, swaptions are a combination of a swap and an option. They give the holder the option to become involved in a swap, i.e. they are a derivative of a derivative. They are similar to traded and over-the-counter options but are less flexible as, once the option to swap is exercised, the company is locked into a particular exchange or interest rate and can no longer benefit from subsequent favourable

Exhibit 12.7	An example of a currency swap indicating (a) the initial and on-going payments, and (b) the payments made on the swap's maturity. The chronological order of payments is indicated by the stages in brackets.

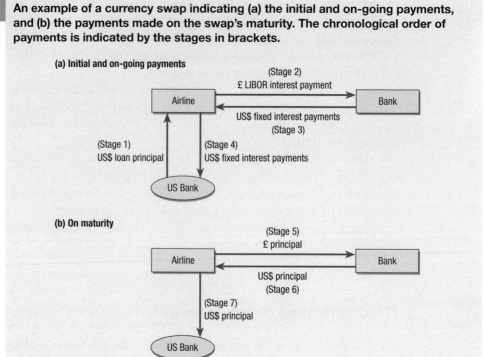

movements in rates. Swaptions represent a cheaper way in which to hedge risk as the premiums paid on them tend to be lower than the premiums charged for options.

12.6.4 Advantages and disadvantages of hedging with swaps

The major advantage of swaps is that they allow companies to hedge interest and exchange rate exposures for relatively long periods compared to other derivatives. The arrangement fees are usually much less than the premiums paid on options, while swaps are more flexible from a principal and duration point of view than stand-ardised derivatives such as traded options and futures.

Swap agreements are not without their risks, however. Once entered into, a swap prevents a company from benefiting from favourable movements in exchange and interest rates, unless of course it defaults on the agreement. If a counterparty to a swap defaults on interest payments, the other party is still legally required to make the servicing payments as it originally took out the loan. This risk of interest default is called *counterparty risk*. Since the company will not be hedged, it will be exposed to interest rate and exchange rate risk while a replacement swap party is found. It is therefore advisable that companies entering into swap agreements do so only with counterparties of an acceptable credit standing.

12.7 | Issues in risk management

12.7.1 The need for a risk management strategy

Hedging interest rate and exchange rate risk is a complicated and dynamic process. Hedging strategies and the techniques and instruments used will vary from company to company, depending on the markets the companies operate in, their attitudes towards risk and their awareness and understanding of the techniques available. When formulating hedging strategies, it is important for companies to be clear about their objectives, to identify and quantify their likely exposures and to select appropriate hedging techniques.

The objectives of hedging policy

Companies must clearly define the objectives of their hedging policy. Is the objective one of securing a certain interest income or interest cost? Is the objective to minimise foreign currency expense, or to maximise or fix the domestic value of foreign currency income? An important determining factor here is whether a company's treasury department is designated as a *cost centre* or a *profit centre*. Within a cost centre, hedging will be seen solely as a means of reducing risk and providing a service to the rest of the company. If the treasury department is seen as a profit centre, however, there will be pressure to use derivatives in a more speculative manner. The consequences of speculating with derivatives can, however, be disastrous.

Cornell and Shapiro (1988) argue that since exchange rate risk affects all aspects of a company's operations, exposure management should not be left solely in the hands of financial managers, but rather should be integrated into the general management of the company as a whole. On this view, exchange rate expectations should inform production, marketing and other operational decisions so that hedging is an anticipatory strategy.

Identifying and quantifying the risk exposure

Companies must identify and quantify their interest and exchange rate risk exposures before they can implement an appropriate hedging strategy. They will have to decide whether they wish to hedge exposures selectively or on a continuous basis. This choice will depend on a company's attitude to risk as well as its expectations concerning future interest rate and exchange rate changes. For example, a company may choose to hedge its interest rate exposure selectively only if it expects interest rates to change significantly.

Time horizon of hedging policy

It is important for companies to consider the time horizon they take when hedging exposures. While some companies hedge expected exposures up to and beyond 12 months others take a more short-term view. The time horizons companies consider when hedging their currency exposures is the subject of Vignette 12.4.

Vignette 12.4

Companies 'too short sighted when hedging'

Companies' currency hedging horizons are often too short to have any real effect in mitigating adverse trends, Citigroup has said after a survey of corporate clients and their foreign exchange hedging practices. The survey showed generally conservative and cautious attitudes to currency risk and the ways in which it could be reduced. Citigroup received responses from 98 of its biggest corporate clients. While increasing cross-border trade has brought new and rising levels of currency risk, companies have been cautious in developing ways of managing those risks.

FX hedging usually hits the headlines only when a company makes a big bet – and in the wrong direction – or when a sharp currency move gives a number of companies in the same region a similar explanation for disappointing results.

Citigroup said many of the survey respondents were keen to see the results, even though the data are presented without company names, to compare their practices with others'. It hopes the survey, the first, will be an annual event.

'Companies don't want to try to do things differently because they're often afraid of being outside the pack – though there's no opposition to being on the front end of it,' said Didier Hirigoyen, global head of corporate risk advisory at Citigroup.

Changes to accounting rules, particularly regarding the treatment of options, have made many corporate treasurers even more wary of hedging FX risks. Only 13 per cent of respondents reported hedging expected transactions beyond 12 months and a third said they used only a six-month horizon. Almost 20 per cent said they did not hedge expected transactions at all.

'When you look at the risk management objectives of companies there's maybe a misconception about how hedging works,' said Mr Hirigoyen. He said: 'Most companies hedge under one year in tenor but since hedging only postpones the impact of a currency move, the shorter the tenor, the more rapidly your performance will get hit by FX moves.

'Companies could achieve a much greater reduction in volatility by adopting two, three or even four-year hedges,' he said. 'With a layering technique such as hedging 100 per cent the first year, 66 per cent the next and 33 per cent the third, you could dramatically lower the volatility of the exchange rate.'

Some companies, usually in highly competitive industries with tight margins, are looking to use FX hedging as a way to gain advantage. 'Companies that are looking to be more innovative are looking at managing risk in more aggressive ways that will help them generate the incremental cash that will help them be more aggressive from a pricing point of view,' said Mr Hirigoyen.

But hedging practices are also dependent on a range of other factors, from interest rates to idiosyncratic business factors. Companies dealing heavily in commodities and energy, for example, frequently said that for them FX risk was a side issue. Habits also change by region. Almost 80 per cent of European respondents put on hedges of more than a year compared with almost 70 per cent of US groups. Asian companies, all of which reported hedging their FX risk, however, had the shortest-term focus because of the wide interest rate differentials with the currency to be hedged.'

Source: Jennifer Hughesin, *Financial Times*, 27 January 2006. Reprinted with permission.

Selection of hedging method

The final component of a company's hedging strategy is the selection of hedging methods appropriate to the nature of its exposure. A sensible strategy is to try to hedge as much of the interest and exchange rate risk as possible by using internal hedging techniques. Any remaining exposure can then be hedged using the most appropriate external techniques. A number of factors restrict a company's ability to hedge internally, however (*see* Section 12.2), increasing the need to use external methods. While there is a wide range of external instruments to choose from, the choice of derivative will depend heavily upon the relative importance to the company of the particular costs and benefits of the derivatives available. Some of the considerations to be taken into account are as follows:

- For exposures of non-standard size and duration, tailor-made derivatives (swaps, FRAs, OTC options) represent more appropriate hedging tools than traded options and futures.
- Options, while costing more, are appropriate when a company is not completely certain of making a transaction or where it is not completely certain about the direction in which interest or exchange rates will move.
- Bank-created products may be more appropriate for smaller companies as their treasury functions are likely to lack the required experience and knowledge needed to use more complex traded derivatives.

12.7.2 The pros of risk management

There is an ongoing debate at both an academic and a practical level about the desirability of hedging by companies. Common sense tells us that a company should hedge an exposure if, and only if, the costs of executing the hedge are outweighed by the benefits. The actions of financial managers would seem to support the importance and benefits of hedging, given the enormous growth in the use of exchange and interest rate management instruments in recent years. It has been known for some time that large UK companies, including Tate & Lyle and Cadbury-Schweppes, have found benefits in adopting such instruments. The potential benefits which may arise from hedging exposures include the following.

Maintaining competitiveness

Adverse changes in interest and exchange rates may reduce the competitive position of a company against those with lower levels of gearing or smaller exchange rate exposures, or compared with companies that have taken the precaution of hedging against rate changes.

Reduction of bankruptcy risk

Adverse movements in interest and exchange rates may jeopardise the continued operation of a company. A classic example is that of a highly geared company with a large proportion of floating rate debt being forced into bankruptcy due to an increase in interest rates.

Restructuring of capital obligations

Interest rate hedging instruments can be used to restructure a company's capital profile by altering the nature of its interest obligations, thereby avoiding the repayment of existing debt or the issuing of new securities. In consequence, considerable savings can be made in respect of call fees and issue costs. At the same time, a wider range of financial sources becomes available to the company.

Reduction in the volatility of corporate cash flows

Reducing the volatility of net cash flows may increase the market rating of the company and will facilitate the process of forward planning.

Enhancement of companies' debt capacity

If interest rate hedging techniques are being used to manage interest rate exposure, companies may be able to increase gearing levels or enhance their debt capacities. Academic research in the USA by Graham and Daniel (2002) substantiated this as a real benefit for companies that hedge.

Tax benefits of hedging

Research in the USA by Graham and Smith (1999) suggests that hedging increases the value of the company if it faces a convex tax function. In this case, income volatility leads to low tax payments in some periods and higher tax payments in others, causing the average tax burden to exceed the average tax the company would have had to pay on an equivalent stable stream of income. Subsequent research by Graham and Daniel (2002) discredited these findings.

12.7.3 The cons of risk management

The benefits of hedging must be balanced against a number of problems which, ultimately, may dissuade some companies from engaging in exposure management.

The complicated nature of hedging instruments

A combination of unfamiliarity with the range of hedging methods available and a belief by potential users that such methods are complex may result in treasurers choosing not to hedge exchange and interest rate exposures.

The costs associated with derivatives

Companies may be dissuaded from using derivatives by the various fees, premiums, margin requirements and transaction costs associated with them.

The risks associated with using external hedging instruments

The perceived risk associated with using hedging instruments can sometimes dissuade potential users. This risk can be illustrated by a number of high-profile derivative disasters. In 1994, Procter & Gamble lost $102m on two interest rate swap agreements with the US bank Bankers Trust. Instead of providing protection from steeply increasing interest rates, the transactions turned out to be highly speculative bets. Procter & Gamble has subsequently taken legal action against Bankers Trust on the grounds that it was misled by the bank.

In February 1995, in a now legendary disaster, Barings Bank went into receivership after making losses in excess of £860m on Nikkei index futures deals on SIMEX in Singapore and the Osaka derivatives exchange in Japan. The losses were accumulated by trader Nick Leeson, who was responsible for both the trading and back office records of his deals, so there was no effective system of monitoring and checking his trading in derivatives.

In more recent years, 1998 saw the near collapse of US hedge fund Long Term Capital Management (LTCM) with nearly $1400 billion of derivatives on its balance sheet despite having investors' funds of only $3 billion. LTCM had been using the steep gearing effect of derivatives to speculate on the pricing of various financial instruments. Derivatives were again cast in an unfavourable light in 2001 by the collapse of US energy giant Enron. While Enron's involvement in the USA's unregulated OTC derivatives market was not the reason for its failure, its questionable operations in the OTC market highlight the dangers of unregulated derivatives trading.

The complicated financial reporting and tax treatments of derivatives

Traditionally, the accounting and tax treatment of derivatives has tended to lag behind the pace of their development owing to the dynamic nature of derivative markets. In the past the major problem regarding the accounting treatment of derivatives was knowing exactly what information to disclose and how to disclose it. This led to companies reporting only superficial information and general strategies rather than disclosing detailed information. Accounting for derivatives has become increasingly more complicated, however, due to the International Accounting Standards Board (IASB) adopting the rule-based approach of FAS 133, the USA's far-reaching accounting standard on derivatives and hedging, in its own standard (IAS 39). Companies must now show any fair value changes in derivative prices in their income statements unless derivatives meet strict criterion on hedge effectiveness.

As far as the tax treatment of derivatives is concerned, it is necessary for companies to seek specialist advice before engaging in the derivatives market. This represents a further cost and may contribute to the reluctance of many companies to use derivatives.

Diversification by shareholders may be superior to hedging

An alternative to hedging by individual companies is for shareholders to diversify away interest and exchange rate risk themselves by holding a diversified portfolio of shares, hence saving the costs associated with hedging at a corporate level. If shareholders hold diversified portfolios, some commentators argue that hedging of exposures by individual companies is motivated purely by management's desire to safeguard their jobs rather than a desire to enhance shareholder wealth.

12.7.4 Managing the use of derivatives

Despite the drawbacks just considered, there can be little doubt that, if used properly, derivatives can and do bring real benefits to the user company. In the cases cited where companies have made huge losses through the trading of derivatives, the problems were not so much with the derivatives themselves but rather with the way that they were used (or misused). Some of these financial disasters have involved unauthorised trading (e.g. the Barings fiasco), raising the possibility that many companies may not have appropriate controls or monitoring procedures in place to regulate their derivatives dealings. The lesson for such companies is that they cannot ignore the need for well-defined risk management policies, which must refer specifically to:

- the types of derivative instrument that can be used;
- limits on the volume and principal amount of derivative transactions allowed;
- the need to calculate regularly the market value of the company's derivative positions;
- systems and procedures to prevent unauthorised dealings.

It is also sensible for companies to outlaw the use of derivatives for speculative purposes. Once such policies are implemented, a company's derivatives transactions should be both more visible and more easily understood.

Spare a parting thought for corporate treasurers who, when it comes to risk management, are effectively in a 'no win' situation. Deciding not to hedge a particular exposure and doing nothing can be construed as speculation if an unfavourable movement in rates occurs. However, should the treasurer hedge the exposure, locking into a particular rate, and the market subsequently moves in what would have been a favourable pre-hedge direction, it is considered bad judgement on the treasurer's part.

12.8 Conclusion

The area of risk management has grown rapidly in importance over the past 30 years and treasurers now find themselves spending an increasing amount of their time engaged in hedging company exposures to risk. This elevation in importance has been mainly due to the increased volatility of interest and exchange rates and to the rapid growth in the risk management tools and techniques available.

Risk can be managed by using both internal and external techniques. Internal techniques allow companies to hedge risk within their own balance sheet by the way in which they structure their assets and liabilities. Alternatively, companies can use one or more of the many external techniques now available, such as swaps, options, futures and forwards. While these derivative instruments give more scope and flexibility to companies to manage their risk, their associated costs and their complicated nature must be taken into account.

There have been a number of huge losses reported by companies in recent years due to the misuse of derivatives. This should not detract, however, from the very real benefits that can be derived from hedging, whether by internal or external methods, provided that these techniques are used in an appropriate manner.

Key points

1 Interest and exchange rate management now plays an increasingly important role within corporate finance owing to recent instability of interest and exchange rates.

2 Interest rate risk is faced by companies regardless of whether they lend or borrow at fixed or floating rates of interest.

3 Exchange rate risk can be classified into transaction, translation and economic risk. Transaction risk and translation risk are faced only by companies with some form of overseas operations, whereas all companies face economic risk.

4 Interest and exchange rate risk can be hedged internally by the way in which companies structure their assets and liabilities, but the degree to which companies can hedge their exposures internally is often limited.

5 The large number of external derivatives available to companies can be subdivided into traded derivatives and over-the-counter (OTC) derivatives.

6 Before the advent of derivatives, external hedging took the form of forward contracts and money market hedges. These techniques remain a popular way of hedging risk.

7 Financial futures are standardised agreements to buy or sell an underlying financial asset. They are traded on exchanges such as Euronext.liffe and allow companies to lock into particular interest or exchange rates for set periods.

8 Options give the holder, on payment of a premium, the right but not the obligation to pay or receive interest, or to sell or buy currency, at a predetermined rate. Traded options are standardised with respect to maturity and principal, whereas OTC options are tailor-made.

9 Interest rate swaps are agreements to exchange interest payments based on a specified principal. They allow companies to hedge interest rate risk over long periods and to raise funds at more favourable rates than if they raised funds directly. Currency swaps are similar to interest rate swaps, but also involve exchanges of principal. They allow companies to hedge translation and transaction risk, and to raise currency more cheaply than if they were to borrow it directly.

10 For companies to hedge effectively, it is important that they have a risk management strategy. This involves specifying hedging objectives, identifying and quantifying exposures and selecting appropriate hedging tools.

11 Advantages of using derivatives include a greater level of certainty with respect to interest rates and currency transactions. Disadvantages include the complicated nature and expense of such instruments.

12 Recent derivatives disasters have stemmed from derivatives misuse rather than from problems with the instruments themselves. If companies have well-defined guidelines to control the use of derivatives, and the required expertise and knowledge to monitor them, then they should benefit from their use.

Self-test questions

Answers to these questions can be found on pages 470–1.

1 In the following cases, state which type of exchange rate risk the company is facing and whether this risk is beneficial or harmful in nature.

   (a) A power-generating company imports coal from Germany, purchasing the coal in euros. The company is expecting the pound to weaken against the euro over the next few months.

(b) A UK toy company supplies only the domestic market. Its only major competitor in this market is a US toy company. The pound is expected to weaken against the dollar over the next year.

(c) A UK company has bought a factory in France, financing the purchase with sterling borrowing. Over the next year the pound is expected to appreciate against the euro.

2 Recommend internal hedging methods that a company can use in order to reduce translation risk and transaction risk.

3 A company is expecting to have to pay $345 000 in three months' time. It is afraid that over this period the pound will depreciate against the dollar. If the current exchange rate is $1.78/£ and the current dollar deposit rate is 8.5 per cent, how can the company use the money markets to hedge the transaction risk it faces?

4 What are the major differences between OTC options and traded options?

5 A company is going to borrow £6m in three months' time for a period of six months. It is afraid that interest rates will rise between now and the time that the loan is taken out. It intends to hedge the risk using futures contracts. Given that the contract size of interest futures is £500 000, which of the following transactions will enable the company to hedge its risk exposure successfully?

(a) Selling 12 futures contracts;

(b) Buying 12 futures contracts;

(c) Selling 24 futures contracts;

(d) Buying 24 futures contracts;

(e) Selling 6 futures contracts.

6 Identify the factors that influence a company's decision to hedge interest rate risk.

7 Which factors determine whether a company, having decided to hedge its interest rate exposure, uses internal hedging methods or external instruments? If it decides to hedge interest rate risk externally, what factors will determine which instruments will be used?

8 Which of the following will *not* help a company to hedge successfully against an *increase* in interest rates?

(a) Selling interest rate futures contracts;

(b) Swapping floating rate interest for fixed interest rate payments;

(c) Buying a bank-created floor;

(d) Splitting borrowing between fixed and floating rate interest loans;

(e) Buying a put option on futures contracts.

9 What are the drawbacks of hedging exchange rate risk by using a swap agreement?

10 Given the following list of US sterling currency options (all with three months to run) and the fact that the current spot rate is $1.55/£, which option do you expect to have the highest market value?

(a) Put option, strike price $1.55;

(b) Call option, strike price $1.66;

(c) Put option, strike price $1.42;

(d) Call option, strike price $1.55;

(e) Put option, strike price $1.71.

Questions for review

Answers to these questions can be found on pages 472–3. Questions with an asterisk (*) are at an intermediate level.

1 Discuss the factors that may persuade a company to hedge an interest rate exposure by using OTC options rather than financial futures contracts.

2* Carrycan plc must make a payment of $364 897 in six months' time. It is currently 1 January. The company is considering the various choices it has in order to hedge its transaction exposure and has collected the following information.

Exchange rates:

$/£ spot rate	1.5617–1.5773
Six-month $/£ forward rate	1.5455–1.5609

Money market rates:

	Borrow (%)	Deposit (%)
US dollars	6	4.5
Sterling	7	5.5

Foreign currency option prices (cents per £ for contract size £12 500):

Exercise price	Call option (June)	Put option (June)
$1.70	3.7	9.6

By making appropriate calculations, decide which of the following hedges is most attractive to Carrycan plc:

(a) forward market (i.e. a forward exchange contract);

(b) cash market;

(c) currency options.

3 Discuss the factors which influence the price of traded options.

4 Two companies, A and B, are considering entering into a swap agreement. Their borrowing rates are as follows:

	Floating rate	Fixed rate
Company A	LIBOR	12%
Company B	LIBOR + 0.3%	13.5%

Company A needs a floating rate loan of £5m and B needs a fixed rate loan of £5m.

(a) Which company has a comparative advantage in floating rate debt and which company has a comparative advantage in fixed rate debt?

(b) At what rate will Company A be able to obtain floating rate debt and Company B be able to obtain fixed rate debt if the two companies agree a swap and the benefits of the swap are split equally between them? Ignore bank charges.

5* Slammer plc has an excellent rating on the corporate bond market and can borrow at a fixed rate of 11.5 per cent, whereas Can plc, which is regarded as riskier, can borrow at a fixed rate of 12 per cent. For floating rate debt, Slammer plc can borrow at LIBOR + 0.2 per cent and Can plc can borrow at LIBOR + 0.4 per cent. If Slammer plc wants a floating rate loan and Can plc wants to lock into current interest rate levels through a fixed rate loan, show how an interest rate swap can benefit both companies. If the benefits from the swap are divided equally between the two companies, calculate their post-swap borrowing rates.

Questions for discussion

Questions with an asterisk (*) are at an advanced level.

1* Goran plc is a UK company with export and import trade with the USA. The following transactions, in the currency specified, are due within the next six months:

Purchases of goods, cash payment due in three months:	£116 000
Sale of finished goods, cash receipt due in three months:	$197 000
Purchase of goods, cash payment due in six months:	$447 000

Data relating to exchange rates and interest rates are as follows:

Exchange rates:	$/£
Spot	1.7106–1.7140
Three months forward	1.7024–1.7063
Six months forward	1.6967–1.7006

Interest rates	Borrow (%)	Deposit (%)
Sterling	12.5	9.5
Dollars	9.0	6.0

(a) Discuss four techniques that a company like Goran might use to hedge against the foreign exchange risk involved in foreign trade.

(b) Calculate the net sterling receipts/payments that Goran might expect for both its three-month and six-month transactions if the company hedges foreign exchange risk using (i) the forward foreign exchange market and (ii) the money market.

2 Give a detailed explanation of how interest rate risk can be hedged using options or swaps. What are the advantages and disadvantages of the hedging method you have chosen?

3 Explain how a company can use financial futures to hedge its interest rate risks and identify any advantages and disadvantages that arise from their use.

4* The monthly cash budget of HYK Communications plc shows that the company is likely to need £18 million in two months' time for a period of four months. Financial markets have recently been volatile, due to uncertainties about the impact of the 'millennium bug'. If severe computer problems occur in January 2000, the finance director of HYK plc fears that short-term interest rates could rise by as much as 150 basis points. If few problems occur then short-term rates could fall by 50 basis points. LIBOR is currently 6.5 per cent and HYK plc can borrow at LIBOR + 0.75 per cent.

The finance director does not wish to pay more than 7.50 per cent, including option premium costs, but excluding the effect of margin requirements and commissions.

LIFFE £500 000 three month futures prices: The value of one tick is £12.50

	December	93.40
	March	93.10
	June	92.75

LIFFE £500 000 three months options prices (premiums in annual per cent)

Exercise price	Calls			Puts		
	December	March	June	December	March	June
92.50	0.33	0.88	1.04	–	–	0.08
93.00	0.16	0.52	0.76	–	0.20	0.34
93.50	0.10	0.24	0.42	0.18	0.60	1.93
94.00	–	0.05	0.18	0.36	1.35	1.92

Assume that it is now 1 December 1999 and that exchange traded futures and options contracts expire at the end of the month. Margin requirements and default risk may be ignored.

Required:
Estimate the results of undertaking EACH OF an interest rate futures hedge and an interest rate options hedge on the LIFFE exchange, if LIBOR:

(i) increases by 150 basis points; and

(ii) decreases by 50 basis points.

Discuss how successful the hedges would have been. State clearly any assumptions that you make.

(ACCA 1999)

References

Buckley, A. (2003) *Multinational Finance*, 5th edn, Harlow: FT Prentice Hall.

Cornell, B. and Shapiro, A. (1988) 'Managing foreign exchange risks', in Chew, D. (ed.) *New Developments in International Finance*, Malden, MA: Blackwell.

Demirag, I. and Goddard, S. (1994) *Financial Management for International Business*, London: McGraw-Hill.

Graham, J. and Daniel, A.R. (2002) 'Do firms hedge in response to tax incentives?', *Journal of Finance*, Vol. 57, pp. 815–39.

Graham, J. and Smith, C. (1999) 'Tax incentives to hedge', *Journal of Finance*, Vol. 54, No. 6, pp. 2241–62.

Winstone, D. (1995) *Financial Derivatives: Hedging with Futures, Forwards, Options and Swaps*, London: Chapman and Hall.

Recommended reading

For two books that both give a clear and easily understandable account of the use of derivatives and the markets upon which they trade from a UK perspective, see:

Chisholm, A. (2004) *Derivatives Demystified: A Step-by-Step Guide to Forwards, Futures, Swaps and Options*, Chichester: Wiley Finance.

Hull, J. (2005) *Options, Futures and other Derivatives*, 6th edn, London: Prentice Hall.

For a US perspective on risk management and derivatives, see:

Cusatis, P. and Thomas, M. (2005) *Hedging Instruments and Risk Management*, New York: McGraw-Hill.

The following two books have sections on risk management which include a number of very readable and interesting articles on the subject of hedging and derivatives:

Chew, D. (ed.) (2000) *The New Corporate Finance: Where Theory Meets Practice*, New York: McGraw-Hill.

Stern, J. and Chew, D. (eds) (2003) *The Revolution in Corporate Finance*, Malden, MA: Blackwell.

Important and informative books, papers and articles recommended for further reading include the following:

Baird, S. (2004) 'What do rising interest rates mean for treasurers?', *www.gtnews.com*, November.

Bank of England (1995) 'The pricing of over-the-counter options', *Bank of England Quarterly Bulletin*, November, pp. 375–81.

Bank of England (1996) 'The over-the-counter derivatives market in the UK', *Bank of England Quarterly Bulletin*, February, pp. 30–36.

Black, F. and Scholes, M. (1973) 'The pricing of options and corporate liabilities', *Journal of Political Economy*, Vol. 18, pp. 637–59.

Hull, J. (2002) *Fundamentals of Futures and Options Markets*, 4th edn, Upper Saddle River, NJ: Prentice Hall.

Walsh, D. (1995) 'Risk management using derivative securities', *Managerial Finance*, Vol. 21, No. 1, pp. 43–65.

Useful websites of derivatives exchanges from around the world include:

http://www.cboe.com: Chicago Board Options Exchange
http://www.cme.com: Chicago Mercantile Exchange
http://www.euronext.com: Euronext.liffe
http://www.sgx.com: Singapore Exchange

Chapter 13

International investment decisions

Learning objectives

After studying this chapter, you should have achieved the following learning objectives:

- an appreciation of the different reasons, strategic or otherwise, for a company to undertake foreign investment;

- the ability to describe the various methods by which a company may internationalise its trading activities, including exporting, licensing, joint venture and subsidiary, and the reasons why direct investment may be preferred;

- an understanding of the various risks associated with foreign direct investment and how they can be mitigated;

- an understanding of the differences between domestic and international investment appraisal and the ability to evaluate international investment decisions;

- an appreciation of the difficulties involved in determining an appropriate cost of capital for use in appraising foreign direct investments.

Introduction

Many companies now operate internationally, either through exporting goods and services or through setting up operations in foreign countries. This has significant implications for corporate financing and investment decisions. The currency risk arising from trading with foreign countries may need to be hedged (*see* Section 12.1.3). Investing directly in a foreign country raises questions about the source and currency of financing.

The primary financial test in evaluating both international and domestic investment proposals is the extent to which a proposed investment leads to an increase in the wealth of shareholders. Evaluation of international investment proposals is more complex than the evaluation of domestic ones. Exchange rates will need to be forecast and the effect on project cash flows of different taxation systems will need to be considered. The risk arising from the actions and decisions of foreign governments must also be assessed. A company could undertake international operations through licensing, franchising or setting up a foreign branch rather than by investing directly in a foreign subsidiary. This is especially true in the early stages of becoming an international company.

13.1 The reasons for foreign investment

It is rare for foreign investment to be undertaken for a single, overriding motive. It is more likely to occur as a result of the interaction of a number of motives, not all of which are explicit or acknowledged. There has been a great deal of research into the reasons why companies invest directly abroad and into how it is possible for international companies to compete successfully with local companies. We shall look at strategic and economic reasons for foreign investment, but the distinction is essentially for the purposes of discussion since the interaction between corporate strategy and economics is complex. The importance of foreign direct investment to the UK economy can be seen in Vignette 13.1.

13.1.1 Strategic reasons for foreign investment

Strategic reasons for foreign direct investment can be classified as *defensive* or *aggressive* (Brooke 1996). Defensive reasons for establishing a foreign subsidiary are suggested by Brooke as:

- government action on tariff barriers, import controls or legislation;
- demands for local manufacture;
- transport costs and delays;
- problems with agents and licensees;
- technical difficulties abroad, e.g. problems with after-sales service;
- the need to protect patents and intellectual property;
- the need to ensure supplies of raw materials and components;

Vignette 13.1

National news: foreign direct investment almost trebles

Foreign direct investment almost trebled last year amid a revival of activity in mergers and acquisitions, according to official figures published yesterday, writes Scheherazade Daneshkhu. Net direct investment inflows rose to £30.7bn last year from a downwardly-revised £10.3bn in 2003 but still down on 2001, said the Office for National Statistics. The biggest inflow was from companies from the rest of Europe, which invested £27.9bn against £7bn in 2003.

Nigel Wilcock, director of regional development at Ernst & Young, the professional services firm, said the increase reflected economic growth of 3.2 per cent in the UK last year against 1.8 per cent in the eurozone.

'There has been a particular increase in European acquisitions of UK companies,' he said. 'Large UK companies have built market share overseas and represent a relatively cost-effective way for European companies to secure growth whilst their own economies are relatively slow growing.'

Domestic companies invested £51.8bn overseas, up 36 per cent on 2003, mostly in the Americas, Asia, Australia and New Zealand.

There was disinvestment of £3.7bn by the US in the UK, the second time this has happened in the past three years. Mr Wilcock said this reflected more attractive alternative locations where costs were lower than in the UK.

Source: Scheherazade Daneshkhu, FT.com, 14 December 2005. Reprinted with permission.

- the need to internationalise to match competitors, suppliers or customers;
- the need to protect parent company shareholders against recession.

Aggressive reasons for establishing a foreign manufacturing subsidiary suggested by Brooke include:

- the search for more profitable uses for underemployed resources;
- the search for lower factor costs;
- the development of global plans and strategies;
- the desire for access to foreign knowledge;
- the need to expand beyond the domestic arena.

Aharoni (1966) studied 38 US companies which had considered foreign investment in Israel and identified the following *external* reasons for foreign investment:

- invitation from an outside source, such as a foreign government offering incentives for inward investment;
- fear of losing an overseas market;
- the *bandwagon effect*, i.e. the need to match competitors who have already been successful in foreign markets;
- strong competition from abroad in the home market.

13.1.2 Economic reasons for foreign investment

In a *perfect* market, foreign subsidiaries would be unable to compete with local companies because of the additional costs imposed by the distance from their parent companies. In order for a foreign subsidiary to compete successfully, the additional costs

399

of operating at a distance from its parent must therefore be overcome. This means that *market imperfections* must offer compensating advantages which are not available to local companies and which are large enough to make investment in the local market attractive to international companies. Such market imperfections may occur in product differentiation, marketing skills, proprietary technology, managerial skills, better access to capital, economies of scale, financial markets and government-imposed market distortions such as incentives for inward investment (Buckley 2003). After considering *diversification* to reduce earnings volatility and *economies of scale* as examples of compensating advantages, we shall look at reasons why companies may choose particular locations for their subsidiaries.

Diversification to reduce earnings volatility

Companies may undertake foreign investment in order to protect themselves against over-exposure to any one economy. Since different economies are unlikely to move exactly in parallel, a company can reduce the volatility of its cash flows by investing in projects in different countries. Reducing cash flow volatility reduces business risk, so one consequence of international diversification is a reduction of risk. Theoretically, a company's shareholders will not benefit if it reduces the volatility of its cash flows as this represents unsystematic risk which shareholders can eliminate themselves through portfolio diversification (*see* Section 8.2). From a practical point of view, however, a company with volatile earnings may have higher interest costs, a lower credit rating, liquidity problems and a higher cost of capital due to being seen as riskier than similar companies. This will result in lower earnings being available for shareholders. It could be argued, therefore, that international diversification adds value for shareholders. However, a review of the available evidence by Siegel et al. (1995) found that diversification did not appear to increase shareholder returns and the risk advantage of multinational companies appeared to be decreasing over time.

Economies of scale

An economic reason for undertaking foreign investment is economies of scale, whereby profit margins and earnings are improved by decreasing average costs per unit through increasing the scale of operations (*see* Section 11.2.1). Scale economies can arise in any area of business activity, for example in purchasing, production, marketing or finance.

Barclay (1995) notes that economies of scale should be one of the main effects of the economic integration accompanying the development of regional blocs such as the European Union and the North American Free Trade Agreement. These scale economies arise because of access to larger, tariff-free markets and are most marked where a regional bloc integrates a number of smaller domestic markets. Economies of scale are also encouraged by the removal of *non-tariff barriers to trade*, thereby making markets less fragmented. Such non-tariff barriers may be physical, for example border controls and transit documents; technical, for example different connectors for electrical appliances in different countries; or fiscal, for example differences in indirect taxes such as VAT (value added tax) between countries. The progress of the European Union towards economic integration is the subject of Vignette 13.2.

Vignette 13.2

Europe is winning the war for economic freedoms

Economic freedoms, no less than other liberties, are eternally vulnerable, and never more so than when governments are weak or prone to populism. The 'four freedoms' underpinning the European integration project – the free movement of goods, services, labour and capital – are no different. In the aftermath of the rejection of the European Union constitution in referendums in France and the Netherlands in mid-2005, the Union's single market appeared to be at risk if member states interpreted the votes as a rejection of liberalisation. The failure of many member governments to implement reforms and recent efforts by three governments to prevent foreign takeovers have added to concerns that the half-century of (unsteady) progress towards European market integration is going into reverse.

The evidence does not support such a conclusion. Consider first the free movement of capital. Only a handful of cross-border deals have attracted unwanted government attention in recent times, while thousands have not. In 2005, almost 5,000 EU businesses were acquired by non-national firms. This represented a two-thirds increase on 2003 and includes sectors, such as energy, which have until recently seen limited pan-European corporate consolidation. Further restructuring will be facilitated, to some extent at least, when a new takeover directive comes into force in May.

This reflects the balance of forces between vestigial interventionism and market liberalisation. The latter is not only stronger but getting more so.

Businesses are becoming more assertive in exercising their right to move capital freely within the EU. The European Commission, though a shadow of its former self in its influence over policy formulation, has seen its regulatory power strengthen and has never been more ready to stand up to member states that break or bend the rules. More member governments are opposed in principle to interfering in corporate restructuring than those willing to resort to such action.

Today there is no intellectually respectable case for protectionism. This is in contrast with the spirit of 1914, evoked recently by Giulio Tremonti, Italy's finance minister. The decades of global catastrophe that took place after that date, caused in part by protectionism, and the successes of the post-1945 liberal order leave those with protectionist instincts in the uncomfortable position of defending the indefensible.

As a consequence, the forces of protectionism are also failing to prevent freer movement of goods and services. Imports to the EU continue to grow strongly. In 2005 they surged, with 15 of the 25 member states registering a record high in imports as a percentage of gross domestic product.

This deepening import penetration is in part explained by China's emergence as an exporting superpower. Though the rise of the Asian giant has been hindered by the occasional EU resort to protectionist measures, such as last year's ill-judged decision to re-impose quotas on Chinese textiles, these amount to little more than tinkering.

China is set to overtake the US as Europe's largest supplier of merchandise goods in 2006 after years of high double-digit export growth to the EU.

The market-opening trend in the EU's bilateral trade relations is mirrored multilaterally. At the World Trade Organisation's ministerial meeting in December 2005, the EU agreed to phase out its agricultural export subsidies and accepted that its tariffs on such goods must fall further.

Trade in services in Europe is also on the rise, despite measures that hinder cross-border provision. While the services directive has been watered down, it represents a still-significant step towards greater liberalisation.

The freedom to work in other member states was partially denied to citizens from the 10 new members when they joined in May 2004. This was the most egregious case of protectionism in the EU is recent years. But even here there are positive signs. The three member countries that allowed full access to workers from the newly joined 10 – Ireland, Sweden and the UK – show no sign of reversing their decision and three more countries – Finland, Portugal and Spain – have committed to extending the freedom to the newcomers this year.

None of this is to say that the EU single market is not fragile. The risks of opportunistic protectionism are ever-present and vigilance is always necessary. However, the evidence shows that Europe continues to go in the right direction, however slow and hesitating that may be.

Source: Dan O'Brien, FT.com, 31 March 2006. Reprinted with permission.

Vignette 13.3

Foreign investment: competitors turn up the heat

In recent years, Uganda's capital has changed beyond recognition. The skyline has shot upwards. Shops, banks and businesses crowd the main streets, and the hills encircling the city centre are sprouting hundreds of new property developments. Just outside town at the Speke resort is the makings of a new conference centre, where proprietor, Asian business mogul, Sudhir Ruparelia envisages the debate on Africa's future taking shape. Delegates there could be misled into thinking the future has already arrived: a dozen rooms, seating between 12 and 1200, boast state of the art sound technology and a dazzling array of gadgets for presentations. Such multimillion-dollar investments may be a vote of confidence in Uganda's economic performance over the past decade. But in terms of the country as a whole, the picture is misleading. In the past 10 years, Uganda has attracted the lion's share of foreign direct investment (FDI) flowing into east Africa. This has increased from 2 per cent of gross domestic product in 1995/6 to 4 per cent more recently.

Returning Asians who took advantage of President Yoweri Museveni's decision to restore to their original owners businesses seized when Idi Amin Dada expelled them in 1972, helped to drive an initial wave of growth in the 1990s. That decision helped clarify the government's attitude to property rights. South Africans have also been moving in, led by South African Breweries and with mobile phone operator MTN driving a boom in telecommunications. Investment in tourism, manufacturing and agro-industries is flourishing.

But competition is intense. Neighbours on the Indian Ocean coast enjoy advantages for exporters and Uganda, once a pace-setter, is now struggling to keep up with incentives such as tax holidays elsewhere. Tanzania's gradual economic transformation has brought rewards, and political change this year in Kenya is generating an upsurge of interest from abroad.

If Kampala has been transformed, the same has been less true elsewhere. Tourism and tea are among the few sectors that have drawn foreign money beyond a 50 km radius of the capital where much of the investment in manufacturing and agroindustries has been concentrated.

Local businessmen say pressure is mounting on property and land prices around the city and the nearby industrial area at Jinja, raising the overall cost of doing business.

Meanwhile, the construction boom on Kampala's hills is not just a sign of new wealth, but also that that new wealth is going into bricks and mortar for lack of adequate savings mechanisms within the domestic economy. 'The good news is that we can do much better,' says Geoffrey Onegy Obel, trade adviser to Mr Museveni who also manages the national social security fund.

Brought in from the private sector last year, Mr Obel is leading efforts to drive government policy beyond the donor assisted stability of the 1990s when capital inflows were impressive by regional standards but still fell well short of generating the double digit growth that would propel Uganda to middle income status. Part of the answer, says Mr Obel, lies in reforms aimed at increasing domestic savings

through mortgage financing, insurance policies and pension schemes. Another part is in deepening the financial markets and providing businesses with alternatives to high interest loans.

'At present, the longest instrument in the economy is a one-year Treasury bill. This sends a signal to me as an investment banker not to take the long view,' says Mr Obel.

But despite some predictions that foreign enthusiasm for Uganda was tailing off, capital inflows have showed few signs of standing still.

The discovery of oil below Lake Albert, where Canada's Heritage Oil has been exploring, could eventually provide a substantial boost to export earnings while reducing the domestic cost of fuel. The government is finalising plans for an export-processing zone while supporting initiatives aimed at exploiting openings in the US textile market.

A new mining code designed to stimulate exploration for gold and other minerals is already in the bag. And remaining privatisations of electricity distribution and the railways could help ease some of the infrastructure weaknesses constraining expansion outside Kampala. Electricity generation is still tiny. South Africa's Eskom is expected to take over the power distribution network later this year, after reviving and expanding generation at the Owens Fall dam.

The World Bank has approved financing for the construction of a controversial $550m dam at Bujagali, which will provide an additional 200MW of electricity. Provided political stability holds, this should help to generate foreign interest well beyond Kampala's rising skyline.

Source: William Wallis, FT.com, 14 April 2003. Reprinted with permission.

Locational factors

Even if a company has compensating advantages which encourage foreign investment, it will still need to select the location which offers the best overall return. Locational factors to be considered include labour costs, marketing factors, trade barriers and government policy (Buckley, 2003).

In order to maximise the benefits of foreign investment, companies can set up production facilities in locations where land and labour costs are lower or where proximity to growing markets offers a reduction in distribution costs. These opportunities are likely to be features of *emerging markets*. Dawes and Ivanov (1995) suggested the example of exploiting cheap labour by producing goods in Vietnam, coupled with selling not only in Vietnam but also to its Pacific Rim neighbours, such as China and Japan. Madura (1998) cites lower costs of production as a reason why Honeywell established subsidiaries in Mexico, Malaysia, Hong Kong and Taiwan, and notes that the establishment of subsidiaries in Mexico by US-based multinational companies has contributed significantly to the growth of Mexico's economy.

An example of how economic integration and locational factors can encourage foreign investment is given in Vignette 13.3.

Research shows that companies operating internationally, i.e. multinationals, are valued more highly than domestic companies and this higher valuation applies to both the domestic and international operations of multinationals (Garrod and Rees 1998). Possible reasons for the higher valuations of UK multinationals were suggested to be diversification benefits, cost of capital reductions and efficiency synergies, although there was some evidence of mispricing due to over-optimistic future growth estimates.

13.2 Different forms of international trade

It is unusual for a company to use a foreign subsidiary as a first step in internationalising its business operations. There are a number of other methods of conducting operations which may be preferred when a company is taking its first steps on the international stage and which may be preferred to foreign investment, even by established international companies. These methods are illustrated in Exhibit 13.1 and include direct exporting, licensing, setting up an overseas branch and participating in a joint venture. If we assume that companies adopt a risk-minimising process of gradual international expansion, these different methods of conducting international operations could be seen as intermediate stages of increasing risk along the path to setting up a foreign subsidiary. It has been found that, while most companies do begin the process of internationalisation through exporting, they do not necessarily undertake all of the intermediate stages mentioned. As Buckley (2003) points out, this incremental model of the internationalisation process only moves in one direction and cannot therefore explain divestment or reorientation as strategic choices. This is because the model is a simplistic representation of a complex process.

Exhibit 13.1   **Diagram illustrating different ways in which a company may conduct international operations, culminating in the establishment of a foreign subsidiary**

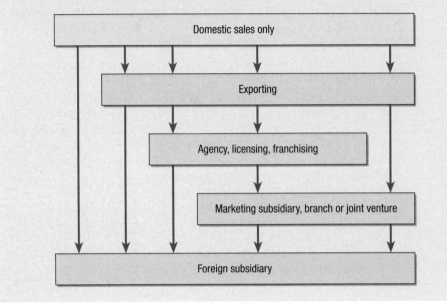

13.2.1   Exporting

Export sales have a lower risk than foreign investment as they offer quick returns and do not require a commitment to substantial capital expenditure. However, selling and distribution costs will be higher with exporting compared to local production and there is also the risk that tariffs may be imposed on imports. Establishing strong business links with foreign customers will be more difficult without a local manufacturing or sales presence, and it will take longer to build up a detailed picture of foreign markets. Furthermore, bulky and perishable goods do not lend themselves to exporting.

Many of the difficulties associated with exporting can be overcome by setting up a branch in the foreign country, perhaps staffed by local employees, as this offers a low-cost way for a company to establish a local presence.

13.2.2   Licensing

Licensing involves a contractual agreement with a local company to manufacture the company's products or offer the company's services in return for a royalty or similar payment and is therefore an example of the trade in knowledge. It offers a way of expanding foreign sales without the need for substantial capital expenditure and it may facilitate penetration of markets where export sales are either not possible or restricted by barriers to trade. It also offers a route by which funds can be remitted back to the parent company even if remittance is restricted, for example by exchange controls. However, the returns from licensing could be small compared with those generated by a foreign subsidiary.

One of the main dangers noted with licensing is the possible creation of a competitor as a result of the transfer of knowledge and expertise. If the licensee terminates the agreement and sets up in competition to the principal company, it may be difficult to restrain them. Difficulties will then arise from competition between the products made by the licensee and the company's existing products.

13.2.3 Joint ventures

A joint venture is a foreign subsidiary company which is jointly owned by a number of independent participants who hold shares in the venture. Each participant will be involved in managing the project and each will have particular resources to offer. These resources may be finance, expertise, local knowledge, local contacts, a distribution network and so on. By pooling financial resources, the participants may be able to undertake a project too big or too risky for an individual company to consider, for example the development and construction of the European Airbus.

There are particular advantages to using a joint venture if one of the participants is based in the foreign country in which it is hoped to trade. Such a participant may have local business knowledge, access to local finance, established distribution channels and access to local raw materials. It is also possible that, if the local participant has political contacts, these could be used to reduce the risk of adverse government action.

The disadvantages of joint ventures are as follows (Brooke 1996):

■ lack of adequate control;
■ the partner may not have the requisite skills and the parent company may find itself doing more work than expected or desired;
■ rigidity, in that the joint venture is difficult to control or amend;
■ division of interest, in that policies that are advantageous to a company as a whole may not be advantageous to an individual subsidiary. Transfer pricing, dividend policy, sourcing of materials and marketing plans are examples of policy areas that may present problems.

13.2.4 Foreign subsidiary

A subsidiary may be established by acquiring an existing company or by setting up a new one. Acquiring an existing company may offer considerable cost advantages if the company has a good reputation, a well-developed distribution network and an established client base, although these advantages will naturally have a price. However, these advantages may be reduced by post-acquisition integration problems due to cultural or operational differences. Whichever method is used, a subsidiary involves a significant commitment of parent company resources.

A subsidiary may be preferred to a branch because it can be financed wholly or in part by local currency debt, allowing both transaction and translation risk to be hedged by matching (*see* Section 12.2.2). A subsidiary is also likely to offer tax advantages over a branch. Since a branch is not a separate legal entity from the parent, its profits are taxed at the home country (domestic) rate as they are earned. The profits of a foreign subsidiary are subject to the local tax system, which may be more or less favourable than the domestic system. Domestic tax liability will not arise until profits are remitted back to the home country.

Vignette 13.4

Positive experience in difficult markets

The experience of pharmaceuticals giant SmithKline Beecham in North Africa is that investment-related export sales may allow a company to consolidate its position even in the most difficult markets. Maghreb countries have been a focus for many years and the company has a joint venture in Algeria, a subsidiary in Morocco, a licensing agreement in Tunisia and operations in Libya.

Investor-friendly Tunisia is 'something of a model in terms of its one-stop investment office that works quite efficiently', says Mr Paul Barrett, director and vice-president for Africa. 'There are plenty of regulatory obstacles,' he says. 'But this tends to be the case with all developing markets.'

Operating is possible even in the most difficult conditions, however, if a company approaches the challenges in an appropriate manner. In Algeria, where tens of thousands have been killed in more than five years of civil conflict, 'the problems attached to security are entirely manageable', says Mr Barrett.

Indeed, SmithKline Beecham's joint venture in Algeria is progressing 'very positively', according to Mr Barrett. 'We have just taken a decision to invest in the second phase of our local manufacturing project, a basic medicines factory at Boudouaou,' he says.

The project was held up by the security situation, but Mr Barrett says SmithKline's Algerian partner built its own factory and demonstrated it was possible to obtain high standards using local staff with only minimal European supervision, 'So we are going ahead with an antibiotic plant on the existing site.'

The Algerian market has shrunk by about half in the last year due to cutbacks on authorized imports by the authorities, which are trying to encourage local manufacturers. Import permits are going to exporters with a firm intent to set up locally or which have an involvement with local manufacturing companies.

Past investments have brought SmithKline's pharmaceutical operations in the region to a stage where they 'are now mature', Mr Barrett says. But this does not mean a lack of new opportunities. Consumer products, particularly healthcare, offer potential. The North African market also needs quality, but affordable, generic materials.

SmithKline has a local manufacturing presence in Morocco and Tunisia, where competition is fierce. Local manufacturers have been operating in the Moroccan market for years, whereas pharmaceuticals investments by Rhône-Poulenc, Roussel Uclaf and others in Tunisia are recent, intensifying competition. 'There are now seven synthetic penicillin plants in Tunisia,' Mr Barrett says.

Morocco is an important market. Here, SmithKline's local subsidiary has an antibiotics facility in production. Pointing to the potential offered by establishing a regional manufacturing base, exports from this plant are expected to start next year.

The company is also a major supplier for Libya, despite the political problems. Libya remains a state-controlled market, where watching closely for public tenders is essential.

Source: Jon Marks, FT Exporter Supplement, *Financial Times*, 10 July 1997. Reprinted with permission.

Selling and distribution costs for goods produced by a foreign subsidiary will be lower than for imported goods, and profit margins will also be improved by avoiding import tariffs and other fiscal penalties attached to imported goods. Business links with foreign customers will be easier to establish and customer loyalty can be fostered by providing after-sales care.

An example of how a multinational company can adopt different forms of international operations to suit local conditions is given in Vignette 13.4.

13.3 The evaluation of foreign investment decisions

Foreign investment may be either foreign direct investment or foreign portfolio investment. Foreign *portfolio* investment occurs when a company makes an international investment but has no control of the business invested in, for example by purchasing a minority of the shares of a foreign company. As a result of such purchases, the investing company receives returns in the form of dividends and capital gains, and may enhance business relationships. We are not concerned here with this kind of foreign investment.

Foreign *direct* investment is a long-term investment in an economy other than that of the investing company, where the investing company has control over the business invested in. The main example of such an investment is the setting up or purchase of a foreign subsidiary.

13.3.1 The distinctive features of foreign direct investment

Foreign direct investment decisions are not conceptually different from domestic investment decisions (*see* Chapters 6 and 7) and can be evaluated using the same investment appraisal techniques, such as the net present value method. However, international investment decisions do have some distinctive features which make their evaluation more difficult:

- project cash flows will need to be evaluated in a foreign currency;
- exchange rate movements create currency risk, which may need hedging;
- foreign taxation systems may differ from the domestic taxation system;
- project cash flows and parent cash flows will be different;
- remittance of project cash flows may be restricted;
- the investment decision may be evaluated from more than one point of view;
- the investment may be subject to political risk.

13.3.2 Methods of evaluating foreign direct investment

The financial evaluation of foreign direct investment proposals can help to eliminate poor projects, check whether marketing assumptions are valid, and give an indication as to the amount and type of finance needed. The academically preferred method of evaluating foreign direct investment proposals is the net present value method (*see* Chapter 6) since shareholder wealth will be increased by the selection of projects with a positive net present value. This also suggests that, as it is shareholders of the parent company whose wealth is of paramount importance, it is the NPV of the after-tax cash flows remitted to the parent company which should be used to judge the acceptability of a foreign direct investment proposal. We should recognise, however, that evaluation at the level of the host country is also possible.

A number of empirical studies of international investment appraisal have been summarised by Demirag and Goddard (1994), Kim and Ulferts (1996) and Buckley (2003). The evidence suggests that, rather than using NPV alone, companies evaluate international decisions using a range of different methods. We can summarise the main findings as follows:

- The majority of multinational companies use discounted cash flow (DCF) methods of investment appraisal as the primary method for evaluating foreign investment projects, with internal rate of return being preferred to net present value.

- There does not appear to have been an increasing use of DCF methods of investment appraisal in recent years.
- A large proportion of companies do not use after-tax cash flows to the parent company as the main measure of income in the evaluation.
- A number of companies appear to base the required rate of return for foreign investment decisions on the cost of debt.
- Smaller firms tend to use less sophisticated investment appraisal methods such as return on capital employed and payback.

This divergence between the methods used by companies and the methods recommended by theory is worth noting.

13.3.3 Evaluation of foreign direct investment at local level

A foreign direct investment project can be evaluated in local terms and in local currencies, for example by comparing it with similar undertakings in the chosen country. This evaluation ignores the extent to which cash flows can be remitted back to the parent company and also ignores the overall value of the project to parent company shareholders. Whether foreign direct investment is evaluated at local level or parent company level, local currency project cash flows need to be determined, however. Local project cash flows can be categorised as follows.

Initial investment

This will be the outlay on fixed assets such as land, buildings, plant and machinery. Funding for this may be from an issue of equity or debt, and debt finance may be raised locally or be provided by the parent company. The initial outlay may also include a transfer of assets such as plant and equipment, in which case transferred assets should be valued at the opportunity cost to the parent company.

Investment in working capital

This may be part of the initial investment or may occur during the start-up period as the project establishes itself in operational terms. Investment in working capital may be achieved in part by transfer of stocks of components or part-finished goods from the parent company.

Local after-tax cash flows

These will be the difference between cash received from sales and any local operating costs for materials and labour, less local taxation on profits. Interest payments may need to be deducted in determining taxable profit to the extent that the investment is financed by locally raised debt, such as loans from banks or other financial institutions. A particular difficulty will be the treatment of goods provided by the parent company, when the price charged to the subsidiary (the transfer price) must be seen by local taxation authorities as a fair one. In cash flow terms, such goods will be an operating cost at local level but a source of revenue to the parent company, and will have tax implications at both levels.

The terminal value of the project

It is necessary to determine a terminal value for the project either because the evaluation will be truncated for ease of analysis or because it is expected that the parent company's interest in the investment will cease at some future date, for example through sale of the subsidiary. The expected market value of the subsidiary at the end of the parent company's planning horizon is one possible terminal value.

Even though evaluating the investment project solely in terms of the cash flows accruing in the foreign country may indicate that it is apparently worth undertaking, making a decision to proceed with the investment on these grounds may be incorrect. The NPV of the project to the parent company depends on the future cash flows which can be transferred to it. If the transfer of funds to the parent company is restricted, this value may be reduced. The effect of the project on existing cash flows, for example existing export sales, must also be considered.

13.3.4 Evaluation of foreign direct investment at parent company level

At the parent company level, project cash flows will be the actual cash receipts and payments in the parent company's own currency, together with any incremental changes in the parent company's existing cash flows. These project cash flows are as follows.

Initial investment

This will consist of cash that has been invested by the parent company and may be in the form of debt or equity. It will also include transferred plant and equipment at opportunity cost.

Returns on investment

The parent company will receive dividends from the project and, if debt finance has been provided, interest payments and repayment of principal.

Receipts from intercompany trade

The parent company may receive a variety of cash payments in exchange for goods and services provided to the project. Goods and components sold to the company will generate income based on agreed transfer prices. Royalties may be received on patents. Management fees may be received in exchange for the services of experienced personnel.

Accumulated contributions

If remittances have been subject to exchange controls, the parent company will at some point receive accumulated (accrued) contributions, perhaps at the end of the project.

Taxation

Cash flows remitted to the parent company will be liable to taxation under the domestic tax system. Tax relief may be given for tax paid overseas.

Cash flows from the overseas investment will need to be converted into the home currency, which means that exchange rates will need to be forecast over the life of the project, probably from forecast differences in inflation rates between home country and host country using purchasing power parity theory (Buckley 2003). A further problem (*see* Section 13.4) is that an appropriate discount rate for the project will need to be determined.

13.3.5 Taxation and foreign direct investment

The taxation systems of the host country and the home country are likely to be different. If profits were subjected to tax in both countries, i.e. if *double taxation* existed, there would be a strong disincentive to investment. *Double taxation relief* is usually available, either by treaty between two countries or on a unilateral basis, whereby relief is given for tax paid abroad on income received. The net effect of a double taxation treaty is that the parent company will pay *in total* the higher of local tax or domestic tax on profits generated by the foreign subsidiary. Taxes paid abroad will not affect the total amount of tax paid, but will only affect the division of tax between the two countries. If the local tax rate is greater than the domestic tax rate, no domestic tax is paid.

For computational purposes, the UK tax liability can be assessed from the taxable profits of the foreign subsidiary. This is easier than grossing up receipts from overseas investments and also avoids the possibility of wrongly assessing capital cash flows to domestic profit tax. The domestic tax liability can then be reduced by any tax already paid at the local level to find the domestic tax payable.

Example	Foreign direct investment evaluation

Wobble plc is a UK company which is considering setting up a manufacturing subsidiary in the small republic of Bandanna, whose currency is the Bar (B). The initial investment of £1m in plant and machinery would be payable in sterling. Initial investment in working capital of B500 000 would be financed by a loan from a local bank, at an annual interest rate of 10 per cent. At the end of five years, the subsidiary would be sold as a going concern to a local company for B4 950 000 and part of the proceeds would be used to pay off the bank loan.

The subsidiary is expected to produce cash profits of B1 500 000 per year over the five-year period. Capital allowances are available on the initial investment on a straight-line basis at a rate of 20 per cent per year. As a result of setting up the subsidiary, Wobble expects to lose export sales to Bandanna of £20 000 per year (after tax).

Profits in Bandanna are taxed at a rate of 20 per cent after interest and capital allowances. All after-tax cash profits are remitted to the UK at the end of each year. UK tax of 30 per cent is charged on UK profits, but a tax treaty between Bandanna and the UK allows tax paid in Bandanna to be set off against any UK liability. Taxation is paid in the year in which it arises. Wobble requires foreign investments to be discounted at 15 per cent. The current exchange rate is B4.50/£1, but the Bar is expected to depreciate against sterling by B0.50 per year.

Should Wobble undertake the investment in Bandanna?

Exhibit 13.2 Calculation of the project cash flows for Wobble plc's subsidiary in Bandanna

Year	0 (B000)	1 (B000)	2 (B000)	3 (B000)	4 (B000)	5 (B000)
Operating cash flows		1500	1500	1500	1500	1500
Capital allowances		(900)	(900)	(900)	(900)	(900)
Interest		(50)	(50)	(50)	(50)	(50)
Profit before tax		550	550	550	550	550
Local tax		(110)	(110)	(110)	(110)	(110)
Profit after tax		440	440	440	440	440
Initial investment	(4500)					
Working capital	(500)					
Loan capital	500					(500)
Sale of subsidiary						4950
Add back CAs		900	900	900	900	900
Project cash flows	(4500)	1340	1340	1340	1340	5790

Suggested answer

Initial investment in Bandanna:	£1 000 000 × 4.50 = B4 500 000
Annual capital allowance:	B4 500 000 × 0.2 = B900 000
Annual interest payment:	B500 000 × 0.1 = B50 000

The calculation of the subsidiary's cash flows is given in Exhibit 13.2. Note that a separate tax calculation has not been carried out, but instead the capital allowances have been deducted from operating cash flows to give taxable profit and then added back after local tax has been calculated. The capital allowances must be added back because they are not cash flows. Note also that, as the subsidiary is sold as a going concern, working capital is not recovered.

To determine the acceptability of the project at the local level, project cash flows could be discounted at the average cost of capital of local companies carrying out similar business.

The first step to determining the acceptability of the project at the parent company level is to translate the remitted cash flows into sterling. UK tax payable on the sterling cash flows can then be calculated by applying the UK tax rate to the taxable profits of the Bandanna subsidiary and then deducting local tax paid, as follows:

Year 1 taxable profit (B) = 550 000
Year 1 taxable profit (£) = 550 000/5.00 = 110 000
UK tax liability   = 110 000 × 0.30 = £33 000
Local tax paid   = 110 000 × 0.20 = £22 000
UK tax payable   = 33 000 − 22 000 = £11 000

→

| Exhibit 13.3 | Calculation of the project cash flows and present values for Wobble plc's subsidiary at parent company level | | | | | |

Year	0	1	2	3	4	5
Remitted to UK (B000)	(4500)	1340	1340	1340	1340	5790
Exchange rate (B/£)	4.50	5.00	5.50	6.00	6.50	7.00
	£000	£000	£000	£000	£000	£000
Sterling equivalent	(1000)	268	244	223	206	827
UK tax		(11)	(10)	(9)	(8)	(8)
	(1000)	257	234	214	198	819
Exports lost, after tax		(20)	(20)	(20)	(20)	(20)
Parent cash flow	(1000)	237	214	194	178	799
15% discount factors	1.000	0.870	0.756	0.658	0.572	0.497
Present values	(1000)	206	162	128	102	397

This calculation can be repeated for subsequent years, bearing in mind that the exchange rate changes each year. After incorporating the after-tax value of the lost export sales, the parent company cash flows and their present values can be determined, as shown in Exhibit 13.3.

We have:

$$NPV = -1\,000\,000 + 206\,000 + 162\,000 + 128\,000 + 102\,000 + 397\,000$$
$$= -£5000$$

At the parent company level, the NPV is marginally negative and it appears that the project should be rejected. The project could become viable if the following issues are addressed:

■ Operating cash flows in Bandanna are constant but exchange rates have deteriorated. This deterioration is likely to mean that Bandanna inflation is higher than UK inflation. Why have overseas cash flows not increased with inflation?
■ Can total tax paid be reduced by increasing local debt finance?
■ The discount rate of 15 per cent seems high. Has the risk of the project been taken into account in calculating the discount rate?
■ Are there any benefits that are non-financial in nature or that are difficult to quantify which have not been included in the evaluation, such as the existence of 'real options' like the possibility of continuing in production with different products rather than selling the business to a third party?

13.4 The cost of capital for foreign direct investment

The arguments for and against using the existing weighted average cost of capital or the CAPM as the source of a discount rate for use in investment appraisal were discussed in Chapters 8 and 9. Similar arguments are relevant when considering the appropriate discount rate to be used in evaluating overseas investment. The following alternative suggestions have been made concerning the cost of capital for overseas investment (Stanley 1990):

■ A project-specific cost of capital should be employed since the discount rate should reflect the value to the company of undertaking particular activities.
■ The weighted average cost of capital should be used for projects of similar risk to existing activities, otherwise a project-specific cost of capital should be employed.
■ The appropriate cost of capital is that of local firms in the same industry.

All three suggestions point towards the need for a cost of capital which reflects the risk and characteristics of individual projects. Each suggestion also implies that a single cost of capital can adequately take account of the complex interaction, between sources of finance, taxation, exchange rates, exchange controls and risk, which is a feature of foreign direct investment.

In contrast, the *adjusted present value* (APV) method of investment appraisal suggests that the basic investment project, shorn of taxation and financing aspects, should be discounted at the parent company's ungeared cost of equity, and that taxation and financing implications can be treated as adjustments to this 'base-case NPV' by discounting their cash flows at an appropriate cost of debt. This investment appraisal method has the advantage of being able to deal with project-specific financing from different capital markets, but the disadvantage that estimating the side-effects of adjustments to the base-case NPV and their associated discount rates is difficult, calling for considerable expertise.

The CAPM was recommended (*see* Section 9.4.3) as being the best way of finding the cost of equity for use in investment appraisal, but there are a number of difficulties that arise in the application of the CAPM in foreign direct investment.

■ The risk-adjusted discount rate found by using the CAPM takes account of systematic or market risk, but which market portfolio should be used in determining the project beta?
■ The CAPM is sensitive to financial market prices and these will change frequently. Over what time frame should the cost of equity be determined?
■ What is the value of the market premium? Studies comparing the returns of capital markets of different countries, while offering some evidence of increasing integration, suggest that integration is by no means complete. Should a global risk premium be determined?

While the resolution of these problems is as yet incomplete, steps have been taken towards the development of an *international capital asset pricing model* (ICAPM), for example as discussed by Buckley (2003).

On the question of whether the cost of capital should in general be higher or lower for foreign direct investment than for domestic investment, it could be assumed from a common sense point of view that foreign direct investment, especially in countries regarded as politically unstable, ought to require a higher risk premium. On the other hand, Holland (1990) suggests that, if foreign investment provides otherwise unattainable diversification benefits to parent company shareholders, the cost of capital used could be lower. It seems that the safe course is to assume that the cost of capital for each foreign direct investment may need to be determined individually by selecting from the range of techniques available, depending on the sophistication of the analysis involved. It will be recalled from Section 13.3.2 that internal rate of return was found to be the most common technique for evaluating foreign direct investment. This may not be so surprising, given the difficulties in determining an appropriate cost of capital for such investment, although the question of determining a hurdle rate against which to compare the calculated internal rate of return remains.

13.4.1 The international financing decision

The main objective of the international financing decision is to minimise the company's after-tax cost of capital at an acceptable level of risk since minimising the cost of capital will maximise the market value of the company. A multinational company with access to international capital markets has a greater opportunity to reduce its cost of capital than a domestic company. The financing decision, which has been considered in detail in Chapter 9, will need to consider:

- the relative proportions of equity and debt finance at both parent and subsidiary level;
- the relative proportions of long-term and short-term finance;
- the availability of different sources of funds;
- the effect of different sources of finance on the risk of the company;
- the direct and indirect costs of different sources of finance;
- the effect of taxation on the relative costs of equity and debt.

13.4.2 Factors influencing the choice and mix of finance

Key factors influencing the choice and mix of finance for international operations include gearing, taxation, political risk and currency risk.

Gearing

Both the gearing of the company as a whole and the gearing of each subsidiary must be considered. If the holding company *guarantees* the debts of its subsidiaries, whether formally or informally, then, as long as the group gearing is acceptable, the decision on the gearing of individual subsidiaries can be made independently. Advantage can then be taken of local interest rates, tax rules and subsidised finance as appropriate. If the holding company does not guarantee the debts of its subsidiaries, the gearing of each subsidiary must be considered separately in order to optimise its individual capital structure (*see* Section 9.8).

Taxation

Differences between the treatment in different tax systems of profit, gains, losses, interest and dividends can be exploited through the financing decision. In particular, since interest payments on debt are tax deductible whereas dividends are not, there is an incentive to use debt as the main source of finance for a foreign subsidiary. Some countries counter this tendency by imposing a maximum allowable level of gearing for tax purposes.

Political risk

One kind of political risk is the possibility of *expropriation* or seizure of assets by a foreign government. Expropriation of assets is less likely if foreign direct investment is financed as much as possible from local sources, for example using local debt, and if the financing arrangements involve international banks and government agencies. Buckley (2003) cites the example of investment along these lines by Kennecott in a Chilean copper mine project, on which the company was able to secure returns despite the subsequent coming to power of a regime committed to expropriating foreign-held assets without compensation. Political risk is discussed further in Section 13.5.

Currency risk

The financing mix chosen for foreign direct investment can be used by a company as part of its overall strategy of managing currency risk. The use of local debt finance, for example, will reduce translation exposure and allow the parent company to use the internal risk management technique called matching (*see* Section 12.2.2).

13.5 Political risk

Goddard (1990) defines political risk as 'the possibility of a multinational company being significantly affected by political events in a host country or a change in the political relationships between a host country and one or more other countries'. Multinational companies making direct foreign investments must consider possible political actions. These may be favourable, such as granting investment incentives to encourage inward investment, or unfavourable, such as expropriation or seizure of assets.

Political risk management involves two stages: first, the assessment of political risk and its potential consequences; and second, the development and implementation of policies to minimise political risk.

13.5.1 Assessment of political risk

Demirag and Goddard (1994) point out that, since there is no consensus definition of political risk or political risk events, the development of a reliable method for the measurement and analysis of political risk is not easy. Two approaches to the measurement of political risk are commonly cited: *macro-assessment* and *micro-assessment*. Macro-assessment seeks to assess political risk on a country basis, without considering factors which are business-specific, whereas micro-assessment looks at political risk from the perspective of the investing company's business.

Macro-assessment of political risk is intended to produce risk indices which give an indication of the level of political risk in each country. These indices focus on political stability and look at a range of political and social factors: relative power of political factions; extent of division by language, race or religion; social conditions; internal conflict; bureaucratic infrastructure; and so on. Rankings of countries by political risk indices are produced regularly by financial media such as *Euromoney* and *Institutional Investor*, or are available by subscription.

Individual companies that are considering investing in a particular country can use a number of different methods to assess its political risk from both a micro- and a macro-assessment perspective, including the following.

- *Checklist approach*: this involves making a judgment on all the factors that are thought to contribute to political risk and weighting them to produce a political risk index.
- *Delphi technique*: this calls for the collection of a number of expert opinions, perhaps by use of a questionnaire, and weighting or aggregating them.
- *Quantitative analysis*: quantitative analysis techniques such as sensitivity analysis or discriminant analysis can be used to identify the key factors influencing the level of political risk of a country.
- *Inspection visits*: Also known as the *grand tour*, this involves company staff visiting the country under consideration on a fact-finding visit.

Goddard (1990) found that UK multinationals typically used a subjective rather than a systematic approach to political risk analysis, with little use being made of external advisers. A more recent approach to macro-assessment of political risk involves calculating a country's implied volatility (i.e. the volatility of the value of a country's economy) as a measure of its risk and this technique has shown itself to be a useful one (Clark, 2002). Note that macro-assessment of political risk must be complemented by assessing the impact of political risk on a particular company, i.e. micro-assessment, since one company may be affected favourably by a particular risk factor which affects another company adversely. Import tariffs, for example, could have an adverse effect on an importer but a favourable effect on a host country manufacturer.

13.5.2 Policies to manage political risk

The simplest way to manage political risk is to choose not to invest in those countries which are perceived as having too high a level of political risk. However, this ignores the fact that the returns from such an investment might more than compensate for the risk incurred.

Insurance against political risk

It is possible to insure against political risk through private companies such as Trade Indemnity and NCM, but most insurance of this kind is through government departments or agencies. The government agency responsible for political risk insurance in the UK for trades in excess of six months is the Export Credits Guarantee Department (ECGD).

Negotiation of agreements

Political risk can be addressed by the negotiation of concession agreements with host governments, setting out the rules and restrictions under which the investing company can expect to conduct its business. The weakness of such agreements is that they may be renegotiated or repudiated by the same or subsequent governments, although this is much less likely to occur with developed nations.

Financing and operating policies

It is possible to reduce political risk exposure by appropriate structuring of company operations. *Operating policies* which have been suggested include: locating different stages of production in different countries; controlling the means by which finished goods are exported; concentrating key services such as research and development, marketing and treasury management outside of the host country; and avoiding becoming dependent upon the output of any particular manufacturing facility.

Exposure to political risk can also be reduced by choosing appropriate *financing policies*. As noted earlier, expropriation of assets is less likely if investment is financed locally as much as possible and if international banks and government agencies are involved in financing arrangements. Another financial strategy which could be employed is securing unconditional guarantees from the host government.

13.6 Conclusion

A company may undertake foreign direct investment for a number of strategic and economic reasons, but whether an investment increases the wealth of parent company shareholders remains the primary financial test. The path to foreign direct investment is not necessarily a straight one: a company may progress through a number of different methods of conducting international trade before it decides that creating or acquiring a foreign subsidiary is in the best interests of the company.

Evaluating foreign direct investments is necessarily more complex than evaluating domestic investments. Apart from the difficulty of determining relevant cash flows, exchange rates must be forecast and an appropriate discount rate determined. Calculating a discount rate for use in foreign direct investment is far from easy: we have concentrated here on outlining the problems involved. The solution depends on the information available and the theoretical model preferred by the analyst.

Key points

1. Companies can have defensive and aggressive motives for foreign investment.

2. If the additional costs of operating at a distance are to be overcome, market imperfections must offer compensating advantages to make foreign investment attractive.

3. Foreign investment may be undertaken to achieve economies of scale, which are encouraged by economic integration within regional blocs such as the EU and NAFTA.

4. Foreign investment may be undertaken in order to reduce earnings volatility or exposure to any one market, i.e. to reduce risk. Whether this lower risk adds value for shareholders is debatable.

5. Locational factors to be considered in order to obtain the best overall return include production costs, marketing factors and government policy.

6 A company can conduct international operations through exporting, licensing, an overseas branch, a joint venture or a subsidiary. From one perspective, these represent stages in the internationalisation process.

7 Exporting is low risk, offers quick returns and does not need capital investment, but selling and distribution costs may be high and there is a risk that import tariffs may be imposed.

8 Licensing allows a local company to produce goods in return for royalties. While it may allow entry into difficult markets, returns may be lower than with direct investment. There is also the danger of encouraging the creation of a competitor.

9 A joint venture with a partner based in the target country may be useful, but joint ventures have problems with lack of control and divided interests.

10 A subsidiary can offer tax advantages, lower selling and distribution costs, higher profit margins and stronger business links.

11 Net present value at parent company level should be used to judge a foreign direct investment, but evidence suggests internal rate of return is preferred by multi-nationals. NPV at local level ignores the overall value to the parent company.

12 While the taxation systems of two countries may be different, double taxation relief is usually available.

13 The arguments for and against using the weighted average cost of capital and the capital asset pricing model in domestic investment appraisal also apply to the problem of finding the cost of capital for foreign investment. A cost of capital which reflects the risk of the individual project should be used.

14 The adjusted present value method may be useful in evaluating foreign direct investment.

15 In using the CAPM with foreign investment, problems arise when considering: which market portfolio to use in order to find beta; over which time period to conduct the analysis; and how to find the value of the market premium.

16 The international financing decision seeks to minimise the after-tax cost of capital at an acceptable level of risk. The key factors in this decision are gearing, taxation, political risk and currency risk.

17 Political risk is concerned with the effect on a company's value of political events in the host country. It can be managed by assessing political risk and its consequences, and by developing policies to minimise it.

18 Companies can assess political risk by using the checklist approach, the Delphi technique, quantitative analysis and inspection visits. Many companies use a subjective approach.

19 Political risk can be managed through insurance, negotiation of agreements, and financing and operating policies.

Self-test questions

Answers to these questions can be found on page 474.

1 For what strategic reasons may a company decide to build a manufacturing facility in another country?

2 Briefly describe the economic reasons why a company might choose to undertake foreign direct investment.

3 Explain the advantages and disadvantages of exporting, licensing and foreign direct investment as different ways of conducting international trade.

4 Describe the advantages and disadvantages of joint venture as a way of selling goods to another country.

5 List the ways in which foreign direct investment decisions are different from domestic investment decisions.

6 Discuss whether foreign direct investment should be evaluated at the local level or at the parent company level.

7 What difficulties may be faced by analysts seeking to use the capital asset pricing model to determine a discount rate for foreign direct investment?

8 Describe the main factors influencing the choice and mix of financing used in foreign direct investment.

9 Explain how political risk may be assessed by a company considering foreign direct investment.

10 Describe briefly the policies and strategies that a company could use to mitigate the problem of political risk.

Questions for review

Answers to these questions can be found on pages 475–8. Questions with an asterisk (*) are at an intermediate level.

1* Scot plc is a successful manufacturing company based in the north of England. As a result of the changing relationship between the European Union and eastern European countries, an opportunity has arisen to invest in Glumrovia. The directors of Scot plc have decided that, because of the risky nature of investments in this part of the world, they will require an after-tax return of at least 20 per cent on the project.

The government of Glumrovia is prepared to grant Scot plc a five-year licence to operate in the country. Market research suggests that cash flows from the project, in Glumrovian dollars (G$), will be as follows:

Year	1	2	3	4	5
G$000	250	450	550	650	800

However, much of the increase in the project cash flows is due to expected rates of inflation. The current G$/sterling exchange rate is G$3.00/£1; in subsequent years it is expected to be:

Year	1	2	3	4	5
G$/£	4.00	5.00	6.00	7.00	8.00

The project will cost G$600 000 to set up, but the present Glumrovian government will pay G$600 000 to Scot plc for the business at the end of the five-year period. It will also lend Scot plc the G$250 000 required for initial working capital at the advantageous rate of 6 per cent, to be repaid at the end of the five-year period.

Scot plc will pay Glumrovian tax on the after-interest profits at the rate of 20 per cent. Glumrovian tax is payable at the end of each year, at which time the balance of profits can be remitted to the UK. There is a tax treaty between the two governments and so any Glumrovian tax paid can be offset against UK tax liability. UK tax is payable at the rate of 30 per cent and you should assume that it is payable at the time that the cash is remitted to the UK.

As yet, there is no stock exchange in Glumrovia as the current liberal government has been unable to complete the implementation of necessary economic reforms. A recent press report revealed that the people of Glumrovia are disappointed with the pace of liberal reform and that elections to be held next year might see a significant renewal of communist influence.

(a) Prepare a report for Scot plc that analyses the data available and makes an argued recommendation as to whether the project should be taken on.

(b) Discuss the possible problems that might confront a company making the type of decision facing Scot plc.

2 Redek Mornag plc manufactures mobile telephones in a UK facility which currently has some spare capacity. It exports 20 per cent of its annual production to Laresia, a developing nation which has recently elected a right-wing government after five years of military rule. It is expected that the Laresian market for mobile telephones will increase significantly in the next few years and Redek Mornag plc wants to increase its share of the market. Discuss the relative merits to Redek Mornag plc of the following ways of servicing the Laresian market:

(a) increasing exports to Laresia from the existing UK factory;

(b) licensing a Laresian manufacturer to produce mobile telephones there;

(c) constructing a factory in Laresia.

3 Critically discuss the ways in which international capital investment decisions differ from domestic capital investment decisions.

4* Brinpool plc, a UK manufacturer of machine parts, has been invited to build a factory in the small African state of Gehell by the government of that country. The local currency is the Ked (K) and data on current and expected exchange rates are as follows:

Year	0	1	2	3	4	5
K/£	3.50	4.00	4.40	4.70	4.90	5.00

Initial investment will be £1 500 000 for equipment, payable in sterling, and K1 000 000 for working capital. The Gehell government has offered a loan to cover working capital at 10 per cent per year, repayable in full after five years. The Gehell government has also expressed a wish to acquire the factory from Brinpool plc as a going concern after five years and has offered K4 200 000 in compensation. Their loan would be recovered from the compensation payment.

Brinpool plc estimates that cash profits will be K3 000 000 per year, but also expects to lose current annual export sales to Gehell of £50 000 after tax. All after-tax cash profits are remitted to the UK at the end of each year.

Profits in Gehell are taxed at a rate of 15 per cent after interest and capital allowances, which are available on the £1.5m initial investment on a straight-line basis at a rate of 20 per cent per year. UK taxation of 30 per cent is charged on UK profits and a double taxation agreement exists between Gehell and the UK. Taxation is paid in the year in which it arises.

Other companies with similar business in Gehell have a weighted average after-tax cost of capital of 12 per cent. Brinpool plc feels that, due to the political risk of Gehell, it should apply a cost of capital of 18 per cent.

Advise whether the proposed investment is financially acceptable to Brinpool plc.

5 Discuss the problem of political risk in the context of foreign direct investment, and the difficulties that companies may face as a result of it.

Questions for discussion

Questions with an asterisk (*) are at an advanced level.

1* Lisant Mirrad International (LMI) is evaluating a proposal to build a manufacturing facility in Weland. The initial investment of £1.6m is payable in sterling to UK contractors and LMI expects before-tax operating cash flows of 1 million Welandian dollars (W$) per year. It is expected that the sales from the new facility will reduce existing exports by LMI to Weland by about £17 000 per year in after-tax profits over the life of the project.

Profit tax in Weland is 15 per cent per year. The directors of LMI propose that all of each year's profits be remitted to the UK, where profit tax is 30 per cent per year. Tax paid in Weland is an allowable deduction against the UK tax liability.

In order to reduce the risk of the project, LMI has agreed to sell the factory to the Welandian government after five years of operations for W$1.5m. The Welandian government has agreed that this sum may be remitted to the UK without further taxation.

Assume that cash transfers occur at the end of each year and that tax liabilities are paid in the year that they arise. LMI requires a return of at least 17 per cent on this kind of investment as regards cash flows received in the UK while, in order to compensate for the perceived risk of investing in Weland, it requires a return of 22 per cent at the level of the manufacturing facility.

The current spot rate is W$1.5/£1 and expected exchange rates for the next five years are as follows:

Year	1	2	3	4	5
W$/£	1.620	1.750	1.890	2.041	2.204

Determine whether the project is acceptable:

(a) from the point of view of the manufacturing facility;

(b) from the point of view of LMI.

2 Critically discuss the following statement:

'Net present value is the best way to find out if a foreign investment project is a good one and all the big multinationals are using it now.'

3* Ice plc has decided to expand sales in Northland because of increasing pressure in its domestic market. It is evaluating two alternative expansion proposals.

Proposal 1
Ice plc could increase production from an existing UK site. This would require initial investment of £750 000 and give export sales worth £280 000 per year before tax.

Proposal 2
Ice plc could build a factory in Northland at a cost of N$2 700 000. Annual sales from the factory would initially be N$1 000 000 before tax, but these are expected to increase each year. The actual rate of increase each year will depend on economic conditions in Northland, as follows.

Economic conditions in Northland	Good	Moderate	Poor
Probability of these conditions occurring	25%	60%	15%
Annual increase in sales	6%	5%	4%

Forecast exchange rates

Year	0	1	2	3	4	5	6	7	8
N$/£	3.60	3.74	3.89	4.05	4.21	4.34	4.55	4.74	4.92

Further information
Ice plc pays UK corporation tax one year in arrears at a rate of 30 per cent per year. For investment appraisal purposes the company uses a seven-year planning period and ignores terminal values. Its weighted-average cost of capital is 12 per cent after tax. Any foreign company investing in Northland pays profit tax to the Northland government one year in arrears at a rate of 30 per cent per year.

(a) Using the information provided, advise Ice plc as to which proposal should be adopted, explaining any assumptions that you make.

(b) Critically discuss the evaluation process used in part (a) and suggest what further information could assist Ice plc in the evaluation of the two proposals for increasing sales in Northland.

4* Sanding plc has received an offer of €75m for Carat, its European subsidiary, and has decided to accept the offer. Financial details relating to the subsidiary and the proposed sale are as follows:

Before tax cash flows of Carat:	€10m per year (current price terms)
Expected market value of Carat in 7 years:	€50m (current price terms)
Annual local profit tax for Carat:	25%
Annual UK tax of Carat:	30%
Annual European inflation:	2.1%
Annual UK inflation:	3.0%

Current and forecast exchange rates

Year	0	1	2	3	4	5	6	7
€/£	1.6413	1.6270	1.6127	1.5986	1.5847	1.5708	1.5571	1.5435

Sanding plc has a nominal after-tax cost of capital of 15 per cent per year.

(a) Determine whether the decision to accept the offer is supported by the financial data provided.

(b) Critically discuss the view that market imperfections play a key role in determining the success of multinational companies in foreign direct investment.

References

Aharoni, Y. (1966) *The Foreign Investment Decision Process*, Boston, MA: Harvard Graduate School of Business Administration, Division of Research.

Barclay, J. (1995) 'Regional blocs', in Dawes, B. (ed.), *International Business: A European Perspective*, Cheltenham: Stanley Thornes.

Brooke, M. (1996) *International Management*, Cheltenham: Stanley Thornes.

Buckley, A. (2003) *Multinational Finance*, 5th edn., Harlow: FT Prentice Hall.

Clark, E. (2002) 'Measuring country risk as implied volatility', *Wilmott Magazine*, September, pp. 64–67.

Dawes, B. and Ivanov, D. (1995) 'Emerging markets: characteristics and opportunities', in Dawes, B. (ed.), *International Business: A European Perspective*, Cheltenham: Stanley Thornes.

Demirag, I. and Goddard, S. (1994) *Financial Management for International Business*, London: McGraw-Hill.

Garrod, N. and Rees, W. (1998) 'International diversification and firm value', *Journal of Business Finance and Accounting*, November/December, pp. 1255–81.

Goddard, S. (1990) 'Political risk in international capital budgeting', *Managerial Finance*, Vol. 16, No. 2, pp. 7–12.

Holland, J. (1990) 'Capital budgeting for international business: a framework for analysis', *Managerial Finance*, Vol. 16, No. 2, pp. 1–6.

Kim, S. and Ulferts, G. (1996) 'A summary of multinational capital budgeting studies', *Managerial Finance*, Vol. 22, No. 1, pp. 75–85.

Madura, J. (1998) *International Financial Management*, South-Western College Publishing, Cincinnati, Ohio.

Siegel, P., Omer, K., Rigsby, J. and Theerathorn, P. (1995) 'International diversification: a review and analysis of the evidence', *Managerial Finance*, Vol. 21, No. 9, pp. 50–77.

Stanley, T. (1990) 'Cost of capital in capital budgeting for foreign direct investment', *Managerial Finance*, Vol. 16, No. 2, pp. 13–16.

Recommended reading

A fascinating account of the various forms of international trade is given by:

Brooke, M. (1996) *International Management*, Cheltenham: Stanley Thornes.

The range of services offered by the Export Credits Guarantee Department can be reviewed at www.ecgd.gov.uk/.

A wealth of information on country risk and political risk can be found on the websites of the Institute of International Finance, www.iif.com, and the Economist Intelligence Unit, www.eiu.com.

Appendix:
Answers to end-of-chapter questions

Chapter 1 **Answers to self-test questions**

1 *See* Sections 1.1.2 and 1.1.3.

2 (a) $500 \times (1 + 0.12)^5 = £881$
   (b) $500/(1 + 0.12)^5 \quad = £284$
   (c) $500/0.12 \qquad\qquad = £4167$
   (d) $500 \times 3.605 \qquad = £1803$

3 The financial manager's job normally falls under the control of the financial director. He or she oversees the financial controller, who deals with the accounting side, and the corporate treasurer, who carries out the financial management tasks. These tasks will include the following:

■ investment decisions, capital budgeting and investment appraisal;

■ financing decisions, including raising debt and equity finance;

■ working capital management, including cash management, debtor management and stock control;

■ dividend policy formulation;

■ interest rate and foreign currency management.

4 Examples could include the following:

■ insufficient finance or expensively raised finance, leading to the rejection of investment projects;

■ too high a level of dividends, restricting the amount of retained earnings and therefore increasing the need for external finance;

■ a large number of attractive projects, leading to a higher level of retained earnings and therefore a lower dividend payment.

5 ■ *Profit maximisation*: profit figures can be manipulated, have no time dimension if profits are maximised year after year and also do not take risk into account.

■ *Sales maximisation*: even further off the mark than the above. Market share may be an initial goal in order to obtain a market foothold. Sales maximisation, taken to the extreme, can lead, via overtrading, to bankruptcy.

■ *Maximisation of benefit to employees and the local community*: again, if taken to the extreme, this could lead to cash flow problems. It is important to keep both employees and the local community happy, but this is not a main goal.

■ *Maximise shareholder wealth*: the correct goal, since as owners their wealth should be maximised.

6 How does a financial manager maximise shareholder wealth? Shareholders derive wealth from share ownership through capital gains and dividend payments. The financial manager, then, should maximise the present value of these. If capital markets are efficient, the current market price of a share should be the net present value of all future benefits accruing to the share. Current market share price, then, can be used as a proxy for shareholder wealth. To maximise shareholder wealth, a financial manager should accept all projects with positive net present values as this will maximise the market share price.

7 The agency problem arises because of a divorce of ownership and control. Within a public limited company (plc), there are a number of examples of the agency problem, the most important being that existing between shareholders (principal) and managers (agent). The problem exists because of divergent goals and an asymmetry of information. Managers act to maximise their own wealth rather than the shareholders' wealth. There are various ways to reduce the agency problem:

■ do nothing, if the costs of divergent behaviour are low;

■ monitor agents, if contracting or divergent behaviour costs are high;

■ use a reward/punishment contract, if monitoring costs and divergent behaviour costs are high.

As regards the shareholders/managers agency problem, monitoring costs and divergent behaviour costs are high so shareholders use contracts to reward managers for good performance and could give managers shares in the company they manage, making them shareholders themselves.

8 The correct answer is (d), because the use of restrictive covenants in bond deeds is of relevance to the providers of debt finance as a way of encouraging optimal behaviour by shareholders. It does not then lead to a reduction in the agency problems experienced by shareholders.

9 Some possible managerial goals are given in Section 1.5.1.

10 The size of the agency problem reflects the relative power of shareholders with respect to managers. Since, in the UK, institutional investors now have significant holdings in UK public limited companies, they are able to bring significant pressure to bear on company managers as a way of encouraging goal congruence. As in the USA, shareholder groups are growing as a way of enhancing and focusing this pressure. It can be argued that, for institutional investors in UK companies, the agency problem is being slowly attenuated. For smaller investors, however, this may not be the case.

Chapter 1 Answers to questions for review

1 The definition of wealth is not straightforward, but one method is to consider the returns that investors expect in exchange for becoming shareholders. Such returns will be in the form of regular dividends and any gain made on disposal of the shares, i.e. the returns will be either revenue or capital in nature. The objective of maximising shareholder wealth then becomes the objective of maximising these returns to the shareholder, i.e. maximising the value of dividends paid to shareholders over time, before shareholders receive any gains made on disposal.

Since investors have a required return, which is the opportunity cost of investing in a given company rather than investing elsewhere, future cash flows will need to be discounted. If disposal of the security is distant, we can ignore it, recognising that discounted distant returns are less valuable than those received in the near future. Maximisation of shareholder wealth then becomes maximisation of the present value of the stream of future dividends, and as Gordon and others have shown, the present value of future dividends can be equated to the current ex-dividend share price. Maximisation of the company's share price can therefore be used as a surrogate objective.

2 The maximisation of sales has a number of problems as a measure of maximisation of shareholder wealth:

- sales are measured in revenue rather than cash terms, so maximising sales may not result in cash inflows for a company;
- sales may be maximised by offering goods on extended credit terms or by making sales to disreputable companies who may default on payment;
- sales or turnover is an historical measure and not necessarily a guide to expected future cash flows;
- sales may be maximised but on mispriced goods, leading to losses;
- sales are in theory maximised when marginal revenue is equal to marginal cost, but how do we know when this has occurred?

Sales maximisation is therefore a subjective measure. In contrast, a company's ordinary share price is an objective yardstick provided by the capital markets. It is independent of the company, forward-looking and reflects an assessment of the company's prospects in both financial and strategic terms.

3 You should discuss the following points:

- divergence of ownership and control;
- divergence of goals between principal and agent;
- asymmetry of information, including access to dissimilar information sets and asymmetry of interpretation;
- managers' personal goals may not lead to maximisation of shareholder wealth;
- conflict between investors and managers in terms of investment decisions and risk;
- ways in which principals can monitor the activities of agents;
- agency costs, including monitoring costs, the free-rider problem and contract costs;
- optimal contracts and other ways of encouraging goal convergence.

4 (a) Agency implies that managers (as agents) maximise their own wealth rather than that of their shareholders (the principals) due to asymmetry of information, differing objectives and divorce of ownership and control. Hence we need to look for clear signs that agency problems are present.

The first thing to note is that the company has diversified its activities across a range of different industries. This is often justified in the name of reducing risk for shareholders, but shareholders should have already diversified themselves through the portfolios they hold. Companies tend to diversify their activities for managerial motives, such as to increase job security by diversifying unsystematic risk.

Second, the company is maintaining a gearing ratio significantly below the industrial average. This is another example of the agency problem as shareholders prefer higher levels of debt because of the cheaper cost of debt finance and are prepared to accept higher levels of financial risk because they have a diversified portfolio. Managers, however, prefer equity finance as too high a level of financial risk could jeopardise their job security.

A more obvious example of agency problem is that the directors' average salaries are above the industry norm and they have five-year contracts, contravening corporate governance directives like the Greenbury Report. Managers are likely to become complacent with contracts of such length. There is also a problem with the use and terms of the share options. Given the historical growth rate in share price of 5 per cent, the company's share price five years ago when the directors were given the share options would have been approximately £1.83. For the share price to climb above £2 in less than five years represents a very unchallenging target.

If managers were to exercise the options in a year's time, their gain would be:

$$(2.34(1.05) - 2.00) \times 100\,000 = £45\,700$$

This represents a generous reward for significantly underperforming the sector share price growth rate of 9 per cent.

(b) Given the company appears to have major agency and corporate governance problems, these could be reduced by some of the following actions:

- get managers to refocus the business in one area of specialisation and realise economies of scale and operation;

- instruct managers to increase the level of debt finance as the current level of gearing is unlikely to minimise the company's cost of capital;

- restructure the managers' share options so that gains are achievable if the management stretch themselves;

- monitor managers to ensure they are not maximising their own wealth. The degree of success depends on the monitoring method used and the structure of the company's shareholders as someone must pay for monitoring to take place;

- reduce salaries back in line with industry averages and tie part of the salary to a performance-related variable (e.g. company share price relative to the sector). Introduce one-year rolling contracts to keep managers on their toes;

- examine the constitution of the remuneration committee and the backgrounds of non-executive directors, and make appropriate changes where necessary;

- ultimately, the shareholders might want to exercise their right to vote out directors at the AGM if they think that their performance has been poor.

Chapter 2   Answers to self-test questions

1 This topic is discussed in Section 2.1.3. The main factors influencing the split between internal and external finance are as follows:

- the level of finance required;
- the cash flow from existing operations;

- the opportunity cost of retained earnings;
- the costs associated with raising external finance;
- the availability of external sources of finance;
- dividend policy.

2 The relevance of the efficient market hypothesis for financial management is that, if the hypothesis holds true, the company's 'real' financial position will be reflected in the share price. If the company makes a 'good' financial decision, this will be reflected in an increase in the share price. Similarly, a 'bad' financial decision will cause the share price to fall. In order to maximise shareholder wealth, the financial manager need only concentrate on maximising the NPV of investment projects, and need not consider matters such as the way in which the future position of the company will be reflected in the company's financial statements. The financial manager, then, may use rational decision rules and have confidence that the market will rapidly reflect the effects of those decisions in the company's share price.

3 The incorrect statement is (b) since, if capital markets are strong form efficient, then nobody, not even people with insider information, will be able to make abnormal returns.

4 These terms are discussed in Section 2.3.1.

5 It is hard to test for strong form efficiency directly, i.e. by studying the market's *use* of information, because it can always be objected that investors with access to inside information can make abnormal gains. Tests for strong form efficiency are therefore *indirect*, examining the performance of *users* of information who may have access to inside information or who have special training for share dealing, such as fund managers.

6 Anomalies in share price behaviour are discussed in Section 2.3.6. You could discuss calendar effects, size anomalies and value effects.

7 Financial performance measures and financial ratios mean little in isolation. In order to assess financial performance, we need to compare with benchmarks such as:
- target performance measures set by managers;
- sector or industry norms;
- performance measures and ratios of similar companies;
- performance measures and ratios of the same company from previous years.

All such comparisons should be made with caution due to the problems in analysing financial performance arising from differing accounting policies and creative accounting.

8 The answer to this question is given in Section 2.4.2 and following sections. You should be able to define *all* the ratios. If you cannot, study these sections further until you can. Compare your calculations to the illustrative calculations given.

9 The problems that may be encountered in using ratio analysis to assess the health and performance of companies include:
- all ratios are imperfect and imprecise and should be treated as guidelines;
- ratios are only as reliable as the accounting figures they are based on;

■ no two companies are identical so inter-company comparisons need care;

■ ratios mean little in isolation and need other information to explain them;

■ ratio analysis tends to be performed on historical data and so may not be an accurate guide to either current position or future activity.

10 Economic value added (EVA) is the difference between adjusted operating profit after tax and a cost of capital charge on the adjusted value of invested capital. It can help managers to increase shareholder wealth by directing their attention to the drivers that create value for shareholders, such as increasing net operating profit after tax, investing in projects with a return greater than the company's cost of capital or reducing the cost of capital or the value of invested capital.

Chapter 2 Answers to questions for review

1 The capital markets are markets for trade in long-term negotiable financial securities or instruments. There are essentially three kinds of securities traded on the capital markets: company securities, such as ordinary shares and debentures; public sector securities, such as Treasury bills and gilts; and Eurobonds.

The primary or new issues market enables firms to raise new finance by issuing new shares and debentures. The secondary market is where dealing takes place in previously issued securities. The secondary market plays a very important role in corporate finance, because this market:

■ increases the liquidity of the shares and so increases their value;

■ increases primary market efficiency by providing pricing information;

■ provides a measure of company performance and also of industrial and commercial performance as a whole (FTSE 100, FT All-Share index, etc.).

The stock exchange consists of the 'full' market, the Alternative Investment Market (AIM) and the gilts market.

The desirable characteristics of a primary capital market are as follows:

■ all transaction costs in primary markets should be as low as possible;

■ primary markets should have allocational efficiency, which means that they should direct funds to their most productive uses;

■ activity in the primary market should have only a minimal effect on prices in the secondary market.

Secondary markets will encourage investment if they provide liquidity and flexibility, reduce price volatility and are operationally and allocationally efficient:

■ price volatility is reduced by having an active market with 'depth' and 'breadth';

■ operational efficiency means that transaction costs should be low;

■ allocational efficiency requires both operational and pricing efficiency.

Pricing efficiency will only occur if the prices of securities reflect available information, i.e. if markets are informationally efficient.

2 The solution to this question is given in Section 2.3.6.

3 Hoult is experiencing deteriorating profitability, liquidity, debtors', current and quick ratios, and has a growing reliance on short-term funding. These are signs of overtrading (*see* Section 3.4). The main reason appears to be erosion of the company's capital base due to repayment of the debentures. If this had not been happening, even if fixed asset investment had been occurring, it is likely that the overdraft would have been much lower, a small cash surplus might have arisen and lower interest payments would have led to increased profitability. Overall profitability would still have been low, but management action to improve profitability might have been possible if the focus of the company's activity had not been on redeeming the debentures.

If only long-term debt is considered, gearing is falling due to repayment of the debentures. However, if both short-term debt and long-term debt are considered, the fall in gearing is marginal. Including short-term debt gives a better indication of the financial risk of Hoult in this case. The Year 3 dividend payment cannot be justified in profitability terms. Is the company hoping to influence shareholders prior to a rights issue?

Overall profitability	Year 1	Year 2	Year 3
ROCE (%)	8.0	8.6	10.3
Net profit (%)	3.1	2.8	2.7
Net asset turnover (*n*:1)	2.6	3.1	3.8
Gross profit (%)	30	28	27
EBITDA/capital employed (%)	12.8	12.3	13.8
Asset management			
Current ratio (*n*:1)	2.5	2.4	1.9
Quick ratio (*n*:1)	1.1	1.1	1.0
Stock turnover (days)	109	98	93
Debtor days (days)	61	61	75
Creditor days (days)	41	37	60
Sales/working capital (*n*:1)	4.5	4.7	5.5
Financial risk			
Total debt/capital employed (%)	51	46	47
Long-term debt/capital employed (%)	32	23	13
Total debt/equity (%)	75	59	54
Interest cover (*n*:1)	2.3	2.1	1.8
Investor ratios			
Dividend cover (*n*:1)	–	–	3.5
Increase in turnover (%)		+12.5	+13.0
Increase in overdraft (£000)		10	30

4 The solution to this question is given in Section 2.3.3.

5 The solution to this question is given in Section 2.4.10.

Chapter 3   Answers to self-test questions

1 It is important to match the financing with the life of assets. We can analyse assets into fixed assets, permanent current assets and fluctuating current assets. Permanent current assets, being 'core' current assets which are needed to support normal levels of sales, should be financed from a long-term source. The working capital policy chosen should take account of the relative risk of long- and short-term finance to the company and the need to balance liquidity against profitability. An aggressive financing policy will use short-term funds to finance fluctuating current assets as well as to finance part of the permanent current assets. A conservative financing policy will use long-term funds to finance permanent current assets as well as to finance part of the fluctuating current assets. An aggressive financing policy will be more profitable, but riskier.

2 The components of the cash conversion cycle (CCC) are the inventory conversion period (ICP), the debtor conversion period (DCP) and the creditor deferral period (CDP), and the relationship between them is:

$$CCC = ICP + DCP + (-CDP)$$

Investment in working capital must be financed and the longer the cash conversion cycle, the more capital is tied up and the higher the cost. A company could reduce the working capital tied up by optimising the components of the cash conversion cycle. So, for example, shortening the inventory conversion period could reduce the working capital requirement and increase profitability.

3 The solution to this question is given in Section 3.2.2.

4 Overtrading arises when a company seeks to do too much too quickly, without sufficient long-term capital to support its operations. While a company which is overtrading may well be profitable, it is likely to meet difficulties with liquidity and may be unable to meet its financial obligations to creditors and others as they fall due. Strategies that could be considered by management wishing to address the problem of overtrading include: introduction of new capital, possibly from shareholders; better control and management of working capital; and a reduction in business activity in order to consolidate the company's position and build up capital through retained earnings.

5 Cash flow problems can arise from:
- making losses, since continuing losses will lead to cash flow problems;
- inflation, since historical profit may be insufficient to replace assets;
- growth, since this calls for investment in fixed assets and working capital;
- seasonal business, due to imbalances in cash flow;
- significant one-off items of expenditure, such as repayment of debt capital.

Cash flow problems can be eased in several ways. Examples include postponing capital expenditure (e.g. extending vehicle replacement life), accelerating cash inflows (e.g. offering cash discounts, chasing up slow payers), shelving investment plans, selling off non-core assets and reducing cash outflows. Economies could be found in normal operations as well.

6 There are three reasons why a company may choose to have reserves of cash. Companies need to have a cash reserve to balance short-term cash inflows and outflows: this is the transactions motive for holding cash. The precautionary motive for holding cash refers to the fact that a company may choose to have cash reserves in order to meet unexpected demands. Companies may also build up cash reserves to take advantage of investment opportunities that may occur: this is the speculative motive for holding cash.

7 Short-term cash surpluses should be invested on a short-term basis without risk of capital loss. In selecting investment methods, the finance director should consider: the size of the surplus; how easy it is to get back the cash invested; the maturity, risk and yield of different investments; and any penalties for early liquidation.

   Short-term instruments which could be discussed include money market deposits, Treasury bills, bank certificates of deposit, gilts and bank deposits.

8 The risk of bad debts could be minimised if the creditworthiness of new customers is assessed and reviewed on a regular basis. Relevant information should be obtained from a variety of sources, including bank references, trade references, published information, such as accounts and the press, and credit reference agencies. In addition, the credit analysis system should adopt a cost-effective approach so that the extent of the credit assessment should reflect the size of the order, the likelihood of subsequent business and the amount of credit requested.

9 Proposed changes to credit policy should be evaluated in the light of the additional costs and benefits that will result from their being undertaken. For example, the cost of the introduction of cash discounts can be compared with the benefits of faster settlement of accounts in terms of reduced interest charges, and possibly also the additional business that may result. The change should be undertaken only if the marginal benefits arising from the new policy exceed its marginal costs.

10 Factors offer a range of services in the area of sales administration and the collection of cash due from debtors, including administration of sales invoicing and accounting, collection of cash due, chasing up late payers, advancing cash against the security of debtors due, and offering protection against non-payment via non-recourse factoring. Invoice discounting, however, involves the sale of selected invoices to another company. Its main value lies in the improvement in cash flow that it offers.

Chapter 3 Answers to questions for review

1 Your recommended policy should have been based on the EOQ model.
$F = £100$ per order
$S = 60\,000$ tons per year
$H = £0.10$ per ton per year

Substituting: $Q = (2 \times 100 \times 60\,000/0.10)^{1/2} = 10\,954$ tons per order
Number of orders per year $= 60\,000/10\,954 = 5.5$ orders
Reorder level $= 2 \times 60\,000/50 = 2400$ tons
Total cost of optimal policy = Holding costs + Ordering costs
$$= (0.1 \times 10\,954)/2 + (100 \times 60\,000)/10\,954$$
$$= 547.70 + 547.74 = £1095$$

To compare the optimal policy with the current policy, the average level of stock under the current policy must be found. An order is placed when stock falls to 10 000 tons, but the lead time is two weeks. The stock used in that time is $(60\,000 \times 2)/50 = 2\,400$ tons. Before delivery, inventory has fallen to $(10\,000 - 2\,400) = 7\,600$ tons. Orders are made twice per year and so the order size $= 60\,000/2 = 30\,000$ tons. The order will increase stock level to $30\,000 + 7\,600 = 37\,600$ tons. Hence the average stock level $= 7\,600 + (30\,000/2) = 22\,600$ tons. Total costs of current policy $= (0.1 \times 22\,600) + (100 \times 2) = £2460$ per year.

The recommended policy, then, costs £1365 per year less than the current policy.

2 *Annual costs:*

Raw materials:	$700\,000 \times 0.20 =$	£140 000
Direct labour:	$700\,000 \times 0.35 =$	£245 000
Overheads:	$700\,000 \times 0.15 =$	£105 000

Working capital requirement:

	£	£
Stocks of raw materials: $140\,000 \times (2/52) =$		5 385
Work-in-progress:		
materials: $140\,000 \times (4/52) =$	10 769	
labour: $245\,000 \times (4/52) \times ½ =$	9 423	
overheads: $105\,000 \times (4/52) \times ½ =$	4 038	
		24 230
Finished goods: $490\,000 \times (3/52) =$		28 269
Debtors: $700\,000 \times (8/52) =$		107 692
Creditors: $140\,000 \times (4/52) =$		(10 769)
Working capital required:		154 807

Note that work-in-progress is assumed to be half complete as regards labour and overheads, but fully complete as regards raw materials, i.e. all raw material is added at the start of production.

3 New level of sales will be $1\,500\,000 \times 1.15 = £1\,725\,000$
Variable costs are $80\% \times 75\% = 60\%$ of sales
Contribution from sales is therefore 40% of sales

	£	£
Proposed investment in debtors $= 1\,725\,000 \times 60/365 =$		283 562
Current investment in debtors $= 1\,500\,000 \times 30/365 =$		123 288
Increase in investment in debtors		160 274
Increase in contribution $= (1\,725\,000 - 1\,500\,000) \times 40\% =$		90 000
New level of bad debts $= 1\,725\,000 \times 4\% =$	69 000	
Current level of bad debts $= 1\,500\,000 \times 1\% =$	15 000	

		£
Increase in bad debts		(54 000)
Additional financing costs = 160 274 × 12% =		(19 233)
Savings by introducing change in policy		16 767

The financing policy is financially acceptable.

4

	£	£
Current level of debtors = 1 600 000 × 45/365 =		197 260
Proposed level of debtors:		
Not taking the discount = 60% × 1 600 000 × 45/365 =	118 356	
Taking the discount = 40% × 1 600 000 × 10/365 =	17 534	
		135 890
Change in level of debtors		61 370
Saving in financing costs = 61 370 × 11% =		6 751
Administrative cost savings		4 450
Total savings		11 201

Calculation of maximum discount:

$$1\,600\,000 \times 40\% \times \text{Maximum discount} = 11\,201$$

Hence maximum discount = 11 201/(1 600 000 × 0.4) = 0.0175 or 1.75%

The maximum discount that could be offered is therefore 1.75 per cent.

Chapter 4 Answers to self-test questions

1 In corporate finance, a key concept is the relationship between risk and return. The higher the risk associated with a given investment, the higher will be the return required in exchange for investing in it. Debentures are debt finance paying a fixed annual return and are secured on assets of the company. They therefore have a much lower risk than ordinary equity, which is unsecured and which has no right to receive a dividend. If a company fails, the ordinary shareholders may receive nothing at all. In exchange for this higher risk, ordinary shareholders will require a higher return.

2 Some of the important rights which are available to shareholders in their position as owners of a company are mentioned in Section 4.1.1.

3 A company may obtain such a quotation through a public offer, a placing or an introduction. These are discussed in Section 4.2.2.

4 There are a variety of advantages and disadvantages to be considered by an unquoted company considering seeking a stock exchange listing.

Advantages of obtaining a quotation:

■ opens up new avenues for the company to raise finance;

■ increases the marketability of the company's shares;

■ raises the profile of the company;

- the company may obtain a better credit rating;
- the company can use its shares to fund future takeover activity.

Disadvantages of obtaining a quotation:
- the costs of flotation have to be met;
- the cost of compliance with listing regulations;
- the company may be open to a hostile takeover bid;
- dilution of control will result from wider share ownership;
- the company may have to satisfy increased shareholder expectations.

5 Pre-emptive rights mean that the company has an obligation to offer any new issue of shares to the existing shareholders before making a public offer. The importance to shareholders of pre-emptive rights is that it prevents significant changes in the structure of ownership and control of the company since the shares are offered to existing shareholders (although not necessarily taken up) in proportion to their existing holdings.

6 The advantage to a company of a rights issue is that, depending on market conditions, it may be a cheaper method of raising equity finance than a public offer. This is partly because the issue costs of a rights issue are lower than in the case of a public offer. A disadvantage is that, if insufficient funds are raised from the rights issue, the company must take further steps to secure the finance that it needs. This will be a more expensive and lengthy process than would be the case with a single placing of shares.

7 Rights issue price = £2.50 × 0.8 = £2.00

Theoretical ex-rights price = $((4 \times 2.50) + 2.00)/5 = £2.40$

Value of rights per existing share = $(2.40 - 2.00)/4 = 0.1$, i.e. 10p per share

The correct answer is therefore (a).

8 The correct answer is (d), a scrip issue, also known as a bonus issue. If you are unsure about this, study Section 4.4 carefully.

9 Preference shares do not enjoy great popularity as a source of finance because they are less tax efficient than debt. They are also riskier than debt since there is no right to receive a preference dividend, although cumulative preference shares will preserve the right to receive unpaid dividends. More recently, more exotic varieties of preference shares have enjoyed an increased popularity, such as auction market preferred stock, a type of variable rate preference share.

10 You should have chosen (c), that a cumulative preference share carries forward the right to receive unpaid preference dividends. The right to be converted into ordinary shares at a future date (a) is carried by convertible preference shares, and the right to receive a share of residual profits (b) is carried by participating preference shares. All three types of preference share entitle their holders to a fixed dividend rate (d). Voting rights at the company's AGM (e) may be attached to preference shares, but it is very unlikely.

Chapter 4 **Answers to questions for review**

1   The shares of Brand plc have a nominal value of 50p and a book value of £200 000 so there are 400 000 shares.

	£
Current market value of Brand = 400 000 × 1.90=	760 000
Funds raised through rights issue	160 000
Final market value	920 000

	£
Earnings before rights issue = 600 000 × 0.15 =	90 000
Earnings from new funds = 160 000 × 0.15 =	24 000
Total earnings after rights issue	114 000

Issue price of £1.80
Number of new shares = 160 000/1.80 = 88 889
Total shares in issue = 400 000 + 88 889 = 488 889
Theoretical ex-rights price = 920 000/488 889 = £1.88
New EPS = 100 × (114 000/488 889) = 23.3 pence
Form of rights issue = 400 000/88 889 = 4.5, i.e. 2 for 9

Issue price of £1.60
Number of new shares = 160 000/1.60 = 100 000
Total shares in issue = 400 000 + 100 000 = 500 000
Theoretical ex-rights price = 920 000/500 000 = £1.84
New EPS = 100 × (114 000/500 000) = 22.8 pence
Form of rights issue = 400 000/100 000 = 4, i.e. 1 for 4

Issue price of £1.40
Number of new shares = 160 000/1.40 = 114 286
Total shares in issue = 400 000 + 114 286 = 514 286
Theoretical ex-rights price = 920 000/514 286 = £1.79
New EPS = 100 × (114 000/514 286) = 22.2 pence
Form of rights issue = 400 000/114 286 = 3.5, i.e. 2 for 7

It is to be expected, since the return on shareholders' funds has not changed, that the theoretical ex-rights price would be below the current share price, and the calculations have confirmed this. Why were the proposed rights issue prices set at discounts of 5, 10 and 16 per cent to the current share price, i.e. less than the commonly quoted discount of 20 per cent? Anyway, the actual share price after the rights issue would also depend on other factors, such as the view taken by the market of the use to be made of the new funds and the effect of the issue on EPS. The current EPS is (90 000/400 000) × 100 = 22.5p and two of the proposed issue prices give an increase on this figure. Only when the issue price falls below the current shareholders' funds per share (600 000/400 000 = £1.50) does dilution of earnings per share occur.

2 The key point here is that Maltby's P/E ratio remains unchanged.

Current number of shares = £4m/0.5 = 8m shares
Current EPS = (£7m/8m) × 100 = 87.5 pence
Current PER = (3.50/0.875) = 4
Rights issue price = 3.50 × 0.8 = £2.80
The rights issue is a 1-for-4 issue, so the total number of shares post rights issue is 10m
Theoretical ex-rights price = ((3.50 × 4) + 2.80)/5 = 16.80/5 = £3.36
Funds raised = £2.80 × 2m = £5.6m

Redemption of debentures
Debentures redeemed = £5.6m/1.12 = £5m
Interest saved = 5m × 0.12 = £600 000
Tax saving lost = 600 000 × 0.30 = £180 000
Net saving = 600 000 − 180 000 = £420 000
New earnings = 7 000 000 + 420 000 = £7 420 000
New EPS = (7.42m/10m) × 100 = 74.2 pence
New share price = 74.2 × 4 = 297 pence

Investment project
Earnings on new funds = 5.6m × 0.2 = £1.12m
New earnings = 7m + 1.12m = £8.12m
New EPS = (8.12m/10m) × 100 = 81.20 pence
New share price = 81.20 × 4 = 325 pence

Conclusion
Both options result in a share price which is less than the theoretical ex-rights price. The theoretical ex-rights price, provided rights are either used or sold, results in no change in shareholder wealth. Both options, then, result in a reduction in shareholder wealth. Since the fundamental financial objective of the company is the maximisation of shareholder wealth, neither option can be recommended as being in the best interests of shareholders.

3 The answer to this question can be found in Section 4.4.2.

Chapter 5 Answers to self-test questions

1 The answer to this question can be found by referring to the discussion at the start of Section 5.1.

2 (a) A restrictive covenant places limitations on the actions of managers in order to safeguard the investment made by providers of debt finance.

(b) Refinancing involves the replacement of existing finance with new finance. This may occur at redemption, if existing debt is replaced by a new issue of debt, or as part of a restructuring of a company's capital structure in line with financial plans.

(c) A redemption window is a period of time during which debentures or loan stock can be redeemed.

3 (a) Deep discount bonds are loan stock issued at a large discount to par value, which will be redeemed at or above par on maturity. They may be attractive to companies which need a low servicing cost during the life of the bond and which will be able to meet the high cost of redemption at maturity. Investors might be attracted to the large capital gain on offer, which will have tax advantages for some.

(b) Zero coupon bonds are bonds issued at a discount to par value which pay no interest. The investor obtains a capital gain from the difference between the issue price and the redemption value. Attractions for companies are similar to those for deep discount bonds.

(c) A warrant is a right to buy new shares at a future date at a fixed, predetermined price. Warrants are usually issued as part of a package with unsecured loan stock in order to make them more attractive. They are detachable from the stock and can be sold and bought separately. Investors may find them attractive because they offer potentially high gains compared with investing in the underlying shares.

(d) Convertible bonds are loan stock which can be converted into ordinary shares at the option of the holder. The interest rate on convertibles is therefore lower, since the holder has the option to participate in the growth of the company, unlike the holder of ordinary loan stock.

4 The answer to this question can be found by referring to Section 5.3.1.

5 The conversion premium is the premium per share on converting a convertible security into equity. The rights premium is the premium per share of a convertible security over equivalent loan stock with a similar coupon, reflecting the option to convert carried by the convertible security. The relationship between conversion premium, rights premium and market value of a convertible bond can be illustrated by a diagram (*see* Exhibit 5.3).

6 The company will consider: the length of time remaining to maturity; the general level of interest rates and the term structure of interest rates; the rate of return on other securities, especially ordinary equity; expectations of likely movements in interest rates and inflation rates; and the required return of investors in debentures.

7 *Advantages*:

- convertibles may be attractive to particular investors;
- interest rates on convertibles are usually lower than on straight debentures;
- interest charges on debentures are tax allowable;
- debentures increase gearing but might decrease the cost of capital;
- convertible debentures can be self-liquidating;
- conversion will not harm the capital structure and may even help it.

Disadvantages:

- there may be restrictive covenants attached to convertible debentures;
- issuing debentures decreases debt capacity;
- dilution of EPS may occur on conversion;
- conversion may cause dilution of control of existing shareholders.

8 As the price of the underlying share changes, there is a larger proportionate movement in the price of the warrant than in the price of the underlying share. In consequence, it is possible to make a greater proportionate gain (or loss) by investing in warrants than by investing in the underlying share. This is called the gearing effect of warrants.

9 Current ex interest market value = $(9 \times 2.487) + (100 \times 0.751) = £97.48$

If the stock is irredeemable, ex-interest market value = $£9/0.1 = £90$

10 For an explanation of the difference between a finance lease and an operating lease, *see* Section 5.8.1. As for the importance of the distinction for corporate finance, operating leases are useful where equipment is required for a short time or where there is risk of obsolescence. The lessee may also be relieved of the cost of servicing and maintenance. Finance leases may be cheaper than purchase, especially if the lessee pays little or no tax. The lessor can obtain tax relief on the capital cost of the leased asset and pass the benefits on to the lessee in the form of lower lease payments. Other benefits claimed for leasing include the 'off-balance-sheet' nature of some kinds of lease finance and access for small firms to expensive equipment.

Chapter 5   Answers to questions for review

1 We can calculate what Bugle plc considers a fair price for each bond, given that it requires a 15 per cent rate of return.

(a) *Stock 1*:

Fair price = $(12 \times 0.870) + ((100 + 12) \times 0.756) = £95.11$

Since the market price is £95, the bond is worth buying.

(b) *Stock 2*:

Fair price = $(8 \times 0.870) + ((110 + 8) \times 0.756) = £96.17$

Since the market price is £95, this bond is also worth buying.

2 The answer to this question can be found by referring to Exhibit 5.3.

3 (a) (i) If converted now: $3.20 \times 25 =$ £80.00

If sold in the market: £93.00

(ii) Convert in two years:

expected share price = $3.20 \times 1.14^2 =$ £4.16

value if converted = $25 \times 4.16 =$ £104.00

present value = $104 \times 0.797 =$ £82.89

interest received = $10 \times 1.690 =$ £16.90

total present value = $82.89 + 16.90 =$ £99.79

(iii) If held until maturity: $(10 \times 5.650) + (100 \times 0.322) = £88.70$

On these figures, the investor will convert in two years since this gives the greatest present value of returns.

(b) In explaining the importance of the distinction between convertibles and warrants to investors, the following points could be discussed.

- With a warrant, the bondholder keeps the original loan stock, whereas with a convertible the loan stock must be given up if conversion is chosen.

- Warrants can be detached from the underlying stock and sold, but conversion rights on convertible loan stock are not detachable.

- Both warrants and convertibles allow investors to participate in the future growth of the company.

- Warrants entitle the holder to obtain shares whether or not any loan stock is held. The right to convert is only held if the stock is held.

- Because of the gearing effect of warrants, they can be used for speculative investment in return for a small outlay.

4 The answer to this question is contained in Sections 5.8.2 and 5.8.3.

5 The appropriate discount rate is the after-tax cost of borrowing, which is 14% × (1 − 0.30) = 9.8% ≈ 10%.

Leasing:

Year	Cash flow	£	10% discount factor	Present value (£)
1–3	Lease payments	(320)	2.487	(795.84)
2–4	Tax savings	96.0	(3.170 − 0.909) = 2.261	217.06
				(578.78)

Buying (assuming Turner is not tax exhausted):

Year	Cash flow	£	10% discount factor	Present value (£)
0	Purchase	(1000)	1.000	(1000)
2	Tax saving	75.00	0.826	61.95
3	Tax saving	56.25	0.751	42.24
4	Tax saving	168.75	0.683	115.26
				(780.55)

The cost of leasing is £587.78 and the cost of borrowing is £780.55 so Turner should lease rather than buy the machine.

Chapter 6 Answers to self-test questions

1 The payback method cannot be recommended as the main method used by a company to assess potential investment projects because it has serious disadvantages. These include the following:

- payback ignores the time value of money;
- payback ignores the timing of cash flows within the payback period;
- payback ignores post-payback cash flows;
- the choice of payback period is arbitrary;
- payback does not measure profitability.

2 *Project A*

Average annual accounting profit = $(13\,000 - 10\,000)/4 = £750$

Average annual investment = $10\,000/2 = £5000$

Return on capital employed = $(750 \times 100)/5000 = 15\%$

Project B

Average annual accounting profit = $(30\,000 \times 15\,000)/5 = £3000$

Average annual investment = $15\,000/2 = £7500$

Return on capital employed = $(3000 \times 100)/7500 = 40\%$

Project C

Average annual accounting profit = $(24\,000 - 20\,000)/4 = £1000$

Average annual investment = $20\,000/2 = £10\,000$

Return on capital employed = $(1000 \times 100)/10\,000 = 10\%$

Project	ROCE(%)	Ranking
A	15	2
B	40	1
C	10	3

If the target ROCE is 12 per cent, projects A and B will be accepted.

3 The shortcomings of return on capital employed (ROCE) as an investment appraisal method are: it ignores the time value of money; it ignores the timing of cash flows; it uses accounting profits rather than cash flows; and it does not take account of the size of the initial investment. However, ROCE gives an answer as a percentage return, which is a familiar measure of return, and is a simple method to apply. It can be used to compare mutually exclusive projects, and can also indicate whether a project is a 'good' one compared to a target ROCE. For these reasons, it is used quite widely in industry.

4 *Project A*

Year	Cash flow (£)	12% discount factor	Present value (£)
0	(10 000)	1.000	(10 000)
1	5 000	0.893	4 465
2	5 000	0.797	3 985
3	2 000	0.712	1 424
4	1 000	0.636	636
		Net present value	510

Project B

Year	Cash flow (£)	12% discount factor	Present value (£)
0	(15 000)	1.000	(15 000)
1	5 000	0.893	4 465
2	5 000	0.797	3 985
3	5 000	0.712	3 560
4	10 000	0.636	6 360
5	5 000	0.567	2 835
		Net present value	6 205

Project C

Year	Cash flow (£)	12% discount factor	Present value (£)
0	(20 000)	1.000	(20 000)
1	10 000	0.893	8 930
2	10 000	0.797	7 970
3	4 000	0.712	2 848
4	2 000	0.636	1 272
		Net present value	1 020

Summary

Project	NPV (£)	Ranking
A	510	3
B	6205	1
C	1020	2

Since all three projects have a positive NPV, they are all acceptable.

5 The advantages of the net present value method of investment appraisal are that it:

- takes account of the time value of money;
- takes account of the amount and timing of cash flows;
- uses cash flows rather than accounting profit;
- takes account of all relevant cash flows over the life of the project;
- can take account of both conventional and non-conventional cash flows;
- can take account of changes in discount rate during the life of the project;
- gives an absolute rather than a relative measure of the desirability of the project;
- can be used to compare all investment projects.

6 If an investment project has positive and negative cash flows in successive periods (non-conventional cash flows), it may have more than one internal rate of return. This may result in incorrect decisions being taken if the IRR decision rule is applied. The NPV method has no difficulty in accommodating non-conventional cash flows.

7 There is no conflict between the NPV and IRR methods when they are applied to a single investment project with conventional cash flows. In other situations, the two methods may give conflicting results. In all cases where this conflict occurs, the project with the highest NPV should be chosen. This can be proven by examining the incremental cash flows of the projects concerned. The reason for the conflict between the two methods can also be viewed graphically.

8 The answer to this question is contained in Section 6.4.

9 If a company is restricted in the capital available for investment, it will not be able to undertake all projects with a positive NPV and is in a capital rationing situation. Capital rationing may be either soft (owing to internal factors) or hard (owing to external factors). Soft capital rationing may arise if management adopts a policy of stable growth, is reluctant to issue new equity or wishes to avoid raising new debt capital. It may also arise if management wants to encourage competition for funds. Hard capital rationing may arise because the capital markets are depressed or because investors consider the company to be too risky.

10 If projects are divisible and independent, they can be ranked by using the profitability index or cost–benefit ratio. If projects are not divisible, then combinations of projects must be examined to find the investment schedule giving the highest NPV.

Chapter 6   Answers to questions for review

1 (a) *Payback*

$$A = 5 + (500/900) = 5.5 \text{ years}$$
$$B = 5 + (500/1200) = 5.4 \text{ years}$$
$$C = 2 + (1000/2000) = 2.5 \text{ years}$$

Net present value

$NPV_A = (-5000) + (900 \times 6.145) = (-5000) + 5530.5 = £530.5$

NPV_B is calculated as follows:

Year	Cash flow (£)	10% discount factor	Present value (£)
0	(5000)	1.000	(5000)
1	700	0.909	636
2	800	0.826	661
3	900	0.751	676
4	1000	0.683	683
5	1100	0.621	683
6	1200	0.564	677
7	1300	0.513	667
8	1400	0.467	654
9	1500	0.424	636
10	1600	0.386	618
			1591

$NPV_C = (-5000) + (2000 \times 2.487) + (1000 \times 0.683) = £657$

Internal rate of return

If $NPV_A = 0$, present value factor of IRR over 10 years $= 5000/900 = 5.556$

From tables, IRR $\approx 12.5\%$

IRR_B

Year	Cash flow (£)	10% discount factor	Present value (£)	20% discount factor	Present value (£)
0	(5000)	1.000	(5000)	1.000	(5000)
1	700	0.909	636	0.833	583
2	800	0.826	661	0.694	555
3	900	0.751	676	0.579	521
4	1000	0.683	683	0.482	482
5	1100	0.621	683	0.402	442
6	1200	0.564	677	0.335	402
7	1300	0.513	667	0.279	363
8	1400	0.467	654	0.233	326
9	1500	0.424	636	0.194	291
10	1600	0.386	618	0.162	259
			1591		(776)

Interpolating: $IRR_B = 10 + \dfrac{1591 \times 10}{(1591 + 776)} = 10 + 6.72 = 16.72\%$

IRR_C

Year	Cash flow ($£$)	15% discount factor	Present value ($£$)	18% discount factor	Present value ($£$)
0	(5000)	1.000	(5000)	1.000	(5000)
1	2000	0.870	1740	0.847	1694
2	2000	0.756	1512	0.718	1436
3	2000	0.658	1316	0.609	1218
4	1000	0.572	572	0.516	516
			140		(136)

Interpolating: $IRR_C = 15 + \dfrac{140 \times 3}{(140 + 136)} = 15 + 1.52 = 16.52\%$

Return on capital employed

$ROCE_A$:

Average capital employed = 5000/2 = £2500

Average accounting profit = (9000 − 5000)/10 = £400

$ROCE_A$ = (400 × 100)/2500 = 16%

$ROCE_B$:

Average accounting profit = (11 500 − 5000)/10 = £650

$ROCE_B$ = (650 × 100)/2500 = 26%

$ROCE_C$:

Average accounting profit = (7000 − 5000)/4 = £500

$ROCE_C$ = (500 × 100)/2500 = 20%

Summary of results

Project	A	B	C
Payback (years)	5.5	5.4	2.5
ROCE (%)	16	26	20
IRR (%)	12.5	16.7	16.5
NPV (£)	530.5	1591	657

(b) *Comparison of rankings*

Method	Payback	ROCE	IRR	NPV
1	C	B	B	B
2	B	C	C	C
3	A	A	A	A

Given that Project B comes top of three of the four investment appraisal methods, including, most importantly, the NPV method, it is this project that should be accepted.

2 Summary of answers:

	Project Alpha	Project Beta
Payback	2.8 years	3.2 years
NPV	£142 000	£210 000
IRR	25%	20%
ROCE	33%	25%

Project Beta appears to be preferable, as it has the higher NPV.

3 The first step is to work out the net cash flows:

Contribution = $(3.00 - 1.75) \times 50\,000 = £62\,500$

Fixed costs = $40\,000 - (125\,000 - 30\,000)/5 = £21\,000$

Year	Capital (£)	Contribution (£)	Fixed costs (£)	Adverts (£)	Net cash flow (£)
0	(100 000)				(100 000)
1	(25 000)	62 500	(21 000)	(10 000)	6 500
2		62 500	(21 000)	(15 000)	26 500
3		62 500	(21 000)		41 500
4		62 500	(21 000)		41 500
5	30 000	62 500	(21 000)		71 500

The net cash flows can now be discounted to find the net present value.

Year	Net cash flow (£)	10% discount factor	Present value (£)
0	(100 000)	1.000	(100 000)
1	6 500	0.909	5 909
2	26 500	0.826	21 889
3	41 500	0.751	31 167
4	41 500	0.683	28 345
5	71 500	0.621	44 402
			31 712

The net present value of the project is £31 712.

4 (a) NPV of Project A:

Year	Cash flow (£m)	PV factors	PV (£m)
0	(150)	1	(150)
1	40	0.893	35.7
2	50	0.797	39.9
3	60	0.712	42.7
4	60	0.636	38.2
5	80	0.567	45.4
		NPV	51.9

NPV of Project B:

Year	Cash flow (£m)	PV factors	PV (£m)
0	(152)	1	(152)
1	80	0.893	71.4
2	60	0.797	47.8
3	50	0.712	35.6
4	40	0.636	25.4
5	30	0.567	17.0
		NPV	45.2

Using the NPV, Project A is preferred as it has the higher NPV.

(b) IRR_A: NPV @ 20% = £15.9m
Therefore IRR = 12% + ((20% − 12%) × 51.9)/(51.9 − 15.9) = 23.5%
IRR_B: NPV @ 20% = £16.6m
Therefore IRR = 12% + ((20% − 12%) × 45.2)/(45.2 − 16.6) = 24.6%

Using IRR, Project B is preferred as it has the higher IRR.

(c) Revised Year 5 PV for Project A = 80 × 0.530 = £42.4m
Revised NPV for Project A = 51.9 − 45.4 + 42.4 = £48.9m
Revised Year 5 PV for Project B = 30 × 0.530 = £15.9m
Revised NPV for Project B = 45.2 − 17.0 + 15.9 = £44.1m

A decision based on IRR would not change as IRR ignores changes in the cost of capital.
Project A would still be recommended using NPV, rather than Project B, as it has the higher NPV.

5 Net present values of the different projects:

$NPV_A = -1000 + (3000 \times 0.467) = £401$
$NPV_B = -800 + (200 \times 0.909) + (300 \times 0.826) + \cdots = £451$
$NPV_C = -750 + (300 \times 3.791) = £387$
$NPV_D = -500 + (150 \times 4.868) = £230$
$NPV_E = -800 + (350 \times (4.868 - 0.909)) = £586$

Project	A	B	C	D	E
Profitability index	1.401	1.564	1.516	1.462	1.732

(a) Non-capital rationing situation: accept all projects.

(b) Projects are divisible and only £2500 is available:
Investment schedule: £800 in project E
£800 in project B
£750 in project C
£150 in project D
Total NPV = £1493

(c) Projects are indivisible and only £2500 is available:
Investment schedule: £800 in project E
£800 in project B
£750 in project C

Total NPV = £1424
Surplus funds = £150

Chapter 7   Answers to self-test questions

1 The cash flows which are relevant to an investment appraisal calculation are those which will arise or change as a result of undertaking the investment project. Direct costs incurred, such as purchased raw materials, are relevant, as are changes in existing cash flows (incremental cash flows), such as additional fixed costs. The opportunity cost of labour and raw materials which have alternative uses may be a relevant cost. Tax liabilities are also relevant.

2 The answer to this question can be found by referring to Section 7.2.1 and Exhibit 7.1.

3 The real cost of capital can be found by deflating the nominal (or money terms) cost of capital. Nominal project cash flows can be obtained by inflating estimated cash flows to take account of inflation which is specific to particular costs and revenues. Real project cash flows can be obtained by deflating nominal project cash flows to take account of general inflation. The NPV of the project can then be found either by discounting nominal cash flows by the nominal cost of capital (the nominal or money terms approach) or by discounting real cash flows by the real cost of capital (the real terms approach). The NPV will have the same value whichever method is used.

4 Evaluating investment projects is made more difficult by the existence of inflation. While it may be possible to forecast general inflation into the near future, it is much harder to forecast specific inflation rates for individual costs and revenues. If specific inflation forecasts can be obtained and used, it is likely that the evaluation of an investment project will be more accurate than if account were taken only of general inflation. The incremental benefit of this increased accuracy would need to be weighed against the cost of obtaining and processing the necessary data, however. Failure to take account of inflation at all might lead to unrealistic estimates of the value of an investment project.

5 The answer to this question can be found by referring to the discussion at the start of Section 7.4, focusing on the relationship between risk and the variability of returns.

6 Sensitivity analysis examines how responsive the project's NPV is to changes in the variables from which it has been calculated. There are two methods: in the first, variables are changed by a set amount and the NPV is recalculated; in the second, the amounts by which individual variables would have to change to make the project's NPV become zero are determined. In both methods, only one variable is changed at a time.

Both methods give an indication of the key variables within the project. These variables may merit further investigation and indicate where management should focus attention in order to ensure the success of the project. However, sensitivity analysis gives no indication of whether changes in key variables are likely to occur, or are even possible.

7 Several recent surveys have shown that payback is widely used in practice. Drury et al. (1993) showed that 63 per cent of firms surveyed used it often or always. However, their survey also indicated that only 14 per cent of firms used the payback method exclusively and did not combine it with a method that took account of the time value of money. More recently, Arnold and Hatzopoulos (2000) found that 68 per cent of all companies used payback in conjunction with one or more investment appraisal methods. The reasons why payback is commonly used to deal with risk in investment projects are as follows:

- it is a useful test for companies concerned about short-term liquidity;
- it focuses attention on the short term, which is more certain and hence less risky than the long term;
- it guards against unforeseen changes in economic circumstances.

8 The answer to this question can be found by referring to Section 7.4.4.

9 The answer to this question can be found by referring to Section 7.4.6.

10 The answer to this question can be found by referring to Section 7.5.

Chapter 7 Answers to questions for review

1 (a) 100 per cent first-year capital allowances available:

Year	Capital (£)	Tax saving (£)	Net cash flow (£)	8% discount factor	Present value (£)
0	(100 000)		(100 000)	1.000	(100 000)
2		30 000	30 000	0.857	25 710
					(71 290)

The present value of the cost of borrowing is £71 290.

(b) Straight-line basis capital allowances over life of asset:

Year	Capital (£)	Tax saving (£)	Net cash flow (£)	8% discount factor	Present value (£)
0	(100 000)		(100 000)	1.000	(100 000)
2		7 500	7 500	0.857	6 428
3		7 500	7 500	0.794	5 955
4		7 500	7 500	0.735	5 513
5		7 500	7 500	0.681	5 108
					(76 996)

The present value of the cost of borrowing is £76 996.

(c) 25 per cent reducing balance capital allowances, zero scrap value:

Year	Capital (£)	Tax saving (£)	Net cash flow (£)	8% discount factor	Present value (£)
0	(100 000)		(100 000)	1.000	(100 000)
2		7 500	7 500	0.857	6 428
3		5 625	5 625	0.794	4 466
4		4 219	4 219	0.735	3 101
5		12 656	12 656	0.681	8 619
					(77 386)

The present value of the cost of borrowing is £77 386.

2. *Machine A:*

Year	0 (£000)	1 (£000)	2 (£000)	3 (£000)	4 (£000)	5 (£000)	6 (£000)
Additional sales		116.60	123.60	131.01	138.87	147.20	
Labour costs		(10.50)	(11.03)	(11.58)	(12.16)	(12.76)	
Power costs		(9.27)	(9.55)	(9.83)	(10.13)	(10.43)	
Net operating cash flow		96.83	103.02	109.60	116.58	124.01	
Capital allowances		(50.00)	(37.50)	(28.13)	(21.09)	(63.28)	
Net taxable cash flow		46.83	65.52	81.47	95.49	60.73	
Taxation			(14.05)	(19.66)	(24.44)	(28.65)	(18.22)
Add back capital allowances		50.00	37.50	28.13	21.09	63.28	
Capital	(200)						
Net project cash flows	(200)	96.83	88.97	89.95	92.14	95.36	(18.22)
Discount factors	1.000	0.870	0.756	0.658	0.572	0.497	0.432
Discounted cash flows	(200)	84.24	67.26	59.18	52.70	47.39	(7.87)
Net present value, m/c A	102.90						

The NPV for machine A is £102 900.

Machine B:

Year	0 (£000)	1 (£000)	2 (£000)	3 (£000)	4 (£000)	5 (£000)	6 (£000)
Additional sales		116.60	123.60	131.01	138.87	147.20	
Labour costs		(7.35)	(7.72)	(8.10)	(8.51)	(8.93)	
Power costs		(4.12)	(4.24)	(4.37)	(4.50)	(4.64)	
Net operating cash flow		105.13	111.64	118.54	125.86	133.63	
Capital allowances		(62.50)	(46.88)	(35.16)	(26.37)	(54.09)	
Net taxable cash flow		42.63	64.76	83.38	99.49	79.54	
Taxation			(12.79)	(19.43)	(25.01)	(29.85)	(23.86)
Add back capital allowances		62.50	46.88	35.16	26.37	54.09	
Capital	(250)					25.00	
Net project cash flows	(250)	105.13	98.85	99.11	100.85	128.78	(23.86)
Discount factors	1.000	0.870	0.756	0.658	0.572	0.497	0.432
Discounted cash flows	(250)	91.46	74.73	65.21	57.69	64.00	(10.31)
Net present value, m/c B	92.78						

The NPV for machine B is £92 780. Machine A should be chosen as it has a higher NPV.

3 (a) The worst likely return is £10000 per annum for five years.

10 000 × 3.791 = £37 910. This has a probability of 12%.

The best possibility is £50 000 per annum for seven years.

50 000 × 4.868 = £243 400. This has a probability of 12%.

(b) £10 000 per year for five years = 10 000 × 3.791 = £37 910

Probability = 0.2 × 0.6 = 12%, so EV = 37 910 × 0.12 = £4549

£10 000 per year for seven years = 10 000 × 4.868 = £48 680

Probability = 0.2 × 0.4 = 8%, so EV = 48 680 × 0.08 = £3894

£30 000 per year for five years = 30 000 × 3.791 = £113 730

Probability = 0.6 × 0.5 = 30%, so EV = 113 730 × 0.3 = £34 119

£30 000 per year for seven years = 30 000 × 4.868 = £146 040

Probability = 0.6 × 0.5 = 30%, so EV = 146 040 × 0.3 = £43 812

£50 000 per year for five years = 50 000 × 3.791 = £189 550

Probability = 0.2 × 0.4 = 8%, so EV = 189 550 × 0.08 = £15 164

£50 000 per year for seven years = 50 000 × 4.868 = £243 400

Probability = 0.2 × 0.6 = 12%, so EV = 243 400 × 0.12 = £29 208

Total EV = 4549 + 3894 + 34 119 + 43 812 + 15 164 + 29 208 = £130 746

4 (a) Try 17 per cent: $((((20\,000 \times 5) - 24\,875) \times 4.659)) - 350\,000 = 7$

Hence IRR = 17%.

(b) If cost of capital is 15 per cent, the project life giving zero NPV can be found from tables, using the cumulative present value factor of 4.659 determined while calculating the IRR. This project life is between eight and nine years, and so interpolating:

Project life = 8 + ((4.659 − 4.487)/(4.772 − 4.487)) = 8.6 years

This is a decrease of 1.4 years or 14 per cent.

(c) If sales price = S

$((((20\,000 \times (S - 3.50)) - 24\,875)) \times 5.019) - 350\,000 = 0$

Hence S = (((350 000/5.019) + 24.875)/20 000) + 3.50 = £8.23

This is a reduction of 27 pence or 3.2 per cent.

5 The answer to this question can be found in Section 7.4.

Chapter 8 Answers to self-test questions

1 Risk may be divided into systematic risk and unsystematic risk. Systematic risk refers to the extent to which a company's cash flows are affected by factors not specific to the company. It is determined by the sensitivity of the cash flows to the general level of economic activity and by its operating gearing.

Unsystematic risk refers to the extent to which a firm's cash flows are affected by company-specific factors, such as the quality of its managers, the level of its advertising, the effectiveness of its R&D and the skill of its labour.

By careful choice of the investments in a portfolio, unsystematic risk can be diversified away. Systematic risk, however, cannot be diversified away, since it is experienced by all companies. The risk of a well-diversified portfolio will be similar to the systematic risk of the market as a whole.

2 Investments may not perform as expected. In a well-diversified portfolio, investments that perform well will tend to balance those that do not, and only systematic risk will remain. The systematic risk of the portfolio will be the same as the average systematic risk of the market as a whole. If an investor wants to avoid risk altogether, he or she must invest in risk-free securities.

A company's managers may feel that shareholders' interests will be best served by spreading risk through diversification. A shareholder with a well-diversified portfolio, however, will already have eliminated unsystematic risk. For such shareholders, diversification at the company level is of no value.

For a shareholder who does not hold a well-diversified portfolio, and who has not eliminated unsystematic risk, such diversification may be of some value.

3 If the set of all possible portfolios that can be formulated from a large number of given securities is considered, there are a large number of portfolios which are the most desirable to a rational investor. These are the portfolios that offer the highest return for a given level of risk, or the lowest risk for a given level of expected return. Such portfolios are known as efficient portfolios and lie along the efficient frontier of the set of all possible portfolios in a graph of portfolio returns against portfolio risk. However, it is not possible to say which portfolio an individual investor would prefer as this would depend solely on his or her attitude to risk and return.

The efficient portfolio which is best suited to the risk–return characteristics of a particular individual investor is an optimal portfolio for that investor. It represents a tangency point of the individual investor's utility or indifference curve on the efficient frontier.

4 Risk-free assets are important to portfolio theory as they allow the market portfolio, the optimum combination of risky investments, to be identified. If a line is pivoted clockwise about the risk-free rate of return until it touches the efficient frontier, the point of tangency represents the market portfolio. The line linking the risk-free rate of return and the market portfolio is known as the capital market line. Subsequently, investors can distribute their funds between the risk-free assets and the market portfolio and move along this line. This allows investors to attain higher levels of utility compared with the situation where no risk-free assets are available and investors are limited to investing along the efficient frontier. Hence, the identification of risk-free assets is of vital importance to portfolio theory.

5 The risk-free rate is approximated in practice by using the yield on government securities such as Treasury bills. As for the capital market line, it will not be a straight line in practice because investors, while being able to lend at the risk-free rate, cannot borrow at the risk-free rate. Therefore, the CML will kink downwards to the right-hand side of the market portfolio.

6 The limitations of portfolio theory as an aid to investment are:
- the assumption that investors can borrow at the risk-free rate is unrealistic;
- transaction costs deter investors from making changes to portfolios;
- the composition of the market portfolio is difficult to determine;
- should not the market portfolio include all securities in all capital markets?
- securities are not divisible in practice;
- how can we determine the expected risks and returns of securities?
- how do investors make choices from the wide variety of possibilities?
- how can investors determine their own utility function?

7 The answer to this question can be found by referring to Section 8.5.

8 The answer to this question can be found by referring to Section 8.6.1.

9 The answer to this question can be found by referring to Section 8.6.2.

10 $R_m = 10$ per cent, $R_f = 4$ per cent, $\text{Cov}_{ls,m} = 7.5$, $\sigma_m^2 = 4.5$
$\beta_{ls} = \text{Cov}_{ls,m}/\sigma_m^2 = 7.5/4.5 = 1.67$
$E(R_{ls}) = R_f - \beta_{ls}(R_m - R_f) = 4 + (1.67 \times (10 - 4)) = 14\%$
The required rate of return on Lime Spider's shares is therefore 14 per cent.

Chapter 8   Answers to questions for review

1 If a risk-free asset is combined with a multi-asset portfolio, the best combination of risky and risk-free assets occurs along a line which begins with a portfolio containing only the risk-free asset and which is tangential to the efficient frontier of portfolios containing only risky assets. This line is called the capital market line.

The point of tangency with the efficient frontier is called the market portfolio since it contains all risky assets. This is because, if we assume that all investors make the same forecasts and therefore come to the same conclusions, all investors will choose to hold this risky portfolio. The conclusion, then, is that all investors will want to hold a slice of the market portfolio, in combination with the risk-free asset. The number of shares that an individual investor needs to hold in order to have a well-diversified portfolio is only about twenty. It is therefore practical for an individual investor to obtain an efficient portfolio which maximises their utility. The optimal portfolio for the investor will be located on the capital market line at the point of tangency with the investor's personal utility curve.

Portfolio theory therefore provides a framework for the investor to construct a market portfolio that diversifies away unsystematic risk and then, by combining the market portfolio with the risk-free asset, maximises utility.

2 (a) Return of X alone $= (30 \times 0.3) + (25 \times 0.4) + (20 \times 0.3)$
$= 9 + 10 + 6 = 25\%$

Return of Y alone = $(50 \times 0.2) + (30 \times 0.6) + (10 \times 0.2)$
$$= 10 + 18 + 2 = 30\%$$

Return of 60% X and 40% Y = $(0.6 \times 25) + (0.4 \times 30) = 15 + 12 = 27\%$

(b) Risk can be measured by the standard deviation of the returns.

Standard deviation of X			
Probability	Return (%)	$(R_i - \overline{R})$	$P_i \times (R_i - \overline{R})^2$
0.3	30	5	7.5
0.4	25	0	0.0
0.3	20	−5	7.5
			15.0

The standard deviation of X = $\sqrt{15}$ = 3.873%

Standard deviation of Y			
Probability	Return (%)	$(R_i - \overline{R})$	$P_i \times (R_i - \overline{R})^2$
0.2	50	20	80
0.6	30	0	0
0.2	10	−20	80
			160

The standard deviation of Y = $\sqrt{160}$ = 12.649%

Standard deviation of 60% X and 40% Y:

Using the portfolio theory expression for σ_P as follows:

$\sigma_P = [(0.6^2 \times 15) + (0.4^2 \times 160) + (2 \times 0.6 \times 0.4 \times 3.873 \times 12.649 \times 0.15)]^{1/2}$
$= [5.4 + 25.6 + 3.527]^{1/2} = 5.876\%$

3 (a) The portfolio beta is the weighted average of the individual security betas.

Share	No. shares	Share price (£)	Market value (£)		Beta	Weighted beta
Rasiak	70 000	3.75	262 500	×	1.27	0.1697
Johnson	150 000	4.25	637 500	×	1.53	0.4964
Smith	100 000	2.50	250 000	×	1.01	0.1285
Bisgaard	80 000	4.50	360 000	×	0.95	0.1740
Idiakez	130 000	3.50	455 000	×	0.82	0.1899
			1 965 000			1.1585

Since β_p = 1.16 and so is greater than 1, the portfolio is riskier than the market.

(b) We need to compare the returns predicted by the CAPM with expected returns (*see* table below). Shares with expected returns less than those predicted by their betas are underperforming and should be disposed of.

Company	Beta	E(R$_j$)%	E(R)%	E(R) – E(R$_j$)%	Advice
Rasiak	1.27	13.89	12.0	(1.89)	Sell
Johnson	1.53	15.71	16.0	0.29	Hold
Smith	1.01	12.07	14.0	1.93	Hold
Bisgaard	0.95	11.65	9.5	(2.15)	Sell
Idiakez	0.82	10.74	15.0	4.26	Buy

4. (a) First we need to find the current return of the market:

FTSE 100 return = $((5153 - 4753)/4753) + 4.55\% = 12.97\%$

The risk-free rate, R$_f$, can be approximated by using the current yield on short-dated

Treasury bills, e.g. 3.78%

For Aardvark:
Required return (R$_j$) = $3.78 + (1.3 \times (12.97 - 3.78)) = 15.72\%$
Actual return = $(224 - 201)/201 + (8/201) = 15.42\%$
Here the actual return of the share is very close to the required return so a *hold* decision would be appropriate.

For Bear:
Required return (R$_j$) = $3.78 + (0.87 \times (12.97 - 3.78)) = 11.77\%$
Actual return = $(307 - 260)/260 + (9/260) = 21.53\%$
Here the actual return of the share is greater than the required return so a *buy* decision would be appropriate.

(b) There are a number of potential problems associated with using the analysis in part (a) to make portfolio management decisions. These include the following:

- Taking one period to calculate the market return is subject to error – a rolling average would iron out any short-term fluctuations in the index.
- Does the FTSE 100 represent the market return accurately?
- The reliability of the estimate of the risk-free rate may be questioned.
- The accuracy of the equity betas used may be suspect – they may also be unstable over time.
- The fact that the rates for the actual return on the shares are calculated over a single discrete time period can lead to problems. The investor may have purchased the shares a year earlier when the share price was higher.

Answers to self-test questions

1 Market value of equity, $E = 500\,000 \times 1.50 = £750\,000$
Market value of debt, $D = $ nil
Cost of equity capital, $K_e = $ dividend/market value of share $= 27/150 = 0.18$
Since there is no debt capital, WACC $= K_e = 18\%$

2 $K_d = 12/94 = 12.8\%$
K_d (after tax) $= 12.8 \times (1 - 0.3) = 9.0\%$

3 $E = 1\,000\,000 \times 0.49 = £490\,000$
$D = 100\,000 \times 72/100 = £72\,000$
$K_e = 9/49 = 0.1837$ and so K_e is 18.37%
$K_d = $ Interest/Market value $= 10/72 = 0.1389$ and so K_d is 13.89%

$$WACC = ((K_e \times E) + (K_d \times D(1 - t)))/(E + D)$$
$$= ((18.37 \times 490\,000) + (13.89 \times 72\,000 \times 0.7))/562\,000$$
$$= 17.3\%$$

4 When we mention the WACC in this context, we can assume we are talking about an historical WACC, i.e. one referring to the cost of funds already raised. There are certain conditions that must be met in order for it to be appropriate to use a historical cost of capital to appraise new projects, as follows:

■ The new project must have a similar level of business risk to the average business risk of a company's existing projects.

■ The amount of finance needed for the new project must be small relative to the amount of finance already raised.

■ The company must be intending to finance the new project by using a similar financing mix to its historical financing mix.

5 The asset beta is the weighted average of the betas of equity and debt. Since the simplifying assumption is made that the beta of debt is zero, but the market value of debt is non-zero, the asset beta will always be lower than the equity beta unless the company is all-equity financed.

6 The answer is (c). This company will have the highest level of *financial* risk due to the high level of gearing and the highest level of *business risk*, given the nature of the building material industry.

7 The answer is (c). The total risk of a company can be split into unsystematic and systematic risk. The company in question may have a very high level of specific risk but only a low level of systematic risk and hence a low equity beta.

8 Currently, $\beta_e = 1.30$, $D = 0.25$, $E = 0.75$

$$\text{Hence: } \beta_a = \beta_e \times (E/(E + D(1 - C_T)))$$
$$= 1.30 \times 0.75/(0.75 + (0.25 \times 0.7))$$
$$= 0.975/0.9125 = 1.0541$$

If, now, $D = 0.33$ and $E = 0.67$ then:

$$\beta_e = \beta_a \times (1 + (D(1 - t)/E)) = 1.0541 \times 1.345 = 1.42$$

The new equity beta is therefore 1.42.

9 The correct answer is (c). If capital markets are perfect and taxation does not exist, we are in a world corresponding to Miller and Modigliani's first model. As the company increases its level of debt, the increase in the cost of its equity finance will be exactly offset by increasing amounts of cheaper debt finance.

10 Here we are assuming that the world of Miller and Modigliani's first paper exists. Therefore the two companies should have similar WACCs. Because York is all-equity financed, its WACC is the same as its cost of equity finance, i.e. 16 per cent. It follows that Johnson should have a WACC equal to 16 per cent also.
Therefore: $(1/3 \times 10\%) + (2/3 \times K_e) = 16\%$
Hence: $K_e = 19\%$

11 The answer is (c). The traditional approach does *not* assume perfect markets and therefore recognises the existence of bankruptcy risk. This is reflected in the upward slope of the cost of debt curve and the steepening of the cost of equity curve at high levels of gearing.

12 The answer depends on how the company has been financed.

- If the company is financed mainly from short-term sources, it cannot ignore an increase in interest rates and may choose to switch to long-term financing. This will be at a higher rate and profitability will be diminished.
- If the company is financed mainly from long-term sources, an increase in interest rates will not affect its profits directly. However, higher interest rates may depress economic activity and its profits may fall accordingly.
- If the company is financed mainly from retained earnings or equity, an increase in the required return of shareholders will lead to pressure for higher dividends. The company may have insufficient funds to meet such demands.

13 The traditional theory of capital structure proposes that an optimal capital exists, and so under this theory a company can increase its total value by the sensible use of gearing. The traditional theory argues that:

- K_e rises with increased gearing due to the increasing financial and bankruptcy risk;
- K_d rises only at high gearing levels when bankruptcy risk increases;
- replacing more expensive equity finance with less expensive debt finance decreases the company's WACC, up to a point;
- once an optimum level of gearing is reached, K_e increases by a rate which more than offsets the effect of using cheaper debt, and so the WACC increases.

14 Miller and Modigliani argued that the weighted average cost of capital remains unchanged at all levels of gearing. The value of a company is dependent on expected performance and commercial risk and so its market value, and hence its cost of capital, are independent of its capital structure. The cost of equity K_e increases in such a manner that it exactly offsets the use of cheaper debt finance, and so the WACC is constant. This can be demonstrated through the arbitrage proof. Arbitrage prevents the possibility of perfect substitutes selling at different prices, and two companies identical except for their capital structures are, for Miller and Modigliani, perfect substitutes. Using the assumption that individuals and companies can borrow at the same rate, they demonstrated how arbitrage would cause the WACC of two such companies to become identical through the buying and selling actions of investors.

Chapter 9 Answers to questions for review

1 $K_e = (7 \times (1 + 0.08)/49) + 0.08 = 0.1543 + 0.08 = 0.2343 \approx 23\%$
$K_p = D_P/P_0 = (0.075 \times 50)/32 = 0.1172 \approx 12\%$
$K_d = I/P_0 = (0.1 \times 100)/92 = 0.1087 \approx 11\%$

A market-based weighting is preferred to one based on book values.

	£
$E = 1\,000\,000 \times 0.49 =$	490 000
$E_p = 250\,000 \times 0.32 =$	80 000
$D = 100\,000 \times 0.92 =$	92 000
	662 000

$$\text{WACC} = [(23 \times 490) + (12 \times 80) + (11 \times (1 - 0.30) \times 92)]/662$$
$$= 19.5\%$$

2 Capital gearing can be determined as (Debt/(Equity + Debt))

(a) Using book values, capital gearing $= (9000/13\,000) \times 100 = 69\%$

(b) Market value of equity $= (4m/0.5) \times 3.50 = £28m$
Market value of debt $= 9m \times 1.12 = £10.08m$
Using market values, capital gearing $= (10.08/38.08) \times 100 = 26.5\%$

A market-based determination of gearing is generally considered to be superior to an estimate based on book values because:

■ book values are historical cost values and so are likely to be out of date;

■ book values reflect decisions taken long ago and may not be relevant;

■ market values reflect current evaluations of the risk of the company;

■ market values reflect current required returns in the capital markets.

3 *Supertronic plc*
$\beta_a = \beta_g \times (E/(E + D(1 - t)))$
$\beta_a = 1.33 \times 0.5/(0.5 + (0.5 \times 0.7))$
$\quad = 0.665/0.85 = 0.782$

Electroland plc

$\beta_a = \beta_g \times (E/(E + D(1 - t)))$

$\beta_a = 1.30 \times 0.6/(0.6 + (0.4 \times 0.7))$

$\quad = 0.78/0.88 = 0.886$

But $\beta_a = 0.886 = (0.8 \times \beta_{a1}) + (0.2 \times \beta_{a2})$

$\quad = (0.8 \times \beta_{a1}) + (0.2 \times 1.4)$

Hence $\beta_{a1} = (0.886 - 0.28)/0.8 = 0.758$

Transelectro plc

$\beta_a = \beta_g \times (E/(E + D(1 - t)))$

$\beta_a = 1.05 \times 0.65/(0.65 + (0.35 \times 0.7))$

$\quad = 0.6825/0.895 = 0.763$

Average proxy asset beta:

$(0.782 + 0.758 + 0.763)/3 = 2.303/3 = 0.768$

Regearing: $\beta_g = \beta_g \times (1 + (D(1 - t)/E))$

$\quad\quad\quad\quad = 0.768 \times (1 + ((0.3 \times 0.7)/0.7))$

$\quad\quad\quad\quad = 0.768 + 1.2786 = 0.998$

$$E(R_i) = R_f + \beta_g (R_m - R_f) = 10 + (0.998 \times (14 - 10)) = 14\%$$

Since the expected return of the project of 18 per cent is greater than the calculated required rate of return, the project should be accepted.

4 First, Kitson should sell his £1000 of shares in Short and borrow enough funds to copy the gearing ratio of Short. Short's gearing ratio is 2000/8000 = 25 per cent, so Kitson should borrow £333, making his gearing 333/1333 = 25 per cent.

The next stage is to invest all the £1333 in Carbon's shares and compare the returns before and after the change.

New dividend income with Carbon shares:

Return: 500 000 × (1333/3 125 000) =	£213.28
Interest on borrowings: 10% of £333 =	(£33.30)
Net return:	£179.98

Old return with Short shares:

Return: 1 000 000 × (1000/6 000 000) =	£166.67

Therefore Kitson makes a net profit of £13.31 on the transaction.

5 *Option (a)*. Income of £2000 is distributed to shareholders who require a return of 9 per cent. The market value of equity is therefore 2000/0.09 = £22 222.

Option (b). Interest on debt of 5000 × 3% = £150 is paid, so dividends to shareholders are 2000 − 150 = £1850. Since the required return of shareholders is 10 per cent, the market value of equity is 1850/0.10 = £18 500. Since the market value of debt is £5000, the total value of the company is 18 500 + 5000 = £23 500.

Option (c). Interest on debt of $9000 \times 6\% = £540$ is paid, so dividends to shareholders are $2000 - 540 = £1460$. Since the required return of shareholders is 13 per cent, the market value of equity is $1460/0.13 = £11\,231$. As the market value of debt is £9000, the total value of the company is $11\,231 + 9000 = £20\,231$.

Since the value of the company is greatest under option (b), this represents the optimal financing choice.

6 There are a number of problems that will be encountered when trying to calculate a WACC for a company.

■ How do we find the cost of equity? There are two alternatives – the dividend growth model and the CAPM – both of which have potential drawbacks.

■ How do we find the cost of debt? Companies have many forms of debt, and company accounts do not always give the appropriate interest that they are paying, for example to their bank. In addition, the maturity date of the debt may not be specified or it may have split redemption dates.

■ The market values of debt and equity may be hard to find. For example, some forms of debt may be tradable, but may not have a continuously trading market, whereas other forms of debt may not be traded.

■ Some debt instruments, for example convertibles and floating rate debt, are rather complex and it may not be possible to find their cost or market value.

■ Should short-term debt be included in the WACC calculation or is it a working capital issue?

■ Company balance sheets may further be complicated by the use of non-sterling debt or currency and interest rate swaps.

7 Problems that could have been discussed in connection with applying the CAPM in investment appraisal include:

■ determining the excess market return;

■ determining the risk-free rate of return;

■ estimation of the equity and overall betas for a company;

■ determination of the beta for a project;

■ the CAPM is a single-period model;

■ the CAPM is an ex-ante model;

■ national surrogates for market return may be internationally inappropriate.

Chapter 10 Answers to self-test questions

1 The answer to this question can be found by referring to Section 10.1.

2 The correct answer is (e). The argument that shareholders could manufacture their own dividends by selling off part of their shareholding was used by Miller and Modigliani in 1961 to argue that the dividend policy of a company was irrelevant. All of the other points can be used to support a case for dividends having an effect on the value of the equity shares of a company.

3 First, convert the share price to ex-dividend: $P_0 = £3.45 - 20p = £3.25$

Using the dividend growth model:

$$£3.25 = (0.20 \times (1 + g)/(0.15 - g))$$

Rearranging:

$$g = 0.2875/3.45 = 8.33\%$$

4 Calculating the cost of equity:

$$K_e = D_0/P_0 = 30/200 = 15\%$$

Value in year 3 of dividend of 40p per year paid in perpetuity $= 40/0.15 = 267.7p$.

Discounting back to the current time: $P_0 = 267.67/(1.15)^3 = 175.3p$

The share price has dropped by $200 - 175.3 = 24.7p$

Option (a) is therefore the correct answer.

5 Option (a) is the correct response. Companies like to keep nominal dividends increasing steadily or, at worst, when profits decrease, to maintain the nominal dividend paid in the previous period.

6,7 Here the discussion should centre around the fact that Miller and Modigliani's assumptions are simplifications of the real world. These assumptions, while not mirroring the real world, do not totally invalidate the model. Given these assumptions, the conclusions made by the model are perfectly logical. The nature of some of the assumptions only weakens the conclusions of the model without actually invalidating the model.

8 Clearly, an increase in institutional share ownership has concentrated control of UK companies. This fact, coupled with the fact that institutional investors require a regular dividend stream from their investments, has led the institutional investors to become involved in trying to influence the dividend policy of companies.

9 (a) *Residual theory of dividends*: dividends may be paid out if the capital investment needs of the company are fully met and there are funds left over. While corporate profits are cyclical, capital investment plans involve long-term commitment, so it follows that dividends may be used to take up the slack.

　　　Financial managers cannot follow both a policy of stable dividends and a policy of long-term commitment to capital investment, unless they are willing to raise new finance in times of need to achieve both. Given the objective of shareholder wealth maximisation, if a company can invest in profitable projects and earn a higher return than shareholders could in their alternative investment opportunities, then shareholders should be willing to subscribe new equity finance.

　　(b) *Clientele effect*: this term refers to the argument that companies attract particular types of shareholder due to their dividend decisions. It states that companies establish a track record for paying a certain level of dividend and that shareholders recognise this. Because of their shareholders' preferences, companies find it difficult to change their dividend policies suddenly.

(c) *Signalling properties of dividends*: with asymmetry of information, dividends can be seen as signals from the company's managers to shareholders and the financial markets. With some exceptions, empirical studies show that dividends convey some new information to the market.

(d) *The 'bird in the hand' argument*: this arises from the existence of uncertainty. If the future were certain and there were no transaction costs, potential dividends retained by a company for the purpose of investment would lead to share price increases reflecting increases in wealth. With uncertainty, however, risk-averse investors are not indifferent to the division of earnings into dividends and capital gains in the share price.

Chapter 10 Answers to questions for review

1 You could have discussed the following factors:

- the need to remain profitable;
- the company's liquidity position;
- the ease with which the company can access further sources of finance;
- investors' preference for a stable dividend policy.

2 (a) Using the dividend growth model, with $D_0 = 20p$ and $K_e = 14\%$

For g: $13 \times (1 + g)^4 = 20$, hence

$$g = \sqrt[4]{\frac{20}{30}} - 1 = 11.4\%$$

$$P_0 = (20 \times (1 + 0.114))/(0.14 - 0.114) = £8.57$$

(b) New value of $K_e = 15.4\%$

$$\text{New } P_0 = (20 \times (1 + 0.114))/(0.154 - 0.114) = £5.57$$

(c) A 10 per cent increase in the required rate of return from 14 per cent to 15.4 per cent has led to a 35 per cent change in share price. This indicates that a small change in the required rate of return for a share leads to a large percentage change in the share price.

3 The answer to this question is given in Section 10.7.1.

4 (a) Company A, which has paid no dividends for five years, is pursuing a sensible policy for a rapidly growing company. All its earnings are being reinvested and so it has reduced its need for external finance to a minimum. Since the company is probably investing a great deal, its tax liability is likely to be small.

Company B's policy of distributing 50 per cent of earnings seems to offer pre-dictability. In fact, its earnings may fluctuate considerably. A dividend cut usually causes a share price fall since the market views it as being a negative signal. If Company B is mature, with low volatility in earnings, its dividend policy may be acceptable.

Company C's policy falls between those of A and B in that a small dividend is paid. The predictability of the dividend will be welcomed by shareholders. It also gives the company the advantage of having retained earnings available for investment. Scrip issues may increase a company's market value by increasing the marketability of its shares. Shareholder concessions are a means of attracting small shareholders who can benefit from them personally and have no impact on dividend policy.

(b) Company A would be attractive to investors who prefer to get a return through capital growth. Company B would be attractive to investors who prefer a high proportion of their return in the form of income, even if it is variable from year to year. A diversified portfolio would reduce the effect of variability in the dividend. Company C would be attractive to private investors, as most of the return is in the form of capital growth and there are shareholder concessions.

Each company *may* maximise the wealth of its shareholders. If Miller and Modigliani are correct, the three companies will maximise shareholder wealth because the value of each company is unaffected by its dividend policy. Alternatively, each company's group of shareholders may favour their particular company's policy, and so maximise their wealth, because the dividend policy of each is appropriate to their tax position.

5 (a) The investor's 1000 shares are initially worth: £4200

For (i) the 20p dividend:
Total dividend: 20p × 1000 = £200
Ex-div share price: 420p – 20p
Value of shares: 1000 × 400p = £4000
Total wealth: £4200
Hence there has been no change in wealth.

For (ii) the 6 per cent scrip dividend:
This means the number of new shares will be: 6% × 40m = 2.4m
Original market value: £4.20 × 40m = £168m
New share value: £168m/42.4m = 396.2p
Shareholder now has 1060 shares at 396.2p, which gives a total value of £4200
Again, no change in wealth has occurred.

For (iii) the share repurchase:
To repurchase 15 per cent of shares would cost: 15% × 40m × 420p = £25.2m
This would be paid out of the company's cash reserves and reduce the company value by: £168m – £25.2m = £142.8
This would reduce the number of shares to 40m × 85 per cent = 34m
New share price: £142.8m/34m = 420p
Again, no change has occurred in the shareholder's wealth.

(b) The following points are relevant.

- The company should accept the project to maximise shareholder wealth.
- The company should take into account that funds are needed for reinvestment.
- This should be taken into account with its dividend policy – out of the three options only (ii), the scrip dividend, allows the company to retain all its current earnings rather than paying cash out to its shareholders.

- However, the scrip dividend is offered as an alternative to a cash dividend and there is no guarantee that shareholders will take the scrip dividend.
- An alternative would be to pay a (reduced) cash dividend and finance the cash shortfall through debt.

Chapter 11   Answers to self-test questions

1 The economic reasons for taking over another company centre on the belief that shareholder wealth will be enhanced by the deal. This increase in wealth can arise from a number of sources, as follows:

- synergy, whereby the value of the combined entity exceeds its parts;
- economies of scale, e.g. in distribution and production;
- the elimination of inefficient management;
- entry into new markets, e.g. instead of starting from scratch;
- to provide critical mass;
- to provide growth;
- to provide market share.

2 The financial benefits that may be gained by shareholders via a takeover will include:

- financial synergy, i.e. a decrease in the cost of capital;
- acquisition of an undervalued target (unlikely if markets are efficient);
- benefit from relative tax considerations;
- increase in EPS or boot-strapping (not accepted as a justification).

3 A number of arguments have been advanced against using acquisitions and mergers as a way of achieving growth:

- the bid might be referred to the Competition Commission and so be delayed and even refused;
- the bid might be contested and result in an unpleasant battle;
- the only beneficiaries from mergers and takeovers are target company shareholders;
- financing a takeover is expensive;
- it is difficult to achieve post-merger integration.

4 There is no consensus view on why mergers and takeovers come in waves, but a number of contributory factors have been identified:

- a bull market can encourage the use of shares to finance takeovers;
- increasing liquidity and profitability can encourage companies to look for acquisition targets;
- deregulation of financial markets has made access to finance easier;
- low levels of gearing allow companies to use debt to finance acquisitions.

5 Using P/E ratios to value companies is a rough rule of thumb and must be used with caution. EPS is an accounting figure that can be subject to manipulation and creative accounting. In addition, earnings will vary over time and not stay at their current level, so the EPS figure may need to be normalised to reflect this. Problems with using the P/E ratio method include the difficulty of selecting an appropriate P/E ratio to apply, and the fact that the ratio combines a current value (share price) with an historical value (EPS).

The accuracy of the dividend growth model relies heavily on forecast future dividend payments and the calculated shareholders' required rate of return. Both of these figures are difficult to estimate with any accuracy. There are also difficulties in using the model in this context because it considers the dividends that flow to individual investors, rather than the company's ability to generate cash flows from its assets.

6 The DCF valuation method is preferred by academics because it is directly related to the ideal of shareholder wealth maximisation. Practical difficulties with this method include:

- estimating future cash flows;
- the choice of an appropriate discount rate;
- the selection of an appropriate time period over which to evaluate;
- how to forecast accurately any economies of scale and synergies;
- taking account of the risk of the target company;
- estimating the future cost of capital.

The appropriate discount rate with which to discount expected cash flows could be the acquiring company's cost of capital or a discount rate reflecting the systematic risk of the target company.

7 The answer to this question can be found in Section 11.5.4.

8 Possible post-bid defences that you could have described include:

- formulation of a defence document;
- announcing forecasts of increased profits;
- announcing an increase in dividends;
- looking for a 'white knight';
- getting rid of the 'crown jewels'.

9 The answer to this question can be found in Section 11.7.1.

10 Possible reasons why the shareholders of acquiring companies rarely benefit from takeovers include the following:

- if the bid is contested, the acquisition can cost the company more than it originally intended to pay, reducing its shareholders' wealth;
- predicted economies of scale and synergy may fail to materialise;
- the acquiring company's managers may lack knowledge and expertise in the business they have acquired;
- the quality of the acquired assets may turn out to be lower than expected;
- cultural problems may be experienced between acquirer and target;
- if the takeover is for cash, the acquiring company may be drained of liquidity and face a high level of gearing. This restricts its ability to accept attractive projects.

Chapter 11 Answers to questions for review

1 (a) The major justifications put forward to explain horizontal takeovers centre on the fact that the merging companies are in the same industry and so are likely to benefit from economies of scale. They may also benefit from synergy between operations as well. Horizontal takeovers can also be justified as a way of breaking into new geographical markets. Market share can also be a viable reason, so that companies can earn monopoly profits, but the bidder must beware of referral to the Competition Commission. There may be financial gains and tax benefits, but increasing EPS is not a valid justification.

(b) In vertical backward or forward takeovers the major justification is that a company can either secure control of vital raw materials or guarantee an outlet for, and control the distribution of, its product. This helps companies to reduce the power of suppliers or to decrease the revenue lost to distributors. Economies of scale or synergy are less likely to occur than with horizontal takeovers.

(c) It is very difficult to see the rationale for conglomerate mergers as there will be few economies of scale or synergy due to the unrelated nature of the merging businesses. The merger cannot be justified from the point of view of risk reduction as shareholders are likely to hold diversified portfolios. Nor can it be justified as the acquisition of a bargain since, if capital markets are efficient, the target's share price will reflect its true value.

2 (a) Calculation of the value of Staygood using Restwell's P/E ratio:

Staygood's share price $= 12 \times 37\text{p} = £4.44$

This assumes that the market will expect Restwell to achieve a level of return on Staygood comparable to that which it makes on its own assets. Hence:

Total market value $= 5\text{m} \times £4.44 = £22.2\text{m}$

(b) To use the dividend growth model we must find g and K_e.

Here g is given by $\sqrt[5]{\dfrac{27}{15}} - 1 = 12.47\%$

K_e for Staygood is 20 per cent higher than Restwell, therefore:

$K_e = 15\% \times 1.20 = 18\%$

Therefore: $P_0 = (27 \times (1.1247))/(0.18 - 0.1247) = £5.49$

Total market value $= 5\text{m} \times £5.49 = £27.5\text{m}$

(c) Using future cash flows and discounting these to infinity using Restwell's WACC as a discount rate:

Present value $= (£2.5\text{m}/(0.12 - 0.05)) + (5 \times 0.797) = £39.7\text{m}$

3 Powell's market value, using its P/E ratio and earnings, is $5.8\text{m} \times 10 = £58\text{m}$
The earnings of Stimac plc will be $(£10\text{m} + £5.8\text{m}) \times 1.08 = £17.06\text{m}$
Using the expected P/E ratio of 9, the value of Stimac is $£17.06\text{m} \times 9 = £153.54\text{m}$
The 10 million shares of Powell will be swapped for 30 million Carsley shares, making 70 million shares in the new company in total. Therefore, the wealth of Powell's shareholders will now be $£153.54\text{m} \times (30\text{m}/70\text{m}) = £65.8\text{m}$.

Powell's shareholders are £7.8m better off (78 pence per share).

4   There are a large number of factors that will influence a company on the way it decides to structure its financing of a takeover bid, as follows.

■ *The tax position of the target company's shareholders*: if they are tax exempt, they may prefer a cash offer as they will not incur capital gains tax. If they are liable for capital gains, they may prefer a share-for-share offer. If there is a range of investors in different tax-paying positions, a mixed bid may be more appropriate.

■ *The acquiring company's level of liquidity and ability to borrow funds*: this will determine whether it can find sufficient funds in order to make a cash offer.

■ *The acquiring company's share price*: if its share price is high compared to the target company's share price, the acquirer will not have to issue too many shares if it makes a share-for-share offer, reducing any potential dilution of EPS and control.

■ *The attitudes and preferences of shareholders*: the acquiring company's shareholders may not want it to borrow for a cash offer because this may increase financial risk beyond what they are prepared to tolerate. A cash offer may be unattractive to the target company's shareholders because they no longer have a participating interest in the company that they originally bought shares in.

5   (a) From the information given the value of the subsidiary can be found by considering the present value of expected earnings:

Equivalent annual earnings growth = $(6.3/6.0)^{0.33} - 1 = 0.0164$ or 1.64%
Present value of expected earnings = $(6.3 \times 1.0164)/(0.14 - 0.0164) = £51.81m$
However, it may be that no earnings growth is expected.
Now the present value of expected earnings = $6.3/0.14 = £45m$
This is higher than the liquidation value of £42m.

We are unable to determine the value of the subsidiary to its buyout team since we do not know its cost of capital and the liquidation value would be reduced by additional long-term debt. It seems that a purchase price of between £45m and £52m would be acceptable to Lissom plc.

(b) The growth in turnover has declined each year over the three-year period. It was 4 per cent in 2000, 3 per cent in 2001 and 2 per cent in 2002. A question that needs to be asked is: will the buyout team be able to improve turnover?

Growth in profit after tax has declined from 3.3 per cent in 2000 to 1.6 per cent in 2001, with no growth at all in 2002. When compared with turnover growth, it is clear that costs have been increasing over the period. Can the buyout team arrest the decline in profit after tax?

The repayment of the £10m debenture in two years will cause significant strains on cash flow. This factor must be considered in the business plan prepared by the buyout team.

(c) The following stages should be discussed:

■ divestment decision is made;

■ management buyout decision is made;

■ financial analysis of the division;

■ purchase price determined;

■ extent of management investment determined;

■ debt investors are assembled;

- additional equity investment is determined;
- cash flow analysis is carried out;
- financing package is agreed.

(d) The answer to this part of the question can be found in Section 11.7.3.

Chapter 12 Answers to self-test questions

1 (a) Here the company is facing transaction exposure. If the pound weakens against the euro, the sterling cost of the company's coal imports will increase. Therefore, the risk here is downside in nature.

(b) The type of exchange rate risk being faced here is economic risk. The UK toy company is facing upside risk here, because a weakening of the pound against the dollar will make the US company's imports less attractive to domestic customers.

(c) Here the UK company faces translation risk. The risk is downside in nature because, as the pound appreciates against the euro, the translated sterling value of the factory will decrease, increasing the value of the company's liabilities relative to its assets.

2 Translation risk is best managed by using matching. For example, if purchasing an asset in a foreign country, a company should raise the funds for the purchase in the foreign currency so both the asset and liability are in the same currency.

There are a number of ways to hedge transaction risk internally. Matching, for example, could mean paying for imports in the same currency that a company invoices its exports in. Alternatively, a company could invoice customers in the domestic currency and find a supplier which does the same. The problem with this method, though, is that the company may lose foreign sales and also restrict the potential suppliers it can purchase from. Companies can also manage transaction risk by leading and lagging payments according to their expectations of exchange rate movements.

3 The company needs to purchase sufficient dollars to deposit on the money markets so that, when the deposit matures, there are exactly enough dollars to pay its $345 000 liability. Therefore:

$$Z \times (1 + 8.5\%/4) = Z \times 1.02125 = \$345\,000$$

Here $Z = \$337\,821$ which at the current spot rate will cost £189 787.

4 The major difference between OTC options and traded options is that the latter come in the form of contracts standardised with respect to amount and duration, whereas the former are non-standardised and negotiable with respect to amount and duration. Traded options are available from LIFFE whereas OTC options are provided by banks. One of the consequences of traded options being standardised is that they can be sold on to other parties. OTC options can be tailor-made to match the characteristics of the exposure a company wants to hedge.

5 If we sell futures contracts and interest rates increase, we close out our position in the future by buying futures contracts at a lower price, thereby making a gain. We therefore need to sell futures contracts to offset the increased cost of borrowing. How many contracts should we sell? Our transaction is equal to 12 contracts, but we are borrowing

for a six-month period, so we need to sell 24 contracts in order to fully hedge our exposure. The correct response is therefore (c).

6 Interest rate risk is concerned with the sensitivity of profit and operating cash flows to changes in interest rates. A company will need to analyse how its profits and cash flows are likely to change in response to forecast changes in interest rates, and take a decision as to whether action is necessary. Factors which could influence the decision to hedge interest rate risk include:

- the expected volatility of interest rates;
- the sensitivity of profits and cash flows to interest rate changes;
- the balance between fixed and floating rate debt in a company's capital structure;
- the financial plans of the company.

7 A company can use internal measures such as matching if it has cash inflows and outflows which can be matched in respect of timing and amount. If it wishes to transfer risk to a third party, however, it will need to use external hedging instruments. The following factors will determine which external hedging instruments will be used:

- whether the company wishes to profit from favourable rate movements or wants to lock into a particular interest rate;
- the view the company takes on future interest rate movements and volatility;
- the timing, nature and duration of the interest rate exposure;
- the extent to which the company wishes to hedge its interest rate exposure;
- the knowledge and experience of the company's treasury staff;
- the relative costs associated with the different derivatives.

8 The correct answer is (c). A bank-created floor is sought only if a company wants to guard against interest rates going down. The rest of the responses will all successfully hedge against interest rate increases.

9 The drawbacks include the following points.

- A company may have difficulty finding a counterparty with equal but opposite requirements to itself (although warehousing reduces this problem significantly).
- Once engaged in a swap agreement it is not possible to benefit from favourable movements in the exchange rate.
- The swap partner has to be vetted so as to reduce the possibility of counterparty default.

10 Put options allow the holder to sell the pound at a fixed rate. If a put has a strike price lower than $1.55 it is out of the money, i.e. option (c). Put option (a) is at the money while (e) is in the money. Call options allow the holder to buy the pound at a fixed rate. If a call has a strike price higher than $1.55 it is out of the money, i.e. option (b). Call option (d) is at the money. Hence, the most valuable option is (e), the $1.71 put option, as it is the only option in the money. The holder of this option can sell sterling at a much more favourable rate than the current spot rate.

Chapter 12 **Answers to questions for review**

1 The factors that you could have discussed include the following.

■ If a company is uncertain as to the direction in which interest rates will move, it could take an OTC option to allow it to take advantage of favourable interest rate movements. This is not possible with a futures contract, which would lock the company into a particular interest rate.

■ While paying a premium for an OTC option, a company will save itself the initial margin required by a futures contract as well as any subsequent variation margin.

■ An OTC option will make it easier for a company to match the hedge to the duration and size of its exposure. The standardised nature of futures contracts may lead the company to have to over- or under-hedge.

■ The company may feel happier dealing with a bank with which it is familiar in order to obtain an OTC option, rather than approaching a new market such as Euronext. liffe to deal in futures contracts.

■ The efficiency of using futures to hedge interest rate changes may be hampered by the existence of basis risk.

2 (a) Using the forward market: $364\,897/1.5455 = £236\,103$

(b) Using the cash market:
Carrycan must make a dollar deposit now.
Six-month dollar deposit rate $= 4.5/2 = 2.25\%$
$Z \times 1.0225 = \$364\,897$
Hence $Z = \$356\,867$
Cost of buying $356\,867 at current spot rate is $356\,867/1.5617 = £228\,512$
Six-monthly sterling deposit rate $= 5.5/2 = 2.75\%$
Six months' interest lost on £228 512 $= (£228\,512 \times 0.0275) = £6284$
Total cost $= 228\,512 + 6284 = £234\,796$

(c) Using currency put options:
Each contract will deliver $1.7 \times 12\,500 = \$21\,250$
Number of contracts required $= 364\,897/21\,250 = 17.17$, i.e. 17 contracts
Cost $= 0.096 \times 12\,500 \times 17 = \$20\,400$
Sterling cost of options $= 20\,400/1.5617 = £13\,063$
Sterling required $= 17 \times £12\,500 = £212\,500$ to deliver $361\,250
Shortfall $= 364\,897 - 361\,250 = \$3647$
Cost in sterling using forward rate $= 3647/1.5455 = £2360$
Total cost of using options $= 13\,063 + 212\,500 + 2360 = £227\,923$
Therefore the foreign currency options are the cheapest method for the company to use to hedge its transaction exposure.

3 You could have discussed the following factors:

■ the time to expiry of the option;

■ interest rates, particularly the risk-free rate of return;

■ the price of the underlying asset, for example, interest rate futures;

■ the exercise price of the option;

- the volatility of interest rates and exchange rates;
- market expectations about future changes in interest and exchange rates.

4 (a) Say for instance LIBOR = 10 per cent. Company B's floating rate is 3 per cent more expensive than Company A's rate ($100 \times 0.3/10$), but its fixed rate is 12.5 per cent more expensive than A's ($100 \times 1.5/12$). Hence Company A has a comparative advantage in fixed rate loans, and Company B has a comparative advantage in floating rate loans.

(b) Net potential gain = (LIBOR − (LIBOR + 0.3)) + (13.5 − 12) = −0.3 + 1.5 = 1.2%, i.e. 0.6% benefit to each company.

Company B pays:
Company A's fixed rate borrowing (12%) + 0.9%, therefore company B's actual fixed rate is 12.9% (compared with 13.5%).

Company A pays:
Company B's floating borrowing rate of LIBOR + 0.3 and also receives 0.9%, therefore Company A's actual floating rate is LIBOR − 0.6 (compared with LIBOR).

5 Slammer plc has a comparative advantage in fixed rates, as it can obtain a fixed rate loan 0.5 per cent cheaper than Can plc, while it can obtain a floating rate loan only 0.2 per cent cheaper than Can plc. If the two companies arranged an interest rate swap, Slammer plc could borrow at a fixed rate of 11.5 per cent and Can plc would pay the fixed rate interest, while Can plc could borrow at a floating rate of LIBOR + 0.4 per cent and Slammer plc would pay the floating rate interest. Since Can plc is saving 0.5 per cent on fixed rates, but Slammer plc is paying 0.2 per cent more than its possible floating rate, the net benefit is 0.3 per cent, which is 0.15 per cent for each company if divided equally. Can plc should therefore have a net cost or effective borrowing rate of 11.85 per cent and so should pay Slammer plc 0.35 per cent. This will make Slammer plc's net cost or effective borrowing rate LIBOR + 0.05 per cent, which is a saving of 0.15 per cent over its opportunity cost. We can show this in table form as follows:

Alternative costs	Slammer plc	Can plc
Fixed rate	11.50%	–
Floating rate	–	LIBOR + 0.4%
Swap: fixed rate	(11.75%)	11.75%
Swap: floating rate	LIBOR + 0.4%	(LIBOR + 0.4%)
Effective borrowing rate	LIBOR + 0.05%	11.85%
Opportunity cost	LIBOR + 0.2%	12.0%
Relative saving	0.15%	0.15%

Chapter 13 Answers to self-test questions

1 The answer to this question can be found in Section 13.1.1.

2 The answer to this question can be found in Section 13.1.2.

3 The answer to this question can be found in Section 13.2.

4 The answer to this question can be found in Section 13.2.3.

5 The answer to this question can be found in Section 13.3.1.

6 The primary objective of the management of a company undertaking foreign direct investment is to maximise the wealth of its shareholders. The evaluation at the parent company level is therefore the key to whether a proposal should be accepted or not.

7 The following difficulties may be encountered by analysts:

- How can they determine an appropriate value of beta?
- With reference to which market should it be calculated?
- What value of the market premium should be used?
- Which risk-free rate should be selected?
- What if the share price of the company changes? Should the cost of capital be recalculated?

8 The main factors influencing the choice and mix of financing used in foreign direct investment are gearing, taxation, political risk and currency risk. The financing decision should aim to minimise the cost of capital in order to maximise the value of the firm.

9 The company can use one of several techniques. It could look at the country's political risk index and compare it with that of other countries. It could use the Delphi technique, statistical analysis or a checklist approach or visit the country concerned. If it seeks to assess political risk in a systematic way, the results of the assessment are more likely to be useful.

10 Apart from doing nothing, one option is insuring against political risk, whether through a private firm or through a government department such as the ECGD. A second option is negotiating a concession agreement with the host government, as long as it can be trusted to keep such an agreement. A third option is using financing and operating policies which reduce the political risk faced in a particular country. An example of such a financing policy is using a significant amount of local debt. An example of such an operating policy is locating different stages of production in different countries to make expropriation less likely.

Chapter 13 Answers to questions for review

1 (a) We need to see if the project is acceptable to the parent company.

Year	0	1	2	3	4	5
Operating profit (G$)		250	450	550	650	800
Interest (G$)		(15)	(15)	(15)	(15)	(15)
		235	435	535	635	785
Taxation (G$)		47	87	107	127	157
		188	348	428	508	628
Capital invested (G$)	(600)					600
Working capital (G$)	(250)					
Loan (G$)	250					(250)
Project after tax (G$)	(600)	188	348	428	508	978
Exchange rate (G$/£)	3	4	5	6	7	8
Payable to UK (£)	(200)	47.0	69.6	71.3	72.6	122.2
UK tax (£)		(5.9)	(8.7)	(8.9)	(9.1)	(9.8)
	(200)	41.1	60.9	62.4	63.5	112.4
20% discount factor	1.000	0.833	0.694	0.579	0.482	0.402
Present value (£)	(200)	34.2	42.3	36.1	30.6	45.2
Net present value (£)	(11.6)					

Since the NPV is negative, the project is not acceptable on financial grounds.

(b) A general discussion of political risk, illustrated by examples from the scenario of the question, is called for.

2 (a) If Redek Mornag chooses to increase exports to Laresia, it will be limited by its current surplus capacity, unless it decides to increase its productive capacity in the UK. Since it currently exports to Laresia, increasing exports is a low-risk strategy as it already has local business contacts and established channels of distribution. However, profitability will be reduced by transport and insurance costs. There is also the possibility that import controls will be introduced if Laresia's balance of trade deteriorates.

(b) Licensing would mean that import and other controls would not present a problem, but the returns are likely to be small. There is also the danger that the licensee could set up in opposition to Redek Mornag, having acquired the necessary knowledge and expertise through operating under licence, and it could be difficult to do much about this.

(c) Constructing a manufacturing facility demonstrates commitment to the country of Laresia, and offers the possibility of higher profits than either exporting or licensing. Government incentives for such a move may be available and it might be possible to take advantage of the latest production techniques. Local wage rates are also likely to be lower.

3 In distinguishing between international and domestic capital investment decisions, the following points could be considered.

- The difference between project cash flows and parent cash flows:
    - the need for a two-stage evaluation process;
    - remittable and distributable cash flows;
    - the nature and type of parent cash flows;
    - the difficulties in identifying relevant cash flows;
    - the effect of investment on other operations.
- Difficulties in valuing investment by the parent company:
    - transfer of capital as equipment and inventory;
    - use of opportunity cost.
- The problem of exchange rates, e.g. estimation difficulties re future exchange rates.
- Taxation:
    - differential tax regimes;
    - withholding taxes;
    - allowances for taxes paid elsewhere.
- Foreign investment and the cost of capital:
    - risk premium;
    - international diversification and systematic risk.
- Restrictions on the repatriation of funds:
    - exchange controls;
    - royalties and management fees.
- International investment decisions and risk:
    - political risk, exchange rate and interest rate risk;
    - risk analysis and risk management methods.

4   At the local level, we have:

Year	0 (K000)	1 (K000)	2 (K000)	3 (K000)	4 (K000)	5 (K000)
Operating cash flows		3000	3000	3000	3000	3000
WDAs		(1050)	(1050)	(1050)	(1050)	(1050)
Interest		(100)	(100)	(100)	(100)	(100)
Profit before tax		1850	1850	1850	1850	1850
Profit tax		(277.5)	(277.5)	(277.5)	(277.5)	(277.5)
After-tax cash flows		1572.5	1572.5	1572.5	1572.5	1572.5
Initial investment	(5250)					
Working capital	(1000)					
Loan capital	1000					(1000)
Sale of subsidiary						4200
Add back WDAs		1050	1050	1050	1050	1050
Project cash flows	(5250)	2622.5	2622.5	2622.5	2622.5	5822.5
12% discount factors	5.000	0.893	0.797	0.712	0.636	0.567
Present values	(5250)	2342	2090	1867	1668	3301

NPV = (5 250 000) + 2 342 000 + 2 090 000 + 1 867 000 + 1 668 000 + 3 301 000
     = K6 018 000

But the NPV at the parent company level is what is important.

Year	0	1	2	3	4	5
Remittances (K000)	(5250)	2622.5	2622.5	2622.5	2622.5	5822.5
Exchange rate, K/£	3.50	4.00	4.40	4.70	4.90	5.00
	£000	£000	£000	£000	£000	£000
Sterling equivalent	(1500)	656	596	558	535	1164
UK tax		(69)	(63)	(59)	(57)	(56)
	(1500)	587	533	499	478	1108
Exports lost, after tax		(50)	(50)	(50)	(50)	(50)
Parent cash flow	(1500)	537	483	449	428	1058
18% discount factors	1.000	0.847	0.718	0.609	0.516	0.437
Parent cash flow	(1500)	455	347	273	221	462

NPV = (1 500 000) + 455 000 + 347 000 + 273 000 + 212 000 + 462 000
     = £258 000

The investment appears to be financially acceptable.

5 Political risk, which is the possibility of favourable or adverse political action, has the following features:

- it is increased if the host nation and the multinational have differing objectives;
- it is increased in areas with political and social instability;
- measuring political and social instability is difficult.

Possible difficulties arising from political risk include:

- exchange controls;
- currency restrictions;
- restrictions on local borrowing;
- expropriation or nationalisation of assets;
- tax discrimination;
- import controls.

Glossary

Accounting rate of return (ARR): the average annual accounting profit generated by an investment relative to the required capital outlay. Also known as return on capital employed.

Accounts payable: money owed by a company to suppliers in return for supplied goods and services. Also known as creditors.

Accounts receivable: money owed to a company by the customers to whom it has supplied goods and services. Also known as debtors.

Acid test ratio: *see* Quick ratio.

Acquisition: the purchase of one company by another.

Agency: the theoretical relationship that exists between the owners of a company and the managers as agents they employ to run the company on their behalf.

Agency costs: the costs arising as a result of an *agency* relationship.

American option: an option that can be exercised at any time up to, and on, its expiry date.

Amortised loan: a loan where interest and principal are paid off through regular, equal payments.

Annuity: a regular payment of a fixed amount of money over a finite period.

Arbitrage: the simultaneous buying and selling of assets or securities in different markets in order to yield a risk-free gain.

Asset beta: the sensitivity to systematic factors of the cash flows accruing to a particular set of productive assets.

Asymmetry of information: the situation where one party is in an advantageous position compared with another due to its access to or possession of privileged information.

Auction market preferred stock (AMPS): a form of preference share where the dividend yield is periodically adjusted by a process of auction.

Authorised share capital: the book value of shares that a company is allowed to issue according to its articles of association.

Balloon repayments: loan repayments that occur towards the end or maturity of the loan period.

Basis risk: the risk that a specific percentage movement in the cash market will not be matched by an equal and opposite move in the futures market when hedging interest and exchange rate risk.

Bear market: a market in which share prices are being driven down by the selling activities of pessimistic investors.

Beta: a measure of the sensitivity of a security's returns to systematic risk.

Bid price: the price at which a market maker or dealer will buy financial assets for.

BIMBO: the combination of a management buyout and a buy-in.

Bonus issue: also known as a *scrip issue*, this is an issue of new shares to existing shareholders, in proportion to their existing holdings, without the subscription of new funds.

Book value: the value allocated to an asset or liability in the financial statements of a company.

Boot-strapping: the practice whereby a company with a high price/earnings ratio can engineer an increase in its earnings per share by taking over a company with a lower price/earnings ratio.

Bull market: a market in which share prices are being driven up by the selling activities of optimistic investors.

Business risk: the variability of a company's operating profits given its business operations.

Called-up share capital: the total book value of shares that a company has issued.

Call option: an option that allows the holder to buy an asset at a predetermined price.

Cap: an agreement that fixes a maximum rate of interest at which a party can borrow.

Capital allowances: a tax allowance given against the purchase of certain fixed assets.

Capital gain: the difference between the original purchase price of a security and its current market price.

Capital gearing: the proportion of a company's total capital that is in the form of debt.

Capital market line: the linear risk/return trade-off for investors spreading their money between the market portfolio and risk-free assets.

Capital markets: financial markets where long-term securities are bought and sold.

Capital rationing: the situation when a company has to limit the number of projects it invests in due to insufficient funds being available to invest in all desirable projects.

Cash conversion cycle: the time period between a company paying cash for its costs of production and receiving cash from the sale of its goods.

Cash market hedge: where a company hedges a risk exposure by making an equal and opposite cash market transaction.

Certificate of deposit: a tradable security issued by banks to investors who deposit a given amount of money for a specified period.

Chartism: the practice of studying past share price movements in order to make future capital gains through the buying and selling of shares.

Clientele effect: the theory that suggests that investors are attracted to companies that satisfy their requirements, for example as regards dividends.

Collar: an agreement that keeps either a borrowing or a lending rate between specified upper and lower limits.

Compound interest: interest which is calculated not only on the initial amount invested but also the accumulated interest from earlier periods.

Concert party: a group of investors acting together under the control of one party to purchase shares in a company.

Conglomerate merger: the combination of two companies who operate in unrelated businesses.

Conversion premium: the amount by which the price of a convertible bond exceeds the current market value of the shares into which it may be converted.

Convertible bonds: bonds that can, at some specified date(s), be converted at the option of the holder into a predetermined number of ordinary shares.

Convertible preference shares: preference shares that can, at some specified date(s), be converted at the option of the holder into a predetermined number of ordinary shares.

Corporate bond: a long-term debt security paying periodic interest with repayment of the principal on maturity.

Corporate governance: the way in which companies are controlled and directed by their stakeholders.

Correlation coefficient: a relative measure of the degree to which the returns of two investments move in the same direction as each other.

Cost of capital: the rate of return required by investors supplying funds to a company and so the minimum rate of return required on prospective projects.

Cost of debt: the rate of return required by the suppliers of debt finance.

Cost of equity: the rate of return required by the suppliers of equity finance.

Counterparty risk: the risk that a counterparty (to a SWAP contract) fails to live up to its contractual obligations.

Coupon rate: the rate of interest paid by a bond relative to its par or face value.

Creative accounting: the practice of manipulating company accounts in order to make a company's performance appear more favourable than it actually is.

Creditor hierarchy: the pecking order in which a company's creditors are paid should it go into liquidation.

Credit rating: an assessment of the creditworthiness of a company's debt securities based upon its borrowing and repayment history, as well as the availability of assets.

Cum dividend market price: the market price of a share whose purchase gives the right to receive a recently declared dividend.

Cum rights price: the market value of a share if the current rights have yet to expire.

Currency futures: derivative instruments that allow companies to lock in to current exchange rates with respect to the future purchase or sale of currencies.

Currency swaps: *see* Swaps.

Current ratio: the ratio of current assets to current liabilities of a company.

Dawn raid: where an acquiring company instructs one or more brokers to purchase as many available shares as possible in a target company as soon as the market opens. The aim is to enable the acquiring company to build a significant position before the target company is aware of the takeover attempt.

Debentures: fixed interest redeemable bonds that are normally secured on the assets of the issuing company.

Deep discount bonds: bonds that are issued at a significant discount to their par value and pay a coupon lower than bonds issued at par.

Default risk: the risk that a borrower will not fulfil their commitments with respect to the payment of interest or repayment of principal.

Demerger: the separation of a company's operations into two or more separate corporate entities.

Derivatives: financial securities whose values are based on the values of other securities or assets such as bonds, shares, commodities and currencies.

Discount rate: the rate used in the process of discounting future cash flows.

Disintermediation: the process whereby companies raise finance and lend through financial markets directly, rather than through financial institutions.

Diversifiable risk: risk that can be avoided by spreading funds over a portfolio of investments.

Dividend cover: the number of times the annual dividend payment can be covered or paid out from current distributable earnings.

Dividend payout ratio: the percentage of distributable earnings paid out as dividends.

Dividend reinvestment plan (DRIP): an offer by companies that allows investors to reinvest their cash dividends via the purchase of additional shares on the dividend payment date.

Dividend yield: dividend divided by current share price.

Drop lock bonds: floating rate bonds that have a minimum interest rate.

Earnings per share: profit after interest and tax divided by the number of shares in issue.

Earnings yield: earnings per share divided by current share price.

Earn-out: a situation where the amount paid by an acquiring company for its target company is dependent on the future performance of its acquisition.

EBITDA: earnings before interest, taxation, depreciation and amortisation.

Economic exposure: the risk of long-term movements in exchange rates undermining the international competitiveness of a company.

Economic profit: amount earned by a business over a given period, after the deduction of operating expenses and a charge representing the company's opportunity cost of capital.

Economies of scale: an increase in production efficiency associated with an increasing number of goods being produced.

Efficient frontier: the set of optimum portfolios when investing in risky securities.

Employee share ownership plans (ESOPs): schemes designed to encourage the ownership of company shares by its employees.

Enhanced scrip dividends: a scrip dividend worth more than the cash dividend alternative.

Envelope curve: the risk/return combinations available to investors when investing in risky assets.

Eurobonds: long-term debt securities denominated in a currency outside of the control of the country of its origin.

Eurocurrency: currency held outside of its home market.

Exchange rate risk: the risk of adverse movements in exchange rates leading to companies experiencing actual or balance sheet losses.

Exercise price: the price at which an option holder can purchase or sell the specified financial asset.

Factoring: the collection of a company's debts by a specialist company, with finance advanced against the security of amounts owed by debtors.

Finance lease: a long-term agreement where the lease period is equivalent to the useful economic life of the leased asset.

Financial engineering: the combining or splitting of different financial instruments to create new or synthetic securities.

Financial risk: the risk interest rate changes causing reductions in a company's after-tax earnings and hence its ability to pay dividends.

Fixed charge security: bonds secured against a specific company asset.

Floating charge security: bonds secured against a pool of company assets.

Floor: similar to a *cap* but here the agreement fixes a minimum rate of interest at which a party can borrow.

Foreign bond: a bond issued in a domestic market by a foreign company, but in the domestic market's currency.

Forward rate agreements (FRA): contracts which allow companies to fix, in advance, future borrowing and lending rates, based on a nominal principal over a given period.

Free riders: parties who enjoy the benefits of corrected management behaviour without contributing to the associated costs.

Fundamental analysis: the use of financial information to determine the 'intrinsic value' of a share and hence profit from shares incorrectly priced by the market.

Futures contracts: an agreement to buy or sell a standard quantity of a specific financial instrument or foreign currency at a future date and price agreed between two parties.

Gap exposure: the exposure to interest rate risk arising when a company has assets and liabilities whose interest rates, though based on similar underlying floating rates, are revised at differing frequencies.

Gilt-edged government securities: low-risk, long-term securities issued by the government.

Goal congruence: the situation where agents and principals have identical objectives.

Golden parachutes: generous redundancy terms for directors of a company, used to deter bidding companies from dismissing them after a takeover.

Hedging: the mitigation of risk exposure by undertaking equal and opposite transactions.

Horizontal merger: the combination of two companies operating in the same industry and at a similar stage of production.

Hybrid finance: a financial security exhibiting the characteristics of both debt and equity.

Initial public offering (IPO): the issuing of shares for the first time in order to obtain a listing.

Indifference curves: a series of curves that join up points of equal utility for an individual investor; also known as utility curves.

Insider dealing: the use of privileged information to buy and sell securities in order to obtain abnormal returns.

Institutional investors: large financial intermediaries, such as insurance companies, unit trusts, investment trusts and pension funds, which invest large amounts of money in company shares.

Interbank market: a money market that facilitates banks' short-term borrowing and lending.

Interest cover: the number of times a company's interest payments can be covered by its profits before interest and tax.

Interest rate risk: the risk of a company's profits being adversely affected by interest rate changes.

Junk bonds: unsecured corporate bonds which pay high interest rates to compensate investors for their high default risk.

Lagging: the delaying of foreign currency payments in order to benefit from favourable exchange rate movements.

Lead time: the delay between placing an order and its delivery.

Leveraged takeover: a takeover, the cost of which is predominantly financed by debt.

Lodgment delay: the delay between paying cash and cheques into a bank account and the account registering the payment.

London Interbank Offered Rate (LIBOR): key interbank money market interest rate.

Long position: the position taken when an investor purchases and holds a security.

Marginal trading: where the share price of a company is determined by the trading of only a small proportion of its issued share capital.

Market capitalisation: the market value of a company's shares multiplied by the total number of its issued shares.

Market portfolio: the optimal portfolio of high-risk assets with which to combine holdings of risk-free assets.

Market risk: *see* Systematic risk.

Matching: an internal hedging technique where liabilities and assets are matched in order to mitigate exposure.

Merchant bank: a bank that specialises in wholesale transactions as opposed to smaller retail transactions.

Mergers: the coming together of two equal organisations to form one unified entity.

Mezzanine finance: debt finance, often used in the finance of takeovers, that has risk and return characteristics somewhere between those of secured debt and equity.

Money markets: markets which specialise in the borrowing and lending of short-term funds.

Netting: the process of offsetting credit balances against debtor balances in order to minimise intercompany indebtedness.

Nominal value: the face value of a financial asset in money terms.

Non-executive directors (NEDs): directors brought in from outside a company to sit on its board and oversee its operations, but who are not involved in its day-to-day operations.

Non-pecuniary benefits: benefits other than those in the form of cash.

Non-recourse factoring: a factoring agreement where the factor, rather than the company, carries the risk of bad debts.

Off-balance-sheet financing: the use of financing, such as operating leases, that does not have to appear on the balance sheet.

Official List: the list of companies that are registered on the London Stock Exchange.

Operating lease: a short-term agreement where the lease period is substantially less than the useful economic life of the leased asset.

Opportunity cost: the benefit forgone by not using an asset in its next best use.

Option: an agreement giving the holder the right, but not the obligation, to buy or sell a specified amount of a commodity or financial instrument over a specific time period and at a specified price.

Over the counter: this term refers to derivatives that are tailor-made by banks to suit the requirements of their customers.

Overtrading: the situation where a company experiences liquidity problems due to its trading beyond the capital resources available to it.

Par value: the face value of a financial security.

Peppercorn rent: the reduced rent paid by a lessee following the conclusion of the primary period of a finance lease.

Permanent current assets: current assets which are maintained at a core level over time, such as buffer stock.

Perpetuity: the payment of equal cash flows at regular intervals which continue into the indefinite future.

Poison pill: a financial transaction, such as a share issue, which is triggered when a bidding company attempts to take over another company, hence making the takeover more expensive.

Political risk: the risk that the political actions of a country will adversely affect the value of a company's operations.

Pre-emptive right: the right enjoyed by existing shareholders of a company whereby they are legally entitled to the first refusal on any new shares that it may issue.

Present value: the value of a future cash flow in current terms, once it has been discounted by an appropriate discount rate.

Primary markets: markets where securities are issued for the first time.

Profitability index: the ratio of a project's net present value relative to its initial investment.

Quick ratio: the ratio of current assets less stock divided by current liabilities.

Real cost of capital: a company's cost of capital which makes no allowance for the effects of inflation.

Recourse: if trade debtors are sold to a factoring company, in the event of the debtor failing to pay the factoring company can return to the vendor for payment.

Redemption yield: the return required by an investor over the life of a security, taking into account both revenue and capital gains.

Refinancing: replacement of one kind of financing with one or more different forms of finance with different characteristics, such as replacing fixed rate long-term debt with floating rate long-term debt or with equity.

Replacement cost: the cost of replacing an asset with one of similar age and condition.

Restrictive covenants: clauses included in bond deeds designed to place restrictions on a company's future financing in order to protect existing creditors' interests. Also known as banking covenants.

Retail price index: the weighted average of the prices of a basket of goods which is taken as a guide to general inflation.

Retained earnings: cash retained by a company for reinvestment purposes.

Risk averse: a term used to describe investors who are not keen to take risk, regardless of the potential returns.

Risk-free rate of return: the yield earned on securities which are considered to be free from risk, such as short-dated government securities.

Risk premium: the return in excess of the risk-free rate that is required by an investor before accepting a high-risk investment.

Running yield: also called interest or flat yield, this is calculated by simply dividing the interest rate of a security by its current market price.

Scrip dividend: an issue of new shares to existing shareholders in lieu of a cash dividend.

Scrip issue: *see* Bonus issue.

Secondary markets: markets where securities are traded once issued.

Securitisation: the process whereby companies, instead of raising finance by borrowing from financial institutions, convert assets into securities for sale in the marketplace.

Security market line: the linear relationship between systematic risk and return as defined by the capital asset pricing model.

Sensitivity analysis: the technique of analysing how changes in an individual project variable affect a project's overall net present value.

Share option schemes: schemes which involve the giving of share options to employees of a company in order to provide an incentive.

Share split: the issuing of a number of new shares in return for each existing share held by investors. Also known as a stock split.

Sinking fund: an amount of money put aside annually for use in redeeming debentures that mature in the future.

Special dividends: a substantial dividend payment that is not expected to be repeated in the near future.

Specific risk: *see* unsystematic risk.

Spot market: a market for immediate transactions, usually in the context of currency purchasing.

Spread: the difference between the buying (offer) price and the selling (bid) price of a financial security.

Stakeholder: any party that has a share or interest in a business.

Sterling commercial paper: short-dated money market instruments that companies can issue to raise finance.

Stock: in the UK, stock is another term for a bond, whereas in the USA it is taken to mean a share.

Stock splits: US terminology for a *share split*.

Strike price: the price at which an option holder can purchase or sell the specified financial asset.

Sunk costs: costs that have already been incurred and therefore cannot be retrieved.

Swaps: an agreement between two parties to exchange interest payments based on an agreed principal.

Swaptions: derivatives which give the holder the option to become involved in a swap agreement.

Synergy: the creation of wealth by the combination of complementary assets.

Systematic risk: also known as *market risk*, this represents the relative effect on the returns of an individual security of changes in the market as a whole.

Tax exhaustion: the position where a company has insufficient profits with which to take advantage of the capital allowances available to it.

Technical analysis: the use of past share price data and statistical analysis to predict future share prices.

Tick: a standardised unit measuring movement in the price of futures contracts, defined as 0.01 per cent of the contract size.

Time value of money: the concept that £1 received in the future is not equivalent to £1 received today due to factors such as risk and opportunity cost.

Traded option: a standardised agreement giving the holder the right, but not the obligation, to buy or sell a specified amount of a commodity or financial instrument over a specific period and at a specified price.

Transaction risk: the risk that the exchange rate will move in an unfavourable direction when transactions are made in a foreign currency.

Transfer pricing: the manipulation of the rate at which one subsidiary charges another subsidiary for its products in order to minimise the company's overall corporate tax bill.

Translation risk: the balance sheet risk on consolidation experienced by companies with assets and liabilities denominated in currencies other than that of the home country. Also known as accounting risk.

Treasury bills: virtually risk-free short-dated debt securities issued by governments.

Unconventional cash flows: a series of cash flows that involve more than one change in sign.

Undercapitalisation: *see* Overtrading.

Underlying: the asset which a derivative security is based upon.

Underwriting: the process whereby companies issuing securities arrange for financial institutions to buy up any unsold securities.

Unique risk: *see* Unsystematic risk.

Unsystematic risk: the risk that is specific to a company and hence can be diversified away by spreading money over a portfolio of investments.

Upside risk: the possibility of a favourable outcome due to the movement of a financial variable.

Utility curves: *see* Indifference curves.

Vanilla: a term often used to describe the purest and most straightforward version of a bond or derivative, i.e. a vanilla swap.

Venture capital: risk capital supplied by specialist organisations to smaller companies that would otherwise struggle to raise capital due to their high risk.

Vertical merger: the combination of two companies operating at different stages of production within the same industry.

Warehousing: the situation where a financial institution acts as an intermediary for a swap deal even though no suitable counterparty has yet been found.

Warrants: tradable share options issued by companies, commonly attached to an issue of bonds.

Weighted average cost of capital: the average rate of return determined from all sources of finance employed by a company, which can be used as a discount rate for investment appraisal decisions and is a key factor to consider in decisions concerning new finance.

White knight: a favourable takeover partner that may be sought by a company that is the subject of an unwanted takeover bid.

Withholding tax: a tax levied by an overseas country on profits repatriated to the home country.

Working capital: the difference between a company's current assets and liabilities, also referred to as net working capital.

Writing down allowance: *see* Capital allowances.

Yield to maturity: *see* Redemption yield.

Zero coupon bonds: bonds issued at a considerable discount to their face value and as a consequence paying no coupon.

Zero sum game: a situation where, for one party to gain by a certain amount, another party must lose by a similar amount.

Present value tables

Table of present value factors

Present values of $1/(1 + r)^n$

					Discount rates (r)					
Periods (n)	1%	2%	3%	4%	5%	6%	7%	8%	9%	10%
1	0.990	0.980	0.971	0.962	0.952	0.943	0.935	0.926	0.917	0.909
2	0.980	0.961	0.943	0.925	0.907	0.890	0.873	0.857	0.842	0.826
3	0.971	0.942	0.915	0.889	0.864	0.840	0.816	0.794	0.772	0.751
4	0.961	0.924	0.888	0.855	0.823	0.792	0.763	0.735	0.708	0.683
5	0.951	0.906	0.863	0.822	0.784	0.747	0.713	0.681	0.650	0.621
6	0.942	0.888	0.837	0.790	0.746	0.705	0.666	0.630	0.596	0.564
7	0.933	0.871	0.813	0.760	0.711	0.665	0.623	0.583	0.547	0.513
8	0.923	0.853	0.789	0.731	0.677	0.627	0.582	0.540	0.502	0.467
9	0.914	0.837	0.766	0.703	0.645	0.592	0.544	0.500	0.460	0.424
10	0.905	0.820	0.744	0.676	0.614	0.558	0.508	0.463	0.422	0.386
11	0.896	0.804	0.722	0.650	0.585	0.527	0.475	0.429	0.388	0.350
12	0.887	0.788	0.701	0.625	0.557	0.497	0.444	0.397	0.356	0.319
13	0.879	0.773	0.681	0.601	0.530	0.469	0.415	0.368	0.326	0.290
14	0.870	0.758	0.661	0.577	0.505	0.442	0.388	0.340	0.299	0.263
15	0.861	0.743	0.642	0.555	0.481	0.417	0.362	0.315	0.275	0.239
16	0.853	0.728	0.623	0.534	0.458	0.394	0.339	0.292	0.252	0.218
17	0.844	0.714	0.605	0.513	0.436	0.371	0.317	0.270	0.231	0.198
18	0.836	0.700	0.587	0.494	0.416	0.350	0.296	0.250	0.212	0.180
19	0.828	0.686	0.570	0.475	0.396	0.331	0.277	0.232	0.194	0.164
20	0.820	0.673	0.554	0.456	0.377	0.312	0.258	0.215	0.178	0.149

					Discount rates (r)					
Periods (n)	11%	12%	13%	14%	15%	16%	17%	18%	19%	20%
1	0.901	0.893	0.885	0.877	0.870	0.862	0.855	0.847	0.840	0.833
2	0.812	0.797	0.783	0.769	0.756	0.743	0.731	0.718	0.706	0.694
3	0.731	0.712	0.693	0.675	0.658	0.641	0.624	0.609	0.593	0.579
4	0.659	0.636	0.613	0.592	0.572	0.552	0.534	0.516	0.499	0.482
5	0.593	0.567	0.543	0.519	0.497	0.476	0.456	0.437	0.419	0.402
6	0.535	0.507	0.480	0.456	0.432	0.410	0.390	0.370	0.352	0.335
7	0.482	0.452	0.425	0.400	0.376	0.354	0.333	0.314	0.296	0.279
8	0.434	0.404	0.376	0.351	0.327	0.305	0.285	0.266	0.249	0.233
9	0.391	0.361	0.333	0.308	0.284	0.263	0.243	0.225	0.209	0.194
10	0.352	0.322	0.295	0.270	0.247	0.227	0.208	0.191	0.176	0.162
11	0.317	0.287	0.261	0.237	0.215	0.195	0.178	0.162	0.148	0.135
12	0.286	0.257	0.231	0.208	0.187	0.168	0.152	0.137	0.124	0.112
13	0.258	0.229	0.204	0.182	0.163	0.145	0.130	0.116	0.104	0.093
14	0.232	0.205	0.181	0.160	0.141	0.125	0.111	0.099	0.088	0.078
15	0.209	0.183	0.160	0.140	0.123	0.108	0.095	0.084	0.074	0.065
16	0.188	0.163	0.141	0.123	0.107	0.093	0.081	0.071	0.062	0.054
17	0.167	0.146	0.125	0.108	0.093	0.080	0.069	0.060	0.052	0.045
18	0.153	0.130	0.111	0.095	0.081	0.069	0.059	0.051	0.044	0.038
19	0.138	0.116	0.098	0.083	0.070	0.060	0.051	0.043	0.037	0.031
20	0.124	0.104	0.087	0.073	0.061	0.051	0.043	0.037	0.031	0.026

Table of cumulative present value factors

Present values of $[1 - (1 + r)^{-n}]/r$

Discount rates (r)

Periods (n)	1%	2%	3%	4%	5%	6%	7%	8%	9%	10%
1	0.990	0.980	0.971	0.962	0.952	0.943	0.935	0.926	0.917	0.909
2	1.970	1.942	1.913	1.886	1.859	1.833	1.808	1.783	1.759	1.736
3	2.941	2.884	2.829	2.775	2.723	2.673	2.624	2.577	2.531	2.487
4	3.902	3.808	3.717	3.630	3.546	3.465	3.387	3.312	3.240	3.170
5	4.853	4.713	4.580	4.452	4.329	4.212	4.100	3.993	3.890	3.791
6	5.795	5.601	5.417	5.242	5.076	4.917	4.767	4.623	4.486	4.355
7	6.728	6.472	6.230	6.002	5.786	5.582	5.389	5.206	5.033	4.868
8	7.652	7.325	7.020	6.733	6.463	6.210	5.971	5.747	5.535	5.335
9	8.566	8.162	7.786	7.435	7.108	6.802	6.515	6.247	5.995	5.759
10	9.471	8.983	8.530	8.111	7.722	7.360	7.024	6.710	6.418	6.145
11	10.368	9.787	9.253	8.760	8.306	7.887	7.499	7.139	6.805	6.495
12	11.255	10.575	9.954	9.385	8.863	8.384	7.943	7.536	7.161	6.814
13	12.134	11.348	10.635	9.986	9.394	8.853	8.358	7.904	7.487	7.103
14	13.004	12.106	11.296	10.563	9.899	9.295	8.745	8.244	7.786	7.367
15	13.865	12.849	11.938	11.118	10.380	9.712	9.108	8.559	8.061	7.606
16	14.718	13.578	12.561	11.652	10.838	10.106	9.447	8.851	8.313	7.824
17	15.562	14.292	13.166	12.166	11.274	10.477	9.763	9.122	8.544	8.022
18	16.398	14.992	13.754	12.659	11.690	10.828	10.059	9.372	8.756	8.201
19	17.226	15.678	14.324	13.134	12.085	11.158	10.336	9.604	8.950	8.365
20	18.046	16.351	14.877	13.590	12.462	11.470	10.594	9.818	9.129	8.514

Discount rates (r)

Periods (n)	11%	12%	13%	14%	15%	16%	17%	18%	19%	20%
1	0.901	0.893	0.885	0.877	0.870	0.862	0.855	0.847	0.840	0.833
2	1.713	1.690	1.668	1.647	1.626	1.605	1.585	1.566	1.547	1.528
3	2.444	2.402	2.361	2.322	2.283	2.246	2.210	2.174	2.140	2.106
4	3.102	3.037	2.974	2.914	2.855	2.798	2.743	2.690	2.639	2.589
5	3.696	3.605	3.517	3.433	3.352	3.274	3.199	3.127	3.058	2.991
6	4.231	4.111	3.998	3.889	3.784	3.685	3.589	3.498	3.410	3.326
7	4.712	4.564	4.423	4.288	4.160	4.039	3.922	3.812	3.706	3.605
8	5.146	4.968	4.799	4.639	4.487	4.344	4.207	4.078	3.954	3.837
9	5.537	5.328	5.132	4.946	4.772	4.607	4.451	4.303	4.163	4.031
10	5.889	5.650	5.426	5.216	5.019	4.833	4.659	4.494	4.339	4.192
11	6.207	5.938	5.687	5.453	5.234	5.029	4.836	4.656	4.486	4.327
12	6.492	6.194	5.918	5.660	5.421	5.197	4.988	4.793	4.611	4.439
13	6.750	6.424	6.122	5.842	5.583	5.342	5.118	4.910	4.715	4.533
14	6.982	6.628	6.302	6.002	5.724	5.468	5.229	5.008	4.802	4.611
15	7.191	6.811	6.462	6.142	5.847	5.575	5.324	5.092	4.876	4.675
16	7.379	6.974	6.604	6.265	5.954	5.668	5.405	5.162	4.938	4.730
17	7.549	7.120	6.729	6.373	6.047	5.749	5.475	5.222	4.990	4.775
18	7.702	7.250	6.840	6.467	6.128	5.818	5.534	5.273	5.033	4.812
19	7.839	7.366	6.938	6.550	6.198	5.877	5.584	5.316	5.070	4.843
20	7.963	7.469	7.025	6.623	6.259	5.929	5.628	5.353	5.101	4.870

Index